Federal Republic of Germany
a country study

Foreign Area Studies
The American University
Edited by
Richard F. Nyrop
Research completed
February 1982

On the cover: Castle at Breisach, upper Rhine region

Second Edition, 1982; First Printing: 1983

Copyright © 1982 United States Government as represented by the Secretary of the Army.   All rights reserved.

Library of Congress Cataloging in Publication Data
Main entry under title:

Federal Republic of Germany.

   (Area handbook series)   (DA pam ; 550–173) Rev. ed. of: Area handbook for the Federal Republic of Germany. 1975.
   Bibliography: p.
   Includes index.
   1.   Germany (West)   I. Nyrop, Richard F.   II. American University (Washington, D. C.). Foreign Area Studies. III. Area handbook for the Federal Republic of Germany.   IV. Series.   V. Series: DA pam ; 550–173.
DD259.F43   1982   943   83–2515

Headquarters, Department of the Army
DA Pam 550–173
Supersedes 1975 Edition

For sale by the Superintendent of Documents, U.S. Government Printing Office
Washington, D.C. 20402

Foreword

This volume is one of a continuing series of books prepared by Foreign Area Studies, The American University, under the Country Studies/Area Handbook Program. The last page of this book provides a listing of other published studies. Each book in the series deals with a particular foreign country, describing and analyzing its economic, national security, political, and social systems and institutions and examining the interrelationships of those systems and institutions and the ways that they are shaped by cultural factors. Each study is written by a multidisciplinary team of social scientists. The authors seek to provide a basic insight and understanding of the society under observation, striving for a dynamic rather than a static portrayal of it. The study focuses on historical antecedents and on the cultural, political, and socioeconomic characteristics that contribute to cohesion and cleavage within the society. Particular attention is given to the origins and traditions of the people who make up the society, their dominant beliefs and values, their community of interests and the issues on which they are divided, the nature and extent of their involvement with the national institutions, and their attitudes toward each other and toward the social system and political order within which they live.

The contents of the book represent the views, opinions, and findings of Foreign Area Studies and should not be construed as an official Department of the Army position, policy, or decision, unless so designated by other official documentation. The authors have sought to adhere to accepted standards of scholarly objectivity. Such corrections, additions, and suggestions for factual or other changes that readers may have will be welcomed for use in future new editions.

> William Evans-Smith
> Director, Foreign Area Studies
> The American University
> Washington, D.C. 20016

Acknowledgments

The authors are indebted to numerous individuals in various agencies of the United States government and in international and private organizations in Washington, D.C. who gave of their time, research materials, and special knowledge to provide data and perspective. The authors also wish to express their appreciation to members of the Foreign Area Studies staff who contributed directly to the preparation of the manuscript. These include Kathryn R. Stafford and Dorothy M. Lohmann, who edited the manuscript with the assistance of Janet B. Connors; Harriett R. Blood, who prepared the graphics with the assistance of Gustavo Arce; and Gilda V. Nimer, who provided valuable bibliographic assistance. The authors appreciate as well the contributions of Ernest A. Will, publications manager.

Special thanks are owed to Marty Ittner, who designed the book cover and the illustrations on the title page of each chapter. The inclusion of photographs in this study was made possible by the generosity of various individuals and public and private organizations. We acknowledge our indebtedness especially to those who provided work not yet published.

Contents

	Page
Foreword	iii
Acknowledgments	v
Preface	xi
Country Profile	xix
Introduction	xxv

Chapter 1. Historical Setting 1
                        Rosalyn Unger

EARLY HISTORY — Roman Period — Medieval Germany — Reformation — Rise of Prussia — GERMAN CONFEDERATION — Liberal Reform Movement — Bismarck and Unification — IMPERIAL GERMANY — Political Consolidation — Bismarck's Fall — Industrial Expansion — Wilhelmine Era — World War I — The War Guilt Debate — WEIMAR REPUBLIC, 1918–33 — Weimar Constitution — Problems of Parliamentary Politics — Stresemann Era — Weimar Culture — Hitler and the Rise of National Socialism — THIRD REICH — Party and State — Domestic Mobilization — Foreign Policy — World War II — FEDERAL REPUBLIC OF GERMANY — The Bonn Democracy — Adenauer Era — Grand Coalition, 1966–69 — Willy Brandt's *Ostpolitik* — Helmut Schmidt's Chancellorship

Chapter 2. Physical and Demographic Setting 59
                        Bruno Steinbruckner

GEOGRAPHY — Topography — Drainage — Climate — POPULATION — EDUCATION — Educational Reforms — Basic Principles of Education — Administration and Finance — The Educational System — Gesamthochschulen — HEALTH AND WELFARE — Health Care Facilities — Medical Personnel — The Welfare System — The Pension System — Health, Accident, and Unemployment Insurance — Child Support — Educational Subsidies — Rehabilitation — Subsidies for War Victims — Housing Subsidies — Other Subsidies — International and Bilateral Agreements on Welfare and Social Security

Chapter 3. The Society 101
Patricia A. Kluck
ETHNICITY — Jews — Romany — Foreign Workers — SOCIAL ORGANIZATION — The Elite — The Middle Class — The Working Class — FAMILY ORGANIZATION — URBANIZATION AND MIGRATION — RELIGION — Protestants — Roman Catholics

Chapter 4. Character and Structure of the Economy 141
Darrel R. Eglin
LEGACIES AFFECTING DEVELOPMENT — ROLE OF GOVERNMENT — Economic Policy — Economic Policy and Problems Since 1970 — Budget — GROWTH AND STRUCTURE OF THE ECONOMY — LABOR — MONEY AND BANKING — Currency — Banking — FOREIGN TRADE — Exports — Imports — BALANCE OF PAYMENTS

Chapter 5. Agriculture 179
Darrel R. Eglin
LAND USE — ORGANIZATION OF AGRICULTURE — AGRICULTURAL POLICY — CROPPING AND PRODUCTION — Cropping Patterns and Production — Livestock — FOREIGN TRADE IN AGRICULTURAL PRODUCTS — FORESTRY — FISHING

Chapter 6. Industry 197
Warrick E. Elrod, Jr.
MAJOR INDUSTRIAL SECTORS — Coal and Lignite — Iron and Steel — Motor Vehicles — Chemicals — Electrical Industry — Engineering — Energy — Transportation — INDUSTRY AND THE FREE MARKET PHILOSOPHY — ORGANIZATIONAL STRUCTURE — Company Supervisory Boards — Industrial Associations — INDUSTRY AND BANKS — BUSINESS PLANNING — LABOR IN THE INDUSTRIAL SECTOR — The Industrial Labor Force: Character, Quality, Skills — Codetermination — Working Conditions, Wages, and Benefits — WEST BERLIN — INDUSTRY AND EAST–WEST TRADE — INDUSTRY AND THE WORLD ECONOMY

Chapter 7. Government and Politics...................... 243
James D. Rudolph
THE CONSTITUTIONAL FRAMEWORK AND FEDERALISM — THE FEDERAL EXECUTIVE — The President — The Government — THE LEGISLATURE — Bundestag — Bundesrat — THE JUDICIARY — THE BUREAUCRACY — STATE AND LOCAL GOVERNMENT — POLITICAL PARTIES AND THE ELECTORAL SYSTEM — Christian Democratic Union/Christian Social Union — Social Democratic Party — Minor Parties — The Electoral System — EXTRA-PARTY POLITICAL FORCES — Traditional Interest Groups — Citizens' Initiative Associations — The Mass Media

Chapter 8. Foreign Relations............................... 287
William C. Cromwell
INSTITUTIONAL FRAMEWORK — THE NORTH ATLANTIC TREATY ORGANIZATION — *OSTPOLITIK* AND DÉTENTE — THE EUROPEAN COMMUNITIES — RELATIONS WITH THE MIDDLE EAST AND EAST ASIA — Middle East — Asia — RELATIONS WITH LATIN AMERICAN STATES — RELATIONS WITH AFRICAN STATES

Chapter 9. National Security.............................. 331
Eugene K. Keefe
ARMED FORCES — Military Traditions — Organization and Mission — Budgetary Problems — Citizens in Uniform — Foreign Military Relations — INTERNAL SECURITY — Federal Police Agencies — State Police Agencies — Criminal Justice — Dissidence and Terrorist Activities

Appendix. Tables 375
Bibliography 399
Glossary 435
Index 437

List of Figures

1	Federal Republic of Germany	xxiv
2	The Carolingian Empire Divided by the Treaty of Verdun	6
3	Germany at the Time of the Protestant Reformation	12 & 13
4	The German Struggle for Unification, 1815–71	15
5	The Weimar Republic, 1918–33	26
6	Extent of Nazi Germany Expansion in 1942	39
7	Topography and Drainage	63
8	Population Density, Late 1970s	71
9	Age–Sex Structure, December 1978	73
10	Model of the Educational System, Early 1980s	80
11	Public and Private Expenditures on Health and Welfare Services, 1978	95
12	Basic Resources and Processing	202
13	Natural Gas Pipeline from Soviet Union	214
14	Transportation	217
15	West Berlin	238
16	System of Government 1981	253
17	Composition of Bundestag by Party, 1949–80	257
18	Foreign and Security Policy Decisionmaking	292
19	Civil and Military Structure of NATO	294
20	Allied Command Europe	296
21	NATO Deployments: West Germany	303
22	Ministry of Defense	341
23	Officers' Rank Insignia	356

Preface

FOR ALMOST THREE decades the Federal Republic of Germany (Bundesrepublik Deutschland—West Germany or Federal Republic) enjoyed with only minor interruptions economic growth and prosperity and political stability. By early 1982, however, an economic downturn that began in the late 1970s had become increasingly troublesome; industrial production and exports were continuing to decline, and inflation and unemployment were continuing to increase. In January 1982 unemployment reached 8.2 percent of the work force, the highest rate since 1954. Partly because of the country's economic woes but also because of foreign policy disputes, Chancellor Helmut Schmidt confronted challenges not only from the opposition political party but also from his political allies.

Federal Republic of Germany: A Country Study replaces the *Area Handbook for the Federal Republic of Germany*, which was published in 1975 and was therefore seriously dated. Like its predecessor, the present country study is an attempt to treat in a compact and objective manner the dominant social, political, economic, and national security aspects of contemporary West German society. Sources of information included scholarly journals and monographs, official reports of governments and international organizations, foreign and domestic newspapers, numerous periodicals, and interviews with individuals who have special competence on West German and West European affairs. Chapter bibliographies appear at the end of the book; brief comments on some of the more valuable sources as possible further reading appear at the end of each chapter. Measurements are given in the metric system; a conversion table is provided to assist those readers who are unfamiliar with metric measurements (see table 1, Appendix). A Glossary is also included, as is a chronology of important events (see table A).

The contemporary place-names used in this study are generally those approved by the United States Board on Geographic Names with the exception that the authors employed the conventional spelling for many place-names. The reader will therefore find Bavaria, Lower Saxony, and Rhineland-Palatinate rather than Bayern, Niedersachsen, and Rheinland-Pfalz, respectively.

Table A. Chronology of Important Events

Periods and Dates	Events

ROMAN PERIOD
ca. 1000 B.C.-A.D.100

Germanic tribes settled in Germania. Roman army defeated by Germans at Battle of Teutoburg Forest in A.D. 9 and routed from central Germania. Romans subsequently reconquered Germania south of the Rhine-Danube and constructed fortified frontiers.

ca. A.D.100–500

Major Germanic tribal migrations into Germania. Collapse of Western Roman Empire; last Roman emperor. Romulus Augustulus, deposed in 476 by German armies led by Odovacar. Frankish tribes settled Gaul (France); Lombards settled northern Italy; Anglo-Saxons settled Great Britain.

FRANKISH PERIOD (431–918)
Merovingian Dynasty (431–751)

Merovingian kings ruled the Frankish tribes. Clovis, Frankish king (482–511), defeated Romans in 486 and ruled over Gaul's mixed Germanic-Roman people. Pepin the Younger, Frankish king (741–68), founded Carolingian Dynasty (752).

Carolingian Dynasty (752–918)

Frankish rule reached from the Spanish marches into central Germany. The "Donation of Pepin" (754–56) established the Papal States. Charles the Great (Charlemagne), Frankish king (768–814), conquered Lombardy in 774. Carolingian Empire (800); Charlemagne crowned Holy Roman Emperor (HRE) by pope. Louis (I) the Pious, HRE (814–40). Treaty of Verdun (843) divided Carolingian Empire among Charlemagne's three grandsons. Germany, France, and Middle Kingdom delineated and imperial title linked with Middle Kingdom. Louis (II) the German ruled East Frankish tribes (843–76). Charles (III) the Fat, German king (876–87) and HRE (881). Arnulf of Carinthia, German king (887–99) and HRE (896). Barbarian invasions weakened Carolingian rule; German duchies of Franconia, Saxony, Thuringia, Swabia, Bavaria rose to power. Louis IV, German king (900–911). Conrad I (of Franconia) elected German king (911–18) following extinction of Carolingian Dynasty in the east.

SAXON DYNASTY (919–1024)

Frankish and Saxon nobles elected Henry (I) the Fowler German king (919–36). Otto (I) the Great, German king (936–73), gained control of Middle Kingdom and proclaimed the "Holy Roman Empire of the German Nation." German empire extended to Elbe and in the

| Periods and Dates | Events |

south to Vienna. Otto II, HRE (973–83). Otto III, HRE (983–1002). Henry (II) the Saint, HRE (1002–24).

SALIAN DYNASTY (1025–1125)

Conrad II, duke of Franconia, founded Salic-Frankish Dynasty, elected HRE (1024–39). Henry III, HRE (1039–56). Henry IV, HRE (1056–1106), challenged Pope Gregory VII. Investiture Controversy and civil war (1075–1122); German empire weakened, and German princes began rise to power. Henry V, HRE (1106–25). The compromise Concordat of Worms (1122) settled papal-imperial struggle. Lothar III, Saxon noble, elected HRE (1125–37).

HOHENSTAUFEN DYNASTY (1138–1250)

Hohenstaufen kings struggled to restore imperial authority. Conrad III elected German king (1138–52). Frederick I (Barbarossa), HRE (1152–90). Italian expeditions to regain imperial control of the Middle Kingdom. Peace of Constance (1183) granted extensive autonomy to Lombard cities. Henry VI, HRE (1190–97). Civil war (1198–1214). Frederick II, HRE (1212–50), restored imperial administration in Italy and Sicily, but German princes gained concessions. Imperial statute (*statutum in favorem principum*) (1232) established the secular and ecclesiastical princes as virtually independent rulers within their own territories (principalities). Great Interregnum (1250–72) anarchy and civil war. German princes gained power and vied for imperial title; Habsburgs of Austria provided all German kings and emperors from mid–15th century.

AGE OF THE PRINCES (1273–1519)

Rudolf of Habsburg elected German king (1273–91), acquired Austria and Styria in 1282, and made Habsburgs the strongest German dynasty. Adolf (of Nassau) elected German king (1292–98). Albert I (Habsburg) elected German king (1298–1308). Henry VII (of Luxemburg), HRE (1308–13); founded dynasty that seriously rivaled Habsburgs from its power base in Bohemia. Louis IV (the Bavarian) of House of Wittelsbach, HRE (1314–47). Charles IV (of Luxemburg), HRE (1355–78), issued Golden Bull of 1356, which granted German princes power to elect emperor and provided basic constitution of German Empire. Wenceslas (of Bohemia), German king (1378–1400). Rupert of Palatinate, German king (1400–10). Sigismund (of Luxemburg), HRE (1410–37); last non-Habsburg emperor until 1742. Habsburgs: Albert II, German king (1438–39). Frederick III, HRE (1440–93); Maximilian I, HRE (1493–1519).

| Periods and Dates | Events |

PROTESTANT REFORMATION AND
RELIGIOUS WARS (1517–1648)
Martin Luther posted his Ninety-five Theses in 1517 in Wittenberg and challenged papal authority. Charles V, HRE (1519–56). Publication in 1520 of Luther's three revolutionary pamphlets. Luther banned in 1521 by church (papal bull, *Decret Romanum*) and empire (Edict of Worms). Charles V's wars against France in 1521–26), 1526–29, 1536–38, 1542–44. Vienna threatened by Turks in 1529. Diet of Augsburg (1530); Protestant "Augsburg Confession" presented, and Protestant League of Schmalkalden formed by German princes. War of Schmalkadlen (1546–47) between Charles V and Protestant princes. Peace of Augsburg (1555); Catholicism and Lutheranism formally recognized in Germany, and each prince given right to decide religion to be practiced in his territory. Ferdinand I, HRE (1556–64). Maximilian II, HRE (1564–76). Rudolf II, HRE (1576–1612). Matthias, HRE (1612–19). Bohemian Revolt in 1618; imperial armies defeated Bohemians at Battle of the White Mountain near Prague in 1620. Thirty Years' War (1618–48). End of Holy Roman Empire as a European power.

RISE OF PRUSSIA (1648–1815)
Frederick William, the Great Elector of Brandenburg-Prussia (1640–88), of Hohenzollern Dynasty, established absolute rule. Frederick III, elector of Brandenburg-Prussia (1688–1713), assumed title of king in 1701. Frederick William I, Prussian king (1713–40), created Prussian civil and military bureaucracy. Frederick (II) the Great, Prussian king (1740–86); Silesian Wars against Austria (1740–42, 1744–45, 1756–65). Frederick William II, Prussian king (1786–97). Frederick William III, Prussian king (1797–1840).

REACTION, REVOLUTION,
GERMAN UNIFICATION (1815–71)
Congress of Vienna (1814–15) after Napoleon's defeat in Wars of Liberation (1813–15) established German Confederation of thirty-nine monarchical states. Prince Metternich, Austrian chancellor and foreign minister (1809–48), headed Confederation. Student unions agitated for democratic reform. Carlsbad Decrees (1819) outlawed radical student organizations. Weimar, Bavaria, Baden, and Württemberg enacted constitutions (1818–19). "July Revolution" in France in 1830 sparked revolutionary movements in Germany; Hesse and Saxony enacted constitutions. Brunswick, Hanover, and Oldenburg enacted constitutions in 1833. Zollverein (Customs Union) created in 1834.

Periods and Dates	Events

March 1848 revolution in Germany. Frankfurt Parliament (May 1848) planned constitutional German nation-state. Frederick William IV, Prussian king (1840–61), refused German crown in 1849, and Frankfurt Parliament dissolved. German Confederation restored in 1851. William I, Prussian king (1861–88); Otto von Bismarck, prime minister (1862–90), united Germany. Constitutional struggle (1862–66): Prussian king versus German liberals in parliament. Schleswig-Holstein War (1864). Seven Weeks' War (1866) between Austria and Prussian; German Confederation dissolved, and Austria excluded from German politics. North German Confederation (1867) headed by Prussia. Franco-Prussian War (1870–71). Second German Empire (1871)—Germany united as nation-state.

IMPERIAL GERMANY (1871–1918)

William I, German emperor (1871–88). Bismarck, chancellor (1871–90). Antisocialist law enacted (1878). Dual Alliance (1879): Germany, Austria-Hungary. Domestic alliance between agrarian and industrial interests. Comprehensive social legislation program (1881). Triple Alliance (1882): Germany, Austria-Hungary, and Italy. German colonies established (1884–85) in South West Africa, Togo, the Cameroons, East Africa, and some Pacific islands. Frederick III, German emperor (March 9–June 15, 1888). William II, German emperor (1888–1918). Bismarck's fall (1890). Leo von Caprivi, chancellor (1890–94). Prince Chlodwig zu Hohenlohe, chancellor (1894–1900). Naval Bill (1898) began naval race against Britain. Bernhard von Bülow, chancellor (1900–1909). Moroccan crisis (1905); Germany intervened in French and British sphere of influence. Theobald von Bethmann-Hollweg, chancellor (1909–17). Moroccan crisis (1911); Germany sent gunboat to Moroccan port of Agadir. New Naval Bill (1912). Balkan Wars (1912–13); nationalist wars against Ottoman rule. Assasination of Austrian Archduke Franz Ferdinand (June 28, 1914) in Sarajevo, Bosnia. World War I (1914–18); Germans defeated.

WEIMAR REPUBLIC (1918–33)

November Revolution (1918): Spartacist League revolt in Berlin on November 9 resulted in William II's abdication. Social Democrats proclaimed republic. German armistice (November 11). Treaty of Versailles (1919). Social Democrat Friedrich Ebert, president (1919–25). Right-wing Kapp Putsch attempted (1920). Communist revolts in central Germany, Hamburg, and Ruhr district (1921). French-Belgian Ruhr occupation (1923), and Hitler's "beer hall putsch" attempted in Munich (November). Gustav Stresemann, chancellor (August-November 1923) and foreign minister until 1929, formulated policy of rapprochement with West. Dawes Plan on reparations (1924). French-Belgian troops withdrawn from Ruhr (1925). Paul von Hindenburg, World War I army commander, elected president (1925–34). Locarno Treaties (1925) and Berlin Treaty with Soviet Union (1926). Germany joined League of Nations (1926). Young Plan on reparations (1929), and Allied troops withdrawn from Rhineland (1930). Depression Years (1929–33) and cabinet crises. Heinrich Brüning, chancellor (1930–32); government by presidential decree (Article 48 of the Weimar Constitution). Franz von Papen, chancellor (May-December 1932); Hitler's National Socialists won 230 Parliament (Reichstag) seats in July 1932 elections and emerged as Germany's strongest political party. Kurt von Schleicher, chancellor (December 1932–January 1933). President Hindenburg appointed Hitler to chancellorship on January 30, 1933.

THIRD REICH (1933–45)

Reichstag fire (February 1933); Hitler demanded presidential emergency decree. Enabling Act (March 1933) accorded Hitler's cabinet full legislative powers. Germany declared one-party National Socialist state (July 1933). Death of Hindenburg (August 1934); Hitler combined offices of president and chancellor, creating dictatorship. German rearmament (1935). Rhineland remilitarized (1936), and Berlin-Rome Axis formed. At secret conference (November 1937) Hitler announced intention to begin eastward expansion. Austrian *Anschluss* (annexation) (March 1938). Czechoslovak Sudetenland annexed (October 1938). Germany occupied Czech-populated provinces of Bohemia and Moravia (March 1939). Poland invaded (September 1939). World War II (1939–1945).

FEDERAL REPUBLIC OF GERMANY (1949–   )

Federal Republic of Germany (West Germany) proclaimed (May 8, 1949) headed by Chancellor Konrad Adenauer (1949–63) and the Christian Democratic Union. West Germany joined NATO (1955); European Economic Community (1957). Berlin Crisis (1958–61). Berlin Wall built by German Democratic Republic (East Germany) (August 1961). Chancellor Ludwig Erhard (1963–66). Grand Coalition (Christian Democratic Union-Social Democratic Party of Germany) headed by Kurt Georg Kiesinger (1966–69). Social Democrat Willy Brandt chancellor (1969–74): Brandt introduced *Ostpolitik* (eastern policy) and concluded détente negotiations with East Germany. Moscow and Warsaw treaties (1970). Four Power Agreement on

Periods and Dates	Events
	Berlin (1971). Basic Treaty between East and West Germany (1972). Joined United Nations (1973). Social Democrat Helmut Schmidt chancellor (1974–).

Country Profile

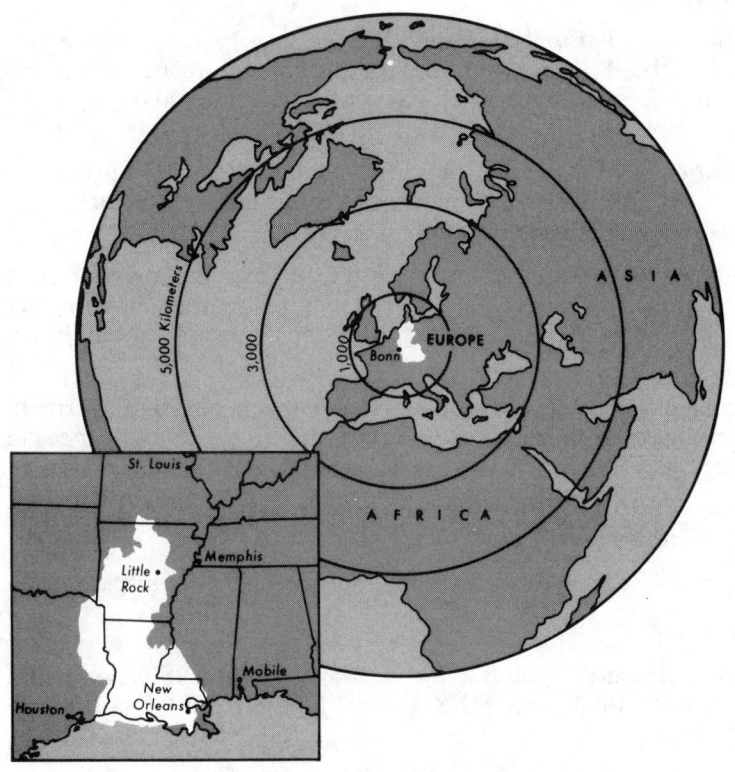

Country

Formal Name: Federal Republic of Germany.

Short Form: West Germany or Federal Republic.

Term for Citizens: West German(s).

Capital: Bonn.

Geography

Size: Approximately 248,630 square kilometers.

Topography: Terrain rises from northern lowlands to a belt of central uplands, descends slightly in the Danube River basin, and rises sharply in the Alpine region of the extreme south. Northward flowing Rhine River is most prominent physical feature.

Climate: Westerly winds and maritime climate predominate, but continental conditions, with greater temperature extremes,

xix

prevail to a degree that increases with the distance inland and to the south.

Society

Population: Estimated in mid-1981 at about 61,760,000; figure includes about 1.9 million in West Berlin and about 4.5 million foreigners. Annual rate of growth variously estimated between 0.1 and 0.3 percent.

Education and Literacy: Full-time education compulsory for nine years; three additional years also compulsory but may be full- or part-time. Virtually all adults literate.

Health and Welfare: Comprehensive and expensive welfare and health programs cover almost all citizens, providing wide range of pensions, accident and health insurance, unemployment insurance, maternity and child care, and similar services.

Language: Standard German (Hochdeutsch or High German) commonly used in public life. Substantial regional differences in dialect.

Ethnic Groups: Primarily German; minority of foreign workers from Mediterranean countries.

Religion: Protestant 44 percent, Roman Catholic 45 percent.

Economy

Gross National Product (GNP): US$826 billion (1980), per capita US$13,410. Real growth 1.8 percent in 1980 and 0.3 percent in 1981.

Agriculture: 2 percent of GNP (1980). Main crops grains, potatoes, and sugar beets. Raising livestock, largely for milk and meat, more important than cropping. Country about 70 percent self-sufficient in foods.

Mining and Manufacturing: 42 percent of GNP (1979); among the world's largest producers of iron, steel, coal, cement, chemicals, and machinery; usually ranked as world's fourth industrial nation.

Exports: US$193 billion (1980), bulk of which was manufactures; machinery and equipment 44 percent. Other members of European Communities (EC) bought 48 percent of exports and other industrialized free market countries an additional 28 percent.

Imports: US$188 billion (1980); fuels 23 percent, machinery and equipment 19 percent, other manufactured goods 36 percent. World's largest importer of agricultural products, which amounted to about 20 percent of total imports. Country heavily dependent on imports for ores and metals, petroleum, rubber, sulfur, cotton, wool, and oils and fats. EC countries supplied 46 percent of imports and other industrialized market economies an additional 27 percent.

Exchange Rate: Average DM2.26 per US$1 in 1981.

Budget: Consolidated expenditures of all levels of government DM698 billion in 1980; consolidated revenues DM646 billion; deficit DM52 billion.

Fiscal Year: Calendar year.

Transportation And Communications

Railroads: 33,453 kilometers, of which 29,032 kilometers in government-owned nationalized system (standard gauge). Nearly 12,500 kilometers double-tracked and over 10,000 kilometers electrified. Systems highly developed and closely integrated with other forms of freight movement locally and abroad. In 1978 railroads carried 31 percent of country's total freight. Over 100 local companies owned and operated the 4,400 kilometers of tracks outside the government system.

Highways: 460,000 kilometers of roads consisting of 6,800 kilometers of superhighways (autobahn), 32,290 kilometers of federal highways, 65,325 kilometers of first-class main roads, 65,725 kilometers of second-class roads, and large network of gravel, dirt, and unclassified roads. In 1978 trucking accounted for 26 percent of nation's freight movement.

Inland Waterways: 4,400 kilometers of rivers and canals link major industrial areas. In 1978 inland shipping accounted for 23 percent of freight carried. In 1980s canal linking Rhine-Main system to Danube River will be completed permitting inland shipping from North Sea to Black Sea.

Ocean Shipping: Ten major and eleven minor ports. In 1978 ocean shipping accounted for 13 percent of total freight movement.

Pipelines: 2,071 kilometers for crude oil; 2,943 kilometers for distribution of refined products; 95,414 kilometers for import, collection from local fields, and distribution of natural gas. In 1978 pipelines accounted for 7 percent of country's freight traffic.

Airports: Eleven civil airports providing passenger and cargo service within country and to rest of world.

Telecommunications: Highly developed modern service to all parts of country and to systems abroad.

Government And Politics

Government: 1949 Basic Law, as amended, functions as constitution. Federalist system whereby federal government shares authority with ten state (*Land*) governments. Dual executive consists of chancellor, who is head of government, and president, who is head of state. Two legislative bodies: forty-one members of Federal Council (Bundesrat) appointed by *Land* governments; 497 members of Federal Diet (Bundestag) popularly elected. Independent judiciary capped by Federal Constitutional Court.

Politics: Two dominant political parties: Social Democratic Party and Christian Democratic Union/Christian Social Union. One important minor party, Free Democratic Party. Federal elections for Bundestag normally held every four years; *Land* and local elections scattered throughout term of federal officeholders. All citizens eighteen and older free to vote; high voter turnout. Extraparty politics secondary.

International Organizations: Member of United Nations and its specialized agencies, North Atlantic Treaty Organization (NATO), and Organisation for Economic Co-operation and Development. Member of EC, which includes European Coal and Steel Community and European Economic Community.

National Security

Armed Forces: Federal Armed Forces (Bundeswehr) consisted of army, navy, and air force, numbering approximately 345,000, 39,000, and 111,000 respectively in early 1982. Conscripts made up almost half of army, about 29 percent of navy, and about 37 percent of air force.

Military Units: Army comprised two major components: Field Army containing combat elements designated as NATO forces and Territorial Army, home defense force. Basic maneuver elements of Field Army were thirty-six brigades, organized in twelve divisions that made up three corps. Navy deployed about 200 warships and 165 aircraft from stations on coasts of North Sea and Baltic Sea. Combat aircraft of air force divided among ground attack, interceptor, and reconnaissance squadrons. Air force also deployed surface-to-surface and surface-to-air missile units.

Equipment: Principal acquisitions ongoing in early 1980s included Leopard II main battle tanks, Tornado and Alpha Jet aircraft, and missile frigates.

Foreign Armed Forces: United States, Britain, France, the Netherlands, Belgium, and Canada deploy military forces in West Germany.

Police: Federal police forces included border police and criminal investigation office in addition to specialized small forces concerned with railways, waterways, shipping. Majority of country's police under control of *Länder*.

Paramilitary: Border police equipped and trained as light infantry but mission did not include military activities. Each *Land* maintained units of Readiness Police similarly trained but also with no military mission. Readiness Police can be moved across *Land* lines if needed for emergency duty, e.g., riot or catastrophe.

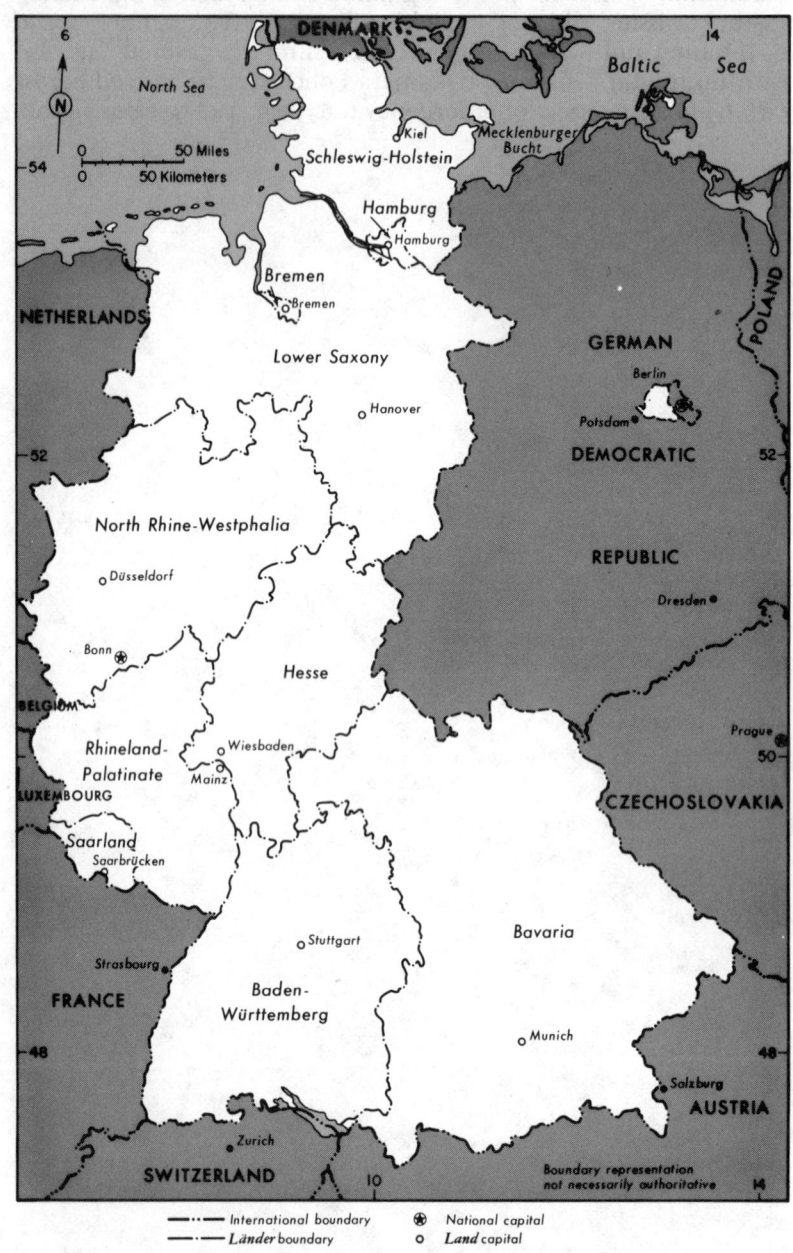

Figure 1. Federal Republic of Germany

Introduction

IN THE LATE spring of 1945 Hitler's Third Reich collapsed in utter defeat; the major cities were devastated, the people destitute, and the land was occupied by foreign armies. On June 8 the Germans surrendered unconditionally, and shortly thereafter the victorious Allies divided the nation into four occupation zones—American, British, French, and Soviet—and placed Berlin under Four Power control. In 1949 Britain, France, and the United States merged their occupation zones to form the Federal Republic of Germany (West Germany or Federal Republic); the Soviet Union converted its zone to the German Democratic Republic (East Germany). Berlin, which lies some 175 kilometers within East Germany, remained under Four Power control, but its western sector was eventually recognized as a part of West Germany, and the eastern sector became the capital of East Germany.

Within a relatively few years West Germany underwent a startling transformation. In early 1982 the economy was experiencing considerable distress, but its industrial production was exceeded only by the United States, the Soviet Union, and Japan. Its military contribution to the North Atlantic Treaty Organization (NATO or the Atlantic Alliance) was second only to the United States, and it continued to be one of the more influential members of the European Communities (EC—see Glossary). Although not a superpower, the Federal Republic was universally recognized as a major economic and military power and therefore possessed political influence on the world scene (see The European Communities, ch. 8; Armed Forces, ch. 9).

The part of the former nation that became West Germany encompasses slightly over 248,630 square kilometers, including the roughly 480 square kilometers of West Berlin. In mid-1981 the government estimated that the population was about 61,760,000, of which over 1.9 million resided in West Berlin. The population estimate included about 4.5 million foreigners, almost all of whom were guest workers (*Gastarbeiter*) and their dependents. In early 1982 the government was seeking to persuade the guest workers to return to their native lands but without much success. Workers from Turkey constituted the largest single foreign community and, because of their Islamic culture, the most conspicuous and least assimilated one (see Foreign Workers, ch. 3).

All but a tiny fraction of the native-born population are ethnic Germans descended from Teutonic tribes that settled the region between the Rhine and Oder rivers a few centuries before the Christian era. The Bavarians, Franks, Frisians, Saxons, Swabians, and Thuringians assimilated lesser tribes and, although differing in some tribal characteristics, these peoples shared a common language that made them the nucleus of a German nation. Many of the regional characteristics and the differences in contemporary dialects resulted from the differences that existed among the ancient Germanic tribes. Despite the existence of the distinctive dialects, the most important unifying factor from the Middle Ages forward was the common language. The use of a standard written language first became widespread after the publication of Martin Luther's voluminous works in the sixteenth century. A standardized spoken language was much slower in developing because of the tenacity with which the people retained their dialects. In modern times—particularly since World War II—the influence of radio, television, the cinema, and the theater has spread the use of standard or High German (Hochdeutsch), and young people have been less interested in retaining distinctive dialects.

About 45 percent of the population claims affiliation with the Roman Catholic Church, and about 44 percent are Protestants. Protestants generally predominate in the north and Catholics in the west and south. Most Protestant churches are associated with the United Evangelical Church in Germany or the Evangelical Church of the Union, both Lutheran. There are also congregations of Methodists, Baptists, Mennonites, and Quakers. Since World War II denominational differences among the Christian churches have become less important in political affairs (see Religion, ch. 3). The Jewish community, which numbered about 530,000 in all of Germany at the beginning of the Hitler period, had about 32,000 adherents in the late 1970s.

The people of West Germany, East Germany, Austria, and German-speaking Switzerland constitute a cultural community that is bound together not only by a common language but also by a common cultural legacy that the members of the community prize highly. German achievements in every field of artistic expression have contributed significantly to the mainstream of Western civilization, and German philosophers and scientists rank among the world's foremost. To list only a few of those who have made an impact on world history necessarily omits the names of many others whose contributions were also of great importance, but seven names serve to highlight past contributions that the modern German-speaking community remembers with fervent pride. The works of Martin Luther, Immanuel Kant, Ludwig van Beethoven, Johann Wolfgang von Goethe, Karl Marx, Sigmund Freud, and Albert Einstein may be expected to last as long as Western civilization.

The two Germanys came into being because the World War II Allies could not agree on reconstituting a government for all of Germany. The assembly that met in 1948 to formulate plans for a federal government in the American, British, and French occupation zones called itself the Parliamentary Council rather than a constitutional convention, and the document produced is known as the Basic Law rather than the constitution. These semantic maneuvers were designed to emphasize that the Basic Law was temporary and that a true constitution would be forthcoming after reunification of the country. The Parliamentary Council, with Konrad Adenauer as chairman, labored through the winter of 1948-49, finally agreeing on the document in late spring. The occupation authorities quickly approved the Basic Law, and it was promulgated on May 23, 1949 (see Federal Republic of Germany, ch. 1).

By means of the Occupation Statute of May 12, 1949, Britain, France, and the United States reserved to themselves rights in the fields of disarmament, displaced persons, foreign affairs, and reparations; in all other respects the new government was to exercise unfettered executive, legislative, and judicial powers. Elections to the Federal Diet (Bundestag) and appointments to the Federal Council (Bundesrat) took place in August 1949, and in September civil government was restored with Theodor Heuss as the first president and Konrad Adenauer as the first chancellor. Bonn was chosen as the capital of the new republic (see The Constitutional Framework and Federalism, ch. 7).

The Federal Republic, as it has since evolved, is made up of ten states (*Länder*, sing., *Land*) plus West Berlin, which is administered separately. The federal executive branch consists of the president as head of state, the chancellor as head of government, and several ministries or executive departments, the ministers of which form the chancellor's cabinet. The bicameral legislature consists of the Bundestag and the Bundesrat. The judiciary is a separate branch consisting of a Federal Constitutional Court and local, regional, and appeals courts. *Land* governments are assigned specific powers and functions by the Basic Law in order to avoid the extreme centralization of the Hitler era.

The president is elected by the Federal Convention (Bundesversammlung), which includes all members of the Bundestag plus an equal number of members chosen by the *Land* legislatures. The Bundesversammlung meets once every five years for the sole purpose of electing the president. The office of president as constituted by the Basic Law has more prestige than power; real political power is in the hands of the chancellor.

The chancellor is nominated by the president and must be confirmed by an absolute majority of the Bundestag. Customarily the chancellor is the leader of the party holding the majority of seats in the Bundestag or the leader of a coalition of parties holding such a majority (see The Government, ch. 7).

Adenauer, as leader of the strongest political party—the Christian Democratic Union (Christlich Demokratische Union—CDU)—ruled with a firm hand from 1949 to 1963 (see Adenauer Era, ch. 1). Reconstruction and economic recovery were the major problems facing the new chancellor, and the rebuilding of the entire country presented a truly monumental task. A combination of currency reform, United States Marshall Plan aid, and German determination brought about the spectacular recovery that the Germans labeled *Wirtschaftswunder* (economic miracle —see Growth and Structure of the Economy, ch. 4). Aside from his interest in the recovery of the domestic economy, Adenauer's special forte was in foreign affairs. Under the auspices of the American, British, and French high commissioners, who retained de jure control of foreign policy until 1955, Adenauer pursued an unwavering policy of making the new country a secure member of the Western economic and military alliances (see The North Atlantic Treaty Organization, ch. 8).

During his tenure as chancellor, Adenauer hewed to a close association with the West as the key to West German policy. As a function of that policy, Adenauer favored the economic integration of Western Europe and the rearmament of the Federal Republic. Under the Hallstein Doctrine, named for one of Adenauer's chief foreign policy advisers, Bonn refused to deal with any government that recognized East Germany. An exception was made in 1955 when Adenauer went to Moscow to establish formal diplomatic ties with the Soviet Union. In the same year, his government was granted full sovereignty by the Western Allies and became a member of NATO.

Under Adenauer's successors—Ludwig Erhard (1963–66), Kurt Georg Kiesinger (1966–69), Willy Brandt (1969–74), and Helmut Schmidt (1974–)—the strong orientation toward the West has continued. Overtures toward Eastern Europe were gradually increased, however, and during Brandt's term as chancellor, *Ostpolitik* (eastern policy) became a major component of the country's foreign policy. Brandt concluded treaties with the Soviet Union, Poland, and East Germany that recognized the de facto boundaries of the post-World War II era. Brandt's government also acknowledged that East Germany was a sovereign state, and in 1973 both Germanys gained admission to the United Nations (see *Ostpolitik* and Détente, ch. 8).

The most outstanding political feature of the Federal Republic has been the stability of its governments. From its founding in the fall of 1949 to early 1982, the country has been governed by only five chancellors. Although Brandt resigned in 1974 after one of his closest aides was exposed as an East German spy, the stability of the government was not threatened. The transfer of power to Schmidt was orderly and peaceful. This remarkable stability is in great contrast to the Weimar Republic, which during its fourteen years had twenty-one governments.

A major reason for the prolonged period of political stability has been the dominance of two major political parties and one minor party, as opposed to the six major parties and a myriad of minor ones that existed during the Weimar era. In early 1982 the larger of the two major parties continued to be the CDU/CSU, which consists of the CDU and the Christian Social Union (Christlich Soziale Union—CSU). The CSU maintains a separate organization and elects its own leadership, but it votes in the Bundestag with the CDU and is referred to as the "sister party" or "Bavarian wing" of the CDU. In the 1980 Bundestag elections the CSU leader, Franz-Josef Strauss, stood as the CDU/CSU candidate for the chancellor's post but was decisively defeated by Helmut Schmidt, the candidate of the other major party, the Social Democratic Party of Germany (Sozialdemokratische Partei Deutschlands—SPD). The SPD first entered the government as the junior member of the Grand Coalition under Kurt Georg Kiesinger (1966–69).

The only minor party to be represented in the Bundestag since 1961 has been the Free Democratic Party (Freie Demokratische Partei—FDP). Over the years it has participated in governing coalitions with one or the other major parties and since 1969 has been in coalition with the SPD. In exchange for its votes in the Bundestag, which provided the majority required to form the government, the FDP was awarded four cabinet positions in the Schmidt government, and in early 1982 the FDP leader, Hans-Dietrich Genscher, continued to serve as vice chancellor and foreign minister, positions he had held since mid-1974.

Another reason for continuing political stability has been the broad areas of agreement among the parties since 1959. Before that time the SPD had espoused a generally socialist economic program and had opposed many aspects of Adenauer's Western-oriented defense and foreign policies. The SPD fared poorly in the 1953 Bundestag election and even worse in the 1957 election. During its 1959 party congress the members therefore drastically altered the SPD political platform. In what became known as the Bad Godesberg Program, the SPD endorsed the concept of a regulated free market economy and the country's existing and expanding role in NATO. Three of the individuals most instrumental in securing the policy shift were Brandt, Schmidt, and Herbert Wehner, who in early 1982 were serving as party chairman, federal chancellor, and SPD leader in the Bundestag, respectively.

A broad political consensus did not preclude strong public political arguments and demonstrations. In October 1981, for example, unprecedentedly large crowds—including several SPD and FDP Bundestag members—participated in peace demonstrations protesting aspects of United States foreign military policy and the Schmidt government's seeming adherence to that policy. And in the aftermath of the December 1981 declaration of martial law in Poland, Schmidt's refusal to impose sanctions either on Poland or the Soviet Union was endorsed by many but also evoked criticism both from his political opponents and members of his own party.

In 1981 and early 1982 the country's economic situation was a serious political issue. Since 1979 a slump in industrial output was accompanied by growing inflation and unemployment. Unemployment had become especially troublesome and by January 1982 had reached 8.2 percent of the work force, which meant that 1.95 million people were out of work, the highest number in more than a quarter century.

In response to the worsening economic plight, Schmidt submitted to the Bundestag a DM12.5 billion (for value of the deutsche mark—see Glossary) program designed to generate employment. Among other things Schmidt's proposal called for bonuses to firms that increased their investments over the levels of the 1979–81 period, low-interest loans to small and medium-sized companies, government construction projects, and measures to stimulate private construction of housing. Schmidt asserted that the DM12.5 billion project, which would be funded by an increase in the value-added tax (VAT) on goods and services (up from 13 percent to 14 percent), would generate as much as DM40 billion in new investment in the 1982–86 period.

Schmidt's proposal elicited strong criticism, and he therefore called for a vote of confidence in the Bundestag, the first since he became chancellor in 1974. He won the vote on February 5 in a straight party-line vote; he received 269 votes—the SPD's 216 and the FDP's 53.

Schmidt's victory did not mean that there will not be further challenges to his government. The Basic Law provides that the Bundesrat may object to all legislation and that its acquiescence is required for money bills. If a majority of the Bundesrat opposes a bill, a majority of the Bundestag suffices to override the objection. If, however, two-thirds of the Bundesrat members oppose a measure, the votes of two-thirds of the Bundestag members are required to override. As the February 5 vote in the Bundestag made clear, the SPD/FDP coalition was far short of the two-thirds required.

The first of four *Land* elections scheduled for 1982 was held in Lower Saxony on March 22, and the results constituted a sharp setback for the SPD. The CDU increased its share of the vote from 48.7 percent in 1978 to 50.7 percent. The surprise of the elections was the success of Die Grünen (the Greens), which secured 6.5 percent of the vote, up from 3.9 percent in 1978 (see Minor Parties, ch. 7). The FDP garnered 5.9 percent compared with 4.2 percent in 1978. Various splinter parties received a few hundred votes each.

The CDU had been expected to win in Lower Saxony, but the poor showing by the SPD at once fueled new speculation about the upcoming elections in Bavaria, Hamburg, and Hesse. Bavaria was generally viewed as safe for the CSU. Before the Lower Saxony election most observers had opined that the June election in Hamburg was too close to call but predicted that the CDU would supplant the SPD in Hesse in September. After the election, observers predicted that the SPD would lose both Hamburg and Hesse, which would provide the CDU/CSU a majority of thirty-three to eight in the Bundesrat.

April 1, 1982

* * *

On September 17 the four FDP ministers in Schmidt's coalition government resigned their cabinet positions. On October 1 the Bundestag engaged in a "constructive vote of no confidence" and thereby replaced Schmidt with Helmut Kohl, who at age 52 became the Federal Republic's sixth and youngest chancellor (see The Government, ch. 7). Kohl at once formed a new cabinet, which consisted of eight members from the CDU, four from the CSU, and four from the FDP. Kohl appointed CDU member Manfred Woerner—a longtime adviser on foreign and defense policy—to the key post of minister of defense. FDP leader Genscher retained his posts of vice chancellor and foreign minister, and two FDP colleagues continued to head the ministries of economics and of food, agriculture, and forests. The FDP lost the powerful ministry of the interior, however. Friedrich Zimmerman, a close ally of CSU leader Strauss, was awarded that position. Zimmerman's first official act was to order the ministry's ten top civil servants to vacate their desks within hours, an act that seriously disturbed the country's press and civil rights advocates.

In his formal "Government Declaration" speech to the Bundestag on October 13, Chancellor Kohl made clear that West Germany's foreign policy would continue to focus on support for the Atlantic Alliance and the European Communities and close relations with the United States. He also stressed the importance of *Ostpolitik*, particularly trade with the Soviet Union and its East European allies.

On October 26 Schmidt announced that he would not be the SPD's candidate for chancellor in the next Bundestag election. Three days later the SPD leadership chose Hans-Jochen Vogel as its candidate. The 56-year-old Vogel had served for twelve years as mayor of Munich, over six years as Schmidt's minister of justice, and one year as the SPD leader in West Berlin. He was the first Roman Catholic, and also the first southerner, to lead the postwar SPD (see Social Democratic Party, ch. 7).

In mid-December Chancellor Kohl instituted the necessary parliamentary process for the calling of Bundestag elections (see The President, ch. 7). President Karl Carstens privately expressed some reservations about the technical constitutionality of the process, but because the political groups within the Bundestag endorsed the procedure, he issued the requisite papers specifying March 6, 1983, as election day. Throughout the fall of 1982 the public opinion polls had indicated countrywide support for the CDU/CSU among the country's approximately 43 million voters. On December 19, however, a special election in Hamburg revealed a resurgence of support for the SPD in that historically SPD state. The SPD candidates gained 51.3 percent of the votes cast, a significant improvement over the 42.7 percent they had garnered in the June 1982 election. The CDU secured 38.6 percent, down from its June 43.2 percent, and the Greens dropped from 7.7 percent to 6.8 percent. The FDP fell from 4.9 percent to 2.6 percent. The disastrous showing by the FDP candidates reflected, among other things, a split within the party and the secession of some members to form a new party. The members of the new party, who dubbed themselves Liberal Democrats, elected Ulrich Krüger as their leader.

Although in January 1983 most observers continued to predict a CDU/CSU victory in the March election, few discounted the possibility of a restoration to power of the SPD. In December 1982 unemployment reached 9.1 percent of the work force, and further increases in that thirty-four-year high were expected in February and March. Industrial workers registered 10.5 percent unemployed, more than double the rate for white-collar workers, and this could redound to the advantage of SPD candidates, who were campaigning vigorously on the jobs issue in an effort to recapture working class support. Foreign policy and related defense issues were widely and fiercely debated, but most observers believed that on March 6 most voters would make their decision on economic issues.

However the elections turn out, the government and the loyal opposition will confront numerous problems in the 1980s. By 1983 over half the population consisted of those born after Hitler's suicide in May 1945. Their expectations and world view differ markedly from those who participated in varying degrees in the policies and practices of the Third Reich. Whereas former Chancellor Schmidt publicly commented that his generation is unable to shed the burden of the past, those citizens born in the postwar period are less certain that they have an obligation to assume that burden.

Richard F. Nyrop

January 1983

Martin Luther

Chapter 1. Historical Setting

Historical Setting

THE FEDERAL REPUBLIC OF GERMANY (West Germany or Federal Republic) was established in May 1949, incorporating the post-World War II American, British, and French occupation zones. Shortly thereafter the German Democratic Republic (East Germany) was created from the Soviet Union's occupation zone. A divided Germany of the cold war era became the European pivot of the East-West conflict. In early 1982 West Germany remained critical to the functioning of the North Atlantic Treaty Organization, and East Germany continued its role as a key member of the Warsaw Pact.

The first West German government was formed by Konrad Adenauer, the leader of the Christian Democratic Union. Adenauer served as chancellor from 1949 to 1963, and throughout that period he remained firmly committed to a Western-oriented foreign policy and to German reunification on a democratic basis. The Soviet Union and its client state, East Germany, posed numerous challenges to Adenauer's policies, culminating in the construction in 1961 of the Berlin Wall, which sealed off East Berlin from the West. The Western powers accepted the Wall as a fait accompli and, consequently, Adenauer's principle of "negotiation from strength" received a serious blow. Willy Brandt and the Social Democrats gained power in 1969; in 1972 Brandt negotiated the Basic Treaty, which recognized the existence of two German states.

As a nation-state, Germany was not united until 1871. Authoritarian and militaristic Prussia subordinated the traditional German monarchical states, creating an empire headed by the Prussian king. Imperial Germany was consolidated politically on the basis of an alliance between landed aristocracy and the financial and industrial bourgeoisie. These groups launched the German pursuit of global politics, establishing overseas colonies and spheres of influence. The nationalistic sentiment of the masses was stirred by promises of world power status, and interest in domestic reform was diverted by the emphasis on foreign policy. Germany competed against Britain, France, and Russia to maintain its place within the European balance of power; competition and conflict culminated in World War I.

The Weimar Republic, established in 1918, represented the original attempt to institute democratic government in Germany. The Social Democrats proclaimed the republic, and in the throes of military defeat, the German people supported a democratic coalition cabinet. The republic's strong presidency, however, reflected the German authoritarian tradition. The Social Democrats allied with the military to suppress the radical-left, and significant social reform was never implemented. Within two years the Weimar coalition had lost its parliamentary majority, and in 1925 the public elected Paul von Hindenburg, former World War I army commander, to the presidency. During the depression years (1929–33) Adolf Hitler's National Socialists (Nazis) acquired a mass following, emerging in November 1932 as Germany's strongest political party. Hindenburg appointed Hitler to the German chancellorship in January 1933, thus enabling him accomplish the "legal revolution" that transformed Germany into a totalitarian dictatorship. The defeat of Hitler's Third Reich in World War II resulted in the division of Germany into the two states that continued to coexist in the early 1980s.

As of early 1982 Helmut Schmidt—member of the Social Democratic Party's conservative wing—had headed the Federal Republic's government since 1974. Social Democrats and Christian Democrats were generally reconciled on two major issues: a commitment to a pro-West foreign policy and to free enterprise. Schmidt introduced the slogan "German Model" (Modell Deutschland), emphasizing West Germany's economic strength and the domestic reform program. The international oil crisis of the mid–1970s, inflation, and slowed economic growth had by the early 1980s resulted in disappointed expectations, however. Manifestations of left-wing extremism, although minor, evoked public concern, as did demonstrations by a growing minority against what its adherents perceived as a present and growing nuclear threat to the nation's survival. These constituted challenges to a pro-Western foreign policy to which the major political parties were officially committed, and many foreign and domestic observers suggested that the country's foreign policy would remain a critical political issue for years to come.

Early History

Roman Period

Germanic tribes originally settled the territories of modern Germany during the final centuries of the pre-Christian era. Migrating from northern Europe, these tribes occupied the lands north of the Roman Empire, and in subsequent centuries German incursions into the empire alternated with Roman attempts to subjugate the people whom the Romans called barbarians. In the first century A.D. the Rhine-Danube was established as truce frontier, and the Romans constructed the limes, a line of fortifications that extended almost 500 kilometers along the frontier.

The collapse of Roman power enabled Germanic tribes to overrun the Western Roman Empire at will. Romulus Augustulus, the last Roman emperor, was deposed in A.D. 476 by Germanic soldiers. By the sixth century Germanic Lombards were settled in northern and central Italy, Anglo-Saxons in Britain, and Franks in

Gaul (France). The Frankish kingdoms later became the seat of a new western European civilization (see table A).

Medieval Germany

In A.D. 768 Charles the Great (Charlemagne) of the Carolingian Dynasty inherited the Frankish crown and a kingdom extending from central Germany to the Pyrenees. During his reign (768–814) Charlemagne subdued Bavaria, conquered Lombardy and Saxony, and established his authority in central Italy. On Christmas Day in the year 800 he was crowned Holy Roman Emperor by the pope in Rome. The Carolingian Empire represented the revival of the tradition of the Western Roman Empire, and in German historiography it later became known as the First Reich.

The Carolingian Empire was based on an alliance between the emperor, a temporal ruler supported by his military retinue, and the pope of the Roman Catholic Church, who granted spiritual sanction for the imperial mission. Charlemagne and his son, Louis the Pious, who reigned from 814 to 840, established centralized authority, appointed imperial counts as administrators, and developed a hierarchical feudal social structure headed by the emperor. Louis' death was followed by internecine warfare, however, and the Treaty of Verdun of 843 divided the empire among his three sons (see fig. 2). The future territories of Germany, France, and the Middle Kingdom (Italy, Burgundy, Provence, and Lorraine) were geographically and politically delineated.

The eastern Carolingians ruled in Germany. The imperial title, however, came to depend increasingly on rule over the Middle Kingdom (primarily Italy), and subsequent German kings struggled to perpetuate the empire. The German kingship was further weakened by the rise of new regional powers, particularly the five great duchies of Franconia, Saxony, Thuringia, Swabia, and Bavaria, which acquired the trappings of petty kingdoms. The ties of legitimacy were broken when the Carolingian line died out in 911, and future German kings faced the problem of asserting their power against the territorial dukes.

The Saxon and Salian (Franconian) dynasties dominated German politics during the tenth and eleventh centuries and reversed the particularist trend. The territorial dukes were subordinated by a monarchy that governed during the tenth century with major assistance from a German church that was subservient to the crown, and during the eleventh century governed through a developing Salian imperial administration. Trade was renewed and, accompanied by cultural advancement, introduced a new sense of affinity among the German provinces. The absorption of the German monarchy in conflicts with the dukes, however, resulted in the neglect of the nobles and freemen—neither bound by feudal ties—who were increasing their power and would later challenge the empire.

Federal Republic of Germany

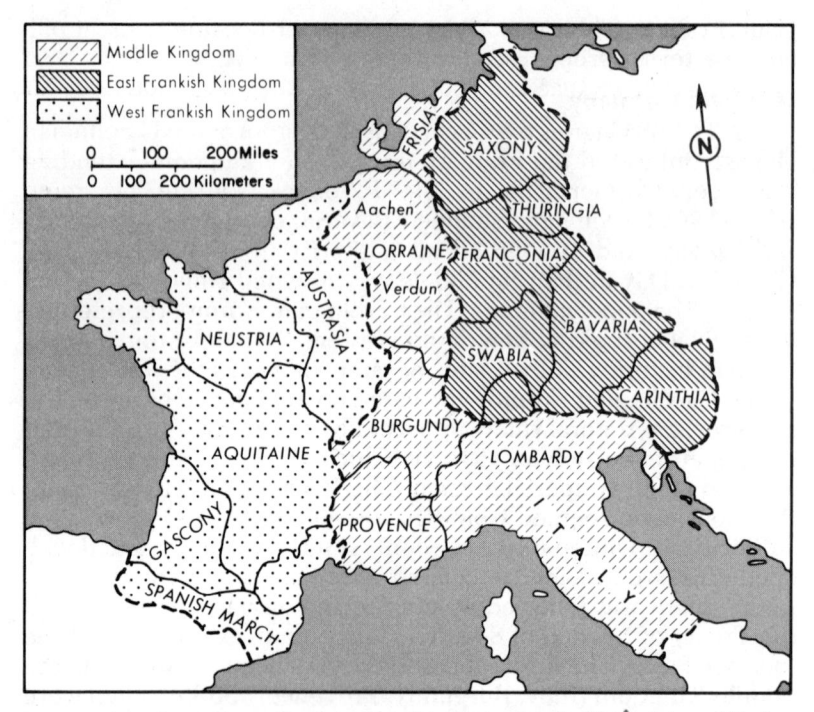

Figure 2. The Carolingian Empire Divided by the Treaty of Verdun

Source: Based on information from Geoffrey Barraclough, *The Origins of Modern Germany*, Oxford, 1949, p. 12.

The Saxon kings, who ruled from 919 to 1024, revived the idea of empire. They established the principle of hereditary succession and increased the crown lands, which were the foundation of monarchical power. They also encouraged eastward expansion and colonization. German rule was extended to the Slavic territories of Poland and Bohemia and to Austria. Otto I (the Great), who had halted the Magyar advance into Europe at the battle of Lech (near Augsburg) in 955, gained control of the Middle Kingdom and in 962 was formally crowned Holy Roman Emperor. Otto proclaimed the "Holy Roman Empire of the German Nation"; the German hold on Italy, however, waned in the eleventh century.

Under the Salian kings (Conrad II, Henry III, and Henry IV, ruling from 1024 to 1106) the German monarchy established itself as a major European power. The main Salian accomplishment was the development of a permanent administrative system based on a class of public officials who served the crown. Salian rule was challenged in 1075, however, by the Investiture Controversy—a

Historical Setting

papal-imperial struggle in which Pope Gregory VII demanded that Henry IV give up his rights over the German church. The pope further attacked the concept of divine right monarchy and gained the support of significant elements of the German nobility interested in delimiting imperial absolutism. Henry was forced to make his famous journey to Canossa in northern Italy in 1077 to do penance and receive absolution from the pope. Henry did not, however, renounce his imperial role as head of the German church, and the papal-imperial struggle was prolonged beyond the death of both opponents.

Because of the papal-imperial struggle, civil war wracked the German lands from 1077 until 1122, and disorder continued until the middle of the twelfth century and the rise of the Hohenstaufen Dynasty. The crown became dependent on the political support of vying aristocratic factions. Control of Italy was lost, and in Germany the princes—powerful nobles who took over administration and organized it around increasing numbers of castles—rose to power. The foundations of the territorial particularism characteristic of subsequent German history were laid during the civil wars. Feudalism advanced rapidly as freemen sought protection by swearing allegiance to a lord. As a result the princes acquired extensive territories and large military retinues. The monarchy lost its preeminence.

The reigns of the Hohenstaufen's Frederick Barbarossa (1152–90) and Henry VI (1190–97), however, were brilliant, but these were followed by a period of decline; the decline of the empire in the thirteenth century left Germany disunited and subject to control by territorial interests. Frederick I and Henry VI, however, were able to restore the empire and to extend it. Frederick pursued a vigorous policy and succeeded in establishing himself as head of a feudal social order. The towns simultaneously gained in economic strength, and eastward expansion was continued. Henry VI continued the Hohenstaufen policy, but his acquisition of Sicily by marriage encouraged later Hohenstaufens to ignore Germany and to focus on Italian politics. Frederick II's absorption in Italian affairs provided an opportunity for the German princes to extract far-reaching concessions. An imperial statute of 1232, for example, established both lay and ecclesiastical princes as virtually independent rulers within their territories. Frederick II's death was followed by the Great Interregnum (1250–72), a period of anarchy in which the German princes vied for control of German politics, and the Middle Kingdom was lost.

With the passing of the Hohenstaufens the empire entered a period of decline that lasted until its final dissolution by Napoleon in 1806. German emperors in the post-interregnum period had their power base in the dynastic principalities. The houses of Luxemburg (Bohemia), Wittelsbach (Bavaria), and Habsburg (Austria) alternated on the imperial throne; from the mid-fifteenth

Federal Republic of Germany

century the Habsburgs retained permanent possession of the imperial title. The Golden Bull of 1356, promulgated by the Luxemburg Emperor Charles IV (1355–78), provided the basic constitution of the German empire during subsequent centuries. The bull acquiesced in the reduction of imperial power by establishing the principle of elective monarchy and confirming the right of seven prince-electors to choose the emperor. The princes received additional protection in that the indivisibility of the principalities was guaranteed, and further, both nobles and towns were prohibited from organizing in opposition to princely hegemony. The Golden Bull paved the way for the political consolidation of the principalities, and by the close of the fifteenth century Germany consisted of a collection of sovereign states.

Reformation

On the eve of All Saints in 1517 Martin Luther, professor of theology at Wittenberg University in Saxony, posted his Ninety-five Theses concerning Vatican corruption—papal grants of mitigation of penalties, including release from purgatory—on the castle church door. Luther's critique of the sale of indulgences consisted of an attack on the secular orientation of the Roman Catholic Church. More fundamentally, Luther challenged the authority of pope and church in matters of faith, affirming instead the authority of holy scripture and ultimately, the word of God.

Luther's theses, posted originally to stimulate debate among academics and clergy, spread rapidly throughout Germany. In 1520 Luther published three revolutionary pamphlets: *Open Letter to the Christian Nobility of the German Nation*; *On the Babylonian Captivity of the Church*; and *On the Freedom of a Christian Man.* In these writings the theologian called for religious reformation and for the establishment of a German national church, independent of Rome. Luther was placed under ban by both Rome and the empire in 1521 but was given sanctuary by friends and supporters among the princes. The oppressed German peasantry read into Luther's religious reform a promise of social reform and rebelled against the princes in the Peasant War of 1524–25. Luther, relying on the nobility for support in his religious revolution, allied himself with the princes in their bloody suppression of the peasant revolt.

The Habsburg Emperor Charles V, who came to the throne in the midst of Luther's religious revolt, had inherited Spain, the Netherlands, southern Italy, Sicily, and the Austrian lands as his patrimony (see fig. 3). Emperor Charles was determined to restore the unity of the empire and to regain imperial control of the Middle Kingdom. Empire and Roman Catholic Church were mutually dependent and indissolubly linked; thus the protection of Rome became Charles' mission. Many German princes, on the other hand, favored Luther's doctrines, hoping to subordinate a

Town square in medieval city of Rothenburg
Courtesy Walter M. Callahan

Federal Republic of Germany

German national church to the authority of the sovereign states and thus further consolidate their power. German princes led the reform movement, creating the Protestant League of Schmalkalden in 1530 to oppose the emperor. By 1545 all northeastern and northwestern Germany and large parts of southern Germany were Protestant. In 1546 Charles V, formerly preoccupied by war against France over the Middle Kingdom and the Turkish menace in the east, declared war on the Protestant princes. The compromise Peace of Augsburg of 1555 represented a victory for the princes. Lutheranism and Catholicism were granted formal recognition in Germany, and each prince gained the absolute right to decide the religion to be practiced within his state.

Religious warfare revived in the early seventeenth century. In 1618 the Bohemian Kingdom, formally ruled by the Imperial House of Habsburg, elected Frederick of the Palatinate, a German Calvinist, to the throne. Imperial armies defeated the Bohemians at the Battle of the White Mountain, near Prague, in 1620. Protestant German princes, however, seized the opportunity to renew their struggle against the emperor. The Thirty Years' War (1618–48) developed into a Europe-wide war: Denmark, Sweden, and France took advantage of the German civil war to attack the empire. By the Peace of Westphalia of 1648 the emperor extended religious toleration to include Calvinism (founded by John Calvin in Geneva, Switzerland, in 1541).

Rise of Prussia

The Thirty Years' War devastated the Holy Roman Empire and effectively completed its disintegration. At the war's conclusion petty despots ruled over an impoverished aristocracy. Commerce, industry, and the middle classes were ruined. Peasant serfs, especially in northeastern Germany, had been subjected to heavy feudal obligations and lived in a state of absolute oppression. The empire ceased to play a role in European politics as Austria and Prussia rose to prominence, the latter to play the leading role in the creation of a German nation-state.

Prussia (officially so named in 1807) was formed as the result of territorial consolidations accomplished during the Thirty Years' War. The Hohenzollerns, a dynasty of the small Electorate of Brandenburg, made a series of agreements and acquired a string of heterogeneous principalities in northern Germany. Frederick William, the Great Elector (1640–88), succeeded in establishing absolute monarchical rule within this territory by making an alliance with the Junkers, the landed aristocracy. The Junkers composed the officer corps of the Prussian army, the buttress of the monarchy, and in turn were guaranteed the perpetuation of an agrarian economy based on serfdom.

The Hohenzollerns developed the Prussian bureaucracy as an organ of administrative centralization. King Frederick William I

(1713–40) formed a collegial General Directory and established both a civil and a military bureaucratic apparatus. The result was the emergence of two new and distinct status groups: the administrative government officials (*Beamtenstand*) and the military officers (*Offizierstand*), the latter recruited almost entirely from among the Junkers. The civil and military bureaucratic elite was able, to some extent, to usurp the local authority of the landed aristocracy.

The Prussian bureaucracy was intended to be completely subordinate to the will of the monarch. In the later eighteenth century, however, the bureaucratic elite, grown increasingly powerful, became concerned with mitigating Hohenzollern absolutism. Frederick II's (1740–86) policy of filling high positions in the civil bureaucracy with nobles made it easier for the Prussian bureaucracy to win the support of the local Junker squirearchy away from the king. During the Napoleonic era the military and civil bureaucracies established themselves as influential and independent political oligarchies.

German Confederation

Liberal Reform Movement

The Congress of Vienna (1814–15), convened after Napoleon's defeat, established a German Confederation of thirty-nine monarchical states, headed by Austria. Prince Klemens von Metternich, Austria's chancellor, presided over a confederation diet composed of monarchical delegates in which he defended a reactionary policy. Within the framework of the absolute states, however, the movement for liberal reform (including constitutional, parliamentary government; economic freedom; and civil liberties) initiated during the Napoleonic era survived: liberal aristocrats and high bureaucratic officials succeeded in obtaining limited reform. The July 1830 French revolution inspired the German liberal intelligentsia—lower government officials, men of letters, professors, and lawyers—to organize local clubs and assume leadership of the reform effort. The particular problem of German liberalism, however, consisted of the absence of a commercial and industrial bourgeoisie. The liberal intelligentsia gained power in March 1848 by means of an alliance with insurrectionary artisans and peasants, but the 1848 "revolution of the intellectuals" failed.

Delegates from all of the German states gathered in May 1848 in Frankfurt am Main—the Frankfurt Parliament—to make preparations for a united and constitutional German nation-state. The Frankfurt constitution, reflecting the majority moderate liberals' attachment to princely authority, established Germany as a federal union headed by a monarch (with imperial title), but Prussia's King Frederick William IV refused the imperial dignity. In the spring of 1849 the German monarchs turned against the liberals. The moderate liberals, who advocated laissez-faire policies, had

Federal Republic of Germany

Figure 3. Germany at the Time of the Protestant Reformation

Historical Setting

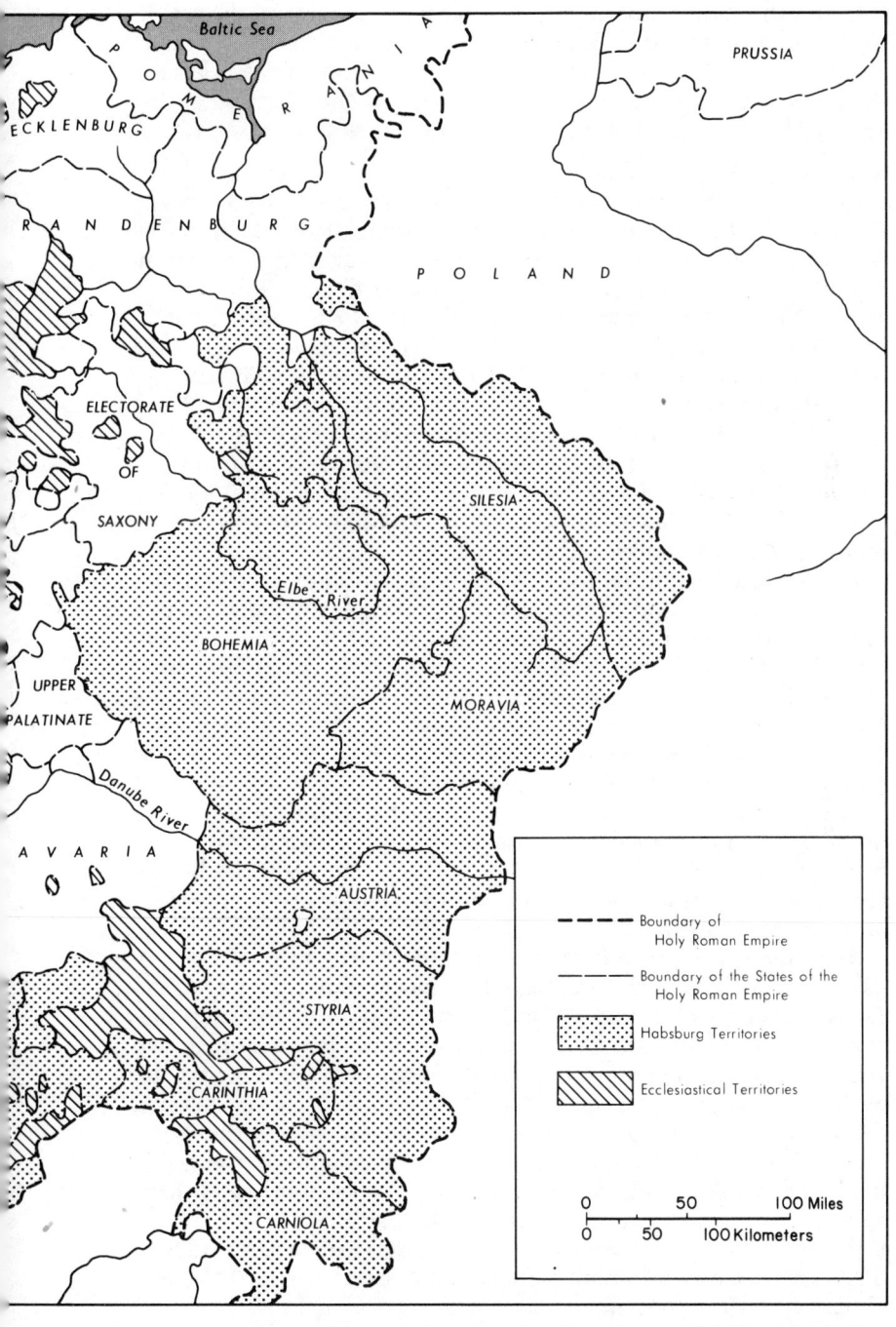

rejected the radical liberals' proposals for social reform; the resulting loss of artisan and peasant support for political liberalism facilitated the restoration of monarchical conservatism. Prussia led the struggle to restore monarchical authority in the German states, and in 1851 the German Confederation was renewed (see fig. 4).

Bismarck and Unification

In 1862 the Prussian King William (Wilhelm) I chose Otto von Bismarck as his prime minister. Of Junker ancestry, Bismarck favored absolutism less than he championed aristocratic hegemony; he was particularly fond of the Junker-dominated Prussian army. Bismarck had been elected to the new Prussian parliament in 1848 and from 1851 served as Prussian delegate to the German Confederation's diet (composed of monarchical representatives). As Prussian prime minister his main task became that of resolving the conflict between crown and parliament on the issue of military reform. Bismarck's solution consisted of a synthesis of Hohenzollern authoritarianism and the liberal program of national unification as the means to win liberal support in parliament. Bismarck's method was the "politics of power."

Upon his accession in 1861 William had announced a military reform to expand and strengthen the Prussian army, leading to a bitter conflict between crown and parliament. By the constitution of 1850, Prussia was established as a dualistic state with power divided between king and parliament, which consisted of the hereditary House of Lords and the elective Chamber of Deputies. The Prussian voting system, based on income, strongly favored upper class representation in the Chamber of Deputies and originally guaranteed Junker control. By the 1860s, however, a financial and industrial bourgeoisie had developed, and the chamber was dominated by liberals. From 1862 until 1866 the liberal faction voted against budget appropriations requisite for the military reform.

As William's prime minister it fell to Bismarck to reaffirm monarchical authority by breaking the parliamentary opposition. Toward that goal he asserted his famous *Lückentheorie* (gap theory), which maintained that in cases of conflict between crown and parliament the will of the former must prevail. During the parliamentary struggle of 1862–66 the *Lückentheorie* enabled the monarch to expend tax monies on the military without the approval of parliament. The enlarged Prussian army enabled Bismarck to initiate a policy of militarism that established Hohenzollern hegemony within a German nation-state.

Bismarck began by declaring war against Austria. As leader of the German Confederation, Austria functioned to protect the sovereignty of the German monarchical states. In June 1866 Bismarck demanded the annexation of Schleswig-Holstein (occupied by Prussia after a recent war) and met with Austrian resistance.

Historical Setting

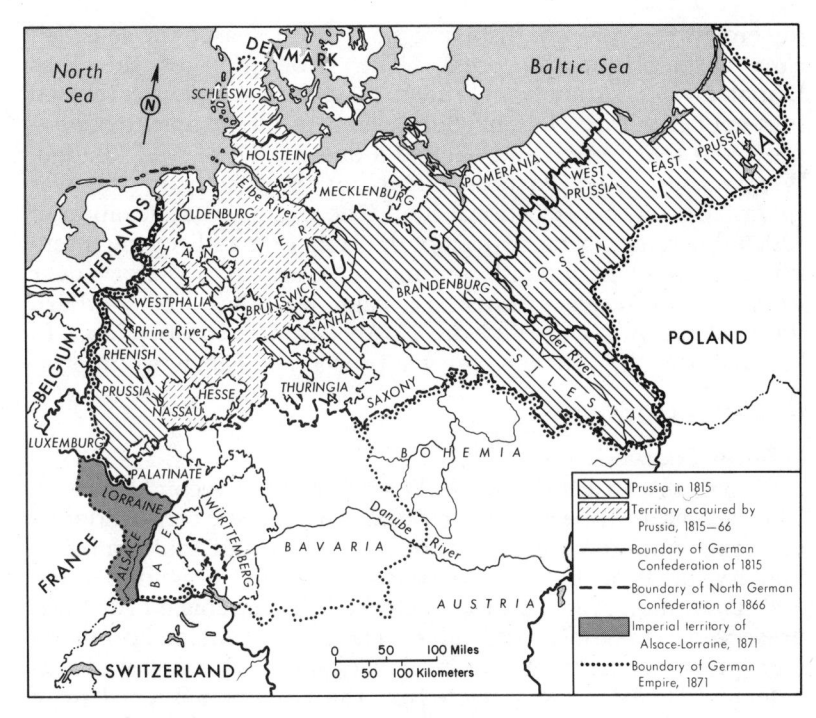

Source: Based on information from Geoffrey Barraclough, (ed.), *The Times Atlas of World History,* London, 1978, p. 216.

Figure 4. *The German Struggle for Unification, 1815–71*

Bismarck made Austria's rejection of Prussian annexationist ambitions into a pretext for war. The Seven Weeks' War, won by Prussia, resulted in the dissolution of the German Confederation and the exclusion of Austria from German politics. A constitutional North German Confederation, headed by the Prussian king, was established. The south German states—Baden, Württemberg, and Bavaria—remained autonomous but promised military allegiance to Prussia in time of war. William presented the Prussian parliament with the Indemnity Bill, which admitted past budgetary impropriety but requested after-the-fact approval. Moderate liberals, impressed by Bismarck's victory, helped pass the bill, thus retroactively approving the crown's illegal military expenditures of 1862–66.

Prussian militarism resumed in 1870. Bismarck deliberately provoked the Franco-Prussian War (1870–71) as the means to incorporate the particularist south German states within a constitutional German nation-state. In July 1870 the Spanish crown was offered to a Hohenzollern prince, but the French protested, and the crown was refused. Bismarck, however, released the so-called Ems Dispatch to the press. The publication of the Ems Dispatch—a telegram from William in which the monarch refused to renounce future Hohenzollern claims to the Spanish throne—provoked the French and elicited a declaration of war. Baden, Württemberg, and Bavaria joined enthusiastically in the war against Germany's traditional foe. The promised annexation of Alsace-Lorraine, formerly part of the Holy Roman Empire, intensified German nationalist sentiment. Germany's victory over France accomplished Bismarck's major war aim: the southern states voluntarily accepted the North German constitution. In January 1871 the Prussian king was proclaimed German emperor.

Imperial Germany
Political Consolidation

Bismarck's constitution of 1871 established the Second Reich—a German nation-state united on the basis of dualistic constitutionalism. The emperor controlled foreign policy and the combined military forces of the German states. Germany remained a federal union, however, and the aristocratic-monarchical order was preserved in the individual states. The Federal Council provided for representation by monarchical delegation. The Imperial Parliament (Reichstag) was elected on the basis of universal male suffrage. The constitution did not include a bill of rights.

Six major political groupings predominated: Conservatives, Free Conservatives, Catholic Center, National Liberals, Progressives, and Social Democrats. The Conservative Party—the party of Prussianism, aristocracy, and landed property—drew its support largely from territories east of the Elbe River (see fig. 7). The Free Conservative Party, pro-Bismarck, represented both nobles and industrialists. The Center Party, Catholic and conservative regarding monarchical authority, was nevertheless progressive in matters of social reform. The National Liberal Party, pro-Bismarck and moderate liberal, advocated constitutionalism, laissez-faire, secularization, and material progress. The Progressive Party, antiauthoritarian and democratic, championed the extension of parliamentary prerogatives. The Social Democratic Party (Marxists) was founded in Gotha in 1875: Ferdinand Lassalle's General German Workers' Association (1863), advocating state socialism, fused with the Social Democratic Labor Party (1869), headed by August Bebel and Wilhelm Liebknecht.

Bismarck's early policies favored the National Liberals who, in coalition with the Free Conservative and Progressive parties, constituted a parliamentary majority in 1871. The federal chancellery published a new commercial code, established a uniform coinage system, and founded imperial banks. The French indemnity payment of 5 billion francs provided capital for military expansion, railroad construction, and building projects. The Kulturkampf (ideological struggle) against the Roman Catholic Church resulted in the subordination of church to state and the secularization of the educational system. German financiers and industrialists, citizens of a potentially powerful nation-state and finally provided with a unified internal market, took ample advantage of investment opportunity. A speculative boom resulted, characterized by large-scale formation of joint stock companies and unscrupulous investment practices. The years 1871–73, known as the *Gründerzeit* (era of speculation), culminated in the stock market crash of 1873.

The crash of 1873 and the subsequent depression signaled the impending dissolution of Bismarck's alliance with the National Liberals. After 1873 the imperial government repudiated liberalism and abandoned free trade. Popular support for German liberalism also waned. Catholic opposition to the Kulturkampf strengthened the Center Party, doubling its popular vote in the Reichstag elections of 1874. In the later 1870s Bismarck began negotiations with the Conservative and Center parties (both protectionist in economic policy) toward the formation of a new government coalition. Conservative electoral gains and National Liberal losses in 1879 brought the Conservative bloc (Conservatives-Center-National Liberals) to power. A political program based on protectionism, primarily agricultural tariffs favoring East Elbian landowners, was drafted. The tariff law symbolized the consolidation of the domestic system on the basis of an alliance between the feudal and industrial classes.

Bismarck's Fall

After 1879 Bismarck struggled to defend the aristocratic-monarchical order. By royal decree in 1882 the king-emperor pronounced himself personally responsible for the direction of government policy. The Military Cabinet and the General Staff, by Bismarck's authorization, were elevated to the status of independent agencies responsible only to the emperor. In the Reichstag, however, the Conservative bloc soon dissolved, and the democratic opposition grew in strength. The dynamic industrialization of Germany after 1871 altered the political scene in the 1880s. German liberals abandoned authoritarianism: the Secessionists left the National Liberal Party and in 1884 united with the democratic Progressives, forming the German Free Thought Party. In addition the Social Democratic Party, led by Bebel, emerged as a political force.

Bismarck's desire to regain German liberal support resulted in the revival of *Machtpolitik* (power politics), and German nationalistic sentiment was stirred with promises of "world power" status. In the mid–1880s Germany joined the European powers in the scramble for overseas possessions, establishing colonies in

South-West Africa, East Africa, Togo, the Cameroons, and the South Sea Islands in the southwest Pacific Ocean. Simultaneously Germany became interested in maintaining its position within the European balance of power. The Bulgarian crisis of 1885–87, a clash between Austrian and Russian interests in the Balkans, provided the opportunity to install a progovernment majority in the Reichstag. Bismarck presented a new armaments bill. When the bill was rejected, he dissolved the Reichstag, called for new elections, and appealed to the German nation, claiming that Germany was threatened by both Austrian and Russian expansionism. In the Reichstag elections of 1887 the pro-Bismarck Conservative, Free Conservative, and National Liberal parties won 220 of 375 seats.

Bismarck's policies relating to the Social Democratic Party reflected the proverbial conservative fear of the masses. The Social Democrats had only minor representation in parliament (twenty-four seats in 1884), but the party grew steadily. Bismarck endeavored simultaneously to pacify and eradicate the Social Democrats. As early as 1878 Bismarck had introduced antisocialist legislation outlawing all Social Democratic workers' clubs, organizations, assemblies, and trade unions. The Social Democrats remained in parliament, however, and by means of the *Sozialdemokrat*, a party newspaper published in Switzerland, continued propaganda activity in Germany. After 1881 Bismarck's comprehensive social legislation (including sickness, accident, old-age, and disability insurance) won the Social Democrats to state socialism. Bismarck nonetheless presented a new antisocialist law in 1889 that included a provision for property expropriation on suspicion of subversive activity. The new German Emperor William (Wilhelm) II and the Reichstag opposed the bill; Bismarck, however, remained adamant. In the February 1890 elections the pro-Bismarck parties were decisively defeated and Bismarck, encouraged by William II, resigned.

Industrial Expansion

Imperial Germany industrialized rapidly, and by 1900 it was the foremost industrial power of Europe. Industrial development was accompanied by significant population growth, increasing from 40.9 million in 1870 to 49.5 million in 1890 and 67.8 million in 1914. Germans migrated to the urban and industrial areas west of the Elbe River, swelling the population of the Rhineland, Westphalia, and Saxony. In East Elbia—East and West Prussia, Pomerania, Brandenburg, Silesia, and the Mecklenburgs—the Junker grain producers engaged in scientific and technological farming and hired migrant workers from Russian Poland and Austrian Galicia to fill their demands for seasonal labor. Employment in the industrial and mining sectors had surpassed employment in agriculture by the turn of the century.

Neuschwanstein Castle, built by "Mad" King Ludwig of Bavaria
Courtesy Walter M. Callahan

German industrialization was sparked by the railroad building of the 1840s and the subsequent development of coal mining. Coal mining created new industrial districts, most significantly in the Ruhr and the Saar, and by 1913 Germany produced 191.5 million tons of coal yearly, far surpassing France's 40.8 million tons.

Iron ore extraction and, concomitantly, iron and steel production accompanied coal mining. Germany's acquisition of Lorraine in 1871, a territory rich in iron ore, doubled steel output between the 1880s and 1890s. By 1910 Germany produced nearly twice as much steel as Britain and almost 50 percent more pig iron than Britain.

Electrochemicals, however, took first place in German industry. Large salt and potassium deposits encouraged chemical manufacture including, by the 1880s, pharmaceuticals, dyestuffs, fertilizers, and ammunition. Hydroelectric power was developed chiefly by two Berlin combines, both formed in the 1880s: the Allgemeine Elektrizitäts-Gesellschaft and Siemens AG. In the last decade before World War I, Germany produced 50 percent of the world's electrical equipment (see Major Industrial Sectors, ch. 6).

Wilhelmine Era

The Wilhelmine Era (1890–1914), characterized by William II's predilection for military dress and military posturing, tells the story of Germany's road to war. Bismarck's successors as German chancellors—Leo von Caprivi (1890–94), Chlodwig zu Hohenlohe (1894–1900), Bernhard von Bülow (1900–09), and Theobald von Bethmann-Hollweg (1909–17)—each emphasized power, to be attained by increased armaments production; the creation of an ocean fleet; and a vigorous global foreign policy as the means to buttress absolutism, encourage political unity, and secure social peace. Colliding with similar designs in other European capitals, these policies culminated in World War I.

The Hohenlohe ministry was supported by the Conservative, Center, and National Liberal parties, the Junker Agrarian League, and the industrialists' Economic Union. All of these groups feared the Social Democrats despite the new revisionist policy adopted by the party. (Marxist revisionism, formulated by Edward Bernstein, advocated gradual socialization by parliamentary means.) *Weltpolitik* (global politics), which included the establishment of overseas colonies and the development of economic spheres of interest abroad, was championed as the means to satisfy German liberals and to divert popular attention from social reform. It was during Hohenlohe's chancellorship that Alfred von Tirpitz, Grand Admiral of the German navy, gained prominence with a new naval policy that increased the commitment to *Weltpolitik* and launched the German naval race against the British.

Tirpitz, founder of the modern German navy, advocated a policy of accelerated battleship construction to protect German interests abroad. Whereas German colonization had ended in the mid–1880s, the extension of German commercial and industrial interests proceeded apace, and Anglo-German conflicts of interest in Africa and the Far East were frequent. Tirpitz identified Britain as the enemy of German economic progress. He converted the Naval Office into a propaganda center, won the support of German industrialists, and made his naval policy into the cornerstone of German foreign policy. In 1898 the Reichstag passed the first Naval Bill. As a result Anglo-German relations deteriorated; overtures from Britain for the peaceful settlement of colonial issues were ignored.

Chancellor Bülow, friend and associate of Tirpitz, pursued *Weltpolitik* on a grand scale and in so doing fomented the formation of a new European alliance system. The Supplementary Naval Act of 1900 further strained relations with Britain. William II proposed a Baghdad Railway through the Ottoman Empire, a project that threatened British as well as Russian interests in the Balkans. Germany precipitated the Moroccan crisis of 1905. William II landed at Tangier and announced German support for Moroccan independence, thus challenging French predominance

Historical Setting

in the area. Britain supported the French claim to a sphere of influence in Morocco, however, and Germany was forced to back down. In 1907 Britain joined France and Russia in an alliance that became known as the Triple Entente.

The Bülow bloc (Conservatives, Free Conservatives, Agrarian League, National Liberals, Economic Union, and Progressives) won 216 parliamentary seats in 1907. Bülow's chancellorship, however, ended soon after, largely in consequence of the *Daily Telegraph* affair, a contest between emperor and chancellor. The *Daily Telegraph* affair raised the issue of imperial versus Reichstag authority. In November 1908 the London *Daily Telegraph* published an interview with William II quoting seriously offensive remarks made by the German emperor regarding Britain and Russia. The German public reacted with alarm, and Bülow confronted William, extracting his promise to consult the Reichstag before issuing public statements. William and the Conservative Party, however, subsequently withdrew their support from Bülow; the Bülow government collapsed.

The militarization of Wilhelmine society peaked during the chancellorship of Bethmann-Hollweg from 1909 to 1917. William II and Bethmann-Hollweg relied increasingly on the counsel of the German military chiefs; in the Reichstag the political weight shifted to the left as the Conservative Party lost influence. A second Moroccan crisis in 1911, involving the dispatch of the German gunboat *Panther* to the Moroccan port of Agadir, heightened tension between Germany and the Entente powers. The European powers nevertheless remained neutral during the Balkan Wars (1912–13), a nationalist rebellion against Ottoman rule. In 1913 the Reichstag, however, passed the new Army Bill, which enlarged the military; the Social Democrats supported the bill, thus indicating the party's decision to support German nationalism and the German pursuit of world power status. When the Austrian Archduke Franz Ferdinand was assassinated in Sarajevo, Bosnia, on June 28, 1914, Germany encouraged its ally, Austria-Hungary, to declare war on Serbia. By early August the European powers were involved in a world war.

Germany's conduct of the war in its early stages adhered to the Schlieffen Plan—the German military strategy prepared by Alfred von Schlieffen, chief of staff (1892–1906). The plan was based on the idea that Franco-Russian rapprochement made a German two-front war inevitable. Schlieffen's successor, Helmuth von Moltke the Younger (1906–14), was firmly committed to the plan. Thus Germany's declaration of war on Russia (August 1), a response to Russian mobilization, was followed immediately by its declaration of war against France (August 3). On August 4 Britain, the third member of the Triple Entente, declared war on Germany. Italy, which had been allied with Germany and Austria-Hungary, switched allegiance and joined the Entente powers in 1915.

Federal Republic of Germany

World War I

The German military implemented the Schlieffen Plan. Its strategy conceived a swift victory in the west wherein German troops entering France via neutral Belgium would envelop the French armies, pinning them against the Swiss frontier. The bulk of the German army would then be free for combat in the east. Total victory within four months was expected. The plan failed, however, leaving German troops stalemated in trench warfare in France. As a result Chief of Staff Moltke, who had at first altered the Schlieffen Plan and later abandoned it, was relieved of his executive position in September 1914 and was succeeded by Erich von Falkenhayn. On the eastern front German armies commanded by Paul von Hindenburg and Erich Ludendorff achieved significant advances. Conflict raged between Falkenhayn, who insisted on continued efforts in the west, and the eastern command.

Bethmann-Hollweg's September Program of 1914 set forth Germany's war aims, which included an expanded German *Mitteleuropa* with Belgium and Poland as vassal states and German colonies in central Africa. The program reflected a domestic political climate in which the German nation had been virtually unanimous in supporting the decision to go to war. When the Reichstag voted in favor of war credits in August 1914, even the Social Democrats voted yea. The Reichstag was controlled during the first years of war by the *Kriegszielmehrheit* (war aims majority), a parliamentary bloc including National Liberal, Center, and Conservative party delegates. The *Kriegszielmehrheit* had pressed for an annexationist war aims program; influential German interest groups like the Pan-German League, the army and navy, agrarian and industrial associations, and the intelligentsia approved. The Social Democratic Party alone remained adamantly opposed to all annexationist claims. Social Democrats and the Center and Progressive parties demanded domestic democratization and the abolition of the Prussian suffrage system (see Bismarck and Unification, this ch.).

By late summer 1916, however, the chances for a definitive German victory seemed remote, and consequently Bethmann-Hollweg considered peace negotiations. He met with opposition from the Army High Command, now headed by Chief of Staff Hindenburg and his adjutant-general, Ludendorff. The chancellor's peace note, drafted in August 1916, which included the renunciation of all German claims against Belgium, was modified at Hindenburg's insistence to leave German war aims undefined. Hindenburg further insisted on the continued exploitation of Belgium and Poland for the German war effort. The Entente powers responded by refusing to start peace negotiations. The Army High Command was determined to fight on and demanded passage of an Auxiliary Service Bill calling for the large-scale militarization of German society; the Reichstag passed a considerably weakened version of the bill. Discord between Bethmann-Hollweg and Hindenburg intensified.

The Army High Command increasingly gained control of political decisionmaking, but in the Reichstag pressure for a peace settlement mounted. In January 1917 Hindenburg and Ludendorff appealed directly to the emperor and won his approval to begin unrestricted submarine warfare. Bethmann-Hollweg attempted to pacify the Reichstag opposition with a renewed pledge of democratic reform. The Russian Revolution of March 1917, however, sparked the first workers' strike in Germany. The United States declared war against Germany in April. William II grew seriously concerned regarding possible social revolution and thus issued his famous *Ostergeschenk* (Easter message) confirming Bethmann-Hollweg's promise of reform. The Social Democrats nevertheless proceeded to issue a manifesto demanding peace without annexations. A group of Independents split from the Social Democratic Party and fomented public demonstrations against the war. (The Independent Party included the revolutionary Spartacist League, led by Karl Liebknecht and Rosa Luxemburg.)

Hindenburg and Ludendorff remained committed to war and annexation, and in April-May of 1917 they met with William II at Kreuznach and persuaded the emperor to draft the Kreuznach claims confirming the goals of the September Program. Bethmann-Hollweg and the Reichstag rejected the Kreuznach claims, however, and an interparty Reichstag committee representing the Center, National Liberals, Progressives, and Majority Socialists drafted a resolution in July demanding peace without annexations. Hindenburg and Ludendorff expressed their opposition by resigning their posts. William II was now compelled to choose between Bethmann-Hollweg and the Army High Command; he supported Hindenburg and Ludendorff and demanded the chancellor's resignation. In July 1917 Hindenburg and Ludendorff gained de facto control of political decisionmaking.

Germany fought on. Russia started peace negotiations after the Bolshevik Revolution of November 1917 and signed the Treaty of Brest-Litovsk in March 1918. On the western front, however, the battle continued to rage. Germany launched a major offensive in the west in the spring of 1918, but by June a German military defeat seemed imminent. Hindenburg and Ludendorff remained enthusiastic, nevertheless, and repeated German annexationist demands. In the early fall of 1918 after the collapse of the German front in the Balkans, the Army High Command finally conceded and called for an armistice. The armistice, however, signed on November 11 after the Social Democrats had proclaimed a republic and formed a government, was subsequently repudiated by the military. The German military—known in the postwar

Federal Republic of Germany

period as the Old Army—invented the legend of the "stab in the back," blaming the World War I defeat on the left-wing November Revolution (see Weimar Republic, 1918–33, this ch.).

The Treaty of Versailles of June 1919 called for German disarmament: (Germany was permitted to retain a small army of 100,000 men and minimal weaponry.) The Rhineland was demilitarized and submitted to occupation by the Western Allied powers for fifteen years. Germany ceded Alsace-Lorraine, the Polish Corridor, northern Schleswig-Holstein, and all overseas colonies. The Allied Reparations Commission was established and assumed responsibility for deciding the total war damage payments to be demanded of Germany. The Versailles Treaty also included the famous "war guilt clause" which, by its implicit suggestion of German responsibility for World War I, evoked German contempt for the treaty.

The War Guilt Debate

The question of Germany's responsibility for the war continues to be debated among German historians. Post-World War I German historians argued that Germany's entry into the war was both accidental and defensive. In 1961, however, German historian Fritz Fischer published *Griff nach der Weltmacht (Germany's Aims in the First World War)*, setting forth a controversial thesis regarding both the origins of World War I and of Germany's continental imperialism. Fischer's thesis, which contradicts the traditional German denial of responsibility for World War I, unleashed a new and continuing "war guilt debate." *Krieg der Illusionen (War of Illusions)*, published by Fischer in 1969, represents an effort to strengthen his original argument.

The Fischer thesis reinterprets the July crisis of 1914; it argues that Germany deliberately exploited the Sarajevo incident to incite an "apparently defensive" major European war. Traditional German historiography, by contrast, maintains that Germany's posture in 1914 was defensive and its entry into war accidental. It offers the following scenario of events: Germany encouraged its ally Austria-Hungary to declare war on Serbia merely in order to preserve its great power status. It anticipated a limited Balkan war. Russian mobilization, however, forced Germany to enter the war. Germany's subsequent declaration of war on France was the result of the Schlieffen Plan and the fear of encirclement by the European powers.

Griff nach der Weltmacht focuses on Bethmann-Hollweg's September Program of 1914 and its imperialist aims. Fischer's affirmation of German "war guilt" is based on the contention that Germany desired war in 1914 in order to realize the *Mitteleuropa* concept. He argues, using documents from the Imperial and Prussian archives, that Germany's commitment to *Weltpolitik* in 1897 included a commitment to establish a Greater Germany. The goal of a Greater Germany, in turn, could be accomplished only by means of war against France and Russia. The Moroccan crises of 1905 and 1911 heightened German nationalist sentiment. William II's War Council of 1912 recommended preparation for a military showdown; Bethmann-Hollweg approved the decision. The Sarajevo incident, Fischer concludes, provided the occasion for war and for the realization of Germany's long-standing goals.

Fritz Fischer, writing in the Western tradition of liberal historiography, is concerned to refute the German school of apologists for the Wilhelmine Empire. He associates German imperialism with the unique conservative-monarchical German social order and suggests continuity between pre-World War I Germany and Hitler's Third Reich. It remains to be shown, however, that Wilhelmine aspirations were indeed qualitatively different from the pre-World War I imperialist ambitions of Britain or France.

Weimar Republic, 1918–33

Weimar Constitution

The Weimar Republic, proclaimed on November 9, 1918, was born in the throes of military defeat and social revolution (see fig. 5). The November Revolution (a succession of bloodless coups) deposed monarchical and state governments throughout Germany, replacing them with revolutionary workers' and soldiers' councils. The November 9 Spartacist revolt in Berlin forced William II's abdication. The Social Democrats in the Reichstag seized the opportunity to demand the reins of government: they then proclaimed the republic, formed a provisional cabinet, and organized the National Assembly. Meeting in Weimar in February 1919, the National Assembly elected Social Democrat Friedrich Ebert to the presidency and drafted a constitution.

The Weimar Constitution of 1919 established a federal republic, headed by a strong president who was to be elected for seven years. The president appointed the chancellor and based on the chancellor's nominations also appointed the cabinet ministers. He retained authority to dismiss the cabinet, dissolve the Reichstag, and veto legislation. The Reichstag's legislative powers were also weakened by the provision for presidential recourse to popular plebiscite. Article 48 (the so-called emergency clause) accorded the president dictatorial rights to intervene in the territorial states for the purpose of enforcing constitutional and federal laws and/or to restore public order.

The constitution provided for the legislative assembly (Reichstag) and the council of German states' representatives (Reichsrat). The Reichstag elected by popular suffrage, voted on legislation introduced by the chancellor. By a vote of no confidence it could, however, call for the dismissal of both chancellor and cabinet ministers. The Reichsrat, established to guarantee state govern-

Federal Republic of Germany

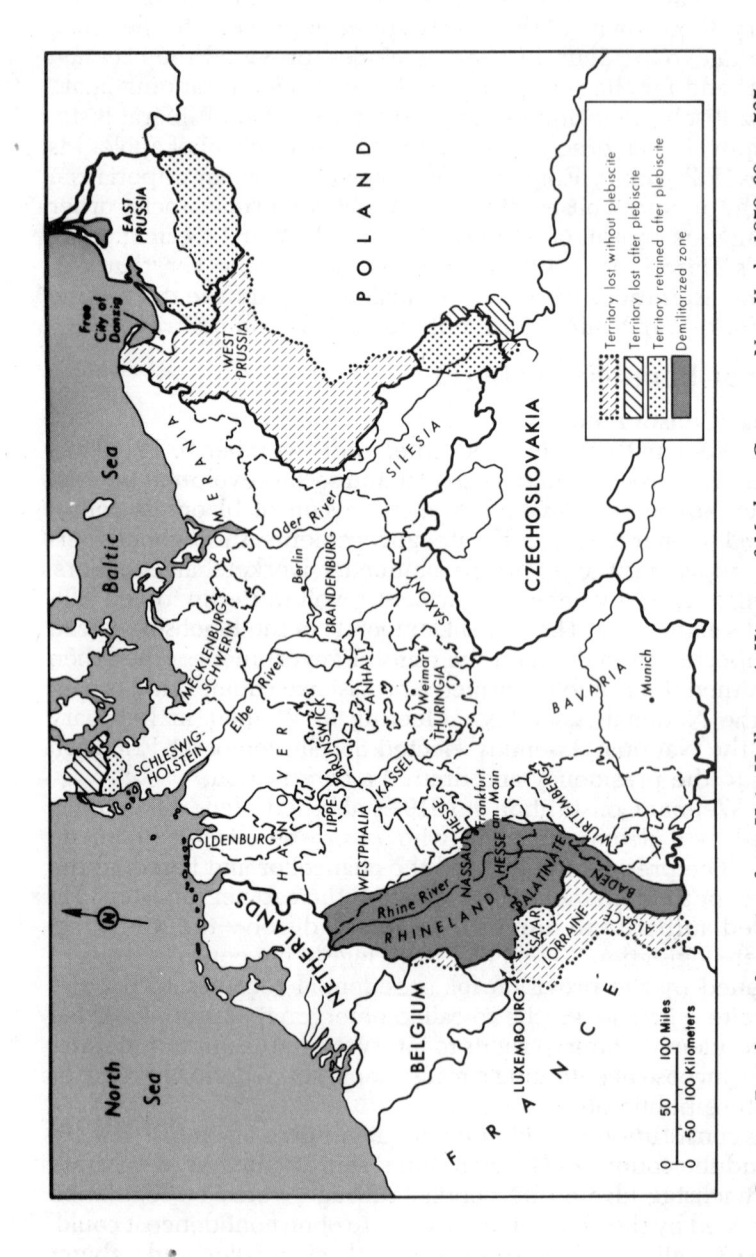

Source: Based on information from Hajo Holborn, *A History of Modern Germany*, New York, 1959–69, p. 535.

Figure 5. *The Weimar Republic, 1918–33*

ment supervision of national legislation, was nevertheless subordinated to national control—members of the Reichstag cabinet convened and presided over Reichsrat sessions. The Reichstag was empowered to override Reichsrat opposition with a two-thirds majority vote.

Thus the constitution established a republic based on a combination of conservative and democratic elements. The strong presidency reflected the nineteenth-century conservative and liberal predilection for monarchical rule. The Old Army and the bureaucracy (the traditional pillars of conservatism) were retained and the territorial states preserved. The Reichstag was strengthened, however, by the democratization of suffrage, and both the military and the bureaucracy were subordinated to cabinet control. The constitution guaranteed civil liberties, but provisions for social legislation, including land reform and limited nationalization, were never implemented.

Problems of Parliamentary Politics

The Weimar Republic represented a compromise—German conservatives and industrialists transferred power to the Social Democrats in order to avert a possible Bolshevik-style takeover; the Social Democrats, in turn, allied with the Old Army to suppress the revolution. The January 1919 National Assembly elections produced the Weimar Coalition, including the Social Democratic Party of Germany (Sozialdemokratische Partei Deutschlands—SPD), the German Democratic Party (Deutsche Demokratische Partei—DDP), and the Center. The democratic Weimar Coalition gained 76.2 percent of the vote (38 percent for the SPD), thus suggesting broad popular support for the republic. The antirepublican conservative German National People's Party (Deutschnationale Volkspartei—DNVP) and German People's Party (Deutsche Volkspartei—DVP), composed of former National Liberals, received only 10.3 percent. Yet the lifespan of the Weimar Coalition was brief, and Weimar politics soon became radicalized, achieving gains for both extreme left and extreme right.

The future of the Weimar Republic was shaped during the critical year separating the National Assembly elections and the June 1920 Reichstag elections. German public opinion was influenced by three major developments. First, the Treaty of Versailles shocked German nationalists and seriously damaged the republic's prestige. The treaty's provisions for Allied occupation of the Rhineland and reparations were considered unduly harsh. Second, the Weimar Constitution disappointed German workers' hopes for social reform. Third, the Kapp Putsch of March 1920 terminated the alliance between the Old Army and the republic and provided impetus for political radicalization. Wolfgang Kapp's right-wing coup was aborted by the communists, thus lending prestige to the Communist Party of Germany (Kommunistische Partei Deutschlands—KPD), which had been formed in December 1918. The army supported the coup and, after it failed, allied with rightist paramilitary groups like the DNVP Stahlhelm (Steel Helmet) and Adolf Hitler's Storm Troops (Sturmabteilung—SA).

In the June 1920 elections the Weimar Coalition lost its majority, polling only 47 percent of the vote. DNVP and DVP electoral success (28.9 percent) reflected German middle-class disillusionment with democracy. SPD strength fell to 21.7 percent as the German working class defected to the extreme left. The Independent Social Democratic Party split as most Independents joined the KPD and the remainder reunited with the SPD.

The Weimar Coalition never regained its majority, and after 1920 the era of unpopular minority cabinets began. Postwar inflation and Allied demands for reparations contributed to political instability. In January 1923 French and Belgian troops occupied the Ruhr district. The occupation of the highly industrialized Ruhr represented sanctions against German defaults in reparations payment. The Weimar government responded by calling the Ruhr population to passive resistance—stopping all industrial activity. In the summer of 1923 Gustav Stresemann (DVP chairman) was asked to form a new cabinet coalition to resolve the crisis.

Stresemann Era

Stresemann typified the Weimar *Vernunftrepublikaner* (commonsense republican); as a former National Liberal and annexationist he supported the republic for pragmatic reasons. During his brief chancellorship (August-November 1923) he headed the "Great Coalition," an alliance including the SPD, Center, DDP, and DVP. When his chancellorship ended, he served as German foreign minister until his death in 1929. The Stresemann era (1923–29) was a period of rapprochement with the West, during which he terminated passive resistance in the Ruhr. As foreign minister he pursued negotiations rather than confrontation with the Allies. His policy, however, was strongly opposed both by DNVP and by the communists.

A plan for German economic recovery prepared by the American financier (and later vice president), Charles G. Dawes, was adopted in 1924. The Dawes Plan attempted to coordinate German reparations payments with a program of economic recovery whereby Germany was required to make only limited payments until 1929. The Reichsbank was founded, and foreign credit, mainly from the United States, was filtered into Germany. As a result German industry and commerce made unprecedented progress between 1924 and 1929, and both living standards and real wages rose steadily. Soon after the adoption of the Dawes Plan, French and Belgian occupation troops left the Ruhr district.

Historical Setting

In 1925 President Ebert died, and the German people elected their national war hero, Paul von Hindenburg.

The Locarno Treaties, signed in 1925 by Germany and the Allied powers, guaranteed the western frontier as defined by the Versailles Treaty and accepted the demilitarization of the Rhineland. Both Britain and Germany, however, preferred to leave open the question of the eastern frontier. The Locarno Treaties were prerequisite for Germany's admission to the League of Nations in 1926. The Treaty of Berlin with the Soviet Union was signed that same year. All Allied troops were withdrawn from the right bank of the Rhine in 1925–26.

The Locarno Treaties, the Treaty of Berlin, and Germany's membership in the League of Nations were successes that earned Stresemann world renown. The Young Plan of 1929, named for American lawyer and businessman Owen D. Young, formulated the final reparations settlement. Germany agreed to a fifty-nine-year schedule of payments averaging approximately 2 billion marks yearly. The Bank of International Settlement was established to facilitate transactions. The Allies, in turn, promised to complete the evacuation of the Rhineland.

Weimar Culture

The Weimar Republic represented the original effort to establish constitutional liberal democratic government in Germany. Symbolically the republic's name evoked memories of Weimar's native son and German literary giant, Johann Wolfgang von Goethe, and of the nation's humanistic cultural traditions. Goethe's Weimar was contrasted with the Prussian Germany of authoritarianism, military swagger, and foreign adventure. The typical German, however, remained attached to the old order and lacked a genuine commitment to republican ideals. Radical opposition resorted to revolutionary tactics. German culture under the republic reflected the ideological diversity of a politically fragmented society. Weimar culture also expressed the German longing for social harmonization.

The Warburg Library (Hamburg), the Psychoanalytic Institute (Berlin), the German Academy for Politics, and the Marxist Frankfurt Institute for Social Research were founded soon after World War I. These institutions, dedicated to the critical analysis of political and social values, reflected the concern of Weimar intellectuals to reconsider the German past. Eckart Kehr's *Schlachtflottenbau und Parteipolitik* (*Battleship Construction and Party Politics*), published in 1930, pursued the same critical objective. Kehr cast Wilhelmine policies in a negative light, revealing the domestic socioeconomic basis for German naval policy.

The cult of the hero nevertheless survived. The poet Stefan George's literary society, known as the George Circle, published poetry and translated the classics. The George Circle's aristocratic mentality, however, displayed itself most ostensibly in a predilection for biography. Ernst Kantorowicz's *Emperor Frederick II*, a biography of the thirteenth-century Hohenstaufen, received widespread public acclaim. Kantorowicz, a former Prussian army officer, described the Weimar Republic as the triumph of mediocrity; his preface spoke of Germany's secret longing for its emperors and heroes. Frederick II was mythically portrayed as a superman defiant of all authority and voraciously eager to taste all of life.

German Expressionism was the movement of radical leftist intellectuals. Expressionists had defended the November Revolution and developed the theme of revolution in terms of the son's rebellion against paternal authority, e.g., Walter Hasenclever's play—*Der Sohn*—published in 1914. Their rejection of realism in painting reflected their repudiation of reason in politics. Wassily Kandinsky's abstract paintings, characterized by bold colors and aggressive lines, are expressionist. In search of a new humanity, the Expressionists made the social outsider the hero—the stranger, the prostitute, the suicide. George Grosz, for example, drew fat industrialists and war profiteers, but also coquettish prostitutes and maimed veterans. The German Expressionist movement subsided after 1924, reflecting the republic's success in suppressing the radical left.

The dilemma of the Weimar intellectual can be approached through the novelist Thomas Mann. Mann was a monarchist before World War I, a commonsense republican after the war, and in the mid–1920s finally made a genuine commitment to the republic. In 1924 he published *Der Zauberberg* (*The Magic Mountain*) a novel describing Hans Castorp's education through life. Castorp visits his tubercular cousin in a Swiss sanatorium, contracts the disease himself, and stays for seven years. The sanatorium represents a simulacrum of European civilization where Castorp is exposed to a variety of political ideologies, including enlightened liberalism. Significantly Castorp (and Thomas Mann) cannot choose liberalism. Love, not reason, the novel concludes, will provide the basis for social reconciliation.

After 1929 Hitler's National Socialism offered a different solution. The Nazi Party took full advantage of political instability and economic depression, launched a large-scale propaganda campaign, and won a mass following. Nazi ideology, authoritarian but promising social revolution, appealed particularly to German youth, who longed for the restoration of order.

Hitler and the Rise of National Socialism

Hitler was born in the Austrian border town of Braunau am Inn in 1889, the son of an Austrian customs official. The family moved to Linz, Austria, in 1894, and at age seventeen Hitler, a mediocre student, sought admission to the Vienna Art Academy and was refused. He remained in Vienna, living a Bohemian existence, until 1917 when he moved to Munich. Hitler joined the German army; he attained the rank of corporal, experienced military authority and discipline, and suffered the disillusionments of defeat. In 1919 Hitler joined the right-wing Bavarian German Workers' Party; the following year the party changed its name to National Socialist German Workers' Party (Nationalsozialistische Deutsche Arbeiterpartei—NSDAP—known as Nazis, a term derived from the German pronunciation of "National"). Hitler assumed the leadership of the NSDAP in 1921.

Hitler established himself as führer (leader) of the NSDAP, reorganized the party on a military command basis, and encouraged the assimilation of other radical right groups. He was assisted in his efforts by Ernst Röhm, Dietrich Eckart, and Alfred Rosenberg. Röhm's SA constituted Hitler's private army. Eckart published the *Völkischer Beobachter*, the official party newspaper. Rosenberg, the party ideologist, developed slogans and symbols and conceived the swastika, the future emblem of the Third Reich. National Socialists denounced the republic and the "November criminals" who had signed the Versailles Treaty. The postwar economic slump won the party a considerable following among unemployed ex-soldiers, the lower middle class, and small farmers; in 1923 membership totaled 55,000. Hitler's "beer hall putsch" of November 1923, an attempt to overthrow the Bavarian government, failed, and the führer was imprisoned until December 1924. In prison he wrote *Mein Kampf*, the Nazi ideological tract.

After the failure of the 1923 putsch, Hitler decided on "legal revolution" as the road to power and then pursued a double aim. First, Nazi propaganda was employed to create a national mass party capable of taking power through electoral successes. Second, the party developed a bureaucratic structure and prepared to assume the functions of the state. From 1924 numerous Nazi cells sprang up in parts of northern Germany—Schleswig-Holstein, Lower Saxony, Brandenburg, Lower Silesia, Saxony, and East Prussia. The northern groups were consolidated with the Munich-Bavarian party core. The NSDAP bureaucracy was established in 1926. It consisted of a Reich directorate (modeled on the Reichstag cabinet) and state-like ministries heading departments. The SA was subordinated to centralized political control and functioned primarily to train party members and to supervise the Hitler Youth (Hitler Jugend). Postwar youth and university students increasingly formed the core of the NSDAP membership. In 1927 the NSDAP organized the first Nuremberg party congress, a mass political rally. By 1928 party membership exceeded 100,000; the Nazis, however, polled only 2.6 percent of the vote in the May Reichstag elections.

The NSDAP, a mere splinter party in 1928, began its rise to power the following year. The original breakthrough was the July 1929 alliance with the DNVP. Alfred Hugenberg, DNVP chairman, arranged the alliance for the purpose of launching a plebiscite against the Young Plan on reparations. Hugenberg considered Hitler a useful drummer who would attract the masses. The DNVP-NSDAP union, however, brought the National Socialists within the framework of a socially influential coalition of the antirepublican right. Hitler's party acquired respectability and—of greater long-range significance—access to financial resources from among the industrialists.

The 1929 economic depression, greatly augmenting political and social instability, assisted the Nazi propaganda effort. German unemployment figures reached 3 million in 1930 and exceeded 6 million during the winter months of 1931–32 and 1932–33. The Nazis exploited the opportunity, making an intensified appeal to the unemployed middle-class urban and rural masses and blaming the Versailles Treaty and reparations for the developing crisis. Nazi propaganda attacked the Weimar political "system," the "November criminals," Marxists, internationalists, and Jews.

Nazi ideology, a blend of conservative and revolutionary elements, consisted of four basic tenets. First, the authoritarian state was glorified. Second, imperialistic nationalism involving continental expansion to acquire living space (lebensraum) constituted the primary Nazi goal. Third, the racist concept of the "superiority" of the so-called Aryan people requiring defense against foreign intrusion, i.e., Jews, was proclaimed. (Austrian and German conservative political parties had emphasized anti-Semitism since the late nineteenth century.) Fourth, the Nazis promised a nationalist-statist form of socialism.

The cabinet crises of the depression years led to increased experimentation with authoritarian methods of rule, which paved the way for Hitler's accession to power. Hindenburg appointed chancellors whose policies favored the right. The electoral decline of the DNVP during the depression left these men with inadequate Reichstag support. They remained in office at the will of Hindenburg and the Army High Command. The SPD, the strongest Reichstag party until July 1932, was never offered the chancellorship.

In the spring of 1930 Hindenburg asked the Center deputy Heinrich Brüning to form a government. As chancellor, Brüning used Article 48 and the presidential decree to implement his policies but met with Reichstag opposition. He dissolved the Reichstag in July and called for new elections in the fall, hoping to form a German Nationalist-Center coalition. The economic depression, however, favored the extremist parties only. The Nazis won 18.3

percent of the vote and emerged suddenly as the second strongest Reichstag party (following the SPD, which had 38.2 percent). The Communist Party polled 13.1 percent of the vote. The DNVP was devastatingly defeated in the elections; in 1931 German Nationalists allied with the Nazis in the Harzburg Front coalition. (The Harzburg Front was named after Bad Harzburg, where the meetings leading to the formation of the coalition were held.) The Brüning government survived feebly until 1932.

Franz von Papen, a Center deputy, succeeded Brüning as chancellor in May 1932. Papen, a strong authoritarian, wished to establish a corporate state under aristocratic leadership and thus circumvent the problems of parliamentary politics. He immediately sought NSDAP-DNVP support for this effort but met with Hitler's refusal. In the July 1932 elections the NSDAP more than doubled its 1930 Reichstag representation and, claiming nearly 40 percent of the vote, was now the strongest German party. Hitler refused Papen's offer to join the cabinet as vice chancellor, and the Nazis remained in opposition in the Reichstag. By the fall of 1932 the economic depression was beginning to abate, and National Socialist popularity began to decline; the NSDAP lost thirty-four of its 230 seats in the November elections. Hindenburg declined Papen's proposal to establish dictatorial rule and dismissed the chancellor in December.

The new chancellor, General Kurt von Schleicher, resumed negotiations with the Nazis and again offered Hitler the vice chancellorship. The führer was determined, however, to hold out for the highest government post. The final outcome of the cabinet crises of the early 1930s was strongly influenced by the intrigues of Papen, Schleicher's arch political opponent. Papen persuaded the aged Hindenburg to concede to Hitler's demand for the chancellorship. On January 30, 1933, Hitler headed a new German government.

Third Reich

Party and State

Hitler proceeded to transform the Weimar Republic into a totalitarian dictatorship. The National Socialist "revolution" was accomplished in gradual steps, using legal and semilegal methods as well as terror and persuasion. The NSDAP endeavored initially to establish National Socialist hegemony within the state. In this process the old conservative-nationalist elite was partially preserved but subordinated to Nazi control. The state bureaucratic apparatus and the army were retained. Germany's economic and social structure remained largely unchanged.

The Reichstag fire of February 27, 1933, presumably started by the Nazis themselves, provided Hitler with the pretext for demanding a presidential emergency decree. The Nazis interpreted the fire as a communist attempt at political subversion and implemented Article 48 of the Weimar Constitution to quash the political opposition. The SA arrested numerous communists as well as socialist and liberal leaders. German state governments lacking a National Socialist majority—Bavaria, Württemberg, Baden, Hesse, Saxony, and the city-states—were dissolved, and the states were subordinated to control by the central government. In March Hitler presented the Reichstag with the Enabling Act. The Reichstag, purged and intimidated, passed the act by a vote of 441 to eighty-four, thereby according Hitler's cabinet full legislative powers, including rights to amend the constitution, for a period of four years.

Hitler used the Enabling Act to implement *Gleichschaltung* (forced political coordination), the policy of subordinating all independent institutions and organizations to Nazi control. The state bureaucracy and the judiciary were purged of "non-Aryans," and all members were obliged to swear an oath of personal loyalty to the führer. The Secret State Police (Geheime Staatspolizei—Gestapo) was created, and a special court, the People's Tribunal, was established to deal with cases of treason. State governments were dismissed and replaced by Reich governors directly responsible to Hitler. Trade unions were dissolved. Political parties other than National Socialist were disbanded. In July Germany was legally declared a National Socialist one-party state.

President Hindenburg died in August 1934, and Hitler promulgated a law that combined the offices of the president and the chancellor. The law violated the Enabling Act but was subsequently sanctioned by national plebiscite. Thus in the pseudolegal fashion characteristic of Nazi tactics, Hitler established himself as German führer. The army swore a special oath of allegiance to the führer, pledging unconditioned obedience. Heinrich Himmler's Guard Detachment (Schutzstaffel—SS) replaced the SA as Hitler's private army.

The National Socialist power and elite structure was consolidated through the efforts of Joseph Goebbels and the Reich Propaganda Ministry. Goebbels formulated the concept of "total propaganda" and established the Reich Cultural Chamber. The chamber extended *Gleichschaltung* to include the educational system, the media, and all cultural institutions. Hitler's *Mein Kampf* and other racist-imperialist literature were widely distributed. The NSDAP focused particularly on "gathering in" the German youth, and the Hitler Youth membership grew to more than 3.5 million.

Domestic Mobilization

National Socialism emphasized authoritarianism but added the political-charismatic combat idea of the "movement," that is, the Third Reich mobilization for war. The attention of the German masses, for whom there was no real social revolution, was diverted ideologically toward the goal of lebensraum. In the economic sphere, domestic mobilization entailed creating a wartime economy. A most significant feature of the Third Reich, however, was the emergence of the SS state.

Nazi economic policy focused on accelerated rearmament. The NSDAP won the support of German industrialists, and consequently the private industrial sector was left intact but was subordinated to party control. The Four Year Plan Office was established in 1936 and under the direction of Hermann Göring assumed responsibility for developing production quotas and market guidelines. Under the Third Reich major industrial enterprises were expanded, particularly such armaments-related firms as Krupp (steel and armaments), I.G. Farben (chemicals), and Siemens (shipbuilding). The enlarged armaments-related industries provided employment opportunities for German labor and were generally permitted to offer preferential wage scales. Large numbers of Germans abandoned agriculture to seek jobs in industry; approximately 1 million persons left the land between 1933 and 1938. During World War II the Nazi regime instituted the labor draft and also utilized disfranchised foreign and slave labor to supply the growing needs of the war economy.

In the mid-1930s Himmler's SS subordinated both the Gestapo and the Nazi concentration camp system, solidifying Hitler's totalitarian control. The SS, or Nazi police state, constituted the truly social revolutionary feature of NSDAP rule that made the formal institutionalization of a system of terror possible. German concentration camps including Dachau (near Munich), Oranienburg and Sachsenhausen (near Berlin), and numerous others became the repository for all "socially undesirable elements." Gestapo arrests, which had focused originally on communists and socialists, were extended to other social groups and, most particularly, to Jews. The Nuremberg Laws of 1935 legalized biological-racist anti-Semitism, disfranchised the Jews, and restricted relationships between Jews and non-Jews. Jews were subsequently subjected to public harassment, pogroms, and Gestapo arrests and increasingly filled the concentration camps. During World War II the concentration camps would provide forced labor for SS-run projects and industries; the camps would also furnish facilities for mass exterminations.

Foreign Policy

As führer, Hitler directed foreign policy. Even his earliest actions reflected National Socialist repudiation of the Versailles and Locarno treaties; Germany withdrew from the League of Nations in 1933. Subsequently Hitler aimed to destroy the League's collective security system and to accomplish German rearmament in preparation for eastward expansion.

Hitler's announcement of German rearmament in March 1935 constituted the Third Reich's first overt violation of the Versailles Treaty. The führer proclaimed a new military draft, stated his intention to expand the army from its legal size of 100,000 officers and men to 550,000, and declared that Germany would create an air force. Britain, France, and Italy responded by sending representatives to a conference in Stresa, Italy, to discuss countermeasures. Hitler succeeded, however, in fomenting the rapid disintegration of the Stresa Front. He approached Britain with the offer of a separate Anglo-German naval agreement that would guarantee British naval superiority. The agreement stipulated, however, that Germany would begin naval construction. The British accepted Hitler's offer without even consulting France and Italy. The Anglo-German Naval Pact of June 1935, itself a violation of the Versailles Treaty, implied tacit British acceptance of German rearmament. France and Italy subsequently abandoned their plans for punitive action against Germany.

Hitler next endeavored to draw Italy away from the Western powers. When Italy invaded Ethiopia in 1935–36, Hitler lent verbal support to fascist leader (Il Duce) Benito Mussolini's action and in March 1936 marched German troops into the Rhineland. The German military presence in the Rhineland violated the Versailles and Locarno treaties and specifically threatened French security. It suggested the forthcoming alliance between fascist Germany and Italy, helped to dissuade Britain and France from taking action against Italian imperialism, and thus displayed the weakness of the Western democracies. The Third Reich and Mussolini's Italy moved increasingly toward rapprochement. The Berlin-Rome Axis was formed during the Spanish Civil War (1936–39); Hitler and Mussolini joined to assist General Francisco Franco in overthrowing Spain's republican government.

Hitler met in secret conference with German military and political advisers in November 1937 and declared his intention to begin eastward expansion. The plan for eventual military aggression was originally discussed at this conference. The führer's immediate aims—the annexation of Austria and the Czechoslovak Sudetenland—would be accomplished by pseudolegal means. These German-populated territories would be claimed on the basis of a national-ethnic revision of the Versailles Treaty.

In February 1938 Hitler summoned the Austrian chancellor Kurt von Schuschnigg to Berchtesgaden, Germany, for consultations. The führer announced his intention to annex Austria and demanded that Schuschnigg cooperate by forming a pro-Nazi cabinet and legalizing the Austrian Nazi party. Schuschnigg returned to Austria and attempted to avert annexation by calling for a national plebiscite to decide the future of the state. Hitler immediately demanded Schuschnigg's resignation and threatened to invade Austria if the chancellor did not comply. Arthur von

Seyss-Inquart, the new Austrian Nazi chancellor, followed Hitler's instructions and invited German troops to enter Austria. On March 13 Austria was declared a province of the German Reich. The Western powers acquiesced.

Hitler prepared to "smash" Czechoslovakia; in April 1938 he instructed Konrad Henlein, the Sudeten Nazi leader, to organize disruptive nationalist agitation in the Sudetenland. Czechoslovakia, cognizant of Hitler's annexationist ambitions, appealed to France and Britain for assistance. British Prime Minister Neville Chamberlain, however, refused to commit his country to defend Czechoslovakia, thus appeasing the Nazi dictator. Chamberlain organized the Munich Conference of September 1938 where Britain and France agreed to German annexation of the Sudetenland; the territory was annexed on October 1. The Czech-populated western provinces of Bohemia and Moravia were occupied by Germany in March 1939, and Slovakia was made a German puppet-state.

When Germany occupied Bohemia-Moravia, Britain and France became convinced, at last, that Hitler's objectives were indeed imperialist-expansionist. The Western powers announced their intention to defend the sovereignty of Poland. In April 1939 Hitler nevertheless approached Poland with demands for Danzig; the führer anticipated war and thus simultaneously instructed the military to prepare invasion plans. In May Germany and Italy signed the Pact of Steel, a formal military alliance. The Soviet Union had endeavored to form an anti-Nazi alliance with the Western powers, but negotiations had stalemated repeatedly. In August the Soviet Union signed a nonagression pact with Germany, thus freeing Hitler to act against Poland. German troops invaded Poland on September 1, 1939. Britain and France declared war on Germany two days later.

World War II

Hitler's armies overran Poland by the end of September and entered Norway and Denmark to "protect" these countries from British and French attack. In May 1940 German troops smashed the western front in a major campaign in Belgium and Holland, leaving more than 300,000 British and French soldiers trapped in Dunkirk on the coast of northern France. The lightning-like strikes (blitzkrieg) of German tanks and planes seemed unstoppable. Chamberlain had resigned as prime minister on May 10, and the king asked Winston Churchill to head the new cabinet. Under Churchill's leadership the British Royal Navy successfully rescued the men in Dunkirk. The fall of France in June 1940, however, brought Hitler to the height of power.

When France fell, Hitler, who had hoped originally that Britain would stay out of the war, approached Churchill with the offer of a separate peace. Churchill was intransigent, however, and the

Federal Republic of Germany

Royal Air Force successfully resisted Hitler's air attack on Britain in August 1940. The führer began to plan the invasion of the Soviet Union. Japan joined the Axis powers in September, and the scene of war was later extended into the Far East. In the meantime Italy had made advances in North Africa and the Mediterranean region. Subsequent Italian setbacks, however, forced Hitler to delay the German attack on the Soviet Union. He sent Field Marshal Erwin Rommel to Africa, and German troops fought their way through the Balkan countries to assist the Italians in Greece. Spain's refusal to join the Mediterranean campaign prolonged the conflict. German successes in Yugoslavia and Greece in the spring of 1941, however, persuaded Hungary, Romania, Slovakia, Bulgaria, and Croatia to join the Axis.

Germany invaded the Soviet Union in June 1941, and by late fall Hitler's armies stood before Moscow. The führer had anticipated victory in the Soviet Union within three months, but the early onset of the Russian winter stopped German advances. Japan attacked Pearl Harbor on December 7, thus bringing the United States into the war. The United States joined Britain and the Soviet Union to form the Grand Alliance. When German troops resumed battle in the Soviet Union in the spring of 1942, the tide of war began to turn against the Axis powers (see fig. 6).

German military victories during World War II were accompanied by the simultaneous consolidation of Himmler's SS state. The SS was expanded to include nearly 150,000 men and came to represent authority within a Greater German Reich. The concentration camps became filled with foreign nationals and non-German Jews. Numerous new camps were opened in 1940 including Auschwitz in Upper Silesia, Neuengamme near Hamburg, Bergen-Belsen and Gross-Rosen in Lower Silesia, Stutthof near Danzig, and Nutzweiler in Alsace. Other concentration camps in East and West Prussia, Styria, and Lorraine served primarily as transit and resettlement camps. The numbers of camps and inmates increased more rapidly after 1941 when the SS began to create extermination camps.

That such acts were occurring in Germany seemed unbelievable. Although an undercurrent of anti-Semitism had always been present in the German society, in no other European society had the Jewish community so completely integrated into the majority community. It was in Germany in the late eighteenth century that Moses Mendelssohn and others launched the movement that became known as the Jewish Emancipation or Enlightenment, which in the nineteenth and twentieth centuries provided the world such personages as Heinrich Heine, Benjamin Disraeli, Karl Marx, Johannes Brahms, Sigmund Freud, Marcel Proust, Franz Kafka, Albert Einstein, J. Robert Oppenheimer, and Yehudi Menuhin. It is true that in 1878 a political party was formed that projected anti-Semitism as a central part of its program, but it is

Historical Setting

- - - European boundaries in 1938
- Germany in 1938
- Allied to Germany
- Annexed territory, 1938-40
- Maximum area of German conquest

Source: Based on information from Eugene K. Keefe, et al., *Area Handbook for the Federal Republic of Germany*, Washington, 1975, p. 43.

Figure 6. *Extent of Nazi Germany Expansion in 1942*

also true that throughout the nineteenth century and up to the advent of Hitler's regime literally hundreds of Jews achieved fame and reknown in almost all facets of German life, particularly in the arts and sciences, and that thousands more secured recognition as prominent and respected members of their communities. An unknown but very large number of Jews so completely assimilated that they had not only ceased to observe the basic precepts of Judaism but also had converted, at least nominally, to Christianity. Assimilation had in fact become so widespread that many Jews predicted that within a few generations most of the Jewish community would disappear.

Federal Republic of Germany

Hitler and his associates and followers, however, subscribed to spurious notions of "racial purity" and "biological superiority" that categorized many groups as "socially undesirable"; specifically targeted were the Jews. By the late 1930s the Nazi leaders had adopted the concept of a "final solution" to the "Jewish problem," a solution that provided for the extermination of all Jews. The scope and methods employed in what came to be known as the Holocaust exceeded anything in recorded history. The term *holocaust* came into general use some years after the event. The English word derives from the Vulgate translation of the Septuagint and that version's translation of the Hebrew word *olah*, from the root meaning "to go up." In the context of the Holocaust the root refers back to an ancient Temple sacrifice in which the sacrifice on the altar is totally consumed by fire and the smoke "goes up" to God.

The scope of Hitler's genocidal efforts, staggering as they were, may be quickly summarized. In 1939 about 10 million of the estimated 16 million Jews in the world lived in Europe. By 1945 almost 6 million had been killed, most of them in the nineteen main concentration camps. Of prewar Czechoslovakia's 281,000 Jews, about 4,000 survived. Before the German conquest and occupation, the Jewish population of Greece was estimated to be between 65,000 and 72,000; about 2,000 survived. Only 5,000 of Austria's prewar Jewish community of 70,000 escaped. And an estimated 4.6 million Jews were killed in Poland and in those areas of the Soviet Union seized and occupied by the Germans. During the 1930s an estimated two-fifths of the Jews in Germany fled the country. Of the estimated 500,000 Jews in Germany in 1939, only about one-fifth survived.

The Allied road to victory started in 1943. The Soviets defeated German troops at Stalingrad in February, and Hitler's armies started their retreat. The Allies gained control of North Africa, and in July Mussolini was deposed in Italy. German cities and industrial centers were bombed with increased intensity. By the end of 1943 Hitler's armies in the Soviet Union had been driven back nearly to the Polish border, and in June 1944 the United States and Britain invaded France.

A number of militant younger German army officers had joined the underground resistance. On July 20, 1944, these men, led by Colonel Claus Schenk von Stauffenberg, attempted to assassinate Hitler and effect a military coup. The coup was planned in cooperation with the civilian resistance, composed largely of socialists but including a diversity of other social groups. Stauffenberg's assassination attempt failed, and the führer was injured only slightly. Military officials waiting in Berlin for news of Hitler's death prepared to seize power. The news of the führer's survival created confusion, however, and the conspiracy fell apart. The military conspirators were subsequently court-martialed, and numerous high-ranking military officers were executed. Approximately 5,000 members of the civilian resistance were executed after civil trials.

American and British troops advanced into western Germany in the fall of 1944. Hitler remained determined to fight on and indeed called for the "total mobilization of all Germans" for the war effort. At the Yalta Conference in February 1945 the United States, Britain, and the Soviet Union discussed arrangements for the postwar control of Germany. American forces reached the Rhine River in March; simultaneously Soviet armies overran most of Czechoslovakia and pressed on toward Berlin. Hitler insisted that every German city, every village, and finally "every square meter" would have to be defended or left behind as "scorched earth." The Western and Soviet armies in Germany made their first mutual contact in Saxony on April 27. Three days later Hitler and his bride, Eva Braun, committed suicide in a Berlin bunker. Berlin fell to the Soviets on May 2. On May 7 the Third Reich surrendered unconditionally.

Federal Republic of Germany

In the aftermath of Hitler's defeat the Allied victors—the United States, Britain, and the Soviet Union—formulated a common German policy. Arrangements for postwar Germany were finalized at the Potsdam Conference of July-August 1945, during which the Allies affirmed the future restoration of a united and democratic German state. German territories east of the Oder and Neisse rivers, however, were ceded to Poland and the Soviet Union. The Allied Control Council in Berlin assumed political authority for all Germany; the American, British, French, and Soviet military occupation zones were considered temporary. Berlin was placed under joint Four Power control. Immediate Allied aims included denazification and demilitarization in preparation for reunification. National Socialist institutions and organizations were disbanded, and the formation of democratic political parties and of trade unions was encouraged.

The International Military Tribunal conducted the Nuremberg Trials held in Nuremberg, Germany, from November 1945 until October 1946. Principal leaders of Nazi Germany and major National Socialist institutions—the Third Reich government, the General Staff, the SA, the SS, and the Gestapo—were arraigned at Nuremberg. Individual members of institutions judged criminal were declared subject to trial by specific tribunals. The military occupation authorities made numerous arrests, totaling by January 1947 some 245,000 persons in the four zones. In addition Nazi sympathizers were dismissed from responsible public and private positions. The Western powers, however, tended to rehabilitate and reinstate the upper echelons of the German administration, economy, and military; the Soviet Union conducted its purge

Federal Republic of Germany

more thoroughly.

The original Allied economic policy in postwar Germany was shaped by the goal of demilitarization and the demand for reparations for war damages. All armaments-related German industries were dismantled and/or appropriated by the victors. The Western powers and the Soviet Union organized confiscations in their respective zones; France and the Soviet Union had suffered large-scale devastation during World War II and thus were most harsh in exacting reparations. The Allies had further agreed to weaken Germany's industrial potential permanently in order to prevent a revival of militarism. Monopolistic trusts and cartels that had formerly controlled two-thirds of all industry were dissolved—the chemical industry, mining, and banking were principally affected (see Legacies Affecting Development, ch. 4). An industrial plan adopted by the Allied Control Council in March 1946 (but never implemented) fixed the permissible level of industrial production at about 50 percent that of 1938, the best prewar year. Such products as gasoline, rubber, and radioactive materials were banned completely; steel production was strictly limited.

At the onset of the cold war in 1947, the Western powers transformed their German policy. In March 1947 President Harry S Truman presented to the United States Congress a proposal of aid to Greece and Turkey, the basis of the Truman Doctrine. The doctrine declared the antithesis between the "free" and "totalitarian" worlds and offered economic aid to nations defending democracy and capitalism. The United States won British and French support for an alliance designed to contain Soviet expansionism; the North Atlantic Treaty Organization (NATO—also referred to as the Atlantic Alliance) was formed in April 1949 (see The North Atlantic Treaty Organization, ch. 8). A decision to include a West German state in the alliance was reached at the same time. Beginning in 1949 the Marshall Plan (named after United States Secretary of State George C. Marshall) provided approximately US$2 billion in financial assistance for the economic reconstruction of the West German zones. Dismantling of industrial plants was halted, and restrictions on industrial production were revoked. A currency reform of June 1948 had helped to stabilize the inflated postwar economy. The war-ravaged German population (including 9 million East European refugees resettled in the Western zones after World War II) was housed and fed.

At the London Six Power Conference of February-June 1948—attended by the United States, Britain, France, and the Benelux states—the conferees formally accepted the American proposal to create a West German state. The Soviet Union left the Allied Control Council and prepared to establish a communist East Germany. Access routes into West Berlin were blockaded by the Soviets in June 1948, an act that became known as the Berlin Blockade. The Soviet Union hoped to starve West Berliners into

*Konrad Adenauer promulgating the Basic Law
in Bonn on May 23, 1949
Courtesy German Information Center*

accepting incorporation into its zone, but the Western powers mounted a massive airlift to furnish the city food and supplies. After several months the city of Berlin was administratively divided, and the blockade was terminated.

The Western powers arranged to convene a Parliamentary Council in Bonn (the future capital) to draft the Basic Law (constitution) that established the Federal Republic of Germany. Both the Basic Law and the West German state were legally defined as provisional, pending reunification. Konrad Adenauer presided over the council (September 1948–May 1949), consisting of sixty-five delegates from the postwar West German states (*Länder*, sing., *Land*) parliaments and West Berlin. It included twenty-seven Christian Democrats (Christlich Demokratische Union—CDU); twenty-seven Social Democrats; and five Free Democrats (Freie Demokratische Partei—FDP). The Basic Law was ratified on May 8, 1949, by a vote of fifty-three to twelve. The United States, Britain, and France, however, by means of the Occupation Statute of April 1949, retained supreme authority in West Germany. Theodor Heuss (FDP) was subsequently elected federal president. Konrad Adenauer (CDU chairman) won the West German chancellorship by a one-vote majority.

The Bonn Democracy

The Federal Republic was constituted as a democratic and federal state (see The Constitutional Framework and Federalism, ch. 7). The Basic Law provides for a federal president elected for five years, but his functions as head of state are largely ceremonial. It was hoped that Weimar authoritarianism could thus be avoided. Executive power is exercised by the federal chancellor (see The Federal Executive, ch. 7). He is formally nominated by the president but is in fact the candidate agreed upon with the Federal Diet (Bundestag). The Bundestag—the popularly elected national chamber—holds extensive rights in federal legislation including foreign affairs, finance, trade, and communications (see The Legislature, ch. 7). The Federal Council (Bundesrat) provides for *Land* representation; it is composed of delegates from the ten *Länder* and West Berlin. (Delegates from West Berlin do not have voting rights in either legislative chamber.) Bundesrat legislative powers are restricted; it possesses an absolute veto, however, in matters of *Land* interest. The Basic Rights section of the constitution guarantees human rights and freedoms. West Germans are guaranteed the right to refuse military service. Trade unions are protected by the constitution, and provisions for nationalization of property are included.

The Federal Constitutional Court was created to defend the democratic principles embodied in the Basic Law. Specifically it possesses the authority to judge the constitutionality of political parties. West Germans remain highly sensitive to the dangers of political extremism. For example the extreme-right Socialist Reich Party (Sozialistische Reichspartei) was declared illegal in 1952, and the Communist Party of Germany (Kommunistische Partei Deutschlands—KPD) was banned in 1956.

Bonn's democracy has its basis in stable government and the political party system. The chancellor and his cabinet play the leading role in deciding legislative policy. A Basic Law provision—the "constructive vote of no confidence"—enables the Bundestag to dismiss the chancellor only by electing a successor. This provision was intended to protect against governmental crises. The stability of the federal government has depended on stable political groups in parliament. (Electoral law restricts parliamentary representation to parties gaining at least 5 percent of the popular vote.) The functioning of the federal government has been marked by competition between the Christian Democratic Union/Christian Social Union (CDU/CSU) and the SPD as major political parties of nearly equal strength. In early 1982 the FDP remained the only other significant political party (see Political Parties and the Electoral System, ch. 7).

Historical Setting

The CDU and Bavaria's CSU are distinct political parties that form a single parliamentary group (*Fraktion*). During the occupation period Allied favor helped to strengthen the bourgeois-conservative CDU/CSU. An interconfessional—Protestant and Catholic—party, the CDU/CSU represents industrial and agrarian interests but includes a small labor wing. The party program advocates free enterprise but also subscribes to Christian social welfare doctrine. Under Adenauer's leadership (1949–63), the CDU/CSU gradually incorporated most small bourgeois parties, including the Center Party, the German Party (Deutsche Partei—DP), and the Refugees' Party.

The SPD re-formed in 1945. Under Allied occupation, the western-zone SPD, which was headed by Kurt Schumacher until his death in 1953, rejected proposals for an SPD-KPD union and thus endorsed the West German alliance with the Western allies. SPD strength declined in consequence of the party's restriction to West German territories; Prussia constituted the former stronghold of German socialism. For most of the period of Adenauer's chancellorship, the opposition SPD took a firm stance against rearmament and in addition pressed for various forms of nationalization. But in 1959 the party adopted the Bad Godesberg Program, which transformed the SPD from a revolutionary, Marxist, working-class party into a reform-oriented "party of the whole German people." From 1959 both the CDU/CSU and the SPD supported NATO and free enterprise. As of early 1982 the SPD had held power since 1969.

The Free Democrats constitute the bourgeois-liberal alternative to the "Christian" and "socialist" parties. Membership reflects the national liberal tradition of north and west Germany but also the progressive liberalism of the south. As West Germany's "third" party, the FDP joined in coalition with Adenauer's CDU/CSU and then with the SPD. The FDP's participation in government has made stable Bundestag majorities possible. Simultaneously the FDP introduced flexibility into German politics and exerted a moderating influence on the major parties.

The success of West Germany's "social market economy" has contributed significantly to its remarkable political stability. Introduced by Ludwig Erhard, minister for economic affairs (1949–63), the "social market economy" is based on "free market" philosophy but permits limited state intervention. The framers of the Basic Law wished to restrict state power, but they also rejected the "laissez-faire" doctrine of nineteenth-century liberalism. State intervention is authorized to prevent monopolization, to encourage small business by means of tax policy and subsidies, and to implement social programs to alleviate hardship. Nonetheless since the mid–1960s West German industry has manifested increasing tendencies toward concentration (see Major Industrial Sectors, ch. 6).

Federal Republic of Germany

Adenauer Era

Adenauer's commitment to a Western orientation shaped his policymaking. The CDU/CSU leader developed a coherent program based on three major objectives. First, West Germany's integration into the Atlantic Alliance was considered essential for security reasons; moreover, NATO membership was expected to entail the much-desired grant of West German sovereignty by the occupation powers. Second, the creation of a West European political union was strongly desired. Adenauer hoped that a united Europe would exercise significant influence within the Atlantic Alliance. Third, the goal of a united and democratic Germany would be pursued on the basis of strength. The Basic Law called for German reunification based on the 1937 frontiers, i.e., including the ceded eastern territories. Britain, France, and the United States had pledged their support for this aim.

The CDU/CSU gained power in August 1949, winning only 31.0 percent of the vote; the SPD followed closely with 29.2 percent. Adenauer negotiated the bourgeois coalition (*Bürgerblock*), however, including the FDP and DP, and thus acquired a stable majority of 208 out of 402 Bundestag seats. Extreme right-wing parties won 10 to 15 percent of the vote; the KPD, only 5.7 percent.

The outbreak of the Korean War in June 1950—the invasion of the Republic of Korea (South Korea) by the Democratic People's Republic of Korea (North Korea)—heightened East-West tensions. As a result the United States made plans to strengthen European defense. Meeting in New York in September, the United States, Britain, and France endorsed proposals for an integrated European Defense Community (EDC), to be subordinate to NATO but to include West Germany. Adenauer and the *Bürgerblock* favored West German rearmament; the oppositionist SPD, however, led an "*ohne mich*" (without me) movement, which prolonged negotiations. West Germany demanded full sovereignty in exchange for EDC participation, and Adenauer argued strongly that the promise of sovereignty would win popular support for rearmament. In March 1951 a revision of the Occupation Statute granted the Federal Republic autonomy in foreign relations. The European Coal and Steel Community (ECSC), established in 1952, represented a victory for Adenauer—who also served as foreign minister—and raised hopes for a European political union. In May 1952 treaties were signed in Bonn and Paris establishing the EDC, and the Bundestag ratified the treaties. The EDC was blocked in 1954, however, when the French National Assembly refused ratification.

Adenauer's CDU/CSU scored a major victory in the September 1953 Bundestag elections. The government party's vote jumped to 45 percent. Postwar economic recovery—attributable largely to Marshall Plan aid—and the promise of sovereignty had popular appeal. The SPD vote remained stable. Not a single extreme

Historical Setting

right-or left-wing party (the KPD vote dropped to 2.2 percent) gained parliamentary representation.

The administration of Dwight D. Eisenhower favored the "Adenauer Boom," an increase in strength of the Atlantic Alliance, and a "roll back" policy toward communism. Treaties signed in Bonn and Paris in October 1954 provided for the Federal Republic's direct membership in NATO and for sovereignty. Popular resistance to West German rearmament, however, remained substantial: the extra-parliamentary opposition movement (*Ausserparlamentarische Oppositionsbewegung*—APO) was joined by the SPD-left. The APO demanded détente negotiations with the post-Stalinist Soviet regime. Adenauer refused APO demands and insisted on free elections in both Germanys. By May 1955 the Bonn and Paris treaties had been ratified by the Bundestag and the Western powers. The Federal Republic acquired sovereign status and joined NATO; East Germany was included in the Warsaw Pact shortly thereafter. As a member of NATO, West Germany's military strength and armaments production were nevertheless subject to restriction. The Allied occupation was terminated, but NATO troops (American, British, and European) remained stationed in West Germany as part of the common defense.

In 1955 West Germany proclaimed the Hallstein Doctrine, which reaffirmed the goal of reunification. (The United States, Britain, and France had restated their pledge to support this aim in the 1954 Bonn and Paris treaties.) The doctrine (named after Adenauer's state secretary, Walter Hallstein) based itself on the Basic Law's *Alleinvertretungsrecht* ("right of sole representation") clause. *Alleinvertretungsrecht* refers to the Federal Republic's claim to represent "all Germans." The Hallstein Doctrine developed the practical implications of the *Alleinvertretungsrecht* by declaring West Germany's intention to sever diplomatic relations with any state other than the Soviet Union that recognized East Germany.

The years 1956–57 were highlighted by rearmament-related issues. The Basic Law was amended, and a compulsory conscription law passed the Bundestag in July 1956 by a clear majority; the SPD opposition was badly defeated. Popular misapprehensions lingered, however, and the response to a 1956 poll showed 40 percent of West Germans in favor of rearmament and 45 percent against. The first conscripts for the Federal Armed Forces (Bundeswehr) were nevertheless called up in early 1957 without incident, and a target of 350,000 men under arms by 1961 was set. From late 1956 political controversy focused on the debate on tactical nuclear weapons. Although West Germany was prohibited from use of the so-called ABC (atomic, biological, chemical) weapons, the United States reserved the right to station tactical nuclear weapons in West Germany. Defense Minister Franz-

Josef Strauss and the Adenauer government defended this right and favored the equipment of the Bundeswehr with nuclear delivery vehicles. The SPD launched a strong campaign opposing the deployment of nuclear weapons in West Germany, but the Bundeswehr was soon equipped with nuclear delivery systems.

By 1957 the CDU/CSU had incorporated all bourgeois parties except the FDP, and in the September 1957 elections the CDU/CSU gained 50.2 percent of the vote and an absolute Bundestag majority. This victory by the Adenauer government may be attributed chiefly to the "economic miracle" (*Wirtschaftswunder*), i.e., the remarkable recovery of the postwar West German economy. Full employment had been attained, and the standard of living equaled that of any European state. The European Economic Community (EEC or Common Market—see Glossary)—established in March 1957—encouraged hopes for further economic progress. In addition the chancellor's dream of European unity seemed realizable (see The European Communities, ch. 8).

The Berlin Crisis of 1958–61, however, challenged the strength of the Atlantic Alliance and finally discredited Adenauer's foreign policy stance. As a result CDU/CSU popularity began to decline. The crisis was sparked by Soviet leader Nikita Khrushchev's ultimatum of November 1958 declaring all Berlin agreements null and void and demanding that West Berlin be transformed within six months into a demilitarized free city. The Soviet Union threatened war. It desired recognition of East Germany by the West and called for détente negotiations between the two Germanys and the establishment of a neutral German confederation. East-West tensions mounted in subsequent months. Eisenhower rejected the Soviet ultimatum and declared the Western military presence in Berlin essential for the security of the free world. The Western powers and the Federal Republic repeated the demand for all German free elections as the prerequisite for détente negotiations. The SPD published the Germany Plan in March 1959, which proposed the demilitarization of East Germany and West Germany and détente negotiations on a parity basis. The plan insisted, however, on the recognition of fundamental human rights. In the end the Soviet Union revoked its original time limit and agreed to a future summit conference.

Although the prospects for a resolution of the American-Soviet impasse seemed negligible, the summit conference opened in Paris on May 16, 1960. Each side resolutely defended its position. Negotiations in Paris concluded abruptly when Khrushchev resumed his bitter complaints about the United States reconnaissance plane that had been shot down over Soviet territory on May 1, denounced the West, and left the conference.

In January 1961 John F. Kennedy took office, and United States foreign policy began a change in orientation. Soviet nuclear parity influenced the policy change. Kennedy restated the United

States' commitment to West Berlin; he announced, however, that NATO interests would be restricted to Western bloc territories, i.e., the goal of incorporating East Germany into West Germany was abandoned. The Berlin Crisis nevertheless escalated. Meeting with Kennedy in Vienna in June, Khrushchev reportedly spoke threateningly of nuclear war. And in August 1961 the East Germans erected the Berlin Wall—a barbed wire and concrete barrier sealing the border between the two sections—an action that took the West by surprise and blatantly violated the Four Power status of the city. The Wall effectively halted East German emigration—which had reached a total of over 3 million—to West Germany, thus making possible the political and economic stabilization of the East German state. The termination of free travel between the two sectors of Berlin obviously separated relatives and friends. The United States and other Western powers grudgingly accepted the Wall as a fait accompli, but West Berliners for the first time staged anti-American demonstrations.

In the September 1961 Bundestag elections the CDU/CSU lost its absolute majority but remained the strongest political group. CDU/CSU and FDP formed a coalition government. At the age of eighty-five Adenauer was reelected chancellor with 259 out of 499 votes, and he continued to champion his cherished diplomatic goals. Khrushchev had seriously challenged the Atlantic Alliance, however, and although unable to impose his demands fully, had succeeded in humiliating it. In consequence Adenauer's principle of "negotiation from strength" suffered a serious blow. Moreover the United States declared the cold war officially ended following the Cuban Missile Crisis of October 1962, and détente and nuclear disarmament became the focus of international discussion. West Germany under Adenauer, however, continued to champion the old goals.

In the fall of 1963 the newsmagazine *Der Spiegel* published an article on the Fallex '62 NATO maneuvers in West Germany. The correspondent, Conrad Ahlers, implicitly attacked Adenauer's foreign policy stance by asserting that the West's nuclear capabilities were insufficient to prevent enemy occupation of a large part of the Federal Republic. Defense Minister Strauss and Adenauer authorized illegal actions against *Der Spiegel*, including raids of its Hamburg and Bonn offices and numerous arrests. The so-called *Spiegel* Affair resulted in a scandal that effected Adenauer's resignation in October. Former Federal Minister of Economics Ludwig Erhard (CDU) finished Adenauer's term (1963–65) and was reelected. Erhard made initial progress toward establishing trade relations with East European states.

Grand Coalition, 1966–69

Erhard resigned in November 1966 following the FDP'S withdrawal from its coalition with CDU/CSU. The FDP with-

Federal Republic of Germany

drew because of an economic recession, which in turn prompted the SPD to join the CDU/CSU in what became known as the Grand Coalition, which was formed in December 1966. Adoption of the Bad Godesberg Program by the SPD—its commitment to NATO and free enterprise—made the coalition possible. The SPD agreed to participate in government in an effort to restore public confidence and prevent the rise of political extremism; the memory of the political impact of the 1929 depression remained strong. Kurt Georg Kiesinger (CDU) was elected chancellor, and Willy Brandt (SPD) was awarded the posts of vice chancellor and foreign minister, indicating the new government's interest in East-West détente. In his inaugural address Kiesinger talked of establishing diplomatic relations with East European nations "wherever possible." West Germany's economic difficulties—the result of government overspending—were quickly brought under control. A new radical-right National Democratic Party (Nationaldemokratische Partei Deutschlands—NPD) made significant gains (average 7.5 percent) in several *Land* elections in 1967 but declined soon after. The main issues confronting the Grand Coalition continued to involve foreign policy.

The Federal Republic restated its commitment to NATO but simultaneously endeavored to establish diplomatic relations with Eastern Europe. The government exchanged diplomatic missions with Romania and Yugoslavia, but negotiations toward détente with East Germany (West Germany suggested trade relations, cultural exchange, and restored personal ties) reached an impasse. Kiesinger reaffirmed his government's adherence to the policy of *Alleinvertretungsrecht* and adamantly refused the Soviet demand for recognition of two sovereign German states. The sovereignty issue split the Grand Coalition. Brandt and the SPD favored recognition and détente as the preliminary to future German reunification. Moreover an extra-parliamentary left wing threatened the republic's stability; the neo-Marxist New Left, formed in mid-1967 in West Berlin, attracted a large number of university students. The New Left attacked the "Bonn system" and identified itself with the international protest movement against United States involvement in the Vietnam Conflict.

The stalemate in East-West détente negotiations and the upsurge of student demonstrations polarized the CDU/CSU-SPD. Kiesinger found it impossible both to defend his foreign policy and to maintain internal order. CDU/CSU Bundestag delegates favored reaffirmation of the Hallstein Doctrine, i.e., nonrecognition of states recognizing East Germany, and harsh legal action to stem political protest. Brandt and the SPD pressed for détente and hoped to secure the allegiance of West German youth. An assassination attempt on New Left leader Rudi Dutschke by a young anticommunist in April 1968 unleashed what were then viewed as massive demonstrations, involving up to 18,000 people in some cities. The Bundestag passed emergency legislation, and numerous arrests followed. A broad propaganda campaign launched by the SPD, however, resulted in amnesty for the political prisoners. Kiesinger's government then approved the German Communist Party (Deutsche Kommunistische Partei—DKP), formed in September 1968. The coalition hoped that the DKP would help integrate protesters into the political system. The New Left, however, continued to gain support. Throughout the 1968–69 election campaign, the ability of the Grand Coalition to perform effectively the functions of government became increasingly suspect.

The election in September 1969 resulted in an SPD increase from 39.3 percent (1965) to 42.7 percent; the CDU/CSU vote dropped from 47.6 percent (1965) to 46.1 percent, and the FDP won 5.8 percent of the vote. Brandt was determined to negotiate an SPD-FDP coalition despite the narrow Bundestag majority of ten seats enjoyed by the two parties and to present himself as chancellor candidate. Sympathetic ties between SPD and FDP had developed following the recent rise of progressive liberals to FDP leadership. (SPD and FDP had joined in supporting Gustav Heinemann's [SPD] election to the federal presidency in March 1969.) Brandt won the chancellorship in October by a three-vote majority; Walter Scheel (FDP) served as vice chancellor and foreign minister, the positions Brandt had held in the Grand Coalition. For the first time, the CDU/CSU constituted the parliamentary opposition.

Willy Brandt's Ostpolitik

Brandt promptly enunciated the new government's *Ostpolitik* (eastern policy)—a new approach to East-West détente. *Ostpolitik* focused on the *Deutschlandproblem* (German problem) and approved recognition of East Germany as the necessary precondition for peaceful relations with Eastern Europe. Normalization of relations between the two Germanys, it was expected, would foster progress toward future reunification. Brandt's proposed formulation—"two states of one German nation"—affirmed the unique relationship of the two German States. The Federal Republic continued to regard the two polities as constituent parts of a single nation, sharing a common language, culture, and tradition. The special category of "inter-German relations"was devised for diplomatic contacts. Negotiation and ratification of the treaties that constitute the heart of *Ostpolitik*—the Moscow and Warsaw treaties, the Four Power Agreement on Berlin, and the Basic Treaty (between East Germany and West Germany)—dominated West German politics until 1973. Throughout the period, however, the West German commitment to NATO remained firm.

The Moscow and Warsaw treaties negotiated in 1970 settled border issues relating to the *Deutschlandproblem* and thus set the stage for an East German-West German agreement. In August 1970 West Germany and the Soviet Union signed the Moscow Treaty, which guaranteed the existing borders of all European states. By recognizing the Oder and Neisse rivers as Poland's western frontier, West Germany renounced its claim to German territory ceded in 1945. In addition the border separating West Germany and East Germany was declared inviolate. The Warsaw Treaty of December 1970 (signed by the Federal Republic and Poland) confirmed recognition of the territorial status quo in Europe, including the Oder-Neisse line.

A struggle over ratification of the eastern treaties followed: the SPD-FDP Bundestag majority was narrow and CDU/CSU opposition strong. The CDU/CSU *Fraktion* unanimously rejected the Moscow and Warsaw treaties and launched a vigorous campaign to block them. By the winter of 1971-72 several SPD-FDP delegates had switched sides. CDU/CSU *Fraktion* Chairman Rainer Barzel decided to challenge Brandt for the chancellorship and called for a "constructive vote of no confidence." Extraparliamentary leftist protest revived; students (and workers) staged massive demonstrations and denounced the CDU/CSU as the party of "reaction." The Baader-Meinhof Gang (an anarchocommunist group led by Andreas Baader and Ulrike Meinhof) introduced terrorist activism in West Germany, including indiscriminate murders and bombings (see Dissidence and Terrorist Activities, ch. 9). Barzel's mandate in April 1972 fell two votes short (247 out of 496) of the necessary absolute majority. Brandt and the Western powers subsequently encouraged Barzel to support ratification. In the end Barzel himself favored conditional approval, but the CDU/CSU *Fraktion* agreed to abstain. The Moscow Treaty passed the Bundestag in May by 248 votes to ten, with 238 abstentions; the Warsaw Treaty, by 248 votes to seventeen, with 230 abstentions.

In the interim the Berlin issue—the final obstacle to a treaty between East Germany and West Germany—had been settled. The Four Power Agreement of September 1971, signed by Britain, France, the Soviet Union, and the United States, guaranteed that ties and links between Bonn and West Berlin would be maintained and developed. The Federal Republic was prohibited, however, from incorporating West Berlin despite the fact that East Berlin had been de facto made part of East Germany. West Berliners were promised the right to visit East Berlin and East Germany and to improve communications with those areas. The Western powers retained authority in West Berlin and responsib-

View of Berlin, 1945
Courtesy German Information Center

View of Berlin, 1982
Courtesy German Information Center

ility for its defense.

Brandt's stature had been enhanced by receipt of the Nobel Peace Prize in October 1971, and *Ostpolitik* was popular among West German citizens. Brandt, hoping to obtain an electoral mandate for *Ostpolitik*, favored new elections to precede the signing of the Basic Treaty. To comply with Basic Law procedure, the chancellor in September 1972 called for a vote of confidence. The Bundestag voted against Brandt and was dissolved. The November 1972 elections brought the SPD-FDP coalition a decisive victory. Brandt's coalition gained 54.3 percent of the vote (SPD–45.9 percent, FDP–8.4 percent) and a majority of forty-six Bundestag seats. The chancellor was reelected by 269 to 223 votes. In the aftermath of the elections the SPD incorporated most of the student protest movement; the majority joined the party's youth wing (Jungsozialisten—Jusos). The Basic Treaty passed the Bundestag in May 1973 by 268 to 217 votes.

In the Basic Treaty West Germany recognized East Germany's existence and territorial integrity. The two Germanys pledged mutual respect for each other's independence and autonomy in the conduct of internal and external affairs. West Germany rejected the idea, however, that East Germany constituted foreign territory. The exchange of diplomatic missions was promised, as were further treaties to establish trade, travel, and communications relations. Both countries joined the United Nations in 1973.

Bavaria's *Land* government, headed by the CSU, appealed to the Federal Constitutional Court in a challenge to the constitutionality of the Basic Treaty. The Basic Law (reunification clause) defends the legal permanence of Germany in its pre-World War II dimensions. West Germany is defined as a temporary political construct that preserves responsibility for all Germany. The Constitutional Court ruled against Bavaria; the Basic Treaty, the Court argued, does not deny the constitutional mandate for reunification, and the federal government retains the prerogative to decide the pragmatically useful approaches to the reunification issue.

After ratification of the Basic Treaty, the stability of Brandt's government—based largely on the *Ostpolitik* consensus—lessened significantly. The SPD domestic reform program (originally introduced in 1969) constituted a new focal point of West German politics. *Politik der inneren Reform* (domestic reform policy) included comprehensive plans for social welfare increases—pensions, health, and unemployment insurance—tax reform, educational reform, and workers' codetermination. The CDU/CSU held a one-vote majority in the Bundesrat and thus was able to challenge domestic reform legislation. In addition the international oil crisis that began in 1973 and the subsequent inflation reduced funds available for domestic reform. The SPD-majority and the FDP favored compromise, but the SPD-left (over

30 percent of total SPD membership) was vocal in its protest. West Germans feared a revival of left-wing extremism, and Brandt was severely criticized for his leniency toward the SPD youth wing. (Walter Scheel [FDP] was elected to the federal presidency in March 1974.) And then in April 1974–in a totally unrelated incident—Günther Guillaume, the chancellor's personal adviser, was arrested as an East German spy. Brandt responded to the scandal by submitting his resignation.

Helmut Schmidt's Chancellorship

Helmut Schmidt, a member of the SPD's conservative wing and deputy leader of the party, headed the new SPD-FDP government. Schmidt, who had held the posts of minister of defense and minister of finance under Brandt, adopted a "no-nonsense" policy toward the SPD-left and succeeded in integrating most members into the party mainstream. With the conclusion of the *Ostpolitik* treaties, the basically conservative character of West German politics reasserted itself, and the SPD and CDU/CSU reconciled on most issues despite the rhetorical bombast of election campaigns. The Soviet Union permitted little genuine progress in détente, and fear of communism remained strong.

Material prosperity made West Germany the envy of Europe in the 1970s. Per capita gross national product (GNP) ranked second only to the United States among larger nations, and the real hourly wage of West German labor exceeded that of American workers. The problems of post–1973 inflation, slowed economic growth, and unemployment nevertheless disappointed expectations. Economic recession in 1975 resulted in over 1 million West Germans unemployed. The Baader-Meinhof terrorist gang (renamed the Red Army Faction [Rote Armee Fraktion—RAF]) frightened West Germans, who were still sensitive to political extremism. The political spectrum shifted to the right, and the SPD was forced to make significant concessions to the CDU/CSU opposition.

The SPD vote fell from 45.9 percent to 42.6 percent in the 1976 elections. The FDP won 7.9 percent of the vote, and Schmidt was reelected, but the SPD-FDP held a slim ten-seat majority in the Bundestag. The CDU/CSU's 48.6 percent represented a significant gain (from 44.9 percent in 1972); the party had campaigned with the slogan "Freedom versus Socialism." Although Helmut Kohl was the CDU/CSU candidate for chancellor, CSU leader Strauss conducted an aggressive campaign, accusing the SPD for doing little against terrorism and communism. Strauss threatened to transform Bavaria's ultraconservative CSU into an independent, national party but was dissuaded by his colleagues in the CSU and by leaders of the CDU.

Schmidt's campaign slogan in 1976–the "German Model"— referred to West Germany's economic strength and the domestic reform program. The chancellor had established good relations

Federal Republic of Germany

with both business leaders and the trade unions. GNP increased from 1976 (although not at pre-1973 rates), and unemployment figures fell slightly. Inflation was mild compared with other industrialized states.

The bogey of political extremism nevertheless continued to haunt Schmidt's government and West German citizens. Although extremist parties won only 0.9 percent of the vote in 1976, thus demonstrating their minimal support, they evoked significant public concern. The various extreme-right groups totaled a membership of some 20,000. Neo-Nazi activism revived in the mid-1970s, and the Hitler cult was especially popular among some uneducated teenagers facing unemployment. The extreme left, however, was the major source of concern. Various Marxist groups (Stalinist, Trotskyist, Maoist) within the university intelligentsia possessed a membership of approximately 80,000; the extreme left had virtually no contact with labor. The university intelligentsia lent sympathetic support to the RAF, and when Ulrike Meinhof committed suicide in prison in the spring of 1976, RAF terrorism (including kidnappings, murders, and hijackings) started afresh in an attempt to gain release of the imprisoned terrorists.

In response to CDU/CSU pressures, Schmidt adopted strict policies against political extremists. These policies were harshly criticized by novelist Heinrich Böll and other prominent West German intellectuals who vigorously defended civil liberties. The ban on employment (*Berufsverbot*) bars political extremists—persons engaged in activities deemed to be hostile to the Basic Law—from civil service positions. The Federal Republic's public sector employs 15 percent of the work force in jobs ranging from high-level positions of responsibility to menial labor tasks. Screening procedures were directed especially against university graduates, two-thirds of whom normally found employment in the civil service. Implementation of the *Berufsverbot* was nevertheless considered mild; a total of 745,000 job applicants were screened in the 1976–77 period, but only 287 were rejected. Schmidt introduced *Politik der inneren Sicherheit* (internal security policy) in late 1977 to root out terrorism. New security legislation declared all terrorist associations illegal. Roadblocks and search warrants were authorized, and legal counsels were restricted and supervised in their communications with clients who were alleged terrorists. (Attorneys were believed to have been used to establish contact with terrorist cohorts on the outside.) An advanced system of citizen surveillance was developed (see State Police Agencies, ch. 9).

In 1979 Karl Carstens (CDU) was elected president. The SPD vote remained stable (42.9 percent) in the 1980 Bundestag elections. The FDP gained significantly, however, polling 10.6 percent of the vote, and Schmidt was reelected chancellor. Many observers attributed the decline of the CDU/CSU in the 1980 election to the choice of CSU leader Strauss as Schmidt's opponent. Strauss had long been a controversial figure whose ultranationalistic speeches over several decades had alienated and frightened many electors, including members of the CDU.

The SPD slogan "Security for the Eighties" had emphasized continuity, stability, and preservation of the status quo. Throughout 1981, however, the country's economic situation continued to worsen, and an increasing number of citizens questioned Schmidt's staunch adherence to NATO and the United States, in particular the positioning of additional American nuclear weapons in West Germany. By early 1982 challenges to Schmidt's leadership from within the SPD and from numerous factions within the electorate had called into question the consensus that had existed for almost two decades. Public opinion polls in late 1981 indicated that a strong majority favored continued association with NATO and the West, but the presence of numerous nuclear warheads—more per square kilometer than any country in the world—was expected to remain a divisive political issue in the early and mid-1980s.

* * * * * *

Alfred Grosser's *Germany in Our Time: A Political History of the Postwar Years* provides a useful synopsis of West German political, economic, and social developments. The reader may enjoy *People and Politics: The Years 1960–1975* by Willy Brandt, the former chancellor. A number of review articles discuss significant recent interpretations of the Federal Republic's history and politics: Peter J. Katzenstein's "Problem or Model? West Germany in the 1980s," in *World Politics*; Wilhelm Bleek's "From Cold War to Ostpolitik: Two Germanys in Search of Separate Identities," in *World Politics*; and Klaus Epstein's "The German Problem 1945–50," in *World Politics*.

For background German history Geoffrey Barraclough's *The Origins of Modern Germany* is a classic study of the late medieval German period. *Germany: 1866–1945* by Gordon Craig represents a recent synthesis of the history of the German nation-state. Fritz Fischer's controversial *Germany's Aims in the First World War* warrants brief perusal: the author reviews a wealth of documentation revealing the political and social context of World War I. *The German Dictatorship: The Origins, Structure, and Effects of National Socialism* by Karl Dietrich Bracher offers an excellent analysis of Hitler's road to power and the Third Reich. (For further information see Bibliography.)

Chapter 2. Physical and Demographic Setting

Houses in Frankfurt

Physical and Demographic Setting

IN EARLY 1982 West Germans enjoyed a high standard of living, although rising unemployment, inflation, and declining economic productivity posed increasingly serious problems. A long tradition of state-sponsored welfare programs, dating from the 1880s, has led Germans to regard security against economic destitution and sickness as an inalienable right. Almost all citizens are covered by social insurance on either a compulsory or voluntary basis. Benefits include pensions, accident and health insurance, unemployment insurance, maternity care, special subsidies for children, and payments to victims of Nazi oppression.

The educational system has a long and excellent reputation for its high standards. The literacy rate has been nearly 100 percent since 1900. In the early 1980s, however, less than 20 percent of the graduates of secondary schools went on to higher education. At about the age of ten, upon completion of elementary school, a child and his or her parents must decide upon a vocational secondary school or a general secondary education; only the latter prepares the student for college and university work.

The federal government and the state (*Land*; pl., *Länder*) provide public education through taxation. Private schools, which coexist with the state schools, are largely financed by private organizations: churches, religious orders, and foundations. Some private denominational schools, however, also are subsidized in part by the state.

Geography

The 248,630 square kilometers within the borders of the Federal Republic of Germany (West Germany or Federal Republic) and West Berlin include a wide variety of terrain. Few of the political boundaries are natural, and the physical regions within the country tend to grow gradually into one another. The flat lowlands of the northwest become rolling green hills to the northeast and inland to the south, where they blend into the uplands of the central part of the country. The low mountains and great forests of the central regions give way to more gentle terrain in the Danube River basin and once again become hilly at the approaches to the Alps. The Bavarian Alps and the Rhine Valley are impressive features of West Germany's landscape—the mountains for their beauty and ruggedness and the Rhine Valley for its importance as a commercial artery and its physical beauty.

Land borders conform roughly to regions that date back to the Holy Roman Empire. Eight of the ten *Länder* divide most of the country's territory. Two of them—Hamburg and Bremen—are large urban complexes requiring so many administrative functions

Federal Republic of Germany

differing from the largely rural areas adjacent to them that they have been made into separate *Länder*. West Berlin is administered separately (see fig. 1).

Topography

For the purpose of topographic discussion, the country is sometimes divided into five major physical regions: the northern lowlands, central uplands, Alpine foothills, Bavarian Alps, and the Rhine Valley and western highlands (see fig. 7). The northern lowlands encompass the territory of three *Länder*—Schleswig-Holstein, Hamburg, and Bremen—and most of a fourth, Lower Saxony. The lowlands are part of a great plain that extends across north-central Europe, broadening from northern Belgium and the Netherlands until, by the time it reaches the Ural Mountains, it has encompassed a large part of Poland and the European portion of the Soviet Union.

South of the northern lowlands, the terrain rises to a hilly region commonly known as the central uplands. The central uplands incorporate the remainder of Lower Saxony, adjacent hills of North Rhine-Westphalia, and most of Hesse. This is a part of the Hercynian Massif, a range of eroded low mountains extending from northern France, through southern Belgium, West Germany, the German Democratic Republic (East Germany), and into southern Poland.

The greatest part of Bavaria and the eastern two-thirds of Baden-Württemberg are hilly or have low, forested mountains that are foothills of the Alps. This Alpine foothill region contains the upper Danube River basin and the country's most beautiful lake area. Where the foothills give way to an abrupt rise in terrain, the Bavarian Alps region begins. This area is part of the Alps proper.

The remainder of West Germany, the western and southwestern section, is largely hilly country and is dominated by the Rhine River, which drains almost all of the area. This section contains the Rhine Valley and most of the terrain beside it from the Swiss border to the Ruhr River. It is a varied region that includes the wide and terraced valley of the upper Rhine, the narrow gorges of the river between Bingen and Bonn, the Saar, the Black Forest (Schwarzwald), and the low mountains on both sides of the river north of the Black Forest.

Northern Lowlands

Hills in eastern Schleswig-Holstein rarely exceed 150 meters in elevation, and those in the central and western parts seldom reach 100 meters. Particularly in the northeast and all along the southern side of the region—wherever there is a little elevation or

Physical and Demographic Setting

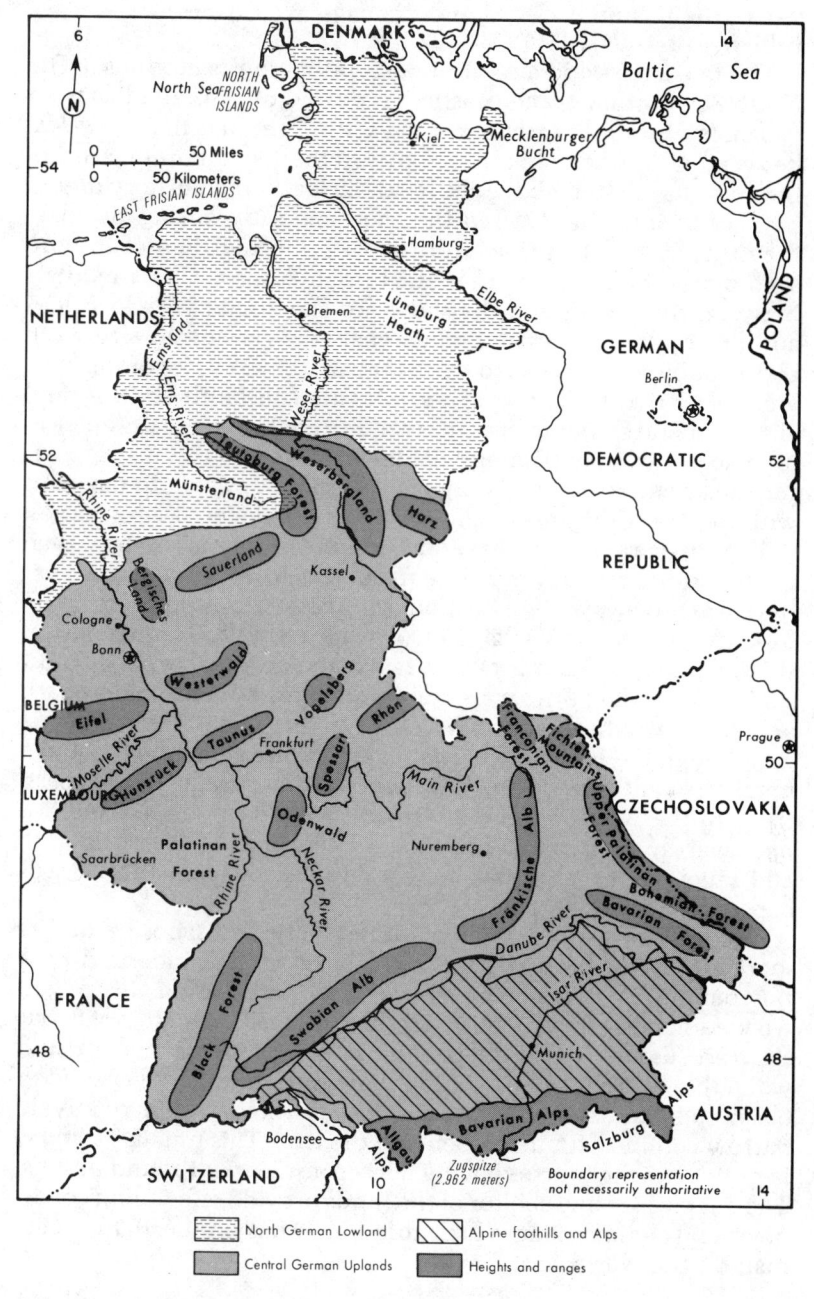

Source: Based on information from Karl Römer (ed.), *Facts about Germany*, Gütersloh, Germany, 1979, p. 11.

Figure 7. *Topography and Drainage*

where the terrain is rolling and drainage is satisfactory—the land is highly productive.

The lowlands slope almost imperceptibly toward the sea. The North Sea portion of the coastline is devoid of cliffs and has wide expanses of sand, marsh, and mud flats. The mud flats (*Watten*) between the Elbe estuary and the Netherlands border are believed to have been above sea level during Roman history and to have been inundated when the shoreline sank during the thirteenth century. In the western area the former line of inshore sand dunes then became the East Frisian Islands. The mud flats between the islands and the shore are exposed at very low tides and are crossed by innumerable channels varying in size from those cut by small creeks to those that are the estuaries of the Elbe and Weser rivers. The mud and sand are constantly shifting, and all harbor and shipping channels require continuing maintenance. Ship access to small fishing villages and even to the major ports remains treacherous, and only pilots familiar on a day-to-day basis with the latest shifting of sands can safely navigate the estuaries.

The offshore islands have maximum elevations of less than thirty-five meters and have been subject to eroding forces that have washed away whole sections during severe storms. In 1854, for example, the only village on Wangerooge, the easternmost of the main East Frisian group, was washed away. Shorelines most subject to eroding tides were stabilized during the late nineteenth and early twentieth centuries.

Although the East Frisian Islands are strung along the coast in a nearly straight line, having long axes roughly parallel to the coast, those in the North Frisian group are irregularly shaped and are haphazardly positioned. They were also a part of the mainland, and much of the mud flat between the islands and the coast is exposed during low tides.

The Schleswig-Holstein coast on the Baltic Sea exposure differs markedly from that on the North Sea side. It is indented by a number of small fjords, which have steep banks, rising abruptly to wooded slopes. Rivers emptying through the fjords are small, but they are usually quite deep because of conditions that existed when they were formed. At that time the land was covered with glacial ice, and the streams, which were held within relatively narrow confines, tunneled beneath the ice. This usually resulted in quite straight courses having fairly constant widths and depths. The deep water and shelter of the fjords provide safe sailing conditions, and fishing villages are more numerous on the Baltic coast than on the North Sea.

Central Uplands

Hundreds of picturesque villages nestle in the hills of Hesse. This region has inspired the legends, children's stories, and folklore of the Grimms' fairy tales and other literature. The lower

Physical and Demographic Setting

hills north of Hesse in Lower Saxony and North Rhine-Westphalia contain a large portion of arable land. The forests thin out, and much of the rich land is sown to wheat and root plants—sugar beets and potatoes—supporting a considerably greater population than either the lowlands to the north or the forests to the south.

Alpine Foothills

All of Bavaria and the eastern portion of Baden-Württemberg, except the Black Forest and the Odenwald, constitute the country's Alpine foothills. Relatively little of this area is forest, and a high proportion is extremely productive crop and pastureland.

Except for small areas in Baden-Württemberg and the part of Bavaria to the north of Nuremberg, most of the region is in the upper Danube River basin. The Danube is not as important a river in West Germany as it is in the countries along its lower courses.

Lakes that range in size from less than half a hectare to a little more than eighty square kilometers were created throughout the region when glacial moraine blocked the valleys. Typical lakes have clear, clean water, are deep, and have steep, heavily wooded banks.

Bavarian Alps

The Bavarian Alps are the small fringe of high mountains that extend in a narrow strip along the country's southern boundary. They range eastward from the Bodensee, a lake on the border shared with Switzerland, to the Austrian border just west of Salzburg. The Bavarian Alps have the same origin, structure, and features as the main Alpine ranges of Switzerland, Austria, Italy, and France, but the western part of the Bavarian portion is separated from the rest of the range by the Inn River Valley.

Valleys are dotted with small cultivated fields, and slopes are usually forested with coniferous trees or are pastureland. The area supports less local population than is average for the country, but it is extremely popular as a holiday resort at all seasons of the year. The highest peak, the Zugspitze (2,962 meters), is near the Austrian border south-southwest of Munich.

The Rhine Valley and the Western Highlands

To many, the Federal Republic is in essence the Rhine River basin. The Rhine is the most important waterway in Europe, and its valley is perhaps the greatest single commercial artery in the world. Although the Rhine rises in Switzerland, and for the final 200 kilometers of its lower course to the sea flows through the Netherlands, the river is nevertheless the single greatest unifying feature of West Germany.

The upper Rhine region consists of a valley plain some thirty to fifty kilometers wide, flanked on both sides by heavily forested mountainous areas. This 300-kilometer portion of the valley is often called the Rhine Rift Valley, because it originated as a result of a sharp fracture of the region's terrain at the same time the Alps were formed. Until then the region had consisted of a single mountain massif that had included the Black Forest and the Vosges range in France.

This upper valley is also referred to as the terraced country. The name derives from the fact that the rift valley has an upper level that is fairly uniform in elevation until it rises to the hilly regions on both sides. This terrace level was formed during glacial periods when ice blocked the river from the lower courses, and sediment was deposited in the valley. As the river established these courses, it cut into the softer sediment, leaving the upper level as a distinctive flat-topped terrace region.

The Black Forest in the extreme southwestern corner of the country is so named both because the fir trees that predominate in its natural forest present a deep green color and because their thick canopies form a cover that shields much of the light from the forest floor, giving an aura of semidarkness. Elevations in the Black Forest approach 1,500 meters, making it the highest of the areas bordering the Rhine.

The Rhine's upper valley ends abruptly in the vicinity of Frankfurt, Wiesbaden, and Mainz, where the river turns sharply to the west. Below Mainz, past Bingen—where it turns northward again—and nearly to Bonn, it flows through narrow gorges.

The Saar region is notable primarily for its rich coalfield and the industry that has developed around it. Located on the French border southeast of Luxembourg, the Saar area has changed hands between France and Germany on several occasions. The coalfield that has made it the source of contention is about forty kilometers long and about thirteen kilometers wide. To the east and north of the coalfield the terrain increases in elevation, and in the north it blends into the Hunsrück mountain range. Across the Moselle River is the considerably steeper, more rugged Eifel region. This area extends from the western border of the country and blends into the lowland region north of Bonn and Aachen. Because of its central location, the high Eifel—known as such only in relation to the surrounding terrain, because its elevations at no point reach 1,000 meters—drains into the Moselle, Rhine, and Meuse rivers.

The Taunus Mountains are low, and their highest point is only 875 meters above sea level. The Westerwald, to the north and northwest of the Taunus, more nearly resembles the Eifel area across the Rhine than it does the uplands adjacent to it on the eastern side of the river. The terrain in the region is lower, as it blends into the northern lowlands, and rarely reaches 600 meters. The most prominent peak, the Drachenfels, is isolated in an area of lower elevation that makes it stand out, even though it reaches a height of only 303 meters. The Westerwald has much forest,

*Entering resort town of Garmisch–Partenkirchen
in the Bavarian Alps
Courtesy Dorothy Lohmann*

steep gorges, and few people; therefore, small pastures and cultivated areas are restricted to land that is reasonably level.

Drainage

The greater part of the country drains into the North Sea via the Rhine, Ems, Weser, and Elbe rivers and by lesser local streams in the northwest. A small area north and northeast of Hamburg drains into the Baltic Sea, and a considerable area in the southeast lies in the Danube River basin. The Danube flows eastward across south-central Europe into the Black Sea.

The divide separating the watersheds of the Danube and Rhine basins winds around Baden-Württemberg and Bavaria in a line that is difficult to define in some places. The Danube basin includes the greater portion of Bavaria and southeastern Baden-Württemberg. Water that it collects from West Germany comes from the Bavarian Alps, the Black Forest, and the Alpine foothills. A small area north of the Bodensee, however, drains into the Rhine River. There are short streams flowing to the lakes, and the area along the Swiss border west of the lake drains directly into the Rhine.

The divide between the Rhine and Danube basins originates at the Bodensee and follows the high ridge of the Black Forest to a point a few miles northeast of Freiburg and then dips to the southeast. After passing between the headwater points of the Neckar and Danube rivers it turns again to the northeast, following the

Federal Republic of Germany

high ridge of the Swabian Alps, and continues in that general direction to the Bohemian Forest (Böhmerwald) and the Czechoslovak border.

Climate

The entire country falls into a climatic zone where westerly winds and a maritime climate prevail most of the year. Maritime influences are effective a greater percentage of the time in the northwest, especially along the coast. Continental conditions and greater temperature extremes between day and night and between summer and winter are experienced increasingly inland, to the south, and to the southeast. The change to an increasing influence from continental weather systems over Europe as a whole is experienced more noticeably from west to east but, because West Germany is narrow in this direction and its north-south axis is more than three times as long, continental climate is more apparent at increasing distances from the sea and in the higher elevations of the south.

In addition to the maritime and continental climates that predominate over most of the country, the Alpine regions in the extreme south and, to a lesser degree, a few of the upland sections of central and western areas, have a so-called mountain climate. This climate is different because temperatures decrease with higher elevations and because precipitation increases when moisture-laden air is forced to lift over higher terrain. Variable local winds develop as high and irregular terrain deflects prevailing winds. Such terrain also creates local areas of differing shelter and exposure, in relation both to winds and sunshine.

The major air masses contributing to the maritime weather are the Icelandic low-pressure and the Azores high-pressure systems. The Icelandic lows originate in the North Atlantic Ocean, rotate in a counterclockwise direction, and tend to move to the east and southeast as they approach Europe. The Azores highs form in the vicinity of the Azores Islands or in their 30° to 40° north latitude band. They move eastward and rotate in a clockwise direction. Both of these air masses furnish Western Europe with moisture-laden clouds propelled by westerly winds.

The northern lowlands frequently experience a situation (more often during the winter months) when they are between these air masses and are simultaneously influenced by both. At such times winds are westerly and usually strong. When only one of the systems is dominant, it is more often the Icelandic low. In spite of their nearly polar origin, the Icelandic lows are warmed by the Gulf Stream, and areas on the country's North Sea coast have midwinter temperatures averaging more than 1.6° C. This is more than three degrees above the average for that latitude, which is shared by central Labrador, the lower part of Hudson Bay, the Aleutian Islands, and some bitterly cold regions in Siberia.

When continental weather systems originating to the east are responsible for the weather, conditions are markedly different. In the winter months these systems have high-pressure air masses that bring bright, clear, cold weather. The local people describe these air masses as Siberian highs and usually expect them to prevail for about two weeks. An occasional condition arises when the center of a low-pressure system deviates to the south of its usual path and crosses the central part of the country. This causes what is called *Föhn* (pl., *Föhne*), or warm wind. Warm tropical air is drawn across the Alps and loses its moisture on the southern slopes of the mountains. The air warms significantly as it compresses during its descent from the northern slopes. In the springtime these winds dissipate the cloud cover and melt the snows. The *Föhne* of Bavaria and Baden-Württemberg rarely are comparable in velocity or in desiccating effect to those that occur in Switzerland or to the mistral winds, which are of the same origin and type, that roar up the Rhone River valley in France.

The yearly mean temperature for the country is about 9° C. It varies with shelter and elevation, but otherwise the annual mean is almost constant throughout the country. Temperature extremes between night and day and summer and winter are considerably less in the north.

During January, the coldest month, the approximately 1.6° C average temperature in the north decreases to less than –2° C in the south. In the higher mountains, where elevation is the dominant factor, the average may be as low as –6° C. In July, the warmest month, the situation reverses, and it is cooler in the north than in the south. The northern coastal region has July temperatures averaging between 16° C and 18° C; at some locations in the south the average is 19.4° C or slightly higher.

Annual precipitation varies from 2,000 millimeters a year in the southern mountains to a low of 400 millimeters in the vicinity of Mainz. Over most of the country it averages between 600 millimeters and 800 millimeters per annum.

Population

The population in early 1982 was estimated at about 61,850,000, including approximately 1,918,000 in West Berlin. The 1970 census—as of early 1982 the most recent complete count—reported a total of 60,650,599 and an annual rate of growth of 0.7 percent. By 1981 the annual rate of growth was variously estimated at between 0.1 and 0.3 percent; the former rate was based on projected crude birth and death rates of 9.6 and 11.6 per 1,000 inhabitants respectively and a net immigration rate of 2.8 per 1,000. The crude birthrate was the lowest since records have been maintained.

Although the area that is now the Federal Republic has existed as that particular entity only since World War II, regional statistics

Federal Republic of Germany

have been maintained in sufficient detail so that the population of the area since early in the nineteenth century can be arrived at with reasonable accuracy. Since 1819 the population of 14.2 million has more than quadrupled. The periods of most rapid growth occurred between about 1880 and 1910 and between 1939 and 1970. The population increased from about 22.8 million in 1880 to about 35.6 million in 1910, an increase of over 55 percent. In 1939 the population was about 43 million; the increase between that date and 1981 amounted to about 43 percent.

The largest factor in that increase was, however, the resettlement in West Germany of great numbers of ethnic Germans from areas to the east. More than 6 million Germans reached the Federal Republic either as refugees or expellees between the end of the war and the fall of 1946. Almost all were from Czechoslovakia, Austria, Hungary, and former German territories east of the Oder and Neisse rivers. Eventually a total of over 9 million entered the country from those areas. In addition before the creation of the Berlin Wall in 1961 an estimated 3 million fled from East Germany to West Germany.

In 1981 the population included about 4.5 million foreigners. The overwhelming majority of the foreigners were guest workers *Gastarbeiter*) and their dependents (see Ethnicity, ch. 3). In 1978 the government reported that one out of every eight live births was to a foreigner.

In the late 1970s about 9 percent of the population lived in the industrial megapolis sometimes called Ruhrstadt (Ruhr City), an area in which major cities merge into each other and in which the population density reaches 5,500 per square kilometer (see fig. 8). Another 8 percent lived in the three largest cities: West Berlin (over 1.9 million); Hamburg (almost 1.7 million); and Munich (almost 1.3 million). Only about 6 percent lived in villages containing fewer than 2,000 inhabitants (see table 2, Appendix).

The composition of the population by age and sex emphasizes the catastrophic events that have occurred in the country during the lifespan of its population (see fig. 9). The bottom of the structure reveals the low and declining birthrate from about 1965 onward. There are in addition "birth gaps" reflecting the events of the two world wars and the economic crisis of the early 1930s. The population also reveals a significant preponderance of females over the age of fifty, reflecting the loss of men in the wars as well as the natural longer life of women. In 1981 life expectancy at birth was given as seventy for males, seventy-six for females.

Education

The origins of the German educational system date back to the era of Charlemagne. A strong educational impetus was exerted during the fourteenth century when the universities of Prague, Vienna, Heidelberg, and Cologne were founded. A small intellec-

Physical and Demographic Setting

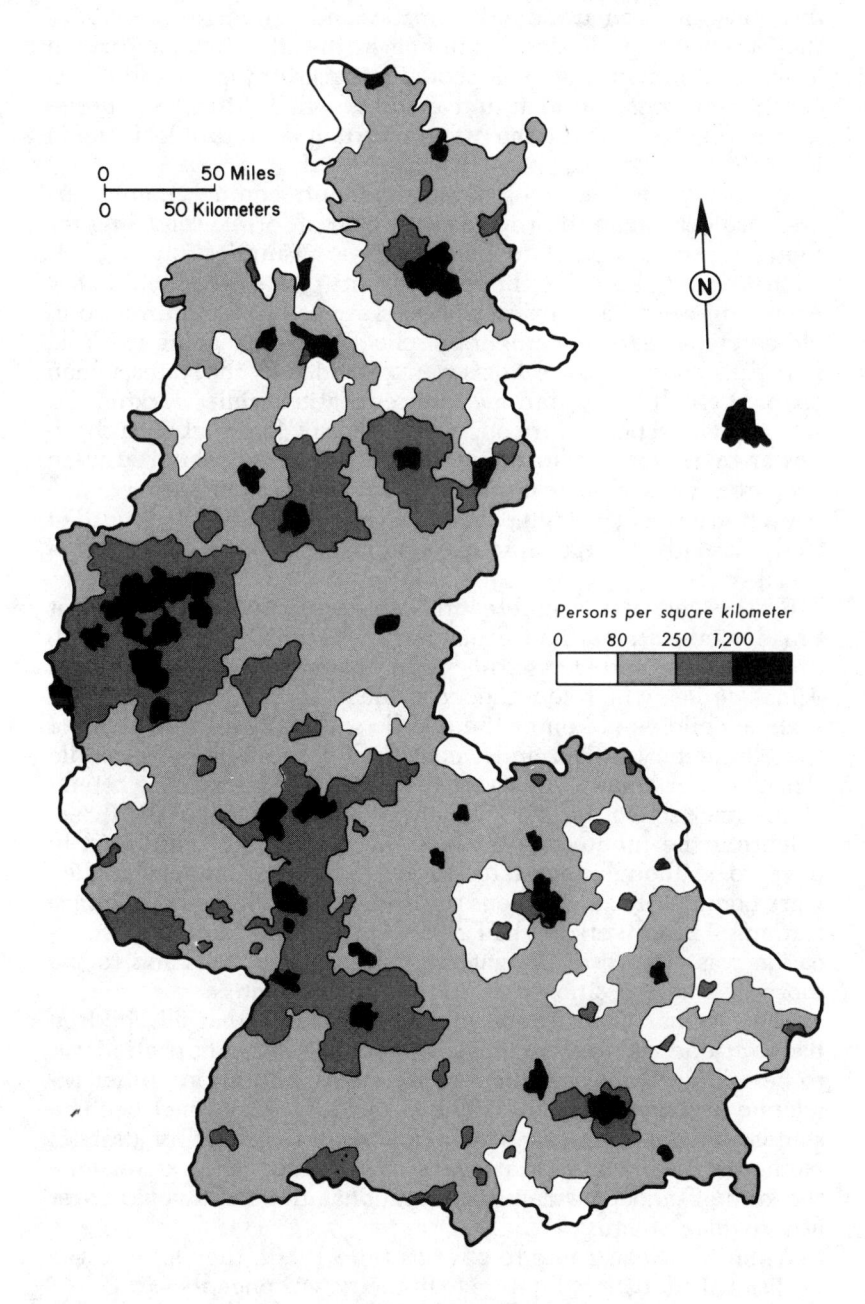

Source: Based on information from Federal Republic of Germany, Press and Information Office, *Territory and Population,* Bonn, 1980

Figure 8. Population Density, Late 1970s

Federal Republic of Germany

tual elite gathered at these universities and in monasteries where they studied the classics; beginning in the fifteenth century an interest in humanism developed. By the seventeenth and eighteenth centuries German universities, which then numbered seventeen, were among the most important centers of learning in Europe.

As early as the beginning of the eighteenth century, many German princes began to provide some kind of formal schooling for the children of their states. At the time of unification in 1871, education still remained the responsibility of the individual states. After unification approximately 90 percent of all children completed eight years of elementary schooling before going to work. Part-time continuation schools were provided by the states, which enabled children to continue their education while working.

Secondary schools were operated either by local public authorities or by private organizations. In these schools children were prepared for professional careers or for entrance into the university. Because of the high educational standards and the length of study, a relatively small number of pupils embarked on this educational route.

By the end of the nineteenth century, many parents sought broader educational and economic opportunities for their children. This attitude led to the establishment of the middle school *Mittelschule*), which lengthened presecondary education. Generally a child would enter the middle school after three years of the elementary school and would then continue in the middle school for six years. An alternative was for the child to attend elementary school for six years and the middle school for three.

During the nineteenth century the universities continued to develop. Although the states supported them financially, they were completely autonomous regarding curriculum and administration. The universities had great prestige, and a university education was viewed as the gateway to the professions and to the more desirable positions within the government.

The Weimar Constitution of 1919 stipulated that all children had to attend school for eight years; this elementary education was to be followed by some form of secondary education, either academic or vocational. By 1925 the middle school had become standardized as a six-year school, following the first four years of elementary school. Parents were required by law to determine the kind of school, academic or vocational, the child would enter at ten years of age.

When the Nazis came to power in the 1930s, they altered the traditional educational system to fit their own concepts. In 1934 a law was promulgated that reorganized the entire educational system, bringing all educational matters under the strict control of the Ministry of Science, Education, and Public Instruction. During the 1930s and 1940s, books were rewritten and censored to

Physical and Demographic Setting

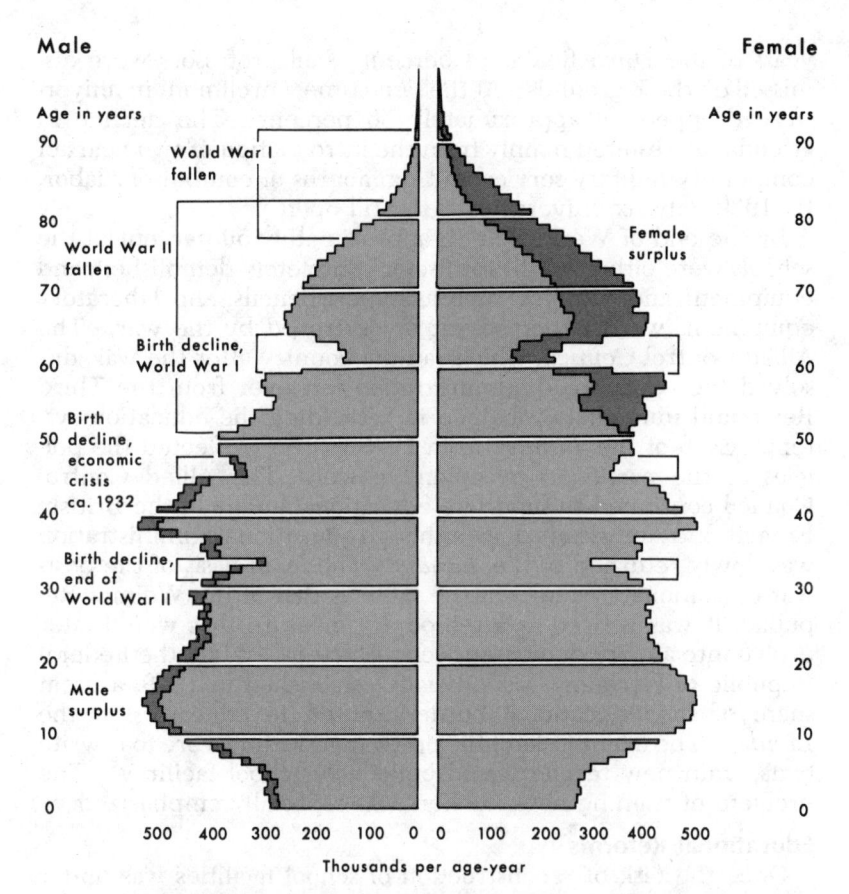

Source: Based on information from Federal Republic of Germany, Statistisches Bundesamt, *Statistisches Jahrbuch, 1979 Für die Bundesrepublik Deutschland,* Stuttgart, 1979.

Figure 9. *Age–Sex Structure, December 1978*

expound only the official views. In 1937 the *Gymnasium* (pl., *Gymnasien*), which had been the preparatory school for the university, was partially replaced by a new form of high school, called the *Oberschule,* which strongly emphasized the official ideology. Another new type of elite school, the so-called NAPOLA (National-politische Akademie), was created. Few students continued on to higher education.

The autonomy of the universities was eliminated. Both administrators and professors, previously elected by their fellows, were appointed by the minister of science, education, and public instruction. Professors were carefully screened for their political views and their ethnic backgrounds, and during the first three years of the Third Reich, 14 percent of all professors were dismissed on those grounds. At the same time, enrollment in universities dropped by approximately 50 percent. The decline in attendance resulted mainly from the introduction of two years of compulsory military service and six months of compulsory labor. By 1939 only six universities were still open.

By the end of World War II, approximately 50 percent of the schools were either not fit for use or completely demolished, and equipment and supplies, such as paper, pencils, and laboratory equipment, were either absent or destroyed by the war. The Allied Control Council, which ran the country after the war, dissolved the educational administration left over from the Third Reich and immediately helped in rebuilding the education system. Each of the *Länder* from 1945 to 1949 reflected the policies of the particular occupying power. The Allied Control Council continued to supervise educational affairs in the British, French, and American zones, although educational administration was slowly returned to the *Länder*. The main basis of the postwar educational system was the same as that of the Weimar Republic. It was viewed as a temporary measure that would later evolve into a more democratic school system. When the Federal Republic of Germany was officially established in 1949, a great share of the educational burden shifted to educators in the *Länder*. The major tasks of the postwar educators were to rewrite texts, train new teachers, and build new school facilities. The problem of training new teachers was especially emphasized.

Educational Reforms

Once the task of reconstruction of school facilities was under way, various reforms were introduced in order to standardize the school system and to infuse into it new elements. In 1953 the Constitution of the German Committee for the Educational System attempted to make the educational system more uniform throughout the *Länder*, and in 1959 the committee published a report on the subject, entitled *General Plan for the Reorganization of the Public School System*. In the 1960s such reforms as apprentice shops and new methods of instruction in vocational training were introduced.

In the 1970s more sweeping reforms were proposed. As the federal government explained: "The desires for improved schooling for children in view of the increasing demands of a workaday world oriented more and more toward science again brought up the question of curricula and basically new structuring of the educational system." Fundamental reforms were proposed in a document called *Structural Plans for the Educational System* which was approved in February 1970 by the German Council of Education and by each *Land* minister of education and cultural affairs (*Kultusminister*).

The broad outlines of these reforms, which were to extend from kindergarten to institutions of higher education, were: the restructuring of the upper level of the *Gymnasium*, an increase in the number of students in institutions of higher learning, and the introduction of the comprehensive school (*Gesamtschule*), which was designed to alleviate and eventually to eliminate the allegedly elitist character of the traditional secondary education system. Another important area included in these proposed reforms was adult education and the vocational sector of the education system.

Nevertheless, because each *Land* is largely autonomous in the field of education, it has been practically impossible to gain consensus regarding uniformity of the school system. In addition educators have disagreed whether the entire educational system needs to be restructured or whether changes should be attempted within the existing structure. Moreover German educators have tended to be reluctant to change traditional and proven educational values that have their roots in the long history of their quality-oriented educational system. Another major hurdle that would have to be overcome is the huge financial burden that quantitative expansion would impose. In the early 1970s it was anticipated that the proportion of the national budget devoted to education would increase roughly 300 percent by the mid-1980s. In order to meet these expenses, taxes would have had to be increased appreciably. Many *Land* officials have been unwilling to commit themselves to reforms until they are assured of an appropriate amount of funding. Also a major factor in the delay or abandonment of some of the reforms was the open resistance of parents in some *Länder* against what they perceived as the lowering of standards in schools in order to provide a broader accessibility of the upper levels of secondary education to some pupils. Budgetary constraints during the late 1970s and increasing doubts about the usefulness of some of the proposed measures made it seem unlikely in the early 1980s that the planned reforms would be fully realized.

Basic Principles of Education

There are three basic principles of the educational system. The foremost principle is to maintain the high quality of education that has served as a model for many other nations, including the Scandinavian countries, most of the East European countries, and the Low Countries, and has significantly influenced the system in the United States, particularly in the area of higher education. The second basic principle is that every individual has the right to an education, which is stated in the Basic Law (constitution) promulgated in 1949. The third essential principle is that the state, in turn, has the right to expect that students going through the system will be prepared for a useful role in society.

Federal Republic of Germany

Among other principles of education are that full-time education should be compulsory for a period of nine years and that literacy should be as nearly universal as possible. Private schools, maintained generally by churches, private associations, and individuals, are frequently subsidized by the state on the principle that they should coexist with state schools. Although traditionally boys and girls were separated within the school system, there has been a growing trend toward coeducation since World War II. Another important principle of German education is to encourage adult education in the working population.

Administration and Finance

Administration

The overall administrator for education is the federal minister of education and science (see The Government, ch. 7). The ministry is in charge of establishing and maintaining state schools and universities, training teachers, supporting private schools, and funding adult education. The federal ministry shares responsibilities, however, with the minister of education and cultural affairs of each of the *Länder*. The *Land* minister is in charge of planning, organizing, managing, promoting, and supervising the entire school system of the state. Other duties include: supervising teachers, administering activities of the schools and various organizations that support them, and supervising boards of education, school committees, and other so-called intermediate bodies at the administrative level. The Commission for Educational Planning ensures that the federal government and the *Länder* cooperate regarding educational policy. This commission also makes long-term plans for educational developments and assesses expenditures.

Although the federal Ministry of Education and Science and the comparable ministries of the *Länder* are the major administrative bodies dealing with education, there are also several ancillary bodies that are involved. Certain federal ministries, such as the Ministry of Agriculture, deal with the administration of appropriate vocational schools. In addition the Council of Education, established in 1965, serves as an advisory committee for the entire educational system, with the exception of the universities. It draws up plans regarding the requirements of the educational system, taking into account the needs of society for people trained in specific areas. The Council on Science and the Humanities, established in 1957, is the advisory body for the universities and performs functions similar to the Council of Education. Institutions of higher learning, especially universities, have the status of corporate bodies with autonomous, self-administering, governmental structures.

The principle of decentralization is rigorously applied throughout the educational system. In this way, despite the fact that the

Ministry of Education and Science and the *Land* ministries have overall control of the system, the administrative body closest to a particular school is the chief administrator of that school. Below the *Land* authorities there are intermediate bodies, such as district presidents, boards of education in the case of state schools, and religious communities and orders in the case of private schools. Their tasks are to supervise the teachers and the activities of other organizations that help maintain the school. Below these intermediate bodies are the so-called lower bodies that include school inspectors, vocational employer organizations, and advisory councils. These bodies generally serve in an advisory capacity rather than as direct supervisors of the system.

Finance

Since the late eighteenth century a major emphasis has been placed on public education, and the government has therefore always given it strong financial backing. Because public education is free, the education system has to be financed almost entirely through federal, state, and municipal taxes. Industrial enterprises and parents' associations also contribute to the financing of education on a voluntary basis. Accredited denominational schools receive financial support from the federal government; the entire budget for private schools—many of which are denominational—amounts to approximately 15 percent of the total expenditures for education.

The educational and research budget is divided into three categories: personnel expenditures, material expenditures, and capital expenditures. During the late 1970s the total amount spent for education and research was approximately 16.2 percent of the total budget of the federal government, the *Länder*, and the districts and communities.

There is also special encouragement of vocational training and retraining through state allowances. The Federal Institute of Labor gives grants and loans to both pupils and adults for vocational training. As an encouragement for vocational retraining by adults who require refresher courses, the Federal Institute of Labor pays living costs of both an individual and his or her family during the period of retraining. The sum normally amounts to about 95 percent of an employee's former income. After retraining, the institute then pays enterprises hiring a retrained worker an "initiation allowance."

In 1970 the total expenses for education were more than DM27.6 billion (for value of the deutsche mark—see Glossary), of which the federal government expended approximately DM1.85 billion, the *Länder* DM19.07 billion, and the local school districts about DM6.67 billion. By 1975 these expenses had risen to a total of DM56.18 billion, with DM4.7 billion expended by the federal government, DM40.05 by the *Länder*, and DM10.98 by the local governments. DM29.79 billion was allocated to personnel expenditures, DM6.9 billion for material expenditures, and DM10.65 billion for capital expenditures.

The Educational System

Kindergarten

Preschool or kindergarten was introduced in Germany in the mid-nineteenth century. Kindergartens are sponsored by churches, communities, private enterprises, and parents' groups and are attended by children from three to six years of age. Attendance is voluntary, but in the late 1970s about 70 percent of all three-, four-, and five-year-olds attended these schools.

The original purpose of the kindergarten was to awaken the child's abilities and interests through participation in games and activities. Although kindergartens still tend to deal with the social aspects of the child's development, the government has sought to emphasize the educational aspects to a greater degree. According to a government source, reforms dealing with the kindergarten level "proceed on the assumption that it is precisely the early years of childhood that are decisive for the development of learning and speaking abilities for the education of creative imagination."

Elementary Education

Attendance at the *Grundschule,* a four-year basic or elementary school, is compulsory. Children attend from the ages of six to ten. Despite the uniformity of the period of attendance, there is some variety in hours and textbooks, depending on the particular city or *Land.* There was a decrease in the number of pupils attending the *Grundschule* between 1975 and 1978, reflecting the declining birthrate (see table 3, Appendix).

When a child finishes the fourth year of the *Grundschule,* the child and the parents must make the decision regarding secondary education. Many educators have asserted that forcing such a decision at age ten is unrealistic and closes higher educational opportunities for those who develop intellectually during their teen years but whose secondary education does not qualify them for university entrance. The child's teachers at the *Grundschule* must concur in the choice. Educators, fearing that too much talent has been lost under the rigidly compartmentalized system, have been experimenting with methods of transferring students at various secondary schools into *Gymnasien,* which have always been the regular route to university education. In the 1970s, a so-called orientation phase (grades five and six) was introduced in all *Länder,* which was designed to extend the period of decision and to make a transition into the appropriate secondary school easier. In 1979 approximately 15 percent of all pupils leaving the elementary schools were enrolled in courses in the orientation phase.

General Secondary Education

There are four forms of general secondary education or continuation schools called: the *Hauptschule,* the *Realschule,* the *Gymnasium,* and the *Gesamtschule* (pl., *Gesamtschulen*) (see fig. 10). The *Hauptschule* is referred to as the secondary modern or short-course school and the *Realschule* as the intermediate school. The *Gymnasium* is called the grammar school or sometimes senior high school. (Great care is to be taken in using such translations of the German terms for the individual types of schools, particularly because in almost all cases the terminology used to describe the German educational system does not correspond to the same terminology as used in the educational system of the United States.) Finally, the *Gesamtschule* is known as the comprehensive school. In recent years some educators have felt that the compartmentalization of secondary education has been restrictive and rigid and has prevented students from exploring various areas of education. The *Gesamtschule*, a radically new kind of school, was introduced to alleviate this situation. It is designed to be a comprehensive school, offering an all-inclusive curriculum for students from ages six to nineteen who are allowed to pursue whatever course they choose. Some of these *Gesamtschulen* have been established as all-day schools, unlike the *Gymnasien*, which have classes only part of the day but which include extensive homework assignments. The degree of acceptance of these schools has varied greatly from *Land* to *Land*, and they have created great political controversies.

Approximately 50 percent of the children who complete an elementary school continue on to a short-course school. They are required to attend this school for five years, from age ten to fifteen. The curriculum stresses preparation for a vocation but also includes mathematics, history, geography, German, and one foreign language. Graduates of this school receive a senior school certificate called the *Hauptschulabschluss.* After graduation they either become apprentices in shops or factories while taking mandatory part-time courses, or they attend some form of full-time vocational school until the age of eighteen.

A much smaller number of elementary graduates, approximately 20 percent, attend the intermediate school, *Realschule*, for a period of six years, or from age ten to sixteen. The intermediate school prepares the student for the middle level of industry and commerce, as well as administrative jobs within the government. The curriculum consists of mathematics, science, German, and two foreign languages; shorthand, typing, and bookkeeping are also stressed. The graduate receives the certificate of medium maturity (*mittlere Reife*) upon completion of the studies. After graduation the student is entitled to attend a higher technical school (*Fachoberschule*) or a specialized grammar school (*Fach-*

Federal Republic of Germany

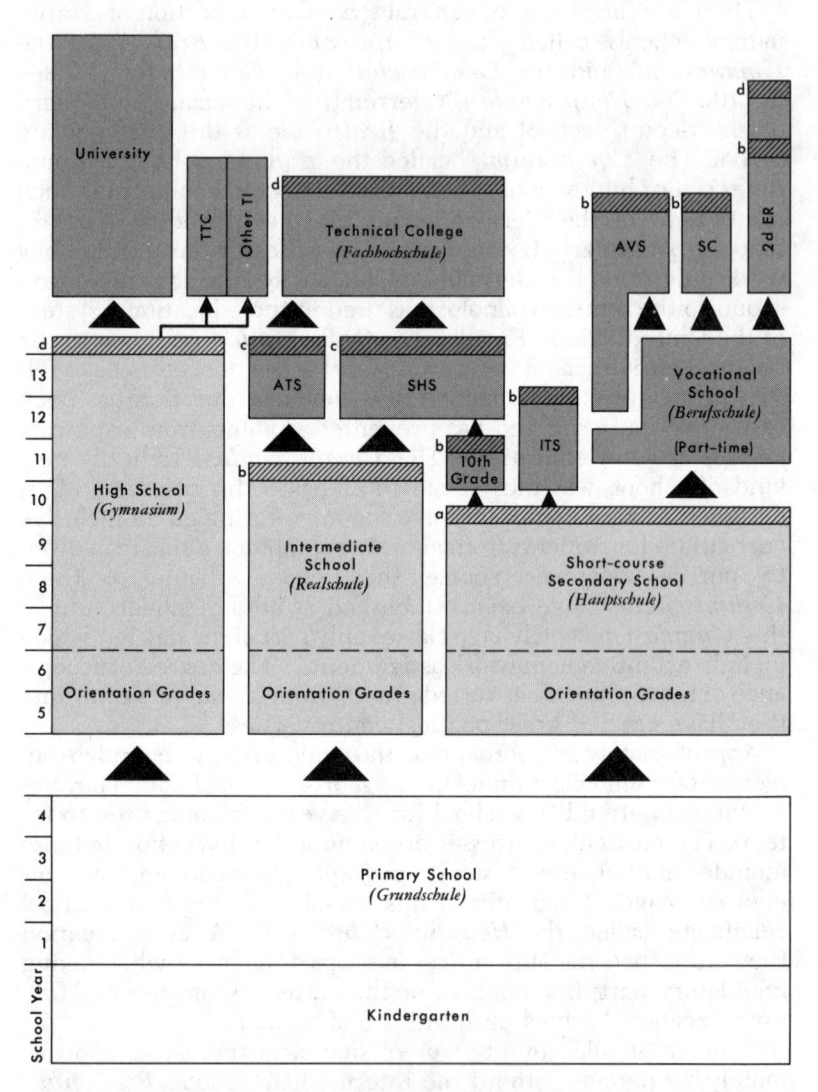

Figure 10. Model of the Educational System, Early 1980s

gymnasium) or to continue education on a part-time basis while serving as an apprentice. Students may also attend an evening intermediate school (*Abendrealschule*) that awards the graduate the medium maturity certificate.

Approximately 30 percent of the elementary graduates continue on to a *Gymnasium*. Pupils attend the gymnasium for nine years, or from the age of ten to nineteen. These schools are the main avenue to higher education and eventually to a professional career. There are three specialized branches of the *Gymnasien*: the classical language *Gymnasium*, which includes nine years of Latin and six years of Greek; the modern language *Gymnasium*, which emphasizes English, French, Spanish, and Russian; and the mathematics and natural science *Gymnasium*. Among the core subjects in all branches are German, English, civics, mathematics, and history. Beginning in 1972 a newly structured type of upper level of the *Gymnasium* (*Neugestaltete gymnasiale Oberstufe*) was gradually introduced on an experimental basis. In this new school the traditional successive classes of the *Gymnasium* have been replaced by college-type basic and intensive courses. The main purpose of this new type of instruction is to adjust *Gymnasium* studies to the need of the individual pupil and to prepare the student more appropriately for a future field of concentration at the university. Between 1961 and 1979 the number of pupils attending the *Gymnasium* increased by approximately 120 percent.

In order to graduate from the *Gymnasium*, a pupil must pass a difficult examination, after which he receives the diploma, or *Abitur*. Of the total number of students who enter the *Gymnasium*, a large portion leaves the school halfway through, receiving the *mittlere Reife*; others transfer to the intermediate or short-course schools, or, if they have gone beyond those levels, they enter full-time technical or vocational schools. Nine out of ten students who receive the *Abitur* enter an institution of higher education, and the others go directly into business or civil service.

There have been two innovations in the *Gymnasium* level that are geared toward making admission to the university more accessible than through the standard *Gymnasium* route. These are referred to as the second route to education or the *Zweiter Bildungsweg*. One is a part-time evening school for people who work, called the *Abendgymnasium*. The minimum age for acceptance at this kind of school is nineteen, and the student must either have completed vocational training or have been employed for three years. The curriculum is similar to the regular *Gymnasium*, emphasizing German, civics, two foreign languages, mathematics, and science. The second school is called the *Studienkolleg*, which is generally affiliated with a university and is primarily for foreign students. Both the *Abendgymnasium* and the *Studienkolleg* grant the *Abitur* or its equivalent.

Federal Republic of Germany

Vocational Secondary Education

There are several kinds of vocational secondary schools that cater to the particular needs of industry and trade. In addition to full-time and part-time secondary vocational schools, there are also evening schools. The part-time vocational school, which is generally combined with work and is therefore known as the dual system, is called the *Berufsschule*. Students are trained in such fields as mining, industry, housecraft (a combination of nursing and general home care), commerce, agriculture, and horticulture. Approximately 40 percent of the instruction in these schools is devoted to general subjects, which include German, social studies, economics, and religion. Of these general subjects, German receives the greatest emphasis, and the other 60 percent of instructions is in an area of specialization.

The full-time secondary vocational school is the *Berufsfachschule*. Enrollment in the school increased by more than 50 percent between 1970 and 1978. This is a specialized vocational school attended by students preparing for a trade or business. There are three main branches of specialization within the school: commerce or business, science and mathematics, and housecraft.

Another kind of vocational school, full-time or part-time, is the *Berufsaufbauschule*, in which the instruction is aimed at a more advanced level. Students who attend this school prepare for higher level jobs and for further schooling. Fields of specialization include: general commercial or industrial, industrial-technical, home economics or nursing, social work, and agriculture. Although specialized courses vary according to the field, the usual curriculum includes: German, a foreign language, history, civics, geography, economic geography, mathematics, physics, chemistry, economics, and management. Teachers in these schools possess the same qualifications as those teaching in the dual-system schools.

Pupils who have graduated from an intermediate school or its equivalent can enter a higher technical school. Training in such schools generally runs for two years, culminating with an examination to be passed at the end of the second year that entitles the graduate to enter studies at a higher technical institute. There are six kinds of higher technical schools: engineering, home economics, business and management, social work, design, and navigation. Instruction is given in three categories: general instruction, specialized instruction, and practical training in a particular field of specialization. The core curriculum for all areas includes German, one foreign language, social studies, mathematics, natural sciences, and physical education.

Pupils who have successfully completed an intermediate school or its equivalent can also enter a dual-system *Gymnasium*, which emphasizes training in economics and technological sciences and at the same time prepares the pupils for future studies at an institution of higher learning.

Advanced Vocational and Technical Education

The society attaches great importance to advanced vocational education. This is clearly reflected in a government publication that pointed out, "With its rapid technological change, the modern industrial country requires the citizens in the Federal Republic always to be prepared to continue to learn and adapt themselves to learning a new profession three or four times in the course of their working life. The Federation, the *Länder*, and the communes have made preparations for this development." Interest in advanced vocational training has increased not only on the part of the government but on the part of the students as well. The number of students in advanced vocational schools (*Fachschulen*) increased significantly between 1970 and 1974, and the subsequent decline reflected demographic changes only.

Graduates of these schools are needed in both the public and private sectors. Since 1966 the Federal Institute of Labor, located in Nuremberg, has been responsible for governmental promotion of advanced vocational training. The federal government and the *Länder*, however, are not the only sponsors. Chambers of commerce, so-called chambers of handicraft, employers associations, trade unions, and private firms have spent large amounts of money on these institutes.

In order to enter an advanced vocational school, a student must be beyond the age of compulsory education and must successfully have concluded the course work at one of the secondary vocational schools and have had some vocational experience. Entrants frequently are practical engineers or lower level administrators. The schools train students for a period of at least one year, and upon graduation they are considered to be medium-level specialists, and many enter such fields as agriculture, industry, and the crafts.

In 1970 the advanced technical colleges (*Fachhochschulen*) were developed and accorded the same status as universities and other institutions of higher learning as a result of an agreement among the *Länder*. Formerly known as advanced technical schools (*Höhere Berufsfachschulen*) and engineering schools (*Ingenieurschulen*), advanced technical colleges provide advanced technical training in forty-seven fields of specialization, among them economics, engineering, health technology, energy technology, computer and information sciences, social work, and other fields in which graduates are greatly in demand.

Federal Republic of Germany

Music and Fine Arts Institutes

The schools of music and fine arts train not only potential artists but also teachers of music and the fine arts. In order to be admitted to these institutes, the applicant is required to take an admission test that determines the level of artistic talent. As far as prior schooling is concerned, the admission requirements vary according to the career objective of the applicant. If one wants to become a teacher of music or the fine arts, he or she must have completed a *Gymnasium* or its equivalent before entering a music or fine arts institute. In 1977 there were eleven academies of fine arts, including an academy of television and motion pictures in Munich.

Teacher Training

The prerequisite for all teacher-training institutions is the *Abitur*. Teachers preparing to teach at the elementary level or in the short-course schools are trained at the *Pädagogische Hochschulen*, or teacher-training institutes. Those who will teach in a *Gymnasium*, an intermediate school, or the various vocational schools attend teacher-training courses at universitites. The length of study varies from six semesters or three years for students at the teacher-training institutes to eight semesters or four years for students at the universities. In the late 1960s and early 1970s the length of study at the universities was increased to as much as twelve semesters or six years. The curriculum for all potential teachers is highly structured, and the emphasis is on pedagogy, educational philosophy, psychology, and a specialized field of concentration. Academic training is followed by two years of practical training. At teacher-training institutes where research in specific fields of education is conducted, diplomas as well as doctoral degrees can be obtained.

Teachers of arts and crafts and technical subjects are generally trained at the *Fachinstitute*. These institutes, unlike the others, do not have university status, and the teachers need not have the *Abitur*. The curriculum includes woodwork, metalwork, domestic science, drawing, and physical education. The period of training varies from two to four years, depending on the field of specialization and the rules of the particular *Land*. After passing the final examination, the student practice-teaches for one year.

Between 90 and 95 percent of all public schoolteachers are public servants, and more than one-half are women. All teachers must take an examination before they can receive status in the civil service (see Glossary), and at the end of five years they receive tenure as public servants. Once given tenure they cannot be dismissed and remain in service until the age of sixty-five, at which time they receive a pension.

Teaching generally is a highly respected profession, not only because of the length of academic training and the relatively good

Interior of Hansa Library, West Berlin
Courtesy German Information Center

pay but also because of long tradition. Although the school systems suffered a painful shortage of teachers in the 1960s and early 1970s, the situation improved markedly thereafter, partly because the number of teachers had increased at a rate of approximately 50 percent between 1970 and 1978, and also because the number of pupils was declining.

Gesamthochschulen

Between 1970 and 1975 ten comprehensive universities (*Gesamthochschulen*) were established—three in Bavaria, one in Hesse, and six in North Rhine-Westphalia, including the so-called correspondence university (*Fernuniversität*) in Hagen. Still largely an experimental type of university, the *Gesamthochschule* is supposed to be a kind of synthesis of the traditional universities, the teacher-training institutes, the advanced vocational schools, and even the fine arts institutes. Besides radically new types of courses—so-called integrated courses that combine course materials from lectures and seminars previously taught independently—the *Gesamthochschule* also offers traditional courses. In order to enter a *Gesamthochschule*, a student must have an *Abitur* or its equivalent.

Universities

Universities and technical universities are considered to be the pinnacle of the educational system. In 1977 there were a total of fifty-one universities, technical universities, and specialized institutions of university standing, among which a *Hochschule für Verwaltungswissenschaften* (college of public administration) in Speyer, a *Sporthochschule* (college of physical education) in Cologne, and two *Hochschulen der Bundeswehr* (colleges of the armed forces), one in Hamburg and one in Munich, were recent additions. In addition there were eight schools of philosophy and theology and five religious institutions of higher learning.

Universities were organized more or less uniformly throughout the *Länder*. Every university had its own rector, who was elected by the members of the university senate and who served as general administrator of the university for a specified time. All university rectors participated in the Westdeutsche Rektorenkonferenz (West German Conference of Rectors), which deliberated on matters of academic policy and administrative concerns at the universities. Its decisions were advisory in nature and, therefore, not binding on individual *Länder* or institutions. Each university had its senate, which functioned as the governing body of the institution. Its decisions on academic and administrative matters were binding for the university. Each of the faculties of the university elected its dean for a specified time. Each academic field in the university was represented by at least one full professor*Ordinarius*), whose initial appointment had to be approved by the minister of education of the appropriate *Land*. The *Ordinarius* enjoyed considerable freedom in staff appointments, which generally consisted of temporary assistants (*Assistenten*) and lecturers (*Dozenten*).

The student body of the university managed its own affairs. It provided for cultural arrangements, located employment for students, and participated in academic affairs. This participation, however, varied from one university to another.

There was no financial barrier for students entering the university, since no tuition was charged. Most students entered the university directly from the *Gymnasium*, although a small portion entered from the so-called second educational route. There was an increase of almost 90 percent in the total number of students at universities between 1970 and 1978. The largest percentage enrolled in subjects belonging to the humanities, followed by economic and social sciences, engineering, mathematics and natural sciences, and medicine.

During the 1960s and 1970s the university system had to deal with a variety of problems. First among them was admittance to the university itself. Unfortunately for the students, a restriction of numbers clause (*numerus clausus*) was imposed on certain preferred fields, such as medicine, pharmacy, psychology, and the natural sciences, primarily because of expanding enrollments and limited staff. The selection process involved the choosing of certain *Abitur* degree students over others. It was severely criticized because the final decisions were based on records, grades, and other factors, rather than admission examinations or essays that might better determine the student's aptitude for a particular field of studies.

A second problem that became quite serious after 1967 was student activism, which frequently took the form of demonstrations and violent clashes between students and the authorities. During several riots, the worst of which took place in Frankfurt in 1968, university property was damaged or destroyed, lectures were disturbed and boycotted, and radical reform measures were demanded. This wave of protest, however, subsided after 1970. In the early 1970s, however, radical students managed to secure seats on several university governing bodies and were therefore able to cast vetoes against professors to whom they were ideologically opposed. Their demands included a reform of the curricula and the examination system, abolition of the *numerus clausus*, better student housing, and an end to the dominant position of the *Ordinarius* within the university.

Although the student riots found no support among the population and the major political parties, the education ministers of the *Länder* and the West German Conference of Rectors began seriously to concern themselves with possible solutions to the problems. After years of deliberations the conference of rectors agreed on the provisions of a new law, the Hochschulrahmengesetz (framework legislation on higher education), which was passed in 1976. This legislation was supposed to give guidance to the *Länder* for the reorganization of higher education. Great stress was placed on the establishment of *Gesamthochschulen*, which were to assure coordination among the traditional institutions and disciplines. The new law also provided for the establishment of a statute of limitations (*Regelstudienzeit*) that was to ensure that students would not waste time during their studies and needlessly delay the taking of final examinations.

Furthermore the traditional faculties of the university were to be reorganized into subject areas (*Fachbereiche*) and were to establish their own councils, consisting of elected members representing not only the professors, but also all groups of employees and the student body. This measure was to introduce a greater degree of democracy, but in many cases it led to a situation in which the professors of a specific subject area saw themselves systematically outvoted by the other representatives on the council. The professors also had to spend a great deal of time on committee work, which took them away from their research and the preparation of lectures.

The loss of control over the academic affairs of the university, which the professors suffered by the measures of reorganization, stirred up particular controversy and led to concerns over the lowering of standards and the loss of research potential. These concerns are taken quite seriously in various *Länder*, and in early 1982 observers expected that the position of the *Ordinarius* within the university would be strengthened.

Special Education

There are a variety of specialized schools (*Sonderschulen*) that provide for children and adults who have physical, mental, and psychological handicaps. The purpose of the specialized schools is to provide an education for handicapped people who could not be trained within the regular school system. Formerly the *Sonderschulen* were called *Hilfsschulen* (auxiliary schools). Traditionally the education of the handicapped has been vigorously supported by the government. In the recommendations made by the conference of education ministers in 1972, the aim of special education practiced in the specialized schools was clearly emphasized: "The *Sonderschulen* are supposed to realize the right of the handicapped person to an education which corresponds to his or her talents and individuality. They [the *Sonderschulen*] are institutions of habilitation and rehabilitation in family, economy, and society. An education which is tailored to the pupils' individuality is supposed to lead them to a social and economic integration and to help them to live a fulfilled life...."

There are specialized schools for the mentally damaged, the hard of hearing, the completely deaf, the blind, those with sight deficiencies, the physically handicapped, the physically ill, those with speech defects, the emotionally disturbed, and juvenile delinquents. The form of schooling depends both on the facilities in the area and the kind of impediment involved. There are individual classes at both the elementary and short-course levels, half-day as well as full-day sessions and boarding schools. There are also teachers who travel from home to home, instructing people who are physically ill. The teachers are graduates of a teacher-training institute, at which they will have taken special courses. There was a steady increase of pupils in schools for the handicapped between 1970, when there were 322,037 pupils, and 1976, when there were 398,176 enrollments. Between 1976 and 1978 enrollments declined to 387,829.

Adult Education

Adult education has existed in Germany since the latter part of the nineteenth century, when adult education centers (*Volkschochschulen*) were set up throughout the country. Modeled after similar institutions in Scandinavian countries, they mainly emphasized education in the traditional disciplines of the humanities that were to enrich the spiritual life of the learning adult. From the 1960s onward, more emphasis was placed on the practical usability of knowledge. During the late 1970s almost 50 per-

Johann Wolfgang Goethe University, Frankfurt
Courtesy German Information Center

cent of all class time was devoted to vocational training. In 1976 there were nearly 1,000 centers offering 210,000 courses. This represented a marked increase in offerings since the late 1960s, when approximately the same number of institutions offered only 95,000 courses. During the same time, enrollments increased from approximately 2 million to 3.7 million. In addition to regular courses, the adult centers sponsored approximately 55,000 onetime educational events in which about 3.4 million persons participated.

The financial outlay for adult education was considerable: whereas DM31.5 million was spent in 1966, the figure rose to approximately DM300 million in 1976, almost a tenfold increase over a period of ten years. The centers were staffed with approximately 2,500 full-time and some 75,000 part-time teachers in 1976.

There were also special schools for military personnel that were sponsored by the Federal Armed Forces (Bundeswehr). Although heavy emphasis was placed on vocational education, servicemen in these schools were also allowed to study other subjects after they had completed their compulsory service. After passing the appropriate examinations, they can obtain the *mittlere Reife*, the final certificate from the intermediate school, or even the *Abitur*.

In the vocational area the Bundeswehr encourages servicemen to pursue various trades and professions in order for them to resume their vocation or pursue a new one when they return to civilian life. The Bundeswehr maintains a variety of specialized schools designed for this purpose, and it also has a Career Promotion Service, which includes working groups and vocational courses. In 1979 there were thirty craft training schools (*Bundeswehrfachschulen*), in which some 200,000 soldiers had obtained craft qualifications.

Other forms of adult education are provided by trade unions, which work in close cooperation with the adult education centers, and the business community, which spends large amounts of money to support educational schemes for its employees. The larger industries maintain educational centers for their own employees. In some of the *Länder*, legislation has been introduced that provides for educational leaves for employees. Both the Roman Catholic and the Protestant churches contribute heavily to adult education, focusing on youth and family matters, development problems, and other topical subjects, as well as on theological matters (see Religion, ch. 3).

Health And Welfare

The crude birthrate in 1978, based on 576,468 live births, was 9.4 per 1,000 population, and the infant mortality rate was 14.7 per 1,000 live births. Life expectancy at birth was approximately seventy for men and between seventy-five and seventy-six for

Physical and Demographic Setting

women. In provisional figures for 1979 live births were at 581,984, and the crude life birthrate amounted to 9.47 per 1,000 population. Between 1970 and 1978 there was a significant shift in the age grouping of the population. Like population patterns in the United States, the total number of persons over sixty-five years of age seems to be increasing at an accelerating stage. At the same time the birthrate has dropped markedly during the same period (see fig. 9).

Since the end of World War II, there has been a dramatic reduction in the incidence of serious disease (see table 4, Appendix). During the years of recuperation from the devastation caused by the war, health and sanitation authorities put a heavy accent on preventive measures. The result was a remarkable drop in the incidence of serious disease during the 1950s. During the following decade a slower but still noticeable decline took place. Since 1970 the national health picture has remained fairly stable: in the late 1970s tuberculosis was still the most common disease, followed by scarlet fever. In the early 1980s continuing problems for health authorities were such diseases as infectious enteritis and dysentery, the incidence of which has steadily risen since the 1950s. There was also a relatively high incidence of infectious hepatitis, although the disease was not on the rise.

One of the causes for the slight but continuing rise in the overall death rate has been an increasing incidence of failings of the circulatory system, among which heart attacks have represented the main cause of deaths (see table 5, Appendix). This trend characterizes most modern societies, and it can be equally applied to the number of deaths from cancer, among which lung cancer and cancer of the stomach claimed most of the lives. Other death-causing diseases have steadily declined, especially pneumonia and children's diseases. Infant mortality during the first year has dropped from 21.1 per 1,000 live births in 1950 to 5.5 per 1,000 in 1978.

Health Care Facilities

In 1978 there were 3,328 hospitals and clinics, 217 fewer than in 1971. The total number of beds, however, increased from 690,236 to 714,879 during the same period of time. The decline in the total number of hospitals is attributable to a drop in health care facilities for the acutely ill. These are institutions in which all types of diseases are treated during a relatively short stay of the patient. Special health care facilities, in which certain diseases are treated for a longer period of time, increased in number, however.

Out of the total number of hospitals and clinics, 1,215 were public facilities, owned and maintained by federal, state, and municipal authorities, containing 373,675 beds (52.3 percent); 1,128 were operated for public benefit by various charitable institutions with 253,239 (35.4 percent) available beds; the remaining 985

Federal Republic of Germany

were private hospitals with 87,965 beds (12.3 percent). There were 11.6 beds available for 1,000 inhabitants. Only about 9 percent of the hospitals and clinics contained more than 500 beds, although these institutions held more than one-third of the total number of beds available. During 1978 there were 11.2 million patients treated in hospitals and clinics. The average hospital stay per patient was about sixteen days in institutions for the acutely ill, but fifty-seven days in special health care facilities. The utilization of available beds was 83.4 percent in hospitals for the acutely ill, and 85.4 percent in special health care facilities. In emergency hospitals the utilization rate was 97.7 percent.

In addition to these hospitals and clinics, there were a large number of sanatoriums and asylums managed by public authorities, charitable organizations, trade unions, industrial enterprises, and private individuals. Because Germans have traditionally placed a high value on the curative powers of mineral waters and fresh mountain or sea air, there were also a great many health resorts and spas. The hotels, inns, and baths at such resorts are usually privately owned and operated.

Medical Personnel

At the end of 1978 there were 130,033 doctors practicing medicine, or one doctor per every 472 inhabitants. This rate compares favorably to other West European countries and the United States. Of the total number of doctors, 45.4 percent were in private practice, 45.5 percent were members of hospital staffs, and 9.1 percent were involved in administration or medical research. Approximately one-fifth of the practicing doctors were women; one-fourteenth were foreigners, of which 83 percent were working in hospitals. The total number of doctors had risen markedly since 1970, when there were 99,654 doctors or one for 612 inhabitants.

About half of all physicians specialized in a specific area of medicine. The most strongly represented areas of specialization were internal medicine (27.4 percent), gynecology (11.3 percent), and surgery (10.9 percent). Among the specialized doctors, 52.1 percent were in private practice, 40.9 percent worked in hospitals, and 6.9 percent were in administration and research.

At the end of 1978 there were 32,482 dentists, or one for 1,888 inhabitants, compared to one for 1,956 in 1970. Dentists in private practice numbered 94.4 percent. There were also 9,277 veterinarians, of which more than half were in private practice.

There were 244,945 nursing personnel at the end of 1978, among which were 175,660 nurses, 24,679 children's nurses, and 44,606 nurses' aides. In the latter category there had been a dramatic increase in numbers since 1970, amounting to more than 100 percent. In addition there were 2,454 persons employed as social workers.

The number of pharmacies has steadily risen for decades. There were 15,340 at the end of 1978, among which 14,965 were public, and 375 were in hospitals. There was one public pharmacy for 4,098 inhabitants.

In 1978 there were 2,996 students of general medicine, 1,081 students of dentistry, 1,035 students of pharmacology, and 542 students of veterinary medicine who concluded their studies successfully. In addition numerous students graduated from advanced vocational schools following training in such fields as medical technology, dietetics, and physiotherapy.

The Welfare System

The welfare system in its present form is based on the first national social insurance system in the world. Its establishment was initiated by an imperial message of November 11, 1881, which constituted an answer to the questions raised by the social movements in Central Europe during the 1860s and 1870s. It was followed by three concrete steps toward a universal social insurance system that were taken by the conservative Chancellor Otto von Bismarck and the Reichstag: the passing and implementation of the Law on Health Insurance of Workers in 1883, the Law on Accident Insurance in 1884, and the Law on Disability and Old-Age Insurance in 1889. In 1911 these three separate laws were synthesized into one piece of legislation, and a bill on white-collar workers was added to these provisions. Although the basic principles of this truly exemplary piece of social legislation—which became the model for many welfare systems in other countries throughout the world—remained valid in early 1982, more than 200 amendments and revisions had been enacted in order to satisfy the changing circumstances of a modern and highly industrialized country. Among these revisions, some are of particular significance. In 1949 the Law on the Adjustment of Social Legislation was passed, which initiated a series of improvements in benefits received by the insured. In 1957 the reform of the pension system began with the indexing of pensions to the development of the national economy. During the following twenty-five years, the network of social legislation was perfected, and in 1982 it covered virtually all situations of a citizen's life.

In order to ensure a consolidation of information of the multitude of needs and requirements of such a vast social welfare system, and to make planning of new legislation easier, a social insurance data bank had been established. All insurance schemes in the social welfare system are self-administered through elected representatives of the employees. Claims and disputes are adjusted by independent courts on local, district, and federal levels.

Federal Republic of Germany

One of the important principles laid down in the Basic Law is the obligation of the government and its institutions to secure the social welfare and well-being of its citizens. The existing social welfare system was created in order to meet this obligation. To ensure its financing, one basic concept had to be accepted: the wage earners support those who are either temporarily or permanently unable to work. Most or all of the social insurance schemes, therefore, had to be accepted as being obligatory, enabling the system to allocate part of the individual salaries or wages toward the temporarily or permanently ill, unemployed, and senior citizens. Together with the social security taxes paid by employers, these contributions constitute the major part of the financing of the social welfare system. The size of the social welfare budget indicates the importance given to this area of public life: in 1978 expenditures totaled DM403 billion, an amount that represented roughly one-third of the country's GNP (see fig. 11).

The laws governing the many diverse areas of welfare and social security have grown enormously in volume and number over the decades. Legal provisions have therefore been compiled into the Code of Social Legislation (Sozialgesetzbuch), which has been published in sections since 1976, consisting in 1981 of ten volumes.

The Pension System

In 1979 a total of approximately 12.5 million persons were receiving old-age pensions. Between 1957, when the so-called dynamic pension (pension indexing) was introduced, and 1979 the individual monthly payments had been raised twenty-one times, thus providing an adequate standard of living for most pensioners.

In 1975 there were 25.5 million persons in the worker's pensions category of the insurance system; 14.2 million were blue-collar workers and 11.3 million were white-collar workers. Approximately 44 percent of the insured were women. The total assets of the system amounted to DM43 million in 1976. After 1972 the system for blue-collar workers operated with a small deficit that had to be compensated for by transfer of funds from the system for white-collar workers. This system also began to operate with a deficit in 1976, and general revenue funds were used to make up for the annual deficit. At the end of 1977 the lowest individual payroll deduction to the system was DM67 per month, the highest DM612.

In 1975 approximately 698,000 persons contributed to the farmer's pension system. Because there had been a steady decline of active contributors and a steady increase of pensioners since 1968, general revenue funds were used to subsidize the system. In 1975 the obligatory monthly contribution paid by each farmer was DM63 and DM31.50 for every member of the family working on the farm.

Physical and Demographic Setting

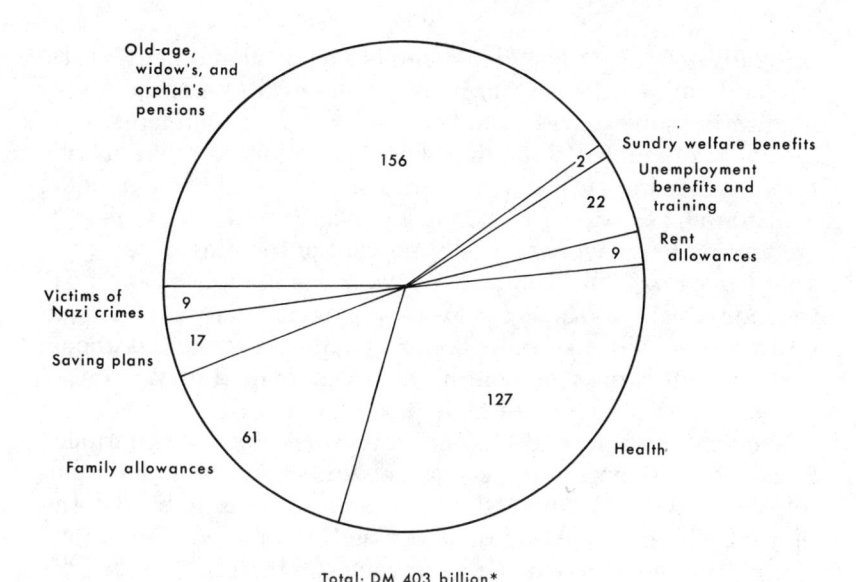

```
            Old-age,
          widow's, and
           orphan's
           pensions
                                              Sundry welfare benefits
                         156        2
                                              Unemployment
                                   22         benefits and
                                              training

                                         9    Rent
                                              allowances
Victims of
Nazi crimes    9
              17
Saving plans
                                  127

                    61                        Health
Family allowances
```

Total: DM 403 billion*

*For value of the deutsche mark—see Glossary.

Source: Based on information from Federal Republic of Germany, Press and Information Office, *Social Services*, Bonn, 1979.

Figure 11. Public and Private Expenditures on Health and Welfare Services, 1978

In 1975 there were approximately 1,574,000 civil servants (excluding members of the armed forces) employed in federal, state, or municipal government agencies (see The Bureaucracy, ch. 7). In addition there were approximately 14,600 judges and 19,400 officials in other government agencies. At the time of retirement, civil servants receive a monthly pension amounting to a maximum of 75 percent of their last salary during active service. Generally the age of retirement is set at sixty-five. There are exceptions for the police, judges, and members of the armed forces, who can retire at an earlier age and still receive the maximum amount of pension set by law. Any civil servant may retire at age sixty-three, but the retiree will not receive the maximum pension. The civil servant's pension system is financed through public funds.

Health, Accident, and Unemployment Insurance

The Health Insurance System represents the oldest branch among all public insurance schemes. Founded in 1883 as part of Bismarck's comprehensive social legislation package, by 1911 it boasted 10 million members organized in 22,000 insurance schemes. By 1980 approximately 90 percent of the population was covered by health insurance under compulsory or voluntary

Federal Republic of Germany

programs. Benefits included complete medical and dental care, free and unlimited hospitalization, full maternity care, the cost of medication and eyeglasses, and medical care for dependents. The system is organized through sickness funds on rural, industrial, trade, or occupational bases. Funds are obtained through equal contributions on the part of the employer and the employee, amounting to an average of 11.3 percent of the employee's gross salary. In case of illness of the employee, every employer must pay the individual's full salary for six weeks per calendar year. Health insurance provides sickness benefit payments for an additional seventy-eight weeks, amounting to a maximum of 85 percent of the individual's salary (see table 6, Appendix).

Accident insurance covers all employees, including farmers. Since 1971 students in regular schools and children in kindergartens have also been insured. It is financed entirely by the employers, whose contributions are assessed on the basis of their total payroll and the degree of danger involved in their business. Funds for Industrial Injuries Insurance are based on a company's expenditure for injuries the previous year. Benefits include cash payments of a percentage of the salary, the size and the duration of the payments depending on the degree of disability; complete medical care, including rehabilitation; and pension and funeral benefits for the survivors. Pensions are annually adjusted to keep pace with the rise in the cost of living. Additionally the accident insurance system is deeply involved in the development and implementation of measures for the prevention of accidents and the supervision of health protection in industry.

In 1977 accident insurance was administered by ninety agencies with approximately 15,000 employees. Among these agencies were industrial, agricultural, and municipal associations that acted as insurance carriers. They were supervised by the Federal Insurance Office in the Ministry of Labor and Social Affairs.

All employees, with the exception of public servants, are eligible for compulsory unemployment insurance. The insurance program was initiated in 1927 and was updated by the Labor Promotion Act of 1969. Benefits usually amount to about 68 percent of the applicant's previous take-home pay. Workers who remain unemployed for more than a year can be granted unemployment assistance. The benefits can amount to a maximum of 58 percent of the applicant's previous take-home pay. Contributions to health insurance and old-age pensions are paid by the local labor exchange while an unemployed worker receives benefits. The system is administered by the Federal Employment Institute and the local labor exchanges. The program is financed through equal contributions by the employer and the employee.

Child Support

Although income tax exemptions for dependent children in the family have been in existence for a long time, the actual payment of allowances for children began in 1954. In 1979 the tax-exempt benefits were DM50 for the first child, DM100 for the second child, and DM200 for each subsequent child. Benefits were paid to the parents irrespective of their income until each child reached the age of eighteen. If the child remained in an accredited educational institution beyond that age, benefits were paid until the age of twenty-seven, in certain cases even longer. Since 1964 the program has been administered by the Federal Employment Institute in Nuremberg and the local labor exchanges. Funds were provided by the federal government.

Educational Subsidies

Although the concept of financial aid given by the state for educational purposes has existed throughout this century, it emerged in its present form after World War II. The latest provisions on educational subsidies are contained in the Federal Training Promotion Act (Bundesausbildungsförderungsgesetz) of 1971. Any pupil enrolled in the senior grades of the secondary or vocational school system or a student in a college or university who can demonstrate the need for financial aid can receive a monthly subsidy. For university students the subsidies will be paid for a maximum period of ten semesters. The amount of the monthly payment usually depends on the income of the parents, on the number of children in the family, and whether or not the educational institution in which the student is enrolled is located in the city or town of the parents' residence. In 1978 the maximum monthly payment was DM620. There are also special scholarships available for students engaged in writing dissertations. In addition student loans are available for students in colleges and universities. These loans are interest-free and can be paid back over a period of twenty years, with payments commencing three years after the end of the individual's studies. In early 1982 the system of educational subsidies was financed at the rate of 65 percent by the federal government and 35 percent by the *Länder*

Rehabilitation

In 1979 there were approximately 4 million persons in the Federal Republic who depended on some form of rehabilitation program. Covered were the physically or mentally handicapped who suffer their illness as a result of war, accident, or disease. Although six agencies were involved in rehabilitation programs, procedures and benefits were coordinated in 1974 by a special act of the Bundestag. The major goal of all rehabilitation programs is the reintegration of the handicapped person into society, starting with treatment in health care facilities and extending to reentry to an active working life. For this purpose special assistance and training centers have been set up. Employers must give special preference to the hiring of handicapped persons, who are entitled to an additional six days of vacation a year and can retire at age sixty. In commercial or industrial enterprises that employ more than fifteen workers, 6 percent of the total number of jobs are required to be open to the seriously handicapped.

Subsidies for War Victims

Since 1945 a number of provisions have been enacted for the care of the war-disabled and the dispossessed. Medical treatment, welfare pensions (indexed since 1970), and employment assistance have been granted to the injured, disabled, widows, and orphans. Included in the provisions are also victims of political persecution, members of the Bundeswehr, conscientious objectors who perform civilian, in lieu of military, service, and former political prisoners in East Germany. In 1952 the Equalization of Burdens Law was enacted in order to compensate for losses of homes and possessions. Payments are made in the form of maintenance allowances, which are fixed amounts depending on the size of the family, or compensation pensions, which constitute a percentage of the goods lost, usually at least 4 percent of the loss. In 1978 subsidies were paid to 2.1 million affected persons. The program is funded by the federal government, but administrative costs are borne by the *Länder*.

Housing Subsidies

In spite of a massive rebuilding program after World War II, which accounted for the fact that in 1979 two out of three houses were no older than thirty-five years, housing problems remained. People with low incomes, some of the senior citizens, and large families sometimes found it difficult to afford the steadily rising rents, especially since the rent controls were relaxed in 1971. To alleviate these problems, in 1977 rent allowances were available to families whose income did not exceed DM9,600. If there was more than one child in the family, DM2,400 annually was added to this limitation for each additional child. A total of DM1,467,000 in rent allowances was paid in 1977. There were also low-cost loans available to people who wanted to build their own house or buy an apartment. One out of four housing units built between 1949 and 1979 were financed this way. The program is funded in equal parts by the federal government and by the *Länder*. Administrative costs are borne by the *Länder* and the communities.

Other Subsidies

In the early 1980s there were a variety of other subsidies available. There was the so-called Social Aid Program, which provided personal and financial aid to people who were unable to provide for themselves, either because they were not sufficiently covered by one of the insurance plans already mentioned or who found themselves in special hardship because of old age or other circumstances. Social aid was provided regardless of the cause of the needy person's predicament. There were also special aid programs for the blind, for persons persecuted for political reasons, for soldiers returning from captivity, for displaced and evacuated persons, and for victims of crimes.

International and Bilateral Agreements on Welfare and Social Security

There were a considerable number of bilateral agreements on welfare and social security between West Germany and other countries. Some of these agreements already existed before World War II. The basic principle of these agreements is reciprocity. In 1977 bilateral treaties existed with over twenty countries, including the United States. The contents of these bilateral treaties vary greatly according to the individual country's welfare and social security system. In the early 1980s efforts were under way within the European Communities that aimed at a unified welfare and social security policy.

* * *

Concise and reliable information on the subjects discussed in this chapter can be found in *Facts about Germany*, edited by Karl Römer and published in 1979. The most detailed treatment of the subject of health and health facilities is given in *Daten des Gesundheitswesens*, published in 1980 under the auspices of the Federal Minister of Youth, Family Affairs, and Health. The most precise and up-to-date information on education is contained in *The Education System*, published in 1980 by the Press and Information Office of the Federal Republic of Germany. An excellent description of the educational and social welfare system is given by David Childs in *West Germany: Politics and Society*, published in 1981. For a detailed account of the social welfare system one could consult *Übersicht über die soziale Sicherung* by Schewe, Schenke, Meurer, and Hermsen, published in 1977 under the auspices of the Federal Ministry for Labor and Social Welfare. (For further information see Bibliography.)

Chapter 3. The Society

The Cathedral, Cologne

The Society

THE WEST GERMAN society of the early 1980s was urban and industrial. The post-World War II economic boom had made it "middle class." There remained extremes of wealth and poverty, but the bulk of the population were middle-income wage earners. Industrial workers were among the most highly remunerated, skilled, and disciplined in the world. Social welfare legislation had had a lengthy history in Germany, and the Federal Republic of Germany (West Germany or Federal Republic) remained a leader among industrial countries in the social benefits provided to the population. The "safety net" was extensive and tightly woven.

Within the broad middle tier of society there was substantial diversity and stratification. Widespread affluence leveled some social distinctions, and post-World War II economic expansion permitted a certain amount of social mobility. Higher education, however, was the principal avenue of upward occupational mobility, and university-level enrollments remained—despite expansion in the 1970s—a small portion of the college-age population.

Economic prosperity engendered a number of trends typical of other European and North American industrial countries. Urbanization—intense since the late nineteenth century—continued, but city growth patterns changed. Increasingly young couples moved to the suburbs and towns surrounding West Germany's numerous urban conglomerates. The need to replace housing lost in World War II and general economic growth fueled a housing boom lasting until the mid–1970s. Prosperity spawned a plethora of consumer goods available to and affordable by many, if not most West Germans. Dietary patterns changed in the midst of a general rise in the level of living.

The people—whose history of industrialization in the nineteenth and twentieth centuries had been as tumultuous as any and whose rising nationalism had been pivotal in two world wars—had enjoyed since the mid–1950s more than a quarter century of unparalleled prosperity and stability. Germany became a nation-state relatively late (1871); for most of their history the German states were regionally and politically divided and religiously fragmented. Confessional differences continued to play a prominent role in social life, but the country was nearly evenly divided between Roman Catholics and Protestants. Despite the persistent significance of religious affiliation, sectarian divisiveness in the post-World War II era was less pronounced than at any time since the Reformation. Efforts to exclude Catholics from political and economic affairs characteristic of Imperial Germany and the Catholics' consequent alienation from Germany's social life found little

Federal Republic of Germany

counterpart in post-World War II society.

The society was largely ethnically homogeneous. Regional differences and loyalties were becoming less pronounced. In the 1950s roughly 12 million German-speaking refugees from the German Democratic Republic (East Germany) and formerly German territories in Eastern Europe had successfully integrated into the Federal Republic's social and cultural life. The single largest ethnically distinct group in the 1970s and early 1980s was the sizable minority of foreign workers amounting to over 7 percent of the total population. Most of these guest workers were from Mediterranean countries; they were culturally and (frequently) religiously alien. The guest worker community included substantial numbers of dependents. In recruiting foreigners for "short-term" labor shortages, West Germany had acquired a foreign population whose presence seemed more and more permanent. It included a generation of guest workers' children whose adaptation either to German society or that of their parents was increasingly questionable. The continued presence of foreign workers and their dependents promised to be problematical for West German authorities in the straitened economic circumstances of the early 1980s.

One of the most prominent points of social cleavage focused not on ethnicity, class, or sex, but simply on age. Much of the stability the country had enjoyed since the republic was established in 1949 reflected a consensus among West Germans who had lived through the chaos and uncertainty of the 1930s and 1940s. By 1981, however, nearly two-thirds of all West Germans had been born after 1945. They were a generation reared in affluence and political stability. The circumstances surrounding their coming of age could hardly have been more divergent from those of their parents. Young West Germans were frequently politically active; they were well represented in the growing peace and ecology movements, and all major political parties courted their allegiance. How they would deal with the 1980s—a decade that augured less political certainty and less economic beneficence—promised to be a major issue in the coming years.

Ethnicity

The country in the early 1980s was largely an ethnic monolith; the overwhelming majority of the population considered themselves Germans—members of a single, howbeit regionally and religiously differentiated, group. The extensive and systematic extermination of those deemed "non-Teutonic" by the Nazis and the post-World War II resettlement of German refugees within West Germany contributed to ethnic homogeneity. Foreign workers and their families, numbering over 4.5 million according to late 1981 estimates, were the single largest non-German ethnic group. There remained a fraction of Germany's pre-World War II

Jewish community and the Gypsy population. A small number of East Frisians along the North Sea coast and the shore of Lower Saxony and Schleswig-Holstein were distinguishable in varying degrees from their Saxon neighbors. They bore substantial similarity to the Dutch West Frisians in livelihood, language, and settlement patterns. An indeterminate number of Danes were concentrated in Schleswig-Holstein, at the base of the Danish peninsula (see fig. 1). The region was traditionally one of mixed Dane and German settlement. Irredentist sentiments on the part of the Danish minority diminished in the general well-being of the 1960s and 1970s. The Danish minority political party polled less than 1 percent of the vote in the 1980 federal elections. The Danish minority commonly used German in daily communications, watched German television, and read the German press. Intermarriage between Germans and Danes was commonplace.

Strong regional loyalties complemented and counterbalanced German national consciousness. Until 1945 regional differences were pronounced and often vied with pan-German sentiment as a focus of the citizen's loyalties. Many Germans considered themselves Rhinelanders, Bavarians, or Prussians first, Germans second. Regional differences were prominent: the values and mores of the Bavarian mountaineer were chasms away from those of the urban Hamburger. East Prussians differed from Westphalians; both found little in common with Rhinelanders or Bavarians. In many ways Germans found greater affinity with neighboring German-speaking populations than with their own countrymen. Catholic Bavarians saw themselves as similar to Austrians; Swabians found they had much in common with German-speaking Swiss.

Food, dress, settlement patterns, and architectural styles marked the myriad German-speaking regions of Central Europe. In the post-World War II era traditional measures of ethnic-regional distinctiveness have declined while national media and widespread migration have had a homogenizing impact on social life. Dialect remained the most pervasive measure of ethnic background. Most Germans spoke both standard German (Hochdeutsch or High German) and their own dialect. The main German dialects were Prussian, Bavarian, and Rhinelander, though each had important variations. Differences in spoken language are sufficient for speakers of widely separated dialects to be nearly mutually unintelligible. Dialectical differences played a central role in the efforts of East German refugees to adapt to West German society. Their use has persisted more in the south, where in the mid–1970s some 80 percent of the population spoke a dialect. National radio and television programming in the post-World War II era reduced the importance of local dialects, even as the greater mobility of the population enhanced the importance of standard German. The use of standard German was commonplace in public life, while dialects were normally reserved for informal communication and home life.

One measure of the dramatic decline in regionalism in contemporary society has been the integration of large numbers of refugees from Eastern Europe and East Germany. Soon after 1945 some 9 million German speakers from former German territories—East Prussia, Silesia, Pomerania, and the Sudetenland—settled or were forcibly resettled in West Germany (see fig. 4). In addition in the 1950s an estimated 3 million—mostly Saxons, Thuringians, Mecklenburgers, and Brandenburgers—fled from East Germany. The Federal Republic absorbed some hundreds of thousands of German speakers from the Soviet Union in the 1970s, though by 1981 the number of these refugees had dwindled to a trickle.

Part of the success with which refugees integrated into the country's social, political, and economic life derived from the government's compensation program that indemnified refugees, in part at least, for lost property. The general prosperity of the 1960s and 1970s benefited former refugees as well as native West Germans. Refugee organizations accustomed to fostering the hope of eventual return to the "homeland" increasingly played a purely social role for their membership. By the early 1970s nearly three-quarters of all refugees indicated they would not return to their regions of origin even if there were an opportunity to do so. Their children, most of whom have been born in West Germany, were overwhelmingly a part of that society.

German nationalism, national consciousness, and ethnic identity are questions that have permeated German thought and social life during the nineteenth and twentieth centuries. German ethnic identity was, for most of European history, transnational or anational. Before the rise of the Prussian-dominated Hohenzollern Empire in the nineteenth century, the German states were politically and religiously fragmented but pluralistic and, within the context of the time, tolerant and cosmopolitan. Prussia itself was a haven for Huguenots, Bohemians, and Jews. Pan-German nationalism as a political force and as an ideology seeking to unite Germans in a nation-state was a nineteenth-century development. It grew in response to the Napoleonic wars, the overweening influence of Habsburg Austria's Klemens von Metternich, and the rising nationalism of the Austro-Hungarian Empire's peoples.

The language from which the word *German* was derived is not known. Julius Caesar, Tacitus, and other Romans wrote about Germania (as the Romans called it) and the peoples known as Germani, but the tribal peoples themselves to which the name was applied did not universally use the term. The name supposedly derived from a single tribe known as Germani from which the name came to be applied to many related tribes in the area. Sometime between the eighth and eleventh centuries A.D., the

The Society

peoples referred to by others as Germani began referring to themselves as *diutisc* (literally, popular), an early form of the word *deutsch*, which eventually became equated with German.

The most revered of stereotypes about Germans, hallowed in political-social commentaries, scholarship, and popular images alike, has been that they are authoritarian. Germans, the received wisdom has it, have little tolerance for deviant behavior of any sort and scant sympathy for pluralism—political or cultural. The quintessential German virtues were "discipline, order, obedience." "You can never make a revolution with the Germans," commented Lenin—who was not unfamiliar with revolutions; "If they were ordered to storm a train station they would first stand in line to buy tickets." Historian Fritz Stern points out that Germans had no history of successful revolution, of creating a new social order by defying the established one. German nationalism, precisely as a reaction against Napoleon and French nationalism, emphasized neither the rights and liberties of the citizenry nor civic virtues such as political participation.

A number of post-World War II developments called the common stereotypes into question. The 1970s saw the flowering of citizen-initiative associations (*Bürgerinitiativen*) organized to fill the gaps left by political parties and civic organizations. They represented their membership on a wide variety of issues from nuclear energy policy to traffic control wherever more conventional avenues failed. *Bürgerinitiativen* borrowed some of their techniques, such as marches and signs, from the student demonstrations of the 1960s and 1970s. Beyond this their activities were diverse: they operated day-care centers and progressive (usually anti-authoritarian) schools and agitated for greater citizens' control of urban planning decisions. Citizen-initiative associations were a major force in the antinuclear peace demonstrations of the early 1980s that were the most massive citizen movements of post-World War II West Germany. All in all they represented a new readiness to take exception with those in authority.

In addition public opinion polls in the 1970s found West Germans committed to the human rights associated with pluralistic and participatory democracy. By an overwhelming percentage they believed that freedom to travel within one's own country, freedom to emigrate, freedom from censorship, freedom of religion, and freedom from arbitrary arrest and imprisonment as well as equal rights for minorities were basic human rights, not state-conferred privileges. Even in the midst of the often violent student demonstrations of the 1970s, more than half of those polled felt even violent demonstrations did not justify abridging the right of assembly. More than half were unwilling to sacrifice any basic freedom for the reunification of Germany, even though reunifica-

Federal Republic of Germany

tion continued to be an issue of overriding importance.

While most were committed to the traditional civic virtues and a number of values not frequently associated with German ethnicity, they viewed the early 1980s with increasing uncertainty. The country's worsening economic situation, although mild by international standards, bred pessimism. According to polls taken by the respected Institut für Demoskopie Allensbach in the summer of 1981, more than 70 percent of those queried viewed the 1980s with "fear or skepticism." Worsening United States-Soviet Union relations and North Atlantic Treaty Organization (NATO—also referred to as the Atlantic Alliance) plans to deploy medium-range nuclear missiles in West Germany fanned a peace movement that was, according to many observers, the most massive, leftist, and nationalist in Europe. Particularly among the young, pacifism, coupled with a general questioning of the country's future role in European and world affairs, was prevalent. It appeared that the general unanimity governing foreign policy for most of the post-World War II era was, if not dissolving, at least being called into serious question by young West Germans. West Germans were increasingly in the process of reworking the country's "sense of national purpose"; what new consensus might emerge was unclear.

Jews

In the late 1970s an estimated 32,000 Jews remained of the half million in Weimar Germany. The contemporary Jewish community included a handful of German Jews who survived the Nazi terror, some East European displaced persons stranded in West Germany following 1945, a number of return emigrants from the United States and Israel, as well as a growing number of Middle Eastern Jews. The generation born after World War II increasingly identified either with Israel or with Marxism. An estimated two-thirds of young Jews marry non-Jewish partners.

The history of anti-Jewish extermination policies in Nazi Germany gave the Jewish community a significance disproportionate to its small numbers. There has been voluminous material about Jewish cultural history, religion, and philosophy published in West Germany since 1945. Nonetheless there was concern that young West Germans be adequately educated about the history of the Third Reich. Overt anti-Semitism was—from all reports—minimal. Racialist sentiments, when they were expressed, had as their targets not the country's small Jewish community but the substantial and ethnically alien guest worker (*Gastarbeiter*) population (see ForeignWorkers, this ch.).

Romany

Estimates of West Germany's Sinti Romany (Gypsy) population range from 30,000 to 50,000 of a pre-World War II population of nearly a half million. In early 1980 Gypsies protested that the

Bavarian authorities continued to harass them. Protesters charged that the Ministry of the Interior monitored Romanies' movements through the use of information files collected by the Nazis; some fifteen to twenty Romany began a hunger strike at Dachau. The protesters were concerned not only with police harassment, but also compensation claims of Romany who were victims of Nazi persecution. Gypsies' frequent illiteracy had hampered victims in applying for restitution. In mid-1980 the Federal Diet (Bundestag) set up a fund for Nazi victims who had not yet received any compensation; Romanies were among those expected to benefit. The Bavarian government denied that they had maintained files on Romanies for any purpose but awarding restitution, but it conceded that the Gypsies had indeed suffered discrimination since 1945 as well as under the Nazis. Certainly the Romany tradition of nomadism violated the traditional German staid sense of order. Thomas Mann in his novella, *Tonio Kröger*, has as the ultimate condemnation of inappropriate behavior: "We aren't Gypsies in green wagons."

Foreign Workers

The presence of several million *Gastarbeiter* and their families was the major change in West Germany's ethnic composition in the 1970s. Immigrant workers began arriving in the mid-1950s, recruited as a short-term response to labor shortages. By the early 1960s there were slightly less than a half million *Gastarbeiter*. In the mid-1970s their numbers stabilized at roughly 2 million workers and perhaps 2.5 million dependents—slightly less than 8 percent of the total labor force and over 7 percent of the total population. Foreign workers were overwhelmingly from Mediterranean countries: Turks, followed by Yugoslavs, Italians, Greeks, and Spaniards were the principal nationalities represented (see table 7, Appendix). The presence of a large, ethnically distinct immigrant population presented a variety of socioeconomic problems, the more so because *Gastarbeiter*, originally recruited as short-term laborers, had by 1980 become a permanent feature of the social landscape.

In the mid-1970s over three-quarters of all foreign workers were unskilled or semiskilled. Yugoslavs were the most highly trained of the main *Gastarbeiter* groups; nearly half of all Yugoslav males were skilled or nonmanual workers—a percentage over twice as great as that of the West German labor force as a whole. Comparable figures for Turks, Italians, Greeks, and Spaniards ranged from 8 to 16 percent. Among women *Gastarbeiter* this trend was even more pronounced: some 90 percent of women in the main immigrant groups were semiskilled or unskilled workers. Guest workers have usually taken jobs most German nationals were unwilling to take; in the late 1970s they were miners and workers in the less desirable aspects of the service sector, construction, and some parts of the automotive industry.

During the economic downturns of the 1970s and early 1980s the federal government tried to limit the number of foreign workers. The government suspended recruitment of foreign nationals in late 1973. Such efforts had limited impact, in part because a substantial portion of guest workers were European Economic Community (EEC or Common Market—see Glossary) nationals and had relatively easy access to the West German labor market. More significantly by the mid-1970s more than 50 percent of all *Gastarbeiter* had been resident in the Federal Republic four or more years, fully 25 percent for seven or more years. Even as recruitment of guest workers declined, more and more long-term foreign workers had families and dependents join them.

The most persistent and complex problem arising from the long-term residence of "temporary" *Gastarbeiter* had to do with the foreigners' children. By the late 1970s one of every six babies born in West Germany was the offspring of foreigners or a mixed German national-foreigner couple. In Frankfurt, a city with a substantial guest worker population, nearly half of all live births were to immigrant families. In the late 1970s there were an estimated 850,000 school-age children of resident foreigners; less than half attended school. In 1974 students from the five largest *Gastarbeiter* groups represented less than 3 percent of elementary and secondary school enrollment.

A variety of government pronouncements delineated the rights of foreign workers' children within the school system. There were provisions for instruction in the students' mother tongues (if all students in a given class were of the same nationality) as well as intensive German language instruction for non-German speakers before entering the formal school system. Despite these efforts, by the early 1980s there was concern that *Gastarbeiter* children were at best marginally educated, inadequate in their command of both German and their mother tongues, and alienated from German society as well as that of their parents. The stratification long a part of West German education was a double handicap for nonnative speakers (see The Working Class, this ch.; Education, ch. 2). German children of working-class background found the gymnasium-university educational hurdle formidable; for foreigners it was virtually insurmountable.

The sheer number of *Gastarbeiter* children was a problem. Concentrated disproportionately in a few large urban centers, southern Bavaria, and the mining areas of the Ruhr, their press on limited employment opportunities promised to be a significant issue in the 1980s. Officials estimated the number of jobs necessary for foreign youngsters entering the work force from 1975 through 1985 at 40,000 a year—half again the number of jobs required for West Germans entering the labor force for the first time. A number of federal and state regulations tried to limit the

*Shops line streets in Rothenburg
Courtesy Walter M. Callahan*

circumstances under which teenage children of *Gastarbeiter* might join their parents and/or obtain work permits. Other regulations stiffened the requirements for a spouse to join a husband or wife working in the Federal Republic and to obtain a work permit.

The concentration of immigrants in older urban centers and certain industrial regions created pressure on housing and social services in those areas. Foreigners often faced discrimination in housing; in addition *Gastarbeiter* families were typically larger than those of West German nationals, thus limiting the availability of newer housing where space codes were strictly enforced. Finally, guest workers themselves were frequently willing to sacrifice comfort in housing in favor of saving a greater portion of their earnings.

Government policy throughout the mid-1970s to early 1980s aimed at curtailing migration to the Federal Republic and encouraging guest workers to return to their countries of origin. *Gastarbeiter* recruitment was officially halted in 1973. By some estimates nearly one-third of all Spanish and Italian guest workers and some 15 to 20 percent of all Yugoslavs, Portuguese, and Greeks returned to their home countries during the 1970s. Few Turks, the single largest national group, left. Overall the number of guest workers ranged from a high of roughly 2.5 million in 1973 to a low of slightly more than 1.8 million in 1978. By the early 1980s the number of foreign workers had stabilized at some 2 million, nearly 8.0 percent of the total work force. Unemployment among *Gastarbeiter* averaged slightly more than a half percentage point higher than the national average from 1973 through 1980 but rose disproportionately more than domestic unemployment between 1980 and 1981.

Social Organization

Many social scientists saw West German society as broadly middle class, characterized by prosperous (and largely skilled) industrial workers merging with the expanding ranks of technical-administrative white-collar employees. West Germans themselves seemed to support such a view of themselves; everyone from factory workers to government officials and business executives classified themselves as "middle class" in response to public opinion queries. The dramatic increase in economic well-being in the late 1950s and 1960s gave rise to a certain social leveling—if only in terms of patterns of consumption.

Sociologist Ralf Dahrendorf identified a variety of social groups: the elite, the service class, the middle-class elite, the working-class elite, clerical and white-collar workers, the working class, and the lower class. These social groups were diverse and certainly difficult to rank with any measure of precision. Society itself remained, however, distinctly hierarchical. The boundaries between the various strata have blurred since 1945; a social pyra-

The Society

mid, nonetheless, persisted—the bottom narrowed slightly, and the top layers expanded.

Social transformations were wrought in post-World War II society, but the principal avenue of social mobility remained, as it had been in the late nineteenth century, the switch from agricultural to nonagricultural employment. By the early 1980s less than 6 percent of the population remained in agriculture. The social transformation that began with nineteenth-century industrialization continued to set the tone for changes after 1945. The rural exodus continued; in the 1960s and 1970s some two-thirds of all farm youth left the countryside for other employment. From the late 1960s through the mid-1970s, the switch from agricultural to nonagricultural employment still accounted for nearly half of all occupational mobility.

Educational achievement has been a major factor in determining occupational attainment and socioeconomic status in the post-World War II era. University education has been virtually essential in gaining access to the most prestigious and remunerative positions. Some of the most enduring social divisions have focused on level of education. Germany's educational system has traditionally served as a funnel, offering universal basic education to the masses, but only the most limited access to higher education. In the 1930s more than 95 percent of all youngsters had completed their formal education by the age of fourteen; by the 1960s the average had risen a scant two years.

For a variety of reasons the educational system reinforced the social hierarchy and limited upward social mobility. The various types of secondary schools were rigidly tracked along academic and vocational courses of study (see Educational System, ch. 2). Children, in conjunction with their parents and teachers, selected their secondary school course of study at approximately ten years of age. The opportunities for those in vocational education programs to switch to university preparatory courses were severely constrained. Few working-class parents had aspirations for their children to continue through the lengthy course of study leading to a university degree. Even the organization of classroom learning with its emphasis on homework (assuming that parents would assist students) put typically less educated working-class parents at a disadvantage. The 1970s educational reforms sought to offer a wider variety of educational opportunities to the population as a whole. By the late 1970s, however, *Gymnasium* and comprehensive school (*Gesamtschule*) enrollment—the two most likely routes to university admittance—amounted to less than one-quarter of the appropriate age-groups.

Those who did attend upper level schools came most often from upper middle- and upper class families. In the mid-1970s students from working-class homes (as defined by the father's occupation) accounted for a scant 6.4 percent of final year *Gymnasium* students. Nearly 60 percent were from self-employed, civil servant, or professional households. In comparison with their portion of the total population, working-class youngsters were grossly underrepresented in *Gymnasium* and university enrollments alike.

Prosperity has played a central role in post–1945 social relations. The experience of economic well-being was pivotal in perhaps the most significant point of cleavage in West German society–the generation gap. The life experience of those born and raised before 1945 was a study in contrasts with that of young adults in the early 1980s. Older West Germans viewed political stability and economic prosperity from the perspective of the economic chaos of the 1920s, Hitler's rise, World War II, and the privations of the early years following Germany's defeat. The central life experience of those born after 1945–50 was, by contrast, one of unparalleled affluence. In 1980 the average thirty-year-old, for example, had entered the labor force when unemployment stood at less than 2 percent. During his or her working life, real earnings had increased every year until 1981. Overall, wages rose nearly 150 percent in the 1960s, and even in the less prosperous 1970s they increased by over 100 percent.

The typical thirty-year-old had known a certain amount of political upheaval. Student political activity in the late 1960s and 1970s had frequently been intense; it took place, however, within the context of a political system generally regarded as a legitimate form of representative government. Except for a tiny minority of young people dedicated to violent revolution, the extreme disaffection with political institutions characteristic of German youth in the 1920s found little echo in the 1970s (see Dissidence and Terrorist Activities, ch. 9). How this generation reared in affluence and political stability would react to the (apparently) less certain 1980s was the focus of much concern. What was clear was that generational differences in world view and life experiences could hardly have anything but a pervasive impact on socialpolitical life.

The Elite

West Germany's elite is a numerically small but highly diverse group of those influential in public administration, politics, the military, economic life, and cultural affairs. It includes highranking civil service (see Glossary) and trade union officials, university professors, the upper echelons of the officer corps, industrial, financial, and political leaders as well as divers writers and artists. In the post-World War II era there was intermingling and a variety of formal and informal contacts between the various elites but, with the exception of civil service officials and political leaders, little overlapping membership among the various strata. In addition, although the elite was certainly varied in its structure, there was, at least until the late 1970s, a significant measure of consensus about the proper modes of sociopolitical action. Party affiliation and ideological differences were salient, but the elite as a whole was committed to stability. Both the political and economic organization of the country possessed a legitimacy that had eluded the Weimar Republic.

Traditionally the elite was nearly a closed caste. Both in Weimar and Nazi Germany, representatives from the lower social orders were virtually nonexistent. A survey of 250 top leadership positions in 1925 and 1940 found individuals of lower class background occupying 5 percent and 2 percent of the slots, respectively. Even this bespoke more mobility than that enjoyed by Imperial Germany's elite, over two-thirds of whom were aristocrats and over three-quarters of whom came from families of top echelon civil servants, military officers, or landowners. A scant 10 percent came from the industrial or mercantile bourgeoisie. In a country where a minute fraction of the total population continued its education beyond primary school, almost all of the elite had taken a secondary school diploma, and two-thirds had their university degrees. Weimar Germany increased the Roman Catholic and Social Democratic presence, limited the Prussian cast, and tolerated labor union leaders. Elite status, nonetheless, remained the preserve of long-entrenched upper middle- and upper class families.

The elite of the post–World War II era was slightly more open than its pre–1945 counterpart. The changes nonetheless were less a matter of restructuring society than the general prosperity of the 1960s and early 1970s. Despite the tumult of the interwar and Nazi eras, the social hierarchy has proved remarkably durable. The elite remained largely university educated, typically in the study of law; more than 80 percent in the mid–1970s had attended postsecondary school. Only trade union leaders, roughly a quarter of whom had university degrees, proved an exception. The elite was more frequently Protestant (57 percent) than Catholic (30 percent). Catholics were most dramatically underrepresented in the leadership of industry, the military, mass media, and trade unions.

The elite's family background—to judge from the father's occupation—represented the narrow upper social strata. Nearly two-thirds of the elite came from the families of the business or civil service (see Glossary) community. In only 10 percent of the cases was an elite member's father a manual worker. Even among trade union leaders nearly one-third had fathers who were businessmen or civil servants.

The captains of industry and finance were, in terms of social background, the elite's most diverse sector. Those who wielded economic power included a remnant of the old aristocracy, the heirs of the nineteenth-century industrialists and financiers, the "salaried rich"—technocrats who ran enterprises (often earning incomes in the seven- and eight-digit range)—and a number of self-made post-World War II multimillionaires. The economic expansion of the 1950s and 1960s offered opportunities to amass fortunes, and though the entrepreneurs who garnered them were few, their rise was truly meteoric. They were the West German rags-to-riches stories. The total number of the economic elite, even including the salaried managers and directors, was minute. Observers suggested something on the order of 600 individuals in a "cobweblike network of interlocking directorates, supervisory boards, and holding companies..." at the helm of the West German economy.

The extent to which economic expansion increasingly concentrated extreme wealth in fewer hands can hardly be overstated. General prosperity contributed to substantial improvements in the working-class standard of living, but it has also permitted the economic elite to increase its share of national income. By the mid–1970s less than 2 percent of West German households controlled roughly 35 percent of all private property. The self-employed have gained relative to wage earners; in 1960 they earned less than two and one-half times as much as the salaried workers, and by 1972 the gap was more than three times as much.

High-ranking civil servants (perhaps 10 percent of the civil service) were the core of the administrative elite. Traditionally a conservative, Protestant, Prussian, and caste-conscious segment of the elite, their relationship to the political order has been complex. The ethos of public service was ostensibly one of apolitical service to the state. Nonetheless in both Nazi and Imperial Germany, those in power made efforts to assure the loyalty of the civil service bureaucracy. Otto von Bismarck eliminated Roman Catholics and Social Democrats; Hitler, the Jews, communists, and more vociferous Weimar adherents.

In addition a political career coupled with one in public service has had a long tradition for upper ranking civil servants. In many ways nineteenth-century civil administrators served as the functional alternative to a politically active bourgeoisie. Individuals with prior civil service experience accounted for some half the delegates of the National Assembly in 1848 and the Prussian Assembly in the 1860s; they were more than 20 percent of the Imperial Parliament (Reichstag) in 1907. In the post-World War II era as well, public service gave the successful bureaucrat a base of operations for acquiring expertise in and familiarity with the workings of government. Civil service could be a stepping-stone in a political career; the number of civil servants elected to the Bundestag has been gradually rising since 1945. In addition the expectation has been that top-ranked bureaucrats would reflect the party affiliation and ideological philosophy of those in power. Finally the trend with Social Democratic Party (Sozialdemokratische Partei Deutschlands—SPD) appointees in the 1970s has been toward individuals whose main career experience has been outside civil service (see The Bureaucracy, ch. 7).

The bureaucratic elite was homogeneous in contrast to the diverse economic leadership. It was overwhelmingly university educated (some 98 percent had university degrees in the mid-1970s), generally male, frequently Protestant. Members of the civil service elite were themselves often the offspring of university-educated civil servants. Economic expansion coupled with the limited number of university graduates made it more difficult, according to some observers, for government to compete with industry for graduates. If there was some dilution in the civil servants' preeminence, it was slight. High-ranking civil servants remained a privileged and prestigious group in the late 1970s and early 1980s.

The Middle Class

The middle class is diverse. Its main components are the petite bourgeoisie; the "old middle class" of merchants, tradesmen, small businessmen, and middling farmers; and a group of more recent origin—middle-range bureaucrats, administrators, and managers as well as upper level white-collar workers. It is as stratified and hierarchical as the elite, though its boundaries are notably diffuse. At the upper end of the scale, the middle class merges with the managerial and professional elite, at the lower end it fades into highly skilled workers, craftsmen, foremen, and clerical employees. Conservative in ethos, it has been traditionally jealous of its privileges and prerogatives.

The middle orders have been transformed in post-World War II society; as the traditional bastion of the middle class—the small-scale merchants and entrepreneurs—declined in number, salaried employees increased. Only those entrepreneurs linked with the expanding service sector reversed the trend. Between 1960 and 1975 the number of independent businessmen dropped by more than 20 percent—a decline that was even more precipitous in agricultural enterprises, which dropped by roughly 40 percent. Throughout the 1970s the number of self-employed dropped at an annual rate of 2.3 percent (see table 8, Appendix). By decade's end they accounted for less than 15 percent of the total labor force (see table 9, Appendix). Those who remained self-employed became wealthier. Between the 1960s and the 1970s, though the overall number of the self-employed dropped, the percentage in the top income brackets increased more than three times.

The Working Class

Roughly one-half to two-thirds of West Germans are of the working class—a group that ranges from skilled workers, craftsmen, factory foremen (who form something of a working-class elite), sales clerks, low-ranking clerical help, transportation

Federal Republic of Germany

workers, and others in the expanding service sector occupations to the mass of semiskilled and unskilled workers in services and industry. The general prosperity of the 1960s and early 1970s diminished the formerly vast gap between the middle and working classes. The barrier between the lower orders and the middle ranges of the social order is by no means easily permeable; but neither is it as insurmountable as it once was.

If education might have offered limited mobility to the children of factory workers or small farmers, the same was not true of the service industry that offered employment to vast numbers with only a primary school education. The move from the working class to the middle class was typically a multigeneration process: one from peasant agriculture to mining or industry, another to nonmanual, lower echelon service industry, still another to the educated, professional middle class. White-collar clerical workers were, according to observers, often middle class in their outlook, values, and aspirations, if not their occupation and life-style.

The bulk of the working class were the skilled, semiskilled, and unskilled workers in industry, mining, and agriculture. The overall proportion of the economically active population in industry, slightly less than half, has been roughly stable since the 1920s. The major change in the composition of the working class in the last half century has been the decline in the farming population since 1945 and the expansion of the service sector. Within industry the workers' level of skill (as measured by the ratio of skilled to unskilled laborers) increased until the late 1970s.

A variety of organizations represented wage earners' interests in the workplace. Legislation throughout the post-World War II era has delineated the ways in which workers can share in an enterprise's decisionmaking. The Works' Constitution Laws (1952 and 1972) provided for works' councils representing workers in matters relating to hiring and firing, factory closures, working conditions, regulations, hours, breaks, and vacations as well as training programs, job safety, and access to company housing. The councils do not negotiate collective wage agreements, but they do have input into job evaluation, proposed piece rates, and wage scales. They function in coordination with unions and employers' associations.

Legislation on codetermination giving workers seats on industries' management boards has had a more uneven history. The original codetermination law (*Mitbestimmungsrecht*), passed in 1951, represented organized labor's first major post-Nazi victory. The law gave workers parity representation on boards of supervisors in coal and steel industries (see Codetermination, ch. 6). Subsequent laws extended codetermination to other industries and enterprises, though none guarantees workers the parity enjoyed under the terms of the 1951 legislation. A 1976 law, passed after years of debate, covers most workers. It provides for codetermi-

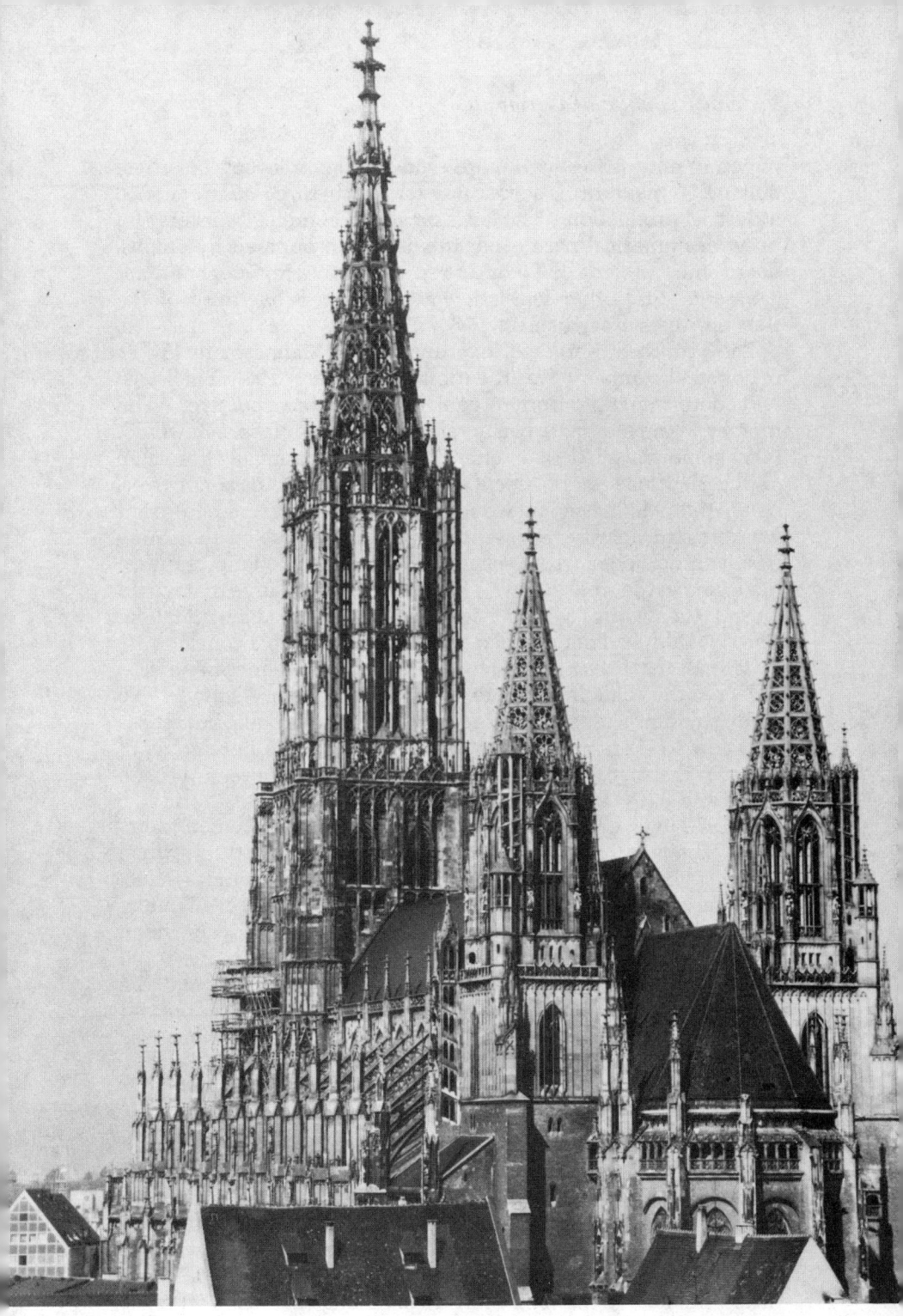

Cathedral in Münster
Courtesy German Information Center

Federal Republic of Germany

nation in enterprises with more than 2,000 employees, i.e., some 600 to 650 major firms accounting for nearly three-quarters of all industrial production. The law's terms are complex; workers end up with numerical parity but, in a stricture opposed by unions, boards must include one worker representative from higher management. Still other legislation gives workers one-third of the slots on supervisory boards.

The proposed merger of two divisions of Mannesmann AG (a major steel company) was the most serious early 1980s challenge to codetermination from organized labor's perspective. The merger would eliminate parity representation for labor. It would, management argued, save some DM25 million annually (for value of the deutsche mark—see Glossary). It would also, however, mean that Mannesmann would no longer be obliged to grant workers strict parity representation. Unions, fearing that Mannesmann's proposal would set an unfortunate precedent for future managers in the steel industry, proposed an alternative that would permit the savings without sacrificing parity codetermination. The two sides had not reached a mutually acceptable compromise by late 1981. It was clear, however, that the Mannesmann case reflected the changing climate of worker-employer relations. No ready solution was forthcoming, and the almost idyllic consensus between workers and management in the 1960s bore signs of strain in the more straitened economic circumstances of the late 1970s and early 1980s.

In 1978 over 40 percent of all wage earners were union members. The largest single representative of labor was the German Trade Union Federation (Deutscher Gewerkschaftsbund—DGB), a federation of seventeen unions including 86 percent of all unionized workers. In addition the German Salaried Employees Union (Deutsche Angestellten Gewerkschaft—DAG) represented slightly less than half a million white-collar managers and the Federation of German Civil Servants (Deutscher Beamtenbund—DBB) accounted for some 80,000 unionized public servants (see Traditional Interest Groups, ch. 7).

DGB's preponderance was significant. In late 1981 one-third of all wage earners were DGB members. The federation's membership accounted for virtually all organized industrial workers (the largest single category in the labor force), roughly half of all unionized civil servants, and two-thirds of organized white-collar employees. I.G. Metall, the metalworkers union (at loggerheads with Mannesmann) having more than 2.5 million members, was the world's single largest autonomous union. Levels of unionization varied significantly among industries; among railroad workers it was close to 100 percent, in agriculture only some 10 percent. In heavy industry and manufacturing, union members were often 70 to 80 percent of the labor force.

DBG's highly organized and cohesive federation stood in marked contrast to the interwar labor movement. Differing political philosophies and allegiances fragmented workers in the Weimar Republic into Christian, socialist, liberal, and communist unions. These splits were, in the view of post–1945 labor leaders, a fatal weakness. Internecine struggles between or among rival unions vitiated workers' attempts to organize. The experience induced union leaders to pursue a different strategy following World War II. Since then West Germany's labor movement has been, at a minimum, more unified. DGB couples a decentralized organizational structure with centralized decisionmaking. Union leaders have generally been responsive to the rank-and-file membership, and workers have characteristically been disciplined and supportive of labor leaders.

Until the early 1970s labor's demands were frequently moderate. The Munich Program of 1949 defined labor's goals as full employment, codetermination in industry, the nationalization of key enterprises, and income redistribution. As the West German "economic miracle" took hold in the 1960s, unions increasingly focused on bread-and-butter issues: wages and job security. For workers the dramatic improvement in their standard of living, particularly in contrast with the privations of the years immediately following World War II, was proof of the virtue of a consensual approach to bargaining in the workplace. Union leaders and workers alike shared a pragmatic orientation as well as a more general concern with order and moderation. Older union leaders, like the membership they represented, were the products of vocational secondary schools. "Radical" leftist views—where they surfaced within unions—were typically held not by elected officials, who generally came from the workplace, but by hired professionals, who were university educated.

Confrontations between labor and management were limited until the mid–1970s. There were major strikes in 1953 and 1954, a few in 1957 and 1964. Wildcat strikes were notably infrequent. Employers facing the possibility of a strike preferred negotiation and settlement to a lockout. Strike threats rather than actual work stoppages were unions' typical negotiating lever in the prosperous 1960s and early 1970s.

The 1970s saw a certain erosion in the consensus governing relations in the workplace. Steelworkers, miners, public service employees, and longshoremen staged a number of wildcat walkouts in late 1969. Low wage agreements were the cause of worker discontent; the rank and file felt that union leaders had been perhaps too ready to hold down wage demands. There were strikes in 1973. Those in printing—an industry hard hit by automation and microprocessing technology—were the first in a half century; those in the chemical industry were the first since the early 1950s. Both the 1969 and the 1973 strikes pushed labor union leaders to higher wage demands in the following years.

By the early 1980s union officials noted a general increase in the frequency of labor disputes. At the same time, management was less reticent about using lockouts to combat strikes. There were three much-touted lockouts involving two major unions (metalworkers and printers) in 1978–79. The courts continued to argue the legality of lockouts in late 1981. Some observers interpreted the increase in labor-management confrontation as the end of the general consensus and moderation governing employer-worker relations in the 1950s and 1960s. The generation that had endured economic chaos in the 1920s, Nazi rule, World War II, and the postwar privations was being gradually replaced by one that had grown up in prosperity. Younger workers were pushing labor leaders into a generally more aggressive bargaining stance. Older union officials were retiring in favor of a younger, more militant generation of leaders.

Much of the impetus for change came simply from the worsening economic scene. Employment and wages both declined in the early 1980s. Real earnings rose three and one-half times between 1950 and 1975 but declined for the first time in the Federal Republic's history in 1981. Unemployment inched upward from a low of 1.0 percent in 1973. It nearly doubled in the 1974–75 recession and did so again in 1980–81. *Gastarbeiter*, women, and those entering the job market for the first time were particularly hard hit. The average duration of a spell of unemployment increased for blue-collar and white-collar workers alike. Some 1.9 million were unemployed in early 1982, a rate of 8.2 percent. There were projections of as many as 2 million out of work in the winter of 1982, with an annual average of 1.6 to 1.75 million jobless. Further the national unemployment average masked significant regional variations. In the heavy industries of the Ruhr Valley, the rate was more than 10 percent. In the Frankfurt metallurgy industry, layoffs reached even skilled workers normally immune from economic fluctuations.

Increased unemployment coincided with the government's 1982 budget battles and a reluctance to increase federal spending with "make work jobs" (see Political Parties and the Electoral System, ch. 7). Approximately 70,000 workers gathered in Stuttgart in November 1981 to protest the budget. It was organized labor's first anti-SPD demonstration in a long time. On a more general level, workers were concerned with long-term employment trends. DGB estimated that automation cost industry roughly 1.5 million jobs in the mid-1970s. Increasing automation decreased the skill levels of many jobs; workers faced not only diminished job opportunities but also job reclassification into less skilled positions. Unions have argued that current pay scales should be maintained despite job reclassification and that early retirement programs with full pensions are a partial solution to high unemployment. Concern with job loss through automation was coupled with worries about flight of capital and jobs abroad. The number of people employed outside the country by West German companies tripled in the decade preceding 1975. In the processing industry, for example, the ratio of domestic to foreign jobs declined from 20:1 to 5:1 in the same period.

Slightly more than one-third of the labor force were women—a percentage that had remained virtually constant since 1950 (see table 10, Appendix). Roughly one-third of women of working age were employed in the late 1970s. Their earnings averaged approximately half those of men. In 1975 female salaried employees received less than two-thirds the income of their male counterparts, and female wage earners received less than half the earnings of male wage laborers. Overall, women were concentrated in the lower reaches of the income scale. In the 1970s some 20 percent of male workers earned less than DM800 per month, but 70 percent of females did; over 90 percent of working women earned less than DM1,200 monthly, yet less than 60 percent of working men fell within that income range.

The skill levels of working women as well as their concentration in the least remunerative sectors of the economy accounted for much of the disparity in earnings. Women found employment primarily in agriculture, commerce, trade, and service industries, where they constituted the majority of the labor force. In the service sector nearly two-thirds of all employees were women. Even within specific branches of the economy men out-earned women, and the difference, at least in industry, increased during the 1970s. Average gross earnings for females in industry were nearly 70 percent those of males in 1970, less than 50 percent in 1978.

Women were frequently part-time workers (some 20 percent of employed women worked a shortened week) and were disproportionately represented in the ranks of less skilled workers. In 1970, for example, less than 2 percent of master craftworkers were females. The chances of a woman worker having training beyond the semiskilled level were one in ten. Where women were trained it was overwhelmingly in the conventional fields of female employment. Women accounted for 95 percent of apprentices in typing, textiles, and sales but only 0.1 percent of all trainees in auto mechanics, concrete work, and masonry.

Unemployment among women rose disproportionate to their share in the labor force in the 1970s. By 1978 women accounted for roughly half of all those out of work. In 1980 the unemployment rate among women was twice that of men. Some observers commented that, in a climate of growing unemployment, there was a resurgence of "back to the kitchen" attitudes toward working women. There was a widely noted hierarchy of the jobless that placed *Gastarbeiter* at the bottom of the heap and women close thereafter. Such feelings reflected general attitudes about women's role in the workplace and the family. Women were not expected to work outside the home; homemakers incurred no disdain, but working mothers, by contrast, were implicitly viewed as neglecting their children. This despite the fact that some 40 percent of women with children under eighteen years of age were employed, and over one-third of all working women had children.

A "three-phase" model of women's careers found wide acceptance. In phase I a woman was educated and trained and then worked for several years; in phase II she was devoted to marriage and childrearing. In phase III, after her children were grown, a woman could reenter the job market. The lack of sufficient childcare facilities contributed to such a view of women's working, as did traditional sex roles within the family (see Family Organization, this ch.). The Work Furthering Act (1969, 1976) provided training and assistance for women entering the labor force after a hiatus of marriage and childrearing.

The scarcity of day-care facilities, especially for children under three years of age, complicated the lot of working parents. In the mid-1970s less than 2 percent of children three years of age attended day nurseries. The number of kindergartens increased rapidly in the 1970s; by mid-decade approximately half of all preschoolers of the appropriate age-group found places in kindergartens. Unfortunately for low-income working parents, most kindergartens were privately run; they therefore were either expensive or required a donation of parent time to the institution. There were a small number of after-school centers for primary-school children of working parents, but these included only a small portion of all primary-school students (see table 11, Appendix). In a number of larger cities, "day mothers" and the elderly filled some of the gap, caring for several hundreds of thousands of youngsters who were unable to find places in conventional childcare facilities.

Family Organization

German society, despite the upheavals of the nineteenth and twentieth centuries, remained strongly family-oriented in the post-World War II era. Families were tightly knit, and cohesive family ties permeated social life. Nineteenth-century industrialization and urbanization wrought profound changes in family composition and kinship. The kinship organization, adapted to a rural, agrarian existence, went through numerous transformations in the social and economic tumult of the nineteenth century. Nonetheless a core of values and customs endured. Even amidst the changing social mores of the 1960s and 1970s, West Germans recognized common elements that were part of a much-respected tradition of family life. Families served as a refuge from confusing and frequently threatening pressures of a rapidly changing world.

The tradition of the home as the center of activity for all family members was strongly instilled in most Germans. Families spend much of their leisure time in shared activities; birthdays, name days, marriages, anniversaries, and holidays are major family affairs. Affective attachments between parents and their children are often strong and lasting. It is not uncommon for several generations of extended families to gather for significant family celebrations.

The nuclear family consisting of a couple and their unmarried children has been the typical family unit since at least the late nineteenth century. Extended families with grandparents or married siblings and their spouses living together were increasingly uncommon. Urbanization and the growing reliance on wage labor for livelihood contributed to their decline. In the 1970s a fraction of young people were involved in communal living arrangements—in part as a form of protest against conventional society, in part as a means of dealing with the urban housing scene. Cohabitation of unmarried couples was increasingly acceptable to young West Germans, though the proportion of consensual unions to formal marriages—even among the young—was minute. Mid–1970s surveys indicated that roughly three-quarters of long-term consensual unions ended in marriage.

The German family was traditionally patriarchal—dominated by the husband and father; ideally he was the unquestioned head of the household. In theory he could, without consulting his wife, determine where the family would live, how it would allocate its income, and how the children would be brought up. He was the disciplinarian, the ultimate arbiter of family disputes, and the household's representative in dealings with the larger society. He was entitled to deference from his wife and children; and although he was supposed to consider the wishes and well-being of all family members, his decisions were final. Ultimately family members had little recourse in the face of paternal authority.

Children customarily remained in the parental household until they married; the age of first marriage was frequently the late twenties (for women) or the thirties (for men). Even mature sons and daughters were treated as legal minors as long as they lived with their parents. Parents, particularly the father, were responsible for their children's well-being, personal property, and conduct in society. The family had the right to its children's labor. Sons were commonly apprenticed in their father's craft with the ultimate objective of carrying on the family business. Parents, through plotting their offspring's course of education, virtually determined their careers (see Social Organization, this ch.). Sons typically followed their father's trade or profession; daughters were educated for marriage and childrearing.

The old saying *"Kinder, Küche, Kirche"* (children, kitchen, church) was probably an accurate and succinct summary of popularly held views of woman's proper domain. Women's admission to institutions of higher education lagged behind that of other West European nations. Early impetus for the emancipation of women had little to do with any overtly German or Prussian influence. It was largely a phenomenon of the southern German states and reflected Catholic efforts to enhance middle- and upper class women's loyalty to the church by admitting them to universities.

Social mores and legal codes alike sanctioned male authority within the family. Women were their husband's legal inferiors in matters of property, sex, marriage, and children. The lot of unmarried working women was scarcely more enviable. Women were denied pensions; marriage constituted legal grounds for firing female workers. Even in the context of the times women were politically disadvantaged; however, the Social Democrats did organize those women within their party's ranks. A budding suffrage movement was profoundly handicapped in most places until it gained the right of assembly in 1908. In 1919 women gained the vote from the Weimar constituent assembly.

Women made some legal and social gains in the Weimar Republic, although its record in promoting women's employment was less than glowing. They suffered reverses under Nazi rule; Nazi philosophy rejected feminism as anti-German (in their view of Teutonic destiny), glorified motherhood along with women's domestic duties, and restricted their activities outside the home. Despite much rhetoric about women's properly feminine, subservient, and maternal role, Nazism's long-term impact on the German hausfrau was other than they might have wished. Their efforts to get women to stop smoking (unfeminine) and using makeup (decadent and bourgeois) fell on deaf ears. Nazis cut enrollments in institutions of higher education, but the proportion of female students in universities remained almost unchanged. The Nazi impact on women in the professions was virtually nil. There were limited numbers of professional women in any event, and those few were concentrated in teaching and medicine—fields "appropriately" maternal and feminine. Overall, women as a percentage of the labor force dropped slightly until 1939. The war effort, of course, increased the female presence in the workplace. Most women workers were in semiskilled and unskilled clerical and industrial positions, but a few found their way into scientific and technical fields that Nazi ideology held them ill-suited for.

Ironically, perhaps the most profound effect Nazi rule had on German family life was the creation of millions of female-headed households. For large numbers of families the wife and mother became the primary authority figure and the source of livelihood.

In another large segment of the population, women and older children shared with the father the responsibility of earning a living under hardship conditions. Although the precise impact such conditions had on German views of marriage and family relationships was not certain, as early as 1951 sociologists noted that nearly three-quarters of the couples questioned considered marriage a partnership of two equals and did not recognize the traditional male prerogatives. Studies throughout the 1960s and 1970s confirmed a dramatic change in husband-wife relationships as well as a decline in authoritarian control of children.

Although the patriarchal, authoritarian family was largely an anachronism in post-World War II society, a sexual division of labor within the family persisted. As in most industrial societies the husband continued to be most frequently considered the breadwinner, charged with seeing to the family's dealing with the society at large and major economic or contractual arrangements. The wife's sphere remained domestic affairs, the running of the household, and childrearing. Nonetheless observers noted a new measure of consensual decisionmaking in West German families and a growing sense of equality and shared authority between spouses. Such attitudes toward marriage were spread unevenly, however; they were more typically urban than rural and characteristic of younger rather than older couples. Acceptance of marriage as a partnership between equals increased with the wife's educational attainments and her involvement in the work force.

The Federal Republic's Basic Law (constitution) guarantees men and women equal rights. 1957 legislation rectified existing inequalities in marriage property law. The Marriage Reform Law, the culmination of a series of reforms affecting child care and custody, marriage, and divorce, took effect in 1977. The law recognizes marriage as a private agreement between equal partners who share responsibility for child care and domestic decisions. Divorce under the new law is no-fault; irreconcilable differences are the only grounds for dissolving a marriage and neither spouse is assigned blame. In case of divorce the economically disadvantaged ex-spouse is due alimony until he or she is able to earn a living.

In common with most West and North European countries, German marriage patterns changed in the late nineteenth-early twentieth centuries. The marriage rate for individuals born circa 1880 dropped dramatically. Of women born at that time, for example, some 10 to 20 percent remained single; those who married did so later in life than previous generations—average age at first marriage was in the late twenties for females. In the early 1960s, by contrast, less than 5 percent of women born about 1940 remained unmarried—most had wed in their early twenties. Not since the eighteenth century had marriage been so universal a part of an individual's life. The increase in the marriage rate was accompanied by a general rise in the number of divorces.

In the 1970s the pattern changed yet again; the number of marriages dropped while divorces continued to rise. The marriage rate (as measured per 1,000 of population) dropped steadily from 1965 until the late 1970s. Further the age-specific marriage rate (for individuals from fifteen through forty-nine years of age) declined much more steeply, by some two-thirds. By contrast the divorce rate doubled from 1960 to 1976, then dropped somewhat in the late 1970s. (It was difficult to determine the effect of the new marriage law on couples contemplating divorce.) In the mid-1970s the divorce rate stood at some 30 percent of new marriages (see table 12, Appendix). Increasingly it was women who began divorce proceedings; in the late 1970s women initiated nearly three-quarters of all divorces. The rising divorce rate obscured the extent to which most marriages and families were stable. According to a 1975 government report, 86 percent of the country's more than 1.5 million married couples were still wed to their first spouses. In only 4 percent of married couples had both spouses been previously married.

Urbanization and Migration

Germany was largely rural and agrarian until the nineteenth century. In the thirteenth and fourteenth centuries, roughly 10 to 15 percent of the population lived in some 3,330 urban centers. Although the estimated populations of Cologne, Lübeck, Frankfurt am Main, and a few other cities exceeded 10,000, most urban settlements were little more than villages or small trading towns. Religious wars and political upheaval contributed to the decline of cities in the sixteenth and seventeenth centuries (see Reformation, ch. 1).

Little more than a quarter of the population lived in cities early in the nineteenth century. Hamburg, a major European seaport, had a population of perhaps 100,000; Berlin, the administrative center of the rising Prussian state, numbered nearly twice that. Otherwise the urban scene remained one of numerous dispersed small towns and villages. The distribution of cities by size had changed little since the fifteenth century. The economy, overwhelmingly rural, was based on small family farms supplemented by cottage industries. Urban dwellers were, almost by definition, the socially and politically fortunate. Cities, notes one fifteenth-century historian, were the haven of "privileged citizens and protected aliens." Property prerequisites for burgher status were notably stringent. Both trade and guild restrictions limited emigration from the countryside.

Industrialization transformed the social and economic life of German cities. Administrative reforms, especially those of the 1871 constitution, cleared away many obstacles to urban growth. The expansion of cities throughout the nineteenth century was astronomical; from 1816 to 1925 the rural population grew by less than 25 percent while cities increased over 5.5 times. Overall more than 10.5 million peasants left the countryside for the city in less than a century—1841–1910. As late as 1871 a scant quarter of the population lived in settlements of 5,000 or more; by 1910 nearly half did. The most substantial population increases were in large cities, i.e., those of 100,000 inhabitants or more, which more than quadrupled their share of total population. Even the number of large cities grew by some 500 percent. Rural dwellers, two-thirds of the population in 1871, were only one-third by the mid–1920s.

If industry was the impetus behind this spectacular urban growth, its influence spread unevenly across the landscape. The expanding industrial and mining towns of Westphalia, the Rhineland, and the Saarland were the most prominent centers of growth. In the east, Upper Silesia, Saxony, and Berlin shared in urban expansion to a lesser extent (see fig. 4). The burgeoning development of towns in the Ruhr coalfields was phenomenal. The main Ruhr cities had an average population of less than 5,000 in 1852; Dortmund, the largest, had approximately 13,500 inhabitants. By 1910 the average was over 53,000; Dortmund, Duisburg, and Essen all had populations in excess of 100,000. Coal towns' growth absorbed the surplus population of the surrounding farming regions, then turned to the wretchedly overpopulated agrarian east. By the 1890s emigrants from eastern Prussia accounted for nearly half the labor force of the newer coal mines.

The onslaught drastically altered traditional urban society. The privileged burghers, guild members, and civil servants were overwhelmed by a sea of businessmen, industrialists, and hordes of laborers. Industrialization spawned subsidiary employment for multitudes of builders, shopkeepers, merchants, and wholesale traders. "Industry," scholar Wolfgang Köllmann points out, "took over the town and reshaped it."

Settlement patterns in the early 1980s bore the imprint of the earlier urban industrial movement. More than one-third of the total population lived in cities of 100,000 or more; another one-fourth resided in mid-sized cities (20,000–100,000 inhabitants), and another one-third in small towns and villages of 2,000 to 20,000 inhabitants. A scant 6 percent of West Germans lived in settlements of less than 2,000 and less than 1 r .cent in those of less than 1,000.

No single urban center has dominated contemporary urbanization; the country lacks a "primate city" to play a role comparable to that of London, Paris, Mexico City, or Lima. Even Berlin at its zenith had shared preeminence with a score of other German cities—Cologne, Munich, Hamburg, and Nuremberg, to name but a few. Immediately before World War II, Berlin still accounted for only 7 percent of the Third Reich's population. In the late

Federal Republic of Germany

1970s West Berlin, with nearly 2 million inhabitants, remained the country's largest city. It represented, however, only 3 percent of total population; by contrast Greater London accounted for some 14 percent of Britain's population and Greater Paris for more than 16 percent of France's. Even among West Germany's thirty-six largest cities, West Berlin accounted for only about 10 percent of the population.

Urbanization was intense, widespread, diverse, and remarkably polycentric. There were, in the late 1970s, thirty-two urban centers having populations over 200,000. Both the political and administrative functions of the federal government were widely dispersed. Although Bonn was the seat of the federal legislature, other cities maintained a significant portion of national agencies. Urban conglomerates that were scattered in an arc from Hamburg in the north to Munich in the south defined urban settlement patterns. (see fig. 8). Each conglomeration consisted of a core city circled by heavily urbanized suburbs and an outer ring of less densely settled commuter towns. Planners looked at the country in terms of some sixty-eight of these urban focuses, core cities surrounded by settlements gradually fading into a rural-urban fringe.

The major post-World War II trend in urbanization has been the growth in conurbations; previously separate cities have expanded and coalesced, and their suburbs have spread further and further from city centers. Already in 1950—despite the devastation of World War II—large urban centers had 2 million more inhabitants than in 1939. The aggregate statistics, however, obscured substantial variation in given city populations. West Berlin, Cologne, and Mainz all lost large numbers of inhabitants, while refugees swelled the population of centers like Lübeck, where the 1950 population was more than 50 percent larger than its 1939 count.

During the 1950s conurbations grew at roughly 2.5 percent per year. Growth slowed in the 1960s, but by the early 1970s conurbations still accounted for half the country's population. Conurbation development patterns changed in the late 1960s and 1970s. The outer rings, suburbs and "bedroom towns," continued to expand rapidly—their annual population increase averaged some 3.0 percent. Central and inner cities, by contrast, grew slowly or stagnated. The arrival of a large number of foreign workers who settled in large cities masked, to an extent, the flight to the suburbs. Further changes in the 1970s in the juridical boundaries of a number of large cities made judging the exact magnitude of population changes complex. Nonetheless since 1960 urban growth has clearly favored the small- to mid-sized city or town within commuting distance of a large urban center. In less than twenty years (1961–79), cities of 10,000–20,000 nearly doubled their portion of total population, and those of 20,000–50,000 increased their share by over two-thirds. During the same period cities of

Vendors in marketplace in Freiburg im Breisgau
Courtesy Dorothy Lohmann

over 100,000, as a percentage of total population, grew by less than 1 percent (see table 13, Appendix).

The Rhine-Ruhr area remained the most populous and densely urban region; in 1978 it represented nearly 10 percent of total population but only 2 percent of total territory. Taken as a whole, North Rhine-Westphalia in 1979 accounted for roughly a quarter of the population. Urban centers in the south and west enjoyed significant growth as well. Their location as the center of much of the expanding electronics and petrochemical industries accounted for most of their increase. Their peak growth was in the 1960s when the population of small- to mid-sized cities grew by roughly one-third.

The most significant migration wave of the late 1940s and 1950s was the movement of German-speaking refugees from the east into the Federal Republic (see Ethnicity, this ch.). The massive rural-urban migration that began in the nineteenth century continued in interwar Germany—more than a million peasants migrated to cities between 1935 and 1939 alone. Since 1945 young rural dwellers have continued to migrate cityward in search of better educational and employment opportunities (see Social Organization, this ch.). Although substantial numbers of rural and urban residents alike migrated—half of all West Germans changed residence in the 1960s, for example—most moves were intraregional. Migrants tend to be young—in the case of rural-urban migrants, overwhelmingly so. A significant proportion of 1960s and 1970s movement from cities to the suburbs consisted of young families exchanging urban apartments for homes in the suburbs.

Urban housing—a perennial concern—was in acutely short supply in the years immediately following World War II. The housing boom in the wake of the war's destruction was little short of incredible. By 1979 more than two-thirds of the country's residential dwellings had been built since 1945. In the 1960s more than a half million units were built per year—an average that was maintained even amid the economic slowdowns of the 1970s. More than 700,000 units were completed in 1973, over 600,000 in both 1972 and 1974. Government programs provided substantial tax breaks for individuals purchasing housing or saving to do so. Other programs allocated subsidies for construction of rental units for low-income individuals, the handicapped, or the elderly. In the late 1970s some 1.5 million annually benefited from housing subsidies (see Housing Subsidies, ch. 2).

Adequate housing in central cities remained a problem in the 1980s. The young, students, and *Gastarbeiter* most frequently experienced problems finding moderately priced accommodations. By the early 1980s numerous squatters were occupying vacant buildings in West Berlin, Hamburg, Frankfurt, and Cologne; West Berlin was the pacesetter. The problem of squatters sparked political controversy. Numbers of rent-controlled apartment buildings stood nearly empty while their owners let them depreciate and anticipated selling them to developers. By late 1981 squatters had occupied nearly 150 buildings. Squatters enjoyed a certain measure of public support; in December 1980 approximately 15,000 West Berliners took to the streets to demonstrate in favor of the squatters. A September 1981 altercation between police and demonstrators resulted in the death of a teenager. Talks between city officials and squatters continued in early 1982 in the midst of a moratorium on evictions of those occupying abandoned apartments.

Religion

In the late 1970s some 44 percent of West Germans were Protestants, 45 percent were Roman Catholics. There were, in addition, a variety of smaller Christian sects: the Old Catholics (who split from Rome over papal infallibility in the 1870s) and a number of Anabaptist groups. There were some seventy Jewish congregations, having a total membership of roughly 30,000, under the umbrella of the Central Council of Jews in Germany. The influx of foreign workers in the 1960s and 1970s gave the country a sizable

Eastern Orthodox presence and a Muslim community estimated at 1.5 million.

The Basic Law guarantees freedom of conscience and religion and freedom from state interference in the practice of religion. Nonetheless the role of confessional differences in German history has meant that religion continued to have a profound impact on social relations in the post-World War II era. Germany was, after all, the home of the Reformation and the center of the devastating religious wars of the sixteenth and seventeenth centuries (see Reformation, ch. 1). Denominational cleavages have played a pervasive role in political and economic life. The evolution of the Reformation made the link between religious and secular authority pivotal. Martin Luther's need for the protection of the German princes set the stage for an altar-throne nexus that lasted four centuries until the twentieth-century Weimar Republic. Temporal and ecclesiastical authority was linked in the German states, and civil rulers historically wielded considerable clout in church affairs. Germans were without the anticlerical tradition typical of much of Europe and Latin America in the nineteenth and early twentieth centuries. Attempts to limit churches' influence were almost exclusively government efforts; they hardly reflected popular aspirations and had a minimal social impact. Religion in the Federal Republic continued to be a matter of public and political import. The country's legal framework combined guarantees of confessional freedom along with a church-state relationship unparalleled among the western democracies in its closeness and complexity.

The experience of Nazi interference in church affairs persuaded Roman Catholic and Protestant clergy alike that safeguards for church autonomy were essential. Beyond accepting freedom of conscience, the federal government simply adopted Weimar's formulation of church-state relations that provided for church autonomy in religious matters. An individual state (*Land*; pl., *Länder*) however, had substantial powers in relation to church affairs, and in early 1982 a number of concordats between the Vatican and various *Länder*—to say nothing of the 1933 Concordat between the Third Reich and the Vatican—remained legally valid. There were, in addition, a series of comparable agreements between various Protestant provincial churches, *Land* governments, and the Evangelical Church in Germany (Evangelische Kirche in Deutschland—EKD) (see Protestants, this ch.).

The interlocking of authority is extensive. *Länder* have a say in the appointment of local bishops, who must be German nationals, have received their higher education in Germany, and have at least three years of theological training. Churches control the hiring of religious instructors in public schools, but these instructors are treated in some respects like public servants, and the state pays part of their salaries. The state finances theological faculties in the universities that are divided along denominational lines. Although churches make recommendations about hiring and firing, theology professors are appointed and granted tenure according to standard university procedures. Ostensibly they cannot be dismissed even for heresy (see Roman Catholics, this ch.).

The most controversial aspect of church-state relations in the early 1980s was the church tax. By law church members pay an 8 to 9 percent surcharge on their income tax that goes to the churches. The tax is collected and disbursed through a variety of arrangements, but generally it is an individual's employer and the tax authorities who collect the revenues and forward them to the churches (see Traditional Interest Groups, ch. 7).

Humanistische Union, a Munich-based civil rights group, has protested the church tax. Other critics charge that, because an employer often knows when an employee refuses to pay, the church tax adds to the social pressure to maintain membership. Other critics focused on the worldliness of the arrangement; quips about "Church & Co." lampooned the church tax. Citizens who do not pay the tax are denied church membership. Heinrich Böll, Nobel Prize-winning novelist and a Catholic, protested the tax in the early 1970s and refused to pay or give up his church membership. The Roman Catholic Church took him to court and won, forcing the author either to pay his back taxes or resign his membership in the church.

Although most West Germans maintained their church membership, there was evidence of increasingly secular attitudes in the 1970s; the growing tendency to question authority had extended to religious authorities as well. Public opinion polls in the early 1970s found a substantial minority of both Protestants and Catholics disenchanted with their religion. Skeptical and/or agnostic attitudes were increasingly common; for example a mid–1970s poll by the Institut für Demoskopie Allensbach found that some 40 percent of respondents did not believe in an afterlife.

Increasing numbers of the faithful severed their formal ties with organized religion. In the mid–1970s perhaps a quarter million Protestants annually left the church. In 1981 declining membership rolls contributed to a DM300 million drop in tax revenues for the Protestant churches. Fewer Catholics chose to leave, and, at least until mid-decade, the number of new church members roughly balanced those leaving. Church-leavers tended to be better educated, white-collar, male workers. Those who remained were less inclined to be regular churchgoers. Church attendance in Germany has historically been high. In late eighteenth-century Bavaria—admittedly an intensely Catholic region—a parish priest could boast that typically no more than ten of his thousand-odd parishioners missed Sunday Mass. In the late 1970s some 33 percent of Catholics and 5 to 7 percent of Protestants attended weekly church services.

Protestants

The country's Protestant population is organized into seventeen geographically defined churches: Lutheran, seven; United, eight; and Reformed. two. The Congress of Vienna (1814–15) set down the territorial divisions of most of the churches, and only in Bavaria and Bremen were church administrative borders coterminous with contemporary state boundaries. A Protestant in Hamburg, for example, could, depending on his or her residence, belong to the Evangelical Church of Hanover, Schleswig-Holstein, or Hamburg. State (or, more accurately, provincial) churches enjoyed substantial autonomy in ecclesiastical matters. They were individually represented (along with the EKD) in the World Council of Churches. In the 1970s the Protestant churches were united in the EKD, an umbrella organization. There were as well some doctrinally defined subgroups: the EKD included the United Evangelical Church in Germany, the Evangelical Church of the Union, and the Reformed Federation of Germany. Reformed churches predominated in the west and in urban areas, Lutheran in the east.

Nazi rule and the subsequent division of Germany were particularly cataclysmic for the Protestant churches. The prominent role given the laity and the largely autonomous provincial church structure combined with a certain theological distance from the affairs of state in interwar German Protestantism. Nazi rule split the Protestant churches into factions: the German Evangelical Church, which had a Nazi party member as bishop, held sway in all but three provincial churches. Nazi interference in church affairs engendered opposition on the part of some clergymen, while, in response to totalitarian rule and disregard of human rights, another group (under the influence of people like Karl Barth and Martin Niemöller) formed the "Confessing Church." Much of the church's post–1945 stance on issues from reunification to nuclear arms reflected the sense of having been compromised under Nazism and a determination never to trim sail in political winds again.

The reunification of divided Germany was the most constant source of concern for the Evangelical church from 1945 until the late 1960s. Soviet- and Western-occupied zones divided Germany's Protestant population almost in half and left West German Protestants—formerly a pronouced majority of the population—confessional coequals with the Roman Catholics centered in southern and western Germany. The psychological impact was the greater because of the numbers of Protestant clergy and theologians from east of the Oder-Neisse Line who came to West Germany as refugees. Wittenberg, the center of the Reformation, is in East Germany.

In the 1950s the East German authorities generally permitted normal contact between churches in both Germanys. Indeed, in

Federal Republic of Germany

the heyday of the cold war the EKD synod maintained a strict ideological neutrality to serve as a link between the two Germanys. Contacts were much more difficult in the 1960s. In 1967—the 450th anniversary of Luther's Ninety-five Theses— East German officials refused to let West German visitors attend the celebration in Wittenberg. East German church leaders resisted pressures to form a separate synod until 1969, when both East German and West German Protestants formed separate ecclesiastical jurisdictions.

The churches' stance on rearmament in the 1950s also reflected a concern for reunification. There was a feeling, especially among the clergy of a socialist bent, that Germans would serve as cannon fodder in a war between the Western nations and the Soviet Union and that Germans fighting against each other was "unthinkable." The exchange between Niemöller and then Chancellor Konrad Adenauer on the subject was both public and acerbic. More extreme opponents of rearmament pleaded: "Don't make sixteen million Protestants in the heartland of the Reformation...wait still longer for the *peaceful reunification of Germany* [emphasis in original]." (The Roman Catholic hierarchy, by contrast, was far readier to defend West Germany against the perils of atheistic communism.) The EKD took a stance more moderate than the more vehement critics of rearmament, noting that there was no theological doctrine resolving the rearmament question. The EKD supported a volunteer army and, failing that, lobbied for liberal grounds for conscientious objector status. Observers widely attributed the legislation governing conscientious objectors to the Protestant churches' influence.

Many of the issues that made rearmament a controversial issue surfaced again when nuclear arms came under consideration in the 1950s; Protestants were divided on whether West Germans should have nuclear weapons. Some felt that if the Federal Republic were to be armed it should be with the most advanced weapons available. Others argued that nuclear weapons so changed the nature of warfare that traditional notions of a "just war" were made wholly untenable. Niemöller held that it should be an article of faith that Protestants should not serve in an army with nuclear weapons. The EKD synod formed a commission to try to reach a consensus. Efforts to work out an agreement among the various points of view were unsuccessful, and the EKD ended the 1950s without denouncing the use of nuclear weapons in self-defense. The resurgence of the peace movement in the early 1980s, however, brought a more unified antinuclear stance from even traditionally conservative Protestants.

Roman Catholics

The country's Roman Catholic population was divided among some twenty-one dioceses and archdioceses, most of which were

Religious paintings on building in Oberammergau
Courtesy Dorothy Lohmann

established by the mid-nineteenth century. Although the Catholic church faced organizational problems because of the division of Germany, reunification was never the issue of overriding concern that it was for Protestants. The Federal Republic held virtually the entire German Catholic population. The status of formerly German dioceses east of the Oder-Neisse Line was an issue in the 1950s and 1960s because the 1933 Concordat between the Vatican and the Third Reich subjected changes in diocese boundaries to state approval. The dioceses went to Polish prelates in the midst of Pope John XXIII's efforts to reach a modus vivendi with the communist regimes of Eastern Europe.

What did concern much of the Catholic hierarchy from 1945 through the early 1970s was the status of denominational schools. Education was historically an ecclesiastical bailiwick in Germany and one the Catholic church had guarded jealously since the Counter-Reformation. Churches had virtually total control of primary and secondary education until 1918. In 1932 more than 80 percent of all elementary schools were still confessional.

The right to denominational schools nationwide was the principal concession the Vatican wrested from the Nazis in the 1933 Concordat. In return the Vatican assured the Nazis that the Catholic clergy would eschew political activity, the government might influence the choice of bishops, and changes in diocese boundaries would be subject to government approval. The Concordat was signed by Eugenio Pacelli—then Vatican secretary of state, subsequently Pope Pius XII—and Hitler's vice chancellor, Franz von Papen. From the Vatican perspective the Concordat was—despite the fact that it was concluded with the Nazis and was never voted on by any German legislative body—a model of the sort of agreement they would have liked with other heavily Protestant European countries. Both sides regretted their partners in the agreement and were, by early World War II, each on the verge of abrogating it. The Nazis had violated the Concordat's terms almost before the ink was dry. Most of the much-coveted denominational schools were eliminated by the late 1930's. Neither side formally withdrew, and the Concordat's status remained a point of contention in occupied Germany as well as in the Federal Republic. A 1957 federal court decided the agreement was legally valid; a 1967 court agreed but indicated that the terms covering confessional schools were not binding on individual *Länder*.

From the perspective of the Catholic hierarchy, confessional schools were easily the most significant aspect of the Concordat. They continued to press for a countrywide system of confessional schools. In each *Land* where the issue came to a vote in the late 1940s, Catholics voted in favor of denominational schools, and Protestants voted against them, with the result that in the Catholic south, confessional schools predominated, and the majority of the republic's Catholic youngsters attended them. In the early 1960s some 40 percent of schools were Catholic, another 40 percent were nonconfessional, less than 20 percent were Protestant.

In the late 1960s and early 1970s, the confessional school system was the subject of educational reform in many predominantly Catholic *Länder*. Confessional school enrollments fell as a result of an increasingly secular society and a reputedly widespread feeling among Catholic parents that confessional schools left their children at a disadvantage in entering the Protestant-dominated universities.

The Catholic hierarchy split on support of denominational schools; liberal bishops were ready to sacrifice the system (in favor of religious instruction in public schools) as outmoded in an ecumenical era, but conservative bishops remained committed to Catholic education as the foremost safeguard of the faith. The debate found conservative bishops increasingly estranged from younger clergy and laity.

Indeed, the split between the faithful and their bishops was not the first in post-World War II Germany; Catholics had failed to respond to the hierarchy's call for a Catholic trade union and had campaigned vigorously for codetermination despite their bishops' reservations. But this difference of opinion was profound and indicative of a changing mood among German Catholics. Public opinion polls—even when limited to practicing Catholics— showed overwhelming support for nondenominational schools. One observer characterized the laity-hierarchy split as "the most severe crisis of confidence between the hierarchy and the faithful since the Reformation." In state after state Catholics voted for some form of nonconfessional schools. Even in North Rhine-Westphalia—a bastion of Catholicism—the vote on postprimary confessional schools left a scant 5 percent of secondary schools with confessional affiliation.

The dichotomies between conservative bishops and those of more liberal ilk, between the former and the younger clergy and laity were the defining features of German Catholicism in the late 1960s and 1970s. German theologians Hans Küng and Karl Rahner were among the most prominent in the world. Küng's 1970 treatise, *Unfehlbar? (Infallible?)*, dealing with papal infallibility, stirred worldwide controversy. A 1978 book, *On Being a Christian*, was likewise controversial. Its publication led to a 1979 Vatican attempt to have Küng barred from his teaching position on the Theological Faculty of Tübingen University. The effort strained Vatican-West German relations and polarized the country's Roman Catholic community. Küng remained a theology professor with the compromise proviso that he not examine candidates for ordination to the priesthood.

West Germans were among the most restive in the ranks of Catholic laity. They were frequently at odds with the Vatican as well as the more conservative members of the German hierarchy. The response at the Eighty-second German Catholic Conference in Essen in 1968 to Pope Paul VI's encyclical condemning artificial means of contraception (*Humanae Vitae*) was little short of rebellion. The bishops demurred playing a taped message from the pope to the conference for fear of the reaction it would provoke. The papal nuncio declined to read the encyclical itself, as did the bishop of Essen. Julius Cardinal Döpfner finally read excerpts from the document.

Other events contributed to Catholics' increased questioning of authority. Rolf Hochhuth's 1963 play *The Deputy*—a virtual indictment of Pope Pius XII for signing the 1933 Concordat—suggested that the pope shared complicity in the Nazis' consolidation of power. Some Catholic leaders pressured local authorities not to have the play produced in Catholic regions, an action that contributed little to general confidence in the Catholic leadership. In the late 1960s *Der Spiegel*, an influential weekly magazine, reported that the auxiliary bishop of Munich, Matthias Defregger, had, as an army officer in World War II, complied with an order to execute seventeen Italian civilians in retaliation for the shooting of four German soldiers. The Catholic hierarchy acknowledged that the incident had taken place and that Defregger had so informed his superiors before entering religious life.

* * *

Federal Republic of Germany

There is a wealth of English-language material available on West German society in the post-World War II era. Ralf Dahrendorf's *Society and Democracy in Germany* and Fritz Stern's *The Failure of Illiberalism* remain classics, albeit somewhat dated. John Dornberg's *The New Germans*, Roy E.H. Mellor's *The Two Germanies*, M.T. Wild's *West Germany: A Geography of Its People*, David Childs' and Jeffrey Johnson's *West Germany: Politics and Society*, and David Binder's "A New Nation" all describe changing social relations in the 1970s. The Institut für Demoskopie Allensbach regularly publishes the results of public opinion polls on a wide variety of subjects.

Andrei S. Markovits and Christopher S. Allen deal with the changing role of trade unions in the late 1970s in "Power and Dissent." Richard Hamilton's and James Wright's "Coming of Age," though its statistical base is somewhat dated, analyzes social mobility in West Germany. Ray C. Rist, in *Guestworkers in Germany*, looks at the socioeconomic impact of foreign workers, as does "Distribution and Migration of Foreigners in German Cities" by John O'Loughlin. Manfred G. Schmidt's "The Politics of Domestic Reform in the Federal Republic of Germany" analyzes politics and social welfare.

Wolfgang Köllmann, in "The Process of Urbanization in Germany at the Height of the Industrialization Period," offers an instructive description of the background of modern urbanization and industrialization. *Migration and Settlement: Federal Republic of Germany* by Reinhold Koch and Hans-Peter Gatzweiler and *Growth Centres in the European Urban System* by Peter Hall and Dennis Hay both offer an analysis of contemporary trends. Frederic Spotts in his *The Churches and Politics in Germany*, details church-state dynamics since 1945. (For further information see Bibliography.)

Chapter 4: Character and Structure of the Economy

The port of Hamburg

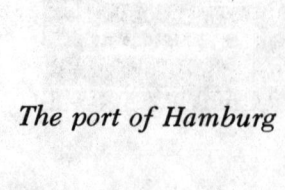

THE FEDERAL REPUBLIC OF GERMANY (West Germany or Federal Republic) possesses a highly industrialized and productive economy and in the early 1980s was usually ranked fourth among the industrial nations of the world. In 1980 the total output of goods and services amounted to the equivalent of US$826 billion, a per capita gross national product of US$13,410—some 16 percent above that of the United States. The population was cared for by extensive and expensive social programs that had been in existence for about a century. Economic growth depended almost completely on private initiative, and management of the economy was largely by free market forces. Foreign trade played a key role. Few natural resources and limited agricultural land required large imports of food, raw materials, and manufactured goods. West Germany was the world's largest importer of agricultural products. A relatively small domestic market and the need to pay for imports required a high level of exports, most of which were manufactured goods of high quality and advanced technology. West German industry competed successfully in world markets, and the deutsche mark remained one of the world's strongest and most stable currencies.

In the 1950s and 1960s the economy expanded rapidly, astounding many inside and outside the country. After the mid–1970s, however, growth slowed and prices increased while unemployment remained high, prompting West Germans to question whether the cause was business cycles, international factors, or structural deficiencies in the domestic economy. In 1981 the debate continued as the economy declined, even if only marginally. By the end of 1981 unemployment reached levels the country had not experienced for nearly three decades, and inflation remained higher than the population was accustomed to. The ruling coalition was strained by differences over economic policy. In the early 1980s observers wondered what effects stagflation (recession or economic stagnation combined with inflation) would have on labor and other groups in the society used to more favorable economic conditions.

Legacies Affecting Development

For more than a century the economy has experienced abrupt changes, including major wars and sudden losses or additions of territory. In the mid–1800s the economy began the transition from a predominantly agrarian society to an industrialized one. Some events and factors retained importance in shaping policies and economic development after 1949.

The industrial revolution came late to Germany, but the new German industrialists found they could compete with established French and British firms by applying scientific advances to industrial processes. A high level of German education and scientific research provided a base for technological innovation in industry. By the late 1800s German industrialists held international rights to many formulas and processes, particularly in chemical fields. German industry and exports earned a reputation for advanced design and technology (see Major Industrial Sectors, ch. 6). The links between scientific research and industry have continued, but by 1982 observers at home and abroad were questioning if industry was introducing new designs and technology fast enough to meet international competition.

Along with and abetted by technological innovations, German industries in the nineteenth century frequently organized production and marketing to avoid destabilizing competition and to enhance profits. In some situations vertical integration accomplished what cartels and cartel-like arrangements did for other industries. The process accelerated after World War I with the formation of additional cartels, one of the more famous being I.G. Farben Industrie, a chemical trust founded in 1925. The government took some steps to preserve competition and to avoid blatant abuses, but officials were tolerant of amalgamation and orderly sales and pricing even when the restructuring of production and marketing often meant greater savings in cost to producers rather than lower prices to consumers. German industry was not unique in its tendency to integrate production and organize markets, but public opinion and official policy were more permissive than in some other industrialized countries, particularly the United States.

The German experience with inflation had a strong impact on subsequent economic policies. World War I was costly for all participants. The Germans financed their war effort largely by public borrowing with the intention of collecting indemnities from the losers at least to cover the debt. The victorious Allies had similar ideas, but after the war the Allies could not agree on a figure for reparations. The view among some of the victors was that Germany should bear the whole cost of the war, however nebulous that concept was. By 1921 the Allies had agreed to a reparations demand of about US$32 billion, approximately the amount of their debts, but there was considerable doubt that collection of such a large amount would ever be accomplished. In any event, Germany was unable to meet the annual payment schedules of the early 1920s, although the Germans, the Allies, and independent unofficial accounting varied widely on the value of the deliveries completed. In 1923 French and Belgian troops took over the Ruhr industrial region to extract reparations directly, claiming Germany had defaulted on its obligations. In 1924 a plan proposed by American financier Charles G. Dawes was worked out. The Ruhr area was returned to German control, adjustments were made in the reparations payment schedule, and a recovery program was planned for the Germany economy (see Stresemann Era, ch. 1). In 1929 the Young Plan—named after Owen D. Young, an American businessman—made major modifications to Germany's reparation payments and annual schedule. The worldwide depression of the early 1930s effectively halted reparation payments. The amount paid by Germany was substantial but was valued differently by the countries involved.

The reparations problems were two: the amount of payment and the means of transfer. The victors desired a cash settlement, such as transfer of gold, but Germany, exhausted by the war, had few reserves left. At the end of the war the Allies took over almost all of the German merchant fleet, German property abroad, and German foreign investments, including extensive patent and licensing rights. In addition the territorial losses of upper Silesia, Alsace-Lorraine and, until 1935, the Saar district, stripped the country of important iron ore and coal resources as well as iron and steel capacity. The German economy had to make major adjustments. Compared with the years before World War I, the economy was forced to rely to a much greater degree on imports. In essence the economy was capable of making reparation payments only through exports, which many of the Allies could not accept because of employment and production problems at home. The Allied reparations demands were basically vindictive with little hope of fulfillment in the existing world conditions. The burden of reparation payments, however, contributed to a deterioration of Germany's balance of payments.

German budget deficits continued after World War I. Energetic tax efforts proved insufficient to raise enough revenue to meet reparation payments, debt service stemming from the war, investments in a disrupted economy, and government expenditures on social needs. The Weimar Republic tried to care for war veterans, widows, and orphans, to compensate civilians for damages, to reconstruct damaged areas, and to finance ongoing programs such as social security.

Germany's rapid and extreme inflation of the early 1920s is the usual textbook example of hyperinflation. Budget deficits and a deteriorating balance of payments began pushing up prices after price and distribution controls were reduced in 1919. Workers began demanding higher wages, and management raised prices. The vicious circle accelerated slowly at first, but between January and November 1923 the index of wholesale prices increased 26 billion times. When the price of a newspaper reached 50 billion marks, wheelbarrows and baby buggies no longer were large enough to transport modest sums of money. In the runaway inflation, money ceased being an adequate unit of account, a means of

Federal Republic of Germany

storing value, or a medium of exchange. The foreign value of the currency fell even more rapidly than the internal value. Hyperinflation was halted in late 1923 by the issue of a new mark (exchanged for 1 trillion old paper marks) and by a severe stabilization program. The middle classes, particularly those holding financial assets, suffered severe losses and in some cases complete ruin from the inflation. This experience, along with milder inflation following World War II, made the population extremely sensitive to increasing prices and falling exchange rates. Economic planners were forced to consider these popular feelings in formulating policies.

The Great Depression was another traumatic experience for the population. Although all major nations were strongly affected, many economists rated the effects most severe in the United States and Germany. Between 1928 and 1932 (the low point of the depression) German national income, retail sales, and industrial production declined by nearly 40 percent. Production of capital goods fell by 50 percent, exports by 55 percent, and gross fixed investment by 70 percent. Unemployment rose from about 7 percent in 1928 to 43 percent in early 1932, by which time 6.1 million workers were without jobs. The worsening economic conditions contributed considerably to Hitler's rise to power.

After World War II a quarter of Germany's eastern area was placed under Polish and Soviet administration, and in the Soviet occupation zone machinery was dismantled and shipped to the Soviet Union. The victors, however, did not make the direct reparations demands they had imposed after World War I. Instead the Allies initially adopted a policy that called for the industrial and technological disarmament of Germany. In the most radical version—usually associated with United States Secretary of the Treasury Henry Morgenthau—the metallurgical, chemical, and electrical industries were to be completely destroyed, and the German economy was to be converted to an agrarian base. The object was to prevent Germans from again waging war. The British and parts of the United States government were against such a harsh policy. Nevertheless agreements reached at the Potsdam Conference of 1945 contained proposals for deindustrialization, and in March 1946 the Allied Control Council, after much discussion, established the so-called level-of-industry plan, which was to reduce the German standard of living to that of 1932. In 1946 industrial capacity was roughly at the 1938 level. More than 1,500 plants were to be dismantled in the Western (British, French, and American) occupation zones to reduce industrial capacity by over 50 percent. A quarter of the equipment from the Western zones and all from the Soviet occupation zone were to be for Soviet use.

The plan stripped Germany of all oceangoing ships, airplanes, and property abroad, including intangible assets, such as some

200,000 patents and licenses. Limits were placed on capacity and production in many industrial branches, and production was prohibited for several products, such as ships, planes, armaments, rubber, ammonia, and heavy machine tools. Scientific and industrial research facilities were to be closed. All of the Allies succeeded in obtaining many of Germany's scientists and high-level technical personnel—thus continuing the brain drain that Hitler started in the 1930s. The flight of so many highly talented people constituted a serious economic and social loss.

The cold war soon began to alter the thinking of the Western Allies. Shipment of dismantled plants to the Soviets was stopped in May 1946. In August 1947 a new level-of-industry plan raised substantially the amount of industrial capacity permitted in the British and American zones and lifted ceilings on consumer goods production. The Western powers had concluded that German industrial production and a strong economy were necessary for reconstruction and a strong Western Europe, which the United States was seeking through large amounts of aid under the Marshall Plan.

Although the deindustrialization policy for Germany was being modified as early as 1946, dismantling of plants continued into the early 1950s. By early 1951 more than 680 plants had been taken apart or destroyed in the Western zones. Even though dismantling affected only about 8 percent of fixed industrial assets (compared with war damage to plants, which was about twice as high), the effects were concentrated in key industrial branches. Capacity in the steel industry in the Western zones, for example, was reduced by nearly 7 million tons or nearly one-third. In addition the breaking up of trusts and cartels was concentrated in banking, chemicals, and heavy industry. The three largest banks were re-formed into thirty institutions to dissolve their close relationship with the economy, particularly industry. The I.G. Farben chemical trust was broken into four companies. The major coal and steel combines were dissolved into many smaller units. The alterations of the structure and capacity of industry frequently ignored or intentionally broke up the intricate relationships that had been the basis for part of the efficiency and the competitive position of German products on world markets.

The Allied efforts to break up the German industrial structure clearly delayed the country's economic recovery efforts. Apart from the actual measures introduced, there was the prolonged uncertainty about new twists that deindustrialization policies might take that restrained investments. In some industrial branches, limits on capacity and production were not lifted until 1955. In addition the denazification process temporarily removed some managers and technicians.

In the years immediately following World War II some 9 million Germans from the East settled in Western occupation zones. At

Federal Republic of Germany

first these refugees were a substantial burden, requiring food, housing, and social services. Many initially settled in rural areas because of the lack of housing and jobs in cities and towns. They contributed to a high rate of unemployment during the late 1940s, but they provided a pool of workers and entrepreneurs for the economic expansion of the 1950s and 1960s.

Immediately after 1945 pent-up demand combined with lack of imported materials and disruptions in the economy to cause strong upward pressures on prices. By mid–1948 industrial production in the American and British zones was still less than half what it had been in 1936. The occupation authorities retained many of the Nazi price and distribution controls, but allocation of materials was far from satisfactory. Production costs soon exceeded controlled prices. Various distortions emerged, such as black markets and graymarkets, in which businesses carried on a form of barter for inputs and outputs, and the population sought commodities, particularly American cigarettes, as a means of storing value and as a medium of exchange. In 1948 a currency reform introduced the deutsche mark, which replaced the Reichsmark on a sliding scale. Shortly thereafter the German authorities removed price and other controls from most commodities, contrary to the injunctions of occupation officials who feared another rapid escalation of prices. The abrupt decontrol required a rationalization in the economy, which was primarily reflected in a surge of unemployment. Prices, contrary to the expectations of many Allied and German economists, remained relatively stable.

Role of Government

Considerable sympathy for socialism existed in Germany following its defeat in World War II. Many of the Nazi economic measures and the high degree of organization in the German economy would have facilitated the transition to widespread public ownership. United States policy, which the British supported in their zone, favored more of a free enterprise system, particularly as the East-West confrontation became more intense. By March 1948 the nationalization issue essentially ended when Ludwig Erhard was appointed the director for economic administration in the American and British zones. Against the advice of most economists and the wishes of the occupation authorities, during 1948 he daringly removed the bulk of price and market controls. The success of decontrol and currency reform that year began the necessary economic adjustments in the three Western occupation zones. These measures also established the base essential for a free market economy that relied largely on private initiative for expansion.

When the Federal Republic was formed in 1949, Erhard became minister for economic affairs, a post he held until 1963 when he became chancellor (1963–66). For eighteen years Erhard was

Wesel on the Rhine, 1945
Courtesy German Information Center

Wesel on the Rhine, 1981
Courtesy German Information Center

in a position to implement economic policies according to the principles of *Soziale Marktwirtschaft*, a term that can be translated as regulated free market economy or socially conscious free market economy. The basic concept is that a market economy provides the most efficient allocation of resources but, if unrestrained, would lead to monopolistic practices and severe business cycles. The role of government thus became one of maintaining a well-functioning market economy and implementing social programs. The government was not to intervene too far toward planning or economic controls, however, because the efficient allocation of resources would be distorted.

Soziale Marktwirtschaft was more an economic philosophy than an economic policy. It was a retreat from the extensive government interference that was practiced by the Nazi regime, and it relied on market forces for primary guidance of the economy. Nonetheless it envisioned an active role by government in guiding the economy in desired directions and in social issues particularly, such as aiding the disadvantaged. By the end of the 1950s this general philosophy and orientation had been accepted by the major political parties.

The constitutional organization of West Germany diffused economic power. Within the republic the states (*Länder*, sing., *Land*) and municipalities retained considerable autonomy. The central government was primarily to formulate broad national policies that the *Länder* and local governments implemented. Most revenue sources were shared, and central government expenditures were smaller than those of the combined *Länder* and municipalities. With few exceptions, the central government lacked offices and staff in the *Länder* (unlike the practice in the United States). Civil service (see Glossary) workers in federal offices were far fewer in number than those placed in the *Land* and local bureaucracies. Having control over their own budgets, *Länder* could and did undertake programs that ran counter to federal fiscal policies.

Economic Policy

Many groups in the population were highly organized in order to articulate their special interest and to influence policy deliberations of government at various levels (see Traditional Interest Groups, ch. 7). Such public law organizations as the chambers of industry and commerce, of handicrafts, and of agriculture had specified but limited governmental functions related to economic policy. Numerous private organizations represented individual groups, such as war victims, consumers, and taxpayers, but their impact was usually minor even though membership in some groups was quite large. In contrast a host of economic associations covering branches or whole sectors, such as the Federation of German Industries (Bundesverband der Deutschen Industrie—

Character and Structure of the Economy

BDI), and the trade unions exerted considerable influence on policy. Trade unions and employers' associations, although private organizations, conducted wage negotiations and participated in such public institutions as social security agencies, labor offices, and labor courts.

Many organizations and associations also exerted influence within and on political parties, which in turn affected economic policy. One of the largest political parties, the Christian Democratic Union (Christlich Demokratische Union—CDU), allied with the Christian Social Union (Christlich Soziale Union—CSU) to encompass a broad range of the population, but the party was usually identified with big business and banking and fiscal conservatism (see Political Parties and the Electoral System, ch. 7). The CDU/CSU, in power from 1949 until 1966, was largely responsible for the basic form of the West German economy and the policies to manage it. The other large political party, the Social Democratic Party of Germany (Sozialdemokratische Partei Deutschlands—SPD) was initially Marxist and advocated extensive nationalization and planning. In 1959 the SPD modified its leftist, worker orientation in order to expand its popular base (see Social Democratic Party, ch. 7). Since 1969 the SPD has headed the federal government in coalition with the Free Democratic Party (Freie Demokratische Partei—FDP). The FDP, much smaller than the other two parties, generally favored liberal, free enterprise economic policies. Since the formation of the Federal Republic, one or the other of the main political parties has usually had to form a coalition with the FDP in order to govern. As a consequence economic policies have tended to be moderate and middle of the road. In the late 1970s and early 1980s this created strains within the SPD from its young, leftist members who objected to the compromise of economic policies that they felt contributed to growing unemployment.

The fundamental goals of economic policy, supported in general by the political parties, have been steady growth, stable prices and foreign exchange rates, and full employment within the free enterprise system. The Basic Law (constitution) of 1949 required a balanced budget, which considerably limited the capacity of the federal government to stimulate economic growth directly. Since the early 1950s the government has relied primarily and extensively on various incentives—such as generous depreciation allowances, benefits for reinvestment of profits, and other tax breaks—to influence the supply of investment funds and their productive employment. These stimulative measures were also selective, guiding the economy in desired directions. In the 1950s the government's efforts to promote investment and to break bottlenecks in production were concentrated in key industries, such as coal, iron, and steel. In the 1970s key industries were nuclear power, other energy sources, and high-technology components for com-

Federal Republic of Germany

puters and communications. Incentives also favored regional policies and the spatial distribution of industry, such as encouraging location in West Berlin and in eastern border areas. Nonetheless while government encouraged investments, the investment decisions and risks were left to the private sector, and policy implementation was largely the responsibility of *Länder* and municipalities.

Although government policy was implemented indirectly on most of the economy, direct intervention was undertaken where it appeared necessary, as in agriculture. For social reasons farmers were provided many forms of aid, such as high commodity support prices, protected markets, and income supplements (see Agricultural Policy, ch. 5). Subsequently major portions of agricultural policy came under rules set by the European Communities (EC—see Glossary), but in 1982 farmers remained sheltered from the international competition that industry had faced since the late 1940s. Although agricultural employment (primarily independent farmers with small holdings) amounted to less than 6 percent of the total labor force in 1980, aid to farmers entailed substantial budgetary costs even though most of the funds were channeled through EC programs.

In 1949 the various levels of the new government inherited many economic enterprises and partial ownership in others. Under the prevailing philosophy, some of these were sold in whole or in part to private investors, but government retained considerable business holdings and even monopolies in such traditional areas as the railroads, airlines, and postal and other communications facilities. One purpose of continuing monopolies in these fields was to influence the tariffs charged and the services rendered in the public interest. For example the railroads required substantial subsidies (reportedly the equivalent of about US$9 billion in 1981), because fares (particularly for commuters) and freight rates were set on the basis of considerations other than operating costs. Local governments operated businesses on a smaller scale, such as local transportation systems, public utilities, hospitals, slaughterhouses, and theaters and orchestras.

Government retained part of its business holdings in order to exert influence on management in key industries. Thus the federal and *Land* governments had partial ownership in several banks. The federal government retained 20 percent, and one of the *Länder* held another 20 percent of the shares in the Volkswagen company, for example. The federal government held 44 percent of the shares in Vereinigte Elektrizitäts und Bergwerks AG (VEBA), the country's largest industrial company, which was, among other things, involved in electrical, petroleum, and chemical activities. Generally the companies, partially or wholly publicly owned, were operated as normal commercial enterprises and were expected to produce a profit.

Character and Structure of the Economy

In the early 1980s the economy remained a mixed one. In a variety of ways and place the government was able to influence investment decisions. For nearly three decades officials successfully promoted a high rate of private investment that contributed to rapid economic expansion. By the early 1980s, however, domestic critics were charging that more encouragement of investment was needed to raise industrial productivity and to create additional jobs for the unemployed.

During the reconstruction and industrial expansion of the 1950s, industry and banking re-formed into large units. Much of the Allied efforts to break up concentrated economic power had not been based on sound technological or organizational understanding of the industries involved. As West Germany gained increasing sovereignty in the early 1950s, industry merged and amalgamated, seeking efficiency and orderly marketing. After years of extensive debate, a law was passed in 1957 regulating cartels to protect competition. In the 1970s the law was strengthened, but in the early 1980s West German industry was dominated by large concerns with interlocking relationships to banks, customers, and suppliers. The West German experience with industrial concentration had not been unfavorable; many of the most efficient firms with international reputations for quality were large organizations. Government economic policy attempted to curb abuses of industrial power, but concentration was not viewed as inherently bad.

The rapid economic expansion of the 1950s helped the government attain another of its primary goals: stability of prices and exchange rates. The government inherited high tax rates instituted by Allied occupation authorities to help control inflation. In the 1950s rapid economic growth under high tax rates produced increasing revenues and budget surpluses. Meanwhile industry reentered foreign markets while producing for domestic consumption, partly because of the growing industrial concentration. A combination of factors, including Marshall Plan aid, contributed to a lack of inflationary pressures and a favorable balance of payments (see Federal Republic of Germany, ch. 1).

By the late 1950s the accumulated government reserves from budget surpluses and diminished requirements for reconstruction allowed for more social expenditures. In 1957 expanded aid to farmers was instituted that became increasingly costly over the years. In the same year the government expanded the old-age pension plan, which also became increasingly costly (see Health and Welfare, ch. 2). Other social programs added to government expenditures as an alternative to reducing taxes. By the 1960s budgetary costs were growing while economic expansion and budget revenues increased more slowly.

In 1963 the Council of Experts for the Evaluation of Overall Economic Development was established to provide independent

Federal Republic of Germany

analyses and recommendations for guidance of the economy. The council, consisting of five nonpolitical, respected, and highly qualified economists (commonly called the five wise men), has drafted a report each fall on overall economic developments. The government is obliged to consider the council's recommendations. Some observers have viewed the recommendations of the council as too divorced from politics to be realistic, however.

In 1967 the country experienced its first recession. The fall in gross national product (GNP) confirmed a growing awareness that the government lacked adequate tools for management of the economy. In 1967 the Law for the Promotion of Stability and Growth of the Economy was passed, followed by a constitutional amendment and some further legislation in 1969. These changes permitted the government to follow a discretionary, anticyclical budget policy to achieve the goals of price stability, full employment, equilibrium in the balance of payments, and steady and adequate growth.

The stabilization law granted the government the right during expansionary phases to freeze up to 3 percent of federal and *Land* revenues of the previous year in the central bank (Deutsche Bundesbank) and then release them during cyclical downswings. The government was also given the right to raise or lower by 10 percent individual and corporate income taxes and to impose temporary surcharges on incomes for use in the anticyclical reserve funds. The government was authorized to limit borrowing by lower levels of government. Although the federal budget frequently incurred surpluses and deficits before 1969, deficits had no legal basis. A constitutional amendment expressly authorized deficit financing by the federal government.

Effective use of fiscal policy in economic management required greater planning and coordination of the autonomous budgetary activities of the federal government, ten *Länder*, West Berlin, and some 9,000 municipalities and local governments. The annual and uncoordinated budgets were replaced by five-year financial plans and medium-term public investment proposals at all levels; the plans for the next five years were revised annually in light of current developments. Each year the government submitted a report of its economic and fiscal policy objectives for the coming year within the framework of the five-year perspective. Two new organizations were established to improve coordination between levels of government. The Financial Planning Council, composed of the finance ministers from the federal and *Land* governments and representatives from lower levels, was to coordinate financial and debt planning between the various levels of government. The Business Cycle Council, composed of the federal and *Land* ministers for economics, was concerned with short-term effects of fiscal activities on the economy. In practice the Financial Planning Council tended to take on both functions because they involved and affected the finance ministers.

The 1967-69 changes substantially added to the management tools and committed the government to anticyclical economic policies. The new tools were used immediately and stimulated the economy to a high rate of growth after 1967, creating considerable optimism for the changes. The optimism faded in the 1970s as economic problems proved less manageable than expected.

Economic Policy and Problems since 1970

Economic problems since the 1970s have not been limited to West Germany but have affected all major industrial nations. The breakdown of the world monetary system created economic difficulties on the international scene. In the late 1970s West Germany joined most of the other members of the EC in establishing the European Monetary System (EMS) to bring order to foreign exchange rates among members. The explosion of prices of crude oil (about a tenfold increase between 1973 and 1979) as well as prices of other raw materials was another major problem. Worldwide recessions followed the 1974 and 1979 oil price increases.

The 1975 recession affected West Germany less severely than a number of other countries, but it was serious and the worst the country had experienced. Real GNP fell by 2 percent, the consumer price index rose by 6 percent, and unemployment doubled, exceeding 1 million. Automatic stabilizers were imposed; tax revenues slowed while budget expenditures increased for unemployment compensation. A tax reform had the unexpected but fortuitous benefit of reducing income taxes in the midst of the recession. Government countercyclical spending consisted of a series of stimulus-investment programs in 1974-75 through public projects concentrated in construction. A substantial federal budget deficit ensued.

The 1975 recession raised important questions for economic policy and generated considerable debate among economists, policymakers, and politicians that was continuing in 1982. Policy adjustments depended on whether the difficulties were ascribed to external causes arising from West Germany's close relationship to the world economy or to domestic structural deficiencies. Many advocates favored the latter position but disagreed about priorities for investment and economic growth, inflation, and unemployment. Politicians usually took positions reflecting their party's economic philosophy and the needs of their constituencies.

Between the 1975 recession and 1981, the economy expanded at a moderate although generally declining rate, unemployment moved downward slowly until 1980, and prices increased gradually. The economy's performance was much better than that in many other industrialized nations, but it was neither what the West German population was accustomed to nor what the politi-

Federal Republic of Germany

cians were comfortable with. Between 1974 and 1979 the government expended about DM50 billion (for value of the deutsche mark—see Glossary) on reflation programs. Large sums were spent on vocational training, increasing labor mobility, and other measures to help the unemployed. Several tax changes were introduced to stimulate consumer spending and private investment. Beginning in 1977 the public deficit was to be reduced gradually to a "sustainable level" by 1980, partly to ease pressure on interest rates caused by public borrowing. A reduction was accomplished in 1977, but from 1978 through 1980 the public deficits again rose as West Germany, like most other industrialized countries, found little flexibility in expenditures and real difficulty in diminishing deficits. The economic policy measures did not return the economy to the high growth, low unemployment, and price stability of earlier times, but they did show a concern for most of the problems troubling the population even if there was a diffusion of effort.

The sharp rise in crude oil prices in 1979–80 caused problems for most countries. In West Germany it contributed to rising prices and difficulties in foreign markets. Economic activity began to slacken in 1980, and unemployment rose. In 1981 real GNP declined by only 0.3 percent, less than expected. Nonetheless the consumer price index rose 5.9 percent, the highest since 1975. Business failings increased rapidly, and in January 1982 unemployment reached 1.95 million (an unemployment rate of 8.2 percent), the worst in twenty-eight years.

Formulating the 1982 federal budget was difficult because of the differing emphases of the economic policies of the three main political parties. Although the economy was in recession or nearly so, there was general agreement among the parties that the federal deficit had to be reduced, not expanded by anticyclical spending. A 1982 federal deficit of DM26.5 billion was agreed to by the SPD-FDP coalition parties in mid–1981, a decline of about DM9 billion from the expected federal borrowing in 1981. The decision to reduce federal borrowing was partly influenced by the country's fiscal conservatism but more specifically by the need to diminish pressures on interest rates. The high cost of credit had contributed to the lower level of business activity.

Although the 1982 budget contained a nominal 4 percent increase in spending, expenditures were to be reduced in real terms. It was an austerity budget that included cuts in such items as defense, social programs, subsidies, and research to support industry. Small increases in minor taxes were included. Agreement on the budget required compromises by all of the political parties. The differing economic philosophies nearly split the ruling coalition, a potential that would remain if economic performance does not improve. The SPD gave up a supplementary levy on income that was to finance government investment to create jobs while accepting some cuts in unemployment benefits and other social programs. The FDP gained some fiscal incentives to stimulate private investment while dropping demands for additional cuts in social spending. The battle over the 1982 budget was just a more intense forum for the compromises that had been necessary to formulate economic policy for the past many years.

Reaction to the proposed 1982 budget became obvious in late 1981. In November labor leaders rallied an estimated 70,000 workers to deplore the government's insensitivity to the plight of the unemployed; they threatened massive demonstrations and indicated wage demands in 1982 would be above the rate of inflation. Bankers believed that the cuts in the deficit were too small to affect interest rates and that some measures, such as reduced reserves in company pension programs and reduced research support, might prolong the stagflation. Business managers complained that the program would neither lower interest rates nor improve the investment climate on which economic growth depended. The general reaction was that the economic policies reflected in the budget were indecisive, a result of the compromises necessary to obtain budget agreement. Whether the government's economic policies were adequate for the times would only be determined in the future, but few economists expected that the economic policies could bring a return of the high growth, price stability, and full employment of the 1950s and 1960s because of the changed internal and external conditions.

Budget

The public sector has considerable importance in the economy. In 1980 the combined expenditures of the federal, state, and local governments, including social security, amounted to 47 percent of GNP. Similar to the trend in most industrial countries, West German public expenditures have been rising faster than the output of goods and services. In 1970 they amounted to 38 percent of GNP. In comparison with other European countries, the 1980 ratio for West Germany was similar to that of France and Italy and below that of Belgium and the Netherlands.

The expenditure pattern of the different levels of government reflected the division of responsibility largely determined by the Basic Law. The two major expenditures of the federal government were defense (19 percent in 1979) and social security and other social programs (35 percent in 1979). Many of the social programs had contributory financing; on a net basis general tax revenues financed only a minor part of social security. Resorting to tax revenues became necessary after 1974 because employer-employee contributions failed to keep pace with benefit payments even though the social security fund had a surplus in 1980 (see The Welfare System, ch. 2). Other federal expenditures included national transportation and communications (14 percent in 1979);

education, science, and research; agricultural programs (such as farm consolidation and coastal protection); housing; internal security; government administration; and foreign aid. Some of these expenditures were grants-in-aid to the *Länder* or funds transferred to local governments to implement federal programs. The federal government could not transfer funds directly to local authorities—only through the *Land* governments. The fiscal year coincided with the calendar year.

Most public services were provided by nearly 9,000 local governments. These supplied such basic needs as water, gas, electricity, garbage disposal, and local road maintenance. The *Länder* cooperated with the local governments in some of these activities as well as in the school systems, cultural programs, and some health services. The main responsibilities of the *Land* were police, education, and public health. About two-thirds of public investment expenditures were carried out by local governments. The federal and *Land* governments each accounted for only about one-sixth of public investments. The bulk of *Land* and local government expenditures were for personnel or were mandated by federal legislation, leaving little flexibility in their spending. For this and several other reasons, countercyclical fiscal measures proved difficult to implement and less successful than expected.

Taxes provided the bulk of revenue for public expenditures apart from social security contributions (see table 14, Appendix). Federal legislation governed major taxes, but the *Länder* were the primary collectors. Although there were several dozen taxes, income, turnover (value-added), petroleum, and trade taxes accounted for about three-quarters of total public tax revenue. In 1980 indirect taxes produced more revenue than direct taxes, a frequent occurrence in the 1970s. In 1978 taxes shared by the administrative units amounted to 71 percent of total tax revenues. Income and value-added taxes were the most productive and the main ones shared between the federal and *Land* governments; a part of the latter's share was passed to local administrations. Strictly federal taxes included those on petroleum products, tobacco, capital transfers, and customs and excise duties (after deduction of the EC share). *Land* taxes included those on motor vehicles, assets, inheritance, and beer. The main local government taxes included those on real estate and on profits and capital—the so-called trading tax that was shared with the *Land*. Shared taxes were distributed according to a format negotiated periodically. The sharing was primarily vertical between levels of government, but horizontal sharing was accomplished between richer and less wealthy *Länder*, partly by the formulas for distribution of turnover tax revenues. In the early 1980s the federal government received about half of all tax revenue.

Although the fiscal changes in 1967–69 expressly authorized deficit financing, public indebtedness was still viewed with distrust by part of the population and many politicians. The growth of the public debt in the 1970s stimulated considerable discussion, particularly after 1975 when indebtedness grew more rapidly. The public debt amounted to nearly DM126 billion at the end of 1970—18 percent of GNP. By the end of 1980 the public debt had increased to DM464 billion—31 percent of GNP. Borrowing by the federal government increased the fastest, rising from 38 percent of total public indebtedness in 1970 to 50 percent in 1980. Nearly all of the public debt was owed domestic creditors; at the end of 1979 the external public debt amounted to the equivalent of only about DM18.5 billion. In 1980 an additional DM20 billion was borrowed abroad—an action that was encouraged in part by a deficit on the current account of the balance of payment. In 1980 interest on the public debt amounted to only 4 percent of total expenditures. Financing the public debt had not become a major burden, and West Germany's public debt, as a share of GNP, was about the lowest of the United States, Japan, and the countries of Western Europe. In the early 1980s, however, West Germans remained sensitive to the dangers of inflation, and the country's fiscal and monetary policies reflected this fact.

Growth and Structure of the Economy

After the Federal Republic was formed, the economy grew rapidly in an expansion that lasted for more than two decades. GNP in constant prices increased an average of 6.4 percent a year between 1950 and 1970. This growth was achieved with remarkable price stability and strengthening of the currency. Many observers at first called it an economic miracle. Some economists adduced several conditions they believed accounted for the rapid growth of output.

The currency conversion and reduction of economic controls in 1948 freed the economy to react to the pent-up demand that had accumulated through the 1940s. After five years of instability and deprivation, the labor force was anxious to work to improve living conditions. A large number of refugees and high unemployment contributed to moderate wage demands and to a labor pool from which industrial expansion could draw. Moreover occupation policies had contributed to a postponement of the industrial and economic recovery that might have taken place in the late 1940s and into the 1950s under expanding West German sovereignty. In addition international aid in excess of US$4 billion, predominantly from the United States, provided needed imports and a saving of foreign exchange while also financing key investments through counterpart deutsche mark funds generated from the sale of aid commodities. High profits, including those from the Korean War boom, were channeled into investments as businesses, helped by fiscal incentives, self-financed much of the industrial expansion of the early 1950s. The German propensity for organization asserted itself in aligning production processes and establishing sales staffs for the postwar conditions in the world. The part of Germany that became West Germany contained about 63 percent of the industrial assets that existed in 1944. The industrial facilities were not balanced, but a strong base of capital goods and basic materials industries enabled West Germany quickly to supply some of the machinery and equipment, vehicles, and electrical and chemical products in demand in world markets. The cold war also facilitated recovery by reducing the Allies' deindustrialization plans and by contributing to political stability.

The interaction of these factors caused real GNP to increase by 7.8 percent a year between 1950 and 1960. Growth was even faster in the first few years of the 1950s. As time went on, however, economic expansion slowed. Between 1960 and 1970 real GNP increased by 4.9 percent a year, including the country's first recession in 1967. Between 1970 and 1980 real GNP increased at an average annual rate of only 2.8 percent, including a more severe recession in 1974-75. Recovery from the 1975 depression saw real GNP rise 5 percent in 1976, 3 percent in 1977, 3.2 percent in 1978, 4.6 percent in 1979, and 1.9 percent in 1980. Real GNP fell 0.3 percent in 1981, and predictions were for very little growth in 1982.

West Germany's rapid economic expansion was confined to the 1950s. In the 1960s the country's growth rate matched the average for all EC members. In the first half of the 1970s West Germany's economic performance was significantly below the average for the EC countries but appreciably better in the last half. Some economists suggested that after the early 1960s the West German economy experienced the same problems that plagued the other industrial nations with about the same results. With an economy as dependent on foreign trade as West Germany's, it would be expected that international developments would impinge strongly on the domestic economy. In the late 1970s, however, the concern of some West Germans was whether private investment, on which the economy was highly dependent for growth, was sufficient in key advanced technology industries to provide for the needed growth and competitive edge in the future.

The expansion of the economy brought relatively little change in its overall structure. Industry dominated (see Industry, ch. 6). In 1980 industry, including mining and construction, accounted for 48 percent of gross domestic product (GDP), a higher proportion than in most countries. In 1979 manufacturing accounted for 38 percent of GDP, mining 4 percent, and construction 7 percent (see table 15, Appendix). The major change over the thirty years was the decline of agriculture and the expansion of services. In 1950 agriculture, including some forestry and fishing, contributed 10 percent of GDP compared with 2 percent in 1980. In contrast, various services rose from 42 percent of GDP in 1950 to 50 percent in 1980.

The West German economy was strongly oriented toward foreign trade. It was the second largest importer and exporter in the world. About a quarter of GNP was exported; roughly every fourth job depended on sales abroad. Exports were primarily manufactured goods (see Foreign Trade, this ch.). In some branches of manufacturing the dependence on foreign markets was quite high. Machine-building firms usually sold about 45 percent of output in foreign countries and those producing vehicles only slightly less. The growth of industry in developing countries required adjustments in West German manufacturing away from mass-produced goods employing less sophisticated technology. West Germany's coal, steel, textile, and shoe industries were contracting and reorganizing because of competition, for example, while the chemical, machine-building, and electrical industries (including nuclear power plants) were expanding. Continual restructuring was required to meet the needs of consumers at home and abroad to ensure the jobs and high income of West German workers.

Labor

In 1980 the labor force numbered nearly 26.7 million, down from its peak of almost 27 million in 1971. The decline encompassed the major factors affecting the labor force. In 1980 only about 3.5 million workers were self-employed or family members helping in a business; farmers made up less than half of the self-employed. In 1980 some 86 percent of the employed labor force were employees working for salaries, wages, or commissions (called dependent labor force in West German statistics). In 1979 industry, which included mining, manufacturing, and construction, employed 45 percent of the labor force while all types of service employment accounted for 49 percent (see table 16, Appendix). In the 1970s industry's and agriculture's share of the labor force declined while service employment increased. Although West Germany's service sector was expanding, by the early 1980s employment in service industries had not reached the proportions of that in some other industrial countries, notably the United States, but observers anticipated significant future growth.

West Germany's rapid economic expansion in the 1950s and 1960s required a growing labor force. Roughly 9 million refugees from Eastern Europe were absorbed into the economy. Until the construction of the Berlin Wall in 1961, perhaps 3 million more refugees from the German Democratic Republic (East Germany) gained employment in West Germany. Between 1950 and 1980 more than 3 million farmers ceased farming, a substantial number of whom entered nonfarm employment. Nevertheless by the early 1960s this flow of workers was insufficient to meet the demands of the expanding economy.

In the early 1960s businesses turned to recruiting foreign workers to supply the economy's needs. West Germany was one of the founding members of the European Economic Community (EEC or Common Market—see Glossary), which was subsequently incorporated into the EC. One of the main goals of the EEC was and has remained the free movement of goods, labor, and capital between members. The first foreign workers to enter West Germany were from EEC countries, primarily Italy. (In the early 1980s workers from EEC countries could still seek employment in West Germany with few obstructions.) When in the early 1960s this supply of workers proved insufficient, West German legislation relaxed the conditions for entry of workers from countries outside of the EEC.

West German firms established recruiting offices in countries outside of the EEC to obtain labor. The result was an increasing flow of workers. The peak was reached in 1973 when some 2.4 million foreign workers (known as guest workers—*Gastarbeiter*) accounted for 9 percent of the labor force. The foreign workers came primarily from the Mediterranean Basin, the largest contingents coming from Turkey and Yugoslavia. They tended to be concentrated in particular areas rather than spread throughout the country. They also tended to be unskilled. The original intention was that they would stay only a few years at most. Many workers have remained much longer and have brought dependents, raised families, and created social problems (see Foreign Workers, ch. 3). Their remittances to their home countries have become substantial (see Balance of Payments, this ch.).

In 1973 rising unemployment caused the government to intervene to halt recruiting and to make it more difficult for foreign workers to enter the country. The number of employed foreign workers gradually declined to 1.9 million in 1978. After that the number again rose, reaching over 2 million in 1980, less than 400,000 below the level in 1973. Foreign workers accounted for 8 percent of the employed labor force in 1980. Part of the increase resulted from children reaching working age and the admittance of some dependents of foreign workers already in West Germany. But as domestic unemployment rose sharply after 1979, officials used various measures to restrict entry of foreign workers.

In the 1970s West Germany's labor market changed radically. During the 1960s the annual unemployment rate was usually below 1 percent, and even during the 1967 recession it was only slightly above 2 percent. In 1970 the "baby boom" of the 1950s began to add to the working-age population (fifteen to sixty-five years). Demographic factors will cause the working-age population to continue to increase until 1985 when it should begin to decrease, reflecting the declining birthrates since the mid–1960s. Besides an expanding pool of indigenous labor, between 1970 and 1973 the number of employed foreign workers increased by about one-third. During the 1970s the supply of labor increased despite the halt to foreign recruitment and a decline in the number of foreign workers.

In spite of the supply of labor, employment peaked in 1971. By 1980 employment was still nearly 1 million below the peak. The economic expansion of the 1970s created few jobs. One reason was the changing pattern of demand away from such labor-intensive activities as construction, shipbuilding, and textiles. Underused capacity and generally poor profit expectations limited plant expansion. Rising relative costs for labor channeled business investment increasingly into the replacement of equipment and rationalization of production, usually accompanied by a reduction of labor inputs.

The mismatch between an expanding supply of and a stagnating demand for labor caused unemployment to rise. Part of the pressure was relieved by falling participation rates, particularly by women, the very young, and older age groups. Lowering the retirement age, for example, helped. Should employment opportunities improve, however, some of the workers who withdrew from the labor force would again seek jobs. The return of foreign workers to their home countries also helped reduce the supply of labor.

Unemployment nearly doubled in 1974 and again in 1975. During the late 1970s the number of unemployed hovered between 900,000 and 1 million. As the slowdown of business activity occurred during 1980, however, unemployment began to rise again. In 1981 unemployment averaged 5.5 percent of the work force, which was still one of the lowest rates in Western Europe. But unemployment continued to increase, and it was a sensitive issue for the population and policymakers. Economists predicted a high rate of unemployment in 1982. Officials were implementing policies to affect both the supply of and demand for labor, and it remained to be seen whether they could reduce unemployment to below 3 percent, which was their goal. By 1985 the reduced birthrates of the 1960s would make the task easier.

Labor was highly organized in order to articulate its interests in unemployment and in other matters, although it was not directly linked to any political party. The largest organization was the German Trade Union Federation (Deutscher Gewerkschaftsbund—DGB), which embraced seventeen industrywide trade unions. Other important organizations included the Federation of German Civil Servants (Deutscher Beamtenbund—DBB) and the German Salaried Employees Union (Deutsche Angestellten Gewerkschaft—DAG) (see Labor in the

Federal Republic of Germany

Industrial Sector, ch. 6). Unions were organized on the basis that one union represented all employees, regardless of kind of work, in an establishment. This eliminated jurisdictional disputes between unions that caused considerable labor strife and aggressive behavior by activitists in other industrialized countries. Workers were free to decide on union membership; there were no closed shops or other devices that compelled workers to belong to a union. In the early 1980s somewhat more than two-fifths of the work force were union members.

Labor unions had a long history in Germany and had contributed to the high level of social legislation the country enjoyed well before the reforms spread to other industrial nations. Nevertheless the unions had been largely impotent. Following World War II the trade union movement unified to overcome the fragmentation and diffused effort of the larger number of unions in the 1920s and 1930s. At the time of the formation of the Federal Republic, labor was accepted as one of the three social partners whose cooperation was needed for economic expansion and the improvement of living standards. Government and management were the other social partners. Government set the legal framework within which labor and management freely negotiated the conditions of work and rates of pay. Legal provisions, for example, defined collective bargaining agreements as binding contracts and subjected violators to heavy fines. Legal provisions also specified certain conditions before a strike could be called. Laws set some conditions of work, such as a maximum regular workweek of forty-eight hours and workers' participation in management. Lockouts by employers and strikes by workers were not prohibited by law and were rights recognized by the courts. Arbitration processes and other safeguards attempted to stimulate settlements short of strikes and lockouts. A system of labor courts handled disputes arising from labor-management controversies.

Within the legal framework established by government, unions and employers' associations negotiated pay and work conditions. The latter were usually contained in a broad agreement that was valid for more than a year. Work conditions were usually more advantageous to workers than those specified by law; the bulk of employees worked forty hours per week or slightly more, for example, rather than the legal maximum of forty-eight hours. Collective bargaining agreements technically applied only to the parties concerned, but in practice the provisions were usually extended to nonunion workers and to all firms engaged in the same activities. Fringe benefits in collective bargaining agreements were extensive and expensive, averaging about 70 percent above strictly wage and salary costs.

In line with the government policy of social partners and because of union pressure, legislation in the early 1950s and amendments in the 1970s established the basis for workers' participation in management decisions affecting them (see Working Conditions, Wages, and Benefits, ch. 6). At the shop or plant level in private firms having five or more employees, a works' council had to be elected by all employees to represent them on an equal basis with management in decisions concerning personnel, the details of wage scales and fringe benefits, working hours, and other matters affecting employees. Works' councils were legally independent of any trade union, but often elected members belonged to the union for that industry and usually worked closely with union officials. The rights and duties of works' councils and the obligations of employers toward the councils were defined by law. At a higher level, workers participated in the supervisory boards of corporate businesses, a system known as codetermination (see Codetermination, ch. 6).

West German labor-management relations have been relatively good. Days lost because of strikes were few compared with most other industrial nations. Although labor and management had conflicting interests, both recognized they had some common interests. Unions, free of the necessity to be constantly aggressive to ward off inroads from other unions, have tended to take a longer term view, which the legal framework encouraged. In the early 1950s wage demands tended to be moderate to facilitate recovery and economic growth. The reward was a rapidly expanding economy that provided workers with an increasing standard of living and wages that were among the highest in the world. Labor's attitude in the more difficult circumstances of the early 1980s will be crucial to the economy's future. In the opinion of many observers, excessive wage demands would reduce the competitiveness of West German goods on world markets, contribute to inflation, and restrain economic growth.

Money and Banking

The country's financial system was large, modern, and intricate. Besides banking, the system included several stock exchanges, many insurance companies (including those for reinsurance), and securities markets handling a variety of financial instruments, both domestic and foreign. In addition the system was closely linked to international financial centers with few restrictions on flows of funds in either direction.

Currency

The deutsche mark, West Germany's currency unit, was introduced during the currency reform of 1948. In September 1949 its value was DM4.20 per US$1, but West Germany, like most European countries in the aftermath of World War II, maintained extensive foreign exchange controls. As the economy and exports expanded, controls were removed in 1958, and since then the deutsche mark has remained freely convertible. At times a few

Federal Republic of Germany

restrictions were placed on certain kinds of transactions, largely to avoid the movement of funds by currency speculators that affected West Germany's money supply and inflation.

Many factors affect the internal and external purchasing power of a currency. West German officials succeeded in maintaining price stability within the country better than most other industrial nations. Expanding exports kept the balance of payments under control at a time when many industrial countries were experiencing less success. As a result the value of the deutsche mark was appreciated several times in terms of the United States dollar, the key currency in the international monetary system before the 1970s. In 1971 the dollar was devalued, and convertibility into gold was officially abandoned. In 1973 the dollar was again devalued, and West Germany stopped using the dollar for the central exchange rate, using instead the market basket of currencies developed by the International Monetary Fund called special drawing rights.

Meanwhile in 1972 EC members set up a European system of controlled currencies called the snake. Other European countries outside the EC subsequently joined. At first fixed parities between the participants' currencies were attempted, but when these proved impossible, limited fluctuations were permitted above and below the fixed parities while each participant allowed its currency to float against all other currencies outside of the snake. Several members dropped out early. A better system was needed, but it was a long time in coming.

In March 1979 the European Monetary System (EMS) came into being after long negotiations, encompassing all EC members except Britain. A basket of participating currencies, called the European Currency Unit (ECU) was calculated against which each member set an exchange rate. Market foreign exchange rates could fluctuate 2.25 percent (6 percent for Italy) above or below that rate before central banks intervened by buying or selling currencies to stay within the prescribed limits. The participating members had no obligation vis-à-vis currencies outside the system where foreign currency markets essentially established the exchange rates. In October 1981 the basic exchange rate of several countries against the ECU had to be adjusted because of differing inflation rates and other monetary developments. West Germany appreciated the value of its currency in the EMS by 5.5 percent.

The purpose of the snake and the EMS was to restore some order to exchange rates after the breakdown of the system that had existed since World War II. In the 1970s large liquid sums were available to speculators to shift around to take advantage of small discrepancies in rates between currencies. These shifting, large sums threatened domestic currency stability and affected exchange rates—and therefore export prices—in many countries.

The broader the system the better for all concerned, but it meant subjugating some control over domestic policies to international developments, which some countries refused to do. The snake and EMS were limited efforts by a group of countries that were close foreign trade partners. West Germany participated in these efforts partly for its own interest and partly to support the EC concept.

In the early 1980s the United States dollar remained the most important currency in international trade, helped in part by the requirement of many crude oil exporters that payment be in dollars. The deutsche mark also remained a very important international currency, which other countries used for currency reserves and as a safe investment. The exchange rate between the two currencies was important to West Germany. In 1980–81 the deutsche mark began to drop in value vis-à-vis the dollar for several reasons. At the end of 1979 the market exchange rate was DM1.71 per US$1 compared with DM2.37 per US$1 in June 1981, a decline of 28 percent. The lower value of the deutsche mark was expected to help West German exports. West German monetary authorities, however, were confronted with an outflow of funds that required action opposite to that needed by the domestic West German economy.

Banking

Banking was the most important part of the financial system. Public, cooperative, and private credit institutions competed in West Germany, and many also conducted business abroad. In 1981 there were more than 5,350 banks with over 44,660 branch offices. In addition the federal postal service operated postal savings banks, which in 1979 had 18 million depositors and DM23 billion of deposits, and there were some 148 private installment credit institutions for consumer loans.

Among the seventeen banks with special functions was the publicly owned Reconstruction Loan Corporation (Kreditanstalt für Wiederaufbau) originally created to handle the Marshall Plan aid for West Germany. In the 1980s it continued long-term loans for domestic development. It also provided long-term credits for exports and handled West German aid to developing countries. It received its funds primarily by bond issues and from the federal government. Other public credit institutions provided special services in industrial, agricultural, and mortgage loans.

In 1981 the main banking organizations included 246 commercial banks, 599 savings banks, twelve central savings institutions *Landesbanken*), thirty-eight private mortgage banks, and 4,225 credit cooperatives. The mortgage banks acquired funds from the sale of long-term bonds, receipts of which financed long-term credits particularly for housing and government projects. The mortgage banks, most of which were owned by the large commercial banks, were a major source of long-term credit. The credit cooperatives had an extensive network of offices and in 1980 accounted for 11 percent of banking business. They were particularly active in lending to individuals but also were important sources of credit to housing and other businesses, including the self-employed. Cooperatives' share of the country's banking business increased rapidly, more than doubling from 1960 to 1980.

Savings banks, usually municipally owned, had a large network of branches, which facilitated rapid growth over the past thirty years. Most savings banks were small, but a few were quite large. In 1980 savings banks accounted for 22 percent of banking business, being an important credit source throughout the economy and the main source for individuals seeking loans. The twelve *Landesbanken* were the regional clearing and reserve institutions for the savings banks, which along with the state government usually owned the *Landesbanken*. By 1981 some of the *Landesbanken* had extended their activities into all phases of commercial banking including operating offices abroad. A couple of the *Landesbanken* were among the largest credit institutions in the country. In 1980 *Landesbanken* accounted for 16 percent of banking business. They were an important credit source for governments, particularly at the state and local level.

The 246 privately owned commercial banks had 6,140 branch offices and accounted for 24 percent of the banking business. They provided customers with a full range of services and extended credit throughout the economy, particularly to corporations. The three largest commercial banks remained the Deutsche Bank, Dresdner Bank, and Commerzbank, which along with a few other large banks provided the bulk of credit to large corporations. The commercial banks had close links with and considerable influence in industry (see Industry and Banks, ch. 6). Many of the commercial banks had branches and subsidiaries abroad. Foreign governments and businesses as well as international institutions issued deutsche mark bonds through West German banks, and the commercial banks participated in many loans abroad. In 1981 West German banks held about DM4.8 billion of Poland's debt, for example.

Banking activity expanded rapidly. The amount of credits extended by West German credit institutions to nonbanks (governments, businesses, and individuals) rose from DM544 billion in 1970 to DM1,543 billion in 1980, while total business increased from DM818 billion to DM2,351 billion for the same years. Considerable competition existed as the various kinds of banks attempted to increase their share of the market. The credit cooperatives, savings banks, and the *Landesbanken* had substantially expanded their shares at the expense of commercial banks over three decades. By 1981 the competition, fluctuating interest rates, and poor judgment had greatly reduced the profits of most banks and pushed some into precarious positions.

By the 1970s several changes in banking laws had been made, and broader reform had been discussed for many years. Draft changes emerged in 1981 only to be scrapped. One object was to include foreign operations in the reporting data of West German banks because some had developed foreign subsidiaries to avoid the closer supervision exercised by West German authorities. Commercial banks feared the proposals would weaken their competitive position internationally. Intense lobbying by the various banking groups sought favorable definitions of equity because loans could not exceed eighteen times equity capital. The reform, when it comes, could have considerable influence on the structure of banking.

Although actual supervision of credit institutions is the responsibility of a federal office, control of credit and monetary policy is lodged with the central bank, the Deutsche Bundesbank, headquartered in Frankfurt but with regional administrations in each of the states (*Landeszentralbanken*). The present form of the central bank dates from 1957 after a reorganization of the former central bank. The government owns the stock of Deutsche Bundesbank and appoints its directors, but the central bank is legally, and often in practice, independent.

The central bank has the exclusive right of note issue, but its main function is the promotion and enforcement of a monetary policy that will ensure economic stability. To this end it has various means at its disposal to regulate the availability of credit and the liquidity of the credit system. The central bank has the power to vary the rediscount rate on commercial paper presented to it and to set limits on the amount of such paper it will discount. The central bank controls the minimum legal reserve requirements that financial institutions must maintain against deposits. By varying the reserve requirements, the central bank can directly influence the supply of liquid funds in the credit system. The central bank also manages the country's foreign currency reserves, buys and sells in foreign currency markets to protect the deutsche mark, and exercises some controls over the movement of funds in and out of the country. In 1981 Deutsche Bundesbank's intervention in foreign exchange markets produced a rare and fortuitously high profit (because of accidental exchange rate movements) expected to be DM10 to DM15 billion, most of which the federal government intended to use to help reduce the 1982 budget deficit.

The central bank is legally required to support the economic policy of the federal government. All too frequently this obligation conflicted with its other main responsibility—to preserve the stability of the currency. In many instances the central bank exhibited its independence by giving priority to maintaining the stability of the currency, in its broad sense, rather than supporting

Federal Republic of Germany

government policy. For example, in 1981 federal officials desired an easing of credit to lower interest rates, but the central bank restricted credit and kept interest rates high most of the year because of the adverse effects lower interest rates would have on internal inflation and the balance of payments. In mid-1981 the head of the central bank publicly responded to government pressure by implying that control of budget expenditures to fit conditions was essential to an economic policy.

Since the 1950s monetary policy has been a major instrument in managing the economy. It generally has tended toward conservatism, leaning toward price stability and stable exchange rates if there was a trade-off in terms of growth or unemployment. Central bank officials have had a variety of tools, however, that have permitted fine adjustments, which they have employed to minimize adverse developments during the course of a year. Bank officials also have had greater discretionary powers since 1973 when West Germany ceased supporting the United States dollar-deutsche mark exchange rate to the degree required in the early 1970s. Since 1974 the central bank has published annual goals for the money supply and other monetary indicators for the coming year to help influence policies and expectations of banks and businesses.

The dilemma of monetary policy was vividly demonstrated in 1980–81 when demand was weakening, the deficit on the current account of the balance of payments was increasing, and high interest rates in other countries were attracting funds from West Germany. If monetary policy was relaxed to expand credit and stimulate domestic demand, capital outflows would exert downward pressure on the exchange rate, which would increase import prices and cause further deterioration in the current account balance. The other extreme—that of keeping domestic interest rates high to encourage an inflow of foreign funds to ease pressure on the exchange rate and to finance the current account deficit—would have a depressive effect on domestic business activity and employment. In 1980 officials selected a middle course to avoid the harshest effects of either extreme with adjustments during the year. By the beginning of 1981, however, external considerations gained importance and domestic interest rates were pushed up, and an informal agreement was arranged with leading commercial banks to halt temporarily long-term loans to foreigners. By the fall of 1981 monetary policy began to relax, and domestic interest rates started to fall as export orders picked up and balance of payments pressures eased. At the beginning of 1982 business activity was increasing, and the expectation was for modest, real economic growth of perhaps 1 percent, although unemployment had reached its highest level since 1953, and prices continued to move up.

Monetary policy, along with other government policy measures, achieved remarkable success over three decades. Exchange rates remained relatively stable, given the sharp changes in international developments. The general trend of the external value of the deutsche mark was upward. The consumer price index increased an average of 1.8 percent a year between 1950 and 1960, 2.6 percent a year between 1960 and 1970, and 6.2 percent a year between 1970 and 1974. The yearly increases in the cost of living index were 6 percent in 1975, 4.3 percent in 1976, 3.7 percent in 1977, 2.7 percent in 1978, 4.1 percent in 1979, and 5.5 percent in 1980. Since 1979 external sources of inflation, partly related to crude oil price increases, have overshadowed those from internal sources. In 1981 prices continued to increase; in September the annual rate reached 6.5 percent, and the average for the year was expected to be above the figure for 1980. Nonetheless West Germany's rate of inflation remained near the lowest among the industrialized nations.

Foreign Trade

West Germany was the world's second largest exporter and importer in terms of value. In 1980 the country exported 23 percent of GNP, the proportion having remained stable since the mid-1970s. Few industrialized countries were as dependent on foreign trade. In 1979 the ratio of exports to GNP was 8 percent for the United States, 10 percent for Japan, 17 percent for France, 23 percent for Britain, 43 percent for the Netherlands, and 51 percent for Belgium. Because it possessed few natural resources and limited agricultural capacity, West Germany also needed many imported goods. In foreign trade, West Germany followed the country's general economic philosophy that competition and free markets provided the best allocation of resources. Few subsidies or other distortions promoted exports, and a liberal trade policy was applied to imports, although the small agricultural sector was protected for social reasons (see Agricultural Policy, ch. 5). In spite of this West Germany was the world's largest importer of agricultural products. Many West German businesses had to face strong international competition whether they produced for export or the domestic market. The result was that the economy was vulnerable to disturbances throughout the world.

West Germany was a founding member of the EC, one goal of which was a common market among members. In 1981 trade among the nine members was duty-free. A common external tariff applied to each member's trade outside of EC. Under the common external tariff, most raw materials had low rates or were duty-free. The exception was agricultural products to which variable levies were applied to equalize the prices of imports with those of commodities produced within the EC. The common external tariff applied duties generally in the range of 5 to 17 percent on manufactured goods, although some processed foods carried substantially higher duties. EC organizations participated in the General Agreement on Tariffs and Trade (GATT) and arranged trade treaties with other trade groups. A treaty with most European countries outside the EC provided for a phased free trade area in industrial goods during the 1980s; free trade had existed for many industrial products since 1977. West Germany applied most-favored-nation treatment to all countries and extended preferential treatment to a number of countries under EC treaties or other schemes.

Exports

Exports increased from DM8.4 billion in 1950 to DM350.4 billion (US$193 billion) in 1980, an annual average increase of 13.2 percent (in current prices). The ratio of exports to GNP was 8 percent in 1950, 16 percent in 1960, 18 percent in 1970, and 23 percent in 1980. Nearly one in four jobs depended on sales abroad. The growth of exports had been primarily in manufactured goods (which probably accounted for nearly 95 percent in 1980)—especially machinery and equipment. In 1980 machinery and equipment alone amounted to 44 percent of total exports (see table 17, Appendix). Other manufactured goods contributed an additional 30 percent, and chemicals 13 percent. Most of the remaining exports were such items as beer, processed foods, tobacco products, and fuel-related products that were surplus to domestic needs.

In 1980 over three-quarters of all exports went to free world industrialized countries. The EC members alone were the markets for 48 percent of exports. France, the Netherlands, Italy, Belgium, and Luxembourg were the largest buyers in order of rank in 1980 (see table 18, Appendix). Although the United States imported about US$11 billion from West Germany in 1980, its share was only 6 percent. West Germany had made an effort to market its manufactures in developing countries. Twelve percent of exports in 1980 went to non-oil exporters and 7 percent to members of the Organization of Petroleum Exporting Countries (OPEC), primarily in the Middle East. Although exports to communist countries, largely the Soviet Union and its East European allies, had expanded considerably and had become particularly important for segments of industry as a result of policies during the 1970s, the communist countries bought only 5 percent of total exports in 1980 (see Industry and East-West Trade, ch. 6).

Exchange of goods with East Germany was considered internal trade and not recorded in foreign trade data. The trade was handled under a bilateral clearing arrangement using a special unit of account instead of either country's currency. A special interest-free swing credit equivalent to about DM850 million a

Hamburg Harbor
Courtesy German Information Center

Bremen Harbor
Courtesy German Information Center

173

Federal Republic of Germany

year permitted a surplus of West German exports for many years. By 1980 East German purchases from West Germany amounted to the equivalent of more than US$2 billion annually, about 2 percent of total exports.

West German exports historically were helped by lower prices but relatively less affected by higher prices. The numerous appreciations of the deutsche mark had a smaller impact on foreign sales, for example, than economists had expected. Buyers were willing to pay the price for West German advanced technology and quality control, deliveries as scheduled, and the availability of after-sales service and parts. Business conditions, particularly in Western Europe and the United States, however, strongly affected West German exports. Exports of machinery, materials used in construction, and chemicals were particularly sensitive to the rise and fall of investment spending in other industrialized countries. Economists attributed part of the West German recessions of 1975 and 1980 to the decline of exports caused by the impact of large crude oil price increases on investments in most industrialized countries.

Imports

The rising price of crude oil and other energy sources has made fuel the country's largest import category. In 1980 energy imports accounted for DM77 billion, 23 percent of total imports. Although coal was imported, natural gas and crude oil (and some refined products), primarily from Britain, Norway, members of OPEC, and the Soviet Union, were the main imported energy sources. Petroleum prices increased 46 percent in 1980. The net oil import bill was nearly DM45 billion in spite of a 10 percent decrease in volume. West Germany, like many other countries finding it difficult to meet rising energy costs, was developing domestic sources while conserving to reduce imports.

Although West Germany was a leading exporter of machinery and equipment, such imports accounted for 19 percent of total imports in 1980 (see table 17, Appendix). West German industry did not attempt to produce all types of machinery but tended to specialize, relying on imports to meet the remainder of total requirements. About 30 percent of imports were various manufactures that included a wide range of consumer goods and substantial amounts of metals and semifinished materials. Prices of metals and raw semifinished materials rose 14 percent in 1980, contributing to the increase of domestic prices. Agricultural products, including some processed foods, were nearly one-fifth of total imports. Imports in 1980 increased only 2 percent in volume but 17 percent in value, amounting to the equivalent of US$187.7 billion.

Western Europe was the main source of imports. Members of the EC supplied 46 percent of total imports in 1980. The Netherlands was the largest source of imports followed by France and Italy (see table 18, Appendix). American exports to West Germany amounted to US$14.1 billion in 1980, accounting for nearly 8 percent of imports. OPEC accounted for 11 percent of imports, and other developing countries an additional 11 percent. Communist countries, primarily the Soviet Union and Eastern Europe, supplied 5 percent of imports. East Germany supplied mainly textiles, petroleum products, food and other agricultural commodities, and machinery under the clearing arrangement. Imports from East Germany amounted to the equivalent of only about US$2 billion, because many of its commodities were difficult to sell in West Germany.

Balance of Payments

Since the 1950s West Germany has relied on a substantial excess of exports over imports to balance international payments. The trade balance increased for more than two decades until 1979 when it began declining, mostly because of increasing prices for imports (see table 19, Appendix). Other items in the current account balance continued to increase in 1979 and 1980, creating the first deficits in fourteen years. The result was pressure on the external value of the deutsche mark and a need for an inflow of capital while high interest rates, particularly in the United States, were attracting funds out of West Germany.

West Germany's current account contained many entries. Although the country's defense expenditures were similar in magnitude to those of its partners in the North Atlantic Treaty Organization (NATO), most defense costs were in domestic currency because few troops were outside of the country. Foreign troops stationed in West Germany, however, required considerable supplies and spent money amounting to the equivalent of nearly US$6 billion in 1980. The federal government made official transfers for various purposes, including payments to the EC and continuing payments to Jews who had suffered losses during the Hitler era. Foreign workers in West Germany continued to send remittances home, although the sums declined from the peak of DM8.2 billion in 1973 to DM6.9 billion in 1980. Net income from foreign investments was small because foreign investments in West Germany were nearly as high as West German investments abroad (see Industry and The World Economy, ch. 6). Net payments for transportation had improved by 1980 but had been negative throughout the 1970s. The passion of West Germans for foreign travel caused a major and increasing outflow of funds that, along with remittances, required an expanding trade surplus to finance it. In 1980 total tourist spending abroad was about US$21 billion (more than twice what American tourists spent), while West Germany's net outflow for tourism amounted to over US$14 billion. The government took no measures to restrict foreign travel, although the balance of payments had become a major concern by 1980.

The current account balance is an alarm signal for many in West Germany. When the balance began to deteriorate in 1979, the alarm bells rang in the form of media coverage. The situation was not nearly as desperate as that which many countries faced, but monthly developments were widely reported. The current account balance went from a positive DM18.4 billion in 1978 to an outflow of DM9.6 billion in 1979, and DM29.1 billion (2 percent of GNP) in 1980. Available statistics for 1981 indicated a probable rise in exports and a smaller current account deficit for the year.

The net capital movements financed only a small part of the current account deficit in 1980. Banks sharply reduced imports of capital, and private funds flowed out because of interest differentials and the declining value of the deutsche mark. Toward the end of 1980 foreign long-term lending and portfolio investment by banks became substantial. In December the central bank obtained the agreement of the leading banks to halt long-term lending abroad until April 1982. Government borrowing became significant for the first time in more than a decade. Direct borrowing by the government occurred largely in Saudi Arabia and the United States. About half of official borrowing abroad was handled by banks. Nearly all of the current account deficit was financed by reducing the reserves of the central bank. At the beginning of 1981 the gross external assets of the Deutsche Bundesbank amounted to DM82 billion, the net value of which was DM67.5 billion.

The 1980–81 recession was troublesome for the West German economy and the population because of the interaction of several factors. Demographic forces were expanding the working-age population while pressures on industry tended toward capital-intensive measures. The business cycle interacted with this longer trend, and both were intensified by price increases for oil and other raw materials. The terms of trade deteriorated for West Germany while high interest rates abroad attracted funds. Economic policy, of which monetary policy was the primary instrument for managing the economy, was severely constrained by the balance of payments to respond to diminishing domestic demand. By early 1982 the economy appeared to be recovering, although unemployment could remain a problem. Many economists believed the West German economy was strong and that its competitiveness had been aided by the decline of the deutsche mark, but the reaction of labor unions in 1982 may play an important role for the country's future.

* * *

Literature on the West German economy is extensive but often narrowly focused. *The Political Economy of Germany in the Twentieth Century* by Karl Hardach presents a comprehensive survey of events and developments up to 1970. *Managing the German Economy* by Jack H. Knott conveys some of the political aspects and techniques of budget formation and economic management at various levels of government. The Organisation for Economic Co-operation and Development publishes an annual economic survey, *Germany,* which reviews recent developments and policies and includes up-to-date key statistics in English. West German official statistical publications are numerous, current, and often in English or with English keys to the tables. The annual *Statistisches Jahrbuch* and the monthly reports, in four separate series, of the Deutsche Bundesbank provide a wide variety of statistics on various aspects of the economy. (For further information see Bibliography.)

Chapter 5. Agriculture

German beer stein

Agriculture

SINCE INDUSTRIALIZATION BEGAN more than a century ago, farming's share in the economy has been declining. In 1980 agriculture, including some forestry and fishing, contributed only 2 percent to gross national product and employed less than 6 percent of the labor force. Most farm activity was oriented toward livestock production; and milk, beef, and pork accounted for over 60 percent of the value of farm output. Small farm size, combined with other structural problems, made it difficult for farmers to support a family by farming alone. The agricultural policies of the government and of the European Communities provided high commodity support prices and a protected market to help maintain farm incomes and improve rural living conditions.

In 1980 the Federal Republic of Germany (West Germany or Federal Republic) was the world's largest importer of agricultural commodities. Large imports were necessary to compensate for deficiencies imposed largely by nature. Cotton and most other natural fibers had to be imported, and more favored areas abroad supplied the bulk or all of the oilseeds, rice, coffee, tea, and spices because domestic commercial cultivation was not feasible. About one-fifth of imports were commodities for livestock feed. The country's degree of self-sufficiency in foods was nearly 90 percent if production from imported feed was included but only 70 percent from purely domestic output.

Land Use

Almost two-thirds of the country is hilly or mountainous, placing narrow limits on land use and on the organization of farming. The country has a variety of soils, most of which have low fertility but respond to careful management. A relatively late spring and summer limit possibilities for crops requiring warm temperatures. Even though natural conditions are not particularly favorable for agriculture, farming is conducted throughout the country. The states (*Länder*) with the largest amounts of agricultural land are Bavaria, Lower Saxony, North Rhine-Westphalia, Baden-Württemberg, and Schleswig-Holstein (see fig. 1). The first three states accounted for about three-fifths of agriculture's contribution to the gross national product (GNP).

The country's total area amounts to nearly 24.9 million hectares, according to the classification system adopted in 1979. Forests and woodland account for 7.3 million hectares, about 30 percent. Urban areas, building sites, wasteland, and lakes and marshes occupy 3.5 million hectares. By the new classifications, in 1980 agricultural land totaled 14.1 million hectares (57 percent of total

Federal Republic of Germany

area) but only 12.2 million hectares on the basis of the former system. Opportunities for bringing new land under cultivation were very limited. Farmers had long ago made the effort to drain and develop areas that would support crops.

In 1980 nearly 4.8 million hectares of the 12.2 million hectares of agricultural land were permanent pasture and grassland. The cropped acreage (called arable in official statistics) was 7.3 million hectares, 29 percent of the total area. In addition vineyards occupied 96,000 hectares, fruit and tree crops 54,000 hectares, and other horticultural uses 75,000 hectares. Since the late 1930s the cropped or arable acreage has slowly declined by nearly 1.5 million hectares, but the figure was imprecise because of changes in definitions over the years. The decline of the cropped area resulted from spreading urbanization, fewer farmers and farms, and withdrawal of some marginal plots from cultivation and a return to grass or woodland.

Organization of Agriculture

West German agriculture has consisted primarily of independent farmers operating very small holdings. Farming has been intensive rather than extensive. In 1980 there were just under 800,000 farms of one hectare or more. The average size of these farms was 15.3 hectares. About 51 percent of farms were between one and ten hectares; only 13 percent of the farms were thirty or more hectares; and less than 0.4 percent of the farms exceeded fifty hectares. In addition there were about 100,000 or more holdings of less than one hectare. The small farm size hampered adoption of modern production techniques and realization of economies of scale. Moreover incomes of farmers with small holdings were usually insufficient to support a family.

Many factors contributed to the problems of agriculture. Over the centuries partible inheritance in several regions of the country reduced farm size and caused considerable fragmentation of holdings. Fragmentation was most severe in the southern and southwestern parts of the country where the Napoleonic Civil Code (Code Napoléon—civil law of France) had become the basis for equal sharing of family land and buildings among all of the children on the death of the head of the household. A study in 1960 showed the average farm consisted of nearly ten separate plots, each averaging 0.8 hectares. Variations from these averages were considerable, however, with a high number of plots and smaller average size on farms with ten hectares or fewer. Fragmentation reduced efficiency because of the time wasted in travel between widely separated plots and difficulties in the use of machinery and the application of chemicals on such small areas.

Compounding the problems of the small farms was the development in the latter part of the nineteenth century of large-scale grain production under far more favorable conditions in parts of

Agriculture

the world such as the United States and Canada. The concurrent growth of the German transportation system facilitated the distribution of imported agricultural products. The needed structural adjustments in German farming to these changing conditions were postponed by various government measures that enabled farmers to survive. Distortions were aggravated under Hitler. Agricultural autarky became government policy, and numerous controls over production, prices, and marketing were instituted. The regime enacted measures to promote and preserve a large farm population but did prohibit the sale and further fragmentation of many of the country's farms.

Even with the small farms, German agriculture introduced modern practices wherever possible as they became available in the twentieth century. Rotation systems, chemical fertilizers, insecticides, and other developments raised yields but also costs. When the Federal Republic was formed in 1949, agriculture was in need of considerable structural adjustment. Many of the controls over agriculture were removed, and market forces began to exert pressures to rationalize farm activities. Nonetheless the government adopted several programs to ease the problems of adjustment for farmers (see Agricultural Policy, this ch.).

Since formation of the republic, the number of farms has fallen by more than one-half, and the average size has risen. In 1949 there were more than 1.6 million farms of one hectare or more. By 1980 there were 797,500 such farms. The average size increased from 8.1 hectares in 1950 to 15.3 hectares in 1980. The number of farms fell most sharply among those of ten hectares or less, while there was an increase in farms of twenty hectares or more. Farmers withdrawing from farming usually did not sell their land, fearing that they might need the land in the future. In earlier years substantial amounts of this land were left uncultivated (called social fallow). In the 1970s such land was increasingly leased to active farmers. By 1981 perhaps as much as one-third of the land utilized on farms of one hectare or more was leased. The agricultural authorities approved the consolidations and increasing farm size but feared that it was not occurring fast enough for the changing conditions in world agriculture.

The decline in the number of farms was accompanied by a fall in agricultural employment by about 3.5 million workers. In 1950 about 20 percent of the employed labor force worked in agriculture. By 1980 the percentage was 5.9, and the number of workers was 1.5 million. The bulk of farm work was done by family members; hired labor made up less than 10 percent of those employed in agriculture. The young in particular sought nonfarm employment, causing the average age of those engaged in farming to rise. Location of industry throughout the country attracted many of the men, leaving women the majority in the agricultural labor force and often the only workers on very small farms.

Federal Republic of Germany

A rising farm output from a declining number of workers meant increased labor productivity. Farming was modern and productive. Research and extension services were readily available and widely used. Greater use of machinery accounted for much of the increase in labor productivity. West German farmers ranked near the top in the world in application of fertilizer per hectare; they achieved yields from many crops substantially above those in the United States, for example. But high productivity did not yield sufficient profitability for many farmers to remain in farming. In the 1980s continuing structural adjustments would be necessary for farm incomes to increase to match those available in other parts of the economy.

Farmers were highly organized to promote their common interests. A number of associations existed, focused on the general welfare of farmers or on specific farm activities. Associations for specific purposes frequently were based on such particular products as sugar beets, fruits, vegetables, or livestock. Federated at the regional, national, and international level, these associations represented members' interests. Cooperatives formed for specialized functions were important farming associations. Cooperatives had a long history in Germany, and in the late 1970s more than three-quarters of the farms were linked in cooperatives. Many farmers belonged to more than one, resulting in cooperative membership substantially exceeding the number of farmers. Credit cooperatives were an important part of the financial system and the major source of funds for agriculture. Cooperative use of machinery helped offset small farm size. Cooperatives played an important role in marketing, although their share varied from one commodity to another. Marketing cooperatives had been traditionally strong in dairy products and grains.

The small holdings of many farmers made part-time farming an important aspect of rural living. In 1980 only about half of the farm households derived at least 90 percent of their income from farming, although they accounted for 77 percent of the farmland. Full-time farms averaged 23.6 hectares each in 1980, nearly one-fifth larger than in 1970. About one-half of all farms were operated as a part-time avocation. Eleven percent of farm households received between 50 and 90 percent of their income from farming; they accounted for 10 percent of farmland, and the average size of their farms was nearly fourteen hectares. Thirty-nine percent of the farm households received 50 percent or less of their income from farming; the average size of their farms in 1980 was five hectares, accounting for 13 percent of farmland. Studies in the early 1970s indicated that less than one-third of farm households lacked some nonfarm income and that for many, farm earnings were only 25 to 33 percent of total income; moreover, farmers working small holdings part-time often had higher total incomes than full-time farmers.

Agriculture

Agronomists considered part-time farming too diversified and labor demanding. Most part-time farmers kept a few dairy cows and pigs as well as attempting some cropping. During the 1970s extension services advised part-time farmers to simplify the production process to reduce management problems and their labor effort. The part-time farmers adopting the suggestions usually reduced the amount of their labor while gaining additional income.

Agricultural Policy

The years immediately following World War II were very difficult for the population. The disruptions in the economy and the industrial policies of the occupation forces limited inputs and contributed to a decline in agricultural output between 1946 and 1948. The flood of refugees, which had increased the population by about one-fifth by the early 1950s, added to the demand for food. The daily food intake between 1945 and 1947 averaged about 1,300 calories, and it varied between about 1,100 and 1,500 calories. The food available was less than half that considered necessary by nutritionists. Underfed workers found it hard to perform heavy physical tasks, and many in the urban population made forays into the countryside to barter or steal food. About one-third of the country's inadequate food supply came from aid imports and food parcels from private individuals. Not until the end of 1948 was the food situation considered adequate, even if barely so.

Immediately after the creation of the republic in 1949, authorities focused primarily on reconstruction of industry and the transportation system. Many controls were retained on food and its distribution to ensure as equitable a supply as possible for consumers because domestic production remained inadequate, and sufficient imports became available only gradually during the early 1950s. Special agencies were created with a monopoly in foreign trade of agricultural commodities. These trading firms at first provided the mechanism to subsidize food imports for consumers when world prices were above those in the domestic market. When international prices fell below domestic prices after the Korean War boom, these agencies shielded domestic farmers from the effects of foreign competition.

In 1955 the government passed an agricultural law that replaced the ad hoc process that had preceded it. The broad aims of agricultural policy were to be a steady increase of farm productivity, a raising of farm incomes and other benefits to the level in the rest of the economy, and an adequate supply of food to consumers at reasonable prices. These policy goals, although desirable, appeared incompatible if not mutually exclusive in view of other economic goals, such as low unemployment. Nonetheless a comprehensive policy framework was established to guide individual steps and to measure progress. In addition the government had to prepare annual statements on agricultural conditions and means to improve them. These annual reports (often referred to as the Green Reports) supplied a valuable source of information on developments in the countryside.

German agriculture had labored for about a century under policies that stressed production with little concern for its costs. These policies contributed to the small farm size, perpetuated the fragmentation of plots, and postponed adjustment of farm operations. In the 1950s officials recognized that changes were long overdue but that abrupt changes would have undesirable social and political consequences. If agricultural imports were freely allowed, in line with the general policy of opening the economy, causing domestic farm prices to fall to the international level, many farmers would have been forced off their farms, and those remaining would have had smaller incomes in the short run. Officials opted instead for a gradual adjustment over time.

It was obvious that the country could not approach self-sufficiency in many agricultural commodities (it produced no cotton, for example) or even in basic foods if prices to consumers were to be kept at reasonable levels. Substantial imports would be necessary to meet consumer demand. The policy options adopted were to import as necessary while supporting farm prices for basic commodities and encouraging structural adjustments and efficiency on farms.

Since the mid-1950s programs have been implemented to achieve the long-term goals. Price supports stimulated production and promoted increased farm incomes. The government at the federal and state levels aided farmers, mostly through financial means, in consolidating plots and adding to their holdings, although the high costs of land acquisition combined with budget constraints to keep consolidation and expansion slower than planned. Subsidized loans and tax incentives encouraged various farm investments and modernization. Social legislation promoted retirement of older farmers, provided job training for farmers seeking nonfarm employment, incorporated farmers in the national health system and other programs, and made education more accessible to rural residents (see Health and Welfare, ch. 2). Government expanded such infrastructure as roads and water systems while encouraging industry to locate away from established centers in part to provide alternative employment for farmers. Farmers received direct (such as income supplements for some) and indirect subsidies. Rail freight rates, for example, subsidized the movement of grains from the southern region to consumption centers to support production and incomes in the south, and fuel taxes were less for farmers.

Since the formation of the Federal Republic the government has supported joint action by the West European countries, including the creation of the European Economic Community (EEC or Common Market—see Glossary), which subsequently became part of the European Communities (EC—see Glossary). A basic objective of the EEC was the free movement of goods, labor, and capital between members after a period of adjustment by each. In the bargaining on common policies for specific sectors, each of the founding members sought favorable treatment for those sectors more economically and politically important to them. Thus West Germany was primarily concerned with industry, the Benelux nations with commerce and transit trade, and France with the formulation of the Common Agricultural Policy (CAP). West German farmers also favored high support prices and protected markets, and their associations effectively lobbied for such measures. Since the early 1960s West Germany's agricultural policy has been increasingly regulated by CAP (see The European Communities, ch. 8).

The founding members of the EEC were modern industrialized nations. The role of the agricultural sector in each country, although minor, varied. The national policies toward the social, political, and economic needs of the rural population also varied. The basic goal of CAP was to harmonize and unify the six different national farm policies so that agricultural commodities could move freely between them without advantages occurring from policy measures. Additional objectives, original or subsequently added, included: increased farm incomes, an adequate supply of food to consumers at reasonable prices, stability in markets, advantage to EEC exporters over those from outside countries, consolidation of farms toward an optimum size, modernization of farming techniques, and alternative employment opportunities or retirement for the farmers whose land was needed in the consolidation process.

The so-called basic pillars of the CAP were common pricing, community preference, and common financing. Common pricing meant a regulated system of prices for major agricultural commodities, in essence support prices, that would permit dismantling of import restrictions in member countries and the free flow of farm produce from the main EEC producing areas to members requiring agricultural produce. EEC preference meant that prices and levies would ensure that EEC products had an advantage over imports from outside. Common financing meant that the costs of agricultural support would be paid by all members.

In the early 1960s CAP began formulating a complex pricing system for various commodities that would support production of major produce, promote intra-community imports but not from nations outside, and help stabilize and increase farm incomes of EEC farmers. Implementation of the pricing formulas was held up for a number of years while some members made major adjustments to the new pricing. West German support prices for grains, for example, had been considerably above those of CAP; even three years after the CAP grain price system became effective in 1967, West Germany was still permitted to make compensation payments to its farmers to avoid excessive hardship. Later, when the international monetary system experienced wide fluctuations, CAP organizations developed mechanisms to maintain the uniform pricing system, partly by using accounting units and administrative exchange rates—the so-called green rates of exchange. The CAP programs effectively stimulated productivity and intracommunity trade of agricultural commodities. Between 1968 and 1976 real incomes of EEC farmers increased an average of 2.8 percent a year, matching the rise in other branches of the EEC economy.

Although CAP achieved notable results, it was strongly criticized almost from the beginning, including its efforts at restructuring. One failing had been the lack of a mechanism to match production to consumption. The success in stimulating production through stable support prices resulted in mounting stocks of surplus commodities, particularly milk, beef, processed fruit and vegetables, cereals, and sugar. Support, storage, and disposal costs of stocks were expensive. By 1981 support prices had been reduced for production above specific levels for a few commodities such as milk and sugar to bring output closer to demand. Another major criticism had been that commodity support prices had been high to support production and incomes of inefficient farmers, with a corresponding high level of protection from imports from nonmembers of the EEC. The result was high consumer prices, accompanied by large support payments to well-to-do and relatively efficient farmers.

By 1981 pressure for revamping CAP was again strong; CAP's difficulties contributed to a growing disillusionment with the program in member countries. One criticism was the excessive and mounting costs of CAP. Of total EC spending in all fields in 1980 of about US$25 billion, two-thirds was spent on CAP programs (74 percent in 1979). Community budget revenues came from a 1 percent value-added tax (VAT), agricultural levies, and custom duties; by the late 1970s total EC spending was approaching the revenue limits. In 1979 West Germany supplied 30 percent of the total EC revenues, by far the largest contributor. More important, however, was the net position, i.e., the funds a country turned over less what it received. West Germany and Britain were the only net contributors to the EC budget. West German net payments reportedly were US$2 billion or more annually in 1980 and 1981. West German leaders accepted the fact that their country would be the largest net contributor to the EC, but they argued that controls and limits had to be imposed on CAP costs

Farm in southern Germany
Courtesy German Information Center

because of constraints on the West German budget.

In mid–1981 EC officials drafted reform measures for CAP. The main features included a slowing of price increases and a narrowing of the gap between EC and world agricultural prices, reduced support for production above specified limits for nearly all commodities, and direct income subsidies for poor farmers hit by the reduced support programs. In November a meeting of EC heads of government failed to reach agreement on guidelines for revising CAP. Officials anticipated that discussions about CAP reforms would continue in 1982 and that differing national interests would make reform difficult to achieve.

The combined national and EC agricultural policies had been effective. The size of West German farms was increasing. West German farmers were better educated and more able to handle the complex management required in modern farming. Amenities were more available to rural inhabitants. Farm incomes were increasing. During the 1970s incomes more than doubled, averaging a 7 percent rise each year. In 1980 and 1981 real farm incomes fell somewhat however, because of a faster increase of prices for inputs than for farm products. Moreover the averages

Federal Republic of Germany

hid considerable variation between regions and between kinds of farming. Generally farmers in the south and those relying primarily on pastures and fodder crop to support livestock had lower incomes. National policy narrowed the gap between farm income and that for nonfarm employment. In the 1970s the rise of farm incomes matched that in other parts of the economy but a gap remained. In 1980 income of full-time farmers averaged about DM24,300 a year (for value of the deutsche mark—see Glossary), about 18 percent below wages of industrial workers. Parity in earnings was still a goal to be achieved in the future.

In spite of the progress achieved under national and community policies since the 1950s, basic structural changes in farming had been largely postponed by these policies. The long tradition on small farms was a mixed operation in which some cropping, usually of grains, was accompanied by raising a few cows for milk, a few pigs for family consumption, and whatever else space and climate allowed. Farming tended to be diversified as a hedge against price and climatic uncertainties. For nearly a century government policy had shielded farmers from the adjustment necessary for efficiency. Except on commercial pig and chicken farms, where techniques approached the industrial process, farmers moved slowly toward the specialization in production practiced in many parts of the world. Several observers thought that farmers in some neighboring West European countries under similar climatic conditions were more efficient than most in West Germany. Continuation of a policy of high support prices and a protected market appeared unlikely to alter appreciably the existing pattern of farming.

Cropping and Production

During the 1970s real growth of the value added by agriculture increased an average of 1.4 percent a year. Most of the increase resulted from improved techniques, such as greater use of fertilizers, high-yield seeds, and machinery, as well as qualitative and quantitative improvements in livestock stimulated by high support prices and a protected market. The amount of agricultural land changed slowly, but cropping patterns were more dynamic. In 1979 about two-thirds of the value of agricultural production came from animal products. An even higher proportion of cropping was associated with livestock. In normal years approximately three-quarters of coarse grains, about two-fifths of bread grains, about half of the potato crop, and all of the fodder beets were consumed by livestock; the acreage for these crops plus pasture and permanent grasslands approached three-quarters of total agricultural land. Farming was strongly oriented toward the raising of livestock.

Cropping Patterns and Production

Grains occupied the bulk of cropped land (see table 20, Appendix). Rye had been the traditional German bread grain, but after World War II wheat became the most important. By 1981 rye acreage and production had dropped substantially below that of the 1950s (see table 21, Appendix). Wheat is largely a winter crop and does well in the rotation system after clover, rapeseed, and root crops. Although it is grown in many places, the central and southeastern parts of the country are the main producing areas. The wheat acreage grew fairly continuously after the 1950s, but production expanded even faster as a result of high-yield seeds and the increased applications of fertilizers. Yields were about double that in the United States because farming was more intensive. Peak production in 1980 was an estimated 8.2 million tons. Although some wheat was exported, the country was usually a net importer of small amounts of wheat.

By the 1980s coarse grains, primarily for livestock feed, exceeded bread grains in both area and production. Barley had become the largest cereal crop, used partly for livestock feed and partly for malt to make beer. In the 1950s barley, which has the shortest growing season of all the grains, was primarily a spring crop. Winter barley largely replaced the acreage in rye and oats, partly because of higher yields when sufficient fertilizers were used. Acreage and production of corn had increased from a very small base in the 1950s; by 1980 corn had become an important crop in the preparation of livestock feed. The total area planted in grains expanded slowly after World War II, but because of greater yields, production increased more rapidly.

Potatoes remain an important crop, although area and production has fallen by more than two-thirds since the 1950s, partly because of changing dietary habits. Sugar beets exhibited the opposite trend because of the growing affluence of consumers. Since the 1950s sugar beet acreage expanded slowly, but increased yields greatly expanded production. By the end of the 1970s, sugar production from beets amounted to about 3 million tons (in raw equivalent), permitting exports of about one-quarter of sugar production. For many years the country has had a serious deficiency of fats and oils, the so-called fat-gap. Largely since World War II, rapeseed has been added in the crop rotation, stimulated by the prices under CAP. By 1980 oil from rapeseed supplied the raw material for 12 percent of domestic requirements of vegetable oils, but it was almost the only source of domestic vegetable oils. The climate largely excluded cultivation of other sources of vegetable oils. A small amount of tobacco was

Federal Republic of Germany

grown, accounting for only 4 percent of that used in tobacco products in 1980.

In 1980 vineyards occupied about 96,000 hectares, close to the limit imposed by a federal law that took effect in December 1981. The harvested area was 19,000 hectares. Nearly all of the vineyards were along the banks of the Rhine River and its tributaries (see fig. 7). Domestic grapes were used to make wine; table grapes were imported. West Germany was the northernmost of the major wine growing countries, and vintners faced extreme growing conditions. In the 1970s considerable investment went into introducing new varieties better adapted to the country's short growing season and relatively cool climate. Production of wine was 4.2 million hectoliters in 1980, a poor year, compared with 10.4 million hectoliters in 1977. The new varieties were expected to have higher yields, permitting wine production to increase.

A small area was devoted to fruits, vegetables, flowers, and ornamental plants, some of which were grown in greenhouses. Flowers and ornamental plants were more important in value, reflecting an affluent society's interest in essentially luxury goods. Production of the major fruits, such as pears, cherries, and plums, was rather widespread. Fruit growing usually was only one of the activities on mixed farms, rather than the main activity on a specialized farm. Growing vegetables for commercial sale was a minor farm activity, although many small plots were used to raise vegetables for home consumption. Since the 1950s, commercial vegetable growers shifted toward such vegetables as asparagus and peas and away from the more traditional ones, such as cabbage. Commercial fruit and vegetable growers found it difficult to compete with producers in favored regions such as the Mediterranean Basin and the highly organized and efficient growers in the Netherlands.

Livestock

Farming was primarily oriented toward producing livestock products, largely milk and pork meat. In 1979 milk accounted for 24 percent of the value of total farm production and 36 percent of the value of the livestock products produced; milk was substantially ahead of all other farm produce in value. Hog raising was next, accounting for 19 percent of the value of all farm production in 1979, followed by cattle raising, which contributed 18 percent. About three-fifths of the value of agricultural activities were associated with raising cattle and pigs.

Historically cattle served three functions for the farmer—as a draft animal, as a producer of milk, which could be turned into cheese for storing, and as meat when the animal became old. Fodder was available on grasslands and from crop stubble. Many centuries ago it became a widespread practice for small German farms to keep one or more cows. Tradition dies hard, particularly under the high support prices for milk and beef that have prevailed since World War II. In the 1980s many small farms still kept a few cows although only rarely were they used as draft animals. West German beef and dairy industries showed little propensity to specialize with large beef or dairy herds. The dispersion of milk production among many small producers reflected the social, economic, and political difficulties in the larger European community of adjusting support prices to match production of dairy and beef products to demand; it affected many small farmers in northern Europe.

In the 1960s and 1970s the number of cattle increased slowly, from 12.9 million in 1960 to 15 million in 1980. These included milk cows, which declined in number from 5.9 million to 5.4 million over the same years. Despite fewer milk cows, milk production increased from 19.2 million tons in 1960 to 24.8 million tons in 1980. Upgraded herds and improved feed raised average milk production per cow from 3.4 tons annually in 1960 to nearly 4.6 tons in 1980. Most milk was marketed for processing into cheese, cottage cheese, butter, and nonfat dried milk. In 1980 West Germany was able to reduce its surplus butter stocks to normal trade levels through CAP export subsidies, which could amount to 80 percent of the purchase costs. CAP subsidies also permitted substantial reduction of stocks of surplus dried milk, largely through its use in livestock feed mixtures. The growth in the number of cattle primarily reflected greater efforts to increase meat production to meet consumer demand. Production of beef and veal rose from 926,000 tons in 1960 to nearly 1.6 million tons in 1980.

Pork was the usual meat in most diets, probably reflecting a pattern set long ago when Germans were predominantly farmers, and nearly all households kept pigs for family consumption. Although many of today's farmers still raise hogs, since the 1950s pork production has shifted toward a highly specialized commercial operation similar to that of modern chicken farming. The number of pigs increased from 15.8 million in 1960 to 22.4 million in 1980, whereas pork production went from 1.8 million tons to 2.7 million tons in the same years. Consumers preferred low-fat meat, which was reflected in breeding; four breeds predominated.

Several other kinds of animals were slaughtered for meat, including sheep, goats, and horses, but they were minor and declining sources. Poultry, however, had become an important meat source since the 1960s as highly specialized chicken farms, similar to those in the United States, were established. In 1980 production of poultry meat amounted to 370,000 tons, primarily from chickens. Before the development of modern chicken farms, poultry were raised largely for eggs on small to medium-sized farms.

Foreign Trade in Agricultural Products

In 1978–80 West Germany averaged nearly 90 percent self-sufficiency in food products. This calculation, however, included livestock production from imported feed components. Excluding imported feedstuffs, domestic food production in 1980 amounted to 70 percent of internal consumption. In 1980 self-sufficiency was 127 percent for sugar, 103 percent for bread grains, 105 percent for beef, and 116 percent for milk and dairy products, making the country a net exporter of these commodities. Self-sufficiency was 89 percent for pork and 62 percent for poultry. German farms were only able to satisfy domestic demand in fats and oils by 12 percent, in fruits and vegetables by 34 percent, and in feed grains by 77 percent. In addition there was complete dependence on imports for such warm climate commodities as coffee, tea, cocoa, rice, and many spices.

In 1980 West Germany was the world's largest importer of agricultural products, amounting to US$25.8 billion. Imports were largely products of plant origin (see table 22, Appendix). About one-fifth of imports were associated with livestock feed. Imports included more than food products. West Germany imported all of its cotton and most other natural fibers, for example. Moreover part of its agricultural imports were reexported after processing, such as cocoa products, vegetable oils, and some livestock feed mixtures. The CAP fostered a major shift in West Germany's trade in agricultural products toward other EC members. The proportion of West Germany's agricultural trade with the members of EC amounted to 34 percent for imports and 40 percent for exports in 1955 compared with 51 percent for imports and 63 percent for exports in 1980. The large deficit in total agricultural trade, however, (exports only amounted to US$10.8 billion in 1980) contributed to the deterioration of the country's balance of payments in the late 1970s and the weakening of the deutsche mark against other currencies.

Forestry

In 1978 forests covered about 7.3 million hectares—over 29 percent of the total area—but only about 5.3 million hectares were considered commercial timberland. The states with the largest forests were Bavaria, Baden-Württemberg, Hesse, and North Rhine-Westphalia. Public forestland amounted to nearly 4 million hectares, and the rest was privately owned. Public afforestation programs expanded the government-owned forests. The government, acknowledging the environmental and recreational aspects of forests, passed a law in 1975 to preserve and promote forested areas. The law required approval by the states for clearing of forested land and established principles for forest management. Private companies were required to replant trees after cutting. In 1978 a total of 28 million cubic meters of wood was cut, 70 percent of which was conifers. West Germany also imported large quantities of logs, sawn lumber, and pulp to meet domestic requirements.

Fishing

Fishing is a minor and diminishing activity. In the 1970s the fishing fleet and its catch declined. In 1979 the fish catch totaled 343,200 tons, compared with 591,400 tons in 1970. The main fishing grounds were in the North Sea and around Greenland, although West German fishing boats operated in the Baltic Sea and the South Atlantic Ocean. Overfishing by many countries and the expanded claims to exclusive fishing rights throughout the world hampered fishermen. In 1970 the EC established a joint policy for fishing and a common market for fish products. A 200–nautical-mile fishing zone in the North Atlantic and the North Sea was established for use by members, but by the late 1970s quotas and other regulations had not been negotiated among members.

* * *

Agriculture is such a small part of the economy that relatively little is written about it in English. The primary German-language source of information is the annual report on the status of agriculture: *Agrarbericht der Bundesregierung.* The government's annual *Statistisches Jahrbuch für die Bundesrepublik Deutschland* provides current statistical data on many aspects of agriculture. The Organisation for Economic Co-operation and Development periodically publishes a survey, the most recent of which in early 1982 was *Agricultural Policy in Germany* (1974). The EC publishes various materials concerning the CAP and its operation. Readers interested in the mechanics of the CAP with respect to the pricing and protection of EC grain production should consult the United States Department of Agriculture's publication titled "European Community Grain Policies and Development," (For further information see Bibliography.)

Chapter 6. Industry

Frankfurt skyline

Industry

INDUSTRY IN EARLY 1982 faced a somewhat uncomfortable future, at least for the near term. The economy had reached a cyclical turning point in mid–1980. At that time it turned sharply downward after a little more than two years of robust, almost boom, expansion. The economic decline in the Federal Republic of Germany (West Germany or Federal Republic) was part of a world economic decline, especially in Western industrial nations, which was caused to a marked degree by the 1979–80 increases in petroleum prices. The major impact of the petroleum price spiral on industry was twofold: production costs rose significantly as petroleum products became ever more expensive because the United States dollar, in which oil was priced, appreciated rapidly against the deutsche mark; and export markets, a vital aspect of industry, weakened for West German goods as the increased petroleum prices forced trading partners to shift from other imports in order to meet the higher petroleum prices.

Industrial investment activity was mixed, but there were some favorable expectations that investment spending would blunt the economic decline. The construction industry was hard hit, in part because of rising interest rates as the German central bank (Deutsche Bundesbank) reluctantly used a higher interest rate policy to stem the flow of capital to American markets where significantly higher interest rates prevailed. With stimulative policy desirable in the face of over 1 million unemployed, the Bundesbank action was forcing restrictive actions.

The depressed iron and steel industry faced severe problems of oversupply and competition as suppliers faced weakening worldwide demand for steel. As the only steel-producing member of the European Economic Community (Common Market) not granting export subsidies to its industry (practically all privately owned), West Germany considered the competition basically unfair and had given notice of intention to try to change the community's pricing system for steel. It was the only member country to oppose a Common Market quota system, which it considered protective of inefficient producers.

In August 1981, however, the government made a major change in its position and approved the equivalent of US$560 million as an aid package for its domestic steel industry and announced that it had prepared plans for levies on imports of subsidized steel from other Common Market countries and had taken administrative measures to impose the levies quickly should it become necessary. Although the European Coal and Steel Community was still trying to eliminate by 1985 all state aid to the steel industries of member states, West Germany felt it had to take steps to counteract "massive distortions of competition" abroad that had begun to threaten domestic jobs and the survival of its steel industry. The aid package, to run from 1982 to 1985, had four major components: grants of up to 10 percent of investment costs to support major restructuring and modernization without expansion of capacity; a federal research program for modernization; investment grants to those federal states with areas heavily dependent on steel that were undertaking job-creation programs; and fostering parallel, independent investment planning among steel companies to avoid creation of new production capacity.

Consumption goods industries were expected to show low levels of investment; but fast-growth industries, including data processing, office machines and equipment, aircraft, and chemicals, were expected to show offsetting increases. Surprisingly the automotive industry, suffering as were manufacturers in other major automobile-producing countries from a worldwide slump in sales as severe as in 1974–75, expected investment to remain strong. Channeling of funds into technical improvements was motivated by the need to meet Japanese competition. Energy conservation was also a strong motive for investment in the automotive as well as in other industries. Overall, investment remained strong in fast-growth industries, in industries seeking to apply new technology and expand research and development, and in industries where conservation of energy had become paramount.

In 1981 West Germany remained the largest exporter of manufactured goods in the world. During the 1970s exports averaged about 25 percent of gross national product and foreign trade (exports and imports) almost 50 percent. The industrial sector was especially vulnerable to conditions of worldwide demand and needed at all times to keep pace with international competition. A worldwide slowdown can therefore be damaging to West German export growth to the extent that world incomes stagnate or rise at a significantly slower rate. From mid–1979 to mid–1981 the deutsche mark had declined by almost 25 percent against the United States dollar, thereby making West German goods cheaper for American buyers. But the full effect of this favorable turn in lowering prices of West German exports could be months in coming, given the lag in international trade adjustments in response to changes in foreign exchange rates.

Industrial recovery in 1982 and later will depend very much upon wage negotiations. Average wage increases on the order of 5 percent were the rule in settlements in 1981. Continuation of such agreements would represent a moderation of the settlements in most preceding years. With productivity likely to grow at a much lower rate during a period of slow industrial growth, the 1981–82 pattern of settlements would aid in maintaining some degree of price stability as cost pressures on prices would ease. Management and labor seemed readier to discuss macroeconomic

Industry

issues that affected both than at any time since the 1977 unraveling of the concerted economic action program, or social partnership (*Sozialpartnerschaft*), after many years in existence.

Major Industrial Sectors

Coal and Lignite

Coal has been the country's most important natural resource, in large part making possible the industrial leadership attained in the late nineteenth century. Earlier of great value in the chemical industry, in powering the steam engine, as fuel for the superb rail transport system, as coke for smelting and refining iron, and as a raw material for numerous other industries, coal in the early 1980s remained vital to the metallurgical and electric industries.

The chief locations of hard coal production are the Ruhr district—the largest coalfield in Europe—and the Saar (see fig. 12). Reserves are estimated at about 70 billion tons, an amount sufficient for about 800 years at the 1980 rate of production of 87 million tons, slightly above the levels of 1977–79, but below production levels of 1976 and earlier. The post-World War II peak was reached in 1956 (102.5 million tons); the decline in annual production since that date has been due to competition from petroleum—in 1981 being slightly reversed—and the lower cost of imported coal. West Germany produces approximately 5 percent of coal mined the world over but is projected to produce only a little over 2 percent by the year 2000. Its own production is expected to rise by only 25 percent, while coal production in such countries as Australia, Canada, China, India, United States, and the Soviet Union will rise by 100 to 400 percent.

The metallurgical (63 percent) and electric industries (22 percent) accounted for about 85 percent of all coal used in 1981; the same percentages were projected for the year 2000. Increased amounts will be used to produce synthetic fuels (from 1 percent in 1981 to 14 percent in 2000), with diminishing amounts (from 12 percent to 5 percent) used in the residential and commercial sectors. Of all Organisation for Economic Co-operation and Development (OECD) countries, West German expenditures on energy research and development are second only to those of the United States—being more than double the expenditures of the governments of Britain and Italy and approaching one-third those of the United States. In large part the West German expenditures were directed toward the ultimate production of synfuels from coal.

The coal industry developed late, following Britain and France, but gained as a result by organizing firms that operated efficiently on a large scale. The coal producers of the Ruhr Valley developed the most remarkable of all European cartel syndicates. The cartel

201

Federal Republic of Germany

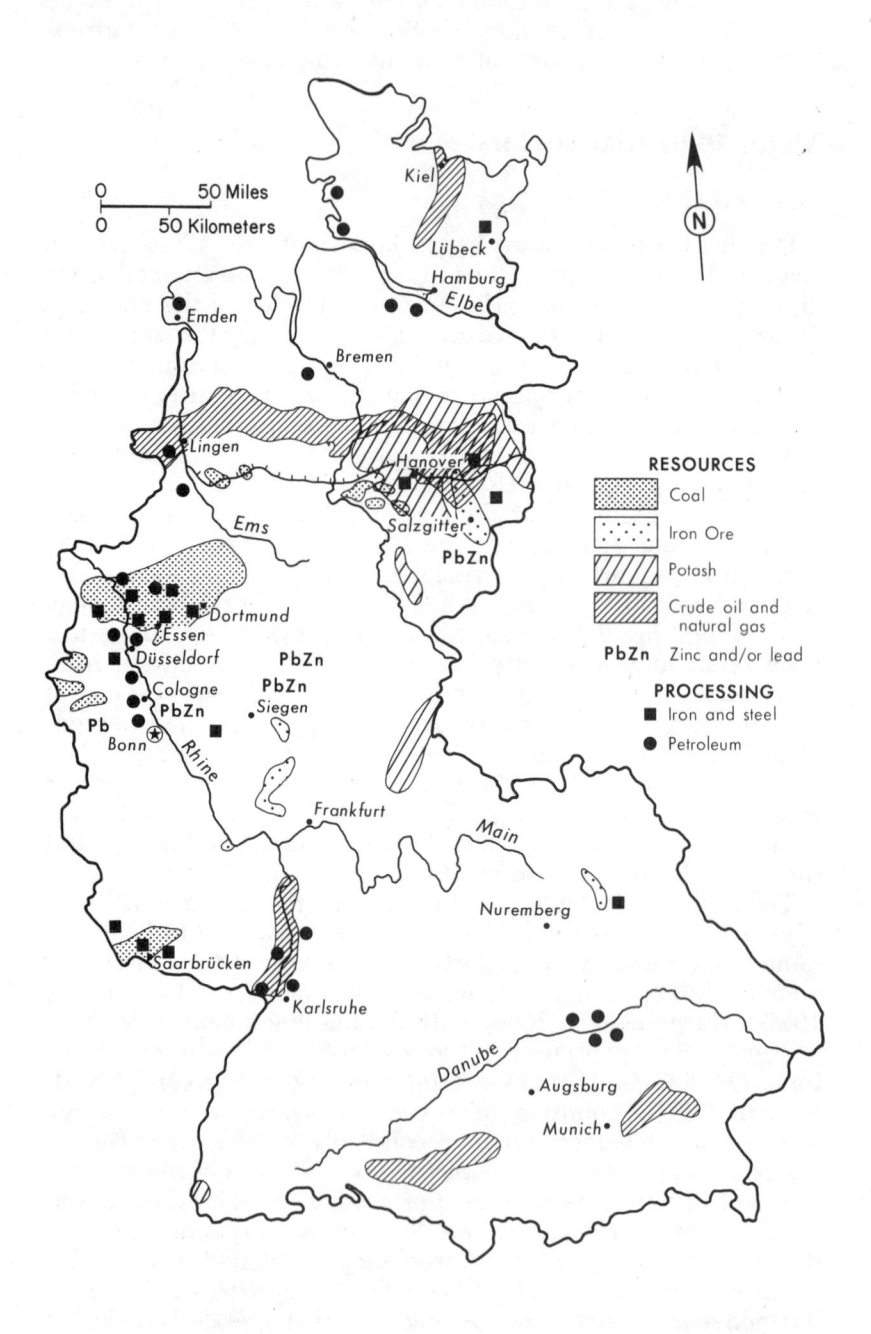

Figure 12. Basic Resources and Processing

Industry

was an outstanding example of a successful attempt by German industry to establish a monopoly in order to avoid price fluctuations and other insecurities that are often found in freely competitive markets, especially those operating under conditions of large-scale production. Such cartel arrangements were anathema to authorities of the occupying powers after World War II, but the federal government nevertheless took steps to aid the coal industry. Through premiums for mine-closing and tax incentives, the coal mines of the Ruhr were concentrated and rationalized and reorganized into a single corporation. Labor productivity rose, in large part because of superior technological equipment. Import duties on coal; limitation of imports from outside the Common Market (see Glossary); subsidies, including one on the transport of coal and another for coal exports; and a fuel oil tax were other measures designed to support the industry. Miners were given protection against unusual hardship arising from structural change. Federal funds covered two-thirds of all costs; the coal-mining states contributed the other third.

Lignite, or brown coal production, was 120 million tons in 1980. West Germany produces annually about one-half as much lignite as the German Democratic Republic (East Germany). Brown coal, a low-grade fuel, intermediate between bituminous coal and peat, is found in vast quarries and generally is used near the mining sites to fuel thermoelectric power plants and as a raw material for chemical plants producing synthetic nitrates and oils. Little labor is needed in the mining of lignite, as it is obtained from the vast open pits with huge excavators. Rid of water and waste, the material either is used for the production of briquettes, which are fed directly as fuel into furnaces for the generation of electricity and the manufacture of chemicals, or is distilled by carbonization processes for the production of tar, oil, and chemicals. Production centers are sufficiently near to the Ruhr to have developed a close economic association with it.

Iron and Steel

Iron has been the basis of all modern industry, but in West Germany iron and nonferrous minerals are found in small quantities in scattered areas. The iron ore is generally of low quality with a metal content averaging 32 percent. Mines are small, most are distant from the Ruhr metallurgical industry, and costs of extraction and transportation are high. Domestic production declined continuously throughout the 1970s, down from 6.1 million tons in 1972 to a little less than 2 million tons in 1980. The country, therefore, must import iron ore, principally from Sweden, Brazil, and the Lorraine area of France.

The iron and steel industries are located in the Ruhr and the surrounding Rhine area. As in the case of the coal industry, the steel industry developed after the industries in Britain and

Federal Republic of Germany

France. It was efficiently organized, used the newest and most advanced methods of production, developed a cartel, the German Steelwork Union (Stahlwerksverband), second only to the Ruhr coal cartel, and formed for the same purpose—to stabilize prices by allocating production of standardized products where destructive competition presented threats to an industry requiring enormously expensive plants and facing heavy fixed costs. Ties to the great German banks were strong and indispensable, given the need to raise large amounts of money capital to finance the great steel plants (see Industry and Banks, this ch.). Mixed coal and steel companies developed as steel companies sought to gain an advantage by owning coal mines where the cost of coal production would be well below prices on the open market.

Steel firms were rationalized and modernized in the 1920s. In the 1930s firms successfully participated in the European steel cartel and enjoyed an increased average efficiency of production when incorporated into the European Coal and Steel Community (ECSC—see Glossary; see The European Communities, ch. 8). Surrendering some of its control by being part of the ECSC was viewed by the steel industry as being far preferable to the internationalization of the Ruhr or to similar proposals made in the early postwar period.

By the mid-1960s steel cartels had returned in Europe as a result of overcapacity. Thirty-one West German steel producers formed four marketing cartels, thus eliminating competition among cartel members. The French and Italian steel industries had earlier sought similar organization as protection against declining sales, falling prices, and the reduced profits that come with overcapacity. West German steelmakers were late in cartel-like rationalization, because they had been able for more than ten years to invest in greater capacity and had no difficulty in finding ready markets for their exports; but a decline in the rate of return on investment prompted action to joint planning. The problems of the mid-1960s in the steel industry were again present in 1982.

In 1980 production of pig iron and ferroalloys reached 34 million tons, the highest production since 1974 (40.5 million tons) except for 1979 when production was 35.4 million tons. Crude steel production in 1980 was 43.8 million tons, the highest level reached since the record high level of 1974 (53.2 million tons) except for 1979 when production was 46 million tons.

Rolled steel products naturally followed the same general trend of the raw metals; the production of sheet steel, steel rods, wire, hot-rolled band steel, and seamless steel tubes declined in 1980 to 31.1 million tons, down slightly from the 32.7 million tons produced in 1979. In 1981 the steel firms faced the problems associated with declining steel demand worldwide, some obsolescence of producing plants, competition from companies subsidized or owned by governments, and resulting declines in returns on in-

Industry

vestment. Ostensibly to combat subsidized competitors, West Germany in August 1981 announced a change in its policy in order to aid its steel industry.

Motor Vehicles

In mid-May 1981 in Puebla, Mexico, Volkswagen produced its 20 millionth car, thereby surpassing the 15 million "Tin Lizzies" produced by Ford. A basically good Volkswagen car design had been improved over the years to meet new tasks, new conditions, and new challenges. Although certainly a symbol of success for West Germany—in 1981 the third largest automobile-producing nation in the world after Japan and the United States—it reflected past sales, not future prospects.

From 1973 through 1980 domestic automobile production averaged 3.4 million cars annually, while production of commercial vehicles (light and heavy trucks, buses, delivery vans, and special vehicles) had an annual average level of 305,000. The peak year for motor cars was 1979, when production was just under 4 million vehicles, and for commercial vehicles 1980, when production reached slightly over 390,000. Car production increased in every year from 1973 through 1979, dropping slightly in 1980 when a total of a little over 3.5 million passenger cars and 380,000 commercial vehicles were produced. The 1973-79 increases matched the performance of the Japanese car industry, which increased production in every year over the same period and achieved a 6.7 million passenger car production in 1980. Meanwhile American production fell in every year from 1977 through 1980 when 6.4 million passenger cars were produced.

In 1981, however, the West German automobile industry, except for its luxury car production, was beset by problems similar to those faced by the American motor industry: Japanese competition, inflated wage costs, stagnant productivity, diminishing markets, and especially, continuing losses in export markets. Japanese exports to the Federal Republic tripled from 1978 to 1980, reaching 251,990 in 1980, or 10.4 percent of the total West German market. Nevertheless in 1981 manufacturers continued to refrain from declaring themselves officially in favor of protectionist measures. The executives of Daimler-Benz and the Bavarian-based BMW were strongly antiprotectionist. Daimler-Benz sales in the United States and Canada increased in 1980 by 2 percent over 1979 to 56,000, reflecting, in Daimler's opinion, a North American trend to diesel cars. BMW became the first West German firm with its own Japanese importing subsidiary in order to expand its sales in Japan from the 1980 level of 3,200. In late 1981 Volkswagen was still exploring a possible production and technological arrangement with Nissan, which could lead to production in Japan of a medium-class Volkswagen or Audi. Volkswagen, only marginally profitable in 1980, was going ahead with an ambitious investment program at home and abroad that would cost some US$5.5 billion for 1981–83.

The automobile industry obviously has depended heavily on export markets to maintain employment in the industry. In 1980 Volkswagen exported slightly over half of the 1.6 million cars it produced domestically. The Japanese not only have increased their share of the West German market, but in 1980 also increased their share of the Latin American market by 81 percent, of the Middle East market by 44 percent, of the Southeast Asian market by 41 percent, and of the African market by 32 percent. Much of the Japanese increase in the overseas market was at the expense of the West German car exports, as well as of American exports. In the United States, German cars faced increasing competition from the smaller American cars that had price advantages.

The need to cut costs in the automobile industry has been paramount as wages in the industry have spiraled. The annual per capita income of the Volkswagen worker has exceeded the equivalent of US$15,000. As in the United States, automobile workers in West Germany have consistently earned the highest industrial wage (see Working Conditions, Wages, and Benefits, this ch.). West German car producers have bought Japanese components to cut the cost of such components by 10 to 20 percent below costs of domestic production. Location of plants abroad has been motivated not only by such location being an aid to holding or increasing market shares, but also as a means of cutting production costs. In 1980–81 Daimler-Benz opened a truck production plant in Hampton, Virginia; Daimler acquired facilities in San Francisco to produce above-fifteen-ton freightliners; and Maschinenfabrik Augsburg-Nürnberg (MAN) established a bus assembly plant in Cleveland, North Carolina. MAN had under consideration acquisition of plants in the Philippines and India in addition to plants it already operated in South Africa, Turkey, and Australia. Although many reasons have gone into the decision of West German car producers to locate plants abroad, cutting production costs has been a major factor.

Higher costs have also resulted from the decline of productivity in the car industry. In 1981 each West German worker in the automobile industry produced 16.5 cars a year, compared to twenty-six by an American worker and thirty-three by a Japanese worker. Although production of luxury cars has accounted in part for fewer cars a year being produced by the West German worker, the decline in average yearly output per worker since the mid-1970s has been evidence of a general decline in productivity in the industry.

Chemicals

Europe was the original home of the chemical industry. Such industries flourished especially in Germany, which achieved

*Industrial robots on assembly line
in Daimler–Benz factory in Stuttgart
Courtesy German Information Center*

world leadership in applying the science of chemistry to industrial technology. Before World War I Germany produced large amounts of inorganic chemicals and held a virtual monopoly on valuable synthetic dyestuffs and on most pharmaceutical chemicals. Although these monopolies were broken after the war, Germany recovered strongly and retained leadership in chemical technology. Under the domination of a giant combination, I.G. Farben Industrie, German chemical industries were streamlined into highly efficient operations. Obsolete plants were closed, products were standardized, production was specialized by plants, research was concentrated, and patents and markets were pooled.

In 1981 the Federal Republic had the world's three largest chemical firms: Hoechst, Bayer, and BASF. The country's chemical industry enjoyed the reputation of being the largest exporter and importer of chemicals in the world. In 1980 total turnover reached US$55 billion, a nominal rise of 5 percent, although overall production declined 4 percent from the record level of 1979. The 1980 figure included exports of US$23 billion and imports of US$13 billion. Included in imports were purchases from the United States of US$1.3 billion, an increase of 20 percent from the year before.

The "Big Three" companies were nearly even in terms of world turnover. Bayer, however, registered a good gain in earnings while Hoechst and BASF experienced declines in profits as American subsidiaries of the latter two firms suffered losses.

As of 1981 West Germany produced more sulfuric acid than any country except the United States, the Soviet Union, and Japan. It produced more caustic soda than any country except the United States and about the same amount as Japan. In the production of plastics and resins, West Germany was a close second to the United States and achieved about the same production as Japan.

The chemical companies in 1981 faced generally depressed markets for their products. Although different companies faced different problems, they shared some problems not limited to West Germany. All firms faced rising costs. They had to pay more for energy and for petroleum and other chemical raw materials. With depreciation of the deutsche mark (for value of the deutsche mark—see Glossary) during 1980 and 1981, purchases abroad inflated costs by more than the basic quoted price increases. Moreover the chemical industry was incurring the expense of meeting the government's increasingly tough environmental regulations. A larger and stable home market would aid chemical firms by reducing dependence on foreign markets where cyclical economic trends have had a destabilizing effect on the industry.

The chemical industry continued its investment abroad, however, and sought to increase overseas market opportunities. Bayer's 1981 worldwide capital investment exceeded US$1 billion even though investment had been greater in 1980 (US$1.06 billion), an increase of almost 19 percent over 1979. Hoechst's capital investment worldwide in 1981 was US$760 million, the same as in 1980. Almost all West German chemical firms, including some smaller ones, increased spending on research and development, considering such expenditures to be essential to maintain competitive shares of markets.

Electrical Industry

No German industry, other than the chemical industry, has given greater evidence of "science in the service of industry" than the electrical industry. The economics of physics found its greatest opportunity in the electrical industry, which, second only to the chemical industry, has offered the most challenging outlet for the society's scientific and organizational talents. German progress in the science of electricity was the foundation of the industry. The basic discoveries of physicists were applied to industry. It is not too much to say that the electrical industry was born and nourished in the research and development laboratories of the universities.

Two great firms concentrated power in the electrical manufacturing industry through their control of inventions and patent rights. The manufacturing industry is distinguished from the generation and sale of electric power on which most other industry depends. The first firm is Siemens AG, the largest industrial firm in Germany, which was founded by Werner Siemens (1816–92). Among his numerous innovations were the invention of the dynamo and the development of the first electric railway system. The second major firm in the industry is the German General Electric Company (Allgemeine Elektrizitäts-Gesellschaft—AEG), which was designed by the organizational genius of Emil Rathenau. The company was formed in the 1880s to exploit Edison's incandescent lamp. The electrical manufacturing industry displayed unusual talent for organizing large-scale business and applying scientific genius; the talent remained evident in 1982.

Electrical manufacturing has maintained rapid and steady growth for over a century. The industry made applications to transportation (tramways), illumination (lamp bulbs), metallurgy (steel production), communications (telephone and telegraph), electrochemical processes (nitrogen fixation from the atmosphere), and countless machines and appliances utilizing electric motors. By 1913 Germany had achieved world leadership in the production of electrical products and equipment, surpassing the United States by a narrow margin, and was preeminently the leading exporter of these products, having no close rival. The renowned British economic historian, John Clapham, wrote of the German electrical manufacturing industry: "Beyond question, the creation of this industry was the greatest single industrial achievement of modern Germany." The industry shared in, in-

Federal Republic of Germany

deed led, the industrial progress of Germany after World War I. Productivity in industrial production rose 25 percent between 1925 and 1929, and real wages and profits also rose.

As should be expected of the fourth largest manufacturing country of the world in 1981, Germany produced more electric power (in kilowatt-hours) than any country except the United States, the Soviet Union, and Japan. It was third in the production of manufactured gas, which was used to produce electricity—not far behind the Soviet Union and the United States.

In the modern electrotechnology industry of the early 1980s West Germany stood among the world leaders. The industry depended heavily upon export markets, accounting in 1980 for almost 10 percent of all exports, i.e., DM30 billion out of DM344 billion. Siemens alone accounted for over DM10 billion. Foreign orders for Siemens' products in the first half of 1981 were up 24 percent over the same period in 1980. Foreign markets were also of importance to AEG, if not to the same degree as to Siemens. Of its total 1980 production of DM15.1 billion, 42 percent or DM6.4 billion was exported. In the first quarter of 1981 new foreign orders were increasing at double the rate of increase in domestic orders.

The country's electrical manufacturing industry has been in the forefront of international cooperation in the rapidly changing world of electronics and electrotechnology. Again, Siemens has been the outstanding example of organizational adaptation to changing needs. In 1980 the company's investments in the United States reached DM269 million, more than double its investments in 1979, making available DM203 million for the acquisition of shares in subsidiaries and associated companies. Siemens' main activity remained medical engineering, but it was increasing its production of power engineering products through Siemens-Allis, a joint venture with Allis-Chalmers, based in Atlanta, Georgia. Siemens also increased its investments in Africa, Asia, and Australia, pointing out that of its total international business sales, 45 percent were generated in the countries where Siemens operated production units. A new switch gear plant in India and a plant to produce communications systems in Australia were among plants going into production in 1981. A joint venture with Fuji Electric that has existed since 1923 has led to the establishment of cooperation between Siemens and Fuji Electric for production of computers.

AEG has begun production of color television in China. AEG-Telefunken was entering a joint venture agreement with Japan Victor Company to produce video recorders in Japan. As manufacturing operations have become increasingly multinational, the industry has sought to preserve the country's electrical manufacturing leadership in world production.

*Turbine factory
Courtesy German
Information Center*

Engineering

The mechanical engineering industry (machine-building) may well be the most important pillar overall of the industrial economy, accounting in 1980 for 20 percent of manufacturing gross domestic product (GDP). In 1980 the industry recorded a turnover of almost DM122 billion, about 11 percent of total industrial production. The industry was of particular importance in the export sector, accounting in 1980 for almost 20 percent of total exports. The industry was a significant contributor to the overall foreign trade surplus. In 1980 sales abroad increased by 7 percent over the previous year to a total of DM63.1 billion. Although imports went up by 12 percent, the total was only DM22.4 billion, which meant that the industry had an overall export surplus of more than DM40 billion. The contribution was all the more remarkable because the overall surplus in foreign trade was about DM9 billion.

The decline in demand in the domestic market, where orders fell 10 percent in the first quarter of 1981, has made the machine builders all the more attentive to markets abroad, even though they were already exporting more than 60 percent of their production. The industry confronted challenges beginning to be posed by manufacturers in Japan and the United States. Although the industry had an export advantage as a result of declines in the

Federal Republic of Germany

exchange value of the deutsche mark, the industry continued to emphasize the need to keep production costs down in order to remain internationally competitive, especially with Japanese manufacturers who were taking increasing shares of foreign markets, particularly in the Far East. As of 1981 Japanese advances had been achieved mainly at the expense of American, British, and French manufacturers, but West German manufacturers had not been unaffected, even though market share losses had been minimal.

An area where West German firms continued to register growth was in turnkey industrial plants. Successful operations of the late 1970s-early 1980s included the completion of a polyester fibers plant in Indonesia by Lurgi, a subsidiary of Metallgesellschaft; a steel mill in the Soviet Union by Schloemann-Siemag; and a power plant in Algeria by Siemens and its subsidiary. Total orders in 1980 for this category of production were almost DM14 billion. Orders from Saudi Arabia reached DM1.5 billion. Other countries placing orders for large-scale plant equipment included China (DM904 million), the Soviet Union (DM822 million), Libya (DM659 million), South Africa (DM654 million), and Indonesia (DM612 million).

The mechanical engineering industry, like the steel industry, has expressed concern over advantages that some foreign competitors hold as a result of being able to offer state-subsidized financing. West German firms seeking contracts abroad for major industrial turnkey projects have reported foreign competitors offering concessional financing. In early 1982 industry, banks, and the government continued to voice their objections to such policies in international forums.

Energy

In 1981 primary energy production was the equivalent of about 2.4 million barrels per day (bpd) of oil. Production had been within a narrow range of this level for the preceding eight years. Of the 2.4 million bpd oil equivalent, 1.7 million bpd were accounted for by coal, 0.3 million bpd by natural gas, 0.3 million bpd by hydroelectric and nuclear power, and only 0.1 million bpd by crude oil. Production of crude oil, excluding natural gas liquids, declined continuously after 1977 when production was 108,000 bpd. In terms of proved reserves, the country had negligible amounts of oil, 6 trillion cubic feet of natural gas, and almost 35 billion tons of coal; the coal reserve, however, was estimated at 70 billion tons.

In the early 1980s the country had a crude oil refining capacity of 3 million bpd, a little above its average daily consumption of 2.7 million bpd in 1979, which was slightly above the average of the preceding three years. Consumption fell significantly in 1980, declining to a daily average of 2.4 million bpd. Reports covering the first six months of 1981 indicated a further decline over 1980. Given the negligible domestic crude oil production, imports of crude oil supplied most of the oil for refining. West Germany is a major importer of oil—importing more oil than any industrial noncommunist nation other than the United States and Japan. Import dependence for energy production is a little under 50 percent, well below the dependence of France (70 percent) and Italy (82 percent).

The Federal Republic had well-distributed sources of oil; Saudi Arabia supplied 25 percent and Libya, Nigeria, and Britain each accounted for about 10 percent of total imports. Other significant suppliers were Algeria, the United Arab Emirates, and until early 1980, Iran. As of the end of 1980 the country had oil stocks exceeding 310 million barrels.

Natural gas production has increased rapidly from only 98 billion cubic feet in 1965 to 670 billion cubic feet in 1980. To supplement domestic production and meet domestic requirements, natural gas has been imported from the Netherlands and from the Soviet Union.

In late November 1981 officials of Ruhrgas AG agreed to buy about US$45 billion of natural gas from the Soviet Union over a twenty-five year period. The transaction represented the largest East-West business agreement of all time. Although no single price for the gas was announced, it was expected to be "tied to the overall trend of heating oil prices" rather than to the price of higher quality crude oil. The Federal Republic will receive 370 billion cubic feet annually, in addition to current deliveries, but Soviet deliveries also to be made to France, the Netherlands, Belgium, Italy, Austria, and Switzerland will bring the annual total of deliveries to Western Europe to 1.4 trillion cubic feet, an energy equivalent of about 700,000 bpd. The gas will be delivered through a 5,760-kilometer pipeline to be built between the Soviet gas fields around Urengoy, in northwestern Siberia, and delivery points along the borders between Czechoslovakia and Austria and the Federal Republic (see fig. 13). The agreement provides for deliveries to begin in 1984.

As of mid-1981 the Soviets were delivering about 425 billion cubic feet of gas annually to West Germany, accounting for about 17 percent of the country's gas supplies and about 3 percent of its primary energy needs. The 17 percent figure will rise to 30 percent and the 3 percent figure to 5 percent when the Siberian pipeline begins delivery. The transaction reflected the underlying philosophy in West Germany, and indeed throughout Western Europe, that East-West trade was business and was not to be politicized. Concern over increased dependency on the Soviet Union as a source of supply was secondary to the economic benefits to be gained. The pipeline, by various estimates costing between US$10 and US$15 billion, will mean jobs and profits for West

Federal Republic of Germany

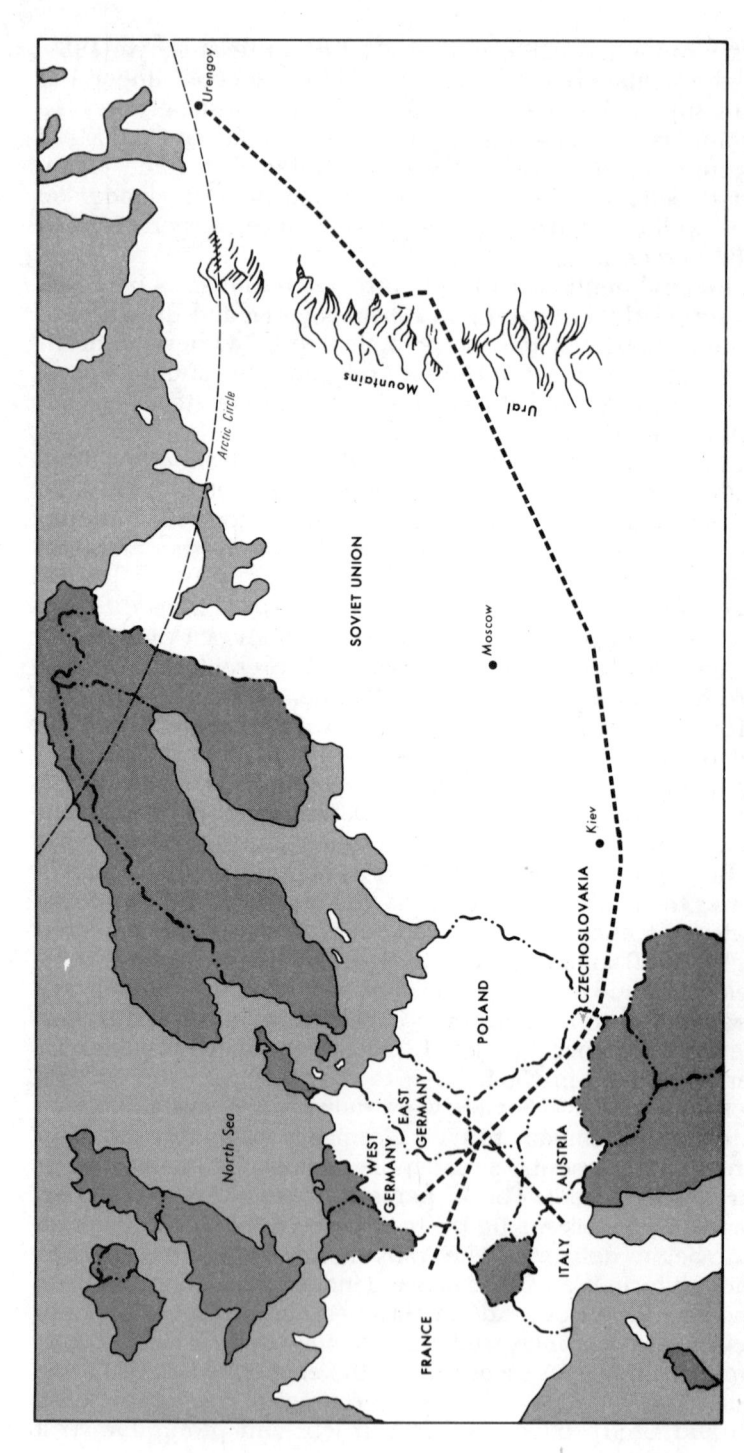

Source: Based on information from *New York Times*, December 30, 1981.

Figure 13. Natural Gas Pipeline from Soviet Union

Industry

German workers and industry, as well as benefits for the other West European countries involved. Orders for the components of the pipeline have been placed with major contractors and subcontractors throughout Europe. The Mannesmann AG steel group had won contracts worth over US$500 million to supply twenty-two compressor stations for the pipeline. In turn, the Soviets stand to earn more than US$7.5 billion annually in convertible currency once the gas starts flowing.

West Germans and other West Europeans minimized the risk of the Soviets cutting off the gas by asserting that such action would damage the pipeline and result in loss of hard currency to the Soviet Union. Moreover the West Europeans believed that their precautions—including alternate systems for switching fuels and for a surge capacity of Dutch gas—would greatly lessen the impact of any cutoff. It was also argued that the Soviets possessed a fine reputation for fulfilling business contracts, an argument that experience has from time to time contradicted. The Soviets, for example, have violated contracts in the past by cutting off petroleum shipments to Yugoslavia (1948), Israel (1956), Finland (1958), and China (1964).

The increased crude oil prices of 1973 did minimal damage to the economy. Remarkably the Bundesbank noted in its July 1974 report that, in a balance of payments sense, the 1973 price increase had been offset by virtue of appreciation of the deutsche mark. (With oil priced in United States dollars, and the deutsche mark appreciating against the dollar and most other currencies, the price increase had been dampened and then offset because in terms of the deutsche mark, industrial and other imports had declined in price.) The increases in oil prices in 1979 and 1980 were damaging, however, in large part because of the depreciation of the deutsche mark and because price rises in the countries that supply industrial imports were greater than those in West Germany.

Production of electricity in 1980 was almost 400 billion kilowatt-hours, or 20 percent more than output in 1974. Of this total almost 44 billion kilowatt-hours were produced by nuclear electricity generation. The electric power industry consumed about 10 percent of the total supplied. Industry consumed about 60 percent and residences 22 percent; the balance was consumed by small trade establishments, transport, and agriculture. West Germany remained a major producer of manufactured gas—gas produced by gasworks and cokeries—producing more than any other country within OECD except the United States and Australia.

The reduction of some 4 percent of total energy consumption in 1980 was attributable to many causes—weather was mild, and the rate of economic growth decreased. There was also an implied increase in energy efficiency and a reduction in the energy coefficient (the incremental amount of energy required to produce an incremental unit of the gross national product [GNP]). Particularly remarkable was a reduction of 10.5 percent in the consumption of petroleum products, especially of light heating oil. As a result oil imports were reduced by about 9 percent as compared to 1979.

Before the 1980–82 glut in the world oil market and the concomitant disarray in the Organization of Petroleum Exporting Countries (OPEC), the government announced details of its energy strategy for the 1980s. The plan had five major elements: phasing out subsidies on oil consumption; more extensive use of domestic coal resources; curtailing the use of natural gas and eliminating oil completely in the generation of electric power; giving priority to finding solutions to the problems of storage and disposal of nuclear waste; and raising the nuclear power share of primary energy generation from 3.4 percent in 1979 to over 10 percent in 1985 and over 16 percent by 1990.

Meanwhile the government and industry made significant progress in obtaining nonnuclear sources of energy. Contracts with Saudi Arabia that were due to expire were renewed, and Saudi Arabia agreed to provide 25 percent of the country's oil imports, up from 17 percent in 1979. Construction was begun on a liquefied petroleum gas terminal at Wilhelmshaven, with completion scheduled for the mid-1980s. Plans were prepared for a nuclear power station at Brockdorf, near Hamburg; political and public reluctance to increase nuclear power generation in the area created continuing difficulties, however. Antinuclear protesters joined in the opposition, and at times clashes with authorities were violent.

Transportation

In the early 1980s the transportation system of West Germany was among the finest in the world. An efficient inland waterway system carried grain, oil, timber, coal, heavy iron and steel products, and countless other goods. The industrial areas remained centers of attraction for both export and import of materials and goods through North Sea ports, especially Hamburg, a center of shipbuilding and marine engineering. The German Federal Railway system, state owned and operated, provided over 29,000 kilometers of rail line carrying fuel and ores, principally coal, stone, and lignite in various forms, as well as other cargo items. High-speed passenger trains connected all major cities. Railway density (length of rail per square kilometer and per capita) was, along with Denmark's, the greatest in Europe. Approximately 4,400 additional kilometers of railways were not federally owned (see fig. 14).

A superior road and highway network served the highest number of road vehicles in any European country. The autobahns, great transcountry motor roads that were developed during the Nazi period, provide limited access express connections of almost

Industry

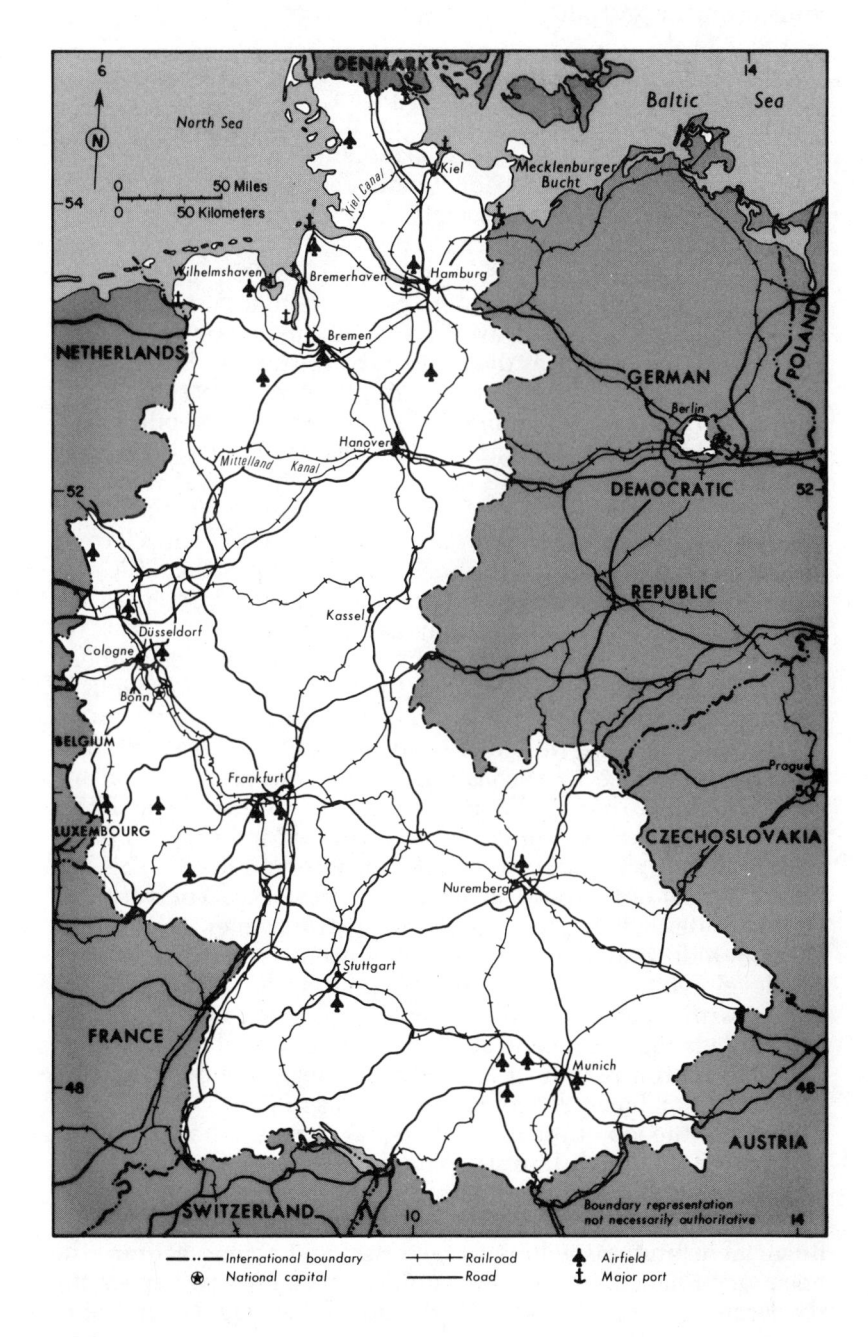

Figure 14. Transportation

217

Federal Republic of Germany

7,000 kilometers, joining all major cities and carrying heavy passenger and cargo traffic.

Industry and the Free Market Philosophy

Following World War II, official policy deliberately set out to reduce the power of the state in the management of the economy—particularly in the management of industry. The effort was personified in Minister for Economic Affairs Ludwig Erhard during the era that took the society through reconstruction to the prosperity and full employment of the late 1950s and early 1960s. Erhard, who later served as chancellor (1963–66), fervently defended private enterprise against governmental power and saw economic liberalism as a way of reducing public power. He believed that free trade was the answer to arbitrary authority. The concept appealed to the new generation ready to cast away the Hitler years of overwhelming state interference (despite which German industry in the Nazi period was never thoroughly and efficiently organized for the war effort). Erhard neatly summarized the point in his book, *Germany's Comeback in the World Market*: "More perhaps than any other economy the German one has had to experience the economic and supraeconomic consequences of an economic and trading policy subjected to the extremes of nationalism, autarchy and government control. We have learned the lesson; and if the basic principles of a liberal economic policy are championed...the reason must be sought in the special circumstances of our recent history."

Although the government's postwar fiscal measures enabled industry to finance its reconstruction and expansion, it did not accept in full Erhard's doctrine of economic liberalism if that doctrine was taken to imply that business and industry would be kept relatively small, divided, and overly competitive. This had been the goal of the postwar occupying powers, particularly the United States. This goal was abandoned, however, when West German industrial power became an obvious asset to the West in the developing cold war. West German industry cooperated to a degree with the Erhard ministry, but it built upon a familiar structural foundation of concentration, and it manifested a strong inclination to centralize industrial decisions. The problem for industry was how to mobilize economic resources and power on the scale required if the job of reconstruction was to be finished in a minimal period of time. Industry saw a need for large enterprises capable of undertaking ambitious investment projects and for large concentrations of venture capital in the hands of powerful financial institutions willing to take risks and able to acquire the necessary financing. Concentration of economic power among the large firms steadily increased, and by the mid-1960s one of every three workers in industry was employed by the 100 largest industrial firms, which produced over 40 percent of total industrial output and accounted for 50 percent of industrial exports.

In the early 1980s industry continued to be highly concentrated, the result of constant efforts to bring together various sources of economic power. Although it is extraordinarily difficult to compare the degree of industrial concentration in different countries, Common Market surveys over the years have suggested that the concentration of industry in the Federal Republic was probably not out of line with that in other member countries.

Tax concessions speeded the postwar recovery of industry. These concessions were used not merely to accelerate overall industrial recovery, but to discriminate purposely between one industry and another. Favored basic industries—steel, coal and iron ore mines, and electric power plants—received special tax benefits throughout the 1950s. Firms in these industries received exceptionally large depreciation allowances for any new investment that they set against the profits, thus sharply reducing taxable profits. A condition of receiving such benefits was that an amount equal to the reduction in taxable profit was to be reinvested in the business, not distributed to shareholders. Thus retained earnings financed industrial expansion through increased research and development, application of technologically advanced methods of production, and reduced cost of capital. Because taxes were purposely set high, the incentive for tax-reducing investment was all the greater. Additionally there was an export tax rebate proportional to the amount exported that was applicable to all industries. It proved to be such an export incentive that by the end of the 1950s West Germany had the strongest balance of payments in the trading world. Domestic consumer demand might, and did, fluctuate, but the continuing boom in world trade kept the export order books filled and the trade balance positive throughout the 1970s despite the worldwide recession of 1974–75. Only in 1980 did imports exceed exports in value—then by only a narrow margin and principally because of the spiraling cost of dollar-priced petroleum, reinforced by depreciation of the deutsche mark against the dollar (see Balance of Payments, ch. 4). Nevertheless demand for exports helped keep industrial employment throughout the 1970s and into 1981 at levels averaging 97 percent of the work force.

Tax incentives also favored the shipbuilding and construction industries. A vast increase in housing contributed to mobility of labor. Availability of housing in the great industrial centers was responsible in part for the low level of unemployment because workers could move from areas of relative unemployment to areas of labor scarcity. By the time the various special incentives were terminated, their intended effect had been achieved with industry reaching higher levels of productivity.

There are many other examples of government support of industry, such as subsidies, low-cost loans provided by the state, and discriminatory tax allowances favoring selected sectors of industrial activity. A free market philosophy does pervade industry, but it is understood as a philosophy restraining state intervention, not as a policy favoring business and industry. And since the early postwar years, moreover, government policy has never been conceived as limiting the concentration in and central direction of industry by industry. Industrial cooperation was achieved by consultation, especially consultative planning within respective industries for future investment.

Organizational Structure

West German civil and commercial laws give legal recognition to a variety of incorporated and unincorporated business forms. The most common forms are the public corporation, *Aktiengesellschaft* (AG), and the limited liability company, *Gesellschaft mit beschränkter Haftung* (GmbH). In addition there are general partnerships, limited partnerships, sole or joint proprietorships, joint ventures, and branches of foreign corporations.

Industrial organization is almost always in the form of a public corporation or a limited liability company. The public corporation is an incorporated business entity. Shareholder liability is limited to the unpaid portion of the nominal value of the shares. Because these shares can, upon application of the corporation, be traded on a stock exchange, the public corporation is the form overwhelmingly favored by large enterprises that have high capital stock requirements. The promoters of the corporation may be citizens or foreign nationals, resident or nonresident. They appoint the supervisory board, *Aufsichtsrat*, which in turn appoints the board of management, *Vorstand* (see Industry and Banks, this ch.).

The share capital (capital stock) of a public corporation must be expressed in deutsche marks with a minimum capital of DM100,000. Shares may be common or preferred (preference shares) and, as in the United States, one share of common stock entitles the holder to one vote; preference shares may be issued without voting rights. Preference shares entitle holders to a preferential dividend or preferential distribution of assets in the event of liquidation. Shareholder approval is required to establish a legal reserve for the protection of shareholders and creditors.

An important difference between a public corporation and a limited liability company is that shares of the latter cannot be traded on a stock exchange. The rules for shareholder representation and for increases and reductions of capital are in principle the same as for the corporation. Registered managers direct the affairs of the limited liability company; a management board oversees the affairs of the corporation. Minimal capital structure for a limited liability company is DM20,000, one-fifth the minimal requirement for a corporation.

The members of the management board are the main corporate officers. Legislation enacted in 1978 requires that a labor director be a member of the management board. This director represents the employer in wage negotiations and is mainly responsible for labor relations, working conditions, personnel, and welfare.

Depending upon the size of a public corporation, or limited liability company, and the number of employees, the supervisory board must consist of from three to twenty-one members—the total number to be divisible by three. Except in the case of a family-owned corporation with fewer than 500 employees, one-third of the members are elected by the employees of the corporation. The supervisory board of a firm with more than 2,000 employees must equally comprise representatives of labor and capital. Shareholders elect representatives of capital, employees elect the labor representatives who may come from the relevant trade union, company-employed wage earners, nonmanagerial salaried employees, and employees with managerial functions.

A limited liability company is legally represented by and managed by one or more registered managers. In addition the company may have a supervisory board or a similar body, but such a body is mandatory only if the company has more than 500 regular employees. Like the workers of a public corporation, employees elect one-third of the board members.

Company Supervisory Boards

Unlike the single-board Anglo-American system, West German companies have two boards: a supervisory board and an executive or management board. The supervisory board generally meets four or five times a year, or more often if conditions necessitate. It analyzes the annual accounts of the company and is responsible for such major policy decisions as overall manpower planning, investment in new plants, closing old facilities, mergers and takeovers, and changes in production methods. The members of the management board are responsible for conducting the day-to-day business of the company and, therefore, work full time. They may not sit on the supervisory board, and members of that board may not sit on the management board.

Since July 1, 1978, one-half of the members of the supervisory board have been representatives of labor. This parity of control with management on supervisory boards was achieved by labor in the iron and steel and coal-mining industries by laws passed in 1956.

Although the supervisory boards appear to have considerable influence, and in fact often do, a management board, so long as it is successful (which means profitable), will exercise dominant control of the firm and will probably have the ultimate word in deciding on the membership of the supervisory board. This is possible because management will have seen that members of the supervisory board represent a mixture of the principal outside interests on whose cooperation the company is normally dependent, i.e., the customers for the firm's products, the providers of finance, or suppliers of materials. This results in a company being represented as a supplier on the supervisory board of another company and having on its own board a representative of the other company as a valued customer. Firms allied in vertical or horizontal structures thus establish long-standing relations by associating the various companies with each other in major decisions, especially on investment. This network is reinforced by the association of banks and companies through interrepresentation on each other's boards (see Industry and Banks, this ch.).

Supervisory boards of major industrial firms thus tend to be highly supportive of management. The members of such boards usually stand in close alliance with each other, and the function of the boards is clearly seen as a device for systematic consultation between firms whose interests are intertwined. A company reform law of 1965 made it illegal for two companies to exchange supervisors and management positions directly, but it is not illegal for a company to have one of its executives sitting on its own supervisory board and on that of another company. The executive must not, of course, be a member of the management board. Interlocking at the supervisory board level is legal, and this is the way that firms of mutual interest—and their banks—do in fact interlock.

It seems, as a matter of practice, that decisions usually considered to be managerial are mainly influenced by management representatives on the supervisory boards. This occurs because trade union members of supervisory boards do not generally intervene adversely in the ordinary conduct of business in the areas of investment and in so-called technical matters. Although informed in these areas, trade union members tend to concentrate their influence on matters that affect employment, wages, and working conditions, the traditional areas of trade union interest.

Industrial Associations

The pervasive industrial associations, and more particularly the central body of associations, the Federation of German Industries (Bundesverband der Deutschen Industrie—BDI), constituted a major force for the organized economic effort and post-World War II reassertion of power by industry. The BDI was established in 1949 with an organizational structure based upon thirty-nine national industrial federations (*Verbände*—also translated as associations). The system is hierarchical to the point that the smaller industrial associations rely heavily upon the support of the so-called top associations (*Spitzenverbände*) to represent their views

Industry

at the center of consultation.

In 1982 this hierarchical structure still seemed to be reinforced by the Basic Law (constitution), which gives the associations an unusual consultative status in the processes of government, even spelling out the general practice in ministries: "Do not bring in for consultation associations which do not exercise a nationwide authority." This collaboration between the state and powerful industrial associations was not new. It was a feature of the Weimar Republic, under which a 1926 law instructed the big associations to provide forums for the views of smaller associations and to take note of such views. The hierarchical principle was not held simply for administrative convenience; it was the basis of the system. Under the Nazi regime the hierarchical system was greatly reinforced. Lines of authority were not to be questioned. Responsibility was concentrated in a small group at the apex of the structure. The Nazi word for their method of organizing industry was *Wirtschaftslenkung* (guided private enterprise). The contemporary practice of developing planned investment programs covering a whole industry and seeking to achieve more collaboration in research to accelerate technical development has its roots in practices of a similar type during the Weimar and Nazi periods.

This is not to assert that industry is rigidly organized. Industry in general recoils from arbitrary procedures, rejects cartel-mongering and compulsory price agreement, and tries to avoid unfair dominance of small industry by large industry. Moreover since 1958 the Federal Cartel Office has prohibited abuse by market-dominating firms, controlled mergers and acquisitions, and applied regulations against unfair competition and unfair trade practices.

The industrial associations were responsible for a marked improvement in the standard of industrial statistics, making them more precise and comprehensive. The steel industry, for example, regularly makes three-to-five-year forecasts of productive capacity on the basis of industry investment plans, including an estimate of future demand for various steel products. Individual steel producers pay particular attention to these industry forecasts, seeking to coordinate long-term supply arrangements for particular products in a conscious effort to avoid creating surplus capacity in the industry as a whole.

The *Verbände* see themselves as exercising a traditional and public role as guardians of national industries. Problems of policy are resolved not by authoritarian decree but by consultation. The associations continue to wield considerable power and influence, but they do so more subtly than in earlier eras. Individual associations vary widely in quality and in importance. As might be expected they are a significant force in the steel, chemical, machine tool, and electrical industries, and supply excellent leadership to these industries, also providing technical assistance and information. The methods used by associations to secure a consensus of industrial decisions in any given direction are distinctly of a high order of sophistication. Technical directors employed by the associations see it as their task to take systematic long-term views of the interests of their industries. As experts in investment and technological development, they are regularly consulted by the government well in advance of presentation of legislation for parliamentary discussion.

Erhard and the ideologues of economic liberalism did not convert West German industrialists from being disciplined members of their particular industrial communities to being passionate adherents of free competitive markets. This does not mean that West German businesspeople are not competitive; in practice they are often extremely responsive to the market and often compete powerfully with each other. There is more competition within West German industry than is sometimes realized.

The BDI has tremendous influence throughout the industrial sector, powerful enough to mobilize industry when deemed desirable. In the 1960s, for example, the BDI persuaded industrial firms to subscribe large amounts of money for government use, thus permitting Bonn greatly to increase its foreign aid to underdeveloped countries. Under leadership of the associations, industry often does voluntarily for the public good what might otherwise require legislation. The methods of industrial associations rest upon the preference of industry leaders for organized and deliberate action, not blind and brutal confrontation (see Traditional Interest Groups, ch. 7).

Industry and Banks

The nation's great industries have been characterized from their beginnings by a high degree of concentration of control. An initial period of strenuous competition in the electrical industry was followed at the turn of the century by curbs on competition and the formation of two giant concerns: AEG and Siemens (see Electrical Industry, this ch.). These two dominant organizations controlled prices and product specialization and allotted spheres of influence. In the chemical industry I.G. Farben emerged as the dominant firm in the late 1920s. Like the great German Steelwork Union (Stahlwerksverband), Farben was a combination of combinations. It dominated the German chemical and dye industry, brought the great chemical companies of Britain and the United States into international cartel agreements, and through its superb research efforts gained a monopoly of chemical formulas, which it used in trade for international market privileges.

Such industrial concentration would likely have been impossible, or certainly far more difficult to achieve, without similar concentration in the banking sector and the intimate association of

Industry

these banks with industry. In steel, chemicals, electrical, engineering, and other great heavy industries, the German banks provided the investment capital, with particular banks adapting their services to particular industries. The pattern of association continued as of 1982, and of all industrialized countries only Japan had gone further in the interlocking of banks and industry.

From the beginning of this close association, the banking industry showed the same concentration as the industries it served. Parent banks tolerated no ruinous competition among their offspring banks. Bank control in industry was exercised by having bank representatives sit on boards of directors of the industrial firms. Often these representatives have served as chairmen and vice chairmen. In 1919 the great English economist, Alfred Marshall, observed that German banks "carried to excess the locking up of their capital in loans which cannot be called in under grave emergency." The banks were overgenerous in their grants of long-term credits and supported to the limit of their strength the issue of industrial shares and bonds. In consequence the banks felt they had a permanent stake in the industries they nurtured. The Dresdner Bank was closely allied with the steel industry, the Deutsche Bank with export and shipping industries, and the Darmstadter Bank with various manufacturing industries, principally chemical and metal production.

In the early 1980s the Deutsche Bank, the Dresdner Bank, and the Commerzbank—the Big Three—remained the three largest banks and continued to exercise bank influence in industry by placing representatives on a company's supervisory board (see Company Supervisory Boards, this ch.). Originally established to give stockholders a more effective voice in management decisions than could be achieved in an annual meeting, the supervisory boards in industry have greatly increased shareholder influence on any major investment decision and on designation of senior management staff.

The power of the banks in industry arises from the fact that banks hold shares in their own names and overwhelmingly control the proxies of shareholders who are their depositors. A government survey in the 1960s found that in companies with aggregate share capital amounting to three-quarters of the nominal value of all quoted industrial shares, 70 percent of the capital was controlled by the banks. Although control depended in part on the banks' direct shareholdings, voting power came principally from the exercise of proxies. This power has increased because the banks as common practice exchange proxies among themselves under a system known as *Stimmenleihe* (loaned votes). An individual bank can thereby increase the weight of its voting power in any firm or industry in which it has particular interest. The Big Three banks collect proxies from smaller banks; it was estimated in 1981 that the Big Three controlled about 70 percent of all shareholders' proxy votes cast at company meetings. Identifying a bank as the exerciser of a shareholder's proxy was difficult as only the name and address of an individual casting a proxy on behalf of a bank need be reported. Banks seem to seek control of at least 25 percent of the shareholding of any company in which the bank has a particular interest.

The power of the banks has been based in part on their roles as agents of investors. Investors generally must go to a bank in order to buy or to sell their shares because, other than specialized brokers who themselves often act as agents of banks seeking to conceal their identities in particular share dealings, bank officials are the only representatives authorized to trade on the floor of the stock exchanges. Banks operate substantial investment departments. Stock market operations are themselves highly centralized, and fifteen large companies account for about 40 percent of the nominal value of all traded shares. The bulk of all share dealings is concentrated in the investment departments of the Big Three banks. A company can trade its shares or bonds on an exchange only after a lapse of one year from registration. During this period it is almost entirely dependent upon bank finance. As a result industrial managers remain quite responsive to bank interests.

The influence exercised by banks, however, is not unrestrained. Management (represented by the management board) represents the executive power of a firm (as contrasted with the supervisory board representing shareholders) and does not easily relinquish control. Thus a firm with excellent management and a successful record of profitability exercises control over company affairs (usually through the management board) and has a major voice in the selection of supervisory board members. In the words of a critic of the practice, however, the banks still succeed in "collecting *Aufsichtsrat* places the way other people collect postage stamps." The Big Three banks hold over half of all supervisory board seats in industry, while the top ten banks hold over three-quarters of such seats.

The major banks thus are represented on the supervisory boards of most of the major industrial companies. Among themselves the banks may compete for positions on a firm's supervisory board. At annual meetings, however, the banks deliver proxy votes to the bank having the greatest representation on the supervisory board of the industry or firm. The West German banks, unlike banks in many other industrialized countries, have technical departments that, on scientific and industrial grounds, can make decisions relating to a company's financing. The banks bring to industry new ideas and techniques that can aid an industry. The banks can, and do, induce management to improve business practices.

The banks conduct their operations with industry on a highly ethical level. Competing concerns that may be clients of the same bank are assured that their business secrets will not be leaked by bank officials who may sit on both their respective supervisory boards. The banks appear to be most concerned to see that management be as efficient as possible in firms where the banks have large investments. The banks are primarily interested in increasing their own profits and thus work closely with the industries they finance to solve problems and evaluate prospects. They do this while respecting the integrity of the individual firm.

The industry-bank relationship is not a one-way street. Directors of the large industrial firms are invited to sit on the banks' supervisory boards—often a firm and a bank will simply exchange representatives for their supervisory boards. Almost all the fifty major industrial firms have bank representatives on their boards. In turn, the representatives of those firms sit on the boards of the Big Three and other banks. It is a form of mutual supervision, a channel of information allowing for diffusion of advanced management techniques. A German industrialist traditionally expected to have his banker intimately informed of all the operations of his business. In return the industrialist received the financial support necessary for large-scale investment required in heavy industry. The tradition continues. Every advanced industrial country presents evidence of close banker-industrial client relationships; in West Germany these relationships are simply closer than most.

Business Planning

From the beginning of the country's industrial development, its business community has been concerned, in some measure, with collective policy planning whether such planning applied to a firm, a group of firms, or to an entire industry. Banks were either organizers or active participants in the process. Influenced in large part by American business practices, West German industry after World War II became increasingly interested in the practice of long-term forecasting, by individual firm or by industry, of investment, production, profits, and other key variables in the operation of industry. Attention to marketing innovations, inventory control, and new methods of working-capital management grew. Industry increasingly used the official national income accounts, which were constantly being refined.

A notable tendency in West German industry has been the extension of the time limit of any business plan. Management in large-scale industrial enterprise found that important decisions, especially in financing and capital investment, required a lengthened perspective. The very large industrial firms have adopted elaborate methods of organizing forecasts in systematic fashion, not believing that modern methods of forecasting are foolproof but rather that they are aids for achieving improved management decisions in the future. A major practitioner of such systematic planning was Siemens; its varied factories developed five-year forecasts at the start of each year. Joint exercises, involving all work managers, occurred every six months, their purpose being to review performance against plan and to analyze the current validity of the long-term plan itself. Both Siemens management and its bankers, the Deutsche Bank, considered such continuing analyses essential to business success. As a seller of heavy electrical machinery, Siemens found it essential to make long-term forecasts of technology changes, thus the elaborate drills of six-month exercises.

The high incremental capital-output ratio achieved in the postwar period has been attributed in large part to industrial planning based on long-term inter-firm agreements designed to aid industries in economizing capital during periods when the pace of demand slackened. The BDI supports the expansion of advanced techniques. The Munich-based Institute of Business Research (Institut für Wirtschafts-Forschung) publishes an extensive series of long-term economic predictive analyses. As the problems faced by the industrialist and businessperson in an increasingly volatile economy become more complex and predictions ever more uncertain, individual firms have found it necessary to compare company plans with the sophisticated industrywide and entire economy forecasts formulated by ever more refined techniques. As significant investment risks markedly increased during the 1970s, firms discovered that industrywide planning may reduce uncertainty about supply and markets. As they have equipped themselves with both business habits and institutions of modern capitalism that could, if necessary, move them toward a greater degree of planning, the possibility exists that should a compelling need arise, a more directed official economic policy might emerge.

Like other industrialized countries, West Germany was faced with the necessity of early identification of the probable beneficial and adverse impacts of the applications of technology. Although lagging behind the United States, West Germany had begun making such indentifications. Technology assessment, as such activity has come to be called, has been for some years a function of the official research and technology policy authorities, e.g., the Ministry for Research and Technology (Bundesministerium für Forschung and Technologie). But these official bodies formulate recommendations that have been taken into account by industry in its planning. As early as the middle 1960s, systems studies on the development and use of nuclear energy were being carried out in the nuclear research centers at Karlsruhe and Jülich. These studies included four projects: man, energy, and the environment; resource exploitation and resource safeguards; communications and society; and transport, land use, and the economy. Increasingly the results of such studies became part of business planning. Among the most important research and development institutions in these four spheres were those of certain major industrial firms that maintained a large systems analysis capability. Industry in its planning undertook studies that were not limited to technical and economic aspects, although the profit motive remained in the foreground.

Labor in the Industrial Sector

Two words may best describe the industrial work force up to the early 1980s: disciplined and moderate. In addition the work force was highly skilled as a result of education and training. Although the workers were not as rigidly disciplined as in pre-World War II years when strict training at home, in school, and in compulsory military service established the fundamental quality of behavior, they have remained more disciplined and more moderate than their counterparts in most Western countries.

The Industrial Labor Force: Character, Quality, Skills

For the first twenty years after World War II, refugees from Eastern Europe kept competition for jobs intense, contributing to energetic performance of labor. This supply of labor from the eastern areas, and later the importation of workers from such countries as Italy, Spain, Portugal, Turkey, Greece, and Yugoslavia, allowed the Federal Republic to keep inflation below levels in other countries. Wages rose constantly but so did productivity, thus offsetting increases in wages in whole or in part. Added to the pressure of competition from other workers, fear of inflation kept worker wage demands moderate for many years because wage increases beyond productivity increases spelled price increases—a problem the West German worker may have feared more than did workers in other countries. For the first twenty years many workers recalled the terrible inflation of the 1920s, and most remembered the immediate post-World War II years, the latter leading to near stagnation of industry and trade until the currency reform of 1948.

In 1980 the total work force was about 26.7 million, slightly above the level of 1979. Of this total, 9.8 million workers were engaged in manufacturing industries. Foreign workers totaled about 2 million. Of the almost 10 million manufacturing industrial workers, 13 percent were in the nonelectrical machinery industry, 12 percent in metal products, 10 percent in electrical machinery, 8 percent in chemicals, 7 percent in basic metals, 5.5 percent in motor car production, 5 percent in nonmetallic minerals, and 2 percent in other transport equipment; the balance was spread over twenty-nine other branches of the manufacturing industry. Guest workers (*Gastarbeiter*) were employed primarily in metallurgy (about 45 percent of the total) and in other manufac-

Federal Republic of Germany

turing (30 percent); most of the balance were in construction. Few were in mining, less than 5 percent of the total.

Of the total labor force, 5.3 percent were in agriculture, 45.3 percent in industry, 17.6 percent in trade and transport, and 31.8 percent in other services. Thus West Germany had about an equal number of workers in the goods-producing sectors and in the service sectors. If this continuing, and inevitable, shift from goods-producing to services sectors follows the pattern of development in the United States (where 68 percent of the work force produces services), productivity overall will fall, but not necessarily in the industrial sector where increased application of technology may sustain productivity increases.

The unemployed numbered about 900,000 in 1980, or 3.8 percent of the total labor force. By late 1981 unemployment had reached 1.5 million, or about 6.4 percent of the work force; in February 1982 unemployment soared to almost 2 million, and government forecasts projected an average for 1982 of close to 1.7 million. Unemployment was especially high among the young as it was elsewhere in Europe and in the United States. The increasing number of new job market entrants, members of the baby boom generation of the early 1960s, was cause for concern because industry had not been able to generate any significant increase in job openings. Overall, the number of vacancies throughout the economy had actually decreased since early 1980. Vacancies in construction had sharply declined, and the decline in manufacturing vacancies accelerated in early 1981. The number of short-time workers was increasing rapidly, reaching 500,000 by mid-1981 the highest level since 1976.

Of the approximately 26.7 million workers almost 9 million were members of unions. In no industry was union membership obligatory. There was no closed shop. All but about 1 million of these unionized workers belonged to one of the sixteen unions in the German Trade Union Federation (Deutscher Gewerkschaftsbund—DGB). The main outsiders were the civil servants' federation and the police union. Unionization was particularly strong in industry, membership being especially high in mining (about 90 percent) and engineering. Among the other more important unions were those for the combined chemical-paper-ceramic industry, the metal industry, and public services.

Otto von Bismarck suppressed the labor movement, and the Weimar Republic's sixty unions were replaced by Hitler's labor front. The country's present sixteen unions, organized under British guidance after the war, have emerged, in the view of some observers, as pillars of the establishment. Founded in 1949, the DGB in 1982 remained committed to free enterprise and social democracy. DGB rules were strict. A decision to strike must be endorsed in a ballot by at least 75 percent of the membership. Union dues averaged about 1 percent of members' monthly pretax

Industry

pay, and unions passed on 11 to 12 percent of this income to the DGB.

In theory West German trade unions were nonpolitical bodies; in practice the trade unions exercised strong political influence, in large part attributable to their considerable finances and their own extensive business interests in both banking and trade (see Traditional Interest Groups, ch. 7). In 1982 the unions owned one large bank as well as a well-financed building society.

Industrial relations in Western Europe continue to be much more varied in the 1980s than is sometimes realized. Some analysts have offered France and Italy as class conflict models of industrial relations while selecting West Germany as the outstanding example of the consensual or integrationist model. Through collective bargaining—supplemented by labor-management cooperation and political action—West German unions have made sufficient progress to accept cooperative reform as the best way to proceed to gain additional worker benefits. In 1982 the unions were extremely well financed and organized and felt secure in exercising their influence. Some critics believed the unions had become too bureaucratic and suggested that for the gradual, though significant, gains achieved, they have paid the price of becoming a part of the establishment. The unions, however, have achieved much. West German industrial workers were among the best paid of Western Europe in 1982. Stability in labor-management relations has contributed much to the economic miracle. Collective bargaining has generally been conducted in a constructive atmosphere, and this has further contributed to general social stability. When agreement cannot be reached directly between the bargaining parties, issues are decided by arbitration. Strikes and lockouts have been rare, and except in 1978 when there was a major dispute in the steel industry, loss of working hours due to labor confrontations has been insignificant.

Fewer workers took part in strikes in 1980 than in 1979. In terms of days lost per 1,000 workers, the figure was only seven in 1980, twenty-five in 1979, and 221 in 1978. The outlook for 1981 was excellent, with days lost per 1,000 workers expected to match the low level of 1980. The optimistic expectation was based upon the wage settlement early in the year in the metalworking industry. I.G. Metall, the country's largest trade union, agreed to a wage increase of 5.3 percent following what was considered to be the most difficult and arduous wage negotiation of 1981. The settlement was important because the metalworkers have tended to set the pattern for industry and for the economy as a whole. The settlement of 5.3 percent was well below the average 6.7 percent of 1980. Later in 1981 over 2.5 million workers in the public sector accepted a modest 4.3 percent increase. Because of high unemployment, settlements were expected to be moderate. The fact that increases were modest should be a help in offsetting inflationary pressures in industry, and in the economy generally, because the prices of industrial inputs, as well as of other imports, have risen as the result of the lowered value of the deutsche mark.

Codetermination

Codetermination (*Mitbestimmungsrecht*) was a unique development after World War II. Against a background of trade union reconstruction and an absence of a collective bargaining tradition within an industrial enterprise, West German unions sought legal establishment of a system of codetermination that would give employees and unions the right to participate in the management of the enterprise, at the lower levels through works' councils and at the highest level through representation on the supervisory boards. The idea of codetermination was in part of British origin and was strongly supported by the Labour Government that in 1945 replaced the Conservative Government.

Actually worker participation has a long tradition in Germany. The first Works' Council Act was passed in 1920. At the same time, the first workers' representatives took seats on company boards, but not in parity with management. As a political demand of industrial workers, codetermination was raised as far back as the March revolution of 1848. Every form of industrial democracy, particularly unions, was repressed under the Nazi government. After World War II the Federal Republic reverted to the best industrial-democracy traditions of the Weimar Republic and reestablished a much-improved system.

It was in the Ruhr area of North Rhine-Westphalia that codetermination, particularly parity codetermination by management and labor, received its first test (see fig. 1). The test came in Mannesmann AG, a major industrial steel-producing firm that had the typical vertical structure of the Ruhr area, i.e., mining, iron and steel production, and processing, all controlled by the one firm. Mannesmann had been subject to decartelization by the Allied Control Council. As early as 1947, in the course of the decartelization, parity codetermination had been introduced in three Mannesmann subsidiaries. At the time the imposition of codetermination had a political, not an economic, motive. The Allies hoped that codetermination would hamper the recovery by the coal and steel industries of their economic (and thus their political) strength, and that ultimately introduction of codetermination in other industries would similarly limit their strength. The political intention of the Allies coincided with the interest of the trade unions in participating in the supervision of heavy industry.

In 1947 companies in the iron and steel industry established supervisory boards based on the principle of parity. Capital owners and employees delegated equal numbers of representatives. Each board additionally had two representatives of the public interest. An *Arbeitsdirektor*, in charge of personnel and social

"Shielded mining" in a Ruhrkohle AG coal mine in Essen
Courtesy German Information Center

affairs, was to be a member of the executive board, along with a commercial and a technical director, and was to be nominated by the trade unions. In the coal and steel industry the two sides, management and labor, selected an independent chairman from outside, an assumed neutral member. In 1951, by threatening to call a general strike, the trade unions brought pressure on the Federal Diet (Bundestag) to pass the so-called codetermination law. By this law, parity codetermination in the iron and steel industry was confirmed and extended throughout the coal-and ore-mining industry. For Mannesmann it meant that Mannesmann AG, the holding company, and all its subsidiaries in the iron and steel industry, as well as in coal and ore mining, had to conform to the new law.

Under the Shop Constitution Act of 1972, a works' council represents exclusively the workers and must be established in any business enterprise having at least five employees. Members of a works' council vary from one, in the case of five employees, to thirty-one and more, in the case of 9,000 and more employees. Duties of works' councils lie in the field of employee welfare and representation of employee interests vis-à-vis the employer. Representatives on the councils need not be union members, but the great majority belong to one of the sixteen industrial unions affiliated with the DGB. Unions exercise influence on the shop floor and in plant bargaining only through membership on a workers' council.

Companies that employ between 500 and 2,000 persons must have supervisory boards with one-third of the members representing labor. If more than 2,000 persons are employed, one-half of the supervisory board must be labor representatives. The law providing for parity of labor and shareholder representation on these company supervisory boards became effective as of July 1, 1978, twenty-two years after parity was established in the coal-mining and iron and steel industries. Similar codetermination rights are enjoyed by workers in the public service, where councils represent workers in all public services including government, courts, and embassies.

Codetermination, both through the works' councils and representation on the supervisory boards, seems to have created a democratic balance between employer and workers; brought about increased industrial peace on the factory floor and, through providing for representation of workers on supervisory boards, raised the level of employee interest in firm and industry.

Working Conditions, Wages, and Benefits

Employer-employee relations continued in 1982 to be regulated through an extensive framework of labor and social security laws (see The Welfare System, ch. 2). The laws regulate maximum weekly working hours (forty-eight), night shift work, Sunday and public holiday work, engagement and dismissal of labor, protection of younger, older, and female workers, training and, in larger enterprises, works' councils and codetermination. Terms of wages and voluntary social benefits are subject to collective bargaining, an annual negotiation between the representatives of the trade unions and employers' associations for industry and other significant sectors of the economy. The resulting wage agreements are normally valid for one year. Labor disputes are subject to the jurisdiction of special labor courts.

Minimum wages and salaries vary—as would be expected among the various branches of industry—and depend upon the degree of skill, knowledge, and age of the worker. Workers in the automobile manufacturing industry are the highest paid of all industrial workers, except for the workers in the much less significant petroleum industry. Wages are roughly equal in the mining, iron and steel, chemicals, and metals industries, at a level just below that of the automobile industry. Wages in the electronics and construction industries are only slightly lower. Wages are considerably lower in wholesale and retail trade, banking, and insurance than in other industry. Wages for women average about 30 to 50 percent below wages for men in the same industry.

A critical element in the concept of a social partnership between labor and management lies in their joint control and joint

Industry

financing of the major manpower and social security programs, Germany having been the first country in the world to introduce comprehensive social security legislation. Adopted during the years 1883 to 1889, this range of jointly sponsored social services includes everything from health insurance and old-age pensions to unemployment insurance and a full range of manpower programs. These services continue to be administered by self-governing public corporations. An example of such a corporation is the Federal Employment Institute, which is governed by an equal number of representatives from labor and management who share the costs through payroll deductions. Only if unemployment rises above a specified level does the government contribute any public funds, and then only to cover additional unemployment insurance payments.

The institute provides as comprehensive a range of manpower services as any similar institution anywhere in the world. It manages the placement and unemployment insurance system and administers adult training, retraining, and upgrading programs. It is responsible for vocational guidance in the schools. The funds involved equal about a quarter of the nation's GNP, the majority of the funds being raised by social security premiums paid by employee and employer. Labor and management jointly administer the funds to enhance benefits in all areas of activity in the belief that in the long run, society's well-being depends upon a skilled, healthy, and socially protected industrial work force and population.

Extensive employee education and training is considered a fundamental basis of industrial democracy. West Germany is a world leader in the training of its industrial labor force, matched only by the Japanese in intensity of effort. Unions participate fully in labor education. For example, I.G. Metall operates a large and impressive residential college, as well as three smaller ones. These colleges provide union members with a variety of courses of varying depth, intensity, and length. Other unions run education and training programs that provide instruction so their members who serve on works' councils or supervisory boards can satisfactorily carry out the duties of their positions.

Industrial workers enjoy fringe benefits that equal those of their counterparts in other West European countries. An annual bonus is not unusual, and almost all industrial firms maintain pension programs financed by employer contributions and by employees if they wish. Many firms create pension reserves out of profits to cover estimated liabilities for future payments under their pension plans, which provide old-age benefits to be paid to employees upon retirement. There is an incentive for management to set up such a reserve because it is, within certain limits, deductible when the firm computes its taxable profits. Employees enjoy various insurance coverages, six weeks of paid sick leave, and severance pay of up to one year's salary or higher if the employee is at least

Federal Republic of Germany

fifty years of age with at least fifteen years' service. Most intermediate-sized and large industrial firms provide job amenities such as subsidized meals, recreation facilities, and health care facilities.

The worker is protected against the risk of loss of wages in the event that a firm goes bankrupt. Compensation for wages and salaries earned is guaranteed by law, as is the refund of contributions made to social and sickness insurance during the three months prior to the bankruptcy. Profit sharing by employees is rarely found, however. Tax incentives are offered to employers and wage earners to participate in limited long-term savings plans, and many wage agreements have incorporated provisions making contributions to such plans compulsory for the employer.

West Berlin

For obvious reasons West Berlin occupies a special position in the West German industrial structure. In late 1981 it still appeared as an isolated center surrounded by East Germany—a difficult to reach, exposed, and potentially perilous place. The Four Power Agreement on Berlin—signed in September 1971—and the Transit Agreement of 1974 have, however, provided stability of relations and of ingress and egress. The agreements have functioned with a minimum of friction and have helped protect an environment for trade and industry. With a population in excess of 1.9 million—thus the country's largest city—West Berlin has required maximum job opportunities for an energetic, trained, and ambitious work force.

In order to strengthen the economy of West Berlin, the Federal Republic has for many years provided considerable incentives to industry and trade to locate in the city. These incentives have included tax-exempt investment subsidies ranging from 10 to 40 percent of costs; low-interest and special government-supported loans; low-cost and long-term property leases; substantially reduced income, corporate, and value-added taxes that can increase profits by as much as slightly over 10 percent of sales; and many other benefits. Companies maintaining permanent establishments in West Berlin could claim a premium of 10 percent of the cost of a new depreciable fixed asset in Berlin. If the fixed asset is used for production in a manufacturing business the premium is increased to 25 percent; if in research and development, to 30 percent.

Employees in West Berlin also have received special benefits, such as a monthly nontaxable payment from the government equal to 8 percent of employee earnings plus nontaxable allowances for dependent children and a 30 percent reduction of the tax on income earned in Berlin. The ability of employers in West Berlin to recover certain costs through special favorable tax treatment specific to their earnings explains in part the industrial har-

Industry

mony found in West Berlin and the resulting thirty-five years of freedom from major industrial strikes.

There were other advantages to industry in West Berlin: a well-developed infrastructure, numerous research and development facilities, nearly 500 square kilometers of area, and a ready market of over 1.9 million people. Moreover the city remained a major center for business and industrial contacts with Eastern Europe. The combination of incentives and advantages had helped make West Berlin the largest industrial center between Moscow and Paris. The GNP of the city was about half that of Denmark or Austria, produced by an economy closely integrated with that of West Germany.

Industry in West Berlin is no new phenomenon. As the prewar capital of Germany, Berlin was responsible for 6 percent of total German industrial production; 41 percent of its population derived their livelihood from industry, as contrasted with 25 percent from commerce and 15 percent from administration and service. The principal industries were the electrical group and textiles. Berlin produced about half of all of Germany's machinery and electrical appliances, two-fifths of its clothing, one-fourth of the precision and optical instruments, and one-fifth of the machine tools. Of industrial commodities produced in the city, 11 percent went abroad. The city nevertheless depended mainly on markets within the country (see fig. 15).

In 1981 West Berlin still depended heavily upon markets in West Germany and in other Common Market countries. It depended upon outside sources for almost all of the necessary industrial inputs—upon the Ruhr for coal and the rest of West Germany, the Common Market countries, and Eastern Europe for vast quantities of foodstuffs and other raw materials.

West Berlin remained a major industrial center in the production of machinery and electrical appliances, machine tools, precision instruments, and electronic equipment, and a major manufacturing location for plastic components. It was a high-technology center with connections to West German industry abroad: electronics was perhaps the major industry, and West Berlin was the computer manufacturing center of West Germany. Daimler-Benz built every Mercedes crankshaft in West Berlin, and Daimler had located its largest assembly plant for truck diesel motors in the city. Every major industry was represented in West Berlin with the exception of iron and steel, coal, and lignite.

Industry and East-West Trade

In the early 1950s West German industries participated in the activities of east committees (*Ostausschusses*), which had many industrial leaders as members and had as their main concern the exploration of possibilities for expanded East-West trade. At the time, the attitude of industry was that the division of Germany

Federal Republic of Germany

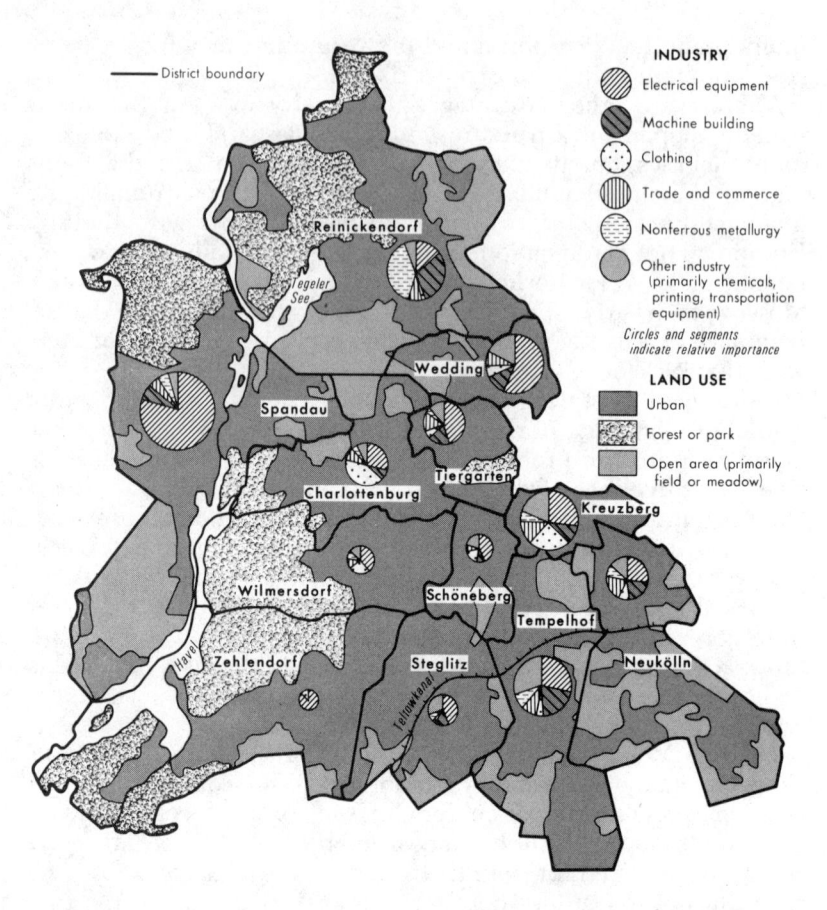

Figure 15. West Berlin

would not be permanent, and traditional ties of trade and commerce should be preserved and strengthened whenever possible, not only to East Germany but also to the Soviet Union and other countries of Eastern Europe, many of them traditional trading partners of prewar Germany. The attitude was in line with the German tradition of keeping politics out of East European trade to the greatest possible degree. This pragmatic line has been consistently followed by successive West German governments and contrasts with policies of the United States and the Soviet Union to politicize business and industrial relationships.

During the period of détente and *Ostpolitik*, various so-called Eastern treaties improved conditions of East-West contacts in social, political, and material terms (see *Ostpolitik* and Détente, ch. 8). More Germans returned from Poland and other eastern territories, travel between East Germany and West Germany was eased, and cultural relations were strengthened. These increased contacts meant increased earnings for East Germany; travel by West Germans to East Germany increased the latter's earnings by over DM1 billion annually.

The signing of the treaties opened a period of startling expansion of trade between West Germany and the members of the Council for Mutual Economic Assistance (Comecon), but especially between West Germany and the Soviet Union. Between 1970 and 1980 West German foreign trade doubled overall in value, but over the same period trade with the Soviets nearly quadrupled in value, and trade with Poland and Hungary increased almost as rapidly. These impressive gains were made despite a falloff in trade during 1977 and 1978. This was followed by a rebound, especially in imports, in 1979 and 1980.

In 1980 the Soviet Union was the tenth largest trading partner of West Germany, accounting for 2.7 percent of West German exports and 2.2 percent of West German imports. The rest of Eastern Europe accounted for 4.9 percent of exports and 4.6 percent of imports. Trade with East Germany, which was considered to be internal trade and was not included in the external trade accounts, consisted of US$2 billion of exports and US$2.2 billion of imports.

The expanding trade between West Germany and the Soviet Union followed the old historic pattern of German-Russian trade. West Germany continued to be by far the largest exporter of any Western country of finished products, almost all manufactures, to the Soviet Union. In return it received important raw materials from the Soviet Union, including significant quantities of its natural gas (see Energy, this ch.). West Germany imported large amounts of industrial metals and minerals, as well as about 40 percent of its enriched uranium imports, from the Soviets. Fuel imports made up more than 50 percent of all imports from the Soviet Union.

The Soviet Union had become critically important as a market for exports for some basic sectors of West German industry and of the economy. Almost half of all West German industrial pipe production went to the Soviets. In 1979 exports to Comecon countries of three major industrial firms—Hoechst, Mannesmann, and Thyssen—reached a value of DM4 billion. Industry thus had a major stake in the cultivation of markets throughout Eastern Europe, but most especially in the Soviet Union. Workers in the exporting and related industries also had a major stake in this trade. Although the Soviets and the West Germans regarded themselves, in some sense, as enemies, they also saw themselves in 1981 as trading partners, the more so after the preceding ten years of good relations. West Germany's economic and technological presence was of great significance to the Soviets who hoped to

Federal Republic of Germany

attract West German technological expertise and financial credit that would help them tap the riches of Siberia. West Germany in return would secure access to newly discovered or exploited energy resources. West German innovation and efficiency impressed the Soviets, and the West Germans were impressed by the vast potential market of the Soviet Union. Not only geography and history, but also deeply embedded economic realities made the West Germans see themselves as both barrier and bridge to the East, and the bridge is trade.

Soviet importers consider four elements decisive when placing orders abroad: product quality and technological standard; punctual delivery and reliability in settlement; price; and financing costs. West Germany has been at the top of the list for the first two. This, in turn, reduced to a degree the importance of price since higher prices of West German goods were accepted because of superior quality. West Germany was the only large Western industrial country other than the United States that did not offer its exporters state subsidies to lower export financing costs. West German exporters have occasionally lost a contract because another foreign competitor offered cheaper export financing. Some West German exporters, in order to stay competitive in the Soviet Union, have routed part of their deliveries from France in order to take advantage of the subsidized instruments of financing provided by French banking. West German firms that can offer export contracts with part delivery from France have an advantage over firms making deliveries with export credits at West German capital market rates. As of late 1981, however, financing had not been a significant deterrent to growing West German trade with the Soviet Union and the other Comecon members.

Industry and the World Economy

West German exports represented 23.3 percent of GNP (fourth largest in the world), and imports represented 22.7 percent, with direct investment abroad—mostly industrial—aggregating about US$35 billion, and direct investment of foreign companies in West Germany aggregating almost US$30 billion. In the early 1980s West Germany was the leading exporter in the world of manufactured goods, which accounted for 87 percent of all goods exported. In manufactured goods, West Germany in 1980 had a positive trade balance of US$63.1 billion, far higher than any other country in the world. West Germany's share of world export markets for manufactures in 1980 was 20.8 percent, again the highest in the world.

Foreign direct investment by West German companies accelerated in 1980, continuing a trend observable in the preceding several years. Total investment abroad was US$3.3 billion compared to US$3.1 billion in 1979. Net capital outflow increased in every year from 1975 through 1980. Direct foreign investment included

Industry

investment in industrial productive capacity and output—plant, equipment, and business inventories. The difference between the direct investment abroad of US$3.3 billion and the amount of net capital outflows in the same year of US$4.5 billion represented direct investment by other than West German industrial firms. The 1980 investment of US$3.3 billion brought total direct investment abroad by West German companies since 1952 to almost US$25 billion. The countries most favored in 1980 for investment by West German industrialists were the United States, Belgium/Luxembourg, Switzerland, France, Canada, and Brazil. Only the United States and Britain invested more abroad.

Three main reasons for this outflow of capital were a need to establish production facilities abroad to produce for foreign markets, motivated by a fear that the West German market had reached a point of saturation; the increase to high levels of West German unit labor costs; and fears of trade protectionism that might be overcome by producing in the foreign market. The decline in the value of the deutsche mark may lessen the importance of domestic labor costs to West German firms, but in early 1982 acceleration of their overseas expansion seemed inevitable. The thrust to place production facilities abroad was normal for a company taking on a multinational status after having satisfied the domestic market and having begun international business relations first through exports followed by the establishment of facilities abroad.

In 1980 direct investment in West Germany by foreign companies was US$1 billion, up from US$.7 billion in 1979, bringing the cumulative total since 1952 to US$25 billion. Net direct capital inflows reached US$1.4 billion in 1980, compared to US$1.1 billion in 1979 and US$1.7 billion in 1978, when direct investment by nonindustrial investors was added. Foreign participation was heaviest in the petroleum industry, followed in order by food, beverages, and tobacco, nonelectrical engineering, instruments, optics, chemicals, and rubber. The United States was the major participator, followed by the Common Market countries and Japan. In 1981 foreign investment in West Germany in value was about 75 percent in wholly owned subsidiaries (95 percent or more ownership), 12 percent in majority ownership (50 to 95 percent), and 13 percent in minority ownership (less than 50 percent). The American share of industries was heaviest in computers, automobiles, and petroleum, with minor shares in electrical-optics, toys, food, machinery, and metal products. American participation in German industry began well before World War I and continues to increase.

Generally West Germany has been receptive to foreign investment, considering such investment, especially when made by Americans, to be accompanied by technology and technical know-how beneficial to industry. Although an occasional critic of in-

Federal Republic of Germany

creasing foreign investment in West German industry has voiced opposition, the attitude of the West German government and industry has, on the whole, remained favorable. West Germany joins the United States and Canada as one of only three countries that allow foreign investors access to their capital markets to secure investment financing without discrimination.

* * *

As of early 1982 regrettably few books had been written since the mid–1960s with specific reference to West German industry. Statistical information is, however, abundant and accurate regarding all areas of industry. Among the best are Graham Hallett's *The Social Economy of West Germany*; the relevant chapters in Dudley Dillard's *Economic Development of the North Atlantic Community*, which are especially useful in explaining the development of the major industries; and the relevant chapters in Andrew Shonfield's *Modern Capitalism*. Robert E. Dickinson's *Germany: A General and Regional Geography* remains a major work describing resource base, industrial location, and the foundations of development of major German industries. Annual publications of the Organisation for Economic Co-operation and Development on West Germany give an overall analysis of economic policy and performance with attention to industrial performance. (For further information see Bibliography.)

Chapter 7. Government and Politics

Residence of the president of the Federal Republic

Government and Politics

IN EARLY 1982 the Federal Republic of Germany (West Germany or Federal Republic) continued to be governed as a stable constitutional democracy under a political system that had changed by degrees, but not in its basic principles, in more than three decades. Political stability was the primary goal of the authors of the 1949 constitution, named the Basic Law; the chaotic German history of unstable democracy and dictatorship sandwiched between two world wars was uppermost in the authors' minds. They selected a federal system of government in light of nineteenth-century German traditions and to avoid the kinds of abuses of centralized structures that had taken place under Nazi rule. The Federal Republic was born in 1949, after four years of Allied occupation, upon ratification of the Basic Law and elections that led to the seating of the first session of the Bundestag, the country's popularly elected federal legislative body. Complete sovereignty was attained in 1955 when responsibility for national security was transferred from the Allies to West Germany's newly organized armed forces, the Bundeswehr.

World War II and the years of Allied occupation created other legacies that continued to loom large in the political system during the early 1980s. Occupation forces had deliberately raised the democratic political parties to a privileged position, and the Basic Law, which was framed by leading party officials, institutionalized the supremacy of the parties in the political system. As a result the Federal Republic became a classic example of the "party state," in which all major government policies are formulated within the organizational structure of the political parties. Another legacy of the era stems from the creation of the German Democratic Republic (East Germany) in 1949. The existence of communist East Germany and the historical experience of Nazism came to define the unacceptable limits of political ideology, and together they have created a consensus in West German society for political moderation, or what some observers call "political centrality" or a system of "limited pluralism."

For nearly two decades this consensus, based on postwar economic recovery and the promise of the European Economic Community, was unimpeded. The rise of leftist student politics in the late 1960s—the so-called student movement or "extraparliamentary opposition"—triggered a brief flourishing of popularity for rightist and reactionary political causes and eventually contributed to the major political transition of the country's first thirty years, the ascendancy to power of the Social Democratic Party in 1969. The consensus returned in the early 1970s as the new government pursued détente in its foreign relations and expanded domestic social welfare programs. In the early 1980s increased East-West strain and incipient economic recession that threatened the government's pervasive and expensive system of social welfare again threatened the consensus that had served as the foundation of political stability for over thirty years. In early 1982 there was considerable speculation of a premature fall from power of the nearly eight-year-old government of Chancellor Helmut Schmidt and a return to power of the Christian Democratic Union/Christian Social Union coalition that had ruled from 1949 to 1966.

A major long-term problem for the government was the recession, which although delayed and less severe than in most Western nations, was politically devastating in West Germany because of the expectations created by three decades of ever-increasing prosperity under successful postwar economic recovery. Differences between Social Democratic Party leaders and those of their coalition partners—the Free Democratic Party—over policies to be pursued to counter rising inflation and unemployment were the major source of strain within the governing coalition during the first two years of the 1980s. A major short-run problem for Schmidt at that time was the sudden and dramatic emergence of the so-called peace movement that arose following United States decisions to manufacture a neutron warhead and to deploy a new generation of nuclear weapons in West Germany. This movement, which also sprang up suddenly in Britain, Italy, the Netherlands, Romania, and other European countries, was organized in West Germany by a wide variety of groups, including Protestant clergy, communists, and factions from within Schmidt's own party. Having strong currents of pacifism, neutralism, and German nationalism, it was able to gather unprecedented numbers of West Germans to demonstrate against nuclear weapons.

These demonstrations pointed to longer term difficulties, however, which stemmed from the increasing remoteness of the legacy of World War II and, related to that fact, the growing fragility of the political consensus. A large majority of the participants in the peace movement had been born in the postwar period and raised in the secure environment of economic prosperity and East-West détente; thus they lacked the perspective of older West Germans who generally viewed political consensus as necessary for both economic and political stability and the umbrella of the North Atlantic Treaty Organization as necessary for military security. Most observers agree that this generational factor will continue to play a role in political dynamics in the future.

The events of the early 1980s brought two further factors of political dynamics into focus. The first points to the importance of external events in domestic politics. Heightened East-West tensions caused by the 1979 invasion of Afghanistan by the Soviet Union, the political strife in Poland, and confrontational statements by the newly installed administration of Ronald Reagan in Washington had a profound impact on West German public opinion. Fears of future nuclear confrontation between the two superpowers in a war not of West Germany's making but fought on its soil spawned the peace movement as a nationalistic response to a feeling of being victimized by external events.

The second factor points to the widespread feeling among West German youth that the existing political institutions that had presided over three decades of peace, stability, and prosperity no longer represented their interests or met the needs of modern society. This concern had been expressed by the student movement, and the political system successfully adapted itself to the rise of grass-roots citizens' initiative associations in the 1970s. Additional adaptation will be called for if the society is to extend its history of political stability further into the 1980s.

The Constitutional Framework and Federalism

The constitution, known as the Basic Law (Grundgesetz), was promulgated on May 22, 1949. At the time, it was viewed as a temporary constitutional framework to serve until Germany was reunited. Its final article states that the Basic Law "shall cease to be in force on the day on which a constitution adopted by a free decision of the German people comes into force." The authors of the Basic Law used the Weimar Constitution of 1919 and the post-World War II constitutions of various states (*Länder* ; sing., *Land*) as models. The framers were determined to avoid a weak multiparty democracy such as that of the Weimar Republic and the authoritarian institutions that could lead to a Third Reich-style dictatorship (see table A). Although amended on some thirty occasions during the first thirty-two years of the Federal Republic, the Basic Law functioned successfully as the country's supreme law during a period of stability—the length of which was unprecedented in modern German history—characterized by democratic political institutions.

Articles 1 through 19 enumerate basic rights that apply to all citizens. These include equality before the law; freedom of speech, assembly, the press, and worship; freedom from prejudice based on race, sex, religion, or political opinions; and the right of conscientious objection to military service. Article 18 provides a caveat to these rights, however: "Whoever abuses freedom of expression of opinion, in particular freedom of the press, freedom of teaching, freedom of assembly, freedom of association, the secrecy of mail, posts and telecommunications, property, or the right of asylum in order to attack the free democratic basic order, forfeits these basic rights." Article 18 was used on two occasions during the 1950s to outlaw political parties of the extreme left and of the extreme right.

Article 20 declares that "the Federal Republic of Germany is a democratic and social federal state." The use of the word "social" in this context has commonly been interpreted as making it the responsibility of the state to provide for the basic social welfare of its citizens (see Health and Welfare, ch. 2). Specific social responsibilities of the state are not, however, enumerated in the Basic Law. Article 20 continues: "All state authority emanates from the people. It is exercised by the people by means of elections and voting and by separate legislative, executive and judicial organs."

The majority of the 146 articles of the Basic Law serve to outline the makeup and functions of the various governmental bodies, as well as the careful system of checks and balances that governs their interaction. Other major areas that are addressed by the Basic Law are the distribution of power between the federal government and the various *Land* governments, the administration of federal laws, government finance, and government administration under emergency conditions. Economic matters are largely ignored in the Basic Law, although Article 14 does guarantee "property and the rights of inheritance" while also stating that "expropriation is permitted only in the public weal."

Amendments to the Basic Law require the affirmative vote of two-thirds of the members in the two federal legislative bodies—the Federal Diet (Bundestag) and the Federal Council (Bundesrat). Provisions of the Basic Law pertaining to the essential structures of federalism, as well as those outlining the division of powers, the principles of democracy, state power based on law, social welfare, and inviolable fundamental rights cannot be amended. The most far-ranging changes made to the Basic Law have been the "defense addenda" of 1954–56, which regulated the constitutional position of the armed forces, and the so-called Emergency Constitution of 1968, which outlined wider executive powers in the event of internal or external emergency.

The system of federalism (as opposed to centralism) laid out in the Basic Law follows a tradition dating back to the founding of the Second Reich in 1871. The Federal Republic is a community of German *Länder*, each having its own constitution and governmental structures, that were formed out of the Western zones of occupation after World War II (see The Bonn Democracy, ch. 1). Sovereignty is vested in the federation. The Basic Law divides authority between the federation and the *Länder*, thus constitutionally guaranteeing a mutual dependence and an ongoing important role for the *Land* governments.

The general principle governing relations between the federation and the *Länder* is set forth in Article 30: "The exercise of governmental powers and the discharge of governmental functions shall be incumbent on the *Länder* insofar as this Basic

Federal chancellors, left to right:
Konrad Adenauer (1949–63)
Ludwig Erhard (1963–66)
Kurt Georg Kiesinger (1966–69)
Willy Brandt (1969–74)
Helmut Schmidt (1974–   )
Courtesy German Information Center

Law does not otherwise prescribe." Thus the federation can exercise authority only in those areas prescribed by the Basic Law. Similarly Article 70 states: "The *Länder* have the power to legislate insofar as this Basic Law does not confer legislative powers on the Federation." The Basic Law enumerates a number of areas, including foreign affairs, defense, citizenship, currency, rail and air transport, and postal services, that come under the exclusive legislative jurisdiction of the federation. Areas of concurrent legislation, found especially in areas related to the economy and the ecology, have increasingly required uniform legislation and therefore have also come under the exclusive jurisdiction of federal authorities. By virtue of their omission from the enumerated exclusive or concurrent powers of the federal government, a large number of matters, including education, cultural affairs, church affairs, police, radio and television, and local government are left primarily to the jurisdiction of the *Länder*. The *Länder* also retain considerable powers of taxation.

Another important strength of the *Länder* within the West German system of federalism lies in their administrative authority. Although most legislative responsibility falls on the federal government, the *Länder* are charged with the implementation of federal law; thus *Land* government officials act as agents of the federal government in the execution of federal, as well as *Land*, law. Most federal taxes, to cite an important example, are collected by *Land* officials.

Another means by which the governments of the *Länder* are assured influence within the federation is through the Bundesrat. Members of the Bundesrat are appointed by the *Land* governments as their representatives in the federal legislative process (see The Legislature, this ch.).

Furthermore an amendment to the Basic Law in 1969 established higher education, regional economic development, and agricultural reform as areas of joint responsibility of the federation and the *Länder*. Henceforth the planning, legislation, and financing of these governmental functions required close cooperation between federal and *Land* authorities.

The special status of West Berlin continues to be, as it has been since 1949, a subject of debate in constitutional and international law. The position of the Basic Law as well as the Berlin Constitution of 1950 is that Berlin is a *Land* of the Federal Republic of Germany. This legal status as an integral part of the Federal Republic is overridden, however, by the 1945 reservations of the Allied powers granted in the so-called Original Rights to Britain, France, the United States, and the Soviet Union following World War II. These "Original Rights," which call for the Allied Kommandatura to govern Berlin, continue to take precedence over West German constitutional law. The ambiguous status of West Berlin was confirmed in the Four Power Agreement, which came into force in June 1972. In that agreement the three Western powers confirmed that West Berlin is not a constituent part of the Federal Republic, while the Soviet Union recognized the close ties between West Berlin and the Federal Republic but confirmed the governing rights of the Allied Kommandatura.

Despite an ambiguous political status, West Berlin is integrated into the legal, economic, and financial system of West Germany. Nevertheless federal laws do not automatically apply to West Berlin; its legislative body—the Abgeordnetenhaus (House of Representatives)—must act on each individual piece of federal legislation that contains a "Berlin clause." West Berlin appoints representatives to the Bundestag and the Bundesrat; its twenty-two nonvoting members of the Bundestag are not popularly elected but are delegated by the House of Representatives (see State and Local Government, this ch.).

The Federal Executive

The President

Within the dual executive created by the framers of the Basic Law, the president, as head of state, has powers clearly subordinate to the federal chancellor, who acts as head of government (see fig. 16). The president's functions are almost all formal or ceremonial. He formally proposes to the Bundestag a candidate for the office of chancellor and formally appoints the chancellor's cabinet ministers, though he relies on the choice of the Bundestag for the former and is bound to the choices of the chancellor in the latter task. He represents the Federal Republic in international relations, and thus signs treaties, receives foreign ambassadors, and represents the country abroad. He appoints federal judges, federal civil servants, and military officers, signs all laws, and has the power to grant pardons, but all these actions require the countersignature of the chancellor or the appropriate cabinet minister. Article 81 of the Basic Law grants the president his sole meaningful source of power: he may dissolve the Bundestag under very special circumstances involving a deadlock between it and the executive branch after declaring a "state of legislative emergency." If such a power were invoked (as of early 1982 it had never been used), the chancellor, not the president, would possess the authority to legislate by decree.

The president is elected indirectly by the Federal Convention, a body that consists of all members of the Bundestag and an equal number of delegates from the legislatures of the *Länder*—over 1,000 persons in all. The Federal Convention is convened every five years solely for this purpose; it may reelect a president for a second, but not a third, five-year term of office. A presidential candidate must be at least forty years of age.

The indirect election of the president is designed to provide an incumbent who is widely acceptable and insulated from popular influence; the president's image is one of nonpartisanship that can be harnessed in the reconciliation of conflicting interests among partisan officials. In July 1979 Karl Carstens became the nation's fifth postwar president. The Basic Law does not provide for a vice president. In the president's absence from the country or if the position should become vacant, the president of the Bundesrat acts as the temporary chief of state. If the president should die in office, a successor is to be elected within thirty days.

The Government

The chancellor plus his cabinet ministers are collectively known as the federal government. The chancellor is the head of government and is the major source of power within the executive branch. His power stems from the authority granted to him in the Basic Law, as well as from his leadership over the party or coalition of parties that holds a majority of the seats in the Bundestag. It is this legislative body that elects the chancellor, upon the recommendation of the federal president and by a majority vote, every four years after the seating of newly elected Bundestag members. The chancellor can be dismissed by the Bundestag only through a "constructive vote of no confidence." This procedure, which was designed to protect the chancellor from shifting and unstable legislative alignments such as those that brought down many chancellors during the Weimar period, demands that the opposition in the Bundestag must have a majority vote both against a chancellor and in favor of a successor in order to remove the head of government. As of early 1982 this procedure had been attempted only once. In April 1972 the opposition Christian Democrats filed a no-confidence vote against Chancellor Willy Brandt and nominated their legislative leader as chancellor. The motion failed, however, as two abstentions led to its being one vote shy of the necessary majority.

The chancellor controls the composition of the cabinet. Although ministers are given considerable freedom of action, the chancellor is responsible for laying the overall guidelines of government policy and is solely responsible to the Bundestag for that policy. Cabinet ministers cannot be censured in the legislature.

The chancellor exercises considerable control over the federal bureaucracy, the distribution of public funds, and the implementation of legislation. He ordinarily needs the approval of the legislature for policy proposals and budgetary requests, but he may legally withhold information from the legislature, ignore its wishes, and veto budgetary appropriations that exceed his requests. In time of war the chancellor assumes supreme command over the armed forces from the minister of defense.

Government and Politics

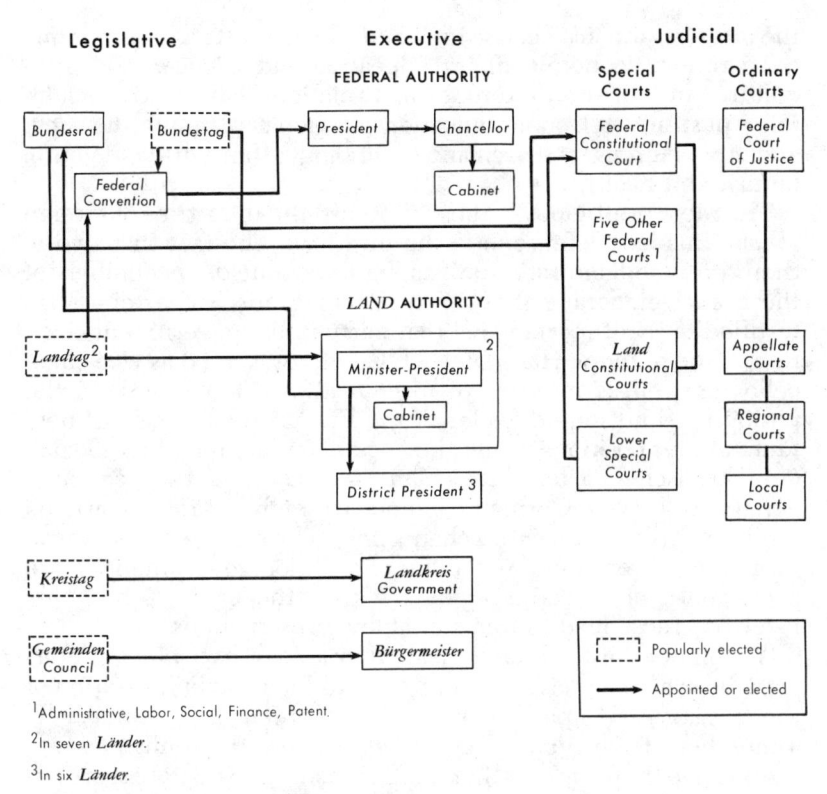

Figure 16. *System of Government, 1981*

[Diagram showing:

Legislative — Bundesrat, Bundestag (popularly elected), Federal Convention, Landtag[2] (popularly elected), Kreistag (popularly elected), Gemeinden Council (popularly elected)

Executive — FEDERAL AUTHORITY: President, Chancellor, Cabinet

Executive — LAND AUTHORITY: Minister-President, Cabinet, District President[3]

Landkreis Government, Bürgermeister

Judicial — Special Courts: Federal Constitutional Court, Five Other Federal Courts[1], Land Constitutional Courts, Lower Special Courts

Judicial — Ordinary Courts: Federal Court of Justice, Appellate Courts, Regional Courts, Local Courts

Legend: dashed box = Popularly elected; arrow = Appointed or elected]

[1] Administrative, Labor, Social, Finance, Patent.
[2] In seven *Länder*.
[3] In six *Länder*.

The majority of the chancellor's staff is found in the Federal Chancellor's Office, which in the late 1970s consisted of about 400 persons headed by a cabinet minister without portfolio. The office's major task is to keep the chancellor informed on current political questions and the workings of the ministries. Its staff prepares cabinet meetings, coordinates the work of the various ministries as well as the intelligence services, and supervises the implementation of the chancellor's policy guidelines. The Federal Chancellor's Office is divided into six departments: law and administration; foreign and inter-German relations and external security; internal affairs; economics, finance, and social policy; planning; and intelligence services.

The number of cabinet ministers is left to the discretion of the chancellor. There have been as many as twenty-two in the Ludwig Erhard government of the mid–1960s and as few as fifteen during the first government of Chancellor Schmidt. In 1980 Schmidt expanded the cabinet by one member. In early 1982 his cabinet consisted of ministers of defense; finance; foreign affairs;

the interior; and justice; also included were ministers for economic cooperation; economic affairs; education and science; food, agriculture, and forestry; inter-German relations; labor and social affairs; post and telecommunications; regional planning, housing, and city planning; research and technology; transport; and youth, family, and health.

The most prestigious of these posts are the ministries of foreign affairs, finance, defense, and the interior. The fact that two of these posts in Schmidt's 1982 cabinet were held by members of the Free Democratic Party (Freie Demokratische Partei—FDP) testified to the importance of that party in the government coalition. One of them, Hans-Dietrich Genscher, served as vice chancellor as well as minister of foreign affairs and thus held the position of undisputed leader of the FDP. In all, the FDP held four cabinet positions, while the Social Democratic Party (Sozialdemokratische Partei Deutschlands—SPD) held twelve. As a general rule West German cabinets are highly stable; nearly all ministers rise and fall with a chancellor. The relative autonomy of cabinet ministers and the realities of coalition government create occasional public disagreements within the cabinet, but only rarely do these lead to ministerial-level resignations.

A cabinet minister's staff is headed by at least two state secretaries, who are career civil servants responsible for administration of the ministry, and a parliamentary state secretary, who is normally a member of the Bundestag and who acts as the ministry's representative there and in other political bodies. The state secretaries normally will serve beyond the tenure of a particular government, whereas the parliamentary state secretary (a political appointee) is considered a junior member of the federal government team whose service ends with that of the minister. Below these officials the ministries are organized functionally to handle specific aspects of federal administrative responsibilities. The ministries tend to be small, because the majority of federal law is administered by *Land* governments, and are staffed almost exclusively by career civil servants (see The Bureaucracy, this ch.)

The Legislature

The federal legislature consists of two chambers, the Bundestag (sometimes called the lower house) and the Bundesrat (sometimes called the upper house). Either chamber may initiate legislation, and most bills must pass through each chamber, as well as the executive branch, in order to become law. Legislation on matters within the exclusive jurisdiction of the federal organs, such as international treaties, does not require the approval of the Bundesrat. In practice the majority of legislation is initiated by the federal government, either the chancellor or one of his ministers. In that case, the bill is first reviewed by the Bundesrat, then passed to the Bundestag. A bill initiated in the Bundesrat is routed to the

Bundestag through the executive branch. A bill initiated in the Bundestag is passed to the Bundesrat (where it may be vetoed) and then passed to the executive. Differences over legislation between the legislative chambers are resolved in a Joint Conference Committee. After a compromise bill has been passed by a majority of both chambers and approved by the cabinet, it is signed into law by the federal president and countersigned by the appropriate cabinet minister.

Bundestag

The Bundestag is the only popularly elected organ at the federal level of government and is by far the more important of the two legislative chambers. It is elected every four years (or more often if a government falls from power); candidates must be at least twenty-one years of age, and there is no restriction on reelection. The size of the Bundestag has gradually increased: the first in 1949 contained 402 deputies, the ninth Bundestag was installed in 1980 with 497 deputies. An additional twenty-two deputies from West Berlin were appointed by West Berlin's own legislative body.

In addition to enacting legislation and acting as the direct representatives of the people, the Bundestag plays an important role in electing the federal chancellor and acting in an important watchdog role over the chancellor and his cabinet. This check on the power of the federal executive can, short of the "constructive vote of no confidence" in the federal government, take the form of binding legislation, publicly aired debates on policy, investigations, and direct questioning of the chancellor and cabinet officials. The Bundestag has the right to summon members of the federal government to appear before the whole chamber or its committees, though it cannot compel them to disclose information. Members of the executive, in turn, often attend plenary or committee sessions to present their views.

Party discipline within the Bundestag is strong—some 90 percent of the votes have followed the dictates of political party leadership. This results from the key role of the *Fraktionen* (sing., *Fraktion*), or parliamentary groups, which are formed by each political party represented in the Bundestag. Throughout the 1970s the Bundestag contained three *Fraktionen*, as the Christian Democratic Union (Christlich Demokratische Union— CDU) and the Christian Social Union (Christlich Soziale Union— CSU) pooled their legislative resources (see Political Parties and the Electoral System, this ch.). The size of a party's *Fraktion* determines the strength of its representation on committees, the number of committee chairmen it can name, and its representation on executive bodies of the Bundestag. The leader of the largest *Fraktion* is named president of the Bundestag. Except for the years 1972–76, the CDU/CSU held down this position; Helmut Kohl became president of the Bundestag in 1980; Herbert

Federal Republic of Germany

Wehner acted as chairman of the SPD *Fraktion* between 1969 and early 1982 (see fig. 17).

Executive bodies within the Bundestag include the Council of Elders and the Presidium. The Presidium, consisting of the president and vice presidents (one from each *Fraktion*), is responsible for administrative matters within the Bundestag, such as the recruitment of clerical and research personnel. The Council of Elders acts as a steering committee, setting the daily agenda of the Bundestag and distributing committee chairmanships according to party representation. The Council of Elders consists of the president, the vice presidents, and twelve to fifteen representatives —the oldest, hence the name—distributed according to the strength of each *Fraktion*.

Most of the legislative work is accomplished within the standing committees. The number of committees has varied over the years to approximate the number of cabinet positions, the titles of which correspond roughly with those of the committees. Between 1972 and 1980 there were nineteen standing committees within the Bundestag. Each contained a chairman and twenty-four to thirty-six other members, depending on the importance and work load of the committee. Committee chairmanships, as well as the membership of each committee, are determined by relative party strengths in the Bundestag. Standing committees have only small ancillary staffs or, in some cases no staff at all.

Bundesrat

The Bundesrat is more than simply a second legislative chamber. It is the federal organ in which the *Land* governments are directly represented and thus a key to the West German federalist system of government. The Bundesrat is not popularly elected, but its members—usually ministers within the *Land* governments—are appointed by their respective *Land* governments. The composition of the Bundesrat changes with each *Land* election, ten times every four years.

The Bundesrat is composed of forty-one voting members, representing the ten *Länder*, plus four nonvoting members representing West Berlin. The least populous *Länder* (Saarland, Hamburg, and Bremen) each have three representatives; those with 2–6 million inhabitants (Schleswig-Holstein, Rhineland-Palatinate, and Hesse) have four each; and the largest *Länder* (North Rhine-Westphalia, Lower Saxony, Bavaria, and Baden-Württemberg) have five representatives each (see fig. 1). Although designed to provide representation according to *Land* population, this system actually gives a greater representation, per inhabitant, to the smaller *Länder*. The presidency of the Bundesrat is rotated yearly among each *Land*. Each *Land* delegation is required, by law, to vote as a bloc according to the instructions from its government.

Government and Politics

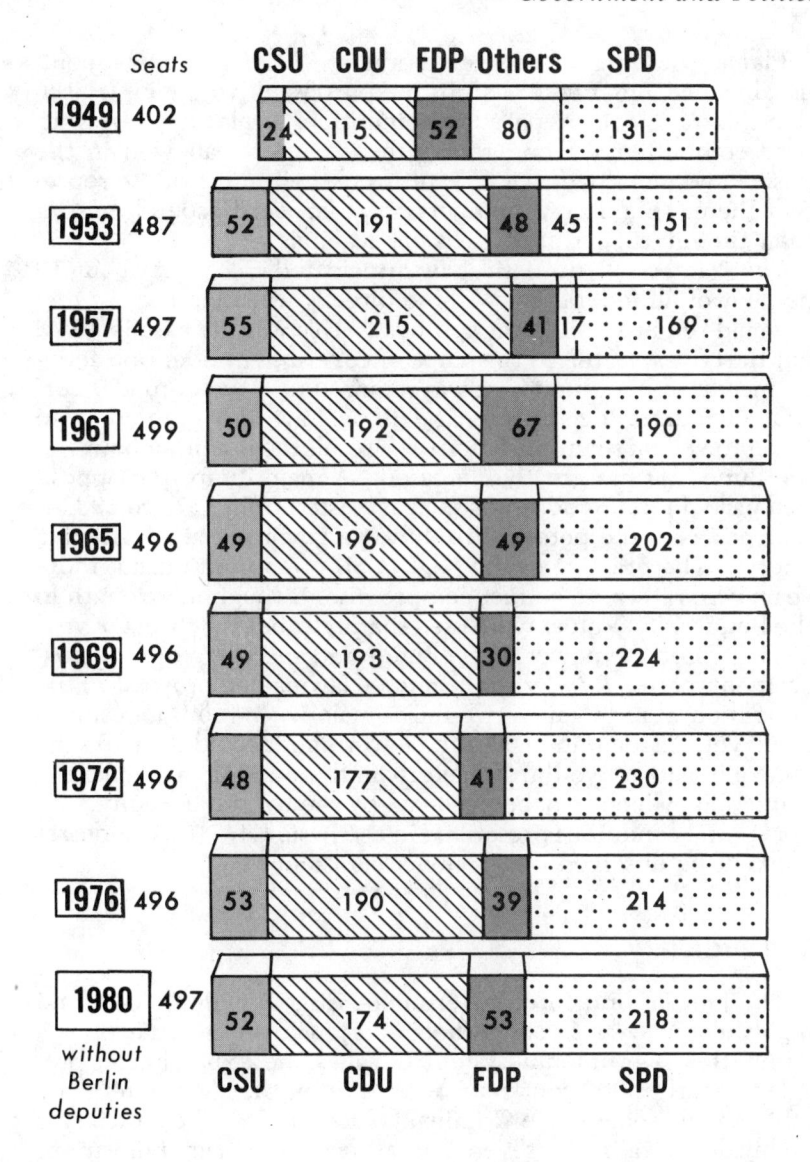

Seats	CSU	CDU	FDP	Others	SPD
1949 402	24	115	52	80	131
1953 487	52	191	48	45	151
1957 497	55	215	41	17	169
1961 499	50	192	67		190
1965 496	49	196	49		202
1969 496	49	193	30		224
1972 496	48	177	41		230
1976 496	53	190	39		214
1980 497	52	174	53		218

without Berlin deputies

CSU — Christian Social Union
CDU — Christian Democratic Union
FDP — Free Democratic Party
SPD — Social Democratic Party

Source: Based on information from *Bulletin* [Bonn], December 12, 1980, p. 11.
Figure 17. Composition of Bundestag by Party, 1949–80

Federal Republic of Germany

Plenary sessions of the Bundesrat are brief and infrequent, usually once a month, called for the purpose of voting on legislation that has been prepared in committee. Delegates rarely attend committee sessions; rather they often—as allowed in the Basic Law—deputize civil servants from their ministries to represent them. Bundesrat members, in other words, spend most of their time in their respective *Land* capitals.

The framers of the Basic Law anticipated that only about 10 percent of all federal laws—those directly affecting the *Länder*—would require Bundesrat approval. This was the case in 1949; but thirty years later, as the scope of government domestic activity increased, the Bundesrat was required to act on some 60 percent of federal legislation. The Basic Law also granted it an absolute veto of such legislation. As a result the potential power of the Bundesrat has greatly increased. A majority for the opposition party in the Bundesrat—such as existed from 1972 to 1982—thus possesses the potential to thwart a government's legislative efforts. The practice of the CDU/CSU opposition during those years was, rather, to extract compromises through its strength in the Bundesrat. Vetoes were used sparingly, but the threat of veto has increased the power of the Bundesrat, and therefore the governments of the *Länder*, in the federal lawmaking process. If the opposition were to gain a two-thirds majority in the Bundesrat, it could veto all legislation, and the government could override the veto only with a two-thirds majority in the Bundestag. Unlike the Bundestag, which may be dissolved by the federal executive under special conditions prescribed in the Basic Law, the Bundesrat may not be dissolved under any circumstances.

The Judiciary

The judicial branch of government is independent, vast, and highly complex, reflecting the importance of the rule of law within the governmental system. In all, some 15,000 judges preside in nearly 1,000 courts of law. As a result the legal system was efficient and speedy (see Criminal Justice, ch. 9). The judiciary is highly decentralized: seven federal courts are located in various cities; the remainder of the courts fall under the administrative responsibility of the *Land* governments.

The judiciary consists of three kinds of courts: ordinary courts, which make up the vast majority of the system, deal with criminal law and most civil cases; specialized courts hear special cases in administrative, labor, social, fiscal, and patent areas; and constitutional courts perform judicial review and constitutional interpretation. The Federal Constitutional Court is the highest court in the land and, over the years, has played an important political role in its interpretations of the Basic Law.

The ordinary courts are organized on four levels. In the late 1970s there were some 600 local courts (*Amtsgerichte*) located in small- and medium-sized towns throughout the country. Most are staffed by a single judge who is assisted by lay judges in criminal cases, but many local courts have two or more professional judges. These courts have jurisdiction over minor civil matters, petty criminal offenses, and related issues. Above the local courts within the system of ordinary courts are regional courts (*Landesgerichte*). The nearly 100 of these courts—each consisting of separate chambers of three to five judges for civil, criminal, and special types of cases—are located in the major towns and cities. Regional courts hold original jurisdiction in most major civil and criminal matters and serve as courts of appeals from decisions of the local courts.

At the next level there are some twenty appellate courts (*Oberlandesgerichte*). Although primarily functioning as courts of appeals, reexamining both facts and procedural matters, they also hold original jurisdiction in cases involving treason and anticonstitutional activity. Appellate courts act as the final appeal for cases originating in the local courts and the second appeal for those originating in the regional courts. Like the regional courts, appellate courts are divided into various chambers, consisting of three to five judges each, specializing in certain types of cases. At the apex of the system of ordinary courts is the Federal Court of Justice (Bundesgerichtshof), located in Karlsruhe. The only federal court among the ordinary courts, the Federal Court of Justice acts as the final court of appeals in all cases that originate above the regional and appellate courts. It holds no original jurisdiction. The Federal Court of Justice contains about 100 judges, divided into some twenty chambers of five judges each.

There are five kinds of specialized courts. Like the ordinary courts, these operate at various levels, and only the highest level of each kind of court falls under the authority of the federal government. Administrative courts exist on three levels: local administrative courts, higher administrative courts, and the Federal Administrative Court in West Berlin. The latter two serve appellate functions similar to those in the system of ordinary courts. Administrative courts allow individuals to seek redress from the government for harm caused by improper administrative actions by officials. Thus they act as a check on the government bureaucracy and as the guardian of administrative procedures.

Labor courts also operate on three levels. Labor and management have equal representation on these tribunals, which deal with disputes arising out of collective bargaining agreements, working conditions, and the like. Social courts, also on three levels, adjudicate matters relating to the system of social insurance, that is, disputes arising from unemployment compensation, workers' compensation, social security payments, and similar matters. Finance courts, because of a smaller case load, are found at only

Federal Republic of Germany

two levels, and deal with tax-related disputes. Finally, a single Federal Patents Court in Munich rules on cases involving industrial property rights.

The final type of court within the judiciary is the constitutional court. There are a total of ten constitutional courts, nine of which are associated with *Land* governments. The Federal Constitutional Court is West Germany's highest court as well as its most important, both because of its judicial authority and its political role. Unlike the other courts, which are administratively tied to the ministries of justice within the federal or the *Land* governments, the constitutional courts are administratively independent and financially autonomous from any other government body. Their ability to draw up their own budgets and hire and fire employees, for example, gives these courts administrative autonomy unique within the government structure. Judges of the Federal Constitutional Court can only be removed upon a motion from the Court itself.

The Federal Constitutional Court consists of sixteen judges who are chosen for twelve-year, nonrenewable terms. Half the judges are selected in the Bundesrat, half in the Bundestag. Thus partisan politics are brought into play, but the need for a two-thirds majority in each case presents the need for compromise of partisan interests in the selection. The Court is divided into two chambers, called senates, of eight judges each. The first deals with cases involving the basic rights covered in Articles 1 through 19 of the Basic Law; the second is responsible for disputes between different levels of government and a variety of other matters.

Any law may be reviewed by the Federal Constitutional Court to determine whether it complies with the Basic Law. The opposition in the Bundestag, when it lacks the legislative means to challenge a government policy, can use the Federal Constitutional Court to challenge it on the grounds of constitutional legality. Thus the SPD attempted to have Chancellor Konrad Adenauer's rearmament policy declared unconstitutional in the early 1950s, and the CSU attempted in 1973 to challenge the Basic Treaty with East Germany on the basis of constitutionality. Both of these efforts failed, but a successful 1975 challenge to the government's abortion reform law in the Federal Constitutional Court was a major victory for the CDU/CSU opposition in the Bundestag. Another overtly political role of the Federal Constitutional Court lies in its rulings on the application of Article 21 of the Basic Law, which allows the banning of extremist political parties. In this role the Court banned a neo-Nazi party in 1952 and a communist party in 1956.

The constitutional courts of the *Länder* are found in each *Land*, with the exception of Schleswig-Holstein. These courts operate, at the *Land* level, in a function that parallels that of the Federal Constitutional Court.

The Bureaucracy

In the early 1980s between 3.5 and 4 million persons, or about 15 percent of the working population, were employed by federal, state, or local government authorities. This figure is exclusive of the nearly 500,000 serving in the armed forces. In addition to the some 1.3 million persons who staff the executive administration of the various government authorities, these figures include, for example, over 800,000 railway and postal workers, some 700,000 public school and university personnel, over 400,000 persons employed in public utilities, and nearly 200,000 policemen. The wide scope of the concept of public service is rooted in a German tradition that places considerable social status on the public servant and has developed a rigid hierarchical system within the bureaucracy to define that status.

Public servants are categorized as either officials (*Beamten*, about 40 percent of the total), employees (*Angestellten*, some 35 percent of the total), or workers (*Arbeiter*, 25 percent). *Beamten*, who are career civil servants possessing special privileges as well as special obligations beyond those of other public servants, are further pegged into one of four "career groups": higher service, executive service, clerical service, and basic service. Only rarely does a public servant jump from one category to another in the course of his or her career.

This rigid hierarchical bureaucratic structure has increasingly been criticized as being ill-suited to the flexible needs of the administration of the modern state; moreover, because of the arbitrary nature of the system of classification, "employees" often perform the same work as "officials." Uniquely, *Beamten* are appointed for life and thus permanently protected from unemployment. Among their other privileges is a noncontributory pension system that has the effect of significantly increasing their salaries compared to public servants in other categories. Only the "official" is charged with the exercise of state authority, and in that capacity he is obliged to obey the orders of his superior, is denied the right to strike, is bound to defend the democratic constitutional order, and is legally responsible for the application of administrative law. Because of these constraints the West German civil servant has often been cited as being a particularly conservative individual because of both the privileges and the legal constraints imposed on the position (see The Elite, ch. 3).

A 1972 executive decree issued by the federal government and the ten minister-presidents of the *Länder* institutionalized the prohibition against antidemocratic extremists being employed in the public service. Under this highly controversial law, known as the *Radikalenerlass* or *Berufsverbot*, all candidates for positions as "officials" are screened, and those already employed may be scrutinized as deemed necessary. These principles are also applied to other public servants "in accordance with the contracts regulating each case." During the first decade of this law's enforcement, well over 1 million persons were thus investigated, and between 1,000 and 4,000 individuals were denied employment or were fired because of their association with radical political groups.

Public servants are not prevented from running for public office. In fact, because of liberal laws that allowed a public official to double or triple his salary while serving in the legislature and return to his former job at the end of his legislative term, over 40 percent of the deputies to *Land* and federal legislatures in the mid–1970s were public servants. Teachers made up the largest component of this group. Laws were subsequently modified, and this figure could be expected to decline somewhat.

Contributing further to the politicization of the bureaucracy is a system of patronage whereby party loyalties are rewarded with appointments to high civil service posts. During the two decades of CDU predominance in the federal government, the upper reaches of the civil service were permeated with CDU/CSU appointees. Since 1969 extensive personnel changes have brought SPD and FDP loyalists in their place.

State and Local Government

Each of the *Land* governments is structured after its own constitutional framework that, by law, must conform to the "principles of republican, democratic, and social government." Except for this one restriction, the ten *Länder* are free to form any type of government structure they deem appropriate. Seven of the *Länder*, in fact, are governed by a cabinet led by a minister-president and have a unicameral legislative body known as a *Landtag*. Bavaria alone has a bicameral legislature. The relationship between the legislature and the executive duplicates the system at the federal level: the legislatures are popularly elected, normally for a four-year term of office, and the minister-president, together with his cabinet, is elected by a majority vote among legislators. The executive branch in the city-state *Länder* —Bremen and Hamburg—consists of a popularly elected senate, the members of which perform functions parallel to those of the ministers in the larger *Länder*. The senate chooses a *Bürgermeister* (mayor) in Hamburg and West Berlin and a senate president in Bremen to act as chief executive. *Land* cabinets contain from eight to ten members; all have ministries of the interior, finance, economy, transport, labor, social security, and education; and each *Land* has additional cabinet positions for its specific needs. For example Rhineland-Palatinate has a minister of wines. The most important cabinet post is the minister of the interior. He is head of the general internal administration of the *Land* and, of critical importance, is in command of the police.

Land governments hold considerable importance, both in a governing capacity under the federal system and in a political

Government and Politics

sense, inasmuch as *Land* politics often have a significant impact on federal political matters. Victories in *Landtag* elections (the ten are scattered throughout the four-year cycle) for parties in opposition in Bonn can erode the strength of the federal government coalition (see table 23, Appendix). The fall of both Adenauer and Brandt from the chancellorship was preceded by a series of opposition victories in *Land* elections. *Land* elections are viewed as polls on the popularity of the Bonn government, and their outcomes also affect the composition of the Bundesrat. In late 1981 the opposition CDU/CSU held twenty-six seats in the Bundesrat, only one vote short of a two-thirds majority that it could use to block any government legislation. This fact reflected the relative success of the CDU/CSU in recent *Land* elections, and this in turn portended badly for the governing SPD/FDP coalition in Bonn.

Three lower levels of government are under the administrative authority of the *Länder*. The six largest *Länder* contain a number of district government structures. Districts decentralize *Land* administration, and each is headed by a district president who is appointed by the minister-president of the *Land* and who operates under the supervision of the *Land* minister of the interior. The district president acts as a representative of *Land* authority.

Each *Land* is divided into *Kreis* (county; pl., *Kreise*) governments. In some 115 cities having populations over 80,000, the *Stadtkreis* acts as the local governing authority. In other areas the *Landkreis* is further divided into *Gemeinden*, or municipal government authorities. The principal government organs in the *Kreis* are an elected council (*Kreistag*) and an executive, variously known as a *Landrat, Kreisrat,* or *Oberkreisdirektor,* who is chosen by the council and whose functions are similar to a county manager who supervises local government administration. The *Landkreise* lack the universal competence of the municipalities, but they do act as the primary administrative authorities in such areas as highways, hospitals, and public utilities.

Gemeinden also contain elected councils, which in turn select an executive, a *Bürgermeister*. In Hamburg and Bremen the mayor is the chief *Land* official as well. In those cases, as well as in West Berlin, the mayor is chosen by the elected legislative body. In some smaller municipalities the mayor is popularly elected. Local governments are autonomous in the provision of such services as fire protection and at the same time carry on social welfare, housing, and other services on behalf of the *Land* government. In order to increase administrative efficiency, the *Gemeinden* have been consolidated, and thus their total number has been drastically reduced, from some 25,000 in the late 1960s to fewer than 9,000 in the mid–1970s.

Federal Republic of Germany

Political Parties and the Electoral System

The stability of the democratic form of government has often been attributed to the pervasiveness of the political parties as stabilizing institutions. "All political decisions in the Federal Republic are made by the parties and their representatives. There are no political decisions of importance in the German democracy which have not been brought to the parties, prepared by them and finally taken by them." This observation by German political scientist Kurt Sontheimer has led him and others to label the country a "party state."

Although most constitutions do not discuss political parties in detail, the framers of the Basic Law envisioned an important role for the parties. Article 21 states that "the political parties shall take part in forming the political will of the people. They must be freely established. Their internal organization must conform to democratic principles. They must publicly account for the sources of their funds." The 1967 Law on Parties further detailed the organization of the parties, the rights of membership, and such procedures as the nomination of candidates for office.

Article 21 also places legal constraints on the ideological orientation of the political parties: "Parties which, by reason of their aims or the behavior of their adherents, seek to impair or destroy the free democratic basic order or to endanger the existence of the Federal Republic of Germany are unconstitutional." Under this provision the neo-Nazi Socialist Reich Party (Sozialistische Reichspartei—SRP) was banned in 1952, and the Communist Party of Germany (Kommunistische Partei Deutschlands—KPD) was banned in 1956. This prerogative of the Federal Constitutional Court was not invoked during the subsequent twenty-five years, however, despite the existence of parties of both the extreme left and right; the electoral process became legitimized and effective in defining limits to the political importance of extremist parties.

The need to regulate the organization and activities of the political parties grew out of the Weimar experience, when a weak multiparty system was abused by antidemocratic parties that were able to hamper seriously the operation of the government (see Weimar Republic, 1918–33, ch. 1). A large number of parties emerged in the aftermath of World War II, but electoral laws that made it difficult for small parties to survive in the federal political arena whittled away at the number of parties (see Minor Parties, this ch.). Between 1961 and early 1982 only four parties were represented in the popularly elected Bundestag: the CDU, the CSU, the SPD, and the FDP. Of these, the CDU and CSU acted as one unit in the Bundestag, and the FDP held minor electoral appeal. The importance of the FDP lay in the fact that the major parties rarely held a majority of Bundestag seats by themselves, and therefore the FDP was able to act as a coalition partner of either the CDU/CSU or the SPD in order to obtain the majority necessary to pass legislation in the Bundestag. This has led to what numerous observers call a "two and one-half party system" in West Germany. Electoral strength outside these four parties in Bundestag elections declined from 28 percent of the vote in 1949 to 2 percent in 1980 (see table 24, Appendix).

The four major parties have gradually incorporated the various specialized interests that had previously been represented in small parties. As a result the major parties became factionalized as they became mass based. Although political party membership grew substantially in the 1970s, it remained a small percentage (about 4 percent) of the total number of voters. Voter turnout is traditionally high, around 90 percent, but active participation in party politics is limited to a small minority of the respective party memberships. Parties are financed through membership dues, corporate and interest association gifts, and, since 1959, public funds. Each party that gains at least 0.5 percent of the national vote receives from the federal treasury the equivalent of about US$1.75 for every vote secured in a Bundestag election. A similar system of public subsidy for political parties exists at the *Land* level.

Christian Democratic Union/Christian Social Union

From 1949 until 1966 the CDU/CSU dominated political life. In 1969, after three years of a coalition with the SPD, the Christian Democrats assumed the position of the opposition political party in the Bundestag (see The Grand Coalition, 1966–69, ch. 1). In early 1982 they retained this position; although their 226-member *Fraktion*, which included the CSU, was the largest single parliamentary group, the governing SPD-FDP coalition held 271 seats. At that time the CDU/CSU was stronger in *Land*-level politics; this was apparent in its holding twenty-six of forty-one seats in the Bundesrat and its holding a plurality of seats in six of the ten *Land* legislatures and in West Berlin, thus acting as the governing party in the majority of the *Länder*. The CSU operated only in Bavaria, whereas the CDU operated in every other *Land* and in West Berlin. Although they acted as one party in the Bundestag, their organizations were entirely separate below the federal level.

The CDU was founded in the wake of World War II by a disparate group of center-left and center-right politicians who, together with Catholic and Protestant laymen, sought a Christian approach to politics and the vital social issues of the day. Early concerns with Christian socialist ideals gave way to the need to differentiate the CDU from the then openly socialist SPD and to the strength of the party's early, free market-oriented leaders, Adenauer and Erhard. Over the years, however, the CDU has avoided an identification with any specific ideology or policy orientation other than

Federal Republic of Germany

an anticommunist foreign policy and a largely capitalist domestic economic policy. As a party in opposition during the 1970s, the CDU has thus sought to accommodate itself, to some extent, to the broadly popular SPD programs of détente with the Soviet bloc and social welfare programs in order to retain the mass appeal that was founded on the electoral strength of Adenauer. Differences of opinions on how to deal with the successes of the SPD, however, led to a rift within the CDU leadership that persisted into the early 1980s. Kohl, party chairman since 1973, continued to be a proponent of a strong North Atlantic Treaty Organization (NATO—also referred to as the Atlantic Alliance) as the key deterrent to the expansionism of the Soviet Union, for example, while others, such as the CDU General Secretary Heine Geissler and the leaders of the party's youth wing, sought a more dynamic approach to foreign policy in response to the rapid rise of the peace movement and the concurrent decline in SPD popularity in the early 1980s. Despite its having distinct right and left wings, the CDU remained the major alternative to the right of the SPD in the political spectrum.

The CDU has traditionally had a decentralized organizational structure, with *Land*-level functionaries assuming the preponderance of party responsibilities over those at the federal level. This reflected the organizational preferences of CDU founders, who chose to name their organization a "union" rather than a "party" to exhibit their distaste for bureaucratic centralization. The transition to the role of opposition party after 1969, however, brought a new emphasis on central party officials, symbolized by its new federal headquarters in the Konrad Adenauer House in Bonn. The annual party congress of some 800 delegates—chosen by party officials at the *Land* level—is nominally the highest authority in the party structure, although an executive committee of some sixty persons acts as the highest body of the CDU between congresses. The executive committee is headed by the party chairman, who is elected for a two-year term, and also contains several deputy chairmen, a general secretary, and a treasurer. Other executive committee members include the party's chief legislative representatives, the leaders of the *Land* party organizations, and the heads of various auxiliary organizations.

CDU organization remains tightly woven at the *Land* level, where the party enjoyed relative electoral success during the 1970s. In each *Land*, with the exception of Bavaria, biannual party congresses are held, and an executive committee is elected. These bodies play the major role in the selection of party candidates for Bundestag elections, and their members comprise a large number of the candidates. It is at the *Land* level that the major recruitment for federal officeholders take place. The larger *Land* organizations are divided into district organizations; all *Land* organizations are divided into local organizations. Grass-

Bundestag building, Bonn
Courtesy German Information Center

Bundestag in session
Courtesy German Information Center

Federal Republic of Germany

roots party work, such as the recruitment of members, publicity campaigns, and fund raising, takes place at the district and local levels.

The CDU incorporates a number of auxiliary organizations whose role is to strengthen the party's appeal within specific socioeconomic groups and to represent their interests within the party. CDU statutes specify seven such organizations, representing youth, women, workers, business and industry, the middle class, municipal politics, and refugees. Other organizations, representing Protestants and students, exist, but they lack the official status of party auxiliary organizations. The most powerful has always been the organization representing business and industry, although in the early 1980s considerable prominence was given the youth organization in an attempt to garner the sizable uncommitted youth vote. The auxiliary organizations are legally autonomous from the CDU, having their own statutes, leadership, and membership roles. In the late 1970s, nevertheless, some 70 percent of their members were also members of the CDU.

In the decade of the 1970s, CDU membership grew dramatically. As the party of opposition, a concerted recruitment drive aimed at broadening its mass appeal increased membership rolls from some 300,000 in 1969 to about 676,000 in 1979. Although recruitment aimed at lessening the historically strong imbalances in the character of the membership, the CDU membership remained biased toward male, rural, Catholic, middle-class, and older voters. In terms of regional strength, the CDU has remained strongest in the southern, rural *Länder* of Baden-Württemberg and Rhineland-Palatinate, while it is weakest in the urban *Länder* of Bremen and Hamburg.

It is the large, southeastern *Land* of Bavaria, however, that has the largest concentration of traditionally conservative, rural, Catholic voters. Here the CDU yields to its Bundestag affiliate, the CSU, which has dominated Bavarian politics since 1957. The two parties form a single *Fraktion* in the legislature, agree on a common candidate for chancellor, and agree not to encroach on the other's territory; otherwise they are completely autonomous political organizations. In the early 1980s the CSU continued to be led by Franz-Josef Strauss, who had first been elected party chairman in 1961.

During the 1970s the CDU/CSU alliance came under some difficulty as a result of differences between the staunchly conservative Strauss and the moderate CDU party chairman Kohl. Following the 1976 CDU/CSU defeat with Kohl as chancellor candidate, Strauss, who contended that the party should pursue a more confrontational stance vis-à-vis the governing coalition in an appeal to conservative voters, announced that the CSU would form a separate Bundestag *Fraktion*. Kohl, in turn, threatened to run CDU candidates against the CSU in Bavaria; but after three weeks of crisis, the two parties were able to resolve their differences. Strauss was given his chance to run as the CDU/CSU chancellor candidate in 1980. The wide margin of the CDU/CSU defeat in that election was a serious blow to the party and particularly to the prestige of Strauss.

Although the flamboyant figure of Strauss has brought the CSU to prominence on the federal level, the party's real source of strength lay in its domination of politics in Bavaria, where it won an absolute majority in every *Land* election between 1957 and 1980. In the 1978 elections the CSU won 129 out of 204 seats in the Bavarian *Landtag*. CSU membership also grew rapidly during the 1970s, from some 70,000 in 1969 to 166,000 in 1979.

Social Democratic Party

The SPD is the oldest political party in West Germany. As of early 1982 it was the largest in terms of membership, and had participated in the governing coalition since 1966. Its chairman, Brandt, had served as chancellor between 1969 and 1974, at which time the SPD deputy chairman, Schmidt, assumed the top federal position, which he retained in early 1982. Because the CDU/CSU consistently outpolled the SPD, the latter had ruled since 1969 through its coalition with the FDP. A gradual decline between 1976 and 1981 in the electoral appeal of the SPD, especially in local and *Land* elections, proved to be a serious threat to the enviable post–1966 SPD record, however. In early 1982 some analysts doubted whether the governing coalition, plagued by dissension from FDP members on the right as well as from the left wing of the SPD, would be able to survive until the scheduled 1984 Bundestag elections.

The SPD was founded in 1875, was suppressed between 1878 and 1890 under the rule of Otto von Bismarck, and participated in government during the Weimar Republic until it was again suppressed, this time by Hitler, in 1933. The SPD retained an organization in exile during the Nazi period, and as the only Weimar-era party to reemerge after World War II, the SPD was expected to be the dominant political party in the nascent Federal Republic. Despite its 1949 membership of nearly 1 million, the SPD was eclipsed by the enormous popularity of Adenauer. The SPD vote declined further in 1953 and 1957.

This string of defeats led the SPD to rethink such basic tenets of its postwar program as socialist economic principles and opposition to the government's Western-oriented defense policies. In an attempt to cast aside its doctrinaire working-class orientation and appeal to a wider range of voters, the SPD announced a remarkable turnabout in its political platform at its 1959 party conference in Bad Godesberg. Calls for the nationalization of the means of production and centralized economic planning were replaced with an acceptance of the established regulated free

Federal Republic of Germany

market economic system, and pro-Western foreign and defense policies were adopted as a fait accompli. Three of the architects of the Bad Godesberg Program—Wehner, Brandt, and Schmidt—continued to lead the SPD within the program's basic guidelines twenty-three years later.

The party adopted modern publicity techniques during its electoral campaigns of the early 1960s and by 1966 had been successful enough to earn a governing role with the CDU/CSU in the Grand Coalition. Further gains in the 1969 Bundestag elections allowed the SPD to govern as chief partner in a coalition with the FDP. The party's successful bid for power at the expense of its time-honored socialist principles was criticized, however, by a sizable portion of the SPD membership, most notably those associated with the SPD youth organization, the Young Socialists (Jungsozialisten—Jusos). Thus was born the factionalism that continued to divide the SPD membership in the early 1980s.

The conservative majority of SPD members in the Bundestag, led by Chancellor Schmidt, generally supported the Bad Godesberg Program but did not otherwise form a cohesive ideological bloc. This dominant SPD faction was known as the Kanalarbeiter (literally, channel workers) because of its less flamboyant political style. The leftist faction in the Bundestag, comprising up to one-quarter of the SPD members, was popularly known as the Leverkusen Circle (after the Ruhr town where they first met) and consisted largely of Jusos, but it also contained a number of trade union leaders and intellectuals. A small center-left SPD faction also operated in the Bundestag as a kind of mediator between the two wings. Small right-wing SPD factions also existed but were not represented in the Bundestag.

The SPD left wing played a more active role during the late 1960s and early 1970s, but it assumed a back seat during the late 1970s as Schmidt proved less tolerant of an active leftist element within his party's delegation in the Bundestag. Beginning in 1980, however, the country's declining economic fortunes and the rise of a pacifist sentiment that often ran counter to Schmidt's defense posture led to a resurgence of pronounced factionalism within the SPD. At that time party chairman Brandt emerged from his relative obscurity since his 1974 resignation from the chancellorship to play a pivotal role between the two factions.

In contrast to the CDU/CSU, the SPD has long been a party of membership. Shortly after World War II it claimed nearly 900,000 members; that figure declined to around 600,000 during the late 1950s, then gradually recovered, and by 1979 the SPD claimed slightly over 1 million paid members. The bulk of the SPD membership had traditionally consisted of urban working-class males. In the 1960s and 1970s, membership became more heterogeneous, as youth, white-collar workers, women, and nonpracticing Catholics contributed to the increased membership rolls in significant numbers. SPD strength was centered in the urban *Länder* of Bremen, Hamburg, and Hesse. In the 1970s party strategists made a particular effort to garner the youth vote. Although that effort met with considerable success, by the early 1980s both the newly formed political party, Die Grünen (the Greens), and the CDU were successfully competing with the SPD for youthful supporters.

The organizational structure of the SPD is more centralized and tightly woven than that of the CDU/CSU. Decisionmaking is generally done in a more top-to-bottom, bureaucratic manner than in the CDU/CSU, although on paper the formal organization of the two major parties varies little. A party congress, which meets biannually, is ostensibly the party's supreme authority. It serves as a symbol of democratic decisionmaking, but in fact its only meaningful function is the election of the thirty-six-member Executive Committee, which acts as the party's chief executive body and policymaker. The heart of the Executive Committee is the nine-member Presidium, the most important members of which during the late 1970s and early 1980s were SPD Chairman Brandt, Deputy Chairman Schmidt, and the SPD *Fraktion* leader in the Bundestag, Wehner. In February 1982 Wehner announced that he was resigning because of poor health.

The SPD organizations at the *Land*, district, subdistrict, and local levels, however, elect their own party officials. All are subordinate to the *Land* executive committees, which direct party policy below the federal level and often exhibit considerable autonomy from federal SPD officials in Bonn. Like the CDU/CSU, the SPD also has specialized groups that represent various professions, youth, refugees, women, trade unions, and sports. These groups are tightly bound to the SPD bureaucracy, however, and with the exception of the Jusos and the trade union group, they have no policymaking role.

Minor Parties

The Free Democratic Party

The FDP wields power in politics far beyond its status as a minor party that has gained as little as 5.8 percent of the vote in federal elections (1969) and whose best federal electoral showing ever netted it 12.8 percent of the vote in the 1961 Bundestag elections. Its pivotal role results from the fact that, 1957 excepted, neither major party has been able to capture a majority of Bundestag seats, thus forcing the formation of a coalition government. As a result the FDP has participated in every government with the exception of those between 1957 and 1961 and the Grand Coalition between 1966 and 1969. The importance of the FDP is augmented further by near-equal electoral strength of the SPD and the CDU/CSU, which allows the FDP to choose which major party will rule. With the clout of an implicit threat to "change partners," the FDP was able to extract large concessions from the primary governing party in both policy and cabinet positons. In early 1982 FDP members held the same four powerful cabinet posts—foreign affairs; economics; the interior; and food, agriculture, and forestry—they had obtained under the first Schmidt government in 1974. The FDP chairman, Genscher, served both as foreign minister and as vice chancellor, making him the most powerful member of the Schmidt cabinet.

The FDP was born in the wake of World War II under the chairmanship of Theodor Heuss, who acted as the first president of the Federal Republic between 1949 and 1954. The party saw itself as the heir of German liberalism, a political movement that from the mid-nineteenth century until the rise of the Third Reich had been divided into two groups, one with conservative, authoritarian views that was strongly allied with big business, and the other with a progressive, parliamentary viewpoint. In a sense this bifurcated tradition continued to be expressed in regional differences within the FDP with respect to policy matters. In the south, for example, the FDP emphasizes personal and cultural freedoms, while in the industrialized central part of the country it stresses its commitment to laissez-faire economic principles.

The major event in the history of the FDP took place in 1969 when the party, under its new chairman, Walter Scheel (who was to serve as federal president from 1974 to 1979), formed a government with the SPD after twenty years of association with the CDU/CSU. The change came both from the perennial FDP need to assert its independence out of fear of losing its identity to its major coalition partner and from a shift to the left among the party leadership. The rupture with the CDU/CSU led to widespread defections of longtime, conservative party members and their replacement by businesspeople, civil servants, and other middle-class elements. The student movement of the time had a considerable impact on the FDP, and the party's leftist youth wing, the Young Democrats (Jungdemokraten—Judos), emerged during the late 1960s. The party's new stance was confirmed at its 1971 party congress, which enacted a program of "social liberalism."

During the 1970s the FDP played a generally moderating role to the right of the SPD in the governing coalition, particularly on economic matters of concern to its business constituency. It forced a moderation of the SPD bill on the reform of codetermination and often argued against increased government spending for social programs. On other subjects, such as *Ostpolitik* and abortion, however, FDP stances coincided with those of their coalition partner. A common campaign ploy of the FDP was "vote for us so that the SPD government cannot go too far to the left." The growing strength of the left wing within the SPD during the early 1980s led observers to note dissatisfaction among the leadership of the FDP, some of whom were reported in 1981 to be considering

Government and Politics

another "change of partners" back to the CDU/CSU. A number of such coalitions had already been formed at the *Land* level.

Although the composition of FDP membership changed markedly after 1969, total membership remained at around the same modest number. In 1979 membership was reported to be 81,000, consisting overwhelmingly of middle- and upper middle-class persons, particularly urbanites associated with business and industrial concerns. FDP voters tended to be those who viewed the CDU/CSU as too religiously oriented, while viewing the SPD as too socialist. Hence the significant increase in the FDP vote in the 1980 Bundestag elections was widely viewed as a protest vote against the major parties.

The organizational structure of the FDP, like that of the CDU, was decentralized and most tightly woven at the *Land* level. This was in line with the varying policy orientations of the party in different regions of the country and has given FDP deputies in the Bundestag more freedom to vote independently than those of the major parties. Governing responsibilities at the federal level, however, have assured the preeminence of central party officials. The party congress meets annually, and every two years it elects a national committee and a federal executive headed by the party chairman. FDP organizations are also found at the local and district levels.

Other Minor Parties

In the years immediately following the birth of the Federal Republic, a number of minor parties representing a variety of groups—such as the neo-Nazi right, the communist left, refugees (people resettled in West Germany following World War II), and Bavarian separatist sentiments—made a considerable impact on federal politics. In the 1949 Bundestag election, seven minor parties garnered 39.8 percent of the popular vote and, as a result, held 133 out of 410 seats in the first session of the Bundestag. Their impact declined steadily, however; after 1961 the FDP was the only minor party to clear the 5 percent threshold necessary to secure Bundestag representation. By the 1980 federal election, parties other than the SPD and the CDU/CSU gained only 12.6 percent of the popular vote, and of this, 10.6 percentage points went to the FDP. Eight other parties competed in that election: one of these, the Greens, gained 1.5 percent, while the National Democratic Party (Nationaldemokratische Partei Deutschlands—NPD) and a new German Communist Party (Deutsche Kommunistische Partei—DKP) each managed only 0.2 percent of the popular vote. The remaining 0.1 percent was divided among five parties. Minor parties have been more effective in *Land* and local elections, but even here their impact had displayed a secular decline. They have continued to show some strength, nevertheless, in certain large cities and regional pockets.

Federal Republic of Germany

The nonpartisan alignments and so-called city hall parties that were quite significant in the postwar years were, by the early 1980s, a factor only in small towns.

The 5 percent clause found in federal, *Land*, and most local election laws was a major but by no means the only reason for the decline of the minor parties in the political system (see The Electoral System, this ch.). A variety of regulations sponsored by the major parties, including federal financing for political parties, procedures for nominating party candidates, and campaign codes have made it difficult for small parties to survive. Media exposure, of course, also aids the two major parties. The success of extremist parties is also limited by what a number of observers have dubbed the "limited ideological space" within the political system. Extreme rightist parties suffer comparison with the Nazis, and extreme leftist parties evoke the specter of the totalitarian system in East Germany. Almost all West Germans are united in rejecting these two systems as inferior to the democratic political structures of the Federal Republic. The Basic Law also holds that such parties may be declared unconstitutional.

The first party to be constitutionally barred was the neo-Nazi SRP. The still insecure Adenauer government saw the party win some 10 percent of the vote in two *Land* elections in 1951 and filed suit against the SRP in the Federal Constitutional Court. The far right was devastated by this action and did not reemerge until 1964 with the founding of the NPD. It gained 2 percent of the vote in the 1965 federal elections and between 1966 and 1968 enjoyed the height of its success, winning between 5 and 10 percent in seven different *Land* elections. In the 1969 federal election, however, it fell short of the 5 percent hurdle, and the NPD dropped into the fringes of political life.

The NPD calls for German reunification and the restoration of former German territories, denounces the decline of traditional morality, charges betrayal by West German communists, and calls for the restoration of discipline and authority. Such reactionary views function to exploit voters' fears during times of uncertainty. Indeed, the rapid rise and fall of the NPD during the late 1960s was widely interpreted as a backlash against the radical student politics of the time. Although the party's electoral votes continued to decline—from 123,000 in the 1976 Bundestag election to 68,000 in 1980, at which time its membership was limited to about 10,000—analysts did not discount the possibility of a rise in NPD electoral strength under similar conditions in the future.

At the other end of the political spectrum, communist parties have suffered a fate remarkably similar to that of the extreme right in a number of respects. The Communist Party of Germany (Kommunistische Partei Deutschlands—KPD) which had been founded in 1918, was reconstituted after World War II, held fifteen seats in the first Bundestag, and was banned under Article 21 of the Basic Law in 1956. The new communist party, the DKP, was founded in 1968 with much the same leadership of the old KPD. As of the early 1980s the DKP had never enjoyed electoral success; it had never been able to poll more than 3 percent in *Land* elections and had consistently received well under 1 percent of the vote in federal elections. The success of the party's organizational efforts among union members, in contrast, was said to be increasing during the early 1980s. The DKP was well financed from East German sources; its membership, undergoing a gradual decline, stood at about 45,000 in 1980.

A number of Maoist and Albanian-oriented communist parties were born out of the student movement of the late 1960s. Consisting of a small number of university students and professors, they were of no political consequence during the 1970s and, at the beginning of the subsequent decade, began to dissolve or further factionalize. At that time it was apparent that a number of members from these various communist parties were gravitating to an active role within the newly formed party, the Greens.

The Greens derived their name from environment-oriented citizens' initiative associations that successfully entered a number of local and *Land* elections during 1978–79 (see Citizens' Initiative Associations, this ch.). The most notable of these had won four seats to the Bremen legislature for the Bremen Green list. In January 1980 some 250 organizations met to constitute formally the Greens as a national political party to enable it to run in federal elections later in the year. Although the party's membership was largely composed of members of environmental associations—the largest being the Green Action Future, the Green List Ecology, and the Action Group of Independent Germans—the Greens decided at their founding party congress to allow simultaneous membership to members of other political parties. As a result the party became radicalized by communist and other leftist members, and three months later it adopted a party program that called for such nonecological concerns as the dissolution of NATO and of the Warsaw Pact, antitrust legislation aimed at large corporations, the introduction of a thirty-five-hour workweek, and an unlimited right to strike.

A number of the party's early leaders, including former CDU Bundestag deputy and best-selling author Herbert Gruhl, opposed the sudden leftist shift of the Greens, and a large number of its early members resigned in protest. August Haussleiter resigned as party chairman and was replaced in June 1980 by Dieter Burgmann. The poor showing of the Greens in the October 1980 Bundestag elections (they had hoped to surpass 5 percent but received only 1.5 percent) was attributed in large part to this early split. In 1981 a new party, the Ecological Democratic Party, was founded by a number of former Greens to counter the leftist orientation of the Greens.

Federal Republic of Germany

In 1981 the Greens made sweeping gains in local elections in Hesse, where the construction of an airport runway in Frankfurt was a major source of protest by environmentalists. In May 1981 a related political grouping in West Berlin, the Alternative List, won 7 percent of the popular vote and assumed nine seats in that city's legislature. In early 1982 the future of these rather amorphous political parties—composed largely of young people wishing to express a wide variety of concerns that they felt were not addressed by the major parties—was highly uncertain (see Introduction).

The Electoral System

The Basic Law grants every citizen eighteen years of age or older the right to vote by secret ballot in direct and free elections. Officials who are popularly elected include Bundestag deputies at the federal level, *Landtag* deputies or senate members at the *Land* level, and council members at the district and local levels. Executive officials are rarely chosen in popular, direct elections; in a minority of municipalities, however, the mayor is elected by a popular vote. At each governing level, elections are normally held every four years, although in unusual cases when a legislative body is dismissed, such as the 1972 Bundestag elections and the 1981 West Berlin Senate elections, they may occur more often. Elections for different level officials are not held simultaneously, as in the United States, but are staggered, and as a result an electoral campaign for either *Land* or local officials in one of the ten *Länder* is almost always in progress, with each viewed as a poll on the popularity of the federal government and the strength of opposition parties. All elections are held on Sunday, and voter turnout is traditionally high at all levels—about 90 percent in federal elections.

The electoral system is a modified version of proportional representation—sometimes called a system of personalized proportional representation—that was slightly altered in 1953 and 1956 and since has been unchanged. For Bundestag elections, the country is divided into 248 constituencies, the sizes of which may not vary by more than one-third from the national average. Following extensive reapportionment in 1976, the size of the constituencies varied between 120,000 and 220,000 voters—their average size being 170,000 voters and 250,000 residents. Each voter casts two ballots; the first is for a named candidate chosen to represent the constituency, the second is for a particular political party. Although the first ballot is designed to reduce the anonymity of a straight proportional representation system—hence the description "personalized"—the number of Bundestag seats obtained by each party is determined solely by the second ballot—the so-called list vote. Each party's total list vote is divided until 496 seats are apportioned, but then the number of seats won by each party in the direct constituency contests (the first ballot) is deducted from the party's total won in the list vote. Thus half the Bundestag seats are for constituency candidates and half for members of party lists. In the unusual case that a party wins more constituency seats than it is entitled to according to its vote in the second ballot, it retains these seats, and the size of the Bundestag is enlarged.

A party must receive a minimum of 5 percent of the list vote or win three constituency seats to be represented in the Bundestag. It is extremely difficult for a small party to win constituency seats; every seat won by the FDP since 1957 has been through its list vote. Although previously rare, voters increasingly have cast "split tickets." During the 1970s this was especially true of those voting the FDP list, while casting their constituency ballot for a candidate of another party. There are no by-elections; if a Bundestag deputy resigns or dies in office, he is replaced by the next candidate down the party's list in the appropriate *Land*.

There are also no primary elections. Constituency candidates are chosen by a local party selection committee, while list candidates are chosen at *Land* party conventions held six to eight weeks before the election. Federal-level party officials therefore have no part in the nominating procedure. Some two-thirds of the candidates run as both constituent and list candidates, thus affording them two ways in which to win. Although the voters are not aware of the names of list candidates, there is considerable bargaining among party factions and various interest groups in the selection and placement of list candidates in each *Land*. A high list position usually requires either incumbency, some other source of political prominence, or support from a key interest group, party faction, or auxiliary party organization. Candidates must be at least twenty-one years old.

Extra-Party Political Forces

Traditional Interest Groups

In a tradition that dates back to the corporate guild system of the Middle Ages, modern West German society remains highly organized into associations that represent the occupational, socioeconomic, religious, and recreational interest of individuals. One study completed in the early 1970s estimated that there were some 200,000 voluntary associations, including local sports clubs and singing societies. The vast majority of these were concerned with local matters, but a considerable number of interest associations were part of a hierarchical structure also organized at the federal level. Some 2,000 interest associations were extended to the federal level and were engaged in lobbying in Bonn. The vast majority were of minor political consequence, but the so-called peak interest associations representing business interests, labor, agriculture, and religion have a major impact on public policy.

The influence of peak interest associations is institutionalized in Bonn in a number of ways. In the Bundestag an estimated one-third of the deputies "represent their occupations in politics." This fact is a product of interest group impact on the nomination process, and as a result many federal legislators are professional interest group employees or are strongly associated with certain interests. Business, agricultural, and religious functionaries tend to be found among CDU/CSU and FDP deputies, while trade union officials are usually associated with the SPD. West German law requires such vested interests to be made public. Major peak interest associations are also required by law to be consulted by the ministerial bureaucracy within the executive branch in the drafting of laws that affect them. Cabinet members themselves, particularly the ministers for labor and social affairs and for food, agriculture, and forestry, often have strong ties to peak interest associations. In addition many permanent ministerial advisory commissions contain a number of interest group representatives who also contribute input into executive branch policymaking. Finally, peak interest associations support members' interests in pertinent legal matters brought before the administrative courts.

Business and industrial interests are represented by three umbrella organizations: the Federation of German Industries (Bundesverband der Deutschen Industrie—BDI), the Confederation of German Employer Associations (Bundesvereinigung der Deutschen Arbeitgeberverbände—BDA),. and the German Industrial and Trade Convention (Deutscher Industrie- und Handelstag—DIHT). Although all three have large staffs in Bonn, by far the most important of these is the BDI (see Industrial Associations, ch. 6). It is made up of thirty-nine individual industrial associations that together have a membership of some 90,000 firms, or some 98 percent of all West German industrial concerns. The BDI maintained close ties to the CDU/CSU government before 1969 and, despite concerns that it would lose its importance as a lobby when the CDU/CSU moved to the opposition, the BDI remained a major and influential voice in the SPD-FDP coalition government during the 1970s.

During that decade BDI's major efforts were aimed against the extension of codetermination laws, which had established worker representation in the governing of firms in certain industries during the 1950s, and against reform of corporate taxation (see The Working Class, ch. 3). It has also lobbied against any expansion of the public sector of the economy, against anticartel legislation, and against any expansion of the social welfare system that would increase employer contributions. The BDI has urged the federal government to pursue moderation in public spending.

During the Weimar Republic labor unions were factionalized along party lines, and there were competing socialist, communist,

*Palais Schaumburg in Bonn,
the former Federal Chancellory
Courtesy German Information Center*

*Government section of Bonn
Courtesy German Information Center*

Catholic, and liberal trade associations. After World War II strong sentiment to form a trade union federation independent of the political parties led to the establishment of the German Trade Union Federation (Deutscher Gewerkschaftsbund—DGB) in 1949. The DGB has retained close ties with the SPD, but it attempts to maintain a nonpartisan posture and maintains representation in the CDU/CSU.

The initial programmatic stances of the DGB, such as the nationalization of key industries and central economic planning, were decidedly leftist. The abandonment of its essentially Marxist positions by 1963 paralleled the ideological moderation that took place within the SPD. By the 1970s the DGB emphasized collective bargaining within existing institutional structures in its representation of workers. It did lobby vigorously, however, in defense of expanding the system of codetermination. The essentially conservative stance of the DGB, compared to counterparts in other West European countries, has been given credit for the relative tranquility of West German labor relations, but the DGB came under attack from the left for its lack of militance in representing the interests of labor. In the early 1980s, in the face of economic recession and rising unemployment, criticism of the aging union leadership became more widespread. In response to growing rank-and-file militance, DGB head Heinz-Oscar Vetter proposed in 1981 to confront the recession with job creation through shorter workweeks, government programs in energy, the environment, and housing, and lowering interest rates in order to stimulate investment.

Headquartered in Düsseldorf, the DGB included sixteen national trade unions with a membership of over 7 million workers under its umbrella. Although this number represented only about 26 percent of the work force, it was almost 86 percent of organized labor. Of all organized workers, nearly all industrialized workers, more than two-thirds of the white-collar employees, and nearly half the public servants were represented by the DGB. By far its largest component was I.G. Metall, representing metalworkers in the steel, automobile, and machinery industries, comprising some 2.5 million members.

There were two important, but much smaller peak interest associations, that represented labor independent of the DGB. The German Salaried Employees Union (Deutsche Angestellten Gewerkschaft—DAG) consisted primarily of high-level technocrats and managers in private enterprise. The Federation of German Civil Servants (Deutscher Beamtenbund—DBB) competed successfully with the DGB among the public servants. Although barred from striking, a large number of public servants were organized. About half of these were in the DGB, the other half (usually those of higher rank) were in the DBB.

Agricultural interests are represented by the so-called Green Front, an informal collaboration of three peak interest associations, the members of which include the vast majority of the country's farmers. These associations—the Association of Agricultural Farmers, the League of German Farmers, and an association of agricultural banks and cooperatives—united under the Green Front, were long known as the best-organized and most successful lobby in Bonn. Strongly associated with the CDU/CSU, however, the power of the Green Front declined under the SPD and as the number of farmers declined rapidly (see Organization of Agriculture, ch. 5). In early 1982 it retained a strong voice in Bonn, nevertheless, in favor of price supports and other government subsidies to agriculture.

The influence of organized religion, the final major arena of traditional West German interest group politics, also witnessed a decline during the 1970s. This resulted both from the pro-CDU/CSU partisanship of the Roman Catholic Church hierarchy and the growing secularization of West German society (see Religion, ch. 3). The Catholic church continued to wield significant influence in the largely Catholic and conservative southern regions, however; in Bavaria clergymen were still appointed to the upper house of the *Land* legislature. Protestant political concerns, presented by the Evangelical Church in Germany, were less conservative, less partisan, and traditionally less actively pursued than those of the Catholic church.

The Catholic church leadership became active following World War II, favoring state support for separate Catholic and Protestant school systems. It ultimately failed in this effort, as it did in campaigns during the 1970s for stiffer divorce laws, strict government controls over pornography, and continued prohibition of abortion. Its positions were put forth in extensive publications that had an estimated 25 million readers. The major policy concerns of the Evangelical Church in Germany at that time were with German reunification, support for codetermination, educational reform, and détente in foreign policy. Protestant clergymen and Protestant youth organizations also played a leading role in the peace movement that resumed prominence in 1981.

Despite a loss in political influence during the 1970s, the Catholic and Protestant churches continued to hold privileged positions in society. A complete separation of church and state seemed highly unlikely to occur. Both churches had large offices in Bonn where representatives maintained close party and governmental contacts. Both churches had representatives on the boards of all radio and television networks as well as on numerous advisory commissions at the *Land* and federal levels. But most important, both churches were recipients of the proceeds from the "church tax," whereby 8 to 9 percent of the income taxes collected by the government from the vast majority of citizens were transferred to the church. These privileges acknowledged the widely held West German view of organized religion as an important factor contributing to the country's postwar political ethos.

Citizens' Initiative Associations

During the early 1970s a novel type of representative force emerged on the political landscape. A decade later the growth of thousands of citizens' initiative associations—loosely and often temporarily organized groups of citizens committed usually to the realization of a specific local goal, although sometimes to the promotion of broader aims—led most observers of West German politics to conclude that this new form of political participation (or nontraditional interest groups) was more than a passing phase in the country's political order. During that decade several million West Germans took part in citizens' initiatives, thus exercising a kind of "direct democracy" that was heretofore unknown in the Federal Republic. This participation represented a widespread dissatisfaction with traditional forms of political participation as well as with the ability of established political institutions to meet the changing needs of society.

Citizens' initiative associations grew out of the increased political awareness created by the 1960s student movement. Its participants continued to be mostly youthful and middle class. White-collar professionals, students, and public servants (especially teachers) predominated. A 1977 study asserted that workers constituted only about 10 percent of the membership of the citizens' initiative associations.

A large majority of the associations were free from any encompassing political ideology, and most concentrated their efforts on one issue. Social and cultural issues, such as the establishment of progressive schools, community recreational facilities, and the provision of services for youth, tenants, and marginal social groups, were common focuses of citizens' initiatives. Their other major area of concern was with environmental issues, such as the planning and limitation of large-scale construction projects, urban planning and renewal, and traffic planning. The common thread of all these issues was a concern with the quality of life as opposed to the issues of material well-being addressed by the traditional political interest groups.

Citizens' initiatives employed a variety of tactics in their political efforts. These included both traditional lobbying techniques, such as the detailing of policy goals and the cultivation of influential government officials, as well as nontraditional tactics borrowed from the student movement, such as petitions, mass demonstrations, and protest marches.

The concerns of citizens' initiative associations were primarily of a local nature, involving political activity only at the local level.

It was not until 1977, at the beginning of a campaign to block construction of a nuclear power facility at Brockdorf, north of Hamburg, that the efforts of a citizens' initiative assumed national significance. Subsequent campaigns against nuclear power, on behalf of squatters in West Berlin and a number of other cities, and to prevent the construction of a new runway at the international airport in Frankfurt increasingly brought the citizens' initiatives into countrywide prominence. These campaigns also served to radicalize a number of the associations.

The Federal Association of Citizens' Initiatives on Environmental Protection has coordinated the activities of a vast number of local environmental lobbies. It also has acted as a federal-level lobbying agent in a variety of concerns. In late 1981, for example, it issued a call for federal legislation to limit the amount of potentially hazardous ingredients in food.

The Mass Media

A highly developed mass media structure has made West Germans among the best politically informed people in the world. In the mid-1970s, 96 percent of West German households had a television, and 97 percent had a radio. Daily newspaper sales exceeded 20 million. Political reporting was generally regarded to be of high quality and generally balanced with respect to public opinion. While the question of whether the mass media formed public opinion was hotly debated, it was widely accepted that the media played a major role in setting the political agenda by defining the issues that entered the public debate. Freedom of the press, which is guaranteed by the Basic Law, was monitored by the German Press Council, consisting of ten publishers and ten journalists.

Radio and television are administered by nine nonprofit public corporations based in, but independent from, *Land* governments. Their decentralized administration is prescribed in the Basic Law intentionally to avoid the abuses of the airwaves such as those committed by Nazi officials. Each corporation is self-governed under the direction of a broadcasting council that consists, by law, of representatives of major "social, economic, cultural, and political forces," including political parties and interest groups. This arrangement has commonly been criticized as producing bland political programming. The broadcasting corporations are funded primarily through monthly fees paid by each household having radio and television receivers and, to a lesser extent, by commercial advertising. The introduction of commercial television was debated during much of the 1970s, and in 1981 a plan by a group of conservative West German publishers to introduce commercial cable television was opposed by the ruling SPD but favored by a number of CDU leaders.

The press is privately owned. Although newspapers owned by political parties were prominent during the Weimar period, in the Federal Republic the only party publications of importance were weeklies—*Vorwärts* of the SPD and *Bayernkurier* of the CSU. The DGB and the Catholic church also published prominent weeklies.

In the early 1980s the most important power of the West German press continued to be Axel Springer, whose chain of daily newspapers, headquartered in Hamburg, produced about one-quarter of the national total. The mass-oriented tabloid *Bild-Zeitung*, having a daily circulation of 3.4 million and a daily readership estimated at 12 million, was far and away the most widely circulated daily. Springer, highly conservative and boldly critical of both the foreign and domestic policy initiatives of the SPD-led government, also owned one of West Germany's four "prestige" or "high quality" dailies, *Die Welt*. The other three rounded out the political spectrum: the *Frankfurter Allgemeine Zeitung* was moderately rightist, the *Süddeutsche Zeitung* was moderately leftist, and the *Frankfurter Rundschau* was decidedly leftist.

The liberal counterpart to Springer was Rudolf Augstein, founder and publisher of the weekly *Der Spiegel*, a highly respected and influential newsmagazine having a circulation of about 1 million. Other political weeklies, such as the liberal *Die Zeit* and the conservative *Deutsche Zeitung* did not approach the importance of *Der Spiegel*.

* * *

The student of West German government and politics, even if confined to the English language, will find an almost overwhelming amount of published material available. The Press and Information Office of the Government of the Federal Republic of Germany publishes a panoply of documents, including the *Basic Law*, that are published in English and available to the public free of charge. These are most useful for their description of the complex system of government and its various institutions. Current events are discussed in *The Week in Germany* and *German Press Review*, both published by that office. The *Financial Times* of London is also particularly thorough in its coverage of West German news.

General English-language studies of the political system are published frequently, and a current bibliography should be consulted. In early 1982 one of the best volumes available, although strictly for the nonspecialist, continued to be *Politics in West Ger-*

many, an updated, second edition of Lewis J. Edinger's 1968 study of *Politics in Germany*. Also most useful as a general text is David P. Conradt's study of *The German Polity*. *Democracy in Western Germany* by Gordon Smith, and *Germany Transformed* by Baker, et al., are more specialized studies of dynamic aspects of modern West German politics. The quarterly journal, *Government and Opposition* has frequent articles of interest to the student of West German politics. (For further information see Bibliography.)

Chapter 8. Foreign Relations

Ludwig van Beethoven

Foreign Relations

THE BASIC CIRCUMSTANCES that shape the foreign relations of the Federal Republic of Germany (West Germany or Federal Republic) are: the existence of two German states and the special position of Berlin, the nation's sensitive location on the East-West dividing line in Europe and resultant security requirements, the critical roles of the North Atlantic Treaty Organization (NATO) and the United States in meeting those security requirements, and the high dependence of the economy on foreign trade. Whereas virtually all states profess a policy of peace, friendship, and cooperation, such aims have special importance for the interests of West Germany. Only in such a climate can the country expect to ensure its security, sustain prosperity through high levels of trade and investment, and keep open the possibility for a future exercise of self-determination by all Germans. Because of its special situation, historical legacy, and economic preponderance in Europe, West Germany has worked to coordinate and gain support for its policies within key multilateral associations such as NATO (also called the Atlantic Alliance), the European Communities (EC), and the United Nations (UN).

Bonn's policy toward the West has been anchored in NATO and the EC. West German officials have emphasized the need to preserve East-West equilibrium and have asserted that the country's security can be ensured only through close partnership between Western Europe and North America. Still, significant opposition has developed in West Germany to some NATO policies, e.g., the 1979 decision to deploy nuclear missiles in Western Europe if negotiations with the Soviet Union to limit such weapons do not succeed. Moreover, West Germany's economic difficulties have led to defense spending increases that are below NATO guidelines.

West Germany has been one of the strongest and most consistent supporters of the EC and the largest contributor to its budget. Trade with other EC countries has represented about half of its total foreign commerce, and it is the principal trading partner for most EC members. Nevertheless economic problems in the early 1980s caused Bonn to seek limits on EC budgetary growth and to advocate measures to reduce the relative size of its own contribution. West Germany has been a major proponent of EC political cooperation and has sought to expand its staff support and scope of consultations. A Europe-wide foreign policy would enable Bonn to exercise a broader and more acceptable influence than would be possible through unilateral action.

The Federal Republic's policy on the issue of national reunification has undergone substantial change since 1949. Although in early 1982 Bonn still proclaimed the goal of eventual German unity in self-determination, its immediate policy sought the expansion and consolidation of ties between the two German states. The German Democratic Republic (East Germany) has sought to strengthen its position as a separate German state, however and has resisted intra-German population contacts that it fears could have destabilizing effects on party and government control. The political crisis in Poland of 1980–82 heightened East German concerns and retarded progress toward normalization in intra-German relations.

The pursuit of détente in Europe remained a major theme of West German policy in the 1970s and early 1980s. The purpose of *Ostpolitik* (eastern policy), a West German aspect of détente, has been to improve relations with the Soviet Union, Eastern Europe, and East Germany in order to establish a climate of confidence and interdependence that would be favorable to progress in intra-German relations. Furthermore détente has been viewed as contributing to strong East-West trade and investment relations that play an important role in the West German economy. Finally, détente has been regarded as an element of its security policy to the extent that it reduces the dangers arising from the East-West military confrontation in Europe. In this sense, in early 1982 West Germany continued to regard support for détente and a leading role in NATO as complementary policy interests.

Another aspect of foreign relations lay in the continuing importance of foreign trade. In 1979 some 27 percent of the nation's gross national product was accounted for by the export of goods and services. Relations with nations of the Third World were especially linked with West Germany's search for export markets and secure sources of energy and other vital inputs into West German industry. By the early 1980s nearly a quarter of the nation's exports were to nations of the Third World; some 40 percent of West Germany's raw material requirements were provided by the less developed countries of Asia, Africa, Latin America, and the Middle East. West Germany's trade dependence has led it to view its own future prosperity as being linked to economic growth among the less developed countries. Thus during the 1970s it substantially increased its foreign aid commitment to nations of the Third World and espoused policies in the UN and other multilateral forums that addressed the problems created by the disparity in wealth between the industrialized "north" and the less developed nations of the "south."

Institutional Framework

Foreign policy is primarily the prerogative of the federal government. The states (*Länder*, sing., *Land*) can conclude agreements with foreign countries in areas of their legislative authority, but such agreements are subject to approval by the federal government. The federal government can require the *Länder* to implement treaty provisions.

The Basic Law, i.e., the constitution, provides that the federal chancellor "determines, and is responsible for general policy." The chancellor enjoys a particularly strong policymaking position since he is not required to seek a parliamentary vote of confidence for his government's program or approval for ministerial appointments. He can be removed from office only through a "constructive vote of no confidence" by the Bundestag (Federal Diet), which then must choose a successor by an absolute majority (see The Government, ch. 7). The once powerful Federal Chancellor's Office (also called the Federal Chancellory) serves essentially to coordinate policy. It has also retained important responsibilities in the area of intra-German relations because of the government's position that relations between the two German states are of a special character and thus not to be handled in the normal manner of interstate relations through the Ministry of Foreign Affairs. The president's functions are largely ceremonial, such as receiving foreign ambassadors and undertaking state visits abroad.

Within the general framework of policy determined by the chancellor, the Basic Law provides that each minister "conducts the business of his department autonomously and on his own responsibility." This has been interpreted to permit a minister considerable latitude in the management of his department without interference from the chancellor. The chancellor can dismiss a minister, however, or compel him to rescind or alter a policy if it is deemed to be inconsistent with established guidelines. Moreover, whereas the minister of defense exercises authority over the armed forces in peacetime, supreme command is transferred to the chancellor in the event of war or similar emergency.

The central department for foreign policy planning, coordination, decisionmaking, and implementation is the Ministry of Foreign Affairs. Most West German representatives to international organizations, e.g., NATO, the EC, and the UN, and conferences are members of the Ministry of Foreign Affairs. Other government departments may also have delegates, though their work is coordinated through the Foreign Ministry. In the area of foreign economic policy, however, its responsibility is limited and is shared with the economic cooperation and finance ministries. Security policies are coordinated with the Ministry of Defense (see fig. 18). The Federal Security Council acts as a committee of the cabinet in the coordination of foreign and security policies among involved agencies. In cases of disagreement following interministrerial negotiations, the issue may be referred to the Federal Chancellor's Office for mediation and resolution.

The Bundestag and Bundesrat (Federal Council) play important roles in the policy process through the ratification of treaties and the approval of most legislation and budgetary provisions pertain-

Federal Republic of Germany

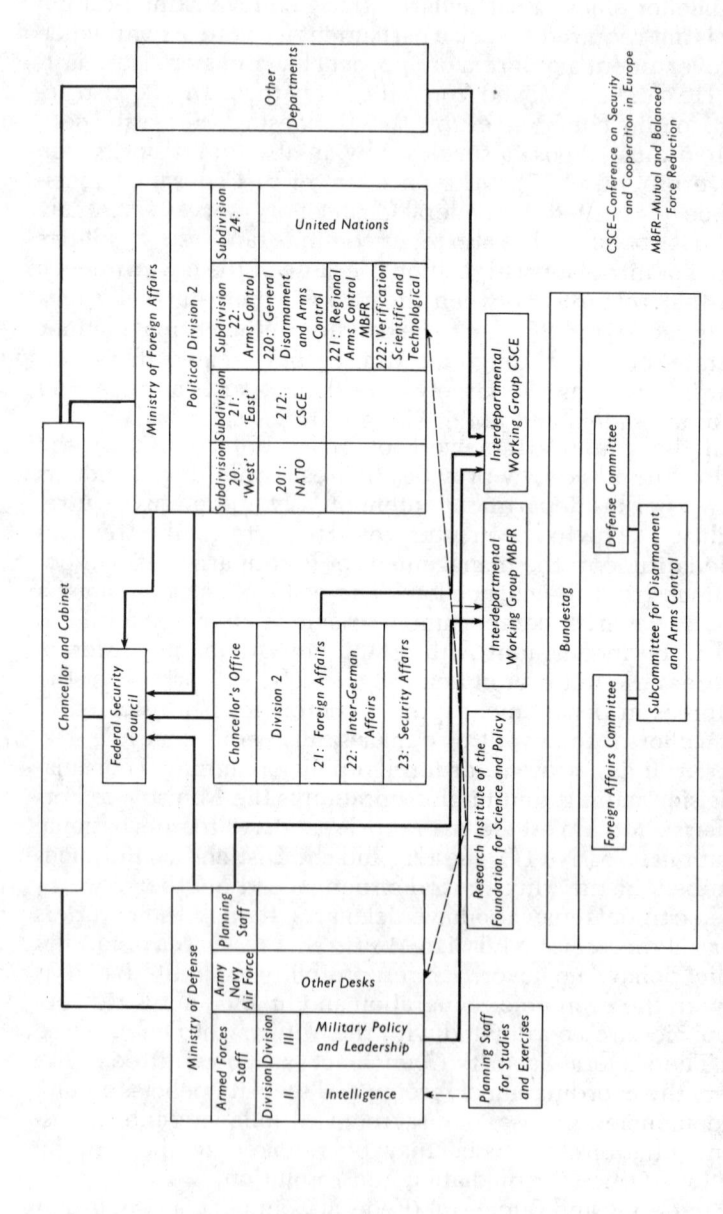

Source: Based on information from Ekkehart Krippendorff and Volker Rittberger (eds.), *The Foreign Policy of West Germany: Formation and Contents*, Beverly Hills, 1980, p. 14.

Figure 18. *Foreign and Security Policy Decisionmaking*

Foreign Relations

ing to foreign commitments. Within the Bundestag, the *Fraktionen* (parliamentary groups) and the committees on foreign affairs, defense, all-German affairs, and budget provide the main organizational structure for participation in policymaking. In practice the parliament generally plays a responsive, rather than initiatory, role and is clearly secondary to the executive in influence on foreign policy (see The Federal Executive, ch. 7).

The North Atlantic Treaty Organization

The North Atlantic Treaty Organization is the foundation of West Germany's foreign and security policy. Moreover the Atlantic Alliance holds a unique importance for the Federal Republic that goes beyond the traditional function of military security by providing vital political anchorage in the West while undergirding Bonn's policies toward the East. Despite changing issues and different emphases over time, all West German governments have regarded NATO as an indispensable element of the Federal Republic's *Westpolitik* and *Ostpolitik*.

The establishment of the two German states in 1949 in a hostile cold war climate necessarily posed the immediate question of West Germany's foreign and security policy orientation. Chancellor Konrad Adenauer's determined commitment to a Western policy, given the improbability of an acceptable accord on reunification, was designed to achieve recovery, sovereignty, and assurance that Germany's interests would not be sacrificed through a Four Power agreement (see Adenauer Era, ch. 1). By becoming a reliable partner and mainstay of the Atlantic Alliance, Adenauer expected consistent Western support of his government's interests in its relations with the East.

In September 1950, five years before West Germany joined it, NATO adopted a "forward strategy" by which aggression would be opposed as far to the east in Europe as possible, thereby implicitly including the Federal Republic within the Western defense perimeter. Though NATO military capabilities at that time were quite limited (a unified command structure had not yet been established), the strategy was intended to provide political and psychological assurance to NATO members and West Germany. In practice, however, a forward strategy was feasible only with a West German defense contribution.

The 1955 agreements providing for West German rearmament and membership in the Western European Union (WEU—see Glossary) and NATO were closely linked with the ending of the Allied occupation and the Federal Republic's acquisition of sovereignty. Indeed partly for this reason, i.e., the termination of occupation, it was politically necessary to establish limitations on West German rearmament as a condition of membership in NATO. This was accomplished through the WEU, which was empowered to establish maximum force levels for its members,

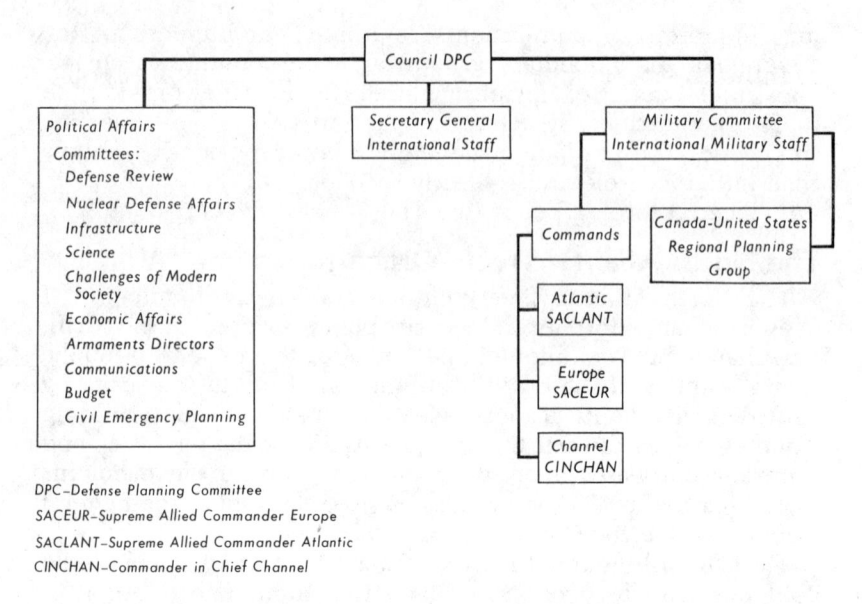

Federal Republic of Germany

```
                        Council DPC
        ┌───────────────────┼───────────────────┐
Political Affairs   Secretary General    Military Committee
Committees:         International Staff  International Military Staff
  Defense Review
  Nuclear Defense Affairs
  Infrastructure                ┌──── Commands ──── Canada-United States
  Science                       │                   Regional Planning Group
  Challenges of Modern          │
    Society                     ├── Atlantic
  Economic Affairs              │   SACLANT
  Armaments Directors           │
  Communications                ├── Europe
  Budget                        │   SACEUR
  Civil Emergency Planning      │
                                └── Channel
                                    CINCHAN
```

DPC–Defense Planning Committee
SACEUR–Supreme Allied Commander Europe
SACLANT–Supreme Allied Commander Atlantic
CINCHAN–Commander in Chief Channel

Source: Based on information from *NATO: Facts and Figures,* Brussels, 1976, p. 204.

Figure 19. *Civil and Military Structure of NATO*

subject to modification based on a recommendation by NATO authorities and having the unanimous consent of the WEU Council. West Germany undertook not to manufacture in its territory atomic, biological, and chemical weapons and not to produce certain armaments, e.g., long-range missiles, bombers, and warships, except on the request of the Supreme Allied Commander Europe (SACEUR) and with the approval of a two-thirds majority of the WEU. (In the case of warships, some production restraints have been loosened or removed. In 1980, for example, the prohibition on West German manufacture of warships was abolished.) With Bonn's consent Allied forces were to remain in West Germany as part of the common defense. West Germany also pledged to pursue the reunification goal only by peaceful means, and the United States, Britain, and France affirmed that any recourse to force that threatened the integrity and unity of NATO would disqualify the offending government from military assistance under the North Atlantic Treaty.

The establishment of the Supreme Headquarters Allied Powers Europe (SHAPE) in 1951, the addition of twelve West German divisions later in the decade, and a substantial increase in United States force levels in Europe strengthened NATO'S deterrence posture and its capability for conducting coordinated defensive operations (see fig. 19; fig. 20). Still, NATO forces-in-being consistently fell short of announced targets. SHAPE'S operational capabilities with conventional forces were inadequate to fulfill NATO'S declared forward defense strategy in Europe. Much of the problem stemmed from differing United States and West European conceptions of the Atlantic Alliance. The United States viewed NATO as the principal instrument for redressing the military imbalance in Europe to deter Soviet aggression and, should deterrence fail, to enable a successful defense. West Europeans, on the other hand, tended to perceive the Atlantic Alliance essentially as a means for committing the United States to their defense. West European governments, responsive to domestic pressures for economic recovery and expanded social services, were prepared to support defense expenditures sufficient to maintain the American presence, but not to a level necessary to create a credible conventional defense against a large-scale attack. Under such circumstances the United States adjusted its military strategy to rely increasingly on tactical nuclear weapons for deterrence in regional conflicts. In December 1954 NATO ministers approved a strategy that anticipated the use of tactical nuclear weapons against even conventional aggression in Europe. Thereafter NATO forces were equipped with tactical nuclear weapons under a "two key" system requiring the consent of both the United States and the host country for the weapons to be used. Conventional forces were to deal with minor incursions and serve a "trip wire" function, signaling the start of an attack that then would be met with nuclear weapons.

The NATO policy of reliance on tactical nuclear weapons was directly related at the strategic level to the United States doctrine of massive retaliation, which implicitly threatened the use of long-range nuclear weapons to repulse an attack against the United States or its allies. By the early 1960s, however, the emphasis on a massive nuclear retaliation strategy had come under heavy criticism in the face of growing Soviet nuclear power. Critics argued that the United States had become vulnerable to Soviet nuclear attack and that a strategy of United States/NATO nuclear use therefore lacked credibility and effectiveness as a deterrent. This concern was reinforced by assertions that an American nuclear response would be disproportional to any but the most serious provocation and therefore lacked credibility. Despite the pronouncements of United States/NATO doctrine, many critics doubted that an American president would risk all-out nuclear war except in response to a direct attack on the United States. Indeed, in April 1959 Christian Herter gave explicit credence to this view during his Senate confirmation hearing for the office of secretary of state. Such widespread concerns seemed to discredit

Federal Republic of Germany

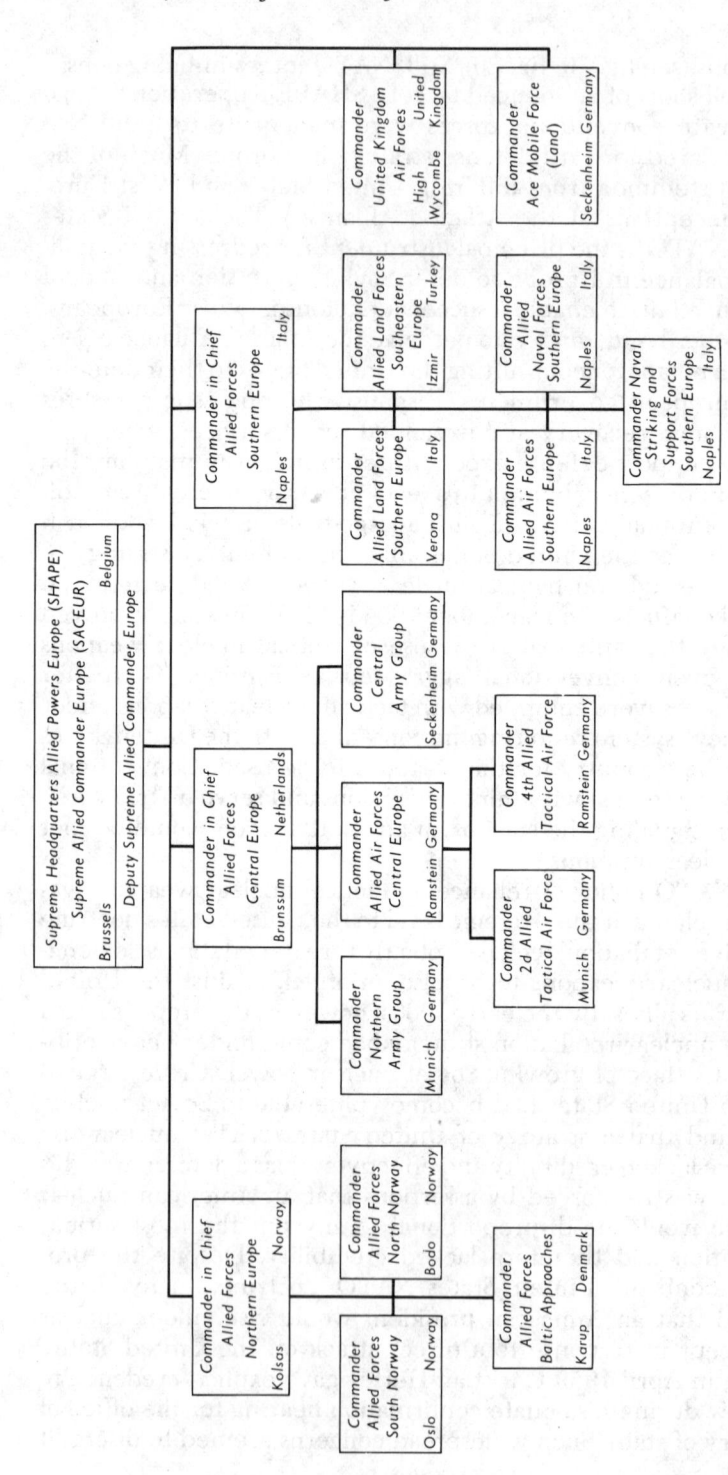

Source: Based on information from *NATO: Facts and Figures*, Brussels, 1976, p. 220.

Figure 20. *Allied Command Europe*

the strategy of massive retaliation less than five years after its formal adoption by NATO.

In the early 1960s the administration of John F. Kennedy inaugurated major changes in United States defense policy with far-reaching implications for NATO strategy. The main feature of the new approach was a reversal of the previous relationship between the nuclear and conventional forms of military power. Whereas the administration of Dwight D. Eisenhower had emphasized NATO's nuclear "sword" and its conventional "shield," the Kennedy administration stressed conventional military power as the most appropriate response to likely forms of aggression, with the threat of nuclear retaliation reserved as an ultimate backup for conventional forces and as a deterrent to first nuclear use by an adversary. Kennedy declared in 1961 that by limiting nuclear weapons to a more restricted role the American objective was to "increase our ability to confine our response to non-nuclear weapons."

The Kennedy administration's emphasis on conventional forces was part of its strategy of developing a capability for a flexible or graduated response to all forms of Soviet aggression. The new approach sought to provide the United States and NATO with a broad spectrum of military measures that could be tailored to the level of provocation. Whereas a full-scale strategic nuclear response was not ruled out, the emphasis was on developing the capability to meet a limited attack, which posed the most likely threat. The range of options included United States tactical nuclear weapons, and those forces were augmented in Europe along with the improvement of strategic nuclear and conventional forces. Yet the administration's concern over the escalatory dangers of tactical nuclear use, i.e., risking a United States-Soviet strategic exchange, led it to stress conventional force preparedness even for a large-scale aggression in Europe. United States defense planners argued that the new posture would strengthen deterrence because a capability for retaliating in proportion to an attack would be more credible and therefore more likely to dissuade any form of aggression. Moreover the new strategy sought to provide a preferred alternative to the threatened use of American strategic weapons, whose credibility had declined in the face of growing Soviet nuclear power. Through the availability of a range of potential NATO responses, the new doctrine promised to maintain the option of military escalation, thus confronting the Soviet Union with the risks of an expanded conflict at any stage of an attack.

The flexible response strategy generated anxiety and misgivings in Western Europe. The emphasis on conventional military options pointed to an American preference for conducting a nonnuclear defense of Europe, whereas an attack upon the United States would be met by instant nuclear retaliation. Thus the new doctrine appeared to introduce a division within the Atlantic Alliance in terms of relative exposure to the risks of war. A conventional war in Europe could leave the North American continent untouched. An American president might be reluctant to commit strategic nuclear forces in such a conflict because of the risk of Soviet retaliation against the United States. Similar considerations could inhibit the use of tactical nuclear weapons because of the escalatory risks involved. Thus there was concern that the emphasis on conventional military responses could weaken NATO's nuclear deterrence strategy while increasing the risk of war in Europe below the nuclear threshold.

Despite these concerns there was general appreciation that the American defense doctrine was a consequence of the changing United States-Soviet Union strategic relationship to which NATO strategy had to adapt. In 1967 the NATO defense ministers formally adopted a flexible response strategy that committed NATO to respond initially to any aggression short of general nuclear attack at the level (conventional or nuclear) of the aggression; to escalate the level of defense if necessary to repulse the aggression and restore the situation; and to initiate a suitable general nuclear response to a major nuclear attack. Despite the consensus reached, the strategy contained ambiguities about its operational meaning, which, however, accommodated the differing American and West European emphases.

The differing United States and West European perspectives on flexible response had both doctrinal and operational implications for NATO strategy. The United States, preferring a relatively high nuclear threshold, i.e., an extensive nonnuclear fighting capability, has stressed the need for augmenting NATO's peacetime supply inventories to sustain a prolonged conventional war. The European allies, on whose territory such a war would be fought, have resisted large peacetime stockpiling and have preferred a low nuclear threshold that anticipated a NATO nuclear intervention at a relatively early stage of a major conflict. In the European perspective, the latter would enhance deterrence of attack at any level by immediately confronting an aggressor with the risk of nuclear war, would avoid the potential loss of vital territory in the early stages of a conventional battle, and would increase the probability of early involvement of American strategic forces.

In the face of continued military modernization by the countries of the Warsaw Pact, the NATO countries in 1978 launched the Long-Term Defense Program (LTDP) to strengthen the Atlantic Alliance's defense posture. The LTDP focused on ten priority categories: enhanced readiness; rapid reenforcement; strengthened European reserve forces; improvements in maritime capabilities; integrated air defenses; command, control, and communications; electronic warfare; rationalized procedures for armaments collaboration; improved logistics coordination and increased war reserves; and theater nuclear modernization. A major feature of the plan was the Rapid Reinforcement Program, which was designed to more than double the American ground forces and triple the American tactical air forces deployed in Europe within two weeks of a reenforcement decision. The success of the LTDP has been dependent upon the provision of adequate European facilities and host nation support and the fulfillment of the allies' pledge in 1977 to increase annual defense expenditures by 3 percent in real terms over the five years covered by the plan.

West German security policy in the early 1980s remained firmly anchored in NATO and in the United States' commitment to the defense of Western Europe, which was regarded as irreplaceable. West Germany's armed forces were more extensively integrated with the NATO command than any other member (see Organization and Mission, ch. 9). Its defense *White Paper* (1979) declared: "Even if Western Europe were to achieve political unity, the nuclear protective function of the United States would still be indispensable." Moreover Bonn rejected the idea of creating a European nuclear force as a possible alternative to existing arrangements. Nevertheless West Germany has encouraged increased West European cooperation on defense and security issues.

In early 1982 West Germany's security policy continued to be based on several interlocking considerations. First, the Soviet Union and the Warsaw Pact have been viewed as the only significant military threats, and the United States and NATO have been essential to counterbalance this power and to deter any form of aggression. Second, military balance has been regarded as vital in order to avoid vulnerability to intimidation and pressures that could gradually nudge Western Europe into the Soviet orbit. Third, a grounding in a strong Western alliance has been necessary to West Germany's continued pursuit of détente with the East. Fourth, NATO backing has been vital to maintain the security and viability of West Berlin and to support Bonn's long-term goal of overcoming the division of Germany.

Given its exposed geographical position in Central Europe, these considerations have unique significance for the Federal Republic. A major war in Europe would likely be fought initially, if not entirely, on West German territory. The country is approximately the size of Oregon, lacks breadth and geographical barriers, and has a high urban area population concentration. A NATO-Warsaw Pact conflict on its territory would produce incalculable destruction. Moreover 30 percent of the Federal Republic's population and 25 percent of its industrial capacity are located within 100 kilometers of the East German border, the initial impact zone of a Warsaw Pact attack.

Thus it is not surprising that West Germany places supreme importance on the deterrence function of NATO. In accordance with official Atlantic Alliance strategy, Bonn has regarded strategic nuclear forces, theater nuclear forces, and conventional forces as forming an inseparable complex, each component being credible alone, and all three closely linked to maintain the threat of escalation. Deterrence is believed to be enhanced by the incalculability of the *manner* of the NATO response to a given level of provocation. An essential element of deterrence has been the NATO principle of forward defense, i.e., the conduct of defensive operations close to the inter-German border with the aim of minimizing territorial loss and recovering any ground that might be lost in the initial stages. Any strategy that would contemplate extensive nonnuclear military operations in West Germany and the acceptance of territorial loss would weaken deterrence by tempting a limited attack and would be unacceptable to the Federal Republic.

Yet while insisting that NATO adhere firmly to a forward defense strategy, Bonn has seen this primarily as an instrument of deterrence rather than as a means for achieving a military decision in war. As explained in the Federal Republic's 1976 defense *White Paper*: "The initial use of nuclear weapons is not intended so much to bring about a military decision as to achieve political effect. The intent is to persuade the attacker to reconsider his intention, to desist in his aggression, and to withdraw." In a similar vein, Helmut Schmidt—who twelve years later became federal chancellor—concluded in his 1962 book, *Defense or Retaliation*: "The use of tactical nuclear weapons...would...lead to the most extensive devastation of Europe....Those who think that Europe can be defended by the massed use of such weapons will not defend Europe, but destroy it." Thus West German thinking has resisted contemplating war-fighting scenarios in Central Europe with conventional or nuclear weapons.

In 1977 the United States proposed the development and deployment of enhanced radiation weapons (ERW—the so-called neutron bomb) in the Federal Republic. The weapons were intended to neutralize the Warsaw Pact advantage in armor and thus shore up NATO's defensive posture. The limited blast feature of the neutron weapons, in contrast to the existing tactical nuclear inventory, would enhance NATO's capability for repelling a major Warsaw Pact assault with significantly less damage to nonbattlefield areas. Yet despite the advantages—indeed because of them—many West German critics argued that such weapons were more likely to be used. By the time Schmidt had mustered a sufficient domestic consensus to agree to accept the weapons, President Jimmy Carter decided to defer indefinitely their further development in the hope of gaining arms control concessions from the Soviet Union. The episode was one of acute embarrassment to Schmidt, who had weathered intense domestic criticism in responding to the United States proposal, and the outcome produced strains in United States-West German relations.

European Community, Brussels
Courtesy German Information Center

In August 1981 the administration of Ronald Reagan announced that it would produce neutron weapons for stockpiling in the United States. Officials stressed that the weapons would not be deployed in Europe without full consultation with the NATO allies. Since the weapons were to be based on American territory, a West German spokesman declared that the production decision was an "exclusively American affair" that did not require consultation with Bonn and that their deployment in West Germany was "at the moment, out of the question." Schmidt stated, however, that under certain conditions the weapons could be stationed on West German soil. The conditions, the same as those adopted in 1978, were that deployment must be a collective NATO decision, that other European NATO members must agree to accept the weapons, and that arms control negotiations with the Soviet Union must have failed to produce positive results.

In early 1982 West Germany continued to be the most important European member of the Atlantic Alliance. In the north-central European region, it provided 50 percent of all NATO ground forces, 50 percent of all ground-based air defense resources, and 30 percent of the combat aircraft, and in the Baltic

Federal Republic of Germany

Sea area, 70 percent of the naval forces and all the naval air forces (see fig. 21).

From 1970 to 1980 Bonn's defense budget more than doubled. In terms of level of expenditures, percentage of total national budget, and per capita outlays for defense, West Germany has generally ranked first or second among the European NATO members. As a percentage of gross domestic product, however, West German defense expenditures have ranked slightly below the average of other members (see table 25, Appendix). As part of a general budget retrenchment program for 1982, the government intended to increase defense expenditures by 4.2 percent in line with overall budget growth. When inflation is taken into account, however, this should produce a decline in defense spending in real terms.

Although a majority of West Germans consistently favored membership in NATO, there was evidence in 1981 of some erosion of support and a greater differentiation in attitudes. In nine different polls over the 1969–80 period, 73 to 88 percent (average 81 percent) believed that NATO was essential to the nation's security, whereas 5 to 13 percent (average 10 percent) regarded it as not essential. A poll conducted in March 1981 found that 62 percent believed that NATO was still essential to their security, 20 percent believed it was not essential, and 19 percent had no opinion. Moreover only 45 percent of West Germans polled expressed confidence in NATO's ability to prevent an attack while 40 percent lacked confidence.

The shift in opinion toward NATO may be related to changed perceptions of the superpower balance. The March 1981 poll disclosed that 18 percent believed that the United States was ahead in total military strength, 35 percent believed that the Soviet Union was ahead, and 33 percent felt that the two were equal. The same or comparable question had been posed in seven different polls over the 1964-77 period, revealing that 15 to 41 percent of the respondents believed the United States was ahead (average 35 percent), 10 to 34 percent believed the Soviet Union was ahead (average 20 percent), and 25 to 38 percent felt the two were equal (average 33 percent).

Interestingly, in view of those findings, West German confidence in the American defense commitment has remained consistent with the average of earlier survey findings. The March 1981 poll revealed that 59 percent had a great or fair amount of confidence that the United States would come to West Germany's defense if attacked. When the same or comparable question was asked in seven different polls over the 1968–80 period, 49 to 72 percent had a great or fair amount of confidence in the United States defense commitment (average 60 percent).

Despite general support for the Atlantic Alliance, however, substantial segments of opinion opposed or were indecisive about

Foreign Relations

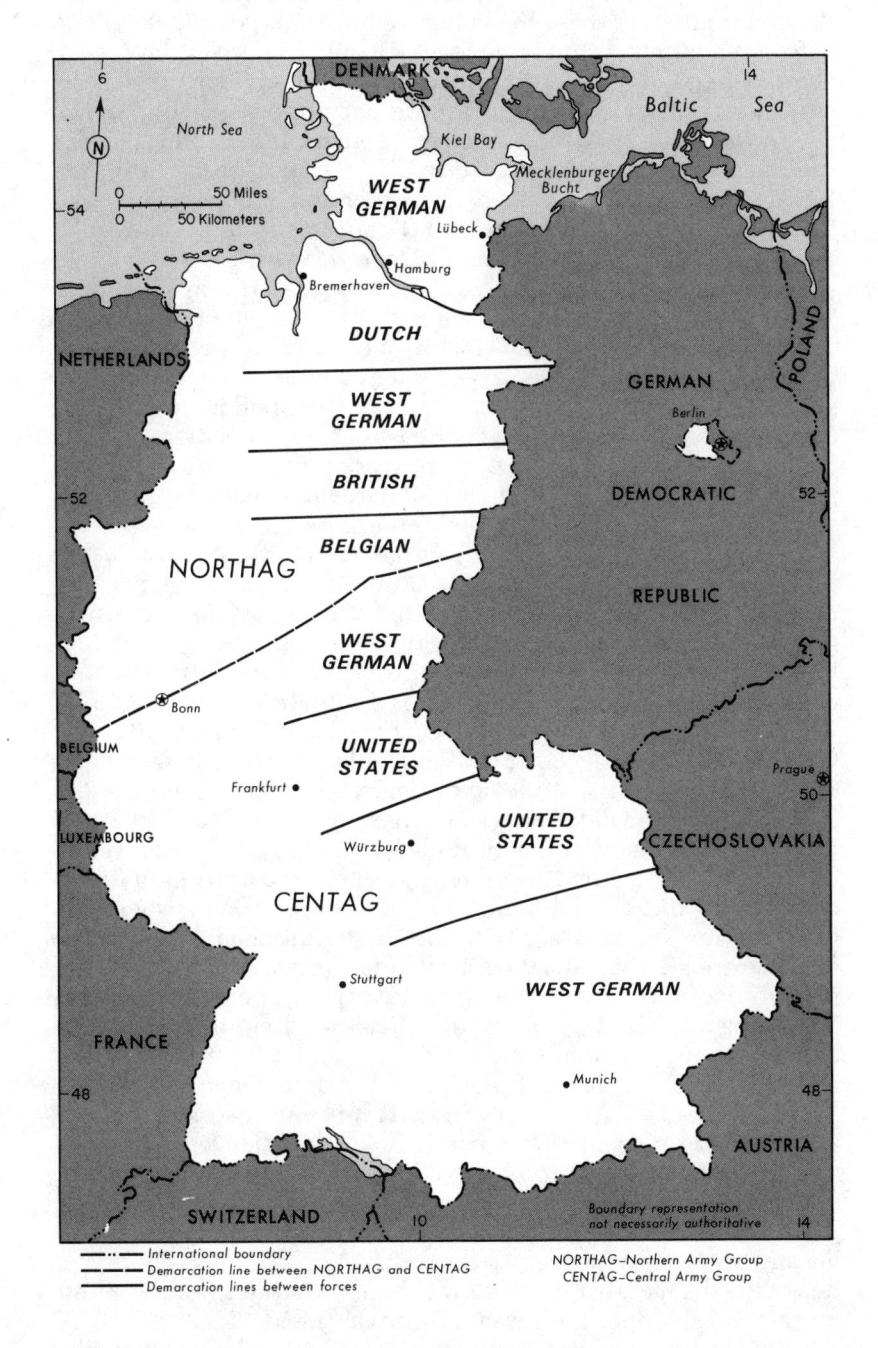

Figure 21. NATO Deployments: West Germany

important aspects of NATO policy. Two polls conducted in 1980 showed that over half the adult population favored keeping defense spending at the same level, 19 and 13 percent favored a decrease, and only 22 and 21 percent favored an increase. These attitudes contrast with the commitment undertaken by NATO governments in 1977 to an annual 3 percent increase in defense spending in real terms as an essential element in fulfilling the LTDP. Public opposition to defense spending increases, a prevalent factor in most European NATO countries, was undoubtedly an important element in Bonn's decision to increase defense spending in 1982 at a rate below the expected rise in inflation.

The NATO decision in December 1979 to deploy Long Range Theater Nuclear Forces (LRTNF) in Western Europe and to propose negotiations with the Soviet Union to limit such weapons has generated intense public debate. A May 1981 poll indicated that 53 percent of West Germans favored the NATO decision, 20 percent were opposed, and 27 percent were undecided. The same poll indicated, however, that only 29 percent actually favored the stationing of the weapons in the Federal Republic.

The most important NATO issue in late 1981 concerned the prospective deployment of LRTNF in Western Europe by the end of 1983. The NATO decision on this matter had its origins in growing West European concerns in the 1970s over the security implications of emerging United States-Soviet Union strategic nuclear parity and the Strategic Arms Limitations Talks (SALT), which were moving toward codifying the balance in a treaty. In October 1977 Chancellor Schmidt publicly acknowledged that SALT neutralized the strategic nuclear capabilities of the United States and the Soviet Union, and thereby magnified East-West disparities at the level of tactical nuclear and conventional weapons. Moreover Schmidt warned that "strategic arms limitations confined to the United States and the Soviet Union would be bound to impair the security of the West European members of the Alliance vis-à-vis Soviet military superiority in Europe if we do not succeed in removing the disparities in Europe parallel to the SALT negotiations." Thus in the official West German view the danger was that United States-Soviet Union parity had removed American strategic forces from a credible deterrence role in Europe. Former Secretary of State Henry A. Kissinger added weight to this view in 1979 when he told an audience in Brussels "what I might not say in office—that our European allies should not keep asking us to multiply strategic assurances that we cannot possibly mean, or if we do mean, we should not want to execute because if we execute, we risk the destruction of civilization....We must face the fact that it is absurd to base the strategy of the West on the credibility of the threat of mutual suicide."

The implications for Europe of United States-Soviet strategic parity drew attention to recent Soviet modernization of medium-range nuclear systems. Beginning in 1977 the Soviet Union began to deploy mobile, multiple warhead SS–20 ballistic missiles possessing a range of from 3,700 to 5,500 kilometers. SS–20 deployment continued at the rate of about fifty a year, resulting in an estimated 250 missiles with 750 warheads (not counting reloading capability) by September 1981. About three-fourths of the total—all reportedly deployed on Soviet territory—were believed to be targeted on Western Europe. The Soviet Union was expected to deploy 1,500 warheads on its SS–20 missiles by the end of 1983. Though the SS–20s were replacements for the older SS–4s and SS–5s, the extended range and improved accuracy, launch, and targeting versatility of the new missiles represented a major strengthening of Soviet theater nuclear capabilities. The SS–20s, together with the Backfire bomber deployed since 1974, posed a significant threat to Western Europe unmatched by comparable NATO forces. Moreover such so-called grey area or European strategic nuclear systems lay outside the framework of existing East-West arms control negotiations, i.e., the SALT negotiations that were confined to United States-Soviet central strategic systems and the Mutual and Balanced Force Reduction [MBFR] negotiations, which were concerned mainly with conventional forces in Central Europe. Thus the limited scope of the SALT and MBFR negotiations had permitted the Soviet Union to expand its advantage in the area of medium-range nuclear weapons in Europe.

Proponents of NATO LRTNF modernization argued that the improved accuracy, reduced warhead yield, mobility, and reload capability of the SS–20s gave the Soviet Union long-range nuclear superiority in the European theater, particularly in selective targeting capability. NATO's long-range aircraft were believed to be vulnerable to preemptive attack and likely to encounter difficulty in penetrating Soviet air defenses. United States submarine missile forces assigned to NATO were criticized by some on grounds of accuracy, flexibility of yield, and their close indentification with United States central strategic forces, which might inhibit an American president from authorizing their use. Critics therefore argued that a deterrence gap had resulted that the Soviet Union might seek to exploit in a crisis by escalating a military attack to a level where NATO would lack a credible response. An actual Soviet attack was believed to be highly unlikely, but the concern was that the perception of Soviet superiority at this force level (taking into account the possible neutralization of American strategic forces) would make Western Europe vulnerable to intimidation and pressure in a crisis.

Following two years of planning, in December 1979 NATO foreign and defense ministers decided to modernize NATO's LRTNF through the deployment in Europe of 108 Pershing II missile launchers (replacing the existing shorter range Pershing

Federal Republic of Germany

I–As) and 464 ground-launched cruise missiles. Taking into account expected public opposition to the action in Europe and strong support for arms control, NATO ministers also endorsed the holding of United States-Soviet Union negotiations to limit LRTNF based on the principle of equality for both sides. Late 1983, the earliest possible deployment date for the missiles, set the time frame for negotiations to succeed. Whereas the NATO "dual decision" was taken unanimously, Belgium and the Netherlands postponed their decisions on accepting the new missiles pending consideration of progress achieved in the arms control negotiations.

The West German position on the NATO decision was unique in several respects, reflecting the country's role as a front-line NATO state and at the same time its keen interest in maintaining a climate of lowered tensions and good relations with the Soviet Union and its East European allies. A major aim of the West Germans was to reconcile the requirements of military security with their interest in continued détente. With more of the missiles to be deployed in West Germany than in any other NATO country, Bonn sought to avoid the label of chief provocateur in an action sure to incite Soviet denunciation and domestic opposition. As a precondition for its own endorsement of the plan, therefore, Bonn insisted that the NATO decision be unanimous and that at least one other continental nonnuclear NATO state agree to accept the missiles (the so-called non-singularity principle). Moreover Bonn reaffirmed its intention not to become a nuclear power and emphasized Washington's leading role in NATO nuclear decisions, including exclusive United States control of the missiles to be deployed in West Germany and primary United States responsibility for negotiating LRTNF limitations with the Soviet Union.

In addition to its strong advocacy of the arms control initiative, Bonn was also instrumental in the NATO decision—taken at the same time—to withdraw 1,000 United States tactical nuclear warheads from Europe as soon as feasible. This action was integral to the LRTNF modernization decision and reflected a numerical shift of emphasis away from shorter range delivery systems. It was also seen, however, as a response to an earlier Soviet announcement of intent to withdraw 20,000 troops from East Germany. Moreover, by linking the withdrawal of older United States nuclear weapons with the deployment of new ones, the aim was to avoid the appearance that the NATO modernization decision was an arms buildup measure. Furthermore the NATO action in effect repudiated any attempt to establish parity or near-parity with the Soviet Union at the European strategic level. The aim instead was to establish a credible NATO deterrence posture at this level while maintaining a further escalation option for United States strategic nuclear forces.

West Germany remained a major political force behind the arms control component of the NATO dual decision. This reflected not only Bonn's commitment to a defense and détente policy for strategic reasons but also the existence of substantial domestic opposition to the deployment decision, including elements within the governing coalition parties. In October 1981 an estimated 250,000 people demonstrated in Bonn to protest the missile deployment decision. In parliament more than one-quarter of the members of the Social Democratic Party of Germany (Sozialdemokratische Partei Deutschlands—SPD) and about one-third of the members of the Free Democratic Party (Freie Demokratische Partei—FDP) endorsed the demonstration.

In May 1981 Schmidt indirectly threatened to resign if the SPD failed to continue its support for the government's position. Later Schmidt declared that "if these [arms control] negotiations turn out to be successful, all that is aspired to under part 1 [NATO's LRTNF modernization decision] need not be fully implemented, perhaps only much less, and in the ideal case, not at all." Thus the optimal objective for West Germany was to achieve a successful United States-Soviet Union negotiation on LRTNF limitation (presumably requiring the removal of all or most of the Soviet SS–20s), which would preclude the need to implement in full or at all the NATO modernization decision. Nevertheless Schmidt told the Bundestag in December 1981 that "if there are no concrete results [to the negotiations] by the summer of 1983, NATO will proceed with the deployment of United States missiles in the Federal Republic of Germany." Preliminary United States-Soviet Union talks on LRTNF limitation began in October 1980 but were suspended as a result of the crisis in Poland. Bonn sought to revive the talks, and in November 1981 the United States and the Soviet Union began negotiations in Geneva on the limitation of European theater nuclear forces.

Ostpolitik and Détente

The Federal Republic's *Ostpolitik* (eastern policy) had its origins in the unsuccessful reunification diplomacy of the 1950s, the absence of strong international support for active reunification efforts by the 1960s, the continued solidification of the division of Germany as symbolized by the Berlin Wall, and the growing interest in East-West détente in Europe (see Adenauer Era, ch. 1). Begun cautiously by Chancellor Ludwig Erhard (1963–66) *Ostpolitik* reached a decisive stage under Chancellor Willy Brandt (1969–74).

The West Germans concentrated on establishing a dialogue with East Germany aimed at normalizing relations, lessening the human hardships resulting from partition, arresting the trend toward separation, and keeping alive the idea of national consciousness. These undertakings were preceded by attempts to improve relations with Eastern Europe and the Soviet Union, particularly in view of the latter's dominant influence over the Eastern bloc's relations with the Federal Republic. With the conclusion of the Four Power Agreement on Berlin in 1971 (the Berlin Accord) and the Basic Treaty in 1972, the two governments acknowledged two German states and pledged respect for each other's independence and autonomy in internal and external affairs. West Germany was guaranteed continued ties with West Berlin (see Grand Coalition, 1966–69, ch. 1; Willy Brandt's *Ostpolitik*, ch. 1).

Conclusion of the Berlin Accord, normalization of relations between the two Germanys, and the Soviet agreement to begin negotiations on military force reductions in Central Europe enabled the opening of the Conference on Security and Cooperation in Europe (CSCE) in Helsinki, Finland in 1972. The Final Act of the CSCE, signed in 1975 by thirty-five countries—including West Germany and East Germany—declared inter alia that the states "will respect each other's sovereignty and equality...including... territorial integrity [and] will refrain...from the threat or use of force against the territorial integrity or political independence of any state." These provisions provided a broader multilateral basis for bilateral accords than had been concluded previously.

The treaties signaled Bonn's preparedness to postpone indefinitely attempts to achieve German unity, a recognition that such unity could come about only as a result of a lengthy historical process of East-West reconciliation. Reversing the sequence of events accepted in the 1950s, West Germany recognized that reunification, in whatever form, could occur only as a result of détente rather than being a precondition for it. West Germany would have to accept the nation's division in order one day to overcome it.

The balance sheet of *Ostpolitik* since the ratification of the treaties has been mixed. On the positive side, the Federal Republic has been relieved of the burden of territorial revanchist positions in Central Europe, which had been a continuing source of suspicion and estrangement in its relations with East European governments. Bonn's acceptance of the territorial status quo and its indefinite postponement of an active reunification policy paved the way for more normalized East-West relations in Europe. The conclusion of the Helsinki Final Act gave multilateral confirmation of territorial frontiers throughout Europe. Berlin was no longer the barometer of East-West tensions, though differences persisted over the implementation of the Berlin Accord. The *Ostpolitik* treaties paved the way for the emigration of about 300,000 ethnic Germans to the Federal Republic, principally from Poland and the Soviet Union. Each year millions of West Germans and West Berliners visit relatives and friends in East Ger-

*Chancellor Willy Brandt and Chairman of the
Council of Ministers of the German Democratic Republic
Willi Stoph in their first meeting, March 19, 1970
Courtesy German Information Center*

*Chancellor Helmut Schmidt and East German leader
Erich Honecker chat at August 1975 Conference on
Security and Cooperation in Europe.
Courtesy German Information Center*

many and East Berlin, though East German travel to the Federal Republic is generally confined to pensioners and family hardship cases. Telephone communications have been restored, and road transportation links have been improved.

The *Ostpolitik* has nonetheless encountered problems and limitations, particularly with respect to West Berlin and intra-German relations. With regard to the former, there has been disagreement over the links between West Berlin and the Federal Republic as provided in the Berlin Accord. The agreement acknowledged that West Berlin was not a "constituent part" of West Germany and was "not to be governed by it" and that specified federal officials and bodies were prohibited from performing "constitutional or official acts" in the city violative of this provision. It also declared, however, that existing ties "will be maintained and developed." Building upon this provision, the Federal Republic sought to strengthen its links with West Berlin, and on several occasions the Soviet Union and East Germany protested that these measures were extensions of West German authority that were prohibited by the treaty.

On another matter, the Berlin Accord states that West Germany's international agreements and arrangements may be extended to include West Berlin provided that such extension is specified in each case. The Federal Republic and the three Western powers—Britain, France, and the United States—interpreted this provision as allowing an automatic extension of Bonn's agreements to encompass West Berlin (in specified instances), whereas the Soviet Union rejected this position. The dispute over this issue blocked conclusion of bilateral treaties between West Germany and the Soviet Union dealing with scientific, technological, and economic cooperation, cultural exchanges, and legal aid. Moscow also protested Bonn's inclusion of West Berlin delegates as part of its total numerical representation in the European Parliament.

In addition, the intra-German dimension of *Ostpolitik* has been limited by the different interests and goals of the two states. West Germany viewed its *Ostpolitik* in general, and intra-German policy in particular, as a means for promoting closer contacts between the two states to advance the long-term goal of overcoming the nation's division. Conversely East Germany regarded the Basic Treaty as the symbol of its international status and legitimacy and as marking the consolidation of the German division into two states with different social systems and international alignments. This view, of course, has been shared by the Soviet Union as one of its major foreign policy aims as represented by the treaty with West Germany, the Berlin Accord, and the security provisions of the CSCE Final Act. As analyst Karl Birnbaum observed, "the consolidation of the GDR...as an equal European state was viewed by Moscow as a necessary precondition for the desired extension of East-West trade and collaboration." Ultimately, therefore, the realization of Soviet détente aims in Europe would depend on "*whether the relations between the two German states could evolve in a fashion that would allow an opening towards the West without jeopardising either the short term stability or the long term viability of a communist regime in East Germany* [emphasis in original]."

Thus *Ostpolitik* in particular and détente in general posed both opportunities and risks for East Germany and the Soviet Union. Whereas East Germany had gained in security and status as a result of the normalization process, it had not persuaded West Germany to accord it formal diplomatic recognition or to abandon its long-term goal of reunification. Moreover the Soviet Union had endorsed the *Ostpolitik* treaties based on this qualified acceptance of East Germany by the Federal Republic. The risk, of course, was that the mood of détente in the 1970s and the expansion of intra-German and East-West contacts as foreseen by the treaties and the Helsinki Final Act could produce destabilizing effects on the East German regime. For example, the so-called Basket III of the Final Act of the Helsinki Accords, in which signatory states pledged to ease travel regulations and facilitate family visits and reunifications, led in 1975–77 to a dramatic upsurge of East German inquiries and applications for travel permits and emigration.

Thus the very process that led to East Germany's increased territorial security and international acceptance carried risks of undermining a regime that still found it necessary to retain its population by means of closely guarded frontiers and tight emigration controls. Nevertheless East Germany stood to realize substantial benefits from increased trade, credits, and technological access in its relations with the Federal Republic.

In the face of these considerations, East Germany responded with a policy of demarcation (*Abgrenzung*) intended to minimize and regulate contacts with West Germany while intensifying party control over all aspects of social and political life. East Germany insisted upon treating West Germany as a foreign state and inculcated the doctrine of a "socialist" German nation, heir to distinctive parts of the German tradition, as opposed to the capitalist Federal Republic. In 1974 the East German parliament formally amended its 1968 constitution to remove references to the goal of German unification. Intensified ideological training, orders restricting persons in politically and socially sensitive positions from meetings with West Germans, restrictions on contacts between West German journalists and East Germans, and suppression of artistic and intellectual expression emerged as practical examples of the demarcation policy. As analyst Peter Christian Ludz observed, such measures "must be understood essentially as an attempt at immunization and legitimization by an ideological and political regime that even today has by no means been stabilized."

Whereas numerous agreements for practical intra-German cooperation have been signed, others have been blocked by differences on the inclusion of West Berlin and the East German demand that Bonn recognize East German citizenship. Predictably East Germany has been more forthcoming in areas of economic cooperation where ties with West Germany have bolstered East Germany's technological and industrial position and provided sorely needed convertible currency to help finance trade with the West. Moreover East Germany has enjoyed tariff-and quota-free access to the West German market on a nonreciprocal basis and has received interest-free credits from West Germany to finance imports.

The deterioration in East-West relations in the wake of the Soviet invasion of Afghanistan in December 1979 did not adversely affect relations between the German states. Indeed, there was mutual expression of interest in continuing intra-German cooperation and limiting the effects of global turbulence elsewhere. In May 1980 West Berlin Mayor Dietrich Stobbe visited East Berlin, the first public appearance by a West Berlin mayor in the East German capital for more than twenty years. In another development, agreement was reached for Bonn to finance major road, rail, and canal improvement projects in East Germany to strengthen transportation links between the two states.

East German interest in intra-German cooperation continued to be almost entirely economic, premised on the simultaneous need to keep the policy of demarcation intact. The Federal Republic continued to be East Germany's most important Western trading partner, accounting for 9 to 12 percent of its total foreign trade. Despite the political climate after the invasion of Afghanistan, trade between the two countries increased by 18.7 percent in 1980, facilitated by a continuation of interest-free credits from Bonn. Moreover West Germany has transferred yearly to East Germany an estimated US$1.6 billion through transportation agreements and private gifts to friends and relatives.

Intra-German relations suffered a serious setback, however, as a result of the political upheavals in Poland beginning in September 1980. East German authorities showed acute concern that widening political, economic, and social unrest in Poland could spread to East Germany. In such circumstances the need for a tighter policy of demarcation took precedence over continued improvement of ties with Bonn. Indeed, West Germany was identified as a major villain in an alleged Western campaign "to liquidate the German Democratic Republic by military and counterrevolutionary means." In October East German party leader Erich Honecker demanded that the Federal Republic recognize East German citizenship and formalize relations through the exchange of ambassadors and the establishment of embassies as a condition for continued normalization of relations. Though these positions were later softened somewhat, they were indicative of East Germany's heightened insecurity as a result of the events in Poland.

Other aspects of the new policy included doubling the foreign exchange requirement for Western visitors to East Germany and abolishing exemptions for children and pensioners, measures that substantially reduced the number of visits by West Germans and West Berliners. Tight controls were imposed on travel between East Germany and Poland, foreign travel by East German performing artists was curtailed, and the Protestant church in East Germany was threatened with restrictions if it continued political criticism. Whereas West German officials strongly denounced the new East German currency exchange rules, the Federal Republic refrained from reprisal measures in the belief that they would be counterproductive and harmful to the continued goal of normalization.

In December 1981 Schmidt met with East Germany's Honecker, the first intra-German summit meeting in eleven years. The main result of the talks was a West German agreement to extend the existing swing credit arrangement to East Germany through June 1982, pending negotiation of a new agreement. Schmidt made clear that there was a "psychological-political" connection between the Federal Republic's extension of the swing credit beyond June 1982, the lowering of the minimum currency exchange requirements for Western visitors to East Germany, and the easing of travel restrictions.

The *Ostpolitik* is an aspect of the Federal Republic's parallel interest in East-West détente. West Germany's détente policy has been rooted in three fundamental conditions: the existence of two German states and the West German goal of normalization of relations and, eventually, some form of reassociation of the German people; the Federal Republic's exposed position on the front line between East and West and thus its special security needs; and the high dependency of the West German economy on exports of manufactured goods and raw material imports.

In the economic sphere exports and imports of goods and services have constituted over half of West Germany's gross national product (GNP), more than any other major industrial country (see Growth and Structure of the Economy, ch. 4). About one in four West German jobs is dependent upon exports. Whereas the bulk of the nation's foreign trade is with other Western industrial countries, West Germany is the largest noncommunist trading partner for Eastern Europe and the Soviet Union. In 1980 almost 9 percent of West Germany's total foreign trade was with the Soviet Union and East European states (including East Germany). Because strong economic relations are encouraged by a favorable political climate (and may be largely dependent upon it), West

Federal Republic of Germany

Germany's exceptional reliance on foreign trade gives it an important stake in maintaining détente with the East.

West Germany's interest in trade with the East has been complemented by other aspects of its economic relations. Bonn played a leading role in negotiations for an agreement with Moscow concluded in November 1981 for supplying Western Europe with some 40 billion cubic meters of natural gas annually by the mid-1980s. The gas is to be extracted with the aid of Western technology and transmitted from Siberia to Europe by Western-built pipelines (see Energy, ch. 6). West Germany, which will receive about 25 percent of the gas deliveries, stands to benefit substantially from the equivalent of at least US$11 billion worth of equipment orders that will be required to complete the project. Under the proposed arrangement, West Germany is expected to increase its dependence on Soviet natural gas from 17 percent in 1981 to approximately 30 percent. In early 1982 the Reagan administration continued to oppose the pipeline project, arguing that it would result in excessive West German dependence on Soviet natural gas and expose the Federal Republic to the risk of political blackmail. Bonn officials have noted that the prospective Soviet gas supply would represent only 5 percent of West Germany's total energy needs and that, in any case, alternative supplies would be available in the event of a cutoff. In another energy area, West Germany was dependent on the Soviet Union for about 50 percent of its enriched uranium supplies, though this was expected to decline to about 23 percent by 1990.

The continuing political and economic uncertainty in Poland in early 1982 posed dangers for West German economic interests. More than one-third of Poland's US$27 billion external debt to the West was owed to West German banks and agencies. Thus Bonn, with a special stake in Poland's stability, was active in promoting food aid shipments and encouraging the rescheduling of Poland's debt repayment obligations to Western creditors.

Détente and *Ostpolitik* also have important meaning for West Germany in human terms. Each year some 7 to 8 million West Germans and West Berliners visit East Berlin and East Germany, and intra-German family ties have been significantly strengthened. Extensive ethnic German emigration from Eastern Europe and the Soviet Union represented another gain. Nevertheless an estimated 3 million remained, in effect, hostages to continued good relations between Bonn and the East. Thus the combined political, strategic, economic, and human dimensions of West German relations with the East comprised a major stake in détente. At the same time they represented sources of potential West German vulnerability in the event of a deterioration of East-West relations in Europe.

Foreign Relations

West Germany's attitude toward détente has continued to be closely related to its policy toward NATO. Bonn has strongly endorsed the Harmel Report, approved by the NATO Council in 1967, which set forth defense and détente as complementary aims. As Schmidt stated in 1979: "If you want to have continuity of détente you have to have continuity of the balance of power, the equilibrium. Continuity of détente cannot persist if you let the military equilibrium deteriorate." In 1980 Schmidt declared: "The decisive prerequisite for the functioning of cooperation between West and East lies in maintaining the military balance." At the same time, détente is viewed as an important element of security policy insofar as it reduces the potential for conflict.

Bonn's dual commitment to defense and détente (though by 1980 the term "dialogue" had come into vogue) has been manifest in specific aspects of West German policy. The Federal Republic's support for the NATO LRTNF deployment decision was balanced by its advocacy of parallel arms control initiatives. Domestic opposition to the deployment decision influenced the Schmidt government to press Washington for an early commencement of LRTNF limitation talks with the Soviet Union. On the neutron warhead issue, Bonn appeared to take some distance from Washington's decision (emphasizing that it was an American affair and that deployment in Europe was not at issue), out of concern that the action could damage the credibility of the United States commitment to arms control and weaken West German public support for the LRTNF deployment decision.

The Soviet invasion of Afghanistan in December 1979 quickly worsened an already deteriorating atmosphere in United States-Soviet relations. The Carter administration interpreted the Soviet action as a dramatic threat to regional stability and as portending possible further Soviet expansionist activity toward the Persian Gulf region. The administration reacted sharply by imposing a partial embargo on American exports to the Soviet Union, declaring the Persian Gulf region to be of vital interest to the United States, announcing plans to create a rapid deployment force to deal with possible military threats to the region, and calling for a boycott of the 1980 Olympic Games scheduled to be held in Moscow.

Whereas the Federal Republic and other West European governments denounced the invasion and called for a withdrawal of Soviet forces, the general tendency was to seek to safeguard détente in Europe from the repercussions of the crisis. As Schmidt declared in June 1980: "We have made great efforts in past months to make sure that, despite intensified tensions in the world, the détente process in Europe would not be damaged but further strengthened." Thus while West Germany and other EC countries agreed "not to undermine or undercut" the United States partial embargo by compensatory increases in their own

Federal Republic of Germany

exports, they nevertheless declined to adopt trade sanctions of their own against the Soviet Union. The Federal Republic, in particular, sought to continue its policy of normalization toward East Germany "without interruption." In line with this position, negotiations were concluded in May 1980 for a new, long-term economic cooperation agreement between West Germany and the Soviet Union.

Moreover the Schmidt government was reportedly critical of what it felt was an American overreaction to the crisis and an excessive emphasis upon confrontation, sanctions, and military preparations. Nevertheless, despite apparent misgivings, the Bonn government was the only major Western country to join the United States in boycotting the Moscow Olympics. West German officials made clear, however, that the government's position was related to the need for United States support in safeguarding the Federal Republic's vital interests. As Foreign Minister Hans-Dietrich Genscher explained: "We expect solidarity from the United States in the Berlin question, and we shall not deny them our solidarity in the question of the Olympic Games."

While stressing the importance of Western cohesion, Bonn also took a broader view of the problem by underlining the need for greater economic and political stability in Third World areas in order to deal with the root causes of conflict that could lead to foreign intervention. In line with this approach, West German officials suggested an agreed division of responsibilities among Western countries whereby each would respond according to its possibilities and individual situation. While eschewing economic sanctions against the Soviet Union and military tasks in the Persian Gulf region, Bonn stated its intention to increase aid to Pakistan and Turkey and to strengthen, jointly with other countries of the EC, diplomatic and economic cooperation with the Persian Gulf states.

West Germany's dual commitment to the Atlantic Alliance and to détente produced tensions in its foreign relations following the establishment of martial law in Poland in December 1981. While condemning the political repression in Poland imposed by the government of Premier Wojciech Jaruzelski, Bonn initially avoided public accusation of the Soviet Union's involvement in the crisis and was unwilling to impose sanctions against either Warsaw or Moscow. Nonetheless the Reagan administration's announcement on December 23 of sanctions against Poland and its warning of steps against the Soviet Union if martial law continued, exerted pressure on the West German government to reconsider its position. A week later the United States announced sanctions against the Soviet Union for its role in the Polish crisis and sought agreement by the NATO allies either to adopt parallel steps or not to take actions that would undermine the American measures. Nevertheless Bonn continued to avoid public accusation of Soviet complicity in the military crackdown and concentrated instead on diplomatic efforts with the Polish government to ease the crisis.

In early January 1982, however, West Germany and the other members of the EC moved significantly closer to the United States position by disapproving "the serious external pressure and the campaign directed by the USSR" in the Polish situation. The EC countries undertook not to undermine United States sanctions against the Soviet Union and indicated that further measures would be considered in light of developments in Poland. Later, following a meeting in Washington between Schmidt and Reagan, the two leaders "noted the responsibility of the Soviet Union for developments in Poland" and insisted that "Poland be allowed to resolve its problems without external interference."

At a special meeting of NATO foreign ministers, West Germany and the other allies (except Greece) agreed to place in abeyance further commercial credits for Poland (other than for food) and to suspend negotiations on the rescheduling of Poland's debt payments due in 1982. In addition each ally agreed to consider, in accordance with its own situation and laws, further measures involving, inter alia, restrictions on the movement of Soviet and Polish diplomats, reduction of scientific and technical activities, and curtailment of commercial relations with the Soviet Union. In line with the NATO position, in February Schmidt's government announced a ban on high-level visits by West German officials to the Soviet Union, postponed the opening of new Soviet consulates in the Federal Republic, imposed travel restrictions on Soviet diplomats, and suspended negotiations for agreements on scientific cooperation and inland shipping. Subsequently West Germany and other members of the EC agreed to restrict imports from the Soviet Union covering a range of luxury goods and manufactured products. Thus by the end of February 1982 there had developed a closer alignment of United States and West European policies with respect to the Polish crisis.

The European Communities

The EC and the Atlantic Alliance represent the Federal Republic's most important institutional commitments to its Western policy orientation. From the country's establishment in 1949, West German policy has sought to transcend the Hitlerian legacy of destructive nationalism and to win confidence in the West through an active policy of promoting European unity. Unique among West European states, the Federal Republic's constitution (Basic Law) provides that sovereign powers may be transferred to international institutions by legislative action.

The EC—including the European Economic Community (Common Market), the European Coal and Steel Community, and the European Atomic Energy Community—was established as a result of the Treaty of Paris (1951) and the Treaties of Rome (1957). In

Federal Republic of Germany

1967 the institutions of the three communities were merged to establish the Council of Ministers of the European Communities, the Commission of the European Communities, the Court of Justice, and the European Parliament. The council of ministers, composed of government ministers representing different functional areas, is the chief decisionmaking body of the EC and can enact regulations and decisions that are binding throughout the EC. The commission, which seeks to represent the EC as a whole, is responsible for initiating legislation to be acted upon by the council, brokering compromise agreements among member governments, overseeing compliance with EC legislation, and enacting regulations on its own under authority of the treaties or in fulfillment of a mandate established by the council. The court is the supreme judicial arm of the EC, possessing final authority to interpret EC law and its meaning in specific cases; EC law takes precedence over national laws in the event of conflict between them. The parliament, directly elected since 1979, is mainly an advisory body, though it must be consulted prior to council action on commission proposals. Since 1975 the parliament has acquired increased power over the EC budget, power that is exercised jointly with the council. As of early 1982 the EC included ten members: West Germany, France, Britain, Italy, Belgium, the Netherlands, Luxembourg, Denmark, Ireland, and Greece.

The chief purpose of the EC is to advance the economic integration of Western Europe through the elimination or reduction of national barriers to the free movement of trade, people, and capital. A major step toward this goal was the gradual introduction of a customs union, achieved in 1968, providing for tariff- and quota-free trade among EC countries and a common external tariff on imports from nonmember states. A Common Agricultural Policy (CAP) has been established through an EC guaranteed and regulated pricing system achieved through levies on imports from nonmember countries and domestic market intervention and export rebate mechanisms. Progress has been made toward perfecting a common internal market through reducing nontariff barriers to trade, for example, by regulating government aids to industries, harmonizing taxes and product performance specifications, and prohibiting monopolistic business practices. In 1978 a European Monetary System was introduced that sought to reduce exchange rate fluctuations among member states through a system of fixed currency relationships that central banks were obligated to support within a narrow margin of variation.

The EC is the most important single market for its members. About half of the Federal Republic's total trade is conducted with other members of the EC. In 1979 and 1980 EC countries occupied the top five places as destinations for West German exports and five of the top six places as suppliers of West German imports. West Germany alone accounted for approximately 30 percent of the total exports of the ten members of the EC.

Despite significant achievements in regional economic integration, the EC experienced serious problems in the 1970s and early 1980s. Many of these difficulties resulted from the oil price shocks of 1973–74 and 1978–79, which produced severe inflationary pressures, stagnating economic growth, and high unemployment. Nevertheless most EC governments sought to maintain their domestic social programs largely intact, which strained national budgets. In 1982 European leaders continued to complain that high United States interest rates were attracting investment funds from Europe and thus further aggravating economic recovery. Moreover the strong position of the United States dollar in relation to European currencies added another dimension to inflation because oil imports were purchased with dollars. In such circumstances EC governments often adopted national solutions to cope with their economic ills, e.g., subsidies to industries and import restrictions, which undermined efforts to maintain common EC policies. Moreover since national economic conditions and needs frequently varied widely, it became more difficult to agree on solutions at the EC level.

The EC method of decisionmaking also burdened the task of agreement on common policies. The Treaties of Rome provide that the council may take most decisions by a weighted majority vote. Some EC members, however, notably France and Britain, have opposed this supranational voting provision and have insisted that on important issues any member may require a unanimous decision. This in effect gives a veto power to any member state. As the EC expands (in 1982 applications were pending from Spain and Portugal), decisionmaking under such a procedure will become increasingly difficult. Moreover the inclusion of additional South European countries may be expected to increase the economic and social disparities within the EC and intensify the competition for distribution of resources in various EC programs.

The CAP has contributed to increased productivity, rising farmer incomes, stabilized markets, and greater self-sufficiency. Yet it has conferred unequal benefits on member states and has absorbed a disproportionate share of the EC budget. CAP guarantees of high prices to farmers have been financed by EC revenues. Chronic surpluses have occurred in some commodities and have resulted in high storage costs and subsidized dumping on foreign markets. Whereas less than 10 percent of EC workers have been engaged in agriculture, about 70 percent of EC revenues have been allocated to support CAP. France, with a large agricultural sector, benefits substantially from the domestic price support and export rebate features of CAP. Conversely Britain and West Germany, with relatively small agricultural populations and high import dependence, gain less benefit from CAP while supporting it heavily through the payment of import levies.

Federal Republic of Germany

The European unity idea has enjoyed wide public support in the Federal Republic since the 1950s. From 1952 through 1980 opinion polls showed that more than 75 percent of the West German public favored the unification of Western Europe. Support for the EC was also broad, as shown by nine polls conducted over the 1973–80 period. An average of 62 percent of West Germans believed that EC membership was "a good thing," while less than 5 percent believed it was "a bad thing." In 1981, however, the same poll revealed that only 49 percent believed that membership in the EC was "a good thing." West Germans have become decidedly less optimistic about the possible emergence one day of a United States of Europe. Moreover when questions were posed in specific terms, e.g., requesting preference of a European currency, flag, or Olympic team compared to a national one, West Germans tended to disapprove of the European alternatives.

Despite popular and governmental support for EC membership, Bonn has become increasingly resistant to cost increases in EC programs. West Germany is the largest contributor to the EC budget and has been displeased with its image as the paymaster of Europe. While West German agricultural minister Josef Ertl has been successful in achieving continued price rises to benefit West German farmers, the economics and finance ministers have expressed growing opposition to large price increases.

In May 1980 the EC resolved a long-simmering crisis over Britain's contribution to the EC budget. Britain had argued that under existing arrangements it would be required to make by far the largest contribution to the EC despite its position as the third poorest member. Prime Minister Margaret Thatcher threatened to withhold part of Britain's value-added tax (VAT) contribution to the EC if an equitable solution were not found. The settlement finally reached provided for an approximate two-thirds reduction in the amount of the British contribution to the budget over three years. Despite initial dissension within the West German cabinet, Bonn endorsed the agreement, which required the Federal Republic to contribute about US$1.4 billion a year additionally to the EC budget. This amount comprised the bulk of the deficit created by the reduced British contribution and made West Germany the largest net contributor to the EC.

The settlement left an unpleasant aftertaste, however, which was aggravated by Britain's later blocking of an EC fisheries agreement with Canada that would have benefited West German trawlers. The growing conviction in Bonn that it was bearing an inequitable share of EC expenses was made more acute by mounting government deficits, slackened economic growth (a 1.3 percent drop in GNP in the first half of 1981), and high interest rates that discouraged capital investment and contributed to the highest level of unemployment in almost thirty years (see Labor, ch. 4). In such a climate, with West Germany's net payments to the

Foreign Relations

EC amounting to one-third of its overall budget deficit, Bonn signaled its determination to limit further EC spending increases. Nevertheless, under EC commission proposals presented in mid-1981, West Germany's EC bill would rise even further in 1982.

The continuing rise of agricultural prices has caused concern that the cost of the EC's budgeted programs (mostly in support of the agricultural sector) may eventually exceed available resources. The EC budget has been financed by agricultural levies on non-EC imports, tariffs on industrial imports, and up to 1 percent of the VAT assessed on products manufactured in the EC. Indicative of its displeasure with the rate of growth of EC spending, Bonn opposed any increase in the percentage of VAT allocated to the EC budget.

On another issue Bonn has been critical of the widespread practice of government subsidies to steel producers in the community (see Iron and Steel, ch. 6). Though such state aids are generally prohibited under EC law, some governments have resorted to support measures to maintain employment and stimulate modernization in an industry that has suffered from slackened demand, overcapacity, insufficient investment, and increased international competition. After voluntary production and price control measures proved inadequate, in October 1980 the EC initiated a system of mandatory production quotas covering most steel products for a nine-month period. West Germany, with an efficient steel industry, reluctantly accepted the quota system as a temporary measure. In June 1981, however, EC governments agreed to extend mandatory production quotas until mid-1982. In a compromise move, partly satisfying Bonn's objections, it was also agreed to terminate state assistance not related to industrial restructuring by mid-1982 and to end all subsidies to the steel industry by the end of 1985.

Although the EC has been concerned primarily with economic integration, political cooperation has become an increasingly prominent focus of its activity. In 1970 the EC foreign ministers agreed "to consult each other on all major questions of foreign policy...[and to work] for a harmonization of views, concertation of attitudes, and joint action when it appears feasible and desirable." In 1973 the ministers further agreed "as a general rule not to take up final positions without prior consultation with its partners within the framework of the political cooperation machinery." In the early 1970s political cooperation was part of the EC's stated determination to transform by the end of the decade "the whole complex of the relations of member states into a European union." This goal proved unfeasible, but progress has been realized in developing common foreign policy positions among EC member states. For example, EC members vote together most of the time on issues at the UN, producing a greater voting convergence than existed before political cooperation was begun. Since 1974 the

Federal Republic of Germany

heads of state or government of the EC countries have met three times a year as the European Council. The representative of the country that holds the presidency of the European Council (a six-month rotating position) addresses the General Assembly and UN committees on behalf of the entire EC. In such ways the EC has enhanced its image as an active and cohesive body in line with its aim to increase its influence on international political issues.

Political cooperation in the EC is carried out through several levels of consultation. The meetings of the European Council are devoted to discussion of EC issues and also to matters of political cooperation. EC foreign ministers meet four times a year, assisted by a political committee composed of the political directors within the respective foreign ministries. The group of correspondents (officials within the foreign ministries) follows through on implementation and coordinates the numerous working groups established to deal with particular issues. The embassies of the ten members in major foreign capitals and their missions to international organizations consult with each other and seek to harmonize foreign policy positions. Although all EC members participate in this political cooperation, it has no basis in treaty obligation and is conducted, largely, independently from the regular institutions of the EC. Close liaison is maintained with EC institutions, however, on matters discussed in political cooperation that have a bearing on EC activities.

Political cooperation produced results when the EC members developed unified positions during the negotiations leading to the conclusion of the Helsinki Final Act in 1975. Similar EC unity was evident in the subsequent review conferences in Belgrade in 1977 and Madrid in 1980–81. Regarding the Middle East, the Venice declaration of the European Council in June 1980 supported the right of the Palestinian people "to exercise fully its right to self-determination" and endorsed participation of the Palestine Liberation Organization (PLO) in negotiations leading to a comprehensive peace settlement and security for all states in the Middle East. Moreover the European Council instructed its presidency to explore with the parties to the Middle East conflict the prospects for a peace initiative along the lines of the Venice declaration. Whereas the EC members had issued earlier statements on the Middle East, this was the first one to include an operational component, and it signaled the growing desire of EC members to exercise collective influence on global and regional issues. With regard to Afghanistan, in June 1981 the European Council proposed a two-stage international conference for the purpose of ending foreign intervention and creating conditions for assuring Afghanistan's independence and nonalignment.

The legacy of German nationalist excesses in the nineteenth and twentieth centuries—reinforced by West Germany's economic preponderance in Europe—has prompted Bonn to seek to harmonize its policies in various multilateral associations such as the UN, NATO, and the EC. By emphasizing a European-oriented foreign policy, Bonn has sought to gain acceptance of its own growing leadership position and to advance its goal of furthering European unity. Moreover European political cooperation has provided a multilateral base of support for West German foreign policy beyond that which might be expected from unilateral action. The Federal Republic has viewed political cooperation as an important means for strengthening support for the EC within member countries, thereby facilitating solutions to the EC's economic and financial problems.

In early 1982 the Federal Republic continued to seek to promote movement toward a joint European foreign policy based on a growing identity of views among EC countries and the need to advance specifically European interests in relation to global problems. Such issues in East-West relations as Afghanistan, Poland, nuclear force levels, and regional tensions in the Middle East and Africa have been seen as affecting vital European interests and requiring a more cohesive European response. Unlike France's policy in the 1960s under President Charles de Gaulle, however, West Germany has rejected the vision of a Europe independent of the United States. On the contrary, Bonn has envisaged continued close cooperation with the United States in a maturing partnership of equals as European unity progresses.

In January 1981 the Schmidt government introduced ideas intended to strengthen and broaden the scope of European political cooperation. Foreign Minister Genscher proposed a "politically binding act" that would join together the EC, European political cooperation, and the European Council. The EC would remain a major forum for activity, whereas political cooperation would be placed on a firm and binding foundation. Genscher proposed extending political cooperation to include security issues and a strengthening of staff resources and consultation arrangements. In September the EC foreign ministers, responding to a British proposal, agreed on the need to create a small support staff and to include representation from the Commission of the EC at all political cooperation meetings. The proposal to include discussion of defense and security issues at such meetings was met with objections from Ireland (the only EC country that is not a member of NATO) as well as other smaller EC countries. The West German goal of extending the scope of political cooperation into sensitive areas may therefore continue to face difficulties in the future.

Relations with the Middle East and East Asia
Middle East

The Federal Republic's policy in the Middle East has sought to develop economic and political cooperation with the oil-producing states, while maintaining Israel's confidence that West

Germany supported its security. The Federal Republic is conscious of the special moral and historical nature of its relations with Israel, yet its heavy dependence on Middle East oil has created incentives for Bonn to establish strong ties with the Arab states.

West Germany's Middle East policy has operated on both multilateral and bilateral levels. With regard to the former, Bonn's policy has been coordinated with its EC partners in the framework of political cooperation. In the aftermath of the October 1973 War and the subsequent rise in oil prices, the EC countries began a sustained attempt to mold a concerted policy for the region. These efforts have led to growing EC interest in playing an active role in the Middle East peace process. Although insisting that a Middle East solution must guarantee Israel's right to exist within secure borders, the EC position has moved toward increased support for the Palestinians. In November 1973 the EC statement on the Middle East affirmed that a just and lasting peace must take account of the legitimate rights of the Palestinians. In June 1977 the Council of Ministers of the EC went further when it supported "the legitimate right of the Palestinian people to give effective expression to its national identity... which would take into account the need for a homeland for the Palestinian people." In June 1980 the council stated that the Palestinian people must be allowed "to exercise fully [their] right to self-determination" within the framework of a comprehensive peace settlement and, for the first time, called for a role for the PLO in the peace negotiations. Mindful of the need to maintain balance in its position, however, the EC member countries abstained on a UN General Assembly resolution in July that for the first time endorsed the right of the Palestinians to found "an independent sovereign state" in the Arab territories occupied by Israel. Under the aegis of the council presidency, in 1980–81 EC members undertook exploratory talks with the parties to the Middle East conflict to determine if there existed a basis for negotiations.

West Germany has also participated in a European-Arab dialogue that was initiated in 1974 as a framework for economic and technological cooperation between the EC and the League of Arab States (the Arab League). Differing Euro-Arab priorities, compounded by intra-Arab divisions and continued Arab-Israeli tensions, prevented significant progress, however. The Europeans have sought to avoid sensitive political questions, e.g., PLO recognition, and have encouraged a climate favorable to the continued flow of oil supplies at stable prices and access to Arab markets, whereas most Arab countries have viewed the dialogue as a means of exerting pressure on Europe to recognize the PLO. The issue was provisionally resolved through the use of two delegations, European and Arab, with the PLO represented in the Arab delegation. As of early 1982 Bonn continued to stipulate that this arrangement did not imply official recognition of the PLO.

The EC position on the Palestinian question has occasioned sharp criticism from Israel and watchfulness for signs of further European movement toward Palestinian recognition. In June 1978 in talks with the Saudi Arabian foreign minister, Schmidt mentioned the right of the Palestinians "to organize a state of their own." Subsequently Genscher sought to reassure Israeli officials that Schmidt's statement did not represent a deviation from the EC position.

The issue of military cooperation has been another delicate aspect of Bonn's Middle East policy. Because of constitutional considerations West Germany has not undertaken military force commitments except in cases related directly to defense (interpreted to embrace NATO obligations). Bonn has rejected suggestions of an extension of Atlantic Alliance responsibilities to include the Persian Gulf and has indicated that it could not accept a military role in the region. Whereas West German units do not participate in UN peacekeeping activities, the government supported a UN presence in the Sinai (1975) and Lebanon (1978) by transporting troops, equipment, and matériel. Moreover Bonn has proposed measures in the UN intended to strengthen the organization's peacekeeping functions in the areas of financial support, training, and designation of available units.

In 1971 the Federal Republic decided to prohibit the sale of West German arms to countries in "crisis zones." This policy was put to a test by Saudi Arabia's reported proposal in 1980 to buy 300 Leopard II tanks and other military equipment from West Germany. The issue was particularly sensitive in light of Bonn's efforts since 1976 to build with Saudi Arabia a close relationship of economic and political cooperation. In early 1982 Saudi Arabia was West Germany's largest foreign creditor and its largest supplier of crude oil—prospectively 40 percent of West Germany's total consumption based on current treaties. Yet the proposed sale of arms to Saudi Arabia provoked heated controversy in West Germany and severe criticism from Israel's Prime Minister Menachem Begin. The Schmidt government eventually declined to approve the sale, but it left open the possibility of later reconsideration.

East Asia

In the early 1980s relations with China and Japan continued to be primarily of an economic nature. West German-Chinese trade was modest, in 1980 amounting to about .05 percent of West Germany's total world trade. In April 1978 the EC concluded a five-year nonpreferential trade agreement with China, placing trade on a most-favored-nation basis. In October 1979 West Germany and China signed bilateral agreements intended to expand economic and cultural ties. China has seen the EC as an important political ally against the Soviet Union. West Germany, for its

Federal Republic of Germany

part, has underplayed this aspect of the relationship so as not to antagonize the Soviet Union and add yet another strain to already troubled East-West relations.

The country's trade with Japan has represented about 2 percent of its total world trade. Whereas in 1980 Japan ranked eighth as a source of West German imports, it was only seventeenth as a market for West German exports. The value of Japanese exports to the country was more than two and one-half times greater than West German exports to Japan, thus increasing Bonn's trade deficit beyond previous levels. In 1980 West Germany imported more than 200,000 Japanese cars, raising the Japanese share of the West German auto market to 10.4 percent compared to 5.6 percent in 1979. The surge of Japanese imports into West Germany and other EC countries, combined with Japanese import restrictions, has led to various protectionist measures in Europe and pressure on Japan to widen its market to foreign suppliers. In June 1981 West Germany and Japan reached agreement on limiting the growth of Japanese automobile exports to West Germany to 10 percent above the 1980 level. Although the arrangement substantially reduced the growth of Japanese imports (which increased 31 percent in the first four months of 1981), it may have forestalled more serious protectionist measures had no action been taken.

Relations with Latin American States

Trade in nuclear power equipment and policies concerning escalating conflict in Central America were the most publicized aspects of West German-Latin American relations in the late 1970s and early 1980s. Both reflected the Bonn government's concern with maintaining and increasing trade with Latin America; both affected and were affected by West German-United States relations.

In 1975 Bonn concluded agreements with Brazil for the sale of eight nuclear power stations and of technology for fuel reprocessing and uranium enrichment. The United States initially opposed the sale because of concern that Brazil, which had not signed the Treaty on the Non-Proliferation of Nuclear Weapons, would be able to produce nuclear weapons if it chose to do so. Washington was particularly concerned about the provision of technology to build a fuel reprocessing plant. The reprocessing of spent fuel rods from a power reactor yields plutonium that can be used either as a reactor fuel or to manufacture nuclear explosives. Brazil argued that uncertainties about its domestic supply of uranium made it necessary to rely on plutonium to fuel its power-generating plants, which are central to its development plan to increase energy self-sufficiency and reduce dependence on imported oil.

The Carter administration temporarily suspended shipments of enriched uranium to West Germany in an effort to pressure the government to cancel the sale. Bonn insisted upon honoring the agreement and argued that it included tight safeguards to prevent misuse of nuclear materials. Nevertheless in June 1977 West Germany announced that while it would fulfill the Brazilian contract, in the future it would not grant licenses for the export of nuclear fuel reprocessing technology.

In January 1978 West Germany and fourteen other nuclear supplier nations announced agreement on a code of safeguards designed to ensure that exported materials and technology would not be diverted to military use. Members of the Suppliers Group agreed not to export nuclear fuel reprocessing equipment, thus providing multilateral reinforcement for the position previously adopted by the Federal Republic. Other provisions included the requirement for arrangements to prevent theft of nuclear materials, recipient government assurances that materials will not be used for weapons production, agreement by recipient countries to international safeguards and periodic inspections by the International Atomic Energy Agency, and agreement not to reexport nuclear materials to third countries except under international safeguards and, in some cases, with the permission of the original supplier. The agreement had no effect on the previously concluded West German supply contract with Brazil but did preclude similar sales in the future.

In 1980 Bonn approved the sale of a heavy water nuclear reactor to Argentina. Although the agreement was consistent with the Suppliers Group export code, the United States sought unsuccessfully to persuade Bonn to insist that Argentina accept "full scope" safeguards as a condition of the sale. These would require that Argentina agree that all of its past, present, and future nuclear facilities be placed under controls and periodic inspection by the International Atomic Energy Agency. The Carter administration's concern was heightened by the fact that Argentina had not signed the Nuclear Non-Proliferation Treaty and had not ratified the Treaty of Tlatelolco, which prohibits nuclear weapons in Latin America (although Argentina indicated its intention to ratify the latter treaty). West Germany argued that the Suppliers Group safeguards code was adequate and that Argentina had agreed to place under international controls not only the new plant but also any future nuclear facilities it might construct based on the West German model.

West German relations with the nations of Central America in the late 1970s and early 1980s were profoundly affected by the ideology of the ruling Social Democratic Party of Germany (Sozialdemokratische Partei Deutschlands—SPD) and the Socialist International, both of which were presided over at the time by Willy Brandt. West Germany was a major aid donor to the revolutionary government in Nicaragua in 1979, 1980, and 1981. In the latter year it provided the equivalent of some US$15 million in unrestricted aid. In addition to being a display of solidarity with social democratic elements within Nicaragua, the aid also reflected competition with the increasingly visible Nicaraguan aid program of East Germany. In 1980 the Federal Republic recalled its ambassador from El Salvador and suspended economic aid to the United States-backed junta, but thereafter West Germany's policy tended to conform more with that of the United States. Political and financial support by the SPD and the Socialist International for the Salvadoran opposition, which had been significant in 1980, dropped off markedly the following year.

Relations with African States

Africa has been the major area of interest for West German policies in the Third World. The chief aim of West Germany's development policy has been to support the nonaligned countries of the Third World with emphasis on combating poverty and meeting basic human needs in the poorer regions of Africa and Asia. West Germany has maintained bilateral and multilateral development assistance programs, the latter including participation in numerous UN activities. In addition West Germany has participated in the Lomé II Convention, which defines an economic association between the EC and over sixty African, Caribbean, and Pacific (ACP) states. The Lomé II Convention provides for nonreciprocal, tariff-free access to the EC for most exports from ACP states and an export stabilization fund that compensates ACP states that experience significant declines in export receipts from primary products. The EC also has provided development assistance to the ACP states, and 28 percent of that assistance has been furnished by West Germany.

A major focus of West German policy in Africa has been its role in attempts to secure the independence of Namibia (South-West Africa) from South Africa. In 1920 South Africa assumed control of the territory under a League of Nations mandate and proceeded to introduce many of its apartheid policies into the region. After World War II, continued South African control of the territory became an increasing source of international contention, particularly in view of the growing numerical representation of Black African states in the UN. In 1966 the UN General Assembly withdrew South Africa's mandate and renamed the territory Namibia. Although South Africa rejected the Assembly's action as illegal, international pressure intensified to bring independence to Namibia.

In 1978 the UN Security Council passed Resolution 435, which called for a phased withdrawal of South African forces from Namibia, the introduction of a UN peacekeeping force, a UN supervised election for a constituent assembly, and independence upon the approval of a constitution and the establishment of a government. South Africa accepted Resolution 435, as did the South-West Africa People's Organization (SWAPO), the principal black African political party recognized by the UN as the only legitimate representative of the Namibian people. South Africa failed to implement the resolution, however, because it doubted the UN's impartiality in overseeing the transition and sought further assurances for the maintenance of democracy and guarantees for the rights of the white minority after independence.

West German policy on the Namibian issue has operated on two planes. The EC, acting through its procedures for political cooperation, adopted a unified position on the Namibian issue, calling for prompt implementation of Resolution 435 by South Africa. The EC countries declined to support mandatory economic sanctions against South Africa, however, in the belief that these would be ineffective and would do serious harm to the Western economies, which are heavily dependent upon raw material imports from South Africa. A West German government report released in 1978 disclosed that a cessation of imports from South Africa would affect several million domestic jobs.

Of greater political import, however, has been Bonn's role as a member of the so-called contact group of five Western countries (United States, Britain, France, Canada, and West Germany), that were on the UN Security Council when Resolution 435 was adopted and have since been seeking agreement on the implementation of the resolution. In an effort to meet South African concerns without imposing formal conditions for a Namibian constitution, West Germany proposed agreement on a general statement of principles that would pledge nondiscrimination, continuation of a multiparty system, an independent judiciary, and other constitutional guarantees to safeguard minority rights. In September 1981 the contact group announced the development of proposals for a timetable for negotiations aimed at implementing Resolution 435 in 1982. This included consideration of possible constitutional principles for the constituent assembly. Preliminary soundings provided a basis for optimism that further negotiations could produce agreement on the implementation of the resolution. In addition to the substance of the proposed constitutional principles, agreement must be reached on arrangements for elections and transfer of power as well as the size, makeup, and mandate of a UN force during the transition.

* * *

A general overview of the country's foreign relations is set forth in *West German Foreign Policy: 1949–1979*, edited by Wolfram

Federal Republic of Germany

F. Hanrieder. William E. Griffith's *The Ostpolitik of the Federal Republic of Germany* and Werner J. Feld's *Germany and the European Community* are excellent sources for those aspects of foreign policy. Also well worth consulting are Hans W. Gatzke's *Germany and the United States*; Helga Haftendorn's *German Foreign Policy*; *West Germany: A European and Global Power* edited by Wilfrid L. Kohl and Georgio Basevi; and *The Foreign Policy of West Germany* edited by Ekkehart Krippendorff and Volker Rittberger. Fritz Stern's article in *Foreign Affairs* is also insightful. (For further information see Bibliography.)

Chapter 9. National Security

Seal of the Federal Republic of Germany

THE FEDERAL ARMED FORCES (Bundeswehr) in 1982 numbered approximately 495,000, and the relative strengths of the army, navy, and air force continued to be at about 70 percent, 8 percent, and 22 percent respectively. The army divides its forces into two major components: the Field Army and the Territorial Army at roughly a four-to-one ratio. The basic combat unit of the Field Army is the brigade, which were being increased in number from thirty-three to thirty-six. The brigades were component parts of the twelve divisions that the government had pledged to commit to the North Atlantic Treaty Organization (NATO or the Atlantic Alliance) when the country was admitted to the alliance in the mid–1950s. The navy operated about 200 warships and a naval air arm, all committed to the NATO mission. The air force, in a state of permanent semialert because of the proximity to the Warsaw Pact forces, had well over 500 combat aircraft, several squadrons of surface-to-surface missiles, and several batteries of surface-to-air missiles, all under NATO command.

The raising and maintaining of armed forces had been forbidden by the Allied powers for several years after World War II; when Britain, France, and the United States authorized creation of the Bundeswehr in 1954, the idea was coolly received by a large segment of the West German public. Many citizens expressed the opinion at the time that the new Federal Republic of Germany (West Germany or Federal Republic) should get along without armed forces, and many feared that their country could become the arena for a war between the superpowers. Although during the next quarter of a century the people grudgingly accepted the need for armed forces, the idea that the country could become a battleground was still a very live issue in the early 1980s. Nevertheless a public opinion poll in October 1981 indicated that approximately 80 percent of those polled favored a continuation of the country's membership in the Atlantic Alliance and close relations with the United States.

The postwar era has been a time when the people have demanded more civil rights and human rights than at any other period in German history. The remembered abuses of the Nazi Reich in the areas of rights and liberties have continued to motivate West Germans to guard zealously the guarantees of their Basic Law (constitution). Traditional German militarism has been tempered in the Bundeswehr, which remains a part of society rather than becoming a society unto itself. Furthermore the officer corps has not become an elite, and every member of the armed

Federal Republic of Germany

forces retains individual rights as a citizen.

The custom of maintaining efficient police forces has been carried on and, as in the past, the police handle an unusually large share of administrative functions at local and state levels. Routine police activities affecting the daily lives of the people are performed by forces at the state (*Land*; pl., *Länder*) level. All nonfederal police forces are supervised and controlled by the ministries of the interior of the *Länder*, a system that has its roots in the post–1871 German Empire. The Western Allies after World War II purposely advocated a return to the *Land* system because of the abuses of Hitler's highly centralized police forces during the Nazi era. For efficiency the border police, some criminal police, and some specialized forces were placed under federal control.

A particularly grievous problem for the police since the late 1960s has been the constant threat of acts of violence by terrorists. The volume of terrorist activity has required that the government perform a delicate balancing act in providing police and prosecutors all means possible to combat terrorism while protecting the civil rights and liberties of ordinary citizens.

Armed Forces
Military Traditions

Probably the first Germans to gain reputations as fearsome adversaries in combat were members of the various tribes who fought the encroachment of Roman legions into their territories. The Roman historian Tacitus praised the leadership and military acumen of Arminius, a chief of the Cherusci who commanded the German forces in the famous battle of Teutoburg Forest in A.D. 9. Three Roman legions were destroyed by the tribal warriors led by Arminius, and that military disaster may well have altered Roman plans for the German lands north of the Danube and east of the Rhine. In any event Roman incursions beyond the frontier created by those rivers were generally sporadic and did not result in permanent occupation. On the contrary, by the time of the fall of the Roman Empire in the fifth century, Germans occupied Roman lands at will. A powerful military tradition has been part of German culture since the earliest times (see table A).

Later the Holy Roman Empire was ruled by Germans, and when the empire had a military arm, it was German. Many of the German kingdoms and principalities that were components of the empire were noted for the emphasis their leaders placed on military might. After the demise of the empire during the Napoleonic period, it was the Kingdom of Prussia that eventually emerged as the dominant power in Central Europe (see Rise of Prussia, ch. 1). Prussia had been colonized and Germanized during the thirteenth and fourteenth centuries by the Teutonic Knights, a military monastic order that pushed back or overran the Slavs in the area.

National Security

The German military heritage was epitomized in the Prussian military establishment of the Great Elector, Frederick William of Brandenburg-Prussia (1640–88), who recognized that a strong army was the keystone to the development of a powerful state in his remote part of the empire. His grandson, Frederick William I, who called himself King of Prussia, developed a standing professional army of 90,000 highly trained, disciplined troops, which was one of the most efficient fighting forces in eighteenth-century Europe. This expensive army was supported by heavy taxes and consumed a large percentage of total state revenues. In 1733 conscription was instituted as the interests of individual citizens were increasingly subordinated to the militaristic interests of the state. The next Prussian king, Frederick the Great, raised the strength of the army to 150,000 and committed it to an almost continuous series of wars from 1740 until 1763, making Prussia one of the most powerful states in Europe and a serious rival of Austria for hegemony over the myriad of German political entities (see German Confederation, ch. 1).

The aristocratic character of the officer corps was established early in the eighteenth century as Prussian kings tried to gain the support of the wealthy landed aristocracy, known as Junkers, by granting them a virtual monopoly over the selection of officers. In 1733 a cadet school was established in Berlin to train the sons of Junkers to be officers. The officer corps was well on the way to becoming the most privileged social class in Prussia. The peasants who made up the rank and file of the army were rigidly trained to accept strict discipline and to be unquestioningly obedient to their superiors.

The chauvinistic militarism of Prussia caused the country to be feared and hated by other European states and peoples. The army under the strong leadership of a self-perpetuating general staff brooked little interference in its affairs by the civil government. In time its extraordinary power earned it the title of "the state within a state," but fighting efficiency declined for various reasons after the death of Frederick in 1786, and twenty years later the army was decisively defeated by Napoleon's forces at Jena.

The Prussian leadership did not concede that their intense concentration on military affairs weakened the economic and social underpinnings of the state but, instead, blamed the defeat on the number of mercenaries in the ranks, which had grown to 50 percent. General Gerhard von Scharnhorst was instrumental in rebuilding the army, which later distinguished itself at the battle of Leipzig in 1813 and again at Waterloo in 1815 where, under command of Field Marshal Gerhard von Blücher, the Prussian army was instrumental in the final defeat of Napoleon.

Federal Republic of Germany

A decline in combat efficiency set in after Waterloo, but the reputation established over two centuries made Prussianism synonymous with militarism. The Prussian War College (Kriegsakademie) became a model for military staff colleges around the world in the early nineteenth century. A book of that era—*On War*—written by Karl von Clausewitz, a Prussian general, became a classic on land warfare. *On War* was translated into several languages and, 150 years after the death of its author, quotations from the book remain commonplace in the military literature of the United States and its allies as well as in that of the Soviet Union. Prussian-German excellence in military matters was accepted as a fact of life, but the excessive accent on militarism led to the disasters of two world wars.

The unification of the many German states into the German Empire of the late nineteenth century followed Prussian-led victories over Denmark in 1864, Austria in 1866, and France in 1870–71. These wars were fought under the guidance and control of Prussia's prime minister, Otto von Bismarck, who then became united Germany's first chancellor (see Imperial Germany, ch. 1). Following unification, the legendary Prussian General Staff became the German General Staff, but Clausewitz's dictum that civilians should control the military was discarded in favor of the exact opposite, which became the German principle. For almost fifty years the highly militaristic regimes of the kaisers William I and William II dominated Central Europe.

Although excessive militarism was a contributing factor to the outbreak of war in 1914, the crushing defeat suffered in World War I did not extinguish the flame. General Erich Ludendorff and Field Marshal Paul von Hindenburg actually took control of the government in 1916 as Ludendorff became virtual dictator of Germany. These leaders sidestepped responsibility for the military catastrophe, however, by returning the government to civilian control in the chaos of 1918. They then fed the rumors that the military had been "stabbed in the back," which had led to defeat rather than, in their words, to the glorious victory Germany deserved.

Under the terms of the Versailles Treaty, the German General Staff was abolished, and the country's right to rebuild an armed force was substantially restricted. The Allies intended that the civilian government of the Weimar Republic completely control the military and that the destruction of the general staff epitomize the end of Prussianism. Nevertheless a general staff continued to function under the sobriquet "Troop Office," and its leaders took advantage of the weak civilian government to reassert their privileged positions. When Hindenburg was elected president of the republic in 1925, the general staff officers regained their hold on the government.

A development of future military significance took place during the 1920s as a result of a clandestine alliance between the armies of the Weimar Republic and the Soviet Union that was arranged in order to circumvent the terms of the Versailles Treaty (see Weimar Republic, 1918–33, ch. 1). The German High Command under General Hans von Seeckt made secret arrangements with the Soviet High Command whereby German officers and specialists would study and train with modern weapons in the Soviet Union in return for German technical assistance in the establishment of Soviet defense industries. This collaboration in the 1920s helped keep alive the military know-how used later as the basis of Hitler's war machine.

By September 1939 when Hitler's invasion of Poland triggered World War II, Germany had a formidable army, an impressive navy, and the best equipped air force in the world. The blitzkrieg, using highly mobile, tank-heavy ground armies assisted by large numbers of close-support aircraft, exhibited tactics never before seen in warfare. In the spring of 1940 the Nazi forces attacked and destroyed the armies of France and Belgium and forced the evacuation of the British Expeditionary Forces at Dunkirk—all in little over one month.

The rapid victories of the early war period did not lead to peace, however. France and the Low Countries were occupied but Britain, which was subjected to unprecedented bombing and rocket attacks, refused to capitulate, thwarting Hitler's plans for the war in the West. When the Nazi invasion of the Soviet Union in June 1941 brought that country into the war and the Japanese attack on Pearl Harbor brought in the United States, the war became global and took on a different complexion. Although the Soviet Union and the United States suffered early defeats, the reservoirs of manpower and resources that each could exploit eventually sealed the fate of Hitler's vaunted "1,000-year Reich," even though the formidable Nazi war machine continued to fight for almost four more years.

When the Soviet forces were able to turn the tide in their favor on the Eastern Front and the Western Allies established themselves in France, there could no longer be any doubt about the outcome of the war. Nevertheless Hitler refused to seek peace. The inevitable result was the destruction not only of the country's armed forces but also of its towns and cities, its industrial capacity, and its transportation systems. Despite this second catastrophic defeat in a thirty-year period, the reputation for military excellence survived. The defeats were frequently attributed to misguided politics, two-front wars, and—in the case of the Nazis—madness and depravity in the top leadership.

The Allies demanded and received the unconditional surrender of Nazi Germany in early May 1945. Two months later at a summit conference held at Postdam (near Berlin), President Harry S Truman of the United States, Prime Minister Clement Attlee of

Britain, and Premier Joseph Stalin of the Soviet Union decreed, inter alia, the demilitarization of Germany. Although the Allies disagreed on many issues discussed at Potsdam, they were in accord concerning the need to prevent a resurgence of German militarism; toward that end they ordered total disarmament. In the immediate postwar years the Allies could not agree on the terms of a peace treaty, and before long they were aligned on opposite sides of the cold war. By 1949 the British, French, and American zones of occupation had become the Federal Republic, and the Soviet zone had become the German Democratic Republic (East Germany). The border between the two republics became the front line of the cold war, or in the words popularized by Winston Churchill, the Iron Curtain. Soon, uniformed Germans carrying weapons were appearing on both sides of the border. By the mid-1950s military units had been organized.

Organization and Mission

In the summer of 1955, ten years after the Nazi surrender and the end of World War II in Europe, the West German Federal Diet (Bundestag) voted to authorize the recruitment of volunteers for the initial formation of the federal armed forces. Later in the year a cadre of about 100 officers and noncommissioned officers (NCOs) was sworn in at a ceremony in Bonn presided over by Theodor Blank, the new republic's first minister of defense. Most of the initial volunteers were veterans of the World War II Wehrmacht who had been serving in the Federal Border Force (Bundesgrenzschutz—BGS) since the inception of that lightly armed organization in 1951 (see Federal Police Agencies, this ch.).

Training facilities and equipment were made available by the United States Army, and 1,500 volunteers had reported for training by January 1956. Chancellor Konrad Adenauer addressed the first contingent of recruits to the newly created Bundeswehr on January 20, 1956, as the first training cycle began. Legislation on compulsory military service was soon promulgated. By the end of the year the force numbered about 65,000, including 10,000 volunteers from the BGS, almost all of whom were war veterans. The reappearance of a German armed force, which would have been inconceivable a decade earlier, had become a reality as a direct result of the cold war.

According to the Basic Law, the sole mission of the Bundeswehr is defense. The forces exist only to deter, in conjunction with NATO allies, a potential enemy attempting to use military force for territorial aggrandizement. The army is charged with repelling the ground forces of an invader; the air force provides close support, air defense, and reconnaissance; and the navy's task is to defend the coasts and deny sea routes to an enemy in the North and Baltic seas.

Leopard tank
Courtesy Krauss Maffei

In fulfilling its constitutional responsibility of defending the country, the Bundeswehr is committed to act as an element of the NATO forces. The NATO mission, as it applies directly to West Germany, is to employ an integrated organization under unified command to face any aggressor encroaching on the territory of the Federal Republic. The Bundeswehr, in its relatively brief history, has become the largest single component of the NATO forces in Europe.

Upon becoming a member of NATO, the Federal Republic committed itself to the raising, training, and equipping of twelve divisions of ground forces, a tactical air force, and a coastal patrol navy. In an effort to allay the fears of those Europeans who were horrified at the idea of once again seeing German soldiers, the new forces were subordinated to NATO command. That subordination of forces continued in effect in the early 1980s, and operational control was maintained by NATO (see The North Atlantic Treaty Organization, ch. 8).

The Bundeswehr grew steadily during its first decade and by 1964 had reached a strength of 435,000 of its authorized 500,000. By 1975 the total strength had reached 495,000 where it remained in early 1982. Conscripts accounted for about 45 percent of the

Federal Republic of Germany

total. When the raising of an army was first discussed and even after enactment of the Obligatory Military Service Law in 1956, the question whether the Bundeswehr should be all-volunteer or conscripted prompted spirited arguments in West Germany. The argument for volunteers was based on the premise that a modern, complex armed force demanded professionals rather than conscripts who would not serve long enough to be properly trained. Those opposed to the volunteer force argued that a professional military establishment could become self-sufficient and independent —the "state within a state" concept that could again bring on military disaster. As matters developed, however, the decision was based primarily on economic factors. An economy beginning to boom dictated the need of a draft law if prescribed manpower levels were to be maintained.

Military policymaking and planning responsibilities are divided between the executive and legislative branches of the government. The president of the republic, who is elected by the Federal Convention and is much like the monarch in the British system, is not the commander in chief of the Bundeswehr (see The Federal Executive, ch. 7). One of the presidential responsibilities, however, is the appointment and dismissal of officers and NCOs. The executive ultimately responsible for the country's defense is the federal chancellor, but in peacetime much of his responsibility is delegated to the minister of defense. The minister, Hans Apel in early 1982, is commander in chief of the Bundeswehr in peacetime, but command reverts to the chancellor in the event of a "state of defense," that is, an outbreak of hostilities.

The Ministry of Defense is traditionally headed by a civilian who is assisted by a parliamentary state secretary and two state secretaries. These four civilians make up the Executive Group of the Ministry of Defense. Directly responsible to the Executive Group are the Organization Office, the Press and Information Office, and the Planning Office. Five military staffs—Bundeswehr, army, navy, air force, and Medical and Health Services,—plus six administrative divisions—personnel, budget, administration and legal affairs, quartering and real estate, social services, and armaments—constitute the remainder of the ministry (see fig. 22).

The top military position in the structure is that of chief of the Bundeswehr Defense Council whose title is General Inspector of the Armed Forces, but he is usually referred to as Bundeswehr chief of staff. As military adviser to the minister and to the federal government, he is responsible for the basic concept of defense of the country and for the implementation of policy after decisions have been taken by the political leadership. In fulfilling overall ministerial responsibilities including defense planning, the Bundeswehr chief of staff is assisted by the chiefs of staff of the army, navy, and air force (also called inspectors) and the surgeon general, who are under his executive authority and who sit as mem-

National Security

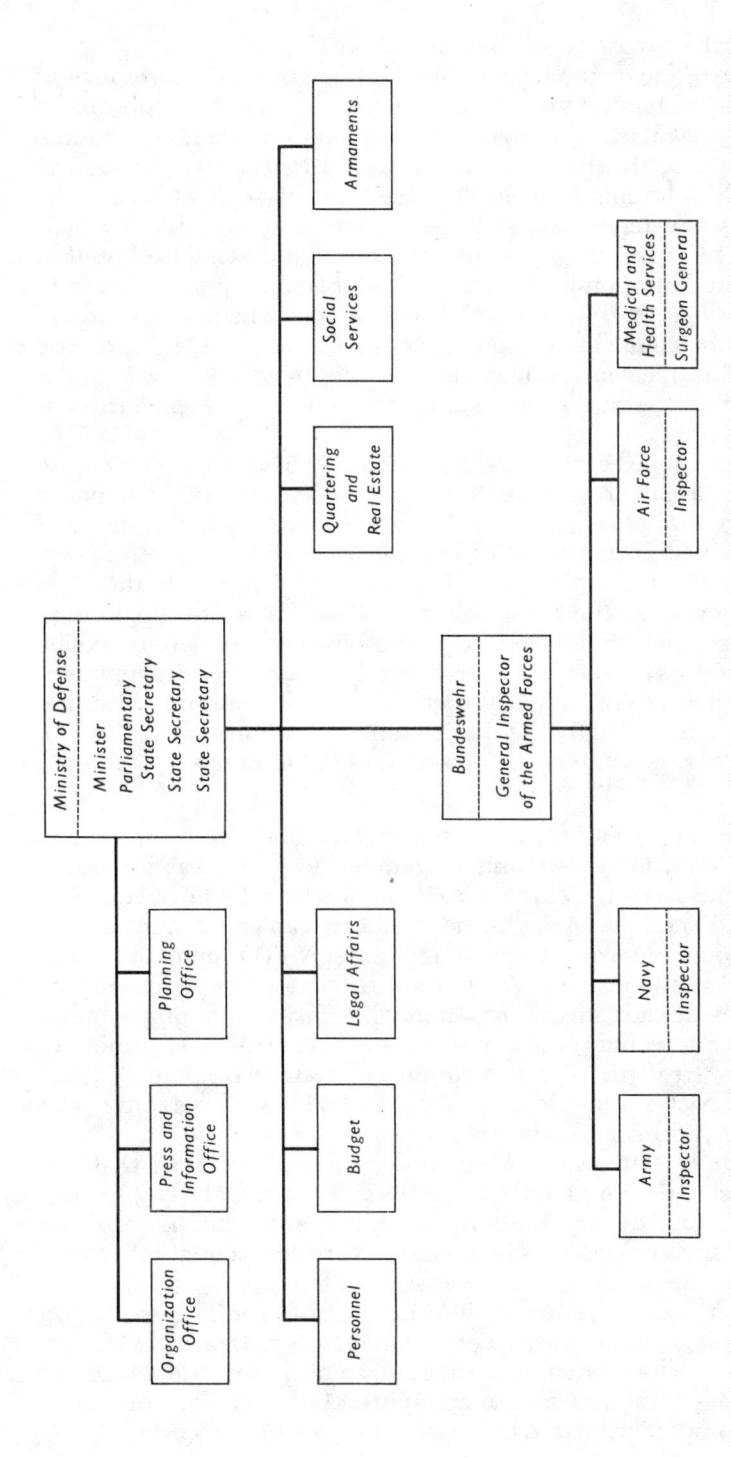

Source: Based on information from Federal Republic of Germany, Press and Information Office, *Jahresbericht der Bundesregierung 1980*, Bonn, 1980.

Figure 22. *Ministry of Defense*

Federal Republic of Germany

bers of the Bundeswehr Defense Council.

There is no general staff in the Bundeswehr. For obvious reasons—its tainted history and condemnation at the Nuremberg trials— that particular structure was omitted when the Bundeswehr was being planned. Nevertheless, of necessity, a comparable body—the Bundeswehr Defense Council—exists to act in the capacity of a general staff. In its responsibilities the Bundeswehr Defense Council may be compared to the Joint Chiefs of Staff in the United States military system, and it is sometimes referred to in English as the Joint Armed Forces Staff. The principal members of the council have dual responsibilities in that they exercise administrative control over their services in addition to acting as advisers to members of the ministry and to other government officials.

Within the executive branch, defense policy and basic defense planning are the responsibilities of the Federal Security Council, a special group of cabinet officers presided over by the minister of defense, who is chairman. The council is also responsible for coordinating the implementation of its plans and policies. In the legislative branch the Bundestag, in addition to legislating appropriations for the defense budget, also debates defense policy and monitors conditions of service and morale. Bundestag members regularly visit military units and installations and maintain regular contact with the Parliamentary Commissioner for the Federal Armed Forces, i.e., the defense ombudsman.

Army

In the early 1980s the army continued to be the largest component of the Bundeswehr and, as from its inception, was composed of the Field Army (Feldheer) and the Territorial Army (Territorialheer). The Field Army is the West German component of NATO's ground forces and would fight under NATO command in the event of hostilities. The Territorial Army is a home defense force that provides administration, training, security, and some combat support but would remain under national control in wartime. Total army strength at the beginning of 1982 was about 345,000 officers, NCOs, and soldiers. About 272,000, or 79 percent of the total, served in the Field Army.

The Field Army was in the process of a reorganization that was expected to be completed during 1982. Primarily the reorganization affected the composition, armament, and equipment of the Field Army's brigades. The brigades were components of twelve divisions, eleven of which were assigned to the I, II, and III corps headquartered respectively at Münster, Ulm, and Koblenz. The three West German corps were components of larger NATO formations. The remaining division, which was deployed in Schleswig-Holstein, was also committed to NATO for operations but was not subordinated to one of the West German corps.

National Security

In developing the new army structure, West German defense officials have stressed that the changes were designed to satisfy NATO requirements, eliminate earlier shortcomings, incorporate improved technologies, and enhance combat readiness. The basic army formations—corps, divisions, brigades, and battalions—remained unchanged after reorganization. As before, there were to be three corps and twelve divisions, but there were to be thirty-six brigades instead of thirty-three; in general, brigades were to be stronger in armored vehicles than their earlier counterparts. Corps support troops were to be heavier in antitank and antiaircraft capabilities. Divisional combat support units were also to be upgraded.

The Territorial Army, in order to perform its assigned defense and support functions, deployed its forces in three geographical areas: Territorial Command North, headquartered in Mönchengladbach; Territorial Command South, Heidelberg; and Territorial Command Schleswig-Holstein, Kiel. The territorial commands were subdivided into military districts that in turn were subdivided into military regions and military subregions. The major maneuver elements of the Territorial Army, which was also undergoing reorganization, were to be six home defense brigades, maintained at varying strength levels, i.e., two at 85 percent, two at 65 percent, and two at 52 percent of authorized strength. The home defense brigades were to be equipped with tanks, armored personnel carriers, artillery, and antitank guns and missiles in order to perform their function of providing security and combat support in the rear areas. It was not contemplated that these brigades would be committed to front-line combat. To fulfill their rear-area missions they were not to be as heavily armed and armored as the brigades of the Field Army. Six additional home defense brigades were to be manned only at cadre strength but would hold equipment to be available for a full-strength brigade upon rapid mobilization.

Navy

The Federal Navy (Bundesmarine) is the smallest of the armed forces and was originally conceived as a coastal patrol service for the country's Baltic and North seas coastlines. When the rearming of West Germany was first contemplated in the early 1950s, the Western European Union (WEU—see Glossary) restricted the navy to ships displacing 3,000 tons or less. Some of the restrictions were lifted in 1980 permitting, for example, the construction of as many as eight destroyers of 6,000 tons and a training ship of up to 5,000 tons. In addition the restriction on auxiliary vessels was raised to 6,000 tons. In July 1981 the remaining restrictions were removed, but the provisions of the 1954 protocol prohibiting, inter alia, the construction of nuclear-powered warships were retained.

Federal Republic of Germany

The Baltic and North seas and the connecting waterways were the principal areas of interest for the navy and would be its primary areas of operations during wartime. The security of the coastlines would also be a wartime mission, but the navy and its air arm could be expected to operate far from German shores in order to perform their functions and fulfill their NATO commitments. From the NATO point of view, denying an enemy easy access from the Baltic Sea to the Atlantic Ocean would be a primary responsibility of the West German navy.

In early 1982 the navy had about 39,000 men, including more than 7,000 in the naval air arm. Approximately 29 percent of the total strength was made up of conscripts who, like their counterparts in the army, served fifteen-month tours of active duty. The complexity of some weapons and equipment and the extended periods needed for training have limited the occupational specialties that conscripts can apply for during their tour.

In early 1982 the ship inventory consisted of about 200 warships and combat craft including destroyers, frigates, submarines, and torpedo boats, plus about ninety auxiliary and support vessels. The air arm had about 165 aircraft including fighter-bombers, reconnaissance planes, utility planes, and helicopters. During the 1970s the navy underwent a program of modernization that involved procurement of new ships and aircraft as well as the reconditioning of older ships. During the first half of the decade, eighteen Type 206 submarines were commissioned, raising the number of submarines in active service to twenty-four. The six older boats were Type 205, all of which had been commissioned during the late 1960s. The navy's largest warships were its eleven destroyers, and four of those (all Hamburg class) had also been reconditioned during the 1970s modernization program.

Air Force

To fulfill its mission of defending against attack, in early 1982 the Federal Air Force (Bundesluftwaffe) maintained its personnel and aircraft at a state of combat readiness that would permit immediate response to any incursion by forces of the Warsaw Pact. In the event of hostilities the air force, working in conjunction with other NATO forces, would interdict enemy ground and air forces, protect friendly forces against air attack, and provide close battlefield support to friendly ground troops. The air force has fighter-bombers and surface-to-surface missiles (SSM) for deep strikes against an attacking enemy, but it has no long-range strategic capability, and the nuclear warheads for its SSMs are retained under United States control.

The air force conducts constant reconnaissance in order to forestall surprise attacks and, if an attack were launched, immediate response would be expected in order to prevent enemy planes

Luftwaffe Tornado armed with MW–1 small bomb ejector being developed for NATO BY Messerschmitt–Bölkow–Blohm. Courtesy Messerschmitt–Bölkow–Blohm

from reaching important targets in the country. At the same time, other air elements would be attempting to inflict as much damage as possible on enemy armored formations in order to deny access to the territory of the Federal Republic or to halt units that have crossed the borders. To perform such combat tasks the air force required a variety of high-performance aircraft as well as trained personnel to operate and maintain them. Also required was the modern electronic equipment for the command and control of units and for communications. Almost from its inception the air force has been known as a well-trained and well-equipped organization, and plans for the 1980s and 1990s indicate that the authorities intend that the reputation will be maintained.

Ground elements of the air force's air defense units were armed with Nike and Hawk surface-to-air missiles (SAM) and 20mm automatic antiaircraft guns. The improved Hawk—known as I Hawk—is a mobile system having a range of forty kilometers. The Nike Hercules, even though it is an older system, is expected to be the 150–kilometer-range SAM throughout the 1980s. The 20mm is a twin-mount gun designed for protection against low-level air attacks, but it will be augmented in that role by the deployment of fully mobile Roland 2 SAMs during the early 1980s.

As part of the Bundeswehr the air force is commanded by the minister of defense in peacetime, and its staff is a component of the Ministry of Defense. The ranking uniformed member is the

Federal Republic of Germany

Inspector of the Federal Air Force (Inspekteur des Bundesluftwaffe) who, as air chief of staff, is a member of the Defense Council and the principal adviser on air force matters to the minister of defense and the government. Operational control is a function of the NATO commander of Allied Air Forces Central Europe (see fig. 20). Combat units are assigned to the 4th Allied Tactical Air Force headquartered at Ramstein, which also controls American and Canadian units, and the 2d Allied Tactical Air Force headquartered at Mönchengladbach, which also controls units from Belgium, Britain, and the Netherlands.

Extensive plans for upgrading the capabilities of the air force during the 1980s include acquisition of 210 Tornadoes and 175 Alpha Jets plus the improvement of the armament and electronic gear of the 120 F–4F Phantom IIs. The Tornado—under development in a joint effort by Britain, Italy, and the Federal Republic—will greatly enhance the NATO capability to repel heavily armored ground forces as well as high-speed, low-flying, all-weather attack aircraft. The Alpha Jet—a joint development enterprise of the Federal Republic and France—was intended to replace the large number of aging Fiat G–91s scheduled to be phased out of the aircraft inventory. The Alpha Jet was designed for rugged and frequent use in the ground support role. Its relatively uncomplicated design and equipment will permit multiple combat sorties with a minimum of maintenance. Ninety Alpha Jets were already in inventory at the beginning of 1982.

Budgetary Problems

Since the creation of the Bundeswehr in the mid-1950s, military issues have received mixed reaction from the public. As a result the military establishment has frequently received greater support from politicians than seemed warranted by the attitudes of their constituents, particularly the generation born after World War II. The dichotomy of attitudes frequently led to difficulties in providing sufficient funding to the Bundeswehr to maintain its personnel and equipment at desired levels even though a consensus did seem to acknowledge the need for defense. Budget problems were compounded in the late 1970s and early 1980s as costs escalated and most Western economies, including West Germany's, entered a period of recession. As a percentage of overall federal spending, the defense budget decreased from 22.4 percent in 1974, to 19.6 percent in 1977, to 18.1 percent in 1980.

In 1978 the Federal Republic made a commitment to NATO to increase its defense spending by 3 percent a year in real terms, but the pledge became difficult for the government of Chancellor Helmut Schmidt as the economy faltered in the early 1980s. As 1982 began, the Schmidt government was drawing criticism from the Christian Democratic political opposition as well as from some NATO partners because of actual cuts in defense spending rather than the pledged 3 percent increase. Schmidt countered with the argument that the Federal Republic should be judged on its overall contribution to NATO, that is, on the efficiency and combat readiness of the Bundeswehr, rather than on the amount of money spent during a particular time period. At the same time, Schmidt opposed members of his own party who wanted to make deeper cuts in the 1982 defense budget.

Citizens in Uniform

Personnel Policies

The overall strength ceiling of 500,000 for the Bundeswehr was set by the Paris Agreements of October 1954. In addition to active duty personnel (495,000), in early 1982 there were approximately 175,000 civilian men and women employed by the forces. Active duty personnel in the three services—army, navy, and air force—comprised three different categories: conscripts, volunteers, and regulars. In accord with standards considered necessary by NATO, the Federal Republic has attempted to maintain a ratio of about 55 percent volunteers and regulars to 45 percent conscripts. Strength figures and ratios remained stable from the early 1970s into the early 1980s, but the number of conscripts often tended to be closer to 50 percent than to the targeted 45 percent. The higher than desired ratio of conscripts to longer service personnel frequently resulted in conscripts serving as junior NCOs, a practice frowned upon because of the rapid turnover of conscripts. Defense officials expressed concern about serious shortages of eligible conscripts that will appear about 1988 and become more severe in the 1990s. Despite the need for specialists of all sorts in the services in the early 1980s and the worry about even being able to conscript enough young men in the late 1980s, the authorities have made little or no effort to recruit women into the armed forces.

At the end of 1978 there were over 62,000 regulars serving in the Bundeswehr, of whom almost 32,000 were officers (including 600 officer candidates) and over 30,000 were senior NCOs. Actually the number of officers was about the same as authorized, but the age distribution bothered personnel specialists. There was a bulge in the age-group from fifty-three to fifty-eight, a noticeable contraction in the forty-five through fifty-two age-group, and an excessive bulge in the thirty-six through forty-four age-group. The poor distribution in age-and rank-groups is expected to lead to personnel management difficulties in the future. Reassignment to desirable posts would be slowed considerably, and a possible promotion barrier would result in officers becoming overage in grade, with the consequence being lowered morale. In 1978 about 42 percent of regular line officers were over forty years old, a figure that was expected to rise to 66 percent in 1985 and 75 percent in 1990. This serious threat to morale, efficiency, and combat readiness was of particular concern to defense officials who ordered special studies be made in an attempt to find remedies. Similar problems affected the senior NCO ranks where solutions were also being sought in order to limit the adverse impact on ambitious younger NCOs who were being stymied in their normal career advancements.

Service Obligations

In July 1956 the Obligatory Military Service Law was enacted stating that all males between the ages of eighteen and thirty-five are subject to conscription for military service. Exemptions are granted to university students and to apprentices in certain vocations but, to maintain force levels, about 210,000 young men must be drafted annually. Conscripts serve fifteen-month tours of active duty after which they have reserve obligations. The Basic Law guarantees the right to refuse military service on grounds of conscience: "No one may be compelled against his conscience to render war service involving the use of arms." Conscientious objectors may be required to serve eighteen months in some alternative civilian capacity. During the 1970s about 35,000 young men annually applied for conscientious objector status. In 1979 the figure had risen to 45,000, and in 1981 the more than 58,000 conscientious objectors alarmed officials who were already concerned about declining numbers of draft eligibles.

Short-term volunteers in the Bundeswehr enlist for periods of twenty-one months to three years. Other volunteers enlist for periods of up to fifteen years. Officers also serve terms of varying lengths. Regular status is conferred on those NCOs and officers who request it, depending on performance records, occupational specialties, and vacancies. The total number of regular NCOs and officers serving on active duty is regulated by law.

The role of women in the Bundeswehr, except in civilian capacities, is practically nonexistent. The Basic Law states: "Women shall not be required by law to render service in any unit of the armed forces. On no account shall they be employed in any service involving the use of arms." Approximately 50,000 women were employed in civilian positions in the Bundeswehr at the end of the 1970s.

In 1970 the federal government appointed a group of prominent citizens to a commission to analyze the Bundeswehr and make recommendations concerning its structure and manpower levels and the options open to the government for the late 1970s, the 1980s, and beyond. Known as the Force Structure Commission, the group stated in its report to the federal government that volunteer forces were highly desirable because of their cost-effectiveness and efficiency and because of the elimination of problems connected with a conscripted force, including the issue of conscientious objectors. The commission, however, said that it could not recommend converting the Bundeswehr to an all-volunteer force because of "security, financial, and manpower reasons" that militated against such a force at that time. The same reasons existed in the early 1980s, and conscription continued. In addition to the very pragmatic reasons of needing conscripts to fill the ranks, the federal government has also stated that universal conscription is a means of keeping the armed forces close to the people and preventing the development of a separated, military elite.

Conditions of Service

When the Federal Republic was founded in 1949 and during the next year or two when the recreation of German armed forces was under public discussion, many of the country's cities were still disfigured by the shells of bombed-out buildings and by huge mounds of rubble. To many Germans the memories of wartime disaster were still too vivid—even the thought of rearming the country was distasteful. But even those citizens who recognized the necessity for defense were convinced that the new armed forces would have to be unlike any that had previously existed in German history. Retired Bundeswehr general Wolf von Baudissin, referring to the intentions of those who planned the new military organization, said, "an awareness of the extent of the military, political and moral disaster marking the period 1933–45 played a decisive role here." The consensus was that the Bundeswehr would have to be a constitutionally legalized institution, designed solely for defense. Futhermore the military would be unequivocally controlled by civilian authorities; citizens serving in the forces would have constitutionally guaranteed rights, thus ensuring that their loyalties would be to the democratically organized republic rather than to a führer or faction.

Thus the earliest conceptions of the Bundeswehr were—for the West Germans—of an entirely new kind of armed forces. The planners wanted to be sure that no images of the Weimar Reichwehr or Hitler's Wehrmacht could be associated with the Bundeswehr. Literature on the subject makes much of the twin concepts of "citizens in uniform" and *"Innere Führung"* (inner leadership). The two ideas are intertwined, and both originated in the strong resolve of many West Germans of the early postwar period to somehow ensure that there could not be a resurgence of the old German militarism. The idea behind the emphasis on citizens in uniform is to remind all West Germans that their servicemen are of the people and work for the people. In this way the founders of the postwar republic hoped to avoid creating a military elite that could lead to the "state within a state" phenomenon. The new concept was also a move to guarantee the constitutional rights of people serving in the armed forces even though those rights might be restricted at times because of the special nature of military duties.

In the Bundeswehr a soldier, sailor, or airman does not give up his political status as a citizen because he has donned a uniform. He continues to be a member of the community from which he entered the service as well as of the West German political community as a whole. He may run for office at the local, state, or federal level and if elected, he would be permitted to resign from the military to take his seat. Regulars and volunteers are permitted to join a servicemen's union or, if they so choose, a national civil servants' union. Conscripts are permitted to retain memberships in trade unions to which they belonged before entering the service. Recognizing the overwhelming importance of discipline as a basic ingredient of the military life, the planners stated their objective of creating "not a democratic army, but an army to serve a democratic society."

The concept of *Innere Führung* charges each serviceman with the responsibility of defending his country according to the dictates of his own conscience rather than because of blind loyalty. The new principle of leadership, that is, self-leadership, applies to everyone in uniform from the most senior general to the conscript entering basic training. For the NCOs, officers, and generals who formed the nucleus of the new forces in 1956, most of whom were veterans of the Wehrmacht or Luftwaffe of World War II, adherence to the new principles meant unlearning those that had guided them in their earlier service. In essence the principles of citizens in uniform and *Innere Führung* are designed to guide relationships between subordinates and superiors, between peers, and between the individual serviceman and the society.

Another innovation that set the Bundeswehr apart from earlier German military organizations was the establishment of the position of the defense ombudsman (Parliamentary Commissioner for the Federal Armed Forces), who is appointed by the Bundestag. The ombudsman is responsible for overseeing the activities of the chief administrators of the services while at the same time guarding the constitutional rights of individual servicemen. All Bundeswehr personnel have the right of direct petition to the ombudsman. Between 6,500 and 7,000 complaints were handled by the ombudsman annually in the late 1970s and early 1980s.

Training

The basic objective of the training program is to maintain the combat readiness of the Bundeswehr in fulfillment of the country's NATO obligations. The program covers everything from basic training to study at a military academy or the Bundeswehr Staff College and aims at imparting the knowledge necessary for technical competence while instilling the discipline required of armed forces in combat situations. The educational opportunities offered to servicemen in accordance with their terms of service

National Security

are designed to meet military requirements but, to the extent possible, this education also aims at easing the eventual transition to civilian life. The Bundeswehr operates thirty technical colleges in which qualified personnel may request training. Qualifications are determined by length of enlistment and educational background.

Basic training and small-unit training are scheduled on a continuing basis. For the conscript the entire fifteen-month tour is devoted to one kind of training or another, but he is not eligible for attendance at service schools unless he voluntarily extends his term of service. In the army about 44,000 conscripts are called up each quarter and begin their military service with three months of basic training in training commands. After basic training the conscripts are assigned to operational commands where they spend a year participating in small-unit training and, possibly, in battalion, brigade, division, corps, and NATO exercises. Naturally conscripts are not on active duty long enough to take part in the field exercises of all levels, but before discharge every conscript will have spent a substantial part of his tour in various training situations. Because requisite facilities are limited in a country as densely populated as the Federal Republic, the West German army must compete with other NATO forces for space in which to conduct large field exercises.

Air force and navy conscripts are also called up quarterly and spend their first three months undergoing basic training. Airmen are then assigned to units where they receive on-the-job training. But even to a greater degree than in the modern army, air force personnel are frequently assigned to highly complex weapons systems, where it is generally accepted that longer experience leads to increased competency. The necessary technical training in the air force is not only expensive but also time-consuming; officials are thus motivated to maintain a lower ratio between conscripts and longer term personnel than can possibly be the case in the army.

Jet pilots and missile personnel of the air force are trained in the United States under long-standing agreements between the two governments. Eighty to 100 West German pilots per year were trained at air bases in the United States during the first twenty-five years of the Bundesluftwaffe. Conversion training for pilots of the new Alpha Jets and Tornadoes was taking place in the early 1980s in Sardinia and England respectively. Training on multi-engine aircraft and helicopters is conducted within the Federal Republic.

Naval conscripts and volunteers receive basic training at shore stations after which they are assigned to ships or shore-based support units for advanced training and routine naval duties. Some volunteers are sent to schools for advanced training before reporting to operational units. As in the army and air force, the culmination of naval training comes in joint exercises with other NATO forces, and the frequency of such exercises makes it unlikely that even a conscript could complete his tour without having participated in such an exercise.

Medical and Health Services personnel also receive basic military training as well as basic medical training in facilities maintained by the army, navy, and air force. On the professional side they receive training in first aid and in basic military medicine. Subsequent training includes emergency lifesaving techniques and procedures for use in responding to disasters. Personnel then progress to specific training in specialties such as hospital orderly, laboratory assistant, anesthetist's assistant, and medical technician.

The training of volunteers varies according to educational background, experience, and length of enlistment. The only educational requirement for enlistment in the Bundeswehr is completion of five years at the secondary school (*Hauptschule*) level (see Education, ch. 2). Recruiters prefer that the enlistee will also have completed some vocational schooling after secondary school, but such training is not a prerequisite. The level of education achieved before volunteering for military service determines whether a recruit enters as a private, a junior NCO, or an officer candidate. A volunteer is given aptitude tests, which aid him and the military counselors in selecting the field of training for which he is best qualified. Long-term servicemen are afforded many educational opportunities during the course of a career that enable advancement within the NCO ranks and, in some cases, promotion to officer rank. In the early 1980s training for promotion into the career NCO ranks of any of the three services required at least twelve months of combined fieldwork and schooling.

An officer candidate in the army, navy, or air force faces a long, arduous training program. Those aspiring to be regular officers, as well as nonpermanent officers who spend up to twelve years on active duty, generally spend about five years in formal training programs. An officer candidate receives basic training like any other recruit after which he attends an officer candidate school operated by the army, navy, or air force. After passing a qualifying examination the candidate is sent to Hamburg Military Academy or to Munich Military Academy for three years of university-level or technical college-level study leading to an academic degree or to a diploma, respectively. After graduation and commissioning, the officer then attends one of several service schools for training in his branch and specialty before reporting to his duty assignment.

The academies at Hamburg and Munich began operations in October 1973 and within four years attained their maximum capacity of 4,570 students. The two academies offer a wide variety of subjects with particular stress on scientific and technical

National Security

courses, but not ignoring the need for study in the social sciences. During the first five years of operation, about two-thirds of those who enrolled in the academies were awarded degrees or diplomas. At about a two-to-one ratio, students opted for curricula leading to academic degrees rather than diplomas.

Attendance at the Hamburg and Munich academies is restricted to officer candidates who sign on for at least twelve years, but nonattendance does not necessarily rule out a career as a regular officer or as a nonpermanent officer provided that an individual has qualifications, e.g., proficiency in computers or another technology, that might be in demand in one of the services. The same applies to a candidate who has not succeeded academically but has the talent and ambition to continue seeking a career as an officer.

Seven years after graduation from one of the academies, a regular line officer would generally be scheduled for attendance at a fourteen-week branch course which, in addition to successful completion of an examination, is prerequisite to promotion to field grade, that is, to major or lieutenant commander. Field grade officers attend courses that train them for general staff assignments. The courses offered at staff colleges are similar to those offered at a comparable level American military college: S–1 courses include studies in personnel matters, public affairs, and *Innere Führung*—a subject given particular stress throughout all levels of the Bundeswehr training and educational structure. S–2 courses are devoted to military intelligence and security; S–3 courses concern operations and training; and S–4, logistics.

Military Medicine

Medical care of Bundeswehr personnel is provided by the Medical and Health Services whose chief, the surgeon general, and his staff form an integral component of the Ministry of Defense. In peacetime the medical services are responsible for preventive medicine and for the care and treatment of military personnel and their dependents. Such care is provided at medical centers that are located near troop formations or, in the case of units in the field, by medical detachments organic to major units. Naval ships have their own assigned medical personnel. Inpatient care is provided by medical centers, station hospitals, and, at times, civilian hospitals. During wartime the Medical and Health Services would become responsible for the evacuation as well as the treatment of casualties.

In planning for a defense emergency, the medical services have divided West Germany into three zones to expedite handling of casualties. In the area that would be expected to be closest to actual combat—the eastern border—mobile field medical detachments and casualty clearing stations would be responsible for lifesaving measures, first aid, classification, and evacuation of casualties to the second medical echelon. The most rapid means

Federal Republic of Germany

of evacuation possible, preferably helicopter, would be given top priority. In the second zone—a strip of territory covering the middle of the country from the Baltic Sea to the Swiss border—200-bed station hospitals would be activated to provide all necessary care, both, emergency and routine, to all casualties. The third medical zone—bordering the Low Countries and France—would have several 1,000-bed hospitals designed to provide in-depth care and recuperation facilities.

The army, navy, and air force have administrative control over the medical services during peacetime and wartime, but technical control and supervision is a function of the surgeon general, who sits as a member of the Defense Council and is the government's chief adviser on military medical affairs. Under the reorganization of the Bundeswehr (in progress in the late 1970s and early 1980s), medical units assigned to corps and divisions were to be restructured in order to provide constant support to the brigades. After completion of the reorganization, the medical battalion of a division will have five companies instead of three, and each company will be equipped to establish a casualty clearing station. The new structure of medical units operating with the three armed services is expected to provide better care to personnel during peacetime and to provide cadres around which wartime units and hospitals could rapidly be activated.

Reserves

The new military structure that has emerged from the reorganization relies on rapid mobilization of reserves to bring the combat support and other support units of divisions and corps up to authorized strength in a declared emergency. Both the Field Army and the Territorial Army have units at cadre strength needing augmentation to reach wartime levels. Many active duty officers and NCOs, whose peacetime assignments are in military schools and other noncombat agencies, are earmarked for positions in combat units to which they would report immediately when so ordered. They would be replaced by members of the Standby Readiness reserve who would also fill positions that are not normally occupied in peacetime.

About 2 million former servicemen constituted the overall reserve pool in early 1982 and, of these, about 1 million would be available for rapid mobilization. Over 200,000 reservists are called up for annual training periods. At this time, those officers and NCOs earmarked for mobilization assignments to combat units join the reservists for field training. Those reservists who have had training within two or three years and all servicemen discharged during the preceding twelve months constitute the Standby Readiness component and are subject to immediate mobilization. Former extended service officers and NCOs are subject to recall until age sixty; regulars until age sixty-five.

National Security

Uniforms, Insignia, and Ranks

As with most armed forces, the Bundeswehr has developed a variety of uniforms for wear on different occasions and in different situations, but the most common for general duty and most off-post activities is the service uniform. The army's service uniform consists of a light gray, single-breasted coat and darker gray trousers, worn with a light blue or a white shirt, black tie, and black shoes. A peaked, visored cap is the common headgear with the service uniform, but berets of solid colors are also worn. Armored troops wear black berets, paratroops maroon, and infantry dark green. Dress uniforms featuring dinner jackets or double-breasted coats are worn by officers for various social occasions.

The traditional arm-of-service colors have been retained by the Bundeswehr and appear as facing on collar flashes or piping on hats and shoulder straps, and as seam stripes on trousers. General officers wear a braided gold piping, other officers wear silver. Piping colors are maroon for general staff, green for infantry, red for artillery, pink for armor, black for engineers, yellow for communications, and various other colors for the remaining branches of service. The national cockade—a gold, red, and black rosette—is worn by all ranks above the cap ornament. All ranks also wear combat uniforms—coveralls or camouflage fatigues—for field duty.

The naval forces wear the traditional navy blue, double-breasted coats and trousers and the summer whites that are common to many of the world's navies. The air forces wear a medium-blue coat and trousers with a light-blue shirt, dark-blue tie, and black shoes.

Officer ranks correspond directly to equivalent ranks in the armed forces of the United States. In the army and air force the company grades are lieutenant, first lieutenant, and captain; field grades are major, lieutenant colonel, and colonel; and the four general officer grades are brigadier general, major general, lieutenant general, and general. Navy officer ranks also correspond, but the terminology differs, and the rank titles do not translate directly as do most of those in the army and air force.

Rank insignia are worn on shoulder straps or, for naval officers, on the lower sleeve and are very similar to equivalent rank insignia in the United States forces (see fig. 23). NCO ranks are based on those used in the Prussian armies of two or three centuries ago, and it is difficult to relate them directly to United States NCO ranks. Enlisted and warrant officer ranks are designated by chevrons and variations of chevrons that are displayed on shoulder straps.

Foreign Military Relations

Since World War II, military forces of several foreign countries have been deployed in West Germany—first as occupation troops

Federal Republic of Germany

ARMY AND AIR FORCE	Leutnant	Oberleutnant	Hauptmann	Major	Oberstleutnant	Oberst	Brigadegeneral	Generalmajor	Generalleutnant	General
UNITED STATES EQUIVALENT	2d Lieutenant	1st Lieutenant	Captain	Major	Lieutenant Colonel	Colonel	Brigadier General	Major General	General	General of the Army or Air Force
NAVY	Leutnant Zur See	Oberleutnant Zur See	Kapitänleutnant	Korvettenkapitän	Fregattenkapitän	Kapitän Zur See	Flottillenadmiral	Konteradmiral	Vizeadmiral	Admiral
UNITED STATES EQUIVALENT	Ensign	Lieutenant Junior Grade	Lieutenant	Lieutenant Commander	Commander	Captain	Commodore	Rear Admiral	Vice Admiral	Admiral

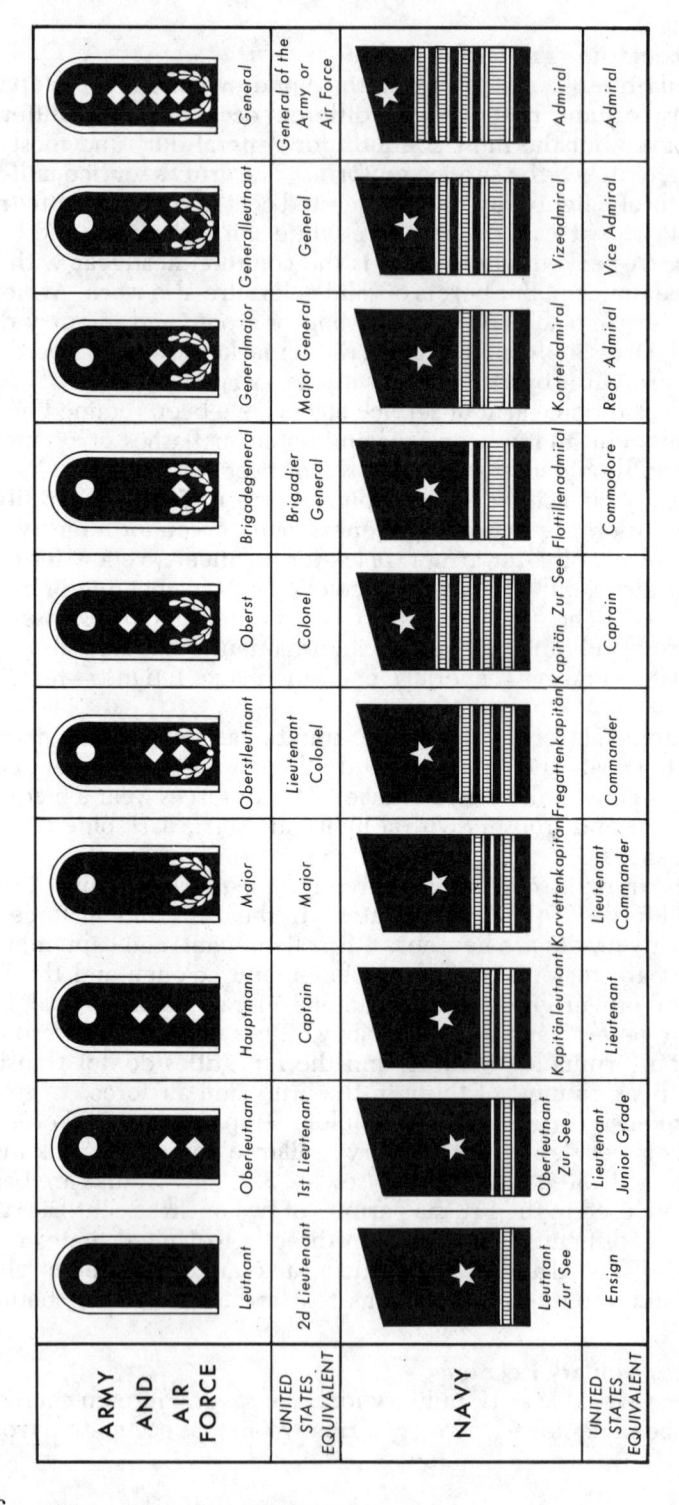

Figure 23. Officers' Rank Insignia

National Security

and since the mid-1950s as allies and members of NATO. The United States has maintained the strongest of the foreign forces, but Britain and France have also deployed sizable contingents. Belgium, Canada, and the Netherlands also maintained troop units there, but the latter two were little more than token forces.

At the beginning of 1982 the United States maintained about 208,000 troops in West Germany and about 4,500 in West Berlin. The various military headquarters included United States Army Europe in Heidelberg, Seventh Army in Stuttgart, V Corps in Frankfurt, VII Corps in Stuttgart, and United States Air Force Europe in Ramstein. Elements of these major formations were deployed throughout the country. In addition there were four army divisions and three brigades in the United States earmarked for emergency deployment to Europe. The United States forces in West Berlin comprised headquarters elements and an infantry brigade. Equipment for United States forces in West Germany included about 3,000 main battle tanks and approximately 300 combat aircraft. Some of the tanks were stockpiled for use by troops who would be airlifted from the United States in an emergency.

British forces in West Germany in early 1982 numbered about 55,000 in the British Army of the Rhine (BAOR), almost 11,000 in air force units, and about 3,000 in a West Berlin infantry brigade. The BAOR deployed a corps consisting of four armored divisions and an artillery division. An additional infantry formation with specialized training and capabilities—the 5th Field Force—was also directly subordinate to BAOR. The British forces operated about 600 main battle tanks and about 150 combat aircraft. Canadian forces in the country numbered only about 3,000, making up one mechanized brigade armed with thirty-nine Leopard tanks.

Because Belgium and the Netherlands share borders with the Federal Republic and because their national armies are committed to NATO, the exact deployment of their forces (whether or not they are in the home countries or in West Germany) is not of major significance. All major combat units of Belgium's 65,000-man army and of the Netherlands' 63,000-man army are integrated into the NATO forces, but Belgium usually maintained a West German garrison of about 25,000; the Netherlands force in West Germany in the early 1980s numbered about 5,000. In an emergency Belgium and the Netherlands could field almost 400 main battle tanks and 140 combat aircraft and 460 main battle tanks and 180 combat aircraft, respectively.

France also maintained about 50,000 troops in the Federal Republic, most of whom were assigned to the French II Corps deployed in Baden-Württemberg, which shares a border with France. The maneuver elements of the corps comprised three armored divisions; support elements included a tactical nuclear missile regiment, but operational control of the nuclear weapons

Federal Republic of Germany

was held by the president rather than by a military commander. France also maintained an infantry regiment and an armored regiment in West Berlin. The position of France among countries maintaining forces in the Federal Republic was unique in that all other non-German forces in the country were committed to NATO, from which France had withdrawn its forces. French forces remained in the country under a bilateral treaty between the two governments.

Internal Security

The West German legal system is the product of many centuries of development from the ancient tribal laws of the first Germans. Those indigenous customs were influenced and changed by Roman law and later by the laws that prevailed in the Holy Roman Empire. German feudal law became a strong influence, and a tradition of multiple legal systems for multiple polities became entrenched. Particularism was the keynote of the Holy Roman Empire, and when the ordering of law and legal institutions became necessary in the eighteenth century, codifications of law and establishment of police systems were left to the individual territorial states. The codes that evolved were mixtures of German, Roman, and ecclesiastical law.

The drive toward political unification during the nineteenth century was accompanied by a trend toward legal unification. The growing interdependence of the many German states, especially in commerce, led to the adoption under the German Confederation of a common law of bills of exchange in 1849 and an all-German Commercial Code in 1861, although both had to be individually ratified by each state. In other than commercial matters, however, legal matters were still the prerogative of each political entity. Prussia was governed by the General *Land* Law that had been codified under Frederick the Great and promulgated in the late eighteenth century. Other states observed the so-called German Common Law and some used the Napoleonic Civil Code. Only after the achievement of political unification under Prussian dominance in 1871 was a start made on drawing up German legal codes (see Political Consolidation. ch. 1).

The codes and laws on police and penal institutions adopted after unification showed in varying degrees the influence of Napoleonic codes. Patterns were established which, despite amendments and modifications, have continued to prevail in the Federal Republic. The most important of the early models were the Penal Code of 1871, defining three classes of imprisonment still in use; the procedural codes of 1877; the law of 1877 establishing a unified court system, the levels of which still survive; and the comprehensive Civil Code, which was begun in 1874 and finally took effect in its full scope of 2,385 paragraphs in 1900. The content of the Civil Code has been amended extensively, but the principles incorporated in it also have survived in West German civil law.

Alongside the courts and laws there developed a structure of penal institutions and a system of police, both characterized by the efficiency for which German administrative organs have long been noted. They were somewhat relaxed during the Weimar period but, like all German bureaucracies, they tended toward rigidity. In their own view of their positions and responsibilities, the police and penal authorities saw the role of serving the state as overshadowing any obligation of service to the people.

When the Nazis came to power they centralized control of the police and administration of the courts and made widespread use of special courts but, superficially, the laws and institutions remained the same. The spirit of the law and the legal system, however, were totally subverted to the dictates of the Nazi leadership. Systems were perverted for purely political purposes and whims, and when "the sound instinct of the people" demanded it (as interpreted, of course, by the Nazis), the rule of law was completely abolished. The impact of Nazi ideology was greatest on the Criminal Code and the Code of Criminal Procedure. The scope of defined criminality (particularly in the area of crimes against the state) and the harshness of punishment were drastically magnified. The Code of Criminal Procedure was made almost unrecognizable by the activities of the Nazi-inspired People's Court in their trying of political cases and by the use of special and summary courts of indeterminate jurisdiction.

The police, whose powers and responsibilities were significantly broadened, became tools of the ruling party under the direct control of the minister of the interior. The regular police agencies included city and town forces; motorized gendarmerie in rural areas; waterways, fire, air-raid warning, and auxiliary police forces; and the administrative police bureaus that enforced welfare, health, and building codes and other such regulations as well as keeping voluminous police records. Much more powerful than the regular police were the Security Police (Sicherheitspolizei—SIPO), which incorporated the Criminal Investigation Police and the Border Police as well as the newly created Secret State Police (Geheime Staatspolizei—Gestapo). In company with two other Hitlerite creations, the Storm Troops (Sturmabteilung—SA) and the Guard Detachment (Schutzstaffel—SS), the Gestapo became infamous as an instrument of terror.

Hitler's reign of terror was a means of pursuing his racial policies in addition to controlling the German people. Millions of persons disappeared into the Nazi concentration camps and gas chambers. Most Germans studiously ignored the terror or were cowed into a stunned acceptance of the regime's insistence that it was necessary to protect and preserve the purity of the German race. At the end of World War II the victorious Allies were determined to eliminate all traces of the terror and horror that the Nazis had imposed on the country during the Third Reich and, to that end, they looked back to the Weimar and empire eras for the codes and institutions that would restore order. Innovation that occurred in the American, British, and French occupation zones aimed at bringing German legal experience into line with that of Western Europe, particularly to protect the rights of the individual from the state.

After the establishment of the Federal Republic in 1949, the Allied authorities (occupation continued until 1955) permitted the formation of West German police forces under specified conditions. The police were to be under *Land* control rather than centralized, and they were forbidden to take on the role of paramilitary units. The missions of the police were to maintain public order and safety and to prevent crime. They were given the power of arrest and were further charged with maintaining local administrative records. Personnel strengths and arms were not to exceed those authorized by local elected governments, and such authorizations were subject to review by the Allied High Commission. Mergers of *Land* police forces were prohibited.

Some early restrictions were lifted within two years as the cold war atmosphere thickened, and some police functions necessitated central rather than local direction. The Federal Border Force (Bundesgrenzschutz—BGS) was created to handle special functions that overlapped *Land* jurisdictions. The Readiness Police (Bereitschaftspolizei) was designed as a paramilitary force, but its purpose was not military. The Readiness Police was intended as a back-up force to assist local or *Land* agencies when a situation demanded, e.g., riot or disaster. Although the Readiness Police remained under *Land* control, agreements permitted forces to be moved to any *Land* in which a situation was out of control and additional forces were required. In addition to the BGS, federal agencies were also created to handle interstate criminal matters and overall security affairs.

Federal Police Agencies

The BGS, established in March 1951, was the first federal police organization permitted by the Allied occupation authorities. The original strength figure authorized for security of the Federal Republic's borders was 30,000, but the actual strength has usually ranged between 20,000 and 25,000 on active duty. The decision to guard the borders with police rather than military forces was taken purposely to reduce the possibility of constant confrontation between NATO and Soviet troops. During the early 1950s incidents were rife on the borders; the East German Volkspolizei (People's Police) and their counterparts in Czechoslovakia were frequently arrogant and belligerent in these areas. In addition the flow of refugees from East Germany, which included large numbers of agents, necessitated the creation of a highly compe-

The Brandenburg Gate, built in 1784 by order of Frederick the Great, is cut off from the West by the Berlin Wall.
Courtesy United Press International

tent border police.

Even though the BGS was organized along military lines, e.g., in battalions, companies, and platoons, and armed as light infantry, it was intended to be and has continued to be a police force controlled by the Ministry of the Interior rather than by the Ministry of Defense. The units of the BGS are supervised through four commands that have headquarters in the four *Länder* bordering East Germany and Czechoslovakia (see fig. 1). Southern Command headquarters is at Munich, Mid-German Command at Kassel, Northern Command at Hanover, and Coastal Command at Kiel.

Border units are equipped and trained as light infantry and, in effect, constitute a highly mobile paramilitary force, albeit highly dispersed. BGS equipment includes armored cars, machine guns, automatic rifles, tear gas, hand grenades, rifle grenades, and antitank weapons. All personnel on border duty wear side arms. Some units have helicopters to facilitate rapid access to remote border areas and for patrol and rescue missions. Units in the Coastal Command are equipped with fast patrol boats. When the Bundeswehr was formed in the mid–1950s, the coastal patrol mission was turned over to the new navy, and the sea police units were abolished. Later, the need for a separate sea police was

Federal Republic of Germany

recognized, and the BGS units were recreated in 1964, relieving the navy of its police functions.

Because of its paramilitary nature and its deployment along the borders, the BGS would very likely be immediately involved with any aggressor. In order to clarify the status of border policemen involved in warfare, the law that established the BGS was amended in 1965 to transfer the entire organization to the Ministry of Defense upon the outbreak of war, thus giving its members the protection given to military personnel under the Geneva Conventions.

Rank structure is similar to that of the Bundeswehr, and personnel are both volunteers and conscripts. The service uniform is green, but field units also wear camouflage fatigues and, at times, steel helmets. Although most field units are deployed near the country's eastern borders, one battalion is stationed in Bonn, where it guards the residences of the president and chancellor and some government buildings. A separate branch of the BGS known as the Individual Services handles immigration and naturalization and customs functions. Its members wear dark-blue uniforms rather than the border police green. They are stationed at all entry points and border crossing points, where they are responsible for customs inspections and passport control.

Another central police agency is the Federal Criminal Investigation Office (Bundeskriminalamt—BKA), which operates nationwide from its headquarters in Wiesbaden. The mission of the BKA is to combat crime, but its jurisdiction is limited to crimes involving two or more *Länder* or when crimes such as gunrunning or drug dealing are international in scope. BKA agents only enter a case that is confined within one *Land* if requested to do so by local authorities. In addition to its investigative functions, the BKA also maintains a major field office in Bonn from which it operates a protective service for government officials similar to the United States Secret Service.

The BKA is a collector and evaluator of intelligence in the continuing war against crime, and it disseminates information to interested police forces and coordinates exchanges of information between them. It also operates a forensic laboratory and makes the facilities available to *Land* authorities when needed. As a central registry of criminal information, the BKA maintains statistics and records including a fingerprint file from which police forces may request information on suspects. The agency also acts as the country's reporting and contact center for the International Criminal Police Organization (INTERPOL) through which it maintains contacts with approximately ninety countries for the exchange of information on criminal activities. The BKA has been heavily involved in combating the terrorist gangs that have plagued the country since the 1960s.

Other federal police agencies include Railways Police, River Police, and Shipping Police. Railroads in West Germany are owned and operated by the federal government, and the Railways Police is a federal force that works exclusively on the railroad lines, stations, and other railroad property to protect installations, cargo, and passengers. River Police maintain the inland waterways and protect canal installations. Shipping Police are responsible for traffic on the waterways and in the country's ports. The Ministry for Transport is responsible for the operation of the railroads and inland waterways. A group often referred to as air police included the air traffic controllers, which consisted of federal and *Land* employees.

Two federal agencies involved in security matters are the Federal Intelligence Service (Bundesnachrichtendienst—BND) and the Federal Office for the Protection of the Constitution (Bundesamt für Verfassungsschutz—BfV). The BND, which is based in Munich, is an intelligence collection and analysis agency as well as a counterintelligence service. If there is a threat to the federal government from outside the country's borders, the BND is supposed to learn about it ahead of time in order to alert the federal authorities. An internal threat falls within the purview of the BfV. The main office is located in Cologne; similar offices exist in each *Land*, and although they cooperate closely with the federal office, they are established by and operate under the control of *Land* authorities.

State Police Agencies

Below the federal level, police forces are organized by the *Länder* and are collectively known as state police (*Landpolizei*). The duties of the police may cover urban or rural areas. The forces may be organized by cities, towns, or rural communities, but they are all integral components of the police forces of the *Land* in which they are located. The *Land* minister of the interior supervises police operations in his jurisdiction. Following German police tradition, the *Landpolizei* handle a great many administrative matters in their areas of jurisdiction. These duties entail maintaining registries of all residents, issuing licenses of various kinds as well as personal identity cards, and other similar administrative tasks.

Although the *Landpolizei* are regulated by eleven different legislatures and are, in fact, eleven different police forces, efforts have been made by the *Länder*, encouraged by the federal government, to standardize laws governing police activities. Until 1977 *Landpolizei* uniforms were distinctive in color and design but have since been standardized throughout the country.

In addition to the general duty police and criminal police in each *Land*, Readiness Police are trained and equipped to reinforce the general duty police whenever ordered to do so by the minister. They may also be called upon to assist the police of other *Länder* for riot duty or other special situations. The Readiness Police of the *Länder* receive their weapons, vehicles, and communications equipment from the federal government, and there is an office in the federal Ministry of the Interior that oversees and coordinates Readiness Police affairs. At the beginning of the 1980s the total strength of the Readiness Police was about 23,000 men.

In contrast to the military services, which do not recruit women, the *Landpolizei* have had policewomen since the forces were reconstituted after World War II. The record indicates, however, that limitations were applied concerning the employment of policewomen—they were usually assigned to cases involving juveniles or women, and they worked in plainclothes and did not carry weapons. Not until the mid–1970s were policewomen used to any large extent in general police duties, but since that time many more policewomen have moved into the uniformed ranks and have been assigned to the same duties as their male counterparts. In the early 1980s women were still not assigned to units of the Readiness Police or the BGS.

Criminal Justice

Law in the Federal Republic is codified and is predominantly federal. Although *Land* laws exist for some cultural and societal matters, they do not deal with criminal justice. The system of criminal justice is derived from the civil law, rather than the common law that provides the basis for the systems used in Britain and the United States. Originating in Europe and developing over many centuries, the civil law (sometimes called continental or Romano-Germanic) is also found in Third World countries that were former colonial possessions of civil law states. In its modern development in Western Europe, including West Germany, the civil law has incorporated ideas of nonconfinement punishments, work-release programs, and other punishments aimed at rehabilitation of criminals rather than simple removal from society. Toward these goals the West Germans in the mid–1970s promulgated the revised Code of Criminal Procedure and the new Federal Prison Act. West Germany also joined several other civil law countries by abolishing the death penalty, which was done in the Basic Law under which the Federal Republic was founded.

It is fundamental to the system that no act is punishable unless its criminality had been established in law before the act was committed, and double jeopardy is also constitutionally prohibited. It is also fundamental that the law will be administered by judges who are independent, that is, they are not subject to removal or transfer except for cause; they are, of course, themselves subject to the law. Criminal cases may be heard for the first time at any of the courts of a three-tiered *Land* system—local courts, regional courts, higher regional (or appellate) courts—and may be taken for appeal or revision from the lowest to the next two levels or from all three to the highest court in the criminal justice system—the Federal Court of Justice (see The Judiciary, ch. 7). Cases heard for the first time in a higher regional court would involve crimes against the Basic Law, such as high treason or sedition. In the late 1970s there were about 11,000 professional judges in the system and, in local and regional courts, professional judges were joined by lay judges to hear cases involving serious crimes. Lay judges may be compared to jury members in common law systems.

Judges are appointed for life or until voluntary retirement and, according to the Basic Law, they cannot be dismissed, suspended, or transferred to another post against their will. Preparation for appointment as a judge is long and arduous. A candidate for such appointment must have a university degree, have followed a law curriculum, have three years legal experience, and pass state qualifying examinations.

The individual rights of citizens are guaranteed in the Basic Law and in the country's statutes. A suspect cannot be forced to talk to the police. If statements to the police have been made, they may be retracted later during a court trial. The law prevents police from subjecting suspects to physical abuse, torture, drugs, deceit, or hypnosis. Only the minimum force necessary for arrest or restraint is authorized, and limitations on a person's freedom can only be those defined in law. A suspect must be brought before a judge no later than the day following arrest, and the judge must issue a warrant of arrest specifying reasons for detention or else release the suspect. A relative or another person selected by the detainee must be notified immediately of detention beyond the day after arrest.

Criminal acts under West German law are classified as felonies or misdemeanors, the latter encompassing less serious crimes but including many acts that would be considered felonies in most common law countries. Crimes categorized as misdemeanors in West Germany include extortion, fraud, larceny, and even negligent homicide. Felonies are punishable by prison sentences of one year or more; misdemeanors may be punished by shorter prison terms, combined imprisonment and fines, or by fines without imprisonment.

During the 1970s the largest number, by far, of persons convicted in West German courts were given fines; a much smaller number received suspended sentences; and a still smaller number were imprisoned. Fines were adjudged in more than 80 percent of the cases, suspended sentences in about 8 to 12 percent, and imprisonment in about 6 to 8 percent. Persons convicted of misdemeanors, if sentenced to imprisonment, do not lose their

Federal Republic of Germany

rights as citizens; convicted felons lose their rights to hold public office or to practice law. Under new prison regimes instituted in the late 1970s, convicts were entitled to vocational training in order that they may be released as productive members of society.

Juveniles are dealt with separately in the criminal justice system. Children under the age of fourteen cannot be held criminally responsible, and cases of those accused of criminal acts are handled in special guardianship courts. Persons between ages fourteen and eighteen are considered responsible but are treated as juveniles insofar as punishments are concerned. Avenues of nonjudicial punishments are fully explored before judicial punishments are imposed on juveniles. Young people between the ages of eighteen and twenty-one are held to be fully responsible for their actions and are tried as juveniles only if adjudged by a court to be mentally immature. Twenty percent of convictions in West German courts in the late 1970s were of persons who had not reached their twenty-first birthdays.

Judges, prosecutors, and counsel concerned with criminal proceedings against juveniles are chosen from among those who have had special education and training in juvenile affairs or who have gained special qualifications through experience. If a court determines that a juvenile must be punished by confinement, the sentence must be carried out in a separate juvenile penal institution. The minimum sentence in a juvenile detention center is three months; the maximum, ten years. Court cases involving juveniles are not open to the public.

Dissidence and Terrorist Activities

Opposition to the government has existed since its inception in 1949 and, in keeping with German tradition, students have been in the front ranks of those opposing the regime. By 1968 when student and youth rebellion had become endemic in many of the world's industrial countries, the leading West German political parties were cooperating in the Grand Coalition (see Grand Coalition, 1966–69, ch. 1). As a result of the decrease in political opposition, student activism (the extra-parliamentary opposition) rose to a much higher level. In addition to the leftist groups opposing the Grand Coalition, right-wing elements also gained strength, and the new National Democratic Party (Nationaldemokratische Partei Deutschlands—NPD), a neo-Nazi organization, gained support in several *Land* elections.

The Grand Coalition was dissolved in 1969, but student groups, e.g., the Socialist Students' League, were well organized and had become radicalized. Among the many causes for protest demonstrations by students were the government's alleged rigidity toward student organization, the resistance to student input to university administration, the supposed undue influence on the government by Axel Springer (owner of several newspapers and radio and television outlets), and United States involvement in Vietnam. Demonstrations led to confrontations between police and students, many of which ended in violence with injuries on both sides leading to further confrontations. Before long, individuals on the fringes of legitimate student organizations had dropped out to form extremist groups, which initiated terrorist activities that remained prevalent through the 1970s and early 1980s.

Citizens have demanded that steps be taken to curb terrorist activities, but new laws intended to curtail them have worried many people who fear the loss of democratic rights. Left-wing extremist groups such as the Red Army Faction (Rote Armee Fraktion—RAF) became internationally known through their bloody exploits in the Federal Republic and through their contacts with terrorist groups in other countries. Right-wing extremism, however, was also a major concern of the political authorities as well as of the police whose job it is to combat terrorists. A particularly heinous act of violence occurred at the Munich Oktoberfest in late 1980 when a right-wing terrorist detonated a bomb that killed and maimed indiscriminately. In 1981 the leftist RAF claimed responsibility for several attacks on United States military installations in West Germany.

The RAF is an outgrowth of the Baader-Meinhof Gang, which came to public attention in the late 1960s and early 1970s with a series of crimes and acts of violence. By 1972 the terrorist activities had alarmed the authorities as well as the people. Even though homegrown terrorists were not involved in the massacre of Israeli Olympic athletes, which was perpetrated by Palestinians, police forces were augmented, and antiterrorist legislation was passed. After the massacre the government decided to create a special force within the BGS (the Grenzschutzgruppe 9 or GSG–9) to be trained as an antiterrorist unit.

Earlier in 1972 a series of crimes including bank robberies, bombings, and murders had been attributed to the Baader-Meinhof Gang and, in June, its co-leaders Andreas Baader and Ulrike Meinhof were captured. Baader, who had been convicted of anarchist activities (arson) in 1968, had escaped from custody (with Meinhof's help) and had gone underground to continue his antigovernment criminal activities. Meinhof, a prominent editor of the left-wing magazine *Konkret*, published by her husband, gave up her profession and her family life to join the underground anarchist group that she and Baader eventually headed.

Taking time out from their terrorist activities in the summer of 1970, some members of the gang, including the two leaders, spent several weeks at a Palestinian camp in Jordan being trained in urban guerrilla tactics. Back in West Germany to apply what they had learned, they began referring to the gang as the Red Army

Federal Republic of Germany

Faction, or RAF, and over the next two years were involved in many acts of terrorism. In early 1972 the RAF claimed responsibility for the bombing of American installations in Frankfurt and Heidelberg, which resulted in the deaths of four American servicemen and the wounding of several others. The gang also took credit for bombings in Augsburg, Hamburg, Karlsruhe, and Munich. In June, Baader and two companions were captured in a shoot-out with Frankfurt police after the most intensive manhunt since World War II. Meinhof was arrested two weeks later and, with the other three RAF members, was held on charges of murder, arson, and armed robbery.

Because of the publicity given to the terrorists and their crimes, the authorities had little trouble in pressuring the Bundestag to push through three bills dealing with internal security, all of which increased the powers of the federal government. One of the new bills gave *Land* authorities permission to call on the BGS for assistance when circumstances seemed to be beyond the control of *Landpolizei*. A second bill upgraded the competence of the BfV and its counterpart offices at *Land* level and provided for closer cooperation and coordination among these offices. The third bill gave the federal government the authority to legislate in the area of gun control, a power that primarily had been a *Land* prerogative.

Despite the fact that the two RAF leaders and other important members were in jail awaiting trail, the RAF remained strong and recruited enough new members to continue a disturbing level of terrorist crimes. Two years later, as Baader, Meinhof, and others still awaited trials, another major police operation resulted in the capture of several more gang members and, by the end of 1974, about ninety RAF members were in custody awaiting trials. Despite police successes, the RAF retained the strength and organization to continue a serious level of operations. When one of the imprisoned terrorists died after a hunger strike, a prominent judge was murdered in retaliation. In the meantime the government was criticized for allegedly poor conditions in prisons where accused terrorists were being held and for the excessive time spent in preparations for trials.

When the long-delayed date for the trial of Baader and Meinhof was finally announced, an armed group took over the West German embassy in Stockholm threatening the lives of several hostages unless the RAF members facing trial were released and flown out of West Germany. The government refused to comply, and before the incident ended, two hostages were murdered. One of the terrorists was also killed, and five others were captured. The intensity of terrorist activities at the time motivated the government to strengthen the BKA and the BfV. The Bundestag passed further legislation making it easier for authorities to combat terrorist groups.

As scheduled, the trial of Baader, Meinhof, Gudrun Ensslin, and Jan-Carl Raspe began on May 21, 1975. All of the defendants had been incarcerated since June 1972 and, in the interim, Meinhof had been tried and convicted of helping Baader escape from earlier custody. For security reasons a special courtroom had been constructed in Stuttgart's Stammheim Prison specifically for this trial. After its long preparation, the prosecution brought forth a 354-page indictment charging the four defendants with five murders and about seventy attempted murders plus several bank robberies, automobile thefts, and assorted other crimes. The trial did not end until April 1977, but a year earlier Ulrike Meinhof had chosen suicide as an end to her bizarre career as a terrorist; her three codefendants received life sentences.

The severe sentences and the permanent removal of the RAF leadership, rather than causing an interruption in terrorist activity, seemed to increase its tempo. The long trial was both complex and controversial. Motions by defense lawyers to have their clients treated as political prisoners rather than common criminals or to have them considered prisoners of war because they had been engaged in partisan warfare against the state delayed the trial as the courts debated those issues. Meanwhile legislation that was passed specifically pertaining to the trial, e.g., that the trial could continue in the absence of the defendants, worried civil libertarians as well as some ordinary citizens who noted that measures to inhibit the activities of terrorists restricted the liberties of everyone.

Three weeks before the trial ended, West Germany's chief federal prosecutor was murdered along with his chauffeur and bodyguard as his car paused at a traffic light in Karlsruhe. In July, after the verdicts had been announced, the terrorists struck again, killing the chief executive of the country's second largest bank during an abortive kidnap attempt. The callers taking credit for the murders identified themselves as the Ulrike Meinhof Commando and the Rote Morgen (Red Morning) respectively. Authorities considered that both were segments of the RAF. In September terrorists kidnapped Hanns-Martin Schleyer, president of the Federation of German Industries and president of the Confederation of German Employer Associations. The kidnappers demanded the release of eleven prisoners including Baader, Ensslin, and Raspe in addition to large payments of ransom.

Almost six weeks after the kidnapping of Schleyer, a Lufthansa passenger plane was hijacked by Arab terrorists who also demanded the release of the same eleven prisoners. After several landings around the Mediterranean area and the Middle East, the plane finally landed at Mogadishu, Somalia, where it was attacked by GSG–9, the specially trained antiterrorist unit. During the

Federal Republic of Germany

spectacular rescue mission, three of the four hijackers were killed, and the fourth was wounded, with no casualties among the eighty-six hostages. Learning of the failure of the effort to free them, Baader, Ensslin, and Raspe committed suicide in Stammheim Prison; Schleyer was then murdered by his kidnappers.

During the remainder of 1977 several terrorists—some associated with the RAF and some not—were captured and tried as the West German crackdown continued. Among those convicted and sentenced to long prison terms were the four survivors of the attack on the embassy in Stockholm. Several lawyers who had defended various accused terrorists came under investigation themselves, and some were charged with having supported a criminal organization by establishing communications links between those in prison and those on the outside. In the meantime the Bundestag voted unanimously for ratification of the European Convention on the Suppression of Terrorism.

Overshadowed by the publicity given to the spectacular and violent acts of the RAF and other leftist terrorist groups from the late 1960s to the late 1970s, a variety of right-wing factions contributed to rising crime statistics with little fanfare. After right-wing groups were accused of using stolen NATO weapons in several bank robberies, the government was criticized for being too lenient with terrorists from that end of the political spectrum. There was also criticism of the expensive computerization of the fight against terrorism because the large quantities of stored information seemingly failed to prevent any of the bloody events of 1977. A few months later, however, the tracking down of several terrorists (including some who had fled to other countries) by using information from the computer bank offset much of the criticism. In a crackdown against the right in 1979, a West Berlin court sent three men to prison and gave several others suspended sentences for establishing a branch of the proscribed Nazi Party.

The federal Ministry of the Interior estimated that incidents by right-wing extremist groups numbered 616 in 1977; increased to 992 in 1978; and numbered approximately 1,500 in 1979. Although the vast majority of these incidents did not involve violence (displaying Nazi flags or distributing Nazi propaganda), the increasing numbers of armed robberies and violent crimes attributed to rightists alarmed officials. The membership in the NPD, however, had dropped considerably by 1979 compared to its strength early in the decade (see Political Parties and the Electoral System, ch. 7). Those harboring neo-Nazi attitudes seemed to prefer the smaller fringe groups rather than the legal political party. During the showing of the American television series "Holocaust," which depicted Nazi genocide, anonymous threats were received by several stations telecasting the programs, and transmitters were bombed in Koblenz and Münster.

On January 30, 1980, the federal Ministry of the Interior banned the organization known as the Hoffmann Military Sport Group (Wehrsportgruppe Hoffmann), which was considered to be an illegal paramilitary unit. Karl-Heinz Hoffmann, founder and leader of the group, had earlier been convicted of attacking left-wing students at Tübingen University and also for wearing Nazi uniforms and insignia. Although membership in the Hoffmann group was small—authorities estimated about 400 members—and the organization was proscribed, the capacity of such extremist splinter groups to cause trouble was underscored in a tragic manner in late 1980 when a terrorist bomb was exploded at the Munich Oktoberfest, killing thirteen people and injuring 200 others. The bomber, who was killed, was identified as a member of the Hoffmann group. Hoffmann and several followers were arrested immediately but had to be released when they could not be connected to the bombing. The fanaticism of the xenophobic rightists was fueled by the large number of foreign workers (many of whom were drawing unemployment benefits) and by the increasing numbers of foreigners asking for political asylum in the country.

Added to the country's problems with terrorism in the late 1970s was the growing number of incidents involving foreign extremists. Demonstrations involving Iranians, Palestinians, Turks, Yugoslavs, and others sometimes turned violent, leading to confrontations with the police. Such troubles caused by foreigners were readily exploited by fanatics among the extreme nationalistic and ethnocentric groups that preached neo-Nazi racist theories.

At the end of 1981 West Germans again looked back at a year marred by terrorist incidents and, whereas the horror of 1980 had generally been caused by the right, in 1981 the left-wing terrorists had again taken center stage, primarily with attacks on American personnel and installations. Although the RAF had been relatively quiet since 1977 (the group was believed, however, to have been responsible for the 1979 attempt on the life of General Alexander M. Haig, then Supreme Allied Commander Europe—SACEUR), the terrorists became active in 1981 taking advantage of widespread citizen unrest over the planned buildup of the United States nuclear arsenal in West Germany. A bombing at the Ramstein Air Force Base in September 1981 that injured eighteen Americans and two West Germans and did considerable damage to the joint United States-NATO headquarters was attributed to the RAF as was the burning of several American-owned automobiles at Wiesbaden. Two weeks later the car in which the commander of the United States Army Europe, General Frederick Kroesen, and Mrs. Kroesen, were riding was hit by an antitank grenade and small arms fire. Because of heavy armor plate on the sedan, the occupants were only slightly injured. A month later an RAF member was arrested in the case and two others of West

Federal Republic of Germany

Germany's "most wanted" terrorists were being hunted.

Adding to police concerns at the end of 1981 were the once-again increasing number of incidents caused by right-wing extremists. Two young neo-Nazis were killed in a shoot-out with Bavarian police, and in the north near Hamburg, police found large quantities of weapons buried in a heath by right-wing terrorists. Led to the caches by a register meticulously kept by a man arrested on terrorist charges, police found thirteen guns including a machine gun, 340 pounds of explosives, 240 bombs, fifty antitank grenade launchers with seventy grenades, 258 hand grenades, 13,000 rounds of ammunition, and large quantities of deadly poisons. Police theorized that the weapons and ammunition had been stolen from Bundeswehr armories.

The right-wing terrorists espouse the same Nazi doctrines that were loathsome when advocated during Hitler's twelve-year reign of crime and terror: extreme nationalism, racism, anti-Semitism, and the like. In the words of Karl-Heinz Hoffmann, the "fatherland needs a dictator." There is probably no shortage of neo-Nazis who like to picture themselves in that role. Many of those attracted to the right are from the lower levels of society, frequently people who work in jobs with no future, or people who are unemployed or only marginally employed; many are school dropouts. Many blame society for whatever evils or imagined evils affect their lives. Some seek the companionship of conspiratorial groups, and others simply seek the thrills of underground activities. Whatever their motivation or circumstances, they seem to be receptive to the extremist ideas put forth by Hoffmann and others of the same ideological mold.

Whereas a Nazi-style dictatorship appears to be the desired goal of the rightists, the leftist terrorist groups do not present any clear ideas of what system they would like to replace the existing establishment. If they adhere to a specific ideology, they are more often than not vague about its dimensions. In fact their words and actions are anarchistic to the point of nihilism. They are usually well educated and frequently well established professionally before entering the terrorist scene. A surprisingly high percentage have been women. The number of women is striking when compared to other West European terrorist groups or to the indigenous right-wing groups. Woman or man, however, the West German left-wing terrorist has not articulated a clear-cut vision of what the future should be like; they seem to dedicate themselves only to the destruction of existing structures rather than to the planning of new ones.

* * *

During the 1970s the Ministry of Defense periodically issued reports on the status of the Bundeswehr. Known as White Papers, these official documents are invaluable, English-language sources on the West German armed forces and their functioning as a part of NATO. Also important to the researcher is the report of the Force Structure Commission which studied the Bundeswehr in the early 1970s. *West Germany: Politics and Society* by Childs and Johnson contains informative chapters on the armed forces and on law and order. A chapter written by Joachim Herrmann in *Major Criminal Justice Systems* is also instructive. *The Military Balance*, published annually by the International Institute for Strategic Studies, and the various Jane's publications are sources of personnel strength and weapons information. (For further information see Bibliography.)

Appendix

Table
1. Metric Conversion Coefficients
2. Population by State *(Land)*, 1978
3. Number of Students in Educational System, 1970, 1975, and 1978
4. Prevalent Diseases, Selected Years, 1950–78
5. Most Common Causes of Death, Selected Years, 1951–79
6. Health Insurance, Selected Years, 1911–76
7. Foreigners in West Germany by Nationality, 1975 and 1981
8. Self–Employed Workers, 1970–80
9. Labor Force, 1970–80
10. Labor Force by Sex, Selected Years, 1950–78
11. Child Care Facilities, 1973–76
12. Marriages and Divorces, Selected Years, 1960–78
13. Population Distribution by Size of Settlement, Selected Years, 1950–79
14. Receipts and Expenditures of General Government, Selected Years, 1970–80
15. Gross Domestic Product by Origin, Selected Years, 1970–80
16. Labor Force and Employment, Selected Years, 1970–80
17. Foreign Trade by Principal Commodity Groups, Selected Years, 1970–80
18. Imports and Exports by Areas, Selected Years, 1970–80
19. The Balance of Payments, Selected Years, 1971–80
20. Area of Major Crops, Selected Years, 1959–80
21. Production of Major Crops, Selected Years, 1959–80
22. Foreign Trade in Agricultural Products, 1979–80
23. State *(Land)* Legislative Elections, 1978–81
24. Federal Election Results, 1949–80
25. Defense Expenditures as Percentage of Gross Domestic Product in Purchasers' Values
26. Equipment Expenditures as Percentage of Total Defense Expenditures
27. Armed Forces

Appendix

Table 1. Metric Conversion Coefficients

When you know	Multiply by	To find
Millimeters	0.04	inches
Centimeters	0.39	inches
Meters	3.3	feet
Kilometers	0.62	miles
Hectares (10,000 m²)	2.47	acres
Square kilometers	0.39	square miles
Cubic meters	35.3	cubic feet
Liters	0.26	gallons
Kilograms	2.2	pounds
Metric tons	0.98	long tons
	1.1	short tons
	2,204	pounds
Degrees Celsius (Centigrade)	9 divide by 5 and add 32	degrees Fahrenheit

Federal Republic of Germany

Table 2. *Population by State (Land), 1978*

Land	Capital	Area (in square kilometers)	Inhabitants Total (in thousands)	Number (per square kilometer)	Including foreigners (in thousands)
Baden-Württemberg	Stuttgart	35,751	9,127	255	827
Bavaria	Munich	70,547	10,811	153	625
Bremen	–	404	701	1,736	42
Hamburg	–	748	1,672	2,237	124
Hesse	Wiesbaden	21,113	5,545	263	446
Lower Saxony	Hanover	47,415	7,226	152	250
North-Rhine Westphalia	Düsseldorf	34,069	17,010	499	1,228
Rhineland-Palatinate	Mainz	19,839	3,634	183	142
Saarland	Saarbrücken	2,568	1,077	419	40
Schleswig-Holstein	Kiel	15,696	2,589	165	75
TOTAL FEDERAL REPUBLIC OF GERMANY*	Bonn	248,150	59,392	247	3,799

* Excudes Berlin.

Source: Based on information from Karl Romer (ed.), *Facts about Germany*, Gütersloh, Germany, 1979, p. 18.

Appendix

Table 3. *Number of Students in the Educational System, 1970, 1975, and 1978*

Kind of School	1970	1975	1978
Elementary and Secondary Schools			
Grund- und Hauptschulen	6,347,451	6,425,116	5,718,124
Realschulen	863,450	147,217	350,721
Gymnasien	1,379,455	1,863,479	2,013,353
Gesamtschulen	n.a	165,812	206,930
Second Educational Route			
Abendrealschulen	6,362	11,942	11,878
Abendgymnasien	9,958	15,167	14,533
Studienkollegs	6,362	11,942	11,878
Secondary Vocational Schools			
Berufsschulen	1,599,840	1,635,968	1,815,724
Berufsaufbauschulen	40,382	27,786	16,115
Berufsfachschulen	205,022	294,964	316,227
Fachoberschulen, Fachgymnasien	58,973	118,675	113,073
Advanced Vocational Schools			
Fachschulen	102,331	116,703	81,937
Higher Education			
Universitäten	411,520	675,946	756,896
Kunsthöchschulen	10,456	15,343	16,228
Fachhochschulen	105,664	144,713	172,773

n.a.—not available.

Source: Based on information from Federal Republic of Germany, Statistisches Bundesamt, *Statistisches Jahrbuch, 1979 für die Bundesrepublik Deutschland*, Stuttgart, 1979.

Table 4. Prevalent Diseases, Selected Years, 1950–78

	Number of Cases			
Disease	1950	1960	1970	1978
Tuberculosis	132,639	70,325	48,262	29,536
Scarlet fever	86,924	28,908	28,262	25,560
Infectious hepatitis	n.a.	n.a.	21,770	20,176
Infectious enteritis (salmonella and other forms)	n.a	3,047	12,847	33,609
Contagious meningitis	n.a.	n.a	6,787	5,809
Dysentery	1,007	3,251	542	2,737
Typhus	n.a.	1,548	477	242
Paratyphoid	5,428	2,406	540	194
Diphtheria	40,584	1,965	57	20
Poliomyelitis	2,830	4,198	15	14

n.a.—not available.

Source: Based on information from Federal Republic of Germany, Der Bundesminister für Jugend, Familie und Gesundheit, *Daten des Gesundheitswesens*, Stuttgart, 1980.

Table 5. Most Common Causes of Death, Selected Years, 1951–79
(per thousand population)

Cause of Death	1951	1958	1971	1979*
Heart disease	178.7	228.1	307.5	410.1
Cancer	175.7	192.6	236.7	252.1
Cerebrovascular disease	131.2	155.1	176.8	167.5
Accidents	49.2	57.9	62.7	46.2
Bronchitis, emphysema, and asthma	n.a.	n.a.	37.5	37.7
Pneumonia	49.2	43.1	26.1	22.4
Cirrhosis of the liver	n.a.	n.a.	24.8	25.2
Suicide	18.4	18.4	20.9	21.4

*Provisional figures.
n.a.—not available.

Source: Based on information from Federal Republic of Germany, Der Bundesminister für Jugend, Familie und Gesundheit, *Daten des Gesundheitswesens*, Stuttgart, 1980.

Appendix

Table 6. Health Insurance, Selected Years, 1911–76

Year	Number of Insured (in millions)	Number of Insurance Plans
1911	10.0	22,000
1914	16.0	13,500
1938	23.2	4,600
1951	20.0	1,992
1960	27.1	2,028
1970	30.6	1,827
1976*	33.5	1,425

*As of August 1976.

Source: Based on information from Dieter Schewe, et al., *Übersicht über die soziale Sicherung*, Bonn, 1977.

Table 7. Foreigners in West Gemany by Nationality, 1975 and 1981
(in percentages)

Nationality	1975	1981
Turks	27	33
Yugoslavs	17	14
Italians	15	14
Greeks	10	7
Spaniards	6	4
Other	25	28
TOTAL	100	100

Source: Based on information from *The Week in Germany*, XI, 37, October 30, 1981, p. 6: and Ray C. Rist, *Guestworkers in Germany*, New York, 1978, p. 66.

Federal Republic of Germany

Table 8. Self-Employed Workers, 1970–80

Year	Self-Employed (in thousands)	Percentage Decrease
1970	4,422	—
1971	4,311	2.5
1972	4,220	2.1
1973	4,148	1.7
1974	4,063	2.0
1975	3,937	3.0
1976	3,800	3.5
1977	3,697	2.7
1978	3,625	1.9
1979	3,565	1.7
1980	3,499	1.9

Source: Based on information from Organisation for Economic Co-operation and Development, *Germany,* Paris, 1981, p. 74.

Table 9. Labor Force, 1970–80
(in percentages)

Year	Self-Employed	Salaried
1970	17	83
1971	16	84
1972	16	84
1973	16	84
1974	15	85
1975	16	84
1976	15	85
1977	15	85
1978	14	86
1979	14	86
1980	14	86

Source: Based on information from Organisation for Economic Co-operation and Development, *Germany,* Paris, 1981, p. 74.

Appendix

Table 10. Labor Force by Sex, Selected Years, 1950–78

	Percentage of Total Labor Force	
Year	Men	Women
1950	64	36
1960	63	37
1965	64	36
1970	64	36
1971	64	36
1972	64	36
1973	64	36
1974	63	37
1975	63	37
1976	63	37
1977	63	37
1978	63	37

Source: Based on information from Harry G. Shaffer, *Women in the Two Germanies,* New York, 1981, p. 57.

Table 11. Child–Care Facilities, 1973–76[1]
(in percentages)

	1973	1974	1975	1976
Pre–kindergarten				
All facilities	6.4	6.6	7.0	7.2
Day–care[2]	0.9	1.3	1.3	1.4
Kindergartens	41.9	46.1	51.2	55.2
After–school Centers	2.3	2.6	2.7	3.0

[1] Enrollment as a percentage of all children of the appropriate age–group.
[2] Day–care for children under three years of age.

Source: Based on information from Harry G. Shaffer, *Women in the Two Germanies,* New York, 1981, p. 104.

Federal Republic of Germany

Table 12. *Marriages and Divorces, Selected Years, 1960–78*
(per 1,000 population)

Year	Marriages	Divorces
1960	9.4	0.9
1965	8.3	1.0
1970	7.3	1.3
1975	6.3	1.7
1976	5.9	1.8
1977	5.8	1.7
1978	5.3	1.2

Source: Based on information from Harry G. Shaffer, *Women in the Two Germanies*, New York, 1981, p. 149; and Federal Republic of Germany, Statistisches Bundesamt, *Statistisches Jahrbuch, 1980 für die Bundesrepublik Deutschland*, Stuttgart, 1980, p. 75.

Table 13. *Population Distribution by Size of Settlement, Selected Years, 1950–79*

Settlement Size by Population	\multicolumn{5}{c}{Percentage of Total Population}
	1950	1961	1970	1975	1979
Under 500	5.8	5.5	4.7	1.4	0.7
500–2,000	21.7	16.7	14.9	6.8	5.4
2,000–5,000	13.1	12.0	12.0	8.7	8.9
5,000–10,000	8.7	9.0	10.0	10.5	10.9
10,000–20,000	6.7	7.2	9.3	13.1	14.0
20,000–50,000	8.7	9.8	10.6	15.0	16.5
50,000–100,000	5.3	6.4	6.4	9.1	9.4
More than 100,000	29.9	33.5	32.2	35.5	34.2
TOTAL*	100.1	100.1	100.1	100.1	100.0

* Totals may not add because of rounding.

Source: Based on information from Federal Republic of Germany, Statistisches Bundesamt, *Statistiches Jahrbuch, 1980 für die Bundesrepublik Deutschland*, Stuttgart, 1980, p. 58; and Roy E.H. Mellor, *The Two Germanies: A Modern Geography*, New York, 1978, p. 196.

Appendix

*Table 14. Receipts and Expenditures of General Government;
Selected Years, 1970–80*
(National accounts basis; in billions of DM[1])

Current Prices	1970	1978	1979	1980
Current Receipts				
Income from property and entrepreneurship	8.63	11.85	13.69	14.29
Indirect taxes	87.18	163.85	179.77	189.82
Direct taxes	72.84	167.49	175.51	187.60
Social security contributions	81.53	198.60	213.53	230.74
Other current transfers received	4.08	15.04	15.31	14.83
Total Current Receipts[2]	254.26	556.83	597.81	637.28
Current Expenditures				
Final consumption expenditure	108.11	257.13	278.58	303.40
Wages and salaries	60.14	141.84	151.93	164.13
Goods and services	47.97	115.29	126.65	139.27
Subsidies	9.63	23.84	24.77	23.64
Interest on public debt	6.60	21.52	24.21	28.68
Current transfers paid	90.16	228.36	242.79	256.66
Total Current Expenditures[2]	214.50	530.85	570.35	612.38
Savings	39.76	25.98	27.46	24.90
Depreciation	3.25	7.46	8.27	9.34
Net Capital Transfers Received	−9.96	−23.76	−25.76	−27.66
Gross Fixed Investment	30.86	44.14	50.92	58.63
Financial Balance (Net Lending)	2.19	−34.46	−40.95	−52.05
In percentage of GNP	0.3	−2.7	−2.9	−3.5

[1] For value of the deutsche mark—see Glossary.
[2] Totals may not add because of rounding.

Source: Based on information from Organisation for Economic Co-operation and Development, *Germany*, Paris, 1981, p. 67.

Federal Republic of Germany

Table 15. *Gross Domestic Product by Origin, Selected Years, 1970–80*
(in billions of DM[1])

	1970	1978	1979	1980
Current Prices				
Agriculture, forestry, fishing	23.1	34.4	32.6	32.2
Mining and quarrying, energy	25.1	47.5	51.0	
Manufacturing	280.0	484.1	525.5	716.6
Construction	55.6	86.5	100.6	
Trade, transport, communications	108.7	199.3	216.4	227.2
Government[2]	63.5	149.5	160.4	173.7
Nonprofit organizations, households	9.1	21.3	23.1	25.3
Other services	113.7	263.8	286.7	319.7
GROSS DOMESTIC PRODUCT AT MARKET PRICES[3]	678.8	1,286.4	1,396.4	1,494.7
1970 Prices				
Agriculture, forestry, fishing	23.1	27.1	26.1	26.5
Mining and quarrying, energy	25.1	31.9	33.7	
Manufacturing	280.0	330.0	346.3	447.6
Construction	55.6	59.4	63.5	
Trade, transport, communications	108.7	133.1	140.6	142.3
Government[2]	63.5	82.6	85.1	87.2
Nonprofit organizations, households	9.1	10.6	10.9	11.2
Other services	113.7	166.3	173.0	181.2
GROSS DOMESTIC PRODUCT AT MARKET PRICES[3]	678.8	840.8	879.3	896.0

[1] For value of the deutsche mark—see Glossary.
[2] Social security, central and local government.
[3] Totals may not add because of rounding.

Source: Based on information from Organisation for Economic Co–operation and development, *Germany*, Paris, 1981, 64.

Appendix

Table 16. Labor Force and Employment, Selected Years, 1970–80

	1970	1975	1978	1979	1980
Number (in millions[1])					
Working-age Population					
(15–64 years)	38.60	39.61	39.94	40.29	40.53
Self-Employed[2]	4.42	3.94	3.62	3.56	3.50
Dependent Employment[3]	22.25	21.39	21.60	22.01	22.30
Nationals	(20.44)	(19.32)	(19.75)	(20.08)	(20.25)
Foreign workers	(1.81)	(2.06)	(1.86)	(1.92)	(2.05)
Total Employed	26.67	25.32	25.23	25.57	25.80
Unemployed	0.15	1.07	0.99	0.88	0.89
Total Labor Force	26.82	26.40	26.22	26.45	26.68
Employment by Sectors (in percentages)					
Agriculture, Forestry,					
and Fishing	8.5	7.2	6.4	6.1	n.a.
Mining, Industry,					
and Construction	48.8	45.6	44.8	44.8	n.a.
Commerce and Communications	17.9	18.5	18.3	18.2	n.a.
Other	24.8	28.7	30.5	30.9	n.a.
Unemployment Rate[4]	0.7	4.7	4.3	3.8	3.8

n.a.—not available.
[1] Totals may not add because of rounding.
[2] Includes family members who help in a business or on a farm.
[3] Workers dependent on wages, salaries, or commissions.
[4] Unemployed as percentage of dependent labor force.

Source: Based on information from Organisation for Economic Co-operation and Development, *Germany,* Paris, 1981, p. 74.

Federal Republic of Germany

Table 17. *Foreign Trade by Principal Commodity Groups, Selected Years, 1970–80[1]*
(Customs basis; in millions of DM[2])

	1970	1978	1979	1980
Imports, c.i.f				
Food and live animals	16,652	29,995	30,653	33,257
Beverages and tobacco	1,477	2,858	3,091	3,405
Crude materials, inedible, except fuels	13,746	19,697	23,100	26,507
Mineral fuels, lubricants, and related materials	9,614	39,173	56,620	76,106
Animal and vegetable oils and fats	860	1,259	1,530	1,445
Chemicals	6,887	17,582	22,682	24,164
Manufactured goods, classified chiefly by material	26,512	46,022	54,141	61,023
Machinery and transport equipment	20,675	50,222	56,382	63,720
Miscellaneous manufactured articles	9,633	29,677	34,077	39,446
Commodities and transactions not classified according to kind	3,549	7,260	9,763	12,186
TOTAL[3]	109,606	243,707	292,040	341,259
Exports, f.o.b.				
Food and live animals	3,501	11,005	12,590	15,102
Beverages and tobacco	402	1,417	1,620	1,795
Crude materials, inedible, except fuels	3,009	5,402	6,564	7,179
Mineral fuels, lubricants, and related materials	3,701	9,118	10,611	13,225
Animal and vegetable oils and fats	407	1,366	1,504	1,541
Chemicals	14,983	33,726	41,044	44,130
Manufactured goods classified chiefly by material	27,392	57,306	64,096	71,190
Machinery and transport equipment	58,192	133,037	140,958	155,254
Miscellaneous manufactured articles	11,645	26,695	29,318	32,645
Commodities and transactions not classified according to kind	2,044	5,836	6,164	8,339
TOTAL[3]	125,276	284,907	314,469	350,400

c.i.f.—cost, insurance, and freight.
f.o.b.—freight on board.
[1] Transactions with the German Democratic Republic not included.
[2] For value of the deutsche mark—see Glossary.
[3] Totals may not add because of rounding.

Source: Based on information from Organisation for Economic Co-operation and Development, *Germany*, Paris, 1981, p. 72.

Appendix

Table 18. *Imports and Exports by Areas, Selected Years, 1970–80*[1]
(Customs basis; in millions of DM[2])

Imports, c.i.f.	1970	1978	1979	1980
OECD				
EEC	54,355	119,777	141,275	157,400
Belgium–Luxembourg	10,388	20,524	23,402	24,468
Denmark	1,506	4,011	4,641	5,739
France	13,899	28,281	33,195	36,591
Ireland	148	962	1,175	1,520
Italy	10,836	23,185	25,804	27,084
Netherlands	13,313	30,748	35,842	39,130
United Kingdom	4,264	12,065	17,216	22,867
Austria	2,313	7,116	8,404	9,826
Japan	2,052	7,179	7,912	10,434
Sweden	3,148	5,147	6,153	7,224
Switzerland	3,336	9,484	10,637	12,138
United States	12,066	17,434	20,274	25,699
Other OECD	10,257	17,685	20,639	25,479
Total OECD	87,527	183,822	215,294	248,200
Non–oil Developing Countries	10,788	27,930	33,759	38,264
OPEC	6,897	19,390	26,966	37,413
Centrally Planned Economies	4,394	12,565	16,021	17,382
TOTAL IMPORTS[3]	109,606	243,707	292,040	341,259

Exports, f.o.b.	1970	1978	1979	1980
OECD				
EEC	58,006	130,566	151,751	168,222
Belgium–Luxembourg	10,294	23,657	26,754	27,483
Denmark	2,911	6,320	6,837	6,668
France	15,480	34,895	39,992	46,615
Ireland	380	1,009	1,303	1,329
Italy	11,172	19,431	24,534	29,935
Netherlands	13,313	28,371	31,298	33,275
United Kingdom	4,456	16,883	21,034	22,917

Federal Republic of Germany

Table 18. (Continued)
(Customs basis; in millions of DM[2])

Exports, f.o.b.	1970	1978	1979	1980
Austria	5,684	14,617	16,461	19,258
Japan	1,957	3,477	4,151	3,970
Sweden	4,688	7,674	9,119	10,127
Switzerland	7,674	14,436	16,398	20,007
United States	11,437	20,180	20,759	21,476
Other OECD	15,525	20,025	21,765	24,621
Total OECD	104,971	210,975	240,404	267,681
Non–oil Developing Countries	11,321	31,772	36,044	40,498
OPEC	3,584	24,525	19,180	22,819
Centrally Planned Economies	5,400	17,635	18,841	19,402
TOTAL EXPORTS[3]	125,276	284,907	314,469	350,400

c.i.f.—cost, insurance, and freight.
f.o.b.—freight on board.
[1] Transactions with the German Democratic Republic not included.
[2] For value of the deutsche mark—see Glossary.
[3] Including South Africa and unspecified transactions. Totals may not add because of rounding.

Source: Based on information from Organisation for Economic Co–operation and Development, *Germany,* Paris, 1981, p. 70.

Appendix

Table 19. The Balance of Payments, Selected Years, 1971–80[1]
(OECD basis; in millions of DM[2])

	1971	1978	1979	1980
Trade Balance	23,538	51,199	32,006	18,945
Exports, f.o.b	138,875	310,791	346,799	410,740
Imports, f.o.b	115,337	259,592	314,793	391,796
Services (net)	−9,153	−15,350	−20,904	−23,913
Foreign travel (net)	−7,300	−19,018	−21,889	−25,762
Transportation (net)	−2,697	−1,498	−2,180	−800
Investment income (net)	760	5,079	4,528	3,194
Receipts from foreign troops	6,732	8,905	9,145	10,273
Other services (net)	−6,648	−8,818	−10,508	−10,818
Transfers (net)	−11,497	−17,431	−20,745	−24,085
Official	−3,944	−8,805	−11,209	−13,528
Foreign worker remittances[3]	−6,450	−5,900	−6,500	−6,900
Other private	−1,103	−2,726	−3,037	−3,657
CURRENT BALANCE[4]	2,888	18,420	−9,644	−29,052
Long−Term Capital (net)	6,293	−2,946	10,826	6,700
Official	−2,166	−3,292	−1,509	21,373
Private (net)	8,458	346	12,334	−14,673
Foreign investment in Germany (net)	12,485	21,205	31,025	12,701
Portfolio	2,008	3,162	5,867	1,003
Direct investment	3,905	3,129	2,062	2,069
Loans and credits	6,658	14,981	23,109	9,776
Other	−85	−66	−14	−147
German investment abroad[3](net)	−4,027	−20,859	−18,690	−27,374
Portfolio	532	−4,204	−2,957	−7,712
Direct investment	−3,656	−7,242	−8,393	−8,249
Loans and credits	−313	−8,769	−6,465	−10,005
Other	−590	−645	−874	−1,407
BASIC BALANCE	9,180	15,473	1,181	−22,352
Nonmonetary Short−Term Private Capital	2,008	−2,859	−4,975	8,539
Nonmonetary Short−Term Official Capital	1,141	1,152	−310	−416
Errors and Omissions	2,854	−4,083	−5,178	−4,319
BALANCE ON NONMONETARY TRANSACTIONS	15,183	9,683	−9,281	−18,548
Private Monteary Institutions Short−Term Capital	1,173	10,089	4,328	−9,346
BALANCE ON OFFICIAL SETTLEMENTS[4]	16,356	19,772	−4,954	−27,894

Federal Republic of Germany

Table 19. *(Continued)*
(OECD basis; in millions of DM[2])

	1971	1978	1979	1980
Miscellaneous Official Accounts	–17	9,430	–21,044	15,582
Allocation of Special Drawing Rights	595	n.a.	534	507
CHANGE IN OFFICIAL RESERVES	16,937	29,202	–25,463	–11,805
Gold	351	29	–3,389	–6
Currency assets	15,305	26,083	–20,330	–10,046
Reserve position in IMF[5]	560	2,640	–2,221	–1,366
Special drawing rights	720	450	477	–387
Memorandum Item Valuation adjustment	–5,996	–7586	–2,868	1,656

f.o.b.—freight on board.
n.a.—not available.
[1] Transactions with the German Democratic Republic not included.
[2] For value of the deutsche mark—see Glossary.
[3] – equals outflow from Federal Republic.
[4] Totals may not add because of rounding.
[5] International Monetary Fund.

Source: Based on information from Organisation for Economic Co-operation and Development, *Germany*, Paris, 1981, p. 68.

Table 20. *Area of Major Crops, Selected Years, 1959–80*
(in thousands of hectares)

Crop	1959–61[1]	1969–72[1]	1979[2]	1980[3]
Wheat	1,378	1,555	1,628	1,668
Rye	1,308	858	583	567
Barley	684	1,510	1,989	2,002
Oats	760	823	919	856
Corn	6	111	115	119
Other Grains	453	390	0[4]	0[4]
Total Grains	4,589	5,247	5,234	5,212
Rapeseed	30[5]	85[6]	127	138
Potatoes	1,023	551	276	258
Sugar Beets	280	316	393	395
Silage Corn	44	238	649	695
Clover	493	276	190	177
Alfalfa	153	88	54	42
Grasslands	n.a.	4,066	4,899	4,857

n.a.—not available.
[1] Yearly average for the period.
[2] Methodology changed from earlier years.
[3] Preliminary figures.
[4] Included under rye and oats.
[5] Average for 1957–60.
[6] 1970–71 agricultural year.

Appendix

Table 21. Production of Major Crops, Selected Years, 1959–80
(in thousands of tons)

Commodity	1959–61[1]	1969–72[1]	1979	1980[2]
Wheat	4,508	5,570	8,061	8,156
Rye	3,397	2,871	2,189	2,184
Barley	2,929	5,508	8,184	8,826
Oats	2,043	2,803	3,697	3,249
Corn	19	555	741	672
Other Grains	1,219	1,288	0[3]	0[3]
Total Grains	14,155	18,595	22,872	23,087
Rapeseed	60[4]	150[5]	321	377
Potatoes	22,920	15,488	8,716	6,694
Sugar Beets	9,916	14,131	18,340	19,122
Fodder Beets	445	333	16,725	14,147
Silage Corn	1,494	10,186	31,765	29,083
Clover	3,388	2,099		
Alfalfa	1,154	695	29,511[6]	28,680[6]
Grasslands	21,335	28,061		

[1] Yearly average for the period.
[2] Preliminary figures.
[3] Included under rye and oats.
[4] Yearly average for 1957–60.
[5] 1970–71 agricultural year.
[6] Expressed in hay equivalents.

Table 22. Foreign Trade in Agricultural Products, 1979–80
(in millions of United States dollars)

Commodity Groups	Imports 1979	Imports 1980	Exports 1979	Exports 1980
Live Animals	370	363	288	328
Animal Products	6,477	7,122	4,063	4,699
Plant Products	13,286	14,643	3,552	4,303
Other[1]	3,499	3,718	1,278	1,447
TOTAL	23,633	25,846	9,181	10,777

[1] Tobacco, tea, coffee, alcoholic beverages.

Federal Republic of Germany

Table 23. *State (Land) Legislative Elections, 1978–81*

Land	Election Date	Total Number of Deputies	CDU[1]	SPD	FDP	Others
Baden–Württemberg	March 1980	124	68	40	10	6[2]
Bavaria	October 1978	204	129	65	10	0
Bremen	October 1979	100	33	52	11	4[2]
Hamburg	June 1978	120	51	69	0	0
Hesse	October 1978	110	53	50	7	0
Lower Saxony	June 1978	155	83	72	0	0
North-Rhine Westphalia	May 1980	201	95	106	0	0
Rhineland–Palatinate	March 1979	100	51	43	6	0
Saarland	April 1980	51	23	24	2	0
Schleswig–Holstein	April 1979	73	37	31	4	1[3]
West Berlin	May 1981	132	65	51	7	9[2]

CDU—Christian Democratic Union.
CSU—Christian Social Union.
SPD—Social Democratic Party.
FDP—Free Democratic Party.
[1] In Bavaria, CSU.
[2] Environmentalists.
[3] One deputy of the minority South Schleswig Voters Association.

Source: Based on information from Karl Römer (ed.), *Facts about Germany*, Gütersloh, 1980, p. 92; "West Berlin Government Formed," *New York Times*, June 12, 1981, p. A8.

Appendix

Table 24. *Federal Election Results, 1949–80*

	1949	1953	1957	1961	1965	1969	1972	1976	1980
Electorate (in millions)	31.2	33.1	35.4	37.4	38.5	38.7	41.4	42.2	43.2
Turnout (in percentages)	78.5	86.0	87.8	87.7	86.8	86.7	91.1	90.7	88.7
				Percentage of List (Second) Vote					
CDU/CSU	31.0	45.2	50.2	45.3	47.6	46.1	44.9	48.6	44.5
SPD	29.2	28.8	31.8	36.2	39.3	42.7	45.8	42.6	42.9
FDP	11.9	9.5	7.7	12.8	9.5	5.8	8.4	7.9	10.6
KPD/DKP	5.7	2.2	–	1.9	1.3	0.6	0.3	0.4	0.2
DRP/NPD	1.8	1.1	1.0	0.8	2.0	4.3	0.6	0.3	0.2
Others	20.4	13.2	9.3	3.0	0.3	0.5	0.0	0.2	1.6

CDU—Christian Democratic Union. KPD—Communist Party of Germany.
CSU—Christian Social Union. DKP—German Communist Party.
SPD—Social Democratic Party. DRP—German Reich Party.
FDP—Free Democratic Party. NPD—National Democratic Party.

Source: Based on information from Gordon Smith, *Democracy in Western Germany*, New York, 1980, p. 105; and *Bulletin* [Bonn], No. 12, December 12, 1980, p. 11.

Federal Republic of Germany

Table 25. *Defense Expenditures as Percentage of Gross Domestic Product in Purchasers' Values*

Country	Average 1970–74	1975	1976	1977	1978	1979	1980[1]
Belgium	2.8	3.1	3.1	3.1	3.3	3.3	3.3
Denmark	2.2	2.4	2.2	2.2	2.3	2.3	n.a.
France[2]	3.9	3.8	3.8	3.9	3.9	3.9	4.0
Germany[3]	3.5	3.6	3.5	3.4	3.4	3.3	3.3
Greece	4.4	6.5	5.9	6.8	6.6	5.8	5.2
Italy	2.7	2.5	2.3	2.4	2.4	2.4	2.3
Luxembourg	0.8	1.0	1.0	1.0	1.1	1.0	1.1
Nertherlands	3.3	3.4	3.2	3.5	3.2	3.4	3.3
Norway	3.2	3.2	3.1	3.1	3.2	3.1	3.0
Portugal	6.9	5.3	4.0	3.5	3.5	3.5	3.4
Turkey	4.2	5.8	6.2	5.8	5.2	4.6	4.7
United Kingdom	5.0	5.0	5.0	4.8	4.7	4.8	5.2
NATO Europe	3.7	3.8	3.7	3.6	3.6	3.6	n.a.
Canada	2.1	1.9	1.9	1.9	2.0	1.8	1.8
United States	6.7	6.0	5.4	5.3	5.2	5.2	5.5
Total NATO	5.2	4.7	4.4	4.4	4.3	4.3	n.a.

n.a.—not available.

[1] Estimate.

[2] France is a member of the Alliance without belonging to the integrated military structure; the relevant figures are indicative only.

[3] These percentages have been calculated without taking into account the expenditures on Berlin; if these expenses were included, the percentages would be as follows: 1975: 4.4; 1976: 4.3; 1977: 4.2; 1978: 4.1; 1979: 4.1; 1980: 4.2.

Source: Based on information from "Documentation," *NATO Review* [Brussels], No. 1, February 1981, p. 33.

Appendix

Table 26. Equipment Expenditures as Percentage of Total Defense Expenditures
(Fiscal Years)

Country	Average 1970–74	1975 or 1975/76	1976 or 1976/77	1977 or 1977/77	1978 or 1978/79	1979 or 1979/80	1980 or 1980/81
Belgium	10.6	9.0	11.0	11.9	13.9	13.1	13.6
Canada	7.3	6.3	8.0	8.5	10.0	12.8	13.7
Denmark	16.8	19.0	19.4	21.8	16.4	16.3	15.4
Germany	11.9	11.8	13.2	12.5	13.0	13.7	14.2
Greece	n.a.	n.a.	n.a.	n.a.	n.a.	n.a.	n.a.
Italy	15.4	13.9	13.1	15.3	16.2	15.1	18.3
Luxembourg	1.6	1.0	3.4	2.0	1.7	2.1	1.9
Netherlands	12.8	15.9	15.5	20.9	18.3	20.1	17.9
Norway	13.5	11.6	11.4	14.2	17.2	18.9	17.0
Portugal	7.5	1.9	1.9	2.1	1.8	3.8	6.7
Turkey	4.0	25.2	28.5	21.9	18.5	9.5	6.1
United Kingdom	17.0	19.3	20.6	22.0	23.0	23.2	24.1
United States	21.1	17.5	17.4	17.5	20.0	19.8	19.5

n.a.—not available.

Source: Based on information from "Documentation," *NATO Review* [Brussels], No. 1, February 1981, p. 33.

Federal Republic of Germany

Table 27. Armed Forces

Country	Military Only (in thousands)						Total Armed Forces[1] as Percentage of Total Labor Force					
	1975	1976	1977	1978	1979	1980[2]	1975	1976	1977	1978	1979	1980[2]
Belgium	103	107	107	118	107	109	2.8	2.9	2.8	3.1	2.8	2.8
Denmark	34	31	32	33	33	35	1.8	1.6	1.6	1.6	1.6	1.7
France[3]	585	585	584	581	578	575	3.2	3.2	3.2	3.1	3.1	3.1
Germany	491	493	495	491	492	495	2.5	2.6	2.6	2.5	2.5	2.5
Greece	185	186	187	186	180	180	6.6	6.7	6.7	6.7	6.5	6.4
Italy	459	455	475	489	490	500	2.5	2.4	2.5	2.5	2.4	2.5
Luxembourg	1	1	1	1	1	1	0.8	0.8	0.9	0.9	0.9	0.9
Netherlands	107	106	103	106	107	107	2.8	2.7	2.7	2.7	2.7	2.7
Norway	38	39	39	40	40	39	2.8	2.8	2.7	2.7	2.6	2.6
Portugal	104	83	79	82	81	83	2.8	2.2	2.1	2.2	2.2	2.2
Turkey	584	674	771	720	698	717	3.9	4.4	4.9	4.6	4.3	4.3
United Kingdom	348	337	326	320	324	328	2.5	2.4	2.3	2.2	2.2	2.2
NATO Europe	3,039	3,097	3,199	3,167	3,131	3,169	2.9	2.9	3.0	2.9	2.9	2.9
Canada	78	78	78	79	79	80	1.2	1.1	1.1	1.1	1.1	1.0
United States	2,098	2,075	2,060	2,033	2,027	2,047	3.3	3.2	3.1	2.9	2.9	2.9
Total NATO	5,215	5,250	5,337	5,279	5,237	5,296	3.0	3.0	2.9	2.9	2.9	2.8

[1] Military and civilian personnel.
[2] Estimate.
[3] France is a member of the Alliance without belonging to the integrated military structure; the relevant figures are indicative only.

Source: Based on information from "Documentation," *NATO Review* [Brussels], No. 1, February 1981, p. 33.

Bibliography

Chapter 1

Arendt, Hannah. *The Origins of Totalitarianism.* New York: Harcourt, Brace, Jovanovich, 1973.

Bainton, Roland H. *The Reformation of the Sixteenth Century.* Boston: Beacon Press, 1952.

Barraclough, Geoffrey. *The Origins of Modern Germany.* Oxford: Basil Blackwell, 1949.

Barraclough, Geoffrey (ed.). *The Times Atlas of World History.* London: Times Books, 1978.

Bleek, Wilhelm. "From Cold War to Ostpolitik: Two Germanys in Search of Separate Indentities," *World Politics*, 29, No. 1, October 1976, 114–29.

Bracher, Karl Dietrich. *The German Dictatorship: The Origins, Structure, and Effects of National Socialism.* (Trans., Jean Steinberg.) New York: Praeger, 1970.

———. *The German Dilemma: The Relationship of State and Democracy.* (Trans., Richard Barry.) New York: Praeger, 1975.

Brandt, Willy. *People and Politics: The Years 1960–1975.* (Trans., J. Maxwell Brownjohn.) Boston: Little, Brown, 1978.

Braunthal, Gerard. "The 1976 West German Election Campaign", *Polity*, 10, No. 2, Winter 1977, 147–67.

Carl-Sime, Carol, and Jane Hall. "The Predictable Germans: 1980 Election Retrospect," *The World Today* [London], 36, No. 12, December 1980, 457–62.

Carsten, F.L. *The Origins of Prussia.* London: Oxford University Press, 1958.

Craig, Gordon A. *Germany: 1866–1945.* New York: Oxford University Press, 1978.

———. *The Politics of the Prussian Army, 1640–1945.* New York: Oxford University Press, 1956.

Epstein, Klaus. "The German Problem 1945–1950," *World Politics*, 20, No. 2, January 1968, 279–300.

Fischer, Fritz. *Germany's Aims in the First World War.* London: Chatto and Windus, 1967.

———. *Griff nach der Weltmacht: Die Kriegszielpolitik des kaiserlichen Deutschland 1914–18.* Düsseldorf: Droste, 1961.

Gay, Peter. *Weimar Culture: The Outsider as Insider.* New York: Harper and Row, 1968.

Grebing, Helga, Peter Pozorski, and Rainer Schulze. *Die Nachkriegsentwicklung in Westdeutschland: 1945–1949.* Stuttgart: Metzler, 1980.

Grosser, Alfred. *Germany in Our Time: A Political History of the Postwar Years*. (Trans., Paul Stephenson.) New York: Praeger, 1971.

Hahn, Walter F. *Between Westpolitik and Ostpolitik: Changing West German Security Views*. (Foreign Policy Papers of the Foreign Policy Research Institute.) Beverly Hills: Sage, 1975.

Hamerow, Theodore S. *Restoration, Revolution, Reaction: Economics and Politics in Germany 1815–1871*. Princeton: Princeton University Press, 1958.

Hillgruber, Andreas. *Deutsche Geschichte 1945–1972*. Frankfurt am Main: Ullstein, 1974.

Holborn, Hajo. *A History of Modern Germany*. 3 vols. New York: Knopf, 1959–69.

Katzenstein, Peter J. "Problem or Model? West Germany in the 1980s," *World Politics*, 32, No. 4, July 1980, 577–98.

Krieger, Leonard. *The German Idea of Freedom: History of a Political Tradition*. Boston: Beacon Press, 1957.

Krieger, Wolfgang. "Worrying about West German Democracy," *Political Quarterly* [London], 50, No. 2, April-June 1979, 192–204.

Lehmbruch, Gerhard. "Party and Federation in Germany: A Developmental Dilemma," *Government and Opposition* [London], 13, No. 2, Spring 1978, 151–77.

Livingston, Robert Gerald. "Germany Steps Up," *Foreign Policy*, 22, Spring 1976, 114–28, 177–79.

Moses, John A. *The Politics of Illusion: The Fischer Controversy in German Historiography*. New York: Barnes and Noble, 1975.

——. *The War Aims of Imperial Germany: Professor Fritz Fischer and His Critics*. Brisbane: University of Queensland Press, 1968.

Nolte, Ernst. *Deutschland und der Kalte Krieg*. Munich: Piper, 1974.

Paterson, W.E. "The Ostpolitik and Regime Stability in West Germany." Pages 23–44 in Roger Tilford (ed.), *The Ostpolitik and Political Change in Germany*. Farmborough, Hampshire, England: Saxon House, 1975.

Pflanze, Otto. *Bismarck and the Development of Germany: The Period of Unification, 1815–1871*. Princeton: Princeton University Press, 1963.

Pridham, Geoffrey. "The Ostpolitik and the Opposition in West Germany." Pages 45–75 in Roger Tilford (ed.), *The Ostpolitik and Political Change in Germany*. Farmborough, Hampshire, England: Saxon House, 1975.

Prittie, Terence. *The Velvet Chancellors: A History of Post-War Germany*. London: Frederick Muller, 1979.

Puhle, Hans-Jürgen. "Conservatism in Modern German History," *Journal of Contemporary History* [London], 13, 1978, 689–720.

Pulzer, Peter. "Responsible Party Government and Stable Coalition: The Case of the German Federal Republic," *Political Studies* [London], 26, No. 2, June 1978, 181–208.

Reinhardt, Kurt F. *Germany: Two Thousand Years*, I and II. New York: Frederick Ungar, 1961.

Roberts, Geoffrey K. "The Ostpolitik and Relations Between the Two Germanies." Pages 77–93 in Roger Tilford (ed.), *The Ostpolitik and Political Change in Germany*. Farmborough, Hampshire, England: Saxon House, 1975.

Rosenberg, Hans. *Bureaucracy, Aristocracy, and Autocracy: The Prussian Experience 1660–1815*. Cambridge: Harvard University Press, 1958.

Rupp, Hans Karl. *Politische Geschichte der Bundesrepublik Deutschland: Entstehung und Entwicklung*. Stuttgart: Kohlhammer, 1978.

Schmidt, Manfred G. "The Politics of Domestic Reform in the Federal Republic of Germany," *Politics and Society*, 8, No. 2, 1978, 165–200.

Shirer, William L. *Berlin Diary: The Journal of a Foreign Correspondent, 1934–41*. New York: Penguin, 1979.

———. *The Rise and Fall of the Third Reich*. New York: Simon and Schuster, 1981.

Smith, Gordon. "West Germany and the Politics of Centrality," *Government and Opposition* [London], 11, No. 4, Autumn 1976, 387–407.

Tilford, Roger. "Introduction." Pages 1–22 in Roger Tilford (ed.), *The Ostpolitik and Political Change in Germany*. Farmborough, Hampshire, England: Saxon House, 1975.

Chapter 2

Bichler, Albert. *Bildungsziele deutscher Lehrpläne*. Munich: Olzog, 1979.

Bruck, Werner Friedrich. *Social and Economic History of Germany from William II to Hitler, 1888–1938*. Cardiff: Oxford University Press, 1938.

Childs, David, and Jeffrey Johnson. *West Germany: Politics and Society*. New York: St. Martin's Press, 1981.

Claessens, Dieter, Arno Klönne, and Armin Tschoepe. *Sozialkunde der Bundesrepublik Deutschland*. Düsseldorf: Econ, 1979.

Dahrendorf, Ralf. *Society and Democracy in Germany*. Garden City, New York: Doubleday, Anchor Books, 1969.

Danton, George Henry. *Germany Ten Years After*. Freeport, New York: Books for Libraries Press, 1971.

Dickinson, Robert E. *Germany: A General and Regional Geography*. New York: E.P. Dutton, 1953.

Federal Republic of Germany

Elkins, T.H. *Germany: An Introductory Geography.* New York: Praeger, 1968.

Federal Republic of Germany. Der Bundesminister für Bildung und Wissenschaft. *Berufsbildungsbericht 1978.* (Schriftenreihe Berufliche Bildung, 9.) Bonn: 1978.

———. *Berufsbildungsbericht 1981.* (Schriftenreihe Berufliche Bildung, 13.) Bonn: 1981.

———. *Grund- und Strukturdaten.* Bonn: 1977.

Federal Republic of Germany. Der Bundesminister für Jugend, Familie und Gesundheit. *Daten des Gesundheitswesens.* Ausgabe 1980. (Schriftenreihe des Bundesministers für Jugend, Familie und Gesundheit, Band 151.) Stuttgart: Kohlhammer, 1980.

———. *Mütter- und Säuglingssterblichkeit.* (Schriftenreihe des Bundesministers für Jugend, Familie und Gesundheit, Band 67.) Stuttgart: Kohlhammer, 1978.

Federal Republic of Germany. Deutscher Bundestag. 8. Wahlperiode. *Bildungspolitik. Antwort der Bundesregierung auf die Grosse Anfrage der Fraktionen von SPD und FDP im Deutschen Bundestag zur Bildungspolitik.* (Berichte und Dokumentationen.) Bonn: 1978.

———. *Sozialbericht 1980.* Bonn: 1980.

Federal Republic of Germany. Press and Information Office. *The Education System.* (Public Document No. 15.) Bonn: 1980.

———. *Higher Education.* (Public Document No. 14.) Bonn: 1979.

———. *Public Health.* (Public Document No. 23.) Bonn: 1980.

———. *Social Services.* (Public Document No. 5.) Bonn: 1979.

———. *Territory and Population.* (Public Document No. 1.) Bonn: January 1980.

Federal Republic of Germany. Statistisches Bundesamt. *Statistisches Jahrbuch, 1979 für die Bundesrepublik Deutschland.* Stuttgart: Kohlhammer, 1979.

Furck, Carl Ludwig. *Das pädagogische Problem der Leistung in der Schule.* Weinheim: Beltz, 1967.

Haarmann, Michael. *Steuerungsprobleme in der medizinischen Versorgung.* Königstein/Taunus: Haim, 1978.

Halbach, Günter, et al. *Übersicht Recht der Arbeit.* Bonn: Der Bundesminister für Arbeit und Sozialordnung, 1981.

Hallett, Graham. *The Social Economy of West Germany.* New York: St. Martin's Press, 1973.

Hearnden, Arthur. *Education in the Two Germanies.* Boulder: Westview Press, 1976.

Heyman, Richard D. *Studies in Educational Change.* Toronto: Holt, Rinehart and Winston, 1972.

Hoffman, G.N. *A Geography of Europe.* New York: Roland, 1953.

Bibliography

Kirsch, Hans Christian. *Bildung im Wandel*. Düsseldorf: Econ, 1979.
Langenberg, Joseph, and Horst Meixner. *Dreissig Jahre Sozialgesetzgebung in der Bundesrepublik Deutschland*. (Schriften der Bundeszentrale für politische Bildung.) Bonn: Bundeszentrale für politische Bildung, 1980.
Manz, Wolfgang. *Schule und Legitimation*. Hamburg: Hoffmann und Campe, 1975.
Milberg, Hildegard. *Schulpolitik in der pluralistischen Gesellschaft*. Hamburg: Leibniz, 1970.
Müller, Detlef K. *Sozialstruktur und Schulsystem*. Göttingen: Vandenhoeck und Ruprecht, 1977.
Organisation for Economic Co-operation and Development. *Classification of Educational Systems: Germany, Finland, Japan*. Paris: 1972.
―――. *Educational Policy and Planning: Germany*. Paris: Directorate for Scientific Affairs, 1972.
―――. *Education Committee Reviews of National Policies for Education: Germany*. Paris: November 4, 1971.
―――. *Education Committee Reviews of National Policies for Education: Germany*. Paris: November 15, 1971.
―――. *Reviews of National Policies for Education: Germany*. Paris: Directorate for Scientific Affairs, November 1971.
―――. *Reviews of National Policies for Education: Germany*. Paris: 1972.
Paulsen, Friedrich. *German Education Past and Present*. New York: AMS Press, 1976.
Plickat, Hans-Heinrich (ed.). *Schulaufbau und Schulorganisation*. Bad Heilbrunn: J. Klinkhardt, 1968.
Reiche-Juhr, Hannelore. *Das Gesundheitswesen in der Bundesrepublik Deutschland und in anderen Ländern 1970–1975*. Bonn Deutscher Bundesverlag, Wissenschaftliche Dienste, 1976.
Römer, Karl (ed.). *Facts about Germany: The Federal Republic of Germany*. Gütersloh, Germany: Lexikon-Institut Bertelsmann, 1979.
Rosenberg, Peter. *Möglichkeiten der Reform des Gesundheitswesens in der Bundesrepublik Deutschland*. Göttingen: O. Schwartz, 1975.
Rust, Val Dean. *German Interest in Foreign Education Since World War I*. Ann Arbor: University of Michigan, Comparative Education Dissertation Service, 1965.
Samuel, Richard H. *Education and Society in Modern Germany*. Westport, Connecticut: Greenwood Press, 1971.
Scheibe, Wolfgang. *Die reformpädagogische Bewegung*. Weinheim: Beltz, 1974.
Schewe, Dieter. *Survey of Social Security in the Federal Republic of Germany*. Bonn: Ministry of Labor and Social Affairs,

1972.
Schewe, Dieter, et al. *Übersicht über die soziale Sicherung.* Bonn: Der Bundesminister für Arbeit und Sozialordnung, 1977.
Schicke, Romuald Karl. *Soziale Sicherung und Gesundheitswesen.* Stuttgart: Kohlhammer, 1978.
Stössel, Jürgen-Peter. *Staatseigentum Gesundheit.* Munich: Piper, 1978.
Teh-wei Hu (ed.). *International Health Costs and Expenditures.* (Proceedings of an International Conference on Health Costs and Expenditures, National Institutes of Health, 1975.) Washington: U.S. Department of Health, Education, and Welfare, 1976.
Thomas, Helga. *Innovation in Education: Germany, Technical Report.* Paris: Organisation for Economic Co-operation and Development, June 1971.
U.S. Congress. 94th, 2d Session. Senate. Committee on Finance. *Cost and Utilization Control Mechanism in Several European Health Care Systems.* Washington: GPO, 1976.
Veraguth, Hans Peter. *Erwachsenenbildung zwischen Religion und Politik.* Stuttgart: Klett, 1976.
Vogel, Martin Rudolf. *Erziehung im Gesellschaftssystem.* Munich: Juventa, 1970.
Walz, John Albrecht. *German Influence in American Education and Culture.* Freeport, New York: Books for Libraries Press, 1969.
Wilhelm, Theodor. *Pädagogik der Gegenwart.* Stuttgart: Kröner, 1977.
Zacher, Hans Friedrich. *Krankenkassen oder nationaler Gesundheitsdienst?* Heidelberg: Decker und Müller, 1980.

Chapter 3

Baker, Kendall L., Russell J. Dalton, and Kai Hildebrandt. *Germany Transformed: Political Culture and the New Politics.* Cambridge: Harvard University Press, 1981.
Beyme, Klaus von. "The Changing Relations between Trade Unions and the Social Democratic Party in West Germany," *Government and Opposition* [London], 13, No. 4, Autumn 1978, 399–415.
―――. "The Politics of Limited Pluralism? The Case of West Germany," *Government and Opposition* [London], 13, No. 3, Summer 1978, 265–87.
Beyme, Klaus von, and Ghita Ionescu. "The Politics of Employment Policy in Germany and Great Britain," *Government and Opposition* [London], 12, No. 1, Winter 1977, 88–107.
Beyme, Klaus von, et al. *German Political Systems: Theory and Practice in the Two Germanies.* (German Political Studies, Vol. 2.) Beverly Hills: Sage, 1976.

Bibliography

Binder, David. "A New Nation," *The Wilson Quarterly*, V, No. 3, Summer 1981, 66–83.
Braunthal, Gerard. "West Germany Moves into the 1980s," *Current History*, 80, No. 466, May 1981, 193–96, 223–24.
———. "West Germany's Thirtieth Anniversary," *Current History*, 77, No. 451, November 1979, 157–61, 182.
Bruse, Rudolf. "Social Mobility and Status Attainment Process of People with Farm Backgrounds in West Germany," *Rural Sociology*, 44, No. 2, Summer 1979, 307–30.
Carl-Sime, Carol, and Jane Hall. "The Predictable Germans: 1980 Election Retrospect," *The World Today* [London], 36, No. 12, December 1980, 457–62.
Castles, Stephen, and Godula Kosack. "How the Trade Unions Try to Control and Integrate Workers in the German Federal Republic," *Race* [London], XV, No. 4, April 1974, 497–514.
Cattani, Alfred. "Germany: From Student Protest to Criminal Violence," *Swiss Review of World Affairs* [Zurich], 28, No. 10, January 1979, 17–31.
Childs, David. *Germany Since 1918*. New York: St. Martin's Press, 1980.
Childs, David, and Jeffrey Johnson. *West Germany: Politics and Society*. New York: St. Martin's Press, 1981.
Cohn, E. "The Land Market in Germany." Pages 56–63 in A.W. Davidson and J.E. Leonard (eds.), *Urban Development in France and Germany*. (Property Studies in the United Kingdom and Overseas.) Reading, England: Centre for Advanced Land Use Studies, College of Estate Management, 1974.
Crew, David F. *Town in the Ruhr: A Social History of Bochun, 1860–1914*. New York: Columbia University Press, 1979.
Crispo, John. *Industrial Democracy in Western Europe: A North American Perspective*. Toronto: McGraw-Hill Ryerson, 1978.
Dahrendorf, Ralf. *Society and Democracy in Germany*. Garden City, New York: Doubleday, Anchor Books, 1969.
Davidson, A.W., and J.E. Leonard (eds.). *Urban Development in France and Germany*. (Property Studies in the United Kingdom and Overseas.) Reading, England: Centre for Advanced Land Use Studies, College of Estate Management, 1974.
Dohnanvi, Klaus von. *Education and Youth Employment in the Federal Republic of Germany*. (Education and Youth Employment in Contemporary Societies series.) Berkeley: Carnegie Council on Policy Studies in Higher Education, 1978.
Done, Kevin. "Immigrant Population at Record Level," *Financial Times* [London], October 27, 1980, VI.
Dornberg, John. *The New Germans: Thirty Years After*. New York: Macmillan, 1975.
Dyson, Kenneth H.F. *Party, State, and Bureaucracy in Western Germany*. (Sage Professional Papers in Comparative Politics.)

Beverly Hills: Sage, 1977.

Edinger, Lewis J. "Post-Totalitarian Leadership: Elites in the German Federal Republic," *American Political Science Review*, LIV, 1960, 58–82.

Elkins, T.H. "Style in German Cities," *Geographical Magazine* [London], XLVIII, No. 1, October 1975, 17–23.

Elliott, John D. "Action and Reaction: West Germany and the Baader-Meinhof Guerrillas," *Strategic Review*, IV, No. 1, Winter 1976, 60–67.

Evans, Richard J. *Society and Politics in Wilhelmine Germany*. New York: Barnes and Noble, 1978.

Federal Republic of Germany. Bundesministerium für Wirtschaft. *Leistung in Zahlen*. Bonn: Referat Presse und Information, 1980.

Federal Republic of Germany. Statistisches Bundesamt. *Statistisches Jahrbuch, 1980 für die Bundesrepublik Deutschland*. Stuttgart: Kohlhammer, 1980.

Fehr, Götz. "The Image of Germany: Constancy and Change." (German Studies Notes.) Bloomington: Institute of German Studies, Indiana University, 1977 (mimeo.).

Festy, Patrick. "On the New Context of Marriage in Western Europe," *Population and Development Review*, 6, No. 2, 1980, 311–15.

Fried, Robert C. "Party and Policy in West German Cities," *American Political Science Review*, LXX, No. 1, March 1976, 11–24.

Geigges, Anita, and Bernhard W. Wette. *Zigeuner heute: Verfolgung und Diskriminierung in der BRD*. Bornheim-Merten: Lamuv, 1979.

Geisseler, Günter. "A German Experience." Pages 155–58 in John S. Marsh, et al. (eds.), *European Economic Issues: Agriculture, Economic Security, Industrial Democracy, the OECD*. New York: Praeger for the Atlantic Institute for International Affairs, 1976.

German Theologians. "We Must Protest," *Cross Currents*, 28, No. 1, Spring 1978, 66–70.

Gershon, Karen (ed., trans.). *Postscript: A Collective Account of the Lives of Jews in West Germany Since the Second World War*. London: Victor Gollancz, 1969.

Glaser, Hermann. "On the Physiognomy of the West German Mind: A Time Exposure with Focusing Difficulties." Pages 17–25 in *Two Essays on Contemporary Culture in America and Germany*. Bloomington: Institute of German Studies, Indiana University, 1978.

Golde, Günter. *Catholics and Protestants: Agricultural Modernization in Two German Villages*. New York: Academic

Press, 1975.

Greiffenhagen, Martin. "The Dilemma of Conservatism in Germany," *Journal of Contemporary History* [London], 14, 1979, 611–25.

Grosser, Alfred. "From Democratic Showcase to Party Domination." Pages 114–41 in Anthony Smith (ed.), *Television and Political Life*. New York: St. Martin's Press, 1979.

Gunlicks, A.B. "Coalition Collapse in Lower Saxony: Political and Constitutional Implications," *Parliamentary Affairs* [London], 29, Autumn 1976, 437–49.

Hall, Peter, and Dennis Hay. *Growth Centres in the European Urban System*. Berkeley: University of California Press, 1980.

Hamilton, Richard, and James Wright. "Coming of Age—A Comparison of the United States and the Federal Republic of Germany," *Zeitschrift für Soziologie* [Stuttgart], 4, No. 4, October 1975, 335–49.

Hardin, Bert. "Living Conditions in the Federal Republic of Germany: Social Change and Welfare Development," *German Studies*, 12, Section 2, 1979, 116–19.

Hartrich, Edwin. *The Fourth and Richest Reich*. New York: Macmillan, 1980.

Hazelrigg, Lawrence E. "Cross-National Comparisons of Father-to-Son Mobility." Pages 469–93 in Joseph Lopreato and Lionel S. Lewis (eds.), *Social Stratification: A Reader*. New York: Harper and Row, 1974.

Heidenheimer, Arnold J. "The Politics of Educational Reform in Sweden and West Germany." Pages 81–111 in Richard Rose (ed.), *The Dynamics of Public Policy: A Comparative Analysis*. Beverly Hills: Sage, 1976.

Helm, Charles. "The German Concept of Order: The Social and Physical Setting," *Journal of Popular Culture*, 13, No. 1, Summer 1979, 67–80.

Hesselbach, Walter. *Public, Trade Union, and Cooperative Enterprise in Germany: The Commonwealth Idea*. London: Frank Cass, 1976.

Hiscocks, Richard. *The Adenauer Era*. (The Lippincott History series.) Philadelphia: J.B. Lippincott, 1966.

Hobson, Irmgard. "Holderlin Our Contemporary: 'Empedokles' and German Intellectuals of the 1970s," *Journal of European Studies* [Chalfont St. Giles, England], 8, No. 31, September 1978, 231–45.

Hoffmann-Nowotny, Hans-Joachim. "Class and Social Structure: Empirical Investigations about the Federal Republic of Germany," *German Studies*, 12, Section 2, 1979, 195–98.

Hofmann, Wolfgang. "West Berlin—the Isolated City in the Twentieth Century," *Journal of Contemporary History* [London], 4, No. 3, July 1969, 77–94.

Hohmann, Joachim S. *Zigeuner und Zigeunerwissenschaft*, 6. (Reihe Metro.) Marburg: Guttandin und Hoppe, 1980.

Holzner, Lutz. "Containing the Metropolis and Saving Downtown: The Case of Munich," *Urbanism Past and Present*, 5, No. 2, Summer 1980, 12–20.

Horchem, Hans Josef. "Rightist Extremism in the Federal Republic of Germany, 1977," *Conflict*, 1, No. 3, 1979, 171–90.

Hulsberg, Werner. "Working Class Seeks an Alternative: Growing Opposition to Austerity and Militarization," *Intercontinental Press*, 19, No. 41, November 9, 1981, 1093–97.

Ing, M. Trieb Dipl. "Land Use Planning and Control in Germany." Pages 64–75 in A.W. Davidson and J.E. Leonard (eds.), *Urban Development in France and Germany*. (Property Studies in the United Kingdom and Overseas.) Reading, England: Centre for Advanced Land Use Studies, College of Estate Management, 1974.

Jarausch, Konrad H. "Perceptions," *The Wilson Quarterly*, V, No. 3, Summer 1981, 56–65.

Kanaar, A.C. "Land Reform in Germany," *The Nineteenth Century and After* [London], CXXXIX, No. 832, June 1946, 284–86.

Knight, Maxwell E. *The German Executive, 1890–1933*, 4. (Elites series.) Stanford: Stanford University Press, 1952.

Knodel, John. "From Natural Fertility to Family Limitation: The Onset of Fertility Transition in a Sample of German Villages," *Demography*, 16, No. 4, November 1979, 493–521.

Koch, Reinhold, and Hans-Peter Gatzweiler. *Migration and Settlement: Federal Republic of Germany*, 9. (Research Reports series.) Laxenburg, Austria: International Institute for Applied Systems Analysis, 1980.

Köllmann, Wolfgang. "The Process of Urbanisation in Germany at the Height of the Industrialisation Period," *Journal of Contemporary History* [London], 4, No. 3, July 1969, 59–76.

Koschnick, Wolfgang J. "Church and State in West Germany," *Church and State*, 30, No. 2, February 1977, 7–11.

———. "West Germany's Witch-Hunt for Radicals," *Contemporary Review* [London], 230, No. 1334, March 1977, 151–55.

Krejci, Jaroslav. *Social Structure in Divided Germany*. New York: St. Martin's Press, 1976.

Kremers, Heinz. "The First German Church Faces the Challenge of the Holocaust: A Report," *Annals of the American Academy of Political and Social Science*, No. 450, July 1980, 190–201.

Lamousé, Annette. "Family Roles of Women: A German Example," *Journal of Marriage and the Family*, 31, February 1969,

145–52.
Lasky, Melvin J. "Journey Among the 'Ugly Germans'," *Encounter*, 159, No. 5, November 1977, 35–45.
Laumann, Edward O., and Franz U. Pappi. *Networks of Collective Action: A Perspective on Community Influence Systems.* New York: Academic Press, 1976.
Lee, W.R. "Bastardy and the Socioeconomic Structure of South Germany," *Journal of Interdisciplinary History*, 7, No. 3, Winter 1977, 403–26.
Lees, Andrew. "Critics of Urban Society in Germany, 1854–1914," *Journal of the History of Ideas*, 40, No. 1, January-March 1979, 61–83.
Lehmbruch, Gerhard. "Party and Federation in Germany: A Developmental Dilemma," *Government and Opposition* [London], 13, No. 2, Spring 1978, 151–77.
Lehr, Ursula, and Hellgard Rauh. "Male and Female in the German Federal Republic." Pages 220–39 in George H. Seward and Robert C. Williamson (eds.), *Sex Roles in Changing Society.* Toronto: Random House, 1970.
Lichter, S. Robert. "Young Rebels: A Psychopolitical Study of West German Male Radical Students," *Comparative Politics*, 12, October 1979, 27–48.
Lowenthal, Richard. "Why German Stability Is so Insecure: On the Self-Awareness of the Bonn Republic," *Encounter*, 51, No. 6, December 1978, 31–37.
Lupri, Eugen. "Contemporary Authority Patterns in the West German Family: A Study in Cross-National Validation," *Journal of Marriage and the Family*, 31, February 1969, 134–44.
"Lutheran Churches in the World: Germany," *Lutheran World* [Geneva], 24, No. 2, 1977, 220–42.
McClelland, Charles E., and Steven P. Scher. *Postwar German Culture: An Anthology.* New York: E.P. Dutton, 1974.
Malhotra, M.K. "The Psychological, Social, and Educational Problems of Primary School Children of Different Nationalities in West Germany," *Ethnic and Racial Studies* [Henly-on-Thames, England], 4, No. 4, October 1981, 486–500.
Markovits, Andrei S., and Christopher S. Allen. "Power and Dissent: The Trade Unions in the Federal Republic of Germany Re-Examined," *West European Politics* [London], 3, No. 1, January 1980, 68–86.
Markovits, Andrei S., and Samantha Kazarinov. "Class Conflict, Capitalism, and Social Democracy: The Case of Migrant Workers in the Federal Republic of Germany," *Comparative Politics*, 10, No. 3, April 1978, 373–92.
Mason, Henry L. "Imponderables of the Holocaust," *World Pol-*

itics, 34, No. 1, October 1981, 90–113.

Mayntz, Renate. "Environmental Policy Conflicts: The Case of the German Federal Republic," *Policy Analysis*, 2, No. 4, Fall 1976, 577–89.

Meier, Reinhard. "The Green Front: Germany's Political Environmentalists," *Swiss Review of World Affairs* [Zurich], 29, No. 10, January 1980, 6–8.

Mellor, Roy E.H. *The Two Germanies: A Modern Geography*. New York: Barnes and Noble, 1978.

Menendez, Albert J. "Church and State in Germany: A Background Sketch," *Church and State*, 30, No. 2, February 1977, 11–14.

Menke-Glückert, Peter. "Media Policy in the Federal Republic of Germany." Pages 22–30 in J. Herbert Altschull and Paula C. Pearce (eds.), *The Mass Media in West Germany and the United States*. (German Studies Notes.) Bloomington: Institute of German Studies, Indiana University, 1978.

Merritt, Anna J., and Richard L. Merritt. *Politics, Economics, and Society in the Two Germanies, 1945–75: A Bibliography of English-Language Works*. Urbana: University of Illinois Press, 1978.

Meulemann, Heiner. "Klassenlage, Entscheidungsfeld und Bildungaspirationen: Ein Versuch zur theoretischen Präzisierung und kausalen Erklärung von Zusammenhängen zwischen sozialer Struktur und individueller Lebensplanung," *Zeitschrift für Soziologie* [Stuttgart], 8, No. 4, 1979, 391–414.

Minnerup, Günter. "West Germany Since the War," *New Left Review* [London], No. 99, September-October 1976, 3–44.

Mooney, Thomas. "A Delicate Balance: Equal Representation for Labor on German Corporate Boards," *Harvard International Law Journal*, 16, Spring 1975, 352–89.

Müller, Peter. "Recent Developments in Land Tenure and Land Policies in Germany," *Land Economics*, August 1964, 267–75.

Müller-Freienfels, W. "The Marriage Law Reform of 1976 in the Federal Republic of Germany," *The International and Comparative Law Quarterly* [London], 28, Part 2, April 1979, 184–210.

Neuloh, Otto. "The German Blue-Collar Worker," *International Journal of Comparative Sociology*, 10, No. 1–2, March-June 1969, 151–60.

Neven-Du Mont, Jürgen. *After Hitler: Report from a German City*. (Trans., Ralph Mannheim.) London: Penguin Press, 1969.

O'Loughlin, John. "Distribution and Migration of Foreigners in German Cities," *The Geographical Review*, 70, No. 3, July 1980, 253–75.

Organisation for Economic Co-operation and Development. *Germany* (OECD Economic Surveys.) Paris: 1981.

Bibliography

―――. *Reviews of National Policies for Education: Germany.* Paris: 1972.
Panitch, Leo. "The Importance of Workers' Control for Revolutionary Change," *Monthly Review*, 29, No. 10, March 1978, 37–48.
Pfaff, William. "Elitists and Egalitarians," *The New Yorker*, September 28, 1981, 120–25.
―――. "Sinking into Materialism," *The New Yorker*, March 30, 1981, 68–81.
Pfeiffer, Ulrich. "Government Initiative in Urban Development in Germany." Pages 76–86 in A.W. Davidson and J.E. Leonard (eds.), *Urban Development in France and Germany.* (Property Studies in the United Kingdom and Overseas.) Reading, England: Centre for Advanced Land Use Studies, College of Estate Management, 1974.
―――. "Market Forces and Urban Change in Germany." Pages 45–52 in Richard Rose (ed.), *The Management of Urban Change in Britain and Germany.* Beverly Hills: Sage, 1974.
Pridham, Geoffrey. *Christian Democracy in Western Germany: The CDU/CSU in Government and Opposition, 1945–1976.* New York: St. Martin's Press, 1977.
―――. "Ecologists in Politics: The West German Case," *Parliamentary Affairs* [London], 31, Autumn 1978, 436–44.
Rist, Ray C. *Guestworkers in Germany: The Prospects for Pluralism.* (Praeger Special Studies series.) New York: Praeger, 1978.
Robinsohn, Saul B., and J. Caspar Kuhlmann. "Two Decades of Non-Reform in West German Education," *Comparative Education Review*, 11, No. 3, October 1967, 311–50.
Rodnick, David. *A Portrait of Two German Cities: Lübeck and Hamburg.* Lubbock, Texas: Caprock Press, 1980.
Rohr, Donald G. *The Origins of Social Liberalism in Germany.* Chicago: University of Chicago Press, 1963.
Römer, Karl (ed.). *Facts about Germany: The Federal Republic of Germany.* Gütersloh, Germany: Lexikon-Institut Bertelsmann, 1979.
Rose, Richard (ed.). *The Management of Urban Change in Britain and Germany.* Beverly Hills: Sage, 1974.
Sandford, John. *The Mass Media of the German-speaking Countries.* London: Oswald Wolff, 1976.
Schalk, Adolph. *The Germans.* Englewood Cliffs: Prentice-Hall, 1971.
Schiller, Günter. "Channelling Migration: A Review of Policy with Special Reference to the Federal Republic of Germany," *International Labour Review* [Geneva], 111, No. 4, April 1975, 335–55.
Schmidt, Manfred G. "The Politics of Domestic Reform in the Federal Republic of Germany," *Politics and Society*, 8, No. 2,

1978, 165–200.

Schnitzer, Martin. *Income Distribution: A Comparative Study of the United States, Sweden, West Germany, East Germany, the United Kingdom, and Japan.* (Praeger Special Studies in International Economics and Development.) New York: Praeger, 1974.

Schofer, Lawrence. *The Formation of a Modern Labor Force: Upper Silesia, 1865–1914.* Berkeley: University of California Press, 1975.

Schreiber, Marion. "We Simply Felt that We Were Stronger." Original article in German, *Der Spiegel* [Bonn], May 11, 1981, 82–108. Reported in English, *Current News*, August 25, 1981, 30–43.

Schweigler, Gebhard Ludwig. *National Consciousness in Divided Germany.* (Sage Library of Social Research series, No. 15.) Beverly Hills: Sage, 1975.

Sereny, Gitta. "Germany: The 'Rediscovery' of Hitler," *Atlantic Monthly*, 242, No. 2, August 1978, 7–14.

Shaffer, Harry G. *Women in the Two Germanies: A Comparative Study of a Socialist and a Non-Socialist Society.* New York: Pergamon, 1981.

Smith, Gordon R. *Democracy in Western Germany: Parties and Politics in the Federal Republic.* New York: Holmes and Meier, 1980.

Smith, Robert J., et al. "When Is a Stereotype a Stereotype?" *Psychological Reports*, 46, April 1980, 643–51.

Sontheimer, Kurt. "Intellectuals and Politics in Western Germany," *West European Politics* [London], 1, No. 1, February 1978, 30–41.

Southern, David. "Radical Thought in Germany," *Contemporary Review* [London], 236, No. 1370, March 1980, 113–17.

Spindler, George D., and Louise Spindler. "A Restudy of Cultural Transmission and Instrumental Adaptation in an Urbanizing German Village," *Anthropology and Education Quarterly*, 9, No. 3, 1978, 235–36.

Spindler, George D., et al. *Burgbach: Urbanization and Identity in a German Village.* (Case Studies in Cultural Anthropology.) New York: Holt, Rinehart and Winston, 1973.

Spotts, Frederic. *The Churches and Politics in Germany.* Middletown, Connecticut: Wesleyan University Press, 1973.

Staeck, Klaus. "Censorship Does (Not) Exist," *Index on Censorship* [London], 9, No. 5, October 1980, 46–51.

Stern, Fritz. *The Failure of Illiberalism: Essays on the Political Culture of Modern Germany.* New York: Knopf, 1972.

Stothard, Baline. "Beyond Berufsverbot," *Index on Censorship*

[London], 7, No. 4, July-August 1978, 21–27.
Szabo, Stephen F. "Social Perspective and Support for Human Rights in West Germany," *Universal Human Rights: A Comparative and International Journal of the Social Sciences, Philosophy, and Law*, 1, No. 1, January-March 1979, 81–98.
Tuppen, J.N. "A Geographical Appraisal of Trans-Frontier Commuting in Western Europe: The Example of Alsace," *International Migration Review*, 12, No. 3, Fall 1978, 386–405.
U.S. Congress. 95th, 2d Session. House of Representatives. Committee on International Relations. *Economic Conditions in the Federal Republic of Germany*. Washington: GPO, 1978.
Vollmer, Rudolf J. "Industrial Democracy in Germany." Pages 159–67 in John S. Marsh, et al. (eds.), *European Economic Issues: Agriculture, Economic Security, Industrial Democracy, the OECD*. New York: Praeger for the Atlantic Institute for International Affairs, 1976.
Walker, Mack. *German Home Towns: Community, State, and General Estate, 1648–1871*. Ithaca: Cornell University Press, 1971.
Weatherford, Jack M. "Millenium of Modernization: A Changing German Village." Pages 35–68 in Priscilla Copeland Reining and Barbara Lenkerd (eds.), *Village Viability in Contemporary Society*. (AAAS Selected Symposium 34.) Washington: American Association for the Advancement of Science, 1980.
Webb, W.L. "Threat of the Backyard Killing Ground Mobilises the German People," *The Guardian* [Manchester], 125, No. 16, October 18, 1981, 18.
Wild, M.T. *West Germany: A Geography of Its People*. Totowa, New Jersey: Barnes and Noble, 1980.
Wildenmann, Rudolf. "Toward a Sociopolitical Model of the German Federal Republic," *Sozialwissenschaftliches Jahrbuch für Politik* [Munich], 4, 1975, 273–301.
Willey, Richard J. "Trade Unions and Political Parties in the Federal Republic of Germany," *Industrial and Labor Relations Review*, 28, No. 1, October 1974, 38–59.
Wollmann, Hellmut. "Cities in West Germany Face Emerging Crisis," *National Civic Review*, 60, No. 9, October 1971, 492–96, 501.
Yondorf, Barbara. "Prostitution as a Legal Activity: The West German Experience," *Policy Analysis*, 5, No. 4, Fall 1979, 417–34.
Zahn, Gordon C. *German Catholics and Hitler's Wars: A Study in Social Control*. New York: Sheed and Ward, 1962.
Zinn, Hermann. "The Influence of Home Environments on the Socialization of Children," *Ekistics* [Athens], 47, No. 281, April

Federal Republic of Germany

1980, 98–102.

(Various issues of the following publications were also used in the preparation of this chapter: *Christian Science Monitor*; *The Economist* [London]; *Financial Times* [London]; Foreign Broadcast Information Service (FBIS) *Daily Report: Western Europe; New York Times; The Week in Germany*; and *World Business Weekly* [London].)

Chapter 4

Allen, Rosemarie. "The European Community: A Superpower in the Making?" *Optima* [Johannesburg], 29, No. 4, January 30, 1981, 204–25.

Artus, Patrick, and Pierre-Alain Muet. "Economic Policy and Private Investment Since the Oil Crisis: A Comparative Study of France and Germany," *European Economic Review* [Amsterdam], 16, No. 1, May 1981, 7–59.

Association of German Economic Research Institutes. "The Economic Situation in the Federal Republic of Germany," *Intereconomics Review of International Trade and Development* [Hamburg], No. 3, May-June 1981, 149–52.

Binder, David. "A New Nation," *The Wilson Quarterly*, V, No. 3, Summer 1981, 66–83.

Böhning, W.R. "Estimating the Propensity of Guestworkers to Leave," *Monthly Labor Review*, May 1981, 37–40.

Braunthal, Gerard. "West Germany Moves into the 1980s," *Current History*, 80, No. 466, May 1981, 193–96, 223–24.

Casper, Ullrich. "Regional Incentives in the Federal Republic of Germany." Pages 82–112 in Douglas Yuill, et al. (eds.), *Regional Policy in the European Community*. New York: St. Martin's Press, 1980.

Childs, David. *Germany Since 1918*. New York: St. Martin's Press, 1980.

Childs, David, and Jeffrey Johnson. *West Germany: Politics and Society*. New York: St. Martin's Press, 1981.

Commission of the European Communities. *European Economic and Monetary Union*. (European Documentation series.) Luxembourg: March 1979.

Commission of the European Communities. Directorate-General for Economic and Financial Affairs. "The European Monetary System," *European Economy* [Luxembourg], No. 3 (offprint), July 1979, 67–111.

Conrad, Wolfgang. "Federal Republic of Germany." Pages 209–38 in Albert A. Blum (ed.), *International Handbook of Industrial Relations: Contemporary Developments and Research*. Westport, Connecticut: Greenwood Press, 1981.

Erhard, Ludwig. *Prosperity Through Competition*. London:

Thames and Hudson, 1962.
Federal Republic of Germany. Deutsche Bundesbank. "The Balance of Payments and Monetary Policy," *Monthly Report of the Deutsche Bundesbank* [Frankfurt am Main], 33, No. 3, March 1981, 5–9.

――――. "The Expenditure of the Central, Regional, and Local Authorities Since the Mid-Seventies," *Monthly Report of the Deutsche Bundesbank* [Frankfurt am Main], 31, No. 1, January 1981, 19–26.

――――. "External Assets and Liabilities of the Federal Republic of Germany at the End of 1980," *Monthly Report of the Deutsche Bundesbank* [Frankfurt am Main], 33, No. 5, May 1981, 24–30.

――――. "The Longer Term Trend of Lending Commitments and Their Use," *Monthly Report of the Deutsche Bundesbank* [Frankfurt am Main], 33, No. 1, January 1981, 12–18.

――――. *Monthly Report of the Deutsche Bundesbank* [Frankfurt am Main], 33, No. 8, August 1981.

――――. "Overall Financial Flows and Total Financial Assets and Liabilities in 1980," *Monthly Report of the Deutsche Bundesbank* [Frankfurt am Main], 33, No. 5, May 1981, 12–18, 31–41.

――――. *Statistische Beihefte zu den Monatsberichten der Deutschen Bundesbank Reihe 3, Zahlungsbilanz Statistik* [Frankfurt am Main], No. 7, July 1981.

――――. *Statistische Beihefte zu den Monatsberichten der Deutschen Bundesbank Reihe 4, Saisonbereinigte Wirtschaftszahlen* [Frankfurt am Main], No. 7, July 1981.

Federal Republic of Germany. Press and Information Office. *Economy*. (Public Document No. 4.) Bonn: December 1978.

――――. *Economy and Society*. (Public Document No. 17.) Bonn: November 1979.

――――. *Employers and Unions*. (Public Document No. 16.) Bonn: December 1979.

――――. *Transport*. (Public Document No. 3.) Bonn: December 1978.

Federal Republic of Germany. Statistisches Bundesamt. *Statistisches Jahrbuch, 1979 für die Bundesrepublik Deutschland*. Stuttgart: Kohlhammer, 1979.

――――. *Statistisches Jahrbuch, 1980 für die Bundesrepublik Deutschland*. Stuttgart: Kohlhammer, 1980.

Frenkel, Jacob A. "The Forward Exchange Rate, Expectations, and the Demand for Money: The German Hyperinflation," *American Economic Review*, 67, No. 4, September 1977, 653–70.

Gordon, Richard L. *An Economic Analysis of World Energy Problems*. Cambridge: MIT Press, 1981.

Gunther, Eberhard. *German Policy Toward the Market Conduct of Powerful Enterprises*. (German Studies Notes.) Blooming-

Federal Republic of Germany

ton: Institute of German Studies, Indiana University, 1977.
Gutowski, Armin, and Hans-Hagen Härtel. "From Shock Therapy to Gradualism: Anti-Inflationary Policy in Germany from 1973 to 1979," *Intereconomics Review of International Trade and Development* [Hamburg], March-April 1981, 90–96.
Hardach, Karl. *The Political Economy of Germany in the Twentieth Century.* Berkeley: University of California Press, 1980.
Hartrich, Edwin. *The Fourth and Richest Reich.* New York: Macmillan, 1980.
International Bank for Reconstruction and Development. *World Tables 1971.* Baltimore: The Johns Hopkins University Press, 1971.
―――. *World Tables 1976.* Washington: 1976.
International Monetary Fund. *Annual Report on Exchange Arrangements and Exchange Restrictions 1980.* Washington: 1980.
―――. "Germany." Pages 235–41 in *Government Finance Statistics Yearbook*, V. Washington: 1981.
Jarausch, Konrad H. "Perceptions," *The Wilson Quarterly*, V, No. 3, Summer 1981, 56–65.
Kindleberger, Charles P. *Germany's Persistent Balance-of-Payments Disequilibrium Revisited.* (German Studies Notes.) Bloomington: Institute of German Studies, Indiana University, 1976.
Knott, Jack H. *Managing the German Economy: Budgetary Politics in a Federal State.* Lexington, Massachusetts: Lexington Books, 1981.
Marsh, John S., et al. *European Economic Issues: Agriculture, Economic Security, Industrial Democracy, the OECD.* New York: Praeger for the Atlantic Institute for International Affairs, 1976.
Mellor, Roy E.H. *The Two Germanies: A Modern Geography.* New York: Barnes and Noble, 1978.
Milward, Alan S. *The German Economy at War.* London: Athlone, 1965.
Neumann, Manfred J.M. *A Study in West German Stabilization Policy, 1956–74.* (German Studies Notes.) Bloomington: Institute of German Studies, Indiana University, 1976.
Organisation for Economic Co-operation and Development. *The Capital Market, International Capital Movements, and Restrictions on Capital Operations in Germany.* Paris: 1969.
―――. *Germany.* (OECD Economic Surveys.) Paris: 1977.
―――. *Germany.* (OECD Economic Surveys.) Paris: 1981.
Parker, Geoffrey. *The Countries of Community Europe: A Geographical Survey of Contemporary Issues.* New York: St. Martin's Press, 1979.
Price Waterhouse. "Doing Business in Germany," *Price Waterhouse Information Guide*, September 1978.

Römer, Karl (ed.). *Facts about Germany: The Federal Republic of Germany.* Gütersloh, Germany: Lexikon-Institut Bertelsmann, 1979.

Schoenbaum, David. "A Place in the Sun," *The Wilson Quarterly,* V, No. 3, Summer 1981, 84–93.

Schweitzer, Arthur. *Big Business in the Third Reich.* Bloomington: Indiana University Press, 1964.

Shapiro, Harvey D. "German Banking Goes Back to Basics," *Institutional Investor,* (International Edition.) June 1981, 139–50.

Speer, Albert. *Infiltration.* New York: Macmillan, 1981.

———. *Inside the Third Reich.* New York: Macmillan, 1970.

"Survey: West German Industry, a Structural Problem," *World Business Weekly* [London], May 11, 1981, 31–37.

"Survey: West Germany, Helmut Schmidt: International Statesman?" *World Business Weekly* [London], December 1, 1980, 29–43.

Tinnin, David B. "The Miracle Economy Hits the Skids," *Fortune,* April 20, 1981, 137–44.

Tran Van Hoa. "Causality and Wage Price Inflation in West Germany 1964–1979," *Weltwirtschaftliches Archiv* [Kiel], 117, No. 1, 1981, 110–24.

U.S. Central Intelligence Agency. National Foreign Assessment Center. *Handbook of Economic Statistics 1981.* Washington: November 1981.

U.S. Department of Commerce. International Trade Administration. *Marketing in the Federal Republic of Germany and West Berlin.* (Overseas Business Reports, OBR80–01.) Washington: GPO, February 1980.

U.S. General Accounting Office. Comptroller General. *Report to the Congress of the United States: The Value-Added Tax in the European Economic Community.* Washington: GPO, December 5, 1980.

"West German Industry," *Financial Times* (Survey) [London], March 18, 1981, XXIX-XXXII.

"West Germany," *Financial Times* (Survey) [London], October 19, 1981, I-XVIII.

"West Germany," *Financial Times* (Survey) [London], October 27, 1980, I-XVIII.

"West Germany, Banking, Finance, and Investment," *Financial Times* (Survey) [London], June 23, 1981, I-VIII.

(Various issues of the following publications were also used in the preparation of this chapter: *Bulletin* [Bonn]; *The Economist* [London]; *Financial Times* [London]; Foreign Broadcast Information Service (FBIS) *Daily Report: Western Europe*; *German Economic Review* [Stuttgart]; *German Press Review*; *International Financial Statistics of the International Monetary*

Federal Republic of Germany

Fund; New York Times; The Week in Germany; and *World Business Weekly* [London].)

Chapter 5

Allen, Rosemarie. "The European Community: A Superpower in the Making?" *Optima* [Johannesburg], 29, No. 4, January 30, 1981, 204–25.

Behrendt, Günther. "The Agrarian Problem in the Federal Republic of Germany," *German Economic Review* [Stuttgart], 2, No. 2, 1964, 111–23.

Bergman, Theodor. "The Agrarian Report, 1972: A Full Account of Farm Policies," *German Economic Review* [Stuttgart], 10, No. 3, 1972, 270–76.

Binder, David. "A New Nation," *The Wilson Quarterly*, V, No. 3, Summer 1981, 66–83.

Breitenlohner, Cynthia A. *The Agricultural Economy of Trade of the Federal Republic of Germany.* (U.S. Department of Agriculture, Economic Research Service, Foreign Agricultural Economic Report, No. FAE 325.) Washington: USDA, 1971.

———. *Structural Changes in West European Agriculture, 1950–70.* (U.S. Department of Agriculture, Economic Research Service, Foreign Agricultural Economic Report, No. FAE 114.) Washington: USDA, 1975.

Childs, David. *Germany Since 1918.* New York: St. Martin's Press, 1980.

Commission of the European Communities. *The Agricultural Policy of the European Community.* (European Documentation series.) Luxembourg: 1979.

———. *Reflections on the Common Agricultural Policy.* (Bulletin of the European Communities, Supplement June 1980.) Luxembourg: 1981.

Dillard, Dudley. *Economic Development of the North Atlantic Community.* Englewood Cliffs: Prentice-Hall, 1967.

Erhard, Ludwig. *Prosperity Through Competition.* London: Thames and Hudson, 1962.

Federal Republic of Germany. Deutscher Bundestag, 9. Wahlperiode. *Agrarbericht der Bundesregierung.* Bonn: Dr. Hans Heger, 1981.

Federal Republic of Germany. Statistisches Bundesamt. *Statistisches Jahrbuch, 1979 für die Bundesrepublik Deutschland.* Stuttgart: Kohlhammer, 1979.

———. *Statistisches Jahrbuch, 1980 für die Bundesrepublik Deutschland.* Stuttgart: Kohlhammer, 1980.

Goldthwait, Christopher E. "Expansion Era Marks German Wine Industry Despite 1980s Downturn," *Foreign Agriculture*, XIX, No. 8, August 1981, 18–20.

Hardach, Karl. *The Political Economy of Germany in the Twentieth Century.* Berkeley: University of California Press, 1980.

Hu, Yao-Su. "German Agricultural Power: The Impact on France and Britain," *World Today* [London], 35, No. 11, November 1979, 453–61.

Jarausch, Konrad H. "Perceptions," *The Wilson Quarterly*, V, No. 3, Summer 1981, 56–65.

Marsh, John S., et al. *European Economic Issues: Agriculture, Economic Security, Industrial Democracy, the OECD.* New York: Praeger for the Atlantic Institute for International Affairs, 1976.

Mellor, Roy E.H. *The Two Germanies: A Modern Geography.* New York: Barnes and Noble, 1978.

Milward, Alan S. *The German Economy at War.* London: Athlone, 1965.

Organisation for Economic Co-operation and Development. *Agricultural Policy in Germany.* Paris: 1974.

——. *Germany.* (OECD Economic Surveys.) Paris: 1981.

Pritchard, Norris T., et al. *Food Marketing in West Germany.* (U.S. Department of Agriculture, Economic Research Service, Foreign Agricultural Economic Report, No. FAE 76.) Washington: USDA, 1972.

Römer, Karl (ed.). *Facts about Germany: The Federal Republic of Germany.* Gütersloh, Germany: Lexikon-Institut Bertelsmann, 1979.

Schiller, Otto. "Cooperative Promotion of Agricultural Production in the Federal Republic of Germany," *The German Economic Review* [Stuttgart], 3, No. 1, 1965, 1–12.

Schmidt, Elsa T. "Key Issues of Land Use Planning in West Germany," *Growth and Change: A Journal of Regional Development*, April 1981, 44–52.

Schoenbaum, David. "A Place in the Sun," *The Wilson Quarterly*, V, No. 3, Summer 1981, 84–93.

Schweitzer, Arthur. *Big Business in the Third Reich.* Bloomington: Indiana University Press, 1964.

Speer, Albert. *Infiltration.* New York: Macmillan, 1981.

——. *Inside the Third Reich.* New York: Macmillan, 1970.

Sposato, Stephen. "West German Agricultural Trade—The Effect of Agricultural Policy on Production and Trade." (U.S. Department of Agriculture.) Washington: 1981 (mimeo.).

U.S. Department of Agriculture. Foreign Agricultural Service. *Agricultural Situation 1980*, I. (Attache Report, No. GY1023.) Bonn: March 13, 1981.

——. *Agricultural Situation 1980*, II. (Attache Report, No. GE1085.) Bonn: July 27, 1981.

——. *The Common Agricultural Policy of the European Community.* (FAS-M-255.) Washington: 1973.

——. *European Community Grain Policies and Development.*

Federal Republic of Germany

(FAS-FG–42–81.) Washington: December 11, 1981.

———. "World Livestock Numbers, Slaughter, Red Meat Production, Consumption and Trade, 1978–82," *Foreign Agricultural Circular*, No. FLM 7–81, December 1981, 1–23.

———. "World Sugar Supplies Plentiful in 1981–82," *Foreign Agricultural Circular*, No. FS2–81, November 1981, 1–15.

"West Germany," *Financial Times* (Survey) [London], October 19, 1981, I-XVIII.

(Various issues of the following publications were also used in the preparation of this chapter: *Bulletin* [Bonn]; *The Economist* [London]; *Financial Times* [London]; Foreign Broadcast Information Service (FBIS) *Daily Report: Western Europe*; *German Economic Review* [Stuttgart]; *German Press Review*; *International Financial Statistics*; *New York Times*; U.S. Department of Agriculture *Circulars*; *The Week in Germany* ; and *World Business Weekly* [London].)

Chapter 6

Baumann, Hans. "Dispute over Terms Holds Up Flow of Russian Gas," *The German Tribune* [Hamburg], No. 999, August 9, 1981, 6.

Boyes, Roger. "Siberian Gas for Europe," *Europe*, No. 225, May-June 1981, 29–30.

Childs, David. *Germany Since 1918*. New York: St. Martin's Press, 1980.

Clapham, John H. *The Economic Development of France and Germany (1815–1914)*. London: Cambridge University Press, 1951.

Commission of the European Communities. "Germany," *The European Community* [Brussels], 14, No. 6, July 1981, 30.

Crispo, John. *Industrial Democracy in Western Europe: A North American Perspective*. Toronto: McGraw-Hill Ryerson, 1978.

Dickinson, Robert E. *Germany: A General and Regional Geography*. New York: E.P. Dutton, 1953.

Dillard, Dudley. *Economic Development of the North Atlantic Community*. Englewood Cliffs: Prentice-Hall, 1967.

The Economist Intelligence Unit, Ltd. "Germany (Federal Republic)," *Quarterly Economic Review* [London], Annual Supplement 1981.

———. "Germany (Federal Republic)," *Quarterly Economic Review* [London], First Quarter 1981.

———. "Germany (Federal Republic)," *Quarterly Economic Review* [London], Second Quarter 1981.

———. "Oil in Western Europe," *Quarterly Economic Review* [London], Annual Supplement 1980.

Erhard, Ludwig. *Germany's Comeback in the World Market*. London: George Allen and Unwin, 1954.

———. *Prosperity Through Competition*. London: Thames and Hudson, 1962.
Financial Times. "Bonn Approves Aid for the Steel Sector," *World Business Weekly* [London], 1, No. 32, August 17, 1981, 7.
"The Gas-Pipeline Arrangement," *German Press Review*, 81, No. 30, July 29, 1981, 3–4.
Geisseler, Günter. "A German Experience." Pages 155–58 in John S. Marsh, et al. (eds.), *European Economic Issues: Agriculture, Economic Security, Industrial Democracy, the OECD*. New York: Praeger for the Atlantic Institute for International Affairs, 1976.
Gordon, Richard L. *An Economic Analysis of World Energy Problems*. Cambridge: MIT Press, 1981.
Hallett, Graham. *The Social Economy of West Germany*. New York: St. Martin's Press, 1974.
International Monetary Fund. *International Financial Statistics*, XXXIV, No. 8, August 1981, 160–61.
Kennet, Wayland (ed.). *The Futures of Europe*. London: Cambridge University Press, 1976.
Milward, Alan S. *The German Economy at War*. London: Athlone, 1965.
Organisation for Economic Co-operation and Development. *Economic Outlook*. Paris: July 1981.
———. *Germany*. (OECD Economic Surveys.) Paris: 1981.
Price Waterhouse. "Doing Business in Germany," *Price Waterhouse Information Guide*, September 1978.
Schweitzer, Arthur. *Big Business in the Third Reich*. Bloomington: Indiana University Press, 1964.
Shonfield, Andrew. *Modern Capitalism*. New York: Oxford University Press, 1965.
Speer, Albert. *Infiltration*. New York: Macmillan, 1981.
———. *Inside the Third Reich*. New York: Macmillan, 1970.
———. *Spandau*. New York: Macmillan, 1976.
U.S. Central Intelligence Agency. National Foreign Assessment Center. *Economic and Energy Indicators*. Washington: August 14, 1981.
———. *Handbook of Economic Statistics 1981*. Washington: November 1981.
———. *International Energy Statistical Review*. Washington: July 28, 1981.
Vollmer, Rudolf J. "Industrial Democracy in Germany." Pages 159–67 in John S. Marsh, et al. (eds.), *European Economic Issues: Agriculture, Economic Security, Industrial Democracy, the OECD*. New York: Praeger for the Atlantic Institute for International Affairs, 1976.
Wallich, Henry. *Mainsprings of the German Revival*. New Haven: Yale University Press, 1955.

Wilson, Carroll L. (ed.). *Coal—Bridge to the Future*. (MIT Report of the World Coal Study.) Cambridge: Ballinger, 1980.

Chapter 7

Altschull, J. Herbert, and Paula C. Pearce (eds.). *The Mass Media in West Germany and the United States*. (German Studies Notes.) Bloomington: Institute of German Studies, Indiana University, 1978.

Arndt, Claus. "The Effects of Détente on the Two German States," *West European Politics* [London], 2, Vol. 2, May 1979, 237–45.

Baker, Kendall L., Russell J. Dalton, and Kai Hildebrant. *Germany Transformed: Political Culture and the New Politics*. Cambridge: Harvard University Press, 1981.

Beyme, Klaus von. "The Changing Relations Between Trade Unions and the Social Democratic Party in West Germany," *Government and Opposition* [London], 13, No. 4, Autumn 1978, 399–415.

———. "The Politics of Limited Pluralism? The Case of West Germany," *Government and Opposition* [London], 13, No. 3, Summer 1978, 265–87.

Billerbeck, Rudolph. "Socialists in Urban Politics: The German Case," *Social Research*, 47, No. 1, Spring 1980, 114–40.

Blair, Philip M. *Federalism and Judicial Review in West Germany*. New York: Oxford University Press, 1981.

———. "Law and Politics in Germany," *Political Studies* [London], 26, No. 3, September 1978, 348–67.

Books, John W. "Social Context and Voting Behavior in West Germany: A Note on Contextual Analysis," *Social Science Quarterly*, 58, No. 3, December 1977, 481–88.

Brandt, Willy. *People and Politics: The Years 1960–1975*. (Trans., J. Maxwell Brownjohn.) Boston: Little, Brown, 1978.

Braunthal, Gerard. "West Germany Moves into the 1980s," *Current History*, 80, No. 466, May 1981, 193–96, 223–24.

Burkett, J.A. "A West German Bundesrat," *Parliamentarian* [London], 59, No. 3, July 1978, 165–70.

Burkett, Tony. "The Federal Republic of Germany." Pages 90–117 in Stanley Henig (ed.), *Political Parties in the European Community*. London: George Allen and Unwin, 1979.

———. *Parties and Elections in West Germany: The Search for Stability*. London: C. Hurst, 1975.

Carl-Sime, Carol. "Bavaria, the CSU, and the West German Party System," *West European Politics* [London], 2, No. 1, January 1979, 89–107.

Carl-Sime, Carol, and Jane Hall. "The Predictable Germans: 1980 Election Retrospect," *The World Today* [London], 36,

No. 12, December 1980, 457–62.

Cerny, Karl H. (ed.). *Germany at the Polls: The Bundestag Election of 1976*. Washington: American Enterprise Institute for Public Policy Research, 1978.

Childs, David. *Germany Since 1918*. New York: St. Martin's Press, 1980.

Childs, David, and Jeffrey Johnson. *West Germany: Politics and Society*. New York: St. Martin's Press, 1981.

Clements, Roger. "A Local Chief Executive Elected by the Citizens: The Oberbürgermeister of Würzburg," *West German Public Administration* [London], 56, Autumn 1978, 321–38.

Conradt, David P. *The German Polity*. (Comparative Studies of Political Life series.) New York: Longman, 1978.

Dyson, Kenneth F. *Party, State, and Bureaucracy in Western Germany*. (Sage Professional Papers in Comparative Politics.) Beverly Hills: Sage, 1977.

———. "Problems of Morality and Power in the Politics of West Germany," *Government and Opposition* [London], 16, No. 2, Spring 1981, 131–48.

Edinger, Lewis J. *Politics in West Germany*. (2d ed.) Boston: Little, Brown, 1977.

Federal Republic of Germany. Press and Information Office. *Berlin*. (Public Document No. 20.) Bonn: 1979.

———. *Constitution and Structure*. (Public Document No. 2.) Bonn: 1980.

———. *Federalism*. (Public Document No. 10.) Bonn: 1980.

———. *Law and the Administration of Justice*. (Public Document No. 24.) Bonn: 1979.

Geddes, John M. "Trouble in Bonn: A Sluggish Economy and Missiles Discord Peril German Stability," *Wall Street Journal*, October 30, 1981, 1, 19.

"German Federal Republic." Pages 357–98 in Amos J. Peaslee (ed.), *Constitutions of Nations*, III—Europe. (3d rev. ed.) The Hague: Martinus Nijhoff, 1968.

Graf, William David. *The German Left Since 1945: Socialism and Social Democracy in the German Federal Republic*. Cambridge, England: Oleander Press, 1976.

Gunlicks, Arthur B. "Campaign and Party Finance at the State Level in Germany: The Case of Lower Saxony," *Comparative Politics*, 12, No. 2, January 1980, 211–23.

Harmon, Robert B. *A Selected and Annotated Guide to the Government and Politics of Germany*. (Exchange Bibliography No. 1474.) Monticello, Illinois: Council of Planning Librarians, 1978.

Hartrich, Edwin. *The Fourth and Richest Reich*. New York: Macmillan, 1980.

Helm, Jutta A. "Citizen Lobbies in West Germany." Pages 576–96 in Peter H. Merkl (ed.), *West European Party Systems*.

New York: The Free Press, 1980.
Hulsberg, Werner. "Working Class Seeks an Alternative: Growing Opposition to Austerity and Militarization," *Intercontinental Press*, 19, No. 41, November 9, 1981, 1093–97.
Johnson, Nevil. "Law as the Articulation of the State in Western Germany: A German Tradition Seen from a British Perspective," *West European Politics* [London], 1, No. 2, May 1978, 177–92.
Katzenstein, Peter J. "Problem or Model? West Germany in the 1980s," *World Politics*, 32, No. 4, July 1980, 577–98.
Keefe, Eugene K., et al. *Area Handbook for the Federal Republic of Germany*. (DA Pam 550–173.) Washington: GPO for Foreign Area Studies, The American University, 1975.
Knoll, Joachim H. *Bildung und Wissenschaft in der Bundesrepublik Deutschland*. Munich: Hanser, 1977.
Kohn, Walter S.E. *Governments and Politics of the German-speaking Countries*. Chicago: Nelson-Hall, 1980.
Kommers, Donald P. *Juridical Politics in West Germany: A Study of the Federal Constitutional Court*, V. (Sage Series on Politics and the Legal Order.) Beverly Hills: Sage, 1976.
Koschnick, Wolfgang J. "Church and State in West Germany," *Church and State*, 30, No. 2, February 1977, 7–11.
Kruse, Wolfgang (ed.). *In Brief—Berlin*. Berlin: Press and Information Office, 1979.
Lehmbruch, Gerhard. "Party and Federation in Germany: A Developmental Dilemma," *Government and Opposition* [London], 13, No. 2, Spring 1978, 151–77.
LoBao, Phil. "A Study in Failure: The Communist Party and Elections in West Germany," *Parliamentary Affairs* [London], 32, Winter 1979, 66–77.
Meier, Reinhard. "The Green Front: Germany's Political Environmentalists," *Swiss Review of World Affairs* [Zurich], 29, No. 10, January 1980, 6–8.
———. "West Germany's Disoriented Left," *Swiss Review of World Affairs* [Zurich], 30, No. 4, July 1980, 20–22.
Merkl, Peter H. "West Germany." Pages 21–60 in Peter H. Merkl (ed.), *West European Party Systems*. New York: The Free Press, 1980.
Minnerup, Günter. "West Germany Since the War," *New Left Review* [London], No. 99, September-October 1976, 3–44.
Nelkin, Dorothy. "Citizens Appeal to the Courts in France and Germany," *Bulletin of Atomic Scientists*, 36, No. 5, May 1980, 36–42.
———. "Political Parties and the Nuclear Energy Debate in France and Germany," *Comparative Politics*, 12, No. 2, January 1980, 127–42.
Norpoth, Helmut. "Choosing a Coalition Partner: Mass Preferences and Elite Decisions in West Germany," *Comparative*

Political Studies, 12, No. 4, January 1980, 424–40.

———. "Dimensions of Preferential Choice in the West German Electorate, 1961–1976," *American Political Science Review*, LXXIII, No. 3, September 1979, 724–36.

———. "Mass Media Use and Electoral Choice in West Germany," *Comparative Politics*, 13, No. 1, October 1980, 1–14.

———. "Party Identification in West Germany: Tracing an Elusive Concept," *Comparative Political Studies*, 11, No. 1, April 1978, 36.

Nova, Fritz. "Political Innovation of the West German Federal Constitutional Court: The State of Discussion on Juridical Review," *American Political Science Review*, LXX, No. 1, March 1976, 114–25.

Paterson, William E. "The German Social Democratic Party." Pages 176–212 in William E. Paterson and Alastair H. Thomas (eds.), *Social Democratic Parties in Western Europe*. New York: St. Martin's Press, 1977.

Pridham, Geoffrey. *Christian Democracy in Western Germany: The CDU/CSU in Government and Opposition, 1945–1976*. New York: St. Martin's Press, 1977.

———. "Ecologists in Politics: The West German Case," *Parliamentary Affairs* [London], 31, Autumn 1978, 436–44.

Pulzer, Peter. "Responsible Party Government and Stable Coalition: The Case of the German Federal Republic," *Political Studies* [London], 26, No. 2, June 1978, 181–208.

Rogowski, Ronald. "Social Class and Partisanship in European Electorates: A Re-Assessment," *World Politics*, 23, No. 4, July 1981, 639–49.

Römer, Karl (ed.). *Facts about Germany: The Federal Republic of Germany*. Gütersloh, Germany: Lexikon-Institut Bertelsmann, 1979.

Scheuch, Edwin K. *Is Germany Becoming Ungovernable?* Glasgow: University of Strathclyde, 1977.

Schmidt, Manfred G. "The Politics of Domestic Reform in the Federal Republic of Germany," *Politics and Society*, 8, No. 2, 1978, 165–200.

Schoenbaum, David. "Dateline Bonn: Uneasy Super Ally," *Foreign Policy*, No. 37, Winter 1979–80, 176–91.

Schweigler, Gebhard Ludwig. *National Consciousness in Divided Germany*. (Sage Library of Social Research series, No. 15.) Beverly Hills: Sage, 1975.

Sheffler, Martin. "Party and Patronage: Germany, England, and Italy," *Politics and Society*, 7, No. 4, 1977, 403–52.

Smith, Gordon R. *Democracy in Western Germany: Parties and Politics in the Federal Republic*. New York: Holmes and Meier, 1980.

———. "West Germany and the Politics of Centrality," *Government and Opposition* [London], 11, No. 4, Autumn

1976, 387–407.
Sontheimer, Kurt. "Intellectuals and Politics in Western Germany," *West European Politics* [London], 1, No. 1, February 1978, 30–41.
Southern, David. "Germany." Pages 107–55 in F.F. Ridley (ed.), *Government and Administration in Western Europe.* New York: St. Martin's Press, 1979.
Stokes, William S., Jr. "Emancipation: The Politics of West German Education," *Review of Politics*, 42, No. 2, April 1980, 167–90.
U.S. Department of State. Bureau of Public Affairs. Office of Public Communication. *Background Notes: Federal Republic of Germany.* Washington: January 1980.
Vinocur, John. "The German Malaise," *New York Times Magazine*, November 15, 1981, 42–125.
Waldman, Eric. "Germany: Federal Republic of Germany." Pages 393–99 in Richard F. Staar (ed.), *Yearbook of International Communist Affairs, 1981.* Stanford: Hoover Institution Press, 1981.
"West Berlin Government Formed," *New York Times*, June 12, 1981, A8.
Willey, Richard J. "Trade Unions and Political Parties in the Federal Republic of Germany," *Industrial and Labor Relations Review*, 28, No. 1, October 1974, 38–59.
Yergin, Angela Stent. "West Germany's Sudpolitik: Social Democrats and Eurocommunism," *Orbis*, 23, No. 1, Spring 1979, 51–72.

(Various issues of the following publications were also used in the preparation of this chapter: *Bulletin* [Bonn], December 1980–December 1981; *Christian Science Monitor*, June 1981–January 1982; *The Economist* [London], September 1981–January 1982; *Financial Times* [London], October 1980–January 1982; Foreign Broadcast Information Service (FBIS) *Daily Report: Western Europe*, March 1980–December 1981; *German Press Review*, June 1981–January 1982; *The Guardian* [Manchester], March 1980–December 1981; *Keesing's Contemporary Archives* [London], 1976–1980; *New York Times*, January 1981–January 1982; *Washington Post*, June 1981–January 1982; and *The Week in Germany*, June 1981–January 1982.)

Chapter 8

Acheson, Dean. "The Practice of Partnership," *Foreign Affairs*, 41, No. 2, January 1963, 247–60.
Adenauer, Konrad. *Memoirs, 1945–1953.* Chicago: Henry Regnery, 1966.
Aron, Raymond. *The Great Debate.* Garden City, New York:

Doubleday, 1965.
Backer, John H. *The Decision to Divide Germany*. Durham: Duke University Press, 1978.
Bark, Dennis L. *Agreement on Berlin: A Study of the 1970–1972 Quadripartite Negotiations*. Washington: American Enterprise Institute for Public Policy Research and Hoover Institution on War, Revolution and Peace, 1974.
Beaufre, André. *NATO and Europe*. New York: Random House, 1966.
Birnbaum, Karl E. *East and West Germany: A Modus Vivendi*. Lexington, Massachusetts: Lexington Books, 1973.
Brandt, Willy. *A Peace Policy for Europe*. New York: Holt, Rinehart and Winston, 1969.
———. *People and Politics: The Years 1960–1975*. (Trans., J. Maxwell Brownjohn.) Boston: Little, Brown, 1978.
Calleo, David P. *The German Problem Reconsidered: Germany and the World Order, 1870 to the Present*. New York: Cambridge University Press, 1978.
Canby, Steven L. "Rethinking the NATO Military Problem." (International Security Studies Program, Working Paper No. 3, 1979, The Wilson Center. Reprinted in *Current News*, No. 432.) Washington: U.S. Department of the Air Force, June 20, 1979.
Catudal, Honoré M., Jr. *The Diplomacy of the Quadripartite Agreement on Berlin*. Berlin: Berlin Verlag, 1978.
Conradt, David P. *The German Polity*. (Comparative Studies of of Political Life series.) New York: Longman, 1978.
Cromwell, William C., et al. *Political Problems of the Atlantic Partnership*. Bruges: College of Europe, 1969.
Czempiel, Ernst-Otto. "Germany and the Third World: The Politics of Free Trade and the Free Hand." Pages 181–96 in Wolfram F. Hanrieder (ed.), *West German Foreign Policy: 1949–1979*. Boulder: Westview Press, 1980.
"Documentation," *NATO Review* [Brussels], No. 1, February 1981, 33.
Doeker, Günther, and Jens A. Bruckner (eds.). *The Federal Republic of Germany and the German Democratic Republic in International Relations*. 3 vols. Dobbs Ferry, New York: Oceana Publications, 1979.
Drath, Viola Herms, and George Schwab (eds.). *Germany in World Politics*. New York: Cyrco Press, 1979.
European Community Information Service. "The European Community Establishes Production Quotas for Steel," (*European Community News*, No. 29/1980.) Washington: November 5, 1980 (mimeo.).
———. "Meeting of the European Council in Luxembourg," (*European Community News*, No. 22/1981.) Washington: June 30, 1981 (mimeo.).

Federal Republic of Germany. Federal Ministry of Defense. *White Paper 1979: The Security of the Federal Republic of Germany and the Development of the Federal Armed Forces.* Bonn: 1979.

Feld, Werner J. *Germany and the European Community.* New York: Praeger, 1981.

———. "Two-Tier Policy Making in the EC: The Common Agricultural Policy." Pages 123–49 in Leon Hurwitz (ed.), *Contemporary Perspectives on European Integration* . Westport, Connecticut: Greenwood Press, 1980.

Gatzke, Hans W. *Germany and the United States: A "Special Relationship?"* Cambridge: Harvard University Press, 1980.

Griffith, William E. *The Ostpolitik of the Federal Republic of Germany.* Cambridge: MIT Press, 1978.

Haftendorn, Helga. *German Foreign Policy: Management of Détente.* New York: Praeger, 1982.

———. "West Germany and the Management of Security Relations: Security Policy under the Conditions of International Interdependence." Pages 7–31 in Ekkehart Krippendorff and Volker Rittberger (eds.), *The Foreign Policy of West Germany: Formation and Contents.* (German Political Studies, Vol. 4.) Beverly Hills: Sage, 1980.

Hanrieder, Wolfram F. *The Stable Crisis: Two Decades of German Foreign Policy.* New York: Harper and Row, 1970.

———. *West German Foreign Policy: 1949–1963.* Stanford: Stanford University Press, 1967.

———. "West Germany: Security and the Western Alliance." Pages 3–26 in Wolfram F. Hanrieder and Graeme P. Auton (eds.), *The Foreign Policies of West Germany, France, and Britain.* Englewood Cliffs: Prentice-Hall, 1980.

Hanrieder, Wolfram F. (ed.). *West German Foreign Policy: 1949–1979.* Boulder: Westview Press, 1980.

Hartmann, Frederick H. *Germany Between East and West: The Reunification Problem.* Englewood Cliffs: Prentice-Hall, 1965.

Hill, Christopher, and William Wallace. "Diplomatic Trends in the European Community," *International Affairs* [London], 55, No. 1, January 1979, 47–66.

Joffe, Josef. "The Enduring Crisis," *Foreign Affairs*, 59, No. 4, Spring 1981, 835–51.

———. "The Foreign Policy of the German Federal Republic." Pages 117–51 in Roy C. Macridis (ed.), *Foreign Policy in World Politics.* (5th ed.) Englewood Cliffs: Prentice-Hall, 1976.

———. "Germany and the Atlantic Alliance." Pages 323–454 in William C. Cromwell, et al., *Political Problems of the Atlantic Partnership.* Bruges: College of Europe, 1969.

Kaiser, Karl. *German Foreign Policy in Transition.* New York: Oxford University Press, 1968.

Kelleher, Catherine McArdle. "Germany and the Alliance." Pages 37–53 in Viola Herms Drath and George Schwab (eds.), *Germany in World Politics.* New York: Cyrco Press, 1979.
———. *Germany and the Politics of Nuclear Weapons.* New York: Columbia University Press, 1975.
Kissinger, Henry. "NATO: The Next Thirty Years," *Survival* [London], XXL, No. 6, November-December 1979, 264–68.
———. *The Troubled Partnership.* New York: McGraw-Hill, 1965.
Kohl, Wilfrid L., and Georgio Basevi (eds.). *West Germany: A European and Global Power.* Lexington, Massachusetts: Lexington Books, 1980.
Krause, Joachim, and Lothar Wilker. "Bureaucracy and Foreign Policy in the Federal Republic of Germany." Pages 147–70 in Ekkehart Krippendorff and Volker Rittberger (eds.), *The Foreign Policy of West Germany: Formation and Contents.* (German Political Studies, Vol. 4.) Beverly Hills: Sage, 1980.
Kreile, Michael. "Ostpolitik Reconsidered." Pages 123–46 in Ekkehart Krippendorff and Volker Rittberger (eds.), *The Foreign Policy of West Germany: Formation and Contents.* (German Political Studies, Vol. 4.) Beverly Hills: Sage, 1980.
Krippendorff, Ekkehart, and Volker Rittberger (eds.). *The Foreign Policy of West Germany: Formation and Contents.* (German Political Studies, Vol. 4.) Beverly Hills: Sage, 1980.
Krisch, Henry. *The German Democratic Republic.* Boulder: Westview Press, 1981.
Kulski, W.W. *Germany and Poland.* Syracuse: Syracuse University Press, 1976.
Ludz, Peter C. "Foreign Policy in Germany: Ideological and Political Aspects of Intra-German Relations." Pages 54–77 in Viola Herms Drath and George Schwab (eds.), *Germany in World Politics.* New York: Cyrco Press, 1979.
McGeehan, Robert. *The German Rearmament Question.* Chicago: University of Illinois Press, 1971.
Merkl, Peter H. *German Foreign Policies, West and East.* Santa Barbara: American Bibliographical Center-Clio Press, 1974.
Milligan, Stephen. "EC-China Trade Pact," *European Community*, No. 207, May-June 1978, 6–7.
Moreton, N. Edwina. *East Germany and the Warsaw Alliance: The Politics of Détente.* Boulder: Westview Press, 1979.
NATO: Facts and Figures. Brussels: NATO Information Service, 1976.
Noelle, Elisabeth, and Erich Peter Neumann (eds.). *The Germans: Public Opinion Polls, 1947–1966.* Allensbach: Verlag für Demoskopie, 1967.
Noelle-Neumann, Elisabeth. "Phantom Europe: Thirty Years of Survey Research on German Attitudes Toward European Integration." Pages 53–74 in Leon Hurwitz (ed.), *Contemporary*

Perspectives on European Integration. Westport, Connecticut: Greenwood Press, 1980.

Noelle-Neumann, Elisabeth (ed.). *The Germans: Public Opinion Polls, 1967–1980.* Westport, Connecticut: Greenwood Press, 1981.

Osgood, Robert E. *NATO: The Entangling Alliance.* Chicago: University of Chicago Press, 1962.

Richardson, James L. *Germany and the Atlantic Alliance.* Cambridge: Harvard University Press, 1966.

Rothman, Stanley, et al. *European Society and Politics: Britain, France and Germany.* St. Paul: West Publishing, 1976.

Rummel, Reinhardt. "Bonn and European Political Cooperation." Pages 73–87 in Wilfrid L. Kohl and Giorgio Basevi (eds.), *West Germany: A European and Global Power.* Lexington, Massachusetts: Lexington Books, 1980.

Schmidt, Helmut. *Defence or Retaliation.* London: Oliver and Boyd, 1962.

Schwarz, Hans-Peter. "Adenauer's Ostpolitik." Pages 127–43 in Wolfram F. Hanrieder (ed.), *West German Foreign Policy: 1949–1979.* Boulder: Westview Press, 1980.

Sinnreich, Richard Hart. "NATO's Doctrinal Dilemma," *Orbis*, XIX, No. 2, Summer 1975, 461–76.

Smyser, W.R. *German-American Relations.* (The Washington Papers, Vol. 8.) Beverly Hills: Sage, 1980.

Stern, Fritz. "Germany in a Semi-Gaullist Europe," *Foreign Affairs*, 58, No. 4, Spring 1980, 867–86.

U.S. Congress. 87th, 1st Session. Senate. Committee on Foreign Relations. *Documents on Germany, 1944–61.* Washington: GPO, December 1961.

U.S. Congress. 92d, 1st Session. Senate. Committee on Foreign Relations. *Documents on Germany, 1944–1970.* Washington: GPO, May 17, 1971.

U.S. Congress. 96th, 2d Session. House of Representatives. Committee on Foreign Affairs. *NATO and Western Security in the 1980s.* (Report of a Staff Study Mission to Seven NATO Countries and Austria, January 2–18, 1980.) Washington: GPO, April 9, 1980.

U.S. Congress. 96th, 2d Session. House of Representatives. Committee on Foreign Affairs. Subcommittee on Europe and the Middle East. *The Modernization of NATO's Long-Range Theater Nuclear Forces.* (Report prepared by the Foreign Affairs and National Defense Division, Congressional Research Service, Library of Congress.) Washington: GPO, December 31, 1980.

––––––. *NATO After Afghanistan.* (Report prepared by Foreign Affairs and National Defense Division, Congressional Research Service, Library of Congress.) Washington: GPO, October 27, 1980.

———. *United States-Western European Relations in 1980.* (Hearings, June 5, July 22, September 9, 15, and 22, 1980.) Washington: GPO, 1980.

U.S. Congress. 96th, 2d Session. Senate. Committee on Foreign Relations. *NATO—A Status Report.* (Report by Senator Howard H. Baker, Jr.) Washington: GPO, October 1980.

Vardamis, Alex A. "German-American Military Fissures," *Foreign Policy*, 34, Spring 1979, 87–106.

Wallace, William, and W.E. Paterson (eds.). *Foreign Policy Making in Western Europe.* New York: Praeger, 1978.

Chapter 9

Baudissin, Wolf von. "Internal Leadership in the Federal German Army," *NATO Review* [Brussels], 26, No. 2, April 1978, 5–10, 29.

Becker, Harold K. *Police Systems of Europe.* (2d ed.) Springfield, Illinois: Charles C. Thomas, 1980.

Brewer, Carey. "The General Staff of the German Army," *United States Naval Institute Proceedings*, LXXXII, February 1956, 157–66.

Carell, Paul. *Hitler Moves East 1941-1943.* New York: Bantam, 1966.

Carr, William. *A History of Germany 1815-1945.* New York: St. Martin's Press, 1969.

Childs, David, and Jeffrey Johnson. *West Germany: Politics and Society.* New York: St. Martin's Press, 1981.

Clark, Alan. *Barbarossa: The Russian-German Conflict 1941–45.* New York: Signet, 1966.

Crozier, Brian. "Political Crime and Terrorism." Pages 219–220 in *Britannica Book of the Year 1976.* Chicago: Encyclopedia Britannica, 1976.

Dudley, Donald R. *The World of Tacitus.* Boston: Little, Brown, 1968.

Federal Republic of Germany. Federal Ministry of Defense. *White Paper 1973/1974: The Security of the Federal Republic of Germany and the Development of the Federal Armed Forces.* Bonn: 1974.

———. *White Paper 1975/1976: The Security of the Federal Republic of Germany and the Development of the Federal Armed Forces.* Bonn: 1976.

———. *White Paper 1979: The Security of the Federal Republic of Germany and the Development of the Federal Armed Forces.* Bonn: 1979.

Federal Republic of Germany. *The Force Structure in the Federal Republic of Germany.* Bonn: Force Structure Commission, 1973.

Federal Republic of Germany. Press and Information Office. *Jahresbericht der Bundesregierung 1980.* Bonn: 1980.

Federal Republic of Germany

Hahn, Walter F. *Between Westpolitik and Ostpolitik: Changing West German Security Views*. (Foreign Policy Papers of the Foreign Policy Research Institute.) Beverly Hills: Sage, 1975.

Herrmann, Joachim. "Federal Republic of Germany." Pages 86–106 in George F. Cole, Stanislaw J. Frankowski, and Marc G. Gertz (eds.), *Major Criminal Justice Systems*. Beverly Hills: Sage, 1981.

———. "Sanctions: German Law and Theory," *The American Journal of Comparative Law*, XXIV, No. 4, Fall 1976, 718–36.

Heymont, Irving. *Analysis of the Army Reserve Systems of Israel, Canada, United Kingdom, Federal Republic of Germany, and the Netherlands*. McLean, Virginia: General Research Corporation, 1977.

Ingleton, Roy. "West Germany." Pages 182–89 in Roy Ingleton (ed.), *Police of the World*. New York: Charles Scribner's Sons, 1979.

Keefe, Eugene K., et al. *Area Handbook for the Federal Republic of Germany*. (DA Pam 550-173.) Washington: GPO for Foreign Area Studies, The American University, 1975.

Keegan, John. "German Federal Republic." Pages 242–54 in John Keegan (ed.), *World Armies*. New York: Facts on File, 1979.

Lellenberg, Jon L. "The Citizen-Army Concept in Germany: Political-Military Implications." (Research paper prepared for the Office of the Deputy Chief of Staff for Military Operations, United States Army.) Menlo Park, California: Strategic Studies Center, Stanford Research Institute, 1974.

McNeill, William H. *The Rise of the West: A History of the Human Community*. New York: Mentor, 1965.

The Military Balance 1981–82. London: International Institute for Strategic Studies, 1981.

NATO Handbook. Brussels: NATO Information Service, 1980.

Nelson, Charles. "Third Force: An International Police Association Scholarship Report," *Police Journal* [Chichester, England], III, No. 2, April 1980, 138–46.

O'Ballance, Edgar. "International Terrorism," *The Retired Officer*, November 1981, 20–23.

Passant, E.J., et al. *A Short History of Germany 1815–1945*. London: Oxford University Press, 1959.

Pinson, Koppel S. *Modern Germany: Its History and Civilization*. New York: Macmillan, 1954.

Radvanyi, Miklos K. *Anti-Terrorist Legislation in the Federal Republic of Germany*. Washington: Law Library, Library of Congress, 1979.

Römer, Karl (ed.). *Facts about Germany: The Federal Republic of Germany*. Gütersloh, Germany: Lexikon-Institut Bertelsmann, 1979.

Rudé, George. *Revolutionary Europe 1783–1815.* New York: Meridian, 1964.

Ruhm von Oppen, Beate (ed.). *Documents on Germany under Occupation 1945–1954.* London: Oxford University Press, 1955.

Silving, Helen. "Discussions of Sanctions," *The American Journal of Comparative Law*, XXIV, No. 4, Fall 1976, 737–53.

Solyom-Fekete, William. "Federal Republic of Germany." Pages 59–74 in *Gun Control Laws in Foreign Countries.* Washington: Law Library, Library of Congress, 1981.

Von Koch, Alexander. "Police Consolidation in Germany," *The Police Chief*, 46, No. 9, September 1979, 46–49.

Wilkinson, Paul. "Terrorism—Weapon of the Weak." Pages 129–37 in James Ertel (ed.), *Britannica Book of the Year 1979.* Chicago: Encyclopedia Britannica, 1979.

Zoll, Ralf (ed.). "Special Issue on Civil-Military Relations in the Federal Republic of Germany," *Armed Forces and Society*, 5, No. 4, Summer 1979.

Glossary

Atlantic Alliance—An alternate designation for NATO (*q.v.*).

CDU/CSU—Christlich Demokratische Union (Christian Democratic Union—CDU) and Christlich Soziale Union (Christian Social Union—CSU) form major political party. CSU, as the "Bavarian wing" or "sister party" of the CDU, maintains a separate organization within Bavaria, but constitutes an integral part of the CDU/CSU in the federal parliament.

civil service—In 1980 some 1.4 million persons, also known as *Beamten* (or "officials"), in public employment, who have a special professional status that carries privileges (such as lifetime guaranteed employment and a pension not requiring employee contributions) and special obligations (such as loyalty to employer and obedience to supervisor). Civil servants are distinct from public servants, a term that refers to all of the 3.5 to 4 million persons in public employment in 1980.

Common Market—European Economic Community, a part of the European Communities (*q.v.*).

CSU—*See* CDU/CSU.

deutsche mark (DM)—The national currency unit, consisting of 100 pfennigs. The value of the deutsche mark fluctuated with international monetary developments—generally upward since its introduction in the currency reform of 1948. The International Monetary Fund's *International Financial Statistics* presents the average value of the mark each year in terms of the dollar and special drawing rights (SDRs). The number of deutsche marks per US$1 averaged 2.46 in 1975, 2.52 in 1976, 2.32 in 1977, 2.01 in 1978, 1.83 in 1979, 1.82 in 1980, and 2.26 in 1981.

EC—European Communities (*q.v.*).

ECSC—European Coal and Steel Community, a part of the European Communities (*q.v.*).

EEC—European Economic Community, a part of the European Communities (*q.v.*).

EURATOM—European Atomic Energy Community, a part of the European Communities (*q.v.*).

European Communities (EC)—A 1965 treaty that entered into force July 1, 1967, joining together the ECSC—created in 1951, operational from July 25, 1952—the EEC or Common Market—established by treaty of March 25, 1957, operational from January 1, 1958—and the EURATOM—also created by a treaty on March 25, 1957, and operational from January 1, 1958. Although the formal name is European Communities, most writers refer to the European Community, and the institution almost always refers to itself as the European Community.

Federal Republic of Germany

European Community—*See* European Communities.

FDP—Freie Demokratische Partei (Free Democratic Party). The only minor party to have won seats in the Bundestag in every national election up to and including 1980 election. In 1982 was junior member of governing coalition with SPD (*q.v.*), a role it had filled since 1969 with SPD and earlier with the CDU/CSU (*q.v.*).

FRG—Federal Republic of Germany (West Germany or Federal Republic). In early 1980s the initials were increasingly used in governmental, academic, and popular publications as a short designation of the country. BRD, from Bundesrepublik Deutschland, also frequently seen.

GDR—German Democratic Republic (East Germany). In early 1980s the initials were increasingly used in governmental, academic, and popular publications as a short designation of the country. DDR, from Deutsche Demokratische Republik, also frequently seen.

NATO—North Atlantic Treaty Organization; frequently called, particularly in official NATO publications, the Atlantic Alliance or the Alliance. In early 1982 membership composed of Belgium, Britain, Canada, Denmark, West Germany, Greece, Italy, Luxembourg, the Netherlands, Norway, Portugal, Turkey, and United States.

SPD—Sozialdemokratische Partei Deutschlands (Social Democratic Party of Germany). One of two major political parties. In early 1982 governed country in coalition with FDP (*q.v.*).

Western European Union (WEU)—In 1948 Belgium, Britain, France, Luxembourg, and the Netherlands concluded and signed the Brussels Treaty, which envisaged a collective security agreement that was at least inferentially a hedge against a resurgent Germany. Instead, in 1949 NATO was formed. In 1954 a nine-power conference in London concluded agreements to include West Germany and Italy in the as yet unformed WEU, to terminate Allied occupation of West Germany, and for the latter to join NATO. These agreements were ratified on May 6, 1955, at which time the WEU came into being. By acceding to the WEU, West Germany accepted limitations on its rearmament and weapons manufacture; in a separate document, West Germany renounced the manufacture of atomic, bacteriological, and chemical weapons. In the early 1980s the WEU, headquartered in London, dealt mostly with intra-union political questions.

Index

Aachen: 66
Adenauer, Konrad: xvi, xxvii-xxix, 3, 44, 46–49, 263, 269; foreign policy, xxviii, 293; rearmament policy, 136, 260, 338; resignation, 49
AEG-Telefunken: 210
Afghanistan, Soviet invasion: 246, 312, 315–316, 322
agriculture (see also *imports*): xx, 64, 181–195; commodity support prices and market protection, 152, 153, 171, 181–193 *passim*, 281, 320; crops, xx, 65, 182, 190–192, 392, 393; farm income, 188, 189–190; farm size, 181, 182, 183, 184, 189; farmers' pensions and accident insurance, 94–95, 186; Green Front association, 281; labor force, 18, 152, 161, 183, 387 (table); land use, 65, 181–182; post-war adjustments, 146, 160–161, 185, 186, 191; production, 160, 181–191 *passim*, 386 (table); shift to nonagricultural urban employment, 35, 113, 118, 129, 131, 183; traditional, 182, 183, 186, 190, 192–193; unionization, 120
airports: xxi, 217; air force, 363
Allied Control Council. *See* post World War II
Alsace-Lorraine: 15, 16, 24, 145
anti-Communism: 47, 50–51, 55, 245, 260, 266
anti-nuclear peace movement: xxix, 4, 107, 108, 136, 216, 246, 247, 266, 281, 283, 371
Apel, Hans: 340
Argentina, German nuclear reactor sale: 327
armed forces (Bundeswehr)(*see also* NATO): xxii, 245, 333–358; age-and-rank-groups distribution, 347–348; air force, xxii, 333, 338, 344–346, 351, 354, 355; budget, 289, 346–347, (tables) 396, 397, 398; Bundeswehr Defense Council (Joint Armed Forces Staffs), 340–342, 354; Career Promotion Service, 90; "citizens in uniform", rights as, 333–334, 347–355; conscientious objectors, 44, 136, 247, 348; conscription, xxii, 47, 338–351 *passim*, 362; defense mission, 338–339, 340, 342, 349; defense ombudsman, 342, 350; deployment, 342, 343, 344; Field Army (Feldheer), 333, 342, 354; Force Structure Commission, 348–349; German General Staff (1851–1945), 17, 27, 41, 336; inner leadership (Innere Führung), 350, 353; manpower, xxii, 261, 333, 339–347 *passim*, 364, 398 (table); Medical and Health Services, 352, 353–354; military traditions, 333, 334–338, 350; NATO integration, xxii, 47, 299, 301–302, 333, 339, 342–343, 344, 350, 351–352; navy, xxii, 20, 294, 333, 338, 343–344, 351–355 *passim*, 361–362; nuclear delivery vehicles, 48, 246; organization, xxii, 338, 340–346, 349; personnel policies, 347–348; reorganization, 1980's, 342–343, 344, 346, 354; reserves, 348, 354; supreme command, 248, 252, 290, 340; terms of service, 348; Territorial Army, xxii, 333, 342, 343, 354; training and equipment, xxii, 338, 343–353 *passim*; U.N. peacekeeping forces, nonparticipation in, 325; under German Empire, 14, 16–17, 20, 21, 336; uniforms, insignia, and ranks, 355, 356 (illustration); vocational and other special schools, 90; volunteer, 136, 338, 340, 347–352 *passim*, 362; women, 347, 348
Arminius: 334
Atlantic Alliance. *See* NATO
Attlee, Clement: 337–338
Augstein, Rudolf: 284
Augustulus, Romulus: xii, 4
Auschwitz concentration camp: 38
Austria: xiii, xv, xxvi, 10, 14–15, 18, 65; *Anschluss*, 1938, xvi, 36–37
Austria-Hungary: 106

Baader, Andreas: 367, 368, 369, 370
Baden: xiv, 15, 16
Baden-Württemberg: 62, 65, 67, 68, 181, 194, 268, 394; French II Corps headquarters, 357
Baghdad railway project, 1900's: 20
Baltic Sea: 64, 67
Bank of International Settlement: 29
banks and banking (*see also* currency): 147, 165, 167–170; central bank (Deutsche Bundesbank), 154, 169–170, 199; central savings institu-

437

tions (*Landesbanken*), 167; commercial banks, 168–169; Commerzbank, 168; Deutsche Bank, 168, 228; Dresdner Bank, 168; government and state partial ownership, 152; industry-bank relations, 147, 153, 204, 220, 222, 224–227; postal savings banks, 167; Reichsbank, 28
Barth, Karl: 135
Barzel, Rainer: 52
BASF company: 208
Basic Law (1949): xxi-xxii, xxvi-xxvii, 247–251; amendment, 248; as provisional constitution, xxi-xxii, 43, 54, 247; balanced budget, requirement, 151; Bundeswehr provisions, 338–339, 348; civil rights provisions, 44, 76, 127, 132, 247–248, 276, 283; extremist political parties banned, 247–248, 264, 273, 274–275; government structure, xx, xxvii, 44–45, 157, 245, 248, 250, 251, 252, 258, 291; interpretation, provisions for, 44, 258, 260; on industrial associations, 223; on judicial systems, 364, 365; on political parties, 264; Parliamentary Council, 1948, xxvi, xxvii, 43; reunification clause, 46, 54, 247; social welfare obligations, 94; status of West Berlin, 250
Baudissin, Wolf von: 349
Bavaria: 62, 65, 67, 108–109, 110, 181, 194; Catholic population, 134, 268, 281; Christian Social Union Party, xxix, 54, 55, 265, 268, 269; church administrative borders, 135; historic, xiv, 15, 16; *Land* government, 262, 266, 268, 394 (table); 1982 election prediction, xxx
Bavarian Alps: 61, 62, 65, 67, 69
Bavarian German Workers' Party. *See* National Socialist German Workers' Party (NSDAP-Nazis)
Bayer company: 208
Bayernkurier, CSU newspaper: 284
Bebel, August: 16, 17
Beethoven, Ludwig van: xxvi
Belgium: German invasion, 1940, 37, 337; military forces in West Germany, xxii, 358
Bergen-Belsen concentration camp: 38
Berlin: 129; Berlin Crisis, 1958–1961, xvi, 48–49; Berlin Wall, xvi, 3, 49, 161, 307, 361 (illustration); cadet school, 1733, 335; Four Power control, xxv, 41; Psychoanalytic Institute, 29; urbanization, 128, 129; West Berlin, communications, 308, 310

Bernstein, Edward: 20
Bethmann-Hollweg, Theobald von: xv, 20, 21, 22, 23, 24–25
Bild-Zeitung: 284
Bingen: 62, 66
Birnbaum, Karl: 310
Bismarck, Otto von: xv, 14–16, 18, 116, 230, 269, 336
Black Forest (Schwarzwald): 62, 65, 66, 67, 68
Blank, Theodor: 338
Blücher, Gerhard von: 335
Bodensee: 65, 67, 68
Bohemia-Moravia, German annexation, 1939: xvi, 37
Bohemian Forest (Bohmerwald): 68
Böll, Heinrich: 56, 134
Bonn: 62, 66; capital, xix, xxvii, 43; CDU party headquarters, 266; police headquarters, 362
boundaries: Austria, 65; East German, recognition, xxviii, 52, 308, 310, 311; Poland, 52; Switzerland, 65
Brahms, Johannes: 38
Brandt, Willy: xvi, xxix, 249 (illustration), 270, 271, 309; chancellorship (1969–1974), xxviii, 3, 51–55, 252, 269, 270, 327; East German policy (*see also Ostpolitik*), 3, 50, 51, 52, 307; Nobel Peace Prize, 1971, 54; resignation, xxviii, 55
Braun, Eva: 41
Brazil, German nuclear power equipment sales: 326–327
Bremen: 61–62, 135, 173 (illustration), 262, 263, 268, 271, 394
Britain (United Kingdom): EC budget contributions, 319, 320; German Empire conflicts of interest, xv, 20; German investment in, 241; military forces in West Germany, xxii, 357; Third Reich relations, 36, 37; World War II, 36, 37–38, 40, 41, 337–338
Brockdorf, nuclear power plant demonstrations: 283
Brüning, Heinrich: xvi, 32, 33
Brunswick: xiv
Bülow, Bernhard von: xv, 20–21
Bundesrat (Federal Council): xxii, xxvii, 250, 263, 265; duties and powers, 44, 249, 254–255, 256, 258, 260, 291–293; legislation, provisions for overriding, xxx, 44, 258; president as temporary chief of state, 252
Bundestag (Federal Diet): xxii, xxvii, 245, 267 (illustration); composition by party, 257, 258, 264–265, 270, 273; Council of Elders, 256, 356; duties

Index

and powers, xxvii, xxx, 44, 248, 249, 251, 252, 254–256, 260, 291–293, 342, 350; 1949 election, 273, 274; parliamentary groups, 255, 256; party discipline, 255, 366; passage of codetermination law, 1951, 233; presidential power to dissolve, 251; West Berlin representation, 44, 251, 255
Bundeswehr. *See* armed forces
Bundeswehr Staff College: 350
Burgmann, Dieter: 275
Business Cycle Council: 154

Canada, military forces in West Germany: xxii, 358
capital: xix, xxvii
Caprivi, Leo von: xv, 20
Carstens, Karl: xxxii, 56–57, 252
Carter, Jimmy: 300
Center Party: 16–23 *passim*, 45
Chamberlain, Neville: 37
Charlemagne (Charles the Great): xii, 5
Charles IV: xiii, 8
Charles V: xiv, 8, 10
China: 212, 325–326
Christian Democratic Union (CDU): 4, 394, 395; Adenauer leadership, xvi, 3, 44, 45; auxiliary organizations, 266; decentralized organization, 266; membership, 268; Parliamentary Council representation, 43; party newspaper, 284
Christian Democratic Union/Christian Social Union coalition (CDU/CSU): xxii, xxviii–xxix, 44–56 *passim*, 246, 263–271 *passim*, 435; as opposition party, 1972–1982, 51, 54, 55, 56, 57, 255, 258, 263, 264–266, 346–347; *Bürgerblock* (coalition with FDP and DP), 46, 48; Free Democratic Party coalition, 45, 49; "Grand Coalition" with Social Democratic Party, 1966–1969, xvi, xxix, 49–51, 66–69, 271, 366; incorporation of smaller parties, 45; Kohl leadership, 255, 268–269; leadership, differences in 1970's (Kohl-Geissler, Kohl-Strauss), 266, 268–269; 1982 election predictions, xxx-xxxi, 246; policy orientation, 151, 266; professional interest groups, 278
Christian Social Union (Bavarian Party). *See* Christian Democratic Union/ Christian Social Union coalition
Churchill, Winston: 37, 338
citizens, term for: xix
citizens' initiative associations: 247, 282–283
civil rights: 333, 365–366, 369; Basic Law, 1949, 44, 127, 132, 247–248, 365; church tax, protests, 134; Weimar constitution, 1919, 27
civil service: 84–85, 150, 261–262, 435; elite, 114, 115, 116–117, 261; patronage for party supporters, 252, 262; pensions, 95, 261, 435; public officials (*Beamten*), 116–117, 261–262; screening for political extremists (*Berufsverbot*), 56, 261–262; unions, 120–121, 163, 230, 280–281
Clapham, John: 209
Clausewitz, Karl von: 336
climate: xix-xx, 68–69, 191
Cologne: 86, 132, 363
colonial expansion. *See* German Empire
Commission for Educational Planning: 76
Common Market. *See* European Economic Community
communism, Weimar Republic: 27–28, 29, 30
Communist Party of Germany (KPD): 28, 33, 44, 46, 47, 51, 275, 395
Confederation of German Employer Associations (BDA): 278
Conference on Security and Cooperation in Europe (CSCE), Final Act: 308, 310; Basket III, 311; EC unified position, 322
constitution. *See* Basic Law, 1949
Council of Education: 76, 77
Council of Experts for the Evaluation of Overall Economic Development, 1963: 153–154
Council on Science and the Humanities: 76–77
Cuban Missile Crisis, 1962: 49
cultural traditions: xxvi, 11, 14, 17, 29–30, 39, 72, 106; German Expressionism, 30
currency (deutsche mark): depreciation, 1980's, xxi, 175, 176, 194, 200, 208, 211–212, 215, 219, 232, 241; exchange rate fluctuations, 143, 153, 165–167, 169–170, 172, 174, 200, 215, 435; introduction, 1948, 148, 159, 165
Czechoslovak Sudetenland annexation, 1938: xvi, 36, 37

Dachau: concentration camp, 35; Romany hunger strike, 1980, 109
Dahrendorf, Ralf: 112
Daimler-Benz Company: 205–207, 237

439

Danube River basin: xix, 61, 62, 65, 67, 68
Dawes, Charles G.: 28, 144
Defregger, Matthias: 139
Denmark, World War II: 37
Deputy, The: 139
Der Spiegel: 49, 139, 284
Deutsche Zeitung: 284
Die Grünen. *See* Greens political party
Die Welt: 284
Die Zeit: 284
Disraeli, Benjamin: 38
dissidents. *See* anti-nuclear peace movement; terrorist activists and dissident groups
Döpfner, Julius Cardinal: 139
Dortmund: 129
Drachenfels: 67
drainage: 63, 64, 67–68
Duisburg: 129
Dutschke, Rudi: 50

Ebert, Friedrich: xv, 25, 29
Eckart, Dietrich: 31
Ecological Democratic Party: 275–276
economy (*see also* banks and banking; currency; industry; labor; trade unions): xx-xxi, 143–177; balance of payments, 153, 159, 166, 170, 175–176, 194, 199, 215, 219, 240, 241, 391–392; Basic Law, 1949, 150, 151; budget, xxi, 122, 145, 153–159 *passim*, 169, 391; consumer price index, 155, 156, 170–171; fiscal policy, 154, 156, 158, 169, 176; foreign investments, 159, 175, 210, 212, 219, 240–242; free market economy, xxix, 45, 148, 150, 171, 218–220; GDP, 211, 386, 396; GNP, xx, 56, 143, 154–161 *passim*, 200, 240, 313; government policies, xxx, 143, 144, 148–159 *passim*; industrialization, 1800's, 16–17, 18–19, 128–129, 143–144; monetary policy, 170–171; recession, 1979–1980's, xi, xxix-xxx, 4, 57, 61, 108, 110, 122, 143, 153, 155–156, 163, 170, 171, 176, 199–200, 219, 246, 280, 319, 320; oil prices, effect, 54–55, 155, 156, 174, 176, 199, 215, 219, 324; post-World War II recovery. *See under* post World War II; private investment, 143, 152–153, 156, 160; public debt, 156, 158–159; public sector, 152, 157–158, 175; special interest groups, effect on government policy, 150–151; stabilization law, 1967, 154; state (*Länder*) local control, 150, 152, 154, 157–158; taxes, xxx, 153, 156, 157, 158; trade-dependent, xx, 143, 145, 160, 161, 171, 200, 218, 289, 290, 313–314
education: xx, 61, 72–90, 108, 379 (table); administration and finance, 61, 72, 75, 76–78, 97, 133–134; adult, 75, 76, 88, 90, 235; basic principles, 75–76; denominational and other private schools, 61, 72, 76, 77, 90, 97, 107, 137–138, 139; educational system, chart, 80; *Gesamtschule*, 75, 79, 113; *Grundschule* (elementary), 78–79; *Gymnasium*, 73, 75, 79, 81–82, 83, 84, 86, 113, 114; *Hauptschule*, 79, 352; historic, 17, 72–74; kindergarten, 78, 124; literacy rate, xx, 61, 76, 109; medical, 93; music and fine arts institutes, 84; Nazi reorganization, 73–74; practical use, 75–83 *passim*, 90; *Realschule*, 79, 81; reforms, 54, 74–75, 87, 138; rural, 186; secondary school, selection of, 61, 72–73, 78–79, 113, 125; special, 88; teacher training, 74, 84–85; vocational and technical training, 72, 74, 76, 77, 79, 81, 82–84, 90, 113, 235, 352, 366; Weimar Constitution of 1919, 72–73
Eifel region: 66
Einstein, Albert: xxvi, 38
Eisenhower, Dwight D.: 48
El Salvador: 328
Elbe River: 64, 67
elite: 11, 112, 114–117; educated elite, 72, 75, 113, 115, 117; military, none, 349
Ems River: 67
energy: 212–216, 386; coal and lignite, 201, 203, 212, 216; crude oil, xxi, 212–213, 215–216; hydroelectric power, 19, 212; Middle East oil dependence, 213, 215, 216, 324; natural gas, xxi, 213, 239; nuclear energy, 212, 215, 216, 228–229, 239, 314; Soviet natural gas pipeline, 213–215, 314
Ensslin, Gudrun: 369, 370
Erhard, Ludwig: xvi, xxviii, 49, 249 (illustration), 307; economic policies, 45, 148, 150, 218
Ertl, Josef: 320
Essen: 129
ethnic groups (*see also* foreign workers): xx, xxv, 104–112; Danes, 105; East Frisians, 105; German, derivation of term, 106–107; gypsies (Romany), 105, 108–109; Jews, 105, 108

Index

Europe, Mutual and Balanced Force Reduction negotiations: 305
European Atomic Energy Community: 317–318
European Coal and Steel Community: xxii, 46, 199, 203, 204, 317–318
European Communities (EC)(*see also* trade): 152, 155, 160, 166, 317–323, 435; African, Caribbean, and Pacific (ACP) economic relations, 328; budget, West German payments, 175, 188–189, 289, 319–321; China, trade agreement, 325; Commission of, 318; common foreign policy positions, 317, 321–325, 329; controlled currencies systems, 166; Council of Ministers, 318, 324; Court of Justice, 318; customs union, 318; decisionmaking process, 318, 319; European Parliament, 318; European unification, 320, 323; fishing policy and common market, 195, 320; membership, xxii, xxv, 171, 289, 318; Persian Gulf states, diplomatic and economic relations, 316; precedence of EC law over national law, 318; United States, relations, 319
European Convention on the Suppression of Terrorism: 370
European Council: 322, 323
European Currency Unit (ECU): 166
European Defense Community, proposed: 46
European Economic Community (Common Market): xxii, 48, 162, 187–190, 199, 389–390; Common Agricultural Policy (CAP), 152, 187–189, 194, 318, 319–320; membership, xvi, 289; steel production, 199, 321
European Monetary System (EMS): 155, 166–167, 318
Evangelical Church in Germany (EKD): 133, 135–136, 381
exports (*see also* trade): xx, 143, 172, 174, 239–240, 388–391; arms sales policy, 325; GNP, 171–172, 200, 240; machinery and equipment, xx, 172, 174

Falkenhayn, Erich von: 22
family organization: 124–128; female-headed households, 126; marriage and divorce, 127–128, 384 (table); partible inheritance, 182; traditional sex roles, 123–124, 125–126, 127
Federal Administrative Court: 259
Federal Association of Citizens' Initiatives on Environmental Protection: 283
Federal Border Force (*Bundesgrenzechutz*-BGS), 338, 360–362; Individual Services branch, 362
Federal Cartel Office: 223
Federal Constitutional Court: xxii, xxvii, 44, 54, 258, 260, 264, 273
Federal Council. *See* Bundesrat
Federal Court of Justice: 259, 365
Federal Criminal Investigation Office (BKA): 362–363
Federal Diet. *See* Bundestag
Federal Employment Institute: 96, 97, 235
Federal Institute of Labor: 77, 83
Federal Intelligence Service (BND): 363
Federal Office for the Protection of the Constitution (BFV): 363, 368
Federal Patents Court: 259–260
Federal Republic of Germany: established (May 8, 1949), xvi, 3, 148, 338; sovereignty (1955), xxviii, 46, 47, 50, 245
Federal Security Council: 291, 292, 342
Federation of German Civil Servants (Deutscher Beamtenbund-DBB): 120, 163, 280–281
Federation of German Industries (BDI): 150, 222, 224, 228, 278
Ferdinand, Archduke Franz: xv, 21
Financial Planning Council: 154
fiscal year: xxi, 158
Fischer, Fritz: 24–25
fishing: 64, 195, 320, 386 (tables), 387 (tables); fishing zone, width, 195
Fohne: 69
foreign relations (*see also* European Communities; German reunification; North Atlantic Treaty Organization): 289–330; African states, 328–329; East Asia, 325–326; East-West detente, xvi, 48, 49, 50, 237–240, 245–246, 290, 299, 306, 307, 310, 311, 313–317; EC members common foreign policy, 317, 321–325, 329; European unification, 46, 48, 320, 323; geographic location, effect, 289, 299, 313; German youth criticisms, 108; international memberships, xvii, xxii, xxv, 54, 289, 323; Latin American states, 326–328; Middle East, 325–326; NATO, importance to, 293, 306, 307; 1949–1955, foreign de jure control, xxvii, xxviii, 41, 43; *Ostpolitik*, xvi, xxviii, 51–55, 238–239, 289, 290, 291, 293, 307–317;

441

Poland, xxix, 314, 316–317; policy making, 290–293; post-war de facto boundaries, recognition, xxviii, 51, 52, 308, 310; pro-West, xxviii, 3, 4, 28, 45, 46, 57, 289, 293, 323; Third World, 290, 316

foreign workers (*Gastarbeiter*): xx, xxv, 18, 104, 108, 132, 229–230; children, problem of, 110, 112; EEC nationals, 110; number of, xxv, 110, 162, 381, 387; recruitment suspended, 1973, 110, 112; remittances sent abroad, 175, 391; unemployment, 112, 122–124, 371; women, 109, 122

forests and forestry: 65, 66, 67, 194–195, 386, 387

France: EC benefits, 187, 319; European Defense Council nonratification, 46; German Empire conflicts of interests, xv, 15–16, 20–21; military forces in West Germany, xxii, 357–358; World War II, 36, 37, 40, 42, 337

Frankfurt: 60 (illustration), 66, 169; demonstrations, 87, 283; foreign workers (*Gastarbeiter*), population, 110; squatters, problem of, 132; unemployment rate, 122; V Corps headquarters, 357

Frankfurt Institute for Social Research: 29

Frankfurter Allgemeine Zeitung: 284

Frankfurter Rundschau: 284

Frederick I (Barbarossa): xiii, 7

Frederick II (the Great): xiv, 11, 335, 358

Frederick II (Holy Roman Empire): xiii, 7, 30

Frederick William, the Great Elector: xiv, 10, 335

Frederick William I: xiv, 10–11, 335

Frederick William IV: xv, 11

Free Democratic Party (*see also* Social Democratic Party/Free Democratic Party coalition)(FDP): xxii, xxix, 44, 56, 271–273, 278, 307, 436; as coalition party, xxix, 45, 46, 55, 151, 254, 264–265, 271–273, 277; at Parliamentary Council, 43; bourgeois-liberalist, 45, 151, 272; cabinet positions, xxix, 51, 254, 272; land and federal representation (tables), 394, 395; lower Saxony election, 1982, xxx

Freiburg: 68, 131 (illustration)

Freud, Sigmund: xxvi, 38

Frisian Islands: 64

Gastarbeiter. See foreign workers

Geissler, Heine: 266

General Agreement on Tariffs and Trade (GATT): 171

Genscher, Hans-Dietrich: xxix, xxxi, 254, 272, 316, 323, 325

geography: xix-xx, 61-69; climate, 68–69; coastline, 64

George, Stefan: 29

German Communist Party (DKP)(*see also* Communist Party of Germany): 273, 275

German Democratic Party (DDP): 27, 28, 275, 436

German Democratic Republic (East Germany)(*see also* Berlin): xxv, 3, 42–43, 338; Basic Treaty, 1972, xvii, xxviii, 3, 51, 54, 308, 310; demarcation policy (*Abgrenzung*), 311–312; inter-German church contacts, 135–136, 137, 313; Polish crisis, effect on relations, 312–313; trade, credits, and technology from West Germany, 174–175, 311, 312, 313–314; travel controls, 49, 135–136, 239, 308, 310, 311, 313; Warsaw Pact membership, 3, 47

German Empire (1871–1918): xv, 3, 15, 16–21; British-German naval race, xv, 20; dualistic constitutionalism, 16–17; elite, 115; European balance of power, xv, 17–18; militarization, xv, 16–17, 20, 21, 336; Morocco crises, 1905, 1911, 20, 21, 25; political parties, 16–23 *passim*; Second Reich, 16; Spartacist revolt, 1918, xv, 23, 25; *Weltpolitik*, xv, 3, 20–21, 24–25

German General Electric Company (AEG): 19, 209, 224

German Industrial and Trade Convention (DIHT): 278

German National People's Party (DNVP): 27, 28, 32, 33

German Party (DP): 45, 46

German People's Party (DVP): 27, 28

German Press Council: 283

German Reich Party (DRP): 395

German reunifications: 3, 43, 49, 50, 107–108, 299, 313; Basic Law, 1949, 43, 46, 54; détente, effect of, 51, 289–290, 294, 307, 308, 310–311, 316; Hallstein Doctrine, 1955, xxviii, 47, 50

German Salaried Employees Union (DAG): 120, 163, 280

German Steelworkers Union: 203–204, 224

German Trade Union Federation (DGB): 120–121, 163, 230, 280–281,

Index

284
Germany Academy for Politics: 29
Goebbels, Joseph: 34
Goethe, Johann Wolfgang von: xxvi, 29
Göring, Hermann: 35
government (Federal) (*see also* Bundesrat; Bundestag; Länder (state) government; politics): xxi-xxii, 44-47, 245-262; Adenauer chancellorship, 1949-1963, xvi, xxvii-xxix, 3, 44-49, 136, 260, 263, 274, 293, 338; Brandt chancellorship, 1969-1974, xxviii, 3, 51-55, 252, 263, 269, 270, 307, 327; budget (tables), 385, 386; bureaucracy, 261-262; cabinet, xxvii, xxix, 44, 251, 252, 253-254, 292; chancellor (head of government), xxii, xxvii, 44, 251-252, 291, 292, 340; citizen-initiative associations, 107; electoral system, 266, 268, 276-277; Erhard chancellorship, 1963-1966, xxviii, 218, 253; Federal Chancellor's Office, 253, 291, 292; Federal Convention, xxvii, 251-252; federalism, xxvii, 44, 130, 150, 245, 248, 250-251; federation-Länder relations. *See under* Land; general support, 114, 115, 246-247; Kiesinger chancellorship, 1966-1969, xxviii; legislature. *See* Bundesrat; Bundestag; 1982 election predictions. xxx-xxxi, 57, 246; "party" state, 45, 245, 264; political stability, xxviii-xxix, 44, 45, 56-57, 160, 245, 247, 254, 264; president (head of state), xxii, xxvii, 44, 251-252, 291, 340; Schmidt chancellorship (*see also* Schmidt, Helmut), xvii, xxviii, xxix, 4, 55-57, 246, 253-254, 269, 271, 315, 325, 346-347; traditional interest groups, 150, 151, 222-224, 277-283; vested interests, 278
Great Depression: 32, 33, 145, 146
Greens, The (Die Grünen): xxx, 271, 273, 275-276, 281
Griff nach der Waltmacht: 24-25
Gross-Rosen concentration camp: 38
Grosz, George: 30
Gruhl, Herbert: 275
Guillaume, Günther: 55

Haig, Alexander M.: 371
Hamburg: 271, 394 (table); administration, 29, 61-62, 262, 263, 268; military academy, 86, 352-353; 1982 election forecast, xxx-xxxi; population, 70, 128, 132; port, 142, 173, 216, 394 (table); terrorist activities, 368,

372
Hanover: xiv, 361
Hasenclever, Walter: 30
Haussleiter, August: 275
health: xx, 61, 91-93, 380 (tables); diet, 185, 191, 193; health and accident insurance programs. *See under* social welfare; health care facilities, 91-92; health resorts and spas, 65, 92; infant mortality, 91; life expectancy, 70, 91; medical personnel, 92-93
Heidelberg, U.S. Army Europe headquarters: 357
Heine, Heinrich: 38
Heineman, Gustav: 51
Henlein, Konrad: 37
Henry IV: xiii, 6, 7
Henry VI: xiii, 7
Hercynian Massif: 63
Herter, Christian: 295, 297
Hesse: xiv, 62, 64, 194, 271, 394; 1982 election predictions, xxx-xxxi
Heuss, Theodor: xxvii, 43-44, 272
Himmler, Heinrich: 34
Hindenburg, Paul von: xvi, 4, 22-34 *passim*, 336
history (*see also* German Empire; Third Reich; Weimar Republic): xii-xvii, 3-57, 334-338; Balkan Wars (1912-1913), xv, 21; Carolingian Dynasty (First Reich), xii, 5, 6; chronology of important events, xii-xvii; Congress of Vienna (1814-1815), xiv, 11, 135; feudalism, 5, 7, 10; Franco-Prussian War (1870-1871), xv, 15-16; Frankish period (431-918), xii, 4-5, 6; German Confederation (1815-1871), xiv-xv, 11, 14-16, 358; Germanic tribal migrations, xii, xxv-xxvi, 4-5; Golden Bull of 1356, xiii, 8; Great Interregnum (1250-1272), xiii, 7; Habsburg Dynasty, xiii, 8, 10, 13; Hohenstaufen Dynasty (1138-1250), xiii, 7, 10-11; Hohenzollern Dynasty (1640-1918), xiv, 10-11, 14-16; Napoleonic Wars, xiv, 7, 335; princes, power of, xiii, 7, 8; Protestant League of Schmalkalden, 1530, xiv, 10; Protestant Reformation and religious wars (1517-1648), xiii-xiv, 8, 10, 12-13, 133; Prussian period (1648-1815), xiv-xv, 10-11, 15, 335-336; Roman period, xii, 4-5, 334; Salian Dynasty (1025-1125), xiii, 5, 6-7; Saxon Dynasty (919-1024), xii-xiii, 5, 6; Seven Weeks' War, 1866, xv, 15; Thirty Years' War (1618-1648), xiv, 10; unification (1815-1871), xiv-

443

xv, 334
Hitler, Adolf (see also Nazi Party; Third Reich): assassination plot against, 1944, 40–41; Beer-hall putsch attempt, Munich, 1923, xv-xvi, 31; foreign policy, 35–37; rise to power, xvi, 4, 31–33, 34, 146; SS (Guard Detachment), as private army, 34; Storm Troops (SA), 28, 34, 41, 359; suicide, 1945, 41
Hochhuth, Rolf: 139
Hoechst company: 208
Hoffmann, Karl-Heinz: 371, 372
Hoffmann Military Sport Group: 370–371
Hohenlohe, Prince Chlodwig zu: xv, 20
Holy Roman Empire: xii-xiv, 5, 6, 10, 13, 61, 334, 358
Honecker, Erich: 309, 312–313
housing: 103, 219; discrimination toward foreign workers, 112, 132
Hugenberg, Alfred: 32
human rights: 48, 107–108, 333, 360
Humanistische Union: 134
Hunsrück mountains: 66

I.G. Farben: 35, 144, 147, 208, 224
I.G. Metall: 120, 231, 235, 280
immigration. See foreign workers; refugees
imports: xx-xxi, 145, 174–175, 240; agricultural, xx, 143, 171, 174, 181, 186, 194, 396 (table); by commodities and area (tables), 388–391; food, xx, 185, 194; fuels, 174, 213, 216, 324; Japanese automobiles, 200, 205, 206, 326; Soviet uranium, 239, 314; wood and wood products, 195
Indonesia: 212
industry (see also economy; energy; post World War II; urbanization; West Berlin): xx, 199–224; advanced technology industries, 144, 151, 160, 200, 210, 228; automotive, 200, 205–206, 207, 237; banks, interrelations, 44, 144, 147, 152, 153, 204, 218–227 passim; capital flow, 220, 228, 241; cartels, 201, 203–204, 215, 218–219, 224; chemicals and electrochemicals, 19, 131, 161, 200–210 passim, 215, 224, 225, 237; coal and lignite, 19, 118, 147, 161, 201–203, 219, 233 (illustration); concentration of, 45, 129, 131, 153, 201, 202 (map), 218–219, 224; corporations and companies, types, 220–224; EEC steel production quota, 199, 321; electrical industry, 209–210, 215, 219, 224; government business holdings, 152; gross domestic product, 160–161, 386 (table); industrial associations (Verbände), 222–224; investment incentives, xxx, 151–153, 199–200, 219, 220; iron and steel, 19, 118, 120, 147, 161, 199–200, 203–205, 215, 219, 225, 233; long-term forecasting and planning, 227–229; mechanical engineering, 211–212; nuclear power plants, 151, 161, 216, 283; plants located abroad, 205, 206, 210, 212; political lobbying groups, 278; post World War II. See under post World War II; supervisory boards, 118, 120, 220–234 passim; technology assessment, 226, 228–229; world rank, xx, xxv, 55, 143, 160, 208
inland waterways: xxi, 216; River Police, 363
Inn River Valley: 65
Institut für Demoskopie Allensbach: 134
Institute of Business Research: 228
internal security (see also terrorist activity and dissidence): 358–372; anti-terrorist legislation, 56, 368–369, 370–371
International Atomic Energy Agency: 327
International Criminal Police Organization (INTERPOL): 362
International Monetary Fund special drawing rights: 166
Ireland: 323
Iron Curtain: 338
Israel: 324, 325
Italy: historic, xiii, 7; World War I, 21; World War II, xvi, 36, 37, 38, 40

Japan: trade relations, 200, 205, 206, 210, 211, 326; World War II, 38, 337
judicial system: xxii, xxvii, 258–260, 364–366; Civil Code, 358–359, 364; criminal justice, 359, 364–366; historic influences, 358, 364; juveniles, 366; rehabilitation, goal, 364; under Third Reich, 359
Jülich, nuclear research center: 228
Junkers: 10, 11, 14, 335

Kafka, Franz: 38
Kandinsky, Wassily: 30
Kant, Immanuel: xxvi
Kantorowicz, Ernst: 30
Kapp, Wolfgang: 27
Karlsruhe: nuclear research center, 228, 259; terrorist activities, 368, 369

Index

Kassel: 361
Kehr, Eckart: 29
Kennedy, John F.: 48–49, 297
Khrushchev, Nikita: 48–49
Kiesinger, Kurt Georg: xvi, xxviii, xxix, 50, 249
Kissinger, Henry A. (quoted): 304
Kohl, Helmut: xxxi, 55, 255, 266, 268
Köllmann, Wolfgang: 129
Konkrat: 367
Korean War: 46, 159
Kroesen, Frederick: 371
Krüger, Ulrich: xxxii
Krupp Company: 35
Küng, Hans: 139

labor (*see also* civil service; foreign workers; social welfare programs; trade unions): automation, effect of, 122–123; codetermination, 54, 118, 120, 121, 138, 165, 232–234, 272, 280; "dependent" labor force, 161, 387 (table); employment abroad, 123; employment by sector (table), 387; industrial labor force, 103, 120–121, 159, 161, 206, 219, 229–236; on supervisory boards, 221–224, 232–233, 234; self-employment, 161 (tables), 382, 387; semiskilled or unskilled, 109–110, 118, 126; service sector, 109–110, 118, 123, 160–161; unemployment, xi, xxx, 122–124, 143, 155, 156, 157, 162, 163, 199, 230, 387 (table); women, 123–124, 126, 383 (table); working conditions, wages, benefits, 164–165, 231–232, 234–236; works' councils, 118, 164–165, 232, 233–234
labor unions. *See* trade unions
Land (state) government: xxii, xxvii, 262–264, 394 (table); Bremen and Hamburg city states, 61, 262; citizens' initiative associations, 247, 275, 282–283; electoral system, 262, 266, 268, 276–277; Federal-Land respective responsibilities, xxii, 44, 150, 152, 158, 248, 250, 256–258, 262–263, 265, 290–291; financing, 158, 250; historic individuality, 7, 8, 61, 106; local and regional courts, 258–260; 1982 election predictions, xxx-xxxi, 57, 246
language: xx, xxv-xxvi, 105–106
Lassalle, Ferdinand: 16
League of Arab States (Arab League): 324
League of Nations: xvi, 29, 35
Lenin, Nikolai: 107
Libya: 212

Liebknecht, Karl: 23
Liebknecht, Wilhelm: 16
livestock: xx, 181, 185, 190, 192–193, 194
Locarno Treaties, 1925: 29, 35
Lome II Convention: 328
Lorraine: 19
Lower Saxony: 62, 65, 394 (table); East Frisian minority, 105; 1982 elections, xxx-xxxi
Lübeck: 130
Ludendorff, Erich: 22, 23, 336
Ludz, Peter Christian: 311–312
Luther, Martin: xiv, xxvi, 2 (illustration), 8, 133
Luxemburg, Rosa: 23

Mainz: 66
Mann, Thomas: 30, 109
Mannesmann A.G.: 120, 215, 232, 233, 239
Marshall, Alfred: 225
Marshall Plan: 42, 147, 153, 167
Marx, Karl: xxvi, 38
Maschinenfabrik Augsburg-Nürnberg (MAN): 206
media: xxvi, 105, 283–284, 366–367
Mein Kampf: 31, 34
Meinhof, Ulrike: 56, 367, 368, 369
Mendelssohn, Moses: 38
Menuhin, Yehudi: 38
metric conversion coefficients (table): 377
Metternich, Prince Klemens von: xiv, 11, 106
Meuse River: 66
Middle East, West German policy: 322, 323–325
mining: xx, 19, 201–203, 212, 216; employment, 18, 387 (table); gross domestic product (table), 386; salt and potassium, 19
Ministries of (*see also* government: cabinet): Agriculture, 76; Defense, 291, 340, 341, 345, 353, 362; Economic Affairs, 218; Education and Science, 76, 77; Foreign Affairs, 291; Interior, 109, 361, 364, 370–371; Labor and Social Affairs, 96; Research and Technology, 228; Transport, 363
Moltke, Helmuth von (the Younger): 21, 22
Morgenthau, Henry: 146
Moselle River: 66
Munich: 70, 259, 361; military academy, 86, 352–353
Mussolini, Benito: 36, 40

445

Federal Republic of Germany

name: xix, 436
Namibia: 328–329
Napoleon Bonaparte: xiv, 7
Napoleonic Civil Code: 182
National Democratic Party (NDP): 50, 273, 366, 370, 395
national security (*see also* armed forces; North Atlantic Treaty Organization): xxii-xxiii, 333–372; defense emergency planning, 248, 353–354, 357; defense expenditures, 157, 175, 396 (table); foreign armed forces, xxii, 47, 175, 355, 358; geographic vulnerability, 299, 305, 306, 313, 338; military policymaking, 291, 292, 340, 342; prohibited weapons, 47, 294, 343–344, 436; rearmament, 1955, 47, 136, 260, 293–294, 333, 343–344; U.S., importance of, 289, 299, 302, 304, 306–307
nationalism: xv, 16, 17, 21, 25, 103, 106, 107, 246; Nazi imperialistic, 32
Nazi Party (National Socialist German Workers' Party-NSDAP) (*see also* Hitler; Third Reich): xvi, 4, 30, 31–33; Hitler Youth (Hitler Jugend), 30, 31, 34; ideology, 32, 34, 35, 359, 372
Neckar River: 68
Netherlands: German invasion, 1940, 37; military forces in West Germany, 357
Neuengamme concentration camp: 38
Nicaragua, German aid: 327–328
Niemöller, Martin: 135, 136
North Atlantic Treaty Organization: xxix, 3, 42, 50, 52, 266, 293–307, 325; civil and military structure, 294; deterrence policy, 295, 297, 299–300, 304–305, 306–307; enhanced radiation weapons (neutron bomb), U.S. proposed deployment (1980's), 57, 246, 300–301, 315; flexible response strategy, 1960's, 297–298, 299–300; forward defense strategy, 1950, 293, 295, 300; German defense spending levels, xxv, 175, 289, 293, 302, 304, 346–347; German security, importance, 46, 289–306 *passim*, 315, 339, 342–343, 344; Long-Term Defense Program (LTDP), 1978, 298–299, 304; LRTNF deployment decision and parallel arms control initiatives, 1979, 57, 108, 246, 289, 300, 304–307, 315; membership, xxi, xxii, xxviii, 47, 436; public opinion, 302, 304, 307, 333, 346–347; Supreme Headquarters Allied Powers Europe (SHAPE), 294–295, 296 (chart); tactical nuclear weapons (1957), 47–48, 295, 297, 298, 300, 306–307; U.S.-Western European differing conceptions, 295, 297–298, 300–301
North-Rhine Westphalia: 62, 65, 139, 181, 194, 394 (table); urbanization, 131
North Sea: 64, 67, 69
Norway, World War II: 37
nuclear power equipment sales policy: 326–327
Nuremberg Trials: 41
Nutzweiler concentration camp: 38

Odenwald: 63, 65
Oldenburg: xiv
Olympic Games, 1980: 315, 316
Oppenheimer, J. Robert: 38
Oranienburg concentration camp: 35
Organization for Economic Cooperation and Development (OECD): xxii, 389–390
Organization of Petroleum Exporting Countries (OPEC): 172, 174, 216, 389, 390
Ostpolitik; xvi, xxviii, 51–55, 238–239, 289, 290, 291, 293, 307–317
Otto I (the Great): xii, 6

Pacelli, Eugenio (Pope Pius XII): 137–138
Pakistan: 316
Palestinian Liberation Organization: EC position, 322, 324–325
Papen, Franz von: xvi, 33, 138
Parliamentary Commissioner for the Federal Armed Forces: 342, 350
Poland: emigration, 18, 238, 308; Nazi invasion, 1939, xvi, 37, 337; Polish Corridor, ceded, 1919, 24; political crisis, 1980–1982, 246, 290, 312–313, 314, 316–317; territorial change, 41, 146; Warsaw treaty, 1970, on border issues, 51, 52
police: xxii, 262, 361–363; border police, xxii, xxiii, 334, 362; Federal Criminal Investigation Office (BKA), 362–363; intelligence services, 362, 363; police union, 230; Readiness Police, xxiii, 360, 363–364
political history (*see also* German Empire; Third Reich; Weimar Republic): administrative centralism, 5, 6, 10–11; dualistic (king-parliament) state, 1850–1918, 14–21 *passim*; elective monarchy provision (Golden Bull of 1356), xiii, 8; Frankfurt Parliament (1848), xv, 11; *Luckentheorie*

446

Index

(gap theory), 1862, 14, 15; Reichstag, 16–32 *passim*; Weimar constitution, 1919, 25–26, 247
politics (*see also* names of political parties): xxii, xxviii-xxix, 264–284; conservatism, 55, 245–246; federal election results (table), 395; five-percent of vote requirement, 274 277; foreign policy issues, 46, 47–49, 50, 51–52, 54, 245–246, 274, 275; opposition parties, effect, 263; political extremists, prohibition of (*see also* terrorist activitists and dissident groups), 44, 247–248, 264, 273, 274; post World War II parties, 41, 43, 45, 245, 264, 273; public subsidy, 265; supremacy of political parties, 45, 245, 264; traditional interest groups, influence, 231, 247, 275, 277–278, 280–282
Pope Gregory VII: xiii, 7
Pope John XXIII: 137
Pope Paul VI: 139
Pope Pius XII: 137–138, 139
population: xx, xxv, 69–71; birth control, position on, 139; by age and sex, 70, 73, 91; distribution, 70, 71, 378 (table), 384 (table); foreign workers (*Gastarbeiter*), xx, xxv, 70, 109, 112, 381 (table); growth rate, xx, 18, 69–70, 162–163, 176
ports and shipping (*see also* names of ports): xxi, 64, 216; Special Police, 361–363
post World War II (see also Berlin; refugees), 1945–1955: xxv, 41–47; Allied Control Council, 41, 42, 146–147; Allied reserved political rights, xxvii, xxviii, 41, 43; brain drain, 147; cold war, effect on lifting restrictions, 42, 147, 160, 218, 360; currency reform, 1948, 42, 148, 165, 229; deindustrialization, 42, 146–148, 153, 159–160, 218, 229, 232; demilitarization, 41, 42, 46, 47, 48, 146; denazification, 41, 147, 359–360; economic recovery (*Wirtschaftswunder*), xxviii, 42, 46, 48, 153, 159–160, 218, 219, 222; education system, rebuilding of, 74; German foreign policy autonomy, 1951, 46; Germany, division of, xxv, xxvi-xxvii, 3, 4, 42, 135, 245, 293, 338; Hallstein Doctrine (reunification goal), xxviii, 47, 50; London Six-Power Conference, 1948, 42–43; Munich Program of 1949, 121; occupation zones, xxv, 41, 135, 146, 147, 338; police forces, restrictions on, 360; Potsdam Conference, 1945, 41, 146, 337–338; Soviet-Allied occupation zone incidents, 1950's, 360
Potsdam Conference, 1945: 41, 146, 337–338
Proust, Marcel: 38
Prussia, historic: xiv, xv, 10–16, 106, 334–336, 358

radio and television: xxi, xxvi, 105, 210, 283–284
Rahner, Karl: 139
railways: xxi, 19, 152, 216, 217; Railway Police, 363
rainfall: 69
Ramstein, U.S. Air Force Europe headquarters: 357, 371
Raspe, Jan-Carl: 369, 370
Rathenau, Emil: 209
Readiness Police: xxiii, 360, 363–364
Reagan, Ronald: 246, 301
Reconstruction Loan Corporation: 167
refugees: from Eastern Europe, 104, 106, 130, 131, 135, 161, 229, 238–239, 308, 311, 314, 360; German intellectuals from Third Reich (brain drain), 147; Jews, 108; 1945–1948, 42, 70, 106, 147–148, 185; political asylees, 37
Refugees' Party: 45, 273
religion (*see also* history: Protestant Reformation): 132–139; Calvinism, 10; church tax, 134, 281–282; division of Germany, effect, 135–136, 137, 313; Eastern Orthodox, 132; freedom of, 133, 247; Jewish, xxvi, 38–39, 132; Lutheran, xiv, xxvi, 10, 135; Muslim, 104, 132; organized religious groups, political influence, 136, 281–282; Protestant, xx, xxvi, 132, 135–136; racism (*see also under* Nazi Party: ideology), 108, 371; Roman Catholic, xiv, xx, xxvi, 10, 17, 103–104, 115, 126, 132, 136–139; under Nazis, 135, 137–138
Rhine-Main-Danube canal: xvi
Rhine River: xix, 61, 62, 67, 203; and Rhine valley, xix, 61–68 *passim*, 192, 203
Rhine-Ruhr area, urbanization: 131
Rhineland, Allied occupation in World War II: 24, 27, 29
Rhineland-Palatinate: 268, 394
Röhm, Ernst: 31
Rommel, Erwin: 38
Rosenberg, Alfred: 31
Rote Morgen (Red Morning): 369
Ruhr: French-Belgian occupation and

withdrawal, 1923, xv, xvi, 28, 144; industrial concentration, 19, 122, 129, 131, 201, 203, 232; labor force, 110, 112
Ruhr River: 62
Ruhrgas AG: 213
Ruhrstadt, population: 70

Saar: 62, 394 (table); coal mining and industry, 19, 66, 129, 145, 201
Sachsenhausen concentration camp: 35
Saudi Arabia: 153, 176, 212, 213, 216, 325
Saxony: xiv, 129
Scharnhorst, Gerhard von: 336
Scheel, Walter: 51, 55, 272
Schleicher, Kurt von: xvi, 33
Schleswig-Holstein: 14–15, 24, 62–63, 64, 181, 394; East Frisian and Danish minorities, 105
Schleyer, Hanns-Martin: 369, 370
Schlieffen, Alfred von: 21
Schmidt, Helmut (*see also* government: Schmidt chancellorship): 249; economic and political problems, xi, xxix-xxx, xxxi, 4, 55, 56, 246, 270, 300, 301, 346–347; "German Model" (Modell Deutschland) campaign slogan, 4, 55–56; German NATO budget cuts, 346–347; meeting with East German leader Honecker, 309, 313
Schmidt position on: detente and security, 315; neutron weapons, xxix, 300, 301; Palestinian state, 325; SALT, 304; sanctions against Poland or Soviet Union, xxix; tactical nuclear weapons (1962), 300
Schumacher, Kurt: 45
Schuschnigg, Kurt von: 36
Seeckt, Hans von: 337
Seyss-Inquart, Arthur von: 36–37
Siemens, Warner: 209
Siemens AEG: 210, 224
Siemens AG: 19, 35, 209, 212, 227–231
Silesia: 145
size: xix, xxv, 61
Slovakia, German puppet state: 37
Social Democratic Party of Germany (SPD)(*see also* Brandt, Willy; government: Schmidt chancellorship): xxii, xxix, 44, 46, 126, 269–271, 436; at Parliamentary Council, 1948–1949, 43; Bad Godesberg Program, 1959, xxix, 45, 50, 151, 269, 270; bureaucracy, 116–117; cabinet positions, 254; Central American policy, 327–328; domestic reform program, 1969, 54; economic policies, 156–157, 246; 1875–1918, 16–23 *passim*, 269; election results (tables), 394, 395; FDP coalition, 55–57, 151, 156, 246, 265–272 *passim*, 436; Grand Coalition, 1966–1969, xvi, xxix; Great Coalition, 1923–1929, 28; left/right wing factions, 270, 272; Marxist beginnings, 16, 151, 269; 1982 election forecast, xxx-xxxi, 246, 269; organization and decisionmaking, 271; political stance, 4, 45, 55–57, 151, 245–246, 266, 307; special interest groups, 271, 278; under Weimar Republic, xv, 3–4, 23–33 *passim*, 115, 269; weekly press, 284; Youth wing (Jungsozialisten-Jusos), 54, 55, 151, 270–271, 272
social welfare programs: xx, 54, 93–99, 103, 107, 124, 132, 143, 234–236, 246, 383 (table); as government obligation, 61, 94, 248; Bismarck legislation, 18, 93, 95; health, accident, and unemployment insurance programs, xx, 61, 93, 95–96, 98, 186, 235–236, 381 (table); pensions, xx, 93, 94–95, 98, 153, 186, 235, 261; social courts, 259; social insurance data bank, 93–94; war victims, subsidies, 61, 98, 106, 109, 145, 175
Socialist International: 327, 328
Socialist Reich Party (SRP): 44, 264, 274
Socialist Students' League: 366
society (*see also* ethnic groups; family organization): xx, 103–132; ethnic intermarriages, 105; generation gap, xxxi, 104, 108, 114, 122, 125, 138, 246; Germans, stereotypes of, 107, 109; Jews, historic position, 38–39; occupational mobility, 103, 113–118 *passim*; pessimism, 108; regional loyalties, 105–106; religious affiliation, effect, 103–104, 115; soical-mobility, 103, 113, 115, 118; standard of living, 61, 103, 116, 121; stratification, 103, 112–113, 114, 117; working class (*see also* labor), 112, 117–124
Sontheimer, Kurt: 264
South Africa: 212, 328–329
Soviet Union: aid for German remilitarization, 1920's, 337; Berlin Blockade, 1948, 42–43; Berlin Crisis, 1958–1961, 48–49; détente, 55, 310–311; diplomatic relations, 1955, xxviii; German Democratic Republic, establishment of, xxvi, xxvi-xxvii, 3, 4, 42, 135, 245, 293, 338; German emigrants, 308, 314; Moscow Treaty, 1970, 51, 52; nuclear weapons

Index

powers, 295, 297, 304–305; occupation zone, post World War II, 41–42, 146, 147; Russian Revolution, 1917, 23; Siberian natural gas pipeline, 213–215, 314; trade, 172, 174, 212, 239–240, 316; Treaty of Berlin, 1926, 29; U.S. sanctions, West German position, xxix, 315–317; World War II, 37, 38, 40, 41, 337
Sozialdemokrat: 18
Spain, World War II: 38
Spanish Civil War, 1936–1939: 36
Spartacist League: xv, 23
Speyer university: 86
Springer, Axel: 284, 366–367
Stalin, Joseph: 338
Stauffenberg, Claus Schenk von: 40–41
Stern, Fritz: 107
Stobbe, Dietrich: 312
Stoph, Willi: 309
Strauss, Franz-Josef: xxix, 47–48, 55, 57, 268–289
Stresemann, Gustav: xvi, 28–29
Stuttgart: 122, 357
Stutthof concentration camp: 38
Suddeutsche Zeitung: 284
suffrage: xxii, 16, 22, 25, 26, 126
Swabian Alps: 68
Switzerland: xxvi, 65

Tacitus: 334
Taunus Mountains: 63, 66
telecommunications: xxi, xxvi, 105, 210, 283–284
temperature: xix-xx, 68, 69, 181
terrorist activists and dissident groups: 56, 334, 362–363, 366–372; anti-American, xxix, 49, 50, 246, 367, 368, 371–372; Baader-Meinhof gang (*see also* Red Army Faction, *infra*), 52, 55, 56, 367; government counter measures, 51, 56, 367–369, 370–371; Hoffmann Military Sport Group, 370–371; left-wing extremists (neo-Marxists), 4, 50, 51, 56, 245, 275–276, 367, 371–372; Lufthansa airplane hijacking, 1977, 369–370; Munich Oktoberfest, 1980, 367, 371; Palestinian massacre of Israeli Olympic athletes, 367; Red Army Faction (RAF), 367–369, 371–372; right-wing extremists (neo-Nazis), 50–51, 56, 274, 367–372 *passim*; Rote Morgen (Red Morning), 369; Ulrike Meinhof Commando, 369; West Germany embassy in Stockholm incident, 368, 370; women activists, 372
Teutonic Knights: 334

Thatcher, Margaret: 320
Third Reich (1933–1945) (*see also* World War II): xvi, 4, 25, 33–41, 126; agricultural policies, 183; Anglo-German Naval Pact of June 1935, 36; anti-Semitism, 32, 35, 38–39, 40; churches, effect on, 135, 137–138, 139; concentration and mass extermination camps, 35, 38, 40, 359; education, restructuring, 73–74; elite, 115; forced and slave labor, 35; forced political coordination (Gleichschaltung), xvi, 34, 269; industrial mobilization, 35, 218, 223, 230; People's Tribunal (Court), 34, 359; rearmament, xvi, 34–35, 36, 74, 337; Reichstag fire, February 27, 1933, 33–34; Secret State Police (Gestapo), 34, 35, 41, 334, 359; SS police state, 35, 38, 116, 359; swastika, 31
Third World, German foreign aid: 290, 316, 327–328
Tirpitz, Alfred von: 20
topography: xix, 62–67
trade (*see also* European Economic Community; exports; imports): 143, 161, 171–175, 218, 237–241; balance of trade, 175–176, 211, 240–242; by principal commodity groups (table), 388; China, Japan, 325–326; Eastern Europe and Soviet Union, 172, 213, 215, 237–240, 290, 311–314; EC countries, xx, xxi, 172, 174, 194, 289, 318–319; gross domestic product, 290, 386 (table); gross national product, 200, 240, 313; import-dependent, xx-xxi, 161, 218, 289, 290, 313–314; OPEC countries, 147, 173; protectionism, 1870's, 17; Third World, 290; Zollverein (Customs Union), 1834, xiv
trade unions (*see also* labor): 120–122, 150–151, 163–165, 230–234, 278–281; banned by Hitler, 34, 230, 232; Basic Law, 1949, 44; labor courts, 164, 234, 259; membership, 120–121, 164, 230; political influence, 176, 222, 230, 278–280; post World War II, 41, 121, 164; SPF members, 270, 271, 278; strikes and lockouts, 23, 121–122, 230–231; union leaders elite, 115
transportation: xxi, 183, 186, 216–218, 386, 391; East German links, 310, 312
Treaty of Verdun, 843: xii, 5, 6
Triple Entente: xv, 21, 22
Truman, Harry S: 42, 337–338

449

Tübingen University, student activism: 371
Turkey: German aid, 316; Turkish workers in Germany, xxv, 109, 112
United Kingdom. *See* Britain
United Nations Organization: EC voting pattern, 321–322; membership, xvii, xxii, xxviii, 54, 289, 323
United States (*see also* North Atlantic Treaty Organization; post World War II; World War I; World War II): Dawes Plan, 1924, xvi, 28, 144; defense policy development, 57, 246, 295, 297–298, 300–301, 304–305, 315; economic and other relations, 159, 176, 241–242, 300, 323, 327; military aid, 338, 351; military forces in West Germany, xxii, 357; Soviet relations, 48–49, 108, 298, 315–317; Strategic Arms Limitations Talks (SALT), 304–305; U.S.-Soviet nuclear parity, 48–49, 247, 302, 304–305, 306–307; Young Plan, 1929, xvi, 29, 32, 145
universities: 61, 75–88 *passim*, 110, 113; *Gesamthochschulen* (comprehensive), 85–86; historic, xiv, 72; student activism, 50, 56, 87, 114, 245, 247, 275, 366, 367; student exemption to conscription, 348; student subsidies, 97; theological professors, 133, 139; under Third Reich, 74; women students, 126
Upper Silesia: 129
urbanization: 70, 125, 128–132, 186; citizen initiative associations, 107; historic, 7, 18, 128–129

Vatican: 139
Vetter, Heinz-Oscar: 280
Vietnam: 367
Vogel, Hans-Jochen: xxxi
Völkischer Beobachter: 31
Volkswagen company: 205–206
Vorwärts: 284:

Wangerooge: 64
Warburg Library: 29
Warsaw Pact: 3, 47, 299
Wehner, Herbert: xxix, 255–256, 270, 271
Weimar, 1818: xiv
Weimar Republic (1918–1933): xv-xvi, 3–4, 25–33, 126, 145, 223, 269; Article 48 (emergency clause of constitution), invocation, 25, 32, 34; cultural values, 29–30; Dawes Plan, 1924, xvi, 28, 144; economic depression, 31, 32, 33, 145–146; elite, 115; Hitler, rise to power, xvi, 4, 31–33, 146; Kapp Putsch, xv, 27–28; labor movement, 121, 232, 278, 280; military, political role, 27, 28–29, 32; November Revolution, 1918, 23–24, 25, 30; political instability, 3–4, 27–28, 32, 252, 264; remilitarization, 336–337; Stresemann government, xvi, 28–29; Weimar constitution, 1919, 25, 27, 247; Young Plan, 1929, xvi, 29, 32, 145
welfare. *See* social welfare programs
Wesel on the Rhine (illustration): 149
Weser River: 64, 67
West Berlin: administration, xxvii, 62, 255, 259, 263; airlift, 1948, 42–43; Alternative List Party, 276; foreign military forces, 357, 358; Four Power Agreement, 1971 (Berlin Accord), xvi, 51, 52, 236, 250–251, 308, 310; industrialization, 151, 236–237, 238; intra-German travel, 52, 308, 310, 312, 314; NATO, importance, 299; New Left Party, demonstrations, 50–51; population, xx, xxv, 69, 70, 130, 132, 236, 283; special status, 44, 52, 54, 250–251, 289, 308, 310; state (Land) elections, 1978–1981, 394 (table)
Western European Union (WEU): 46, 293–294, 343, 436
Westerwald: 63, 66–67
Westphalia: 129
Wiesbaden: 66, 362, 371
William (Wilhelm) I: xv, 14, 15, 336
William (Wilhelm) II: xv, 18, 20–21, 25, 336; *Ostergeschenk* (Easter Message), 1917, 23
Wittenberg, East Germany, Protestant center: 135, 136
Woerner, Manfred: xxxi
women: employment and salaries, 84, 109, 123–124, 146, 234, 364; suffrage, 126; traditional roles, 123–124, 125–126, 127
World Council of Churches: 135
World War I: xv, 3, 20, 21, 22–24, 37, 336; German reparations, xvi, 24–32 *passim*, 144–145; German war aims, 22–25; German war guilt, question, 24–25; Schlieffen Plan, 21, 22, 24; Treaty of Versailles, 1919, 24–36 *passim*, 336–337
World War II (*see also* post World War II): xvi, 37–41, 139; Allied invasion of France, 40; blitzkrieg, xvi, 37, 337; destruction, xxv, 337, 349; Grand Alliance (U.K., U.S., U.S.S.R.), 38; Munich Conference of September 1938,

37; North Africa, 38, 40; reparations, 42; unconditional surrender and demilitarization, xxv, 41, 146–147, 337–338

Württemberg (*see also* Baden-Württemberg): xiv, 15, 16

Yalta Conference, 1945: 41
Young, Owen D.: 29, 145
Yugoslav workers in Germany: 109, 112
Zimmerman, Friedrich: xxxi
Zugspitze mountains: 65

Published Country Studies

(Area Handbook Series)

550-65	Afghanistan		550-151	Honduras
550-98	Albania		550-165	Hungary
550-44	Algeria		550-21	India
550-59	Angola		550-154	Indian Ocean
550-73	Argentina		550-39	Indonesia
550-169	Australia		550-68	Iran
550-176	Austria		550-31	Iraq
550-175	Bangladesh		550-25	Israel
550-170	Belgium		550-182	Italy
550-66	Bolivia		550-69	Ivory Coast
550-20	Brazil		550-177	Jamaica
550-168	Bulgaria		550-30	Japan
550-61	Burma		550-34	Jordan
550-83	Burundi		550-56	Kenya
550-50	Cambodia		550-81	Korea, North
550-166	Cameroon		550-41	Korea, South
550-159	Chad		550-58	Laos
550-77	Chile		550-24	Lebanon
550-60	China		550-38	Liberia
550-63	China, Republic of		550-85	Libya
550-26	Colombia		550-172	Malawi
550-91	Congo		550-45	Malaysia
550-90	Costa Rica		550-161	Mauritania
550-152	Cuba		550-79	Mexico
550-22	Cyprus		550-76	Mongolia
550-158	Czechoslovakia		550-49	Morocco
550-54	Dominican Republic		550-64	Mozambique
550-52	Ecuador		550-35	Nepal, Bhutan and Sikkim
550-43	Egypt		550-88	Nicaragua
550-150	El Salvador		550-157	Nigeria
550-28	Ethiopia		550-94	Oceania
550-167	Finland		550-48	Pakistan
550-155	Germany, East		550-46	Panama
550-173	Germany, Federal Republic of		550-156	Paraguay
550-153	Ghana		550-185	Persian Gulf States
550-87	Greece		550-42	Peru
550-78	Guatemala		550-72	Philippines
550-174	Guinea		550-162	Poland
550-82	Guyana		550-181	Portugal
550-164	Haiti		550-160	Romania

453

Federal Republic of Germany

550-84	Rwanda	550-89	Tunisia
550-51	Saudi Arabia	550-80	Turkey
550-70	Senegal	550-74	Uganda
550-180	Sierra Leone	550-97	Uruguay
550-184	Singapore	550-71	Venezuela
550-86	Somalia	550-57	Vietnam, North
550-93	South Africa	550-55	Vietnam, South
550-95	Soviet Union	550-183	Yemens, The
550-179	Spain	550-99	Yugoslavia
550-96	Sri Lanka (Ceylon)	550-67	Zaire
550-27	Sudan	550-75	Zambia
550-47	Syria	550-171	Zimbabwe
550-62	Tanzania		
550-53	Thailand		
550-178	Trinidad and Tobago		